C000230842

Professional disciplir
healthcare regulators

a legal handbook

Available as an ebook at www.lag.org.uk/ebooks

The purpose of the Legal Action Group is to promote equal access to justice for all members of society who are socially, economically or otherwise disadvantaged. To this end, it seeks to improve law and practice, the administration of justice and legal services.

Dr. Carl Anandan
8. Oct 2012

Professional discipline and healthcare regulators

a legal handbook

Christopher Sallon QC, Jon Whitfield QC,
Gemma Hobcraft, Amanda Hart, Nicole
Ridgwell, Sue Sleeman, Eloise Power,
Louise Price and Steve Broach

 Legal Action Group
2012

This edition published in Great Britain 2012
by LAG Education and Service Trust Limited
242 Pentonville Road, London N1 9UN
www.lag.org.uk

British Library Cataloguing in Publication Data
a CIP catalogue record for this book is available from the British Library.

Crown copyright material is produced with the permission of the Controller of HMSO and the Queen's Printer for Scotland.

This book has been produced using Forest Stewardship Council® (FSC®) certified paper The wood used to produce FSC certified products with a 'Mixed Sources' label comes from FSC certified well-managed forests, controlled sources and/or recycled material.

Print ISBN   978 1 908407 06 1
ebook ISBN   978 1 908407 07 8

Typeset by Regent Typesetting, London
Printed in Great Britain by Hobbs the Printers, Totton, Hampshire

This book is dedicated to the memory of Arsineh Gaspariance, a long-term colleague, staff member and friend of many at Doughty Street Chambers, who sadly passed away this year. There will always be times where despite huge determination, positivity and bravery there is only so much that current medicine can do.

Foreword

by The Hon Mr Justice Collins

As the introduction pertinently points out, the regulation of health-care professionals is in a state of flux. This is described as a practical handbook. So it is, and a very useful one, not only for practitioners who are instructed in hearings before the various disciplinary bodies or on appeal to a tribunal or court but also for those who take part in such hearings or undertake preparatory work for them in various capacities.

The focus is on five regulators. They deal with many thousands of professionals and, since the sanctions which may be imposed can affect the ability of those professionals to work, there is not only a need to act fairly but also a need to comply in particular with article 6 of the European Convention on Human Rights. This should not lead to any real problems provided the legal principles, helpfully set out in the first chapter of this book, are properly applied. But it is essential that all those who are in any way involved in, or are likely to be involved in, the disciplinary processes applicable should be aware of the material principles.

Unfortunately, although the procedures are broadly intended to produce not only fairness to all parties but decisions which are made within a reasonable time, they are not identical in each of the five regulators. However, the legal principles to be applied are common to all. There are now a considerable number of cases in the Administrative Court which have set out those principles. Many of these are unreported and so the citations in chapter one are particularly valuable for anyone who needs to know how to deal with particular issues which may arise in individual cases.

A real concern, which stems from the increase in the workload of the regulatory bodies, is that there are substantial delays and hearings can take far too long. The two problems to an extent go together. But delays and lengthy hearings not only increase costs but also increase the pressure on registrants who are involved, particularly if they are subjected to interim orders or are in fact innocent. All those involved should take all steps which can reasonably be taken to narrow the issues and to avoid prolixity in hearings. A degree of firmness by panel chairs, with an input from legal advisers, is in my view desirable and it is surely in the interest of the various professionals that unnecessary delays and lengthy hearings should be avoided. This handbook gives practical advice which will enable cases to be prepared and presented in as efficient a manner as possible in order to achieve as speedy a process as is compatible with fairness. And the advice deals with the particular requirements of the procedures laid down for the regulatory body in question.

The final chapter deals with the Independent Safeguarding Authority which, albeit not directly regulatory, may make orders against those who work with vulnerable individuals and who have been found guilty of criminal offences or whose conduct has been such that regulatory sanctions have been imposed upon them. It focuses on the barring scheme and provides valuable advice and information.

Whatever changes may be made, the legal principles applicable will remain the same. Furthermore, the advice on how to prepare and present cases will continue to be of the greatest assistance. I have no doubt that this handbook is a necessary aid not only for practitioners but for all who are, or are likely to be, involved in regulatory proceedings. I am accordingly happy to commend it.

Mr Justice Collins
Administrative Court
Royal Courts of Justice
London

July 2012

Introduction

The changing face of healthcare regulation

The regulation of professional discipline for healthcare professionals, commonly referred to as fitness to practise proceedings, is in a constant state of flux. Currently, all regulators have their own specific rules, and their own procedures. The Law Commission's far-reaching consultation *The regulation of health and social care professionals* closed on 31 May 2012 with a report and draft bill not anticipated before February 2014.[1] It aims for consistency in the way health professional regulators are governed. Its most fundamental proposal is that all regulators should be subject to one overarching statute rather than the current patchwork of individual statutes. It contemplates broad powers for regulators to set up, under a single statute, their own processes and structures, and to draft their own rules It also considers a Unified Tribunal Service, and asks whether, following determinations by regulators, there should be a right of appeal other than to the High Court, and whether costs and financial penalties should be more widely available within this jurisdiction. Legislation is promised for 2015, but with no place in the current parliamentary timetable, it may be a long way off. So, while these proposals may appear to provide a skeleton of consistency, real differences in the way that individual regulators operate are likely to remain for some considerable time.

Aims of this book

This book is, first and foremost, a practical handbook setting out the preparation, practice and procedure for professional disciplinary hearings before five healthcare regulators: the General Medical Council (GMC), the Nursing and Midwifery Council (NMC), Health

---

1   Available at http://lawcommission.justice.gov.uk/consultations/closed-
    pending-report.htm.

and Care Professions Council (HCPC), General Dental Council (GDC) and General Optical Council (GOC) (herein, 'the councils'). No significance should be attached to the fact that these regulators have been singled out while four other regulators subject to Council for Healthcare Regulatory Excellence (CHRE) oversight[2] have not been included. Portability and the key experience and expertise of the author group determined its length, and it was simply not practical to address every single health regulator within this edition.

The book is intended for lay advisers, registrants, trade union officials and lawyers new to these areas of disciplinary work, and can be used as a self-contained guide by those seeking practical and tactical advice on how to conduct or provide advice in such a case. The general principles relating to the healthcare regulators that are the subject of this book are fully set out, as well as a chapter on linked litigation and its potential impact on the regulatory process. Other cross-cutting issues are also addressed, and we have included a chapter specifically devoted to the thorny and growing issue of referrals to the Independent Safeguarding Agency (ISA) and appeals from inclusion on the barred lists.

Among the practical difficulties for registrants and those representing them are:

- How to remember whether hearings are conducted in three discrete stages, two stages, or before a Health Committee, a Conduct and Competence Committee or a Fitness to Practise Panel.
- How to get the terminology right. Terminology matters and an understanding of the specific rules is obviously a cornerstone to effective representation of registrants.
- How to go beyond the limited nature of the rules. The rules, as in any area of law, only provide so much detail.
- How a registrant should respond at an investigation stage.
- What a registrant or his or her representative should expect on the first day of a hearing.
- What is meant by 'insight' or 'impairment'?
- What mitigation might be of most use at the sanction stage.

These are just a few of the issues about which registrants and representatives need assistance, and which this book aims to provide.

---

2   The General Chiropractic Council (GCC), General Osteopathic Council (GOsC), General Pharmaceutical Council (GPhC) and Pharmaceutical Society of Northern Ireland (PSNI).

Scope and structure of the book

Each chapter is self-contained. It enables those with more time to spare to read the chapters relevant to their needs in totality, while allowing a busy practitioner to quickly navigate and locate the relevant part of a chapter or chapters. The general chapters (1, 7 and 8) literally envelope the regulator-specific chapters and there are extensive cross-references between chapters 2–6 and 1, 7 and 8. We have contained general applicable law and principles within one chapter, allowing the regulator-specific chapters the space to address the issues as they relate to that regulator but cross-referring back to chapter 1 for a fuller discussion of the general legal principles and general case-law.

Chapter 1 provides the general backbone of the book, addressing general legal principles that cross-cut all the healthcare regulators featured within this book (and others not featured). This chapter contains a detailed account and analysis of current law in this field, relevant extracts from case-law and addresses the applicability of the European Convention on Human Rights (ECHR) to these regulators. The stress of proceedings that can strip an individual of his or her only known profession and livelihood are not to be underestimated, and the importance of substantive and procedural safeguards are fundamental. Among a vast range of topics, there is also guidance on evidence, particularly the approach to hearsay evidence given the recent cases of *R (Bonhoeffer) v General Medical Council*[3] in the regulatory context and *Al-Khawaja and Tahery v UK*.[4]

As indicated, five regulators are the focus of this book, and each has its own chapter.

- Chapter 2: The GMC – responsible for regulating doctors.
- Chapter 3: The NMC – the regulator for nurses and midwives.
- Chapter 4: The HCPC currently regulates 16 professions – arts therapists, biomedical scientists, chiropodists/podiatrists, clinical scientists, dieticians, hearing aid dispensers, occupational therapists, operating department practitioners, orthopists, paramedics, physiotherapists, practitioner psychologists, prosthetists/orthotists, radiographers, speech and language therapists and, as of 1 August 2012, social workers.

---

3   [2011] EWHC 1585 (Admin).
4   [2011] ECHR 2127 (Grand Chamber).

- Chapter 5: The GDC which regulates dentists, dental nurses, dental technicians, clinical dental technicians, dental hygienists, dental therapists and orthodontic therapists.
- Chapter 6: The GOC which regulates optometrists, dispensing opticians, student opticians and optical businesses.

Chapters 2–6 are the regulator specific chapters, with one chapter dedicated to the specific rules and procedures of each council. The book provides a roadmap through GMC (chapter 2), NMC (chapter 3), HCPC (chapter 4) GDC (chapter 5) and GOC (chapter 6) proceedings with reference to rules, practice, convention, tactics and procedure. As indicated above, these can be read as stand-alone chapters, but all provide cross-referencing back to the relevant parts of chapter 1 to allow quick reference to further detail relating to case law and the application of general principles across the regulators.

Linked litigation often goes hand-in-hand with fitness to practise proceedings. For example, where a registrant is referred to their regulator because of a criminal conviction, the issue of parallel criminal proceedings arises. There may be judicial reviews arising out of preliminary decisions by regulators, or issues relating to disclosure of patient information and the compatibility of such actions with data protection laws. When advising on or conducting a regulatory matter the impact of such linked litigation upon the regulatory process must be carefully considered as it may have a significant evidential or tactical impact upon how a registrant should conduct themselves once a referral has been made to a regulator. Chapter 7 provides guidance on these linked litigation issues.

Last, but by no means least, chapter 8, provides the law and guidance on the current barring scheme operated by the ISA which determines referrals for individuals considered to be unsuited to working with children and vulnerable adults. Many registrants facing professional disciplinary proceedings can also face a referral to the ISA. This is a developing area of law, but it is an important one as the ISA does not defer to the decision of a regulator and therefore a registrant could for example, have the case against them dismissed at half-time by their regulator only to find themselves barred on a long-term basis by the ISA and unable to work in their chosen field as a consequence.

Due to the practical emphasis of this book, readers may find that further research may be necessary on the law itself, especially in new, developing, specialist or complex areas.

Acknowledgements

Many thanks to Joanne Howard of Thompsons Solicitors for comments on chapter 4, Mandie Lavin at the General Optical Council for advice on chapter 6 and, of course, enormous gratitude to LAG and particularly Esther Pilger for supporting this publication and all her work on it.

Despite the assistance we have had, all mistakes remain our own and we would be grateful for any comments or corrections via Gemma Hobcraft at g.hobcraft@doughtystreet.co.uk.

The law is stated as at May 2012 although where it has been possible to include further developments we have endeavoured to do so.

We could not let this introduction pass without acknowledging the fact that during the preparation of this book, three of the authors became first time parents – little Benjamin, Leonora and Sebastien have all been very forgiving in allowing the book to reach completion.

While every attempt has been made to ensure the accuracy of the contents of this book, the authors can accept no responsibility for advice given in reliance on its contents

Christopher Sallon QC, Jon Whitfield QC,
Gemma Hobcraft, Amanda Hart,
Nicole Ridgwell,[5] Sue Sleeman, Eloise Power,
Louise Price and Steve Broach

Members of the Professional Discipline and Regulatory Team
Doughty Street Chambers
May 2012

---

5   Nicole Ridgwell is legal officer for the Eastern and South Eastern regions of the Royal College of Nursing (RCN).

Authors

Christopher Sallon QC is the head of Doughty Street Chambers Regulatory and Financial Crime Team. He represents doctors and dentists in professional disciplinary proceedings before the Fitness to Practice Panels of the General Medical Council and the General Dental Council. He undertakes the defence of those doctors and dentists and other professionals charged with criminal offences arising out of their professional activities. He also defends in criminal cases which involve medicine and forensic science, and corporate manslaughter in which issues of health and safety arise.

Christopher represented the Forensic Science Service in the Home Office Review into forensic work carried out during the investigation into the death of Damilola Taylor. He subsequently served as a member of the Independent Advisory Group of the Forensic Science Service, and continues to advise forensic service providers on regulatory matters, data protection and related criminal justice issues. He was a former member of the Professional Conduct Committee of the Bar Council. He is licensed by the Bar Standards Board to accept public access work. Christopher was lead author for chapter 6 on the General Optical Council.

Jon Whitfield QC has specialised in criminal cases of homicide, terrorism and fraud involving issues of mental health, medical and forensic expertise and, professional misconduct. This has led to his advising in medical disciplinary proceedings and sitting as a legal assessor on GMC cases since 2007. Jon has worked with consistent success in some of the most high profile cases of recent times. He responds well to the pressures of work putting in long hours to assimilate the large amounts of information needed to successfully argue cases of this gravity. His style is robust and combative which compliments his intellectual ability to reduce complex evidence to an essential core. Twenty five years of successful work as a junior were rewarded by his taking Silk in 2010. He is licensed by the Bar Standards Board

xvi   *Professional discipline and healthcare regulators / Authors*

to accept public access work and is a member of two professional referral schemes by which those accused of crime or professional misconduct can gain access to advice quickly and efficiently. Jon was lead author for chapter 1 on General legal principles.

Gemma Hobcraft specialises in health law, particularly professional discipline (representing a wide range of medical and health care practitioners, including doctors, nurses, midwives, health visitors, psychologists and physiotherapists in fitness to practise proceedings before their regulators) and health related aspects of public law. Gemma has a particular interest and expertise in reproductive health and rights – for nine years prior to coming to the Bar, Gemma was heavily involved in advocacy for young people's sexual and reproductive rights at the local, national and international level. She has been a lay member of the Human Fertilisation and Embryology Authority (HFEA) since September 2008 and is currently Chair of the Authority's Ethics and Law Advisory Committee. Gemma is a co-opted member of the Executive Committee of the Association of Disciplinary and Regulatory Lawyers (ARDL) and the Bursary Officer of the Human Rights Lawyers Association (HRLA). As of July 2012 she is licensed by the Bar Standards Board to accept public access work. Gemma was lead author for chapter 2 on the General Medical Council.

Amanda Hart is a specialist in regulatory and employment law. She has over five years experience of Health Professions Council and Nursing and Midwifery Council fitness to practise proceedings, and has defended health professionals accused of a wide range of conduct, competence and health issues. She also specialises in employment and discrimination law representing claimants at Employment Tribunals, Employment Appeals Tribunals and the Court of Appeal. She is rated as a tier 3 leading junior in Legal500 for her employment work. Prior to being called to the bar Amanda was a national union official for the National Association of Teachers in Further and Higher Education. Amanda was co-author with Nicole Ridgewell (from the RCN) of chapter 3 on the Nursing and Midwifery Council.

Nicole Ridgwell is Legal Officer for the Eastern and South-Eastern regions of the Royal College of Nursing. She acts for nurses and healthcare assistants in regulatory and public law matters. She regularly appears before and advises clients in relation to referrals to the Nursing and Midwifery Council. Nicole previously worked in immigration law and in a number of voluntary and charitable organisations.

Sue Sleeman is an employment and regulatory law practitioner. She regularly appears before a variety of professional disciplinary tribunals and regulatory bodies, representing individuals facing allegations of misconduct and lack of competence.

While the majority of her regulatory work is on behalf of health professionals, including nurses, midwives, physiotherapists and paramedics she also represents other professionals such as teachers, college lecturers and social workers. Before coming to the Bar, Sue worked in the trade union movement, initially as a lay representative in UNISON and later for the NUT and the Chartered Society of Physiotherapy. Sue's employment practice is claimant based and in the main she acts for trade union members bringing claims in the employment tribunals for unfair dismissal, discrimination and whistleblowing. Sue was lead author for chapter 4 on the Health and Care Professions Council.

Eloise Power is a civil practitioner with a practice focusing on the rights of individuals in the areas of clinical negligence, product liability, personal injury, regulatory law and inquests. She also acts in civil claims for damages against public authorities. Before joining Doughty Street Chambers Eloise practised as a solicitor at South West London Law Centres for several years and also lectured on the Bar Vocational Course at BPP Law School. Eloise was lead author for chapter 5 on the General Dental Council.

Louise Price specialises in regulatory and employment law and in her practice regularly deals with the interplay between employment tribunal claims and professional regulatory proceedings. She also acts in public law matters with a focus on the rights of the individual in community care and education contexts. Prior to joining Doughty Street Chambers, Louise had worked for the International Labour Organisation and domestically as a specialist adviser for the Citizen's Advice Bureaux. Louise was the lead author for chapter 7 on linked litigation and its impact upon the regulatory process.

Steve Broach is a public lawyer whose regulatory practice largely involves judicial review challenges and statutory appeals in relation to decisions of professional regulators and appeals to the Upper Tribunal against decisions of the Independent Safeguarding Authority (ISA). Steve recently succeeded in a judicial review challenge to a decision to re-open a case in which the NMC had previously found no case to answer (*R (B) v NMC* (2012)). Steve acted for the appellant in *PH v ISA* (2012) and was junior counsel for the Royal College of Nursing in its intervention at the Court of Appeal stage in *SB v ISA*, both considered in chapter 8. Prior to coming to Doughty Street Chambers Steve held a number of senior roles with leading voluntary sector disability organisations, including the National Autistic Society and the *Every Disabled Child Matters* campaign. Steve was voted Young Barrister of the Year at the Legal Aid Lawyer of the Year Awards in 2011. Steve was the lead author for chapter 8 on the Independent Safeguarding Authority.

Contents

Table of cases

Table of statutes

Table of statutory instruments

Table of European legislation

Table of guidance

Abbreviations

ADR	alternative dispute resolution
ASBO	anti-social behaviour order
CEA 1995	Civil Evidence Act 1995
CET	continuing education and training
CHRE	Council for Healthcare Regulatory Excellence
CJA 2003	Criminal Justice Act 2003
Copine	Combating Paedophile Information Networks in Europe
CPD	continuing professional development
CPIA 1996	Criminal Procedure Investigations Act 1996
CPS	Crown Prosecution Service
CPSM	Council for the Professions Supplementary to Medicine
CQC	Care Quality Commission
CRB	Criminal Records Bureau
CRHP	Council for the Regulation of Healthcare Professionals
DBS	Disclosure and Barring Service
DPA 1998	Data Protection Act 1998
ECHR	European Convention on Human Rights
ECtHR	European Court of Human Rights
FOIA 2000	Freedom of Information Act 2000
FTP	fitness to practise
GCC	General Chiropractic Council
GDC	General Dental Council
GMC	General Medical Council
GOC	General Optical Council
GOsC	General Osteopathic Council
GPhC	General Pharmaceutical Council
GSCC	General Social Care Council
GTCE	General Teaching Council for England
HCA	healthcare assistant
HCPC	Health and Care Professions Council
HPC	Health Professions Council
IBB	Independent Barring Board
ILEX	Institute of Legal Executives
ISA	Independent Safeguarding Authority
MA 1983	Medical Act 1983
MHPS	Maintaining high professional standards in the modern NHS
MoU	memorandum of understanding

MPS	Medical Protection Society
MPTS	Medical Practitioners Tribunal Service
NCAS	National Clinical Assessment Service
NMC	Nursing and Midwifery Council
NMO 2001	Nursing and Midwifery Order 2001 SI No 253
NPSA	National Patient Safety Agency
OA 1958	Opticians Act 1958
OA 1989	Opticians Act 1989
OCCS	Optical Consumer Complaints Service
OHPA	Office of the Health Professions Adjudicator
PACE	Police and Criminal Evidence Act 1984
PALS	Patient Advisory Liaison Service
PFA 2012	Protection of Freedoms Act 2012
POCA 1999	Protection of Children Act 1999
POCA list	Protection of Children Act list
POVA list	Protection of Vulnerable Adults list
PSNI	Pharmaceutical Society of Northern Ireland
ROA 1974	Rehabilitation of Offenders Act 1974
RPS	Royal Pharmaceutical Society of Great Britain
SGC	Sentencing Guidelines Council
SJP	structured judgment process
SRA	Solicitors Regulation Authority
SVGA 2006	Safeguarding Vulnerable Groups Act 2006

General legal principles

continued

Key points
Key legal issues in fitness to practise proceedings

- *Fit to practise:* Means being competent, respectable, honest, trustworthy, able to work with patients and others, and in sufficiently good health to practice.
- *The European Convention on Human Rights (ECHR):* Applies to regulatory proceedings, although it may not if there is no prospect of a sanction affecting a registrant's ability to practice. The most important articles are article 6 (right to a fair trial) and article 8 (right to privacy).
- *Charges:* A registrant should be informed of the allegation and supporting facts promptly, in plain language, accurately and in sufficient detail to answer them. Serious allegations such as dishonesty, sexual misconduct, etc must be pleaded.
- *Amending charges:* Should be done as soon as practicable but may be done later if no unfairness is caused. A registrant must be given time to reassess and re-prepare his or her case.
- *Delay:* A case should be heard within a reasonable time. If there is delay it will not found an abuse of process unless incurable unfairness is caused. No abuse flows from delay caused by a registrant.
- *Disclosure:* A regulator has a continuing duty to review the unused material it holds and disclose material that may undermine its case or may assist the registrant. There is no duty on the regulator to gather evidence that helps the registrant. However, if a registrant is prejudiced by a lack of access to material a regulator can readily obtain, it should assist if it considers it reasonable so to do.

Interim orders hearing

- *Burden & standard of proof:* The regulator brings the case and while there is no strict burden and standard as understood in for example a full FTP hearing, an Interim Orders Panel may only impose conditions or suspend a registrant when it is *satisfied that there may be impairment* of fitness which poses a *real risk* to the public, the public interest or the profession.
- *Evidence:* Information may be scant. No evidence is called. The registrant is permitted to make representations. The IOP makes no findings of fact.

- *Decision*: Any order must be *necessary* to protect the public, otherwise in the public interest (including upholding confidence in and standing of the profession) or the registrant's interest.
- *Reasons*: Reasons must be given for any order and the length of the order.

Full fitness to practise hearings

- *Evidence:* Hearsay is admissible even if it is the principal evidence, but there should be safeguards and the overall fairness of proceedings should be carefully assessed.
- *Evidence:* Character is now important at *all* stages of a fitness to practise hearing and the panel must be carefully advised on the evidential use and weight of good or bad character.
- *Panel impartiality:* The panel should be, and be seen to be, divorced from any interest in the allegations, the parties or the result. (This also applies to Interim Orders Panels.)
- *Legal assessor:* Is there to advise on law and procedure. The legal assessor plays no part in determining facts. Advice should be given with all parties present. The legal assessor is also there to assist (but not advise) the parties on disputed law or procedure. (This also applies to Interim Orders Panels.)
- *Specialist advisers:* Are present to help interpret expert evidence. Advice should be given with all parties present so they may challenge it if they wish.
- *Legal representation:* A registrant is entitled to be represented at fitness to practise or interim order hearings since these may materially affect the right to practice.
- *Absence of registrant:* Provided all reasonable effort has been made to inform the registrant, the interim order or fitness to practise hearing may proceed in his or her absence.
- *Staged process:* The Fitness to Practise Panel will: a) consider evidence to make findings of fact; b) determine current impairment based upon such misconduct or deficient performance as is proved on the facts; c) consider what sanction is necessary to meet any identified risk.
- *Burden and standard of proof regarding the facts:* The burden is on the regulator. The standard is the balance of probability.
- *Half-time submissions:* May be made in accordance with *Galbraith* (see para 1.348 below).

- *Impairment:* Is a question of *judgment* for the panel. There is no burden or standard of proof. It may be based on past facts but impairment must be *current*. The panel must consider matters looking forward and assess risk whether in misconduct, performance etc.
- *Misconduct:* Difficult to define, but it is a *serious failure* to adhere to accepted professional standards. It means more than just negligence. It is likely to be repeat behaviour but may only be one serious event.
- *Deficient professional performance:* Means conduct in practice or, practice-related activities, that has *fallen far short of the standards expected of a reasonably competent practitioner* and done so on more than one occasion. One exceptionally serious event may suffice. A registrant will be required to undergo assessment.
- *Criminal findings:* Are always treated with the utmost seriousness, may, and frequently do, found a case in misconduct.
- *Adverse health:* Poor health that affects the quality of service to patients or their safety may found a case of impairment. A registrant will be required to undergo assessment.
- *Determination by another professional body:* May also found a case in impairment.
- *Sanctions:* Should be *proportionate and necessary* to meet the risk identified by the panel in their finding of current impairment. The interests of the public, patients and profession come before that of the practitioner albeit the public should not be deprived of a competent registrant longer than is necessary to meet the risk. Cases of dishonesty, sexual misconduct and child pornography are always treated very seriously. Addictions may be met by conditions to facilitate the registrant's safe return to practice. Likewise deficient performance, but the emphasis is on safety and if it cannot be secured then suspension or erasure will result.
- *Jurisdiction:* Matters that occurred outside the UK and before a registrant was registered may nonetheless found a case because the emphasis is on public protection and the profession.
- *Key documents and rules:* The regulator's published guidance will be carefully considered by a panel particularly when considering sanctions based on breaches. Each regulator has its own procedural rules to follow in addition to the matters set out in this chapter.
- *Reasons:* The panel should give *sufficient* reasons on the facts for the registrant to understand what has been proved against

him or her. The panel should give *full and detailed* reasons on impairment and sanction sufficient to be clear to any reviewing tribunal or court.

- *Voluntary erasure:* A process whereby some registrants are able to withdraw from their profession by applying to their regulator for removal from the register. It is only permitted if there are no FTP issues, or no serious FTP issues, and the latter are admitted. The registrant should genuinely be leaving practice and it must be in the public interest to be dealt with in this way (eg, in cases involving serious health problems).

Introduction

1.1   All healthcare regulators that deal with a registrant's[1] fitness to practise (FTP) are concerned with the same broad values – namely, upholding patient safety and maintaining the standards of the professions such that the public may have confidence in healthcare providers. This necessarily involves receiving, investigating and determining matters of complaint. There are a number of fundamental legal principles applicable to these regulatory functions and any proceedings that follow.

1.2   While the principles affect all who serve or care for the public, this book deals with healthcare professionals regulated by the General Medical Council (GMC), Nursing and Midwifery Council (NMC), General Dental Council (GDC), General Optical Council (GOC) and Health and Care Professions Council (HCPC).

1.3   Perhaps the most oft-stated principle is that individuals have a 'right to a fair trial' and, whether this is expressed in terms of European or domestic legislation or case-law, it encompasses several issues including delay, disclosure of information, attendance at hearings, admission of evidence, reasons for decisions, the effect of sanctions and so on. Regulatory proceedings fall somewhere between criminal and civil process and as such guidance on some of these principles and the way they are implemented may be drawn from both branches of the law, albeit with a tendency towards criminal process given the nature of regulatory tribunal hearings.

---

1   The term 'registrant' is used as a generic term to cover healthcare practitioners whose practice and conduct are governed by regulatory bodies.

1.4   However, matters are complicated by the fact that each of the regulators has its own set of procedural rules or 'orders of council'. They are not always the same. This is particularly important when looking at how and why a case has been referred to the relevant panel. Each regulator has its own staged process and some apply slightly different tests. Again it is important to be aware of these differences when considering case-management, since non-compliance with directions may lead to adverse inferences. Furthermore, some regulators control cases by way of a case-manager, while others have management hearings and some a combination of both. The same caution should be applied to reviews post-hearing. While the basic principles of law may be the same, there are nuances of language, procedure and style that may wrong-foot the unwary.

1.5   Examples of differences are:

- Some of the regulators' rules allow service by email whereas others do not, or only some documents or notices and not others.
- Some panels hear submissions, retire and make a decision at each stage of facts, impairment and sanction. Others retire and consider all matters at the same time.
- Some regulators have a Fitness to Practise Panel which hears a variety of cases including matters of conduct and/or health, whereas others have a separate Conduct and Competence Committee (CCC) and a Health Committee (HC).
- As can be seen, regulators have different names for their panels despite fulfilling the same functions.

1.6   In this chapter the term 'panel' is used as a generic term to cover the Fitness to Practise Panel, Interim Orders Panel (IOP) and the other panels or committees operated by the various regulators. Furthermore while reference may be made to the GMC, NMC or other rules to introduce or illustrate a point, *care should be taken to apply the correct council rules/orders of council when arguing matters pertinent to a case.*

1.7   The principles outlined below follow the timeline of proceedings from charge to sanction.

The meaning of fitness to practise

1.8   The following principles are adapted from a policy statement by the GMC.[2] While they are formulated for doctors they set out the basic

---

2   Approved in 2001. The quotes from the GMC's *Good medical practice* are from the 2006 edition.

headings under which the fitness to practise of all healthcare professionals are likely to be assessed. Key words are highlighted.

1.9   To practise safely, registrants must be *competent* in what they do. They must establish and maintain *effective relationships* with patients, respect patients' autonomy and act responsibly and appropriately if they or a colleague fall ill and their performance suffers.

1.10   But these attributes, while essential, are not enough. Registrants have a *respected* position in society and their work gives them privileged access to patients, some of whom may be very vulnerable. A registrant whose conduct has shown that he or she cannot *justify the trust* placed in him or her should not continue in unrestricted practice while that remains the case.

1.11   In short, the public is entitled to expect that their healthcare providers are *fit to practise*, and follow principles of *good practice* published by the relevant regulator.[3] These set out the standards of competence, care and conduct expected of doctors, under the following main headings:[4]

- *Good (clinical) care* – registrants must provide good standards of clinical care, must practise within the limits of their competence, and must ensure that patients are not put at unnecessary risk.
- *Maintaining good (medical) practise* – registrants must keep up to date with developments in their field, maintain their skills and audit their performance.
- *Relationships with patients* – registrants must develop and maintain successful relationships with their patients, by respecting patients' autonomy and other rights.
- *Working with colleagues* – registrants must work effectively with their colleagues.
- *Teaching and training* – where registrants have teaching responsibilities they must develop the skills, attitudes and practices of a competent teacher.
- *Probity* – registrants must be honest and trustworthy.
- *Health* – registrants must not allow their own health condition to endanger patients.

1.12   The healthcare regulators have legal powers to take action where it appears that a registrant's fitness to practise may be affected by poor skills or performance, ill health, misconduct or a criminal conviction or caution.

---

3 See, for example, *Good medical practice* published by the GMC.
4 Drawn from *Good medical practice* but of general application.

The healthcare councils' role in regulation

1.13   All human beings make mistakes from time to time. Healthcare professionals are no different. While occasional one-off mistakes need to be thoroughly investigated and any harm put right by those involved, they are unlikely in themselves to indicate a fitness to practise problem. *Good medical practice* puts it this way:

> Serious or persistent failures to meet the standards in this booklet will put your registration at risk.[5]

1.14   A question of fitness to practise is likely to arise if:

- *A registrant's performance has harmed patients or put patients at risk of harm.* A risk of harm will usually be demonstrated by a series of incidents that cause concern locally. These incidents may indicate persistent technical failings or other repeated departures from good practice which are not being, or cannot be, safely managed locally or local management has been tried and has failed.

- *A registrant has shown a deliberate or reckless disregard of clinical responsibilities towards patients.* An isolated lapse from high standards of conduct – such as an atypical rude outburst – would not in itself suggest that the registrant's fitness to practise was in question. Misconduct, whether criminal or not, which indicates a lack of integrity on the part of the registrant, an unwillingness to practise ethically or responsibly, or a serious lack of insight into obvious problems of poor practice will bring a registrant's registration into question.

- *A registrant's health is compromising patient safety.* The regulator does not need to be involved merely because a registrant is unwell, even if the illness is serious. However, a registrant's fitness to practise is brought into question if it appears that the registrant has a serious medical condition (including an addiction to drugs or alcohol) *and* the registrant does not appear to be following appropriate medical advice about modifying his or her practice as necessary in order to minimise the risk to patients.

- *A registrant has abused a patient's trust or violated a patient's autonomy or other fundamental rights.* Conduct that shows that a registrant has acted without regard for patients' rights or feelings, or has abused his or her professional position as a registrant, will usually give rise to questions about a registrant's fitness to practise.

---

5   *Good medical practice,* page 05.

- *A registrant has behaved dishonestly, fraudulently or in a way designed to mislead or harm others.* The registrant's behaviour was such that public confidence in doctors generally might be undermined if the GMC did not take action.

1.15 The advice above is only illustrative of the sort of behaviour which could call registration into question. *Good medical practice* and other published guidance provide a more complete picture of behaviour of this kind, but even that is not exhaustive. The outcome of any case will always depend on its own particular facts.

1.16 While the above is adapted from the guidance published by the GMC, it encapsulates the issues that should guide all healthcare practitioners. The other professions covered by this work have similar codes of conduct or statements of ethics.

1.17 As the above makes clear, everyone makes mistakes and the majority are dealt with by means other than fitness to practise procedures. It is only when a practitioner falls 'seriously short' of what is expected and this adversely impacts upon patients or the profession that it is appropriate to instigate proceedings.

The European Convention on Human Rights

> It is undoubtedly the case that the European Convention on Human Rights (ECHR) applies to regulatory proceedings, although there may be argument when there is no prospect of suspension or erasure.
>
> The better approach to case preparation and presentation is to adopt the *spirit* of, in particular, article 6 (right to a fair trial), the letter of which is frequently reflected in domestic case-law.

1.18 The two articles of the ECHR which have most relevance to regulatory proceedings are articles 6 and 8. They respectively provide for what are colloquially called the 'right to a fair trial' and 'the right to privacy'.

Article 6

1.19 Article 6 of the ECHR guarantees certain minimum rights when facing a trial and provides as follows:

> 1. In the determination of his civil rights and obligations or of any criminal charge against him, everyone is entitled to a fair and public hearing within a reasonable time by an independent and impartial tribunal established by law. Judgment shall be pronounced publicly

but the press and public may be excluded from all or part of the trial in the interest of morals, public order or national security in a democratic society, where the interests of juveniles or the protection of the private lives of the parties so require, or to the extent strictly necessary in the opinion of the court in special circumstances where publicity would prejudice the interests of justice.

2. Everyone charged with a criminal offence shall be presumed innocent until proved guilty according to law.

3. Everyone charged with a criminal offence has the following minimum rights:

(a) to be informed promptly, in a language which he understands and in detail, of the nature and cause of the accusation against him;

(b) to have adequate time and facilities for the preparation of his defence;

(c) to defend himself in person or through legal assistance of his own choosing or, if he has not sufficient means to pay for legal assistance, to be given it free when the interests of justice so require;

(d) to examine or have examined witnesses against him and to obtain the attendance and examination of witnesses on his behalf under the same conditions as witnesses against him;

(e) to have the free assistance of an interpreter if he cannot understand or speak the language used in court.

1.20   Therefore:

a) A proper hearing should be:
   i)   fair;
   ii) public;
   iii) reasonably timeous.

b) A proper tribunal should be:
   i)   legally empowered;
   ii) impartial;
   iii) independent.

c) A defendant has the right to:
   i)   prompt and proper information;
   ii) time and facility to prepare;
   iii) choose to represent himself or herself or, appoint a lawyer;
   iv) funds for a lawyer if necessary;
   v)   challenge and question his accuser(s);
   vi) an interpreter if one is needed.

1.21   The above all seem quite straightforward and obvious, but the principles have been applied/misapplied and interpreted/re-interpreted through case-law such that they do not always appear to mean what they say. There is also the issue of whether the ECHR applies to regulatory proceedings at all.

1.22   Since the majority decision of the European Court of Human Rights (ECtHR) in *Le Compte, Van Leuven and De Meyere v Belgium*[6] it has been accepted that a decision of a professional tribunal affecting the right to practise the profession is a determination of civil rights and obligations.

1.23   In *Wickramsinghe v UK*[7] it was held that disciplinary proceedings before the GMC constituted a civil rather than criminal case. Similarly in *General Medical Council v Michael Pembrey*[8] it was held that article 6 was applicable to Professional Conduct Committee proceedings since these were civil proceedings within the meaning of the article. This was endorsed by the Privy Council in *Preiss v General Dental Council*.[9]

1.24   The first line of article 6(1) makes it plain that the provisions will apply whenever the outcome of proceedings determines a person's civil rights. This includes a registrant's right to continue to practise in his or her profession. Thus it applies in principle to any disciplinary process where erasure or suspension is possible – see *Ghosh v General Medical Council*,[10] a decision of the Privy Council. There are, however, two lines of approach to this.

1.25   In *R v General Medical Council ex p Kypros Nicolaides*[11] Tucker J said that the question of whether article 6 applies to the proceedings does not arise at the outset but depends on the outcome of the case. This is because the result may not affect his or her right to practice.

1.26   On the other hand, in *Tehrani v United Kingdom Central Council for Nursing Midwifery and Health Visiting*[12] it was said that:

> ... if the petitioner can establish that the disciplinary proceedings *could* result in a finding that would constitute a determination of her civil rights and obligations, the decision to initiate those disciplinary proceedings is open to challenge as being incompatible with the petitioner's convention rights.[13] [Emphasis added.]

1.27   In *R (Johnson) v Nursing and Midwifery Council*,[14] a case before the Professional Conduct Committee, Beatson J approached the case from both the domestic and the ECHR viewpoints. In *R (Madan) v*

6   (1981) 4 EHRR 1.
7   [1998] EHRLR 338.
8   [2002] Lloyd's Rep Med 434.
9   [2001] Lloyd's Rep Med 491.
10 [2000] 1 WLR 1915.
11 [2001] Lloyd's Rep Med 525.
12 [2001] SC 581.
13 Per Lord Mackay of Drumadoon at para [33].
14 [2008] EWHC 885 (Admin).

General Medical Council[15] Richards J accepted that article 6 applied with respect to interim order proceedings where an interim suspension order was made because it substantially affected M's right to practise.

1.28   In *R (Bonhoeffer) v General Medical Council*[16] Stadlen J approached the issue of admitting hearsay evidence under rule 34 of the GMC (Fitness to Practise) Rules 2004[17] (which provide for the admission of evidence provided it is relevant, fair and desirable so to do) by reference to article 6 and both criminal and disciplinary case-law.

1.29   It is perhaps rather artificial to decide whether to apply article 6 principles depending on the possible outcome of a case. In any event, there is considerable overlap between the principles of European law, domestic law, natural justice and many of the regulator's own rules of practise. It is submitted that the better approach is to proceed on the basis that article 6 does in fact apply both by letter and in spirit. That is certainly the approach adopted in this chapter.

Article 8

1.30   Article 8 of the ECHR provides that:

> 1. Everyone has the right to respect for his private and family life, his home and his correspondence.
> 2. There shall be no interference by a public authority with the exercise of this right except such as is in accordance with the law and is necessary in a democratic society in the interests of national security, public safety or the economic well-being of the country, for the prevention of disorder or crime, for the protection of health or morals, or for the protection of the rights and freedoms of others.

1.31   While article 8 is more frequently concerned with the rights of patients infringed by healthcare personnel or regulators through mismanagement or misuse of information, the case of *Bonhoeffer* (above and discussed fully under hearsay evidence at para 1.212 below) demonstrates its applicability to regulatory proceedings.

1.32   The 'right to privacy', as this is frequently called, confers a 'right to respect' for the four areas mentioned (privacy, family, home, correspondence), however the protection is qualified not absolute. The right may be infringed in the circumstances specified under clause 2.

15 [2001] EWHC 577 (Admin).
16 [2011] EWHC 1585 (Admin).
17 Contained in the Schedule to the General Medical Council (Fitness to Practise) Rules Order of Council 2004 SI No 2608.

In regulatory proceedings the most relevant circumstances are: in accordance with the law and *necessary* for public safety, or the protection of health or the rights of others.

1.33   There are two aspects to the right: first a right to protection from interference by public authorities; and second, there may be a duty imposed upon authorities to secure respect for those rights from others.

1.34   Regulatory bodies are entitled to investigate allegations and bring proceedings with the intention of protecting the profession, the public or the practitioner. Proceedings brought for these reasons are clearly capable of satisfying the qualification of article 8 thereby permitting interference with a registrant's rights. However, as with all matters of competing rights such as those between the registrant, the complainant and the public interest, there is a balance to be struck. Three particular criticisms may be levelled at regulatory proceedings: delay, publicity and harsh sanction.

1.35   While these have to date been dealt with as article 6 matters infringing the right to a fair trial, they may also be raised under article 8.

Delay and publicity

1.36   Regulatory proceedings frequently have a devastating effect upon the registrant and his or her practice, family and private life. This effect is magnified if an interim order is imposed which either suspends the registrant or, seriously curtails his or her ability to practice by way of conditions. The damage is further exacerbated by the fact that regulatory proceedings frequently take many months, sometimes years, to come to a final hearing. In the meantime the registrant is expected to deal with the pressures placed upon his or her family, etc.

1.37   Given that serious and complex criminal allegations are now routinely concluded within a very few months (and rarely beyond a year), lengthy delay in regulatory proceedings may be unjustifiable, particularly where there are few or no witnesses or the facts are hardly disputed. Frequently there appears to be little or no justification for such delay. Part of the problem may be the routine imposition of an 18-month interim order granted on the basis that the Interim Orders Panel does not know how long the investigation will take or when the case will come before the Fitness to Practise Panel. Delay, whether caused, contributed to or wholly divorced from an interim order should be examined in the light of the registrant's article 8 rights.

1.38   Article 8 places a duty on the regulator not to interfere and to prevent interference by others. This must necessarily include others acting upon its behalf namely its investigatory and regulatory arm. Given this, article 8 may well be engaged when the delay and/or publicity consequent upon proceedings adversely affects the rights protected.

1.39   In *Bonhoeffer* (para 1.28 above) the court took specific note of the fact that serious allegations would adversely affect B's reputation (and thus his private life) if they were proved at first instance even if he were subsequently acquitted on appeal. The damage is already done. The court held that B's right to respect for his reputation and private life are matters to be considered before the case came to trial.

1.40   This healthy dose of reality may be readily imported into an argument regarding the effect that extended delay and publicity has upon a registrant's article 8 rights even where his or her reputation may not be as eminent as B's.

Sanction

1.41   As regards sanction, much is rightly made of the need to protect the professions and uphold standards. Sanctions are imposed which are *necessary* to meet identified risks. However, where there has been delay, publicity, an interim order or other factor that have already adversely affected the registrant's article 8 rights, there may come a point at which the balance tips in favour of the registrant.

1.42   It is submitted that the adverse affect of sanctions upon a registrant's article 8 rights *should* be considered in the light of the whole proceedings and the effect they have had to date, not just in isolation. In *Selvarajan v General Medical Council*[18] it was held that delay may be a mitigating factor on sanctions. Given this, and the approach in *Bonhoeffer*, there is no reason why the cumulative effect of proceedings upon a registrant's article 8 rights should be ignored in mitigation always allowing for deference to the principle of protecting the profession.

18   [2008] EWHC 182 (Admin).

Charges

The charges

> The particulars of the allegation and the facts upon which they are founded should be clear and settled in advance of any hearing.
>
> If in doubt, clarification and/or further and better particulars should be obtained.
>
> A panel may, having heard from both parties, amend either the allegation or the facts provided no injustice is caused but this should be the exception not the rule.

1.43　Healthcare regulators are public authorities and, as stated above, the ECHR applies to disciplinary proceedings.[19] An important right in this respect is to have sufficient and proper notice of the allegation.

1.44　　Article 6(3) provides that everyone charged with a criminal offence has the following minimum rights:

a) to be *informed promptly*, in a language which he understands and *in detail*, of the nature and cause of the accusation against him;

b) to have adequate time and facilities for the preparation of his defence.

1.45　While disciplinary proceedings are not criminal in nature (see *Wickramsinghe v UK*[20] above) what follows demonstrates the application of the above rights in disciplinary proceedings.

1.46　　Domestic law is clearly supported by the requirements of article 6. In *Albert and Le Compte v Belgium*[21] the ECtHR indicated that this principle should apply to disciplinary proceedings. Subsequent caselaw upheld the requirement to list offences giving the date and place thereof, the relevant articles of the Criminal Code and the name of the victim (see *Brozicek v Italy*[22]).

1.47　　In *Gee v General Medical Council*[23] the court held it to be a requirement that the registrant had fair notice of the nature of the evidence to be led in support of the allegations, time to prepare for his defence and, that the panel should make plain which of the allegations of fact, if any, they had found proved.

19　*Preiss v General Dental Council* [2001] UKPC 36 para [9]; *Ghosh v General Medical Council* [2001] UKPC 29 para [31].

20　[1998] EHRLR 338.

21　(1983) 5 EHRR 533.

22　(1989) 112 EHRR 371.

23　[1987] 1 WLR 564.

1.48   Healthcare regulators have taken cognisance of the Criminal Procedure Rules which require an indictment or charge to contain a statement and description of the offence, the relevant legislation and 'such particulars of the conduct constituting the commission of the offence as to make it clear what the prosecutor alleges against the defendant'.[24]

1.49   In fitness to practise proceedings a document variously entitled 'notice of proceedings', 'notice of hearing' or similar is used to identify both the case brought against the registrant and the alleged facts upon which it is based. It is one of the most important documents in the case and should be drafted with some care. Although amendments may be made, there are limitations. It is only fair and reasonable that both parties and the panel have a firm and settled idea of what the case is about before it is under way.

1.50   Each regulator has its own set of rules[25] but the central requirements are as follows:

a) Regarding notice:
- As soon as reasonably practicable after an allegation has been referred to a panel the council's registrar or appointed officer should serve a notice of hearing on the registrant.
- The notice should particularise the allegation against the practitioner and the facts upon which it is based.

b) Regarding case-management – again the procedures vary. Some regulators employ case managers, others use case-management hearings. However, in general either (or their equivalent) may issue directions including such of the following as are appropriate having regard to the nature of the allegation, any representations made by the parties and all other material factors:
- that each party disclose to or inform the other of:
  - the material they intend to rely upon namely documentary evidence, details of the witnesses (this includes the practitioner if giving evidence), signed witness statements, any expert report and skeleton arguments;
  - time estimates;
  - whether or not the health of the practitioner is to be raised as an issue;
- that the practitioner indicates, so far as is practicable:
  - whether the allegation is admitted;
  - which facts are admitted and which remain in dispute;

---

24 Criminal Procedure Rules 2011 SI No 1709 r14.2(1).
25 See GMC (Fitness to Practise) Rules 2004 rr15 and 16 as a good example.

> – which witness evidence is admitted and which witnesses are required for cross-examination; and
> – whether any preliminary legal arguments are to be made;
> • where the allegation is admitted, a direction that the parties produce a statement of agreed facts.

1.51   The above notices and directions post-date the various stages of investigation, case-correspondence and/or hearings that occur before referral to the panel or, the final hearing. The case is thus already some way (perhaps many months) down the line by the time allegations and notices are drafted. The regulator should be in a position to provide precise particulars of the allegation and the facts. Furthermore, any areas of dispute should be defined and refined in the case-management process. The effect of this is that by the time a case comes before the panel the disputed allegations and facts should be clear but, this is not always the case.

1.52   In recent times, the length and detail of notices has increased. This may reflect the requirement to provide sufficient particulars to the registrant so that he or she understands the case against him or her. However, since 'case' has generally been understood to mean the alleged facts as well as how those facts constitute impairment, the consequence has been the inclusion of peripheral or irrelevant details which obscure the real facts relied upon for the issue of impairment.

1.53   In *R (Wheeler) v Assistant Commissioner House of the Metropolitan Police*[26] it was alleged that W had failed to carry out duties 'to an acceptable standard' thereby breaching the code of conduct. Stanley Burnton J said:

> Vagueness is a ground for judicial review if it leads to unfairness in the proceedings, and the danger with a vague charge is that the parties, and in particular the respondent, do not know with some precision what is alleged against them, and therefore are not fully able to address those matters in the course of a hearing.[27]

His Lordship commented that while the particulars of a disciplinary charge may be refined following an initial draft, it should be sufficiently particularised well before the hearing for the respondent to know what it is alleged he failed to do and, in what respects he failed.

---

26 [2008] EWHC 439 (Admin).
27 At para [6].

1.54   In *Sheill v General Medical Council*[28] Foskett J quashed the panel's finding of dishonesty because the head of charge was unspecific regarding the circumstances in which it was alleged that S had made a false claim. His Lordship stated that when it is alleged that a false or dishonest claim had been made in a document it would be usual for the document to be identified by date or description in the charge. This was not done, neither was there any request for further and better particulars before or at the start of the hearing.

1.55   On the face of it, the lack of a request for further and better particulars is a serious failing by the defence team. Equal criticism can be made of the prosecutor who should provide appropriate details without the need to be asked. If in doubt, particulars should be sought and/or given. It is highly unlikely that anyone will be criticised for such an approach whereas a failure may bring censure.

1.56   It is of particular importance that the allegations are clear both to the practitioner and to the panel, since the proceedings should remain within the factual limits of the allegations unless they are amended. As Pill LJ observed in *Strouthos v London Underground Ltd*[29] 'it is a basic proposition, whether in criminal or disciplinary proceedings, that the charge against the defendant or employee facing dismissal should be precisely framed and that the evidence should be confined to the particulars in the charge'.[30]

1.57   This is made clear from the comment by Silber J in *Cohen v General Medical Council*[31] that findings in relation to a charge at stage one of the process 'must be focused solely on the heads of the charges themselves'.[32] This is of particular relevance when scrutinising the reasons given by the panel. Adverse findings have been quashed in a number of cases where the reasons demonstrate that consideration has been given to extraneous matters.

1.58   In *Roomi v General Medical Council*[33] Collins J allowed R's appeal against a finding of impairment by reason of deficient professional performance (ie lack of competence) on the grounds that the finding by the panel went beyond the allegations contained in the notice of hearing. During the case R called evidence to show that he had taken steps to improve his skills. The panel concluded that the deficiencies

28   [2008] EWHC 2967 (Admin).
29   [2004] EWCA Civ 402.
30   At para [12].
31   [2008] EWHC 581 (Admin).
32   At para [48].
33   [2009] EWHC 2188 (Admin).

identified in the notice had been remedied. However the panel still made an adverse finding relying on managerial matters out-with the original allegations. Not surprisingly His Lordship was critical both of the panel for going beyond the matters alleged and of the legal assessor for failing to advise them of their error.

1.59   Similarly in *Chauhan v General Medical Council*[34] King J allowed C's appeal against findings of dishonesty and impairment because the panel failed to confine itself to the proper ambit of the disciplinary charges and considered prejudicial factual matters outwith the notice of hearing. The panel made findings of fact adverse to the registrant which could have been the subject of professional misconduct but were not within the charges as formulated. King J ruled that the findings of fact could not be properly or fairly used by the panel to support its decision. He further concluded that the panel had considered evidence of behaviour not the subject of a charge when determining the issue of dishonesty. He quoted Silber J from *Cohen* (above) that the process must focus solely on the heads of charge and rejected the GMC's submission that the extraneous material, even if strictly outside the ambit of the charges, could nonetheless be introduced as evidence of C's propensity to dishonestly exaggerate his expertise.

1.60   The approach outlined above is to be contrasted with criminal cases where the time-honoured prohibition on bad-character has now been removed and, previous *or subsequent* misconduct is admitted far more frequently. This may become more important in disciplinary proceedings since character evidence is now admitted at the stage of impairment and not just sanction. (See section on character below, at para 1.225ff.)

1.61   The decision went the other way in *Richards v Law Society*[35] in which the Divisional Court held that the purpose of a rule 4(2) statement (now a rule 5(2) statement under the Solicitors (Disciplinary Proceedings) Rules 2007[36]) is to inform the solicitor in advance of the case he or she has to meet. The tribunal found the case proved on a basis different from that in the statement. However, since the case was made clear in correspondence well before the hearing, R had received advance notice of the point upon which they found against him.

---

34 [2010] EWHC 2093 (Admin).
35 [2009] EWHC 2087 (Admin) (Sir Anthony May P and Saunders J).
36 SI 2007 No 3588.

1.62   In *Hutchinson v General Dental Council*[37] Blair J differentiated between the vagueness of the charges and the specific behaviour clearly alleged. The clearly alleged misconduct was a failure to take adequate care over the sterility of dental instruments but the instances of occurrence described as 'regularly' or 'on occasions' were insufficiently specific to permit a proper response. While the clearly alleged misconduct meant that a fair hearing was possible, he stopped the case on its merits taking account of such matters as the lack of supporting evidence and the possibility of prejudice caused by delay and lack of specificity.

1.63   A final case in point is *R (Johnson) v Nursing and Midwifery Council*[38] in which J and M faced allegations relating to their management of a nursing home. (The facts appear below under 'disclosure' at para 1.150.) They submitted that the charges were so vague as to be unfair and contrary to article 6 arguing that the lack of particularity was evident from the number of unknown dates, the breadth of the period covered by the charges and the unknown number and frequency of the alleged events. The court asked itself two questions: 1) did the charges provide sufficient information for them to know with reasonable clarity the case they had to meet; and 2) is a stay the only possible remedy?

1.64   The court found that neither European nor domestic law required the detail of particulars suggested by J and M and referred to criminal cases, especially those involving historic sexual abuse. It is not always possible to provide details of dates and locations but, the public interest requires that such matters be tried. In accordance with criminal cases the court held that the Fitness to Practise process itself is equipped to deal with many such issues. A stay is an exceptional remedy and it is only to be granted if a fair trial is impossible.

1.65   It is of importance to note that the court took into account the stage at which the application was made, namely at the outset of proceedings. While this was not premature (and in criminal proceedings submissions on the indictment are made at the outset) it did mean that the panel was deprived of any evidence which may help them in their decision. J and M had thus created an even greater hurdle for themselves.

1.66   The above principles can be drawn together when considering the case of *Thaker v Solicitors Regulation Authority*[39] (SRA) in which T

37 [2008] EWHC 2896 (Admin).
38 [2008] EWHC 885 (Admin).
39 [2011] EWHC 660 (Admin) (Jackson LJ and Sweeney J).

appealed against the decision of the Solicitors Disciplinary Tribunal to strike him off. The court ordered a retrial on the basis that the original hearing was unfair owing to the manner in which the case was pleaded and presented by the SRA. A solicitor, faced with being struck off for dishonesty or gross negligence, is entitled to a coherent and intelligible statement of the allegations and the facts relied upon. This is particularly important in complex cases, or when a registrant is said to have known or ought to have known about alleged facts. During their opening it became clear that the SRA's case was far wider than that alleged in the statement of facts. The tribunal refused T's application to adjourn. The court said that while adjourning was a matter of discretion, the fact that the case went far beyond the original allegations meant that time for consideration was the *least that should have been granted*. In addition, by allowing the proceedings to range far and wide with submissions and evidence beyond the identified relevant transactions, the tribunal had caused injustice to T.

1.67   It is submitted that a reasonable rule of thumb is to consider whether the charge provides sufficient information to allow a full and fair response. If it does not, can this be cured by amendment and a reasonable time to adjust? If amendment and time will make no appreciable difference and the respondent is at a disadvantage, is there still an overriding public-interest requirement to look into the allegation? If there is such an overriding requirement, for example in cases of historic sexual abuse, the panel must keep the issue of fairness under review. If it is apparent that even with the flexibility of a trial/tribunal-process a fair hearing cannot be maintained then the case should be stayed.

1.68   As previously stated, the interpretation of the above cases has led to rather verbose allegations that have been treated by both sides in an unnecessarily confrontational way. The latter is perhaps a reflection of the quasi-criminal adversarial system but it is of little assistance to the panel. As to verbosity, rather than pick a representative sample of important alleged facts there has been a tendency to list everything. Additionally there has been a tendency to allege that a registrant has *failed* to do something rather than that he or she 'did not' do something. 'Failed' carries overtones of fault which may result in the defence refusing to admit facts which really do not require dispute. While some cases necessarily require a failure to be alleged, where possible, it is better to allege that a registrant 'did not' do something which fact may then be admitted in whole or in part and leave the issue of fault or failure to legal argument and the judgment of the panel. (See the general drafting guide below.)

1.69   That the concern over particulars had become a problem was clear not just from the cases but from the comments of Dame Janet Smith in the *Fifth Report of the Shipman Inquiry* where she said:

> ... it does appear to me that, in some types of case (for example, one that depends to a large extent upon a performance or health assessment), it would be sufficient if the doctor were to be told (adopting the words of the adjudication stage test proposed by the GMC) that it was alleged that his/her fitness to practise was impaired (to a degree justifying action on registration) by reason of the matters contained in the assessment report. Even in conduct cases, I doubt that the degree of particularity that appears to have been given in the past is necessary for the giving of proper notice to the doctor. Reading some [Professional Complaints Committee] decisions, it appears that the proceedings have been broken down into the consideration of every single element which must be proved in order to support the allegation of [serious professional misconduct]. I do wonder whether this is really necessary; it fosters the impression that these are criminal proceedings, whereas they are not.[40]

1.70   These problems have prompted a move towards more succinct formulation and the prioritisation of allegations. Indeed some charges are now so short that they read more like an indictment and have almost no detail at all other than a two-line description of the offence and the assertion of impairment. This is perhaps taking the matter too far the other way, and it is to be hoped that a middle ground will be reached swiftly. (See the general drafting guide below.) In cases with shorter heads of charge, the accuracy and completeness of the regulator's opening address is important. As with criminal proceedings it should describe and circumscribe the scope of the case. Ordinarily the regulator should not go outside its case as stated in the opening.

Some specific requirements

1.71   In addition to the general principle of knowing the case, the courts have ruled that certain specific allegations must be included in an allegation. Again the accuracy and completeness of the opening is important if the heads of charge are in a shortened form.

Dishonesty

1.72   This must be clearly and unambiguously stated.

---

40 At para 25.273.

1.73   In *Salha and Abusheikha v General Medical Council*[41] the Privy Council held that a fundamental principle of fairness requires a charge of dishonesty to be unambiguously formulated and adequately particularised. It found that there was no justification for findings of dishonesty or lack of integrity against the doctors as it was not alleged against them.

1.74   If a regulator considers that a registrant's conduct was dishonest (as opposed to some lesser degree of culpability) it is essential that this is specifically pleaded. A failure to include such an allegation if the facts may properly support such an inference can amount to a procedural error or 'under-prosecution' on the part of the regulator (see *R (Council for the Regulation of Healthcare Professionals) v (1) The Nursing and Midwifery Council (2) Kingdom*[42]).

1.75   See also *Singleton v Law Society*,[43] in which it was said that: 'It is unacceptable for the Tribunal to make findings of dishonesty when there has been no documentary pleading of such an allegation in a clear and *timeous* way' (emphasis added).[44]

1.76   It is not necessary to allege dishonesty if the allegation is already clearly contained in the words used – for example, 'you stole a bag'. If there are other conclusions that a panel might be asked to reach regarding a registrant's motives or state of mind (eg deliberate, misleading, etc) these should be clearly pleaded (see alternatives below).

Sexual motivation

1.77   This should be spelled out in all relevant cases.

1.78   In *R (Council for the Regulation of Healthcare Professionals) v General Medical Council; Rajeshwar*[45] the court held that it was a serious procedural irregularity and 'under-prosecution' not to plead sexual motivation.

1.79   It is worth noting that an allegation of 'indecency' may be made even where the registrant has been acquitted of indecent assault. However, the better approach is to charge the actions as 'sexually motivated,' not least because there is an element of subjective judgment in what is or is not indecent. On the other side of the coin, the defence and the panel are entitled to rely on the fact that a charge does

---

41 Privy Council 32/2003 and 35/2003.
42 [2007] EWHC 1806 (Admin).
43 [2005] EWCH 2915.
44 At para [13].
45 [2005] EWHC 2973 (Admin).

not contain allegations of indecency or sexual motivation since this sort of decision must be a properly reasoned and appropriate one.

Alternatives

1.80   Lesser alternatives must be included where different interpretations and conclusions can be drawn from the reasons for a practitioner's actions. However, care must be taken to limit these to the most serious allegations. By way of example when alleging dishonesty, a clear and appropriate charge may suggest that an alleged statement was: a) misleading; b) intended to mislead; and c) dishonest.

1.81   In *R (Farag) v General Medical Council*[46] the panel's finding of dishonesty was quashed. The GMC presented the case for dishonesty on the basis that F was not ill despite submitting sick notes to his employer. This was demonstrated by the fact that he was working elsewhere at the time. The panel rejected this, declining to go behind the contents of the sick-note but found F to be dishonest because he had been selective about the information that he had given to the Trust regarding his alternative employment. This was not the way that the GMC had put the case. The court found that the defence had not had an opportunity to answer this alternative case. There are clear parallels to be drawn with the cases regarding consideration of extraneous matters. This illustrates the importance of an accurate opening as discussed above.

Summary or wrap-up clauses and narrative

1.82   These should be limited to those cases where it is absolutely necessary – for example, to indicate the seriousness of alleged events. Narrative that explains the circumstances of events should also be avoided.

1.83   There are two distinct types of summary clause: 'specific aggravating factors' and 'generic summary clauses'. The former are likely to be required when particular factual findings need to be made regarding aggravating features of the alleged misconduct. Examples are when the allegations describe the misconduct as dishonest, misleading or sexually motivated. These are factual issues which must be proved to the required standard. The latter clauses, encompassing terms such as 'not of the standard expected of ...' or 'inappropriate or inadequate', are not factual matters for stage one. However, they may be relevant to the exercise of the panel's judgment when it comes to impairment.

46 [2009] EWHC 2667 (Admin).

Most regulators provide specific guidance on the use of such adjectives in order to be consistent in drafting and presenting cases.

1.84 Catch-all or wrap-up charges should not be included unless there is a specific need in the case. For example, in performance cases it may be necessary to state how far a registrant's fitness to practise has fallen short of an accepted standard.

1.85 In *Williams v General Medical Council*[47] Davis J was critical of what he referred to as a 'summation charge' or 'sweeping-up' charge which added very little to what had gone before. Likewise in *Misra v General Medical Council*,[48] a case concerning professional misconduct, the Privy Council criticised the charges as unnecessary and oppressive when an allegation of dishonesty was seemingly routinely added to each disputed fact.

1.86 The *GMC drafting guide* takes up the points made in *Williams* and *Misra* and advises that:

> ... it is important to ensure that the charges identify the core areas of concern, and relate to matters which are serious enough to justify impairment proceedings. Impairment of fitness to practise is judged 'in the round', so it may be necessary to look at the cumulative effect of a series of faults. However, drafters should consider carefully whether each incident relied on should genuinely attract criticism.[49]

1.87 The principle has equal application to all disciplinary proceedings.

Drafting principles

1.88 The following is a summary of general drafting principles:[50]

- The notice needs to be sufficiently particularised regarding the basis of the alleged impairment, but without unnecessary detail. It is not a narrative of the case, a summary of the evidence, or an opening statement. It should set out the facts which the regulator says indicate impairment.
- Charges should be unambiguously drafted, using succinct plain language, concise and without numerous sub-clauses. They should say what is meant.
- A charge should be chronological.
- A charge should:
  - identify and describe the registrant's practice and location;

---

47 [2007] EWHC 2603 (Admin).
48 [2003] UKPC 7.
49 *GMC Guidance on charge drafting for notices of hearing*, 3 February 2010.
50 Based on the GMC publication on charging principles but of general application.

- – describe the key factual elements of what is alleged avoiding unnecessary narrative detail;
- – indicate what is being criticised and how it is being criticised. Guidance may be obtained from an expert report or from publications such as *Good medical practice* or other specific guidance; it is not necessary to tie allegations to specific provisions in such guidance.

- It should allege that practise is impaired by reason of misconduct or poor performance etc as the case may be.
- When deciding what facts to allege, only those provable through admissible evidence should be included.
- The 'best evidence' rule provides a good starting point such that direct evidence should be used before hearsay. Supporting evidence from another witness or documentation is also desirable but not essential.
- 'Failed' versus 'did not': The term 'you failed' – eg 'You failed to examine patient A' – means that the regulator must prove two elements: first, that the practitioner did not examine patient A, and second that the practitioner *should* have done so. This approach should only be adopted where the *failure to examine is core* to the allegation otherwise the wording should be: 'You did not examine patient A'.

Amending the charges

> The allegations/charges may be amended provided no injustice is caused.
>
> The later and/or more substantial the change, the more likely it is to cause injustice.
>
> If the risk of injustice can be met then charges may be changed late in the proceedings. Some difficulties may be dealt with by adjourning to allow all parties time to prepare the newly altered case or, call or recall witnesses.

1.89   The principles on charging and drafting have equal input to amending charges.

1.90   Article 6(3) ECHR is engaged when there is a change in the nature of an allegation. Since an accused is entitled to proper notification of a charge he or she is also entitled to proper notification of a change and, adequate time and facility to deal with the change. In *Mattoccia v Italy*[51] the ECtHR found that M had been denied the right to proper notification by vague charges the essential details of which were repeatedly altered during trial with no allowance given to him to deal with 'yet another new version of events' late in the hearing.

1.91 In *O'Reilly and Mackman*[52] Lord Diplock stated that:

... the requirement that a person who is charged with having done something which, if proved to the satisfaction of a statutory tribunal, has consequences that will, or may, affect him adversely, should be given a fair opportunity of hearing what is alleged against him ... is so fundamental to any civilised legal system that it is to be presumed that Parliament intended a failure to observe it should render null and void any decision reached in breach of this requirement.[53]

1.92 The regulators' rules each provide for amending the particulars of the allegation or the alleged facts provided it can be done without injustice. Before such amendments are made, the panel must consult with the legal assessor and hear from both parties. However, the timing of amendment is open to further argument given the staged process of regulatory hearings.

1.93 It follows from the requirement of a fair hearing that the registrant is entitled to proper notice of the allegation. That much is uncontroversial. The authorities are, however, less clear on the issues of when notice has to be provided and when it is too late. In *Singleton v Law Society* (above) the High Court held that: 'It is unacceptable for the Tribunal to make findings of dishonesty when there has been no documentary pleading of such an allegation in a clear and *timeous* way'.[54] This was followed in *R (Council for the Regulation of Healthcare Professionals) v (1) The Nursing and Midwifery Council (2) Kingdom* (above) where the High Court ruled that a failure to cite dishonesty was a 'serious procedural error', but Beatson J '[rejected] the submission that the Committee could not reconsider or amend the charge once the facts were proved'.[55]

1.94 From *Singleton* notice must be 'timeous', whereas in *Kingdom* the judge envisaged a serious amendment to an allegation (averring dishonesty) even after the panel had retired to consider the facts. The two are difficult to reconcile, from which it may be said that each case

---

51 Application no 23969/94, (2003) 36 EHRR 47.
52 [1983] 2 AC 237.
53 At p276B–C.
54 At para 13.
55 At para 32.

must be considered on its own facts. The principle consideration is, as ever, fairness.

1.95   Assistance may be gleaned from criminal proceedings in which a defective indictment may also be amended by the judge at any stage before or during trial provided this can be done *without injustice* (Indictments Act 1915 s5). The starting point is that the longer the interval between arraignment and amendment the less likely that it can be done without causing injustice – see *R v Johal and Ram*.[56] However, the courts have given an increasingly liberal interpretation to this section and, amendment may be made if an indictment is bad for duplicity, or it does not accord with the evidence before the committing magistrates, or the evidence given at trial, or when the evidence discloses more than one offence, or when it does not include a defendant who may be properly joined. Finally the court may substitute a different offence or add another – see *R v Radley*[57] and *R v Johal and Ram* (above).

1.96   The clear notion is that unless there is unfairness that cannot be cured by allowing time, or recalling witnesses, charges may be amended at the latter stages of a trial.

1.97   If there is to be a retrial, amendment can again be made but with the same caveat namely that there is no injustice – see *R v Swaine*.[58]

1.98   The limits of these points are met in three cases. In *R v Newington*[59] the Court of Appeal commented per curiam that while a judge had the power to amend an indictment during his summing up it was:

> ... questionable whether it was ever wise to [do so] especially in a long and complex case ... it must inevitably deprive defence counsel, no matter that he does not object strenuously, or at all ... of the opportunity to address the jury on the implications of the amendment. Furthermore, there is a risk to the Judge being unequal to the task of properly adjusting his summing-up to accommodate the change brought about by the amendment.[60]

1.99   By way of contrast, in *R v Bonner*[61] a case of historic indecent assault the Court of Appeal said that an amendment to the date of the alleged offence *after* the summing up was to be discouraged but, if the

56   (1972) 56 Cr App R 348.
57   (1974) 58 Cr App R 394.
58   [2001] Crim LR 166, CA.
59   (1990) 91 Cr App R 247, CA.
60   At page 251.
61   [1974] Crim LR 479.

interests of justice required it, then it should be made only after the defence has been given time to consider recalling witnesses or calling further evidence. This case should be treated with some caution before reliance is placed upon it since the date was not an essential particular of the allegation.

1.100   In *R v Piggott and Litwin*[62] following a successful submission of no case to answer, it was held to be inappropriate to permit amendment of the indictment, discharge of the jury and retrial of P and L on a basis withdrawn by the Crown prior to committal. The initial amendments which included the addition of new counts caused injustice and should not have been permitted. The retrial on the amended indictment was consequently an abuse of process and should have been stayed.

1.101   Referring the criminal principles back to *Singleton* and *Kingdom* and the conflict between the 'timeous' change in the former and the late change in the latter, the following lines of reasoning emerge:

1) major alterations to charges should be made as soon (timeous) as is reasonably practicable after the issue has arisen;
2) late and/or major changes may be made provided there is no injustice *and*, any unfairness can be met by allowing time or opportunity to prepare;
3) each case must be decided on its own facts.

Pre-hearing matters

Delay

> Article 6 ECHR and domestic case-law confer a right to a hearing within a reasonable time however to stay proceedings is an exceptional course and delay is not a ground unless there is material prejudice to the extent that no fair trial is possible.
>
> Where a regulatory body's rules impose a time bar preventing proceedings save in exceptional circumstances, an assessment of those circumstances must be fair, transparent and understandable.

1.102   Both domestic case-law and the ECHR confer a right to the speedy and just resolution of disputes. However, while delay may constitute a breach of the ECHR or the rules of a regulatory body, mere delay is insufficient to stop proceedings. Where the regulatory body has rules

62 [1999] 2 Cr App R 320, CA.

concerning old complaints, this may give rise to further argument concerning the just application of those rules.

1.103   As we have seen, ECHR article 6(1) provides for 'the determination of [civil rights and criminal charges by] a fair and public hearing within a reasonable time'.

1.104   It has been said that article 6 is to be given a broad and purposive interpretation: *Moreiva de Azevedo v Portugal*.[63] Much of the case-law concerning the application of article 6 stems from the criminal jurisdiction and it is instructive to start there.

1.105   In *Porter v Magill; Weeks v Magill*,[64] the House of Lords confirmed that there was no requirement to demonstrate specific prejudice in order to establish a breach of the right to trial within a reasonable time. However, while it may be possible to establish a breach, subsequent case-law makes it clear that this alone is not sufficient to stay proceedings.

1.106   In *Dyer v Watson*,[65] the Privy Council gave the following general guidance:

- Unless the time elapsed, on its face and without more, gave grounds for real concern, it is almost certainly unnecessary to go further.
- If there are grounds for real concern it is (a) necessary for the court to look at the detailed facts and circumstances and (b) necessary for the state to explain and justify the apparently excessive lapse of time.
- Relevant factors include the complexity of the case, the conduct of the defendant, and the manner in which the case had been dealt with by the administrative and judicial authorities.
- The state could not lay the blame on prosecutors, judges, lists, funding etc but neither was the court to shut its eyes to the practicalities of litigation and the organisation of cases.
- A marked lack of expedition, if unjustified, would point towards unreasonable delay.

1.107   The principle issues on delay are to be found in *Attorney-General's Reference (No 2 of 2001)*[66] where it was held that:

---

63   (1990) 13 EHRR 721.
64   [2002] 2 AC 357.
65   [2004] 1 AC 379.
66   [2004] 2 AC 72, HL.

    i) a stay would only be appropriate if a fair trial is no longer possible or if it is for any compelling reason unfair to try the defendant; and

    ii) time runs from the earliest time when the defendant was officially alerted to the likelihood of criminal proceedings being taken against him, which would normally be when he was charged or served with a summons.

1.108   As to i), where there was a breach, there had to be an appropriate remedy which would depend on the nature of the breach and all the circumstances, including particularly the stage at which the breach was established.

1.109   Apart from public acknowledgement of the breach, pre-trial remedies could include expediting the hearing and/or granting bail. Neither the prosecutor nor the court would further breach article 6 by continuing with the prosecution since the breach consisted of the delay which had accrued. Post-trial remedies may include a reduction in sentence or the payment of compensation to an acquitted defendant (see *Selvarajan v General Medical Council*[67] below).

1.110   It was further noted that there could be circumstances which justified a stay even when the fairness of the trial itself was not in question but the delay was such that it would be unfair to try the accused thus.

1.111   Cases where it might be unfair to try the defendant include cases of bad faith, executive manipulation and abuse of process, or where the delay was of such an order, or a prosecutor's breach of professional duty was such as to make it unfair that the proceedings should continue. Such cases would be 'very exceptional [and] a stay would never be an appropriate remedy if any lesser remedy would adequately vindicate the defendant's Convention right'.[68]

1.112   The circumstances where it might be unfair to continue are of the kind illustrated by *R v Horseferry Road Magistrates' Court ex p Bennett*[69] (in which a government agency acted unlawfully to wrongly detain a man and arrange his return to the UK rather than use lawful means) but as is noted such circumstances are exceptional and a stay would never be appropriate if any lesser remedy would adequately protect the defendant's convention rights.

1.113   The following comments of Lightman J in *R (Toth) v General Medical Council*[70] are also particularly pertinent:

---

67 [2008] EWHC 182 (Admin).
68 *Attorney-General's Reference (No 2 of 2001)* [2004] 2 AC 72 at para 25.
69 [1994] 1 AC 42.
70 [2000] EWHC 361 (Admin).

The Act and Rules set out to provide a just balance between the legitimate expectation of the complainant that a complaint of serious professional misconduct will be fully investigated and the need for legitimate safeguards for the practitioner, who as a professional man may be considered particularly vulnerable to and damaged by unwarranted charges against him.[71]

...

The general principles underlying the Act and Rules are that (a) the public have an interest in the maintenance of standards and the investigation of complaints of serious professional misconduct against practitioners; (b) public confidence in the GMC and the medical profession requires, and complainants have a legitimate expectation, that such complaints (in the absence of some special and sufficient reason) will be publicly investigated by the [panel]; and (c) justice should in such cases be seen to be done. This must be most particularly the case where the practitioner continues to be registered and to practise.[72]

1.114   In *R (Gibson) v General Medical Council and another*[73] Elias J relied upon Lightman J's observations in *Toth* (above), summing these up thus:

... both the legitimate expectation of complainants and the public confidence in the regulation of the medical profession require that the complaint should, in the absence of some special and sufficient reason, be publicly investigated. It would undermine that important principle if mere unreasonable delay, absent prejudice, were to require a stay to be granted.[74]

1.115   For the purposes of the ECHR, time runs from when a person is subjected to a 'charge' meaning that they are officially notified of or substantially affected by proceedings (*Deweer v Belgium*[75]; *Eckle v Germany*[76]). In regulatory proceedings this is likely to be the date of the letter notifying the registrant of the allegations.

1.116   While there have been two lines of authority on the application of article 6 to disciplinary proceedings, the better approach is that article 6 does in fact apply. See under ECHR above:

- *Ex p Kypros Nicolaides:* whether article 6 applies to the proceedings does not arise at the outset but depends on the outcome of the case.

---

71   At para [10].
72   At para [14].
73   [2004] EWHC 2781 (Admin).
74   At para 36 of his judgment.
75   (1980) 2 EHRR 439.
76   (1982) 5 EHRR 1.

- *Tehrani v UKCC*: 'if the petitioner can establish that the disciplinary proceedings could result in a finding that would constitute a determination of her civil rights and obligations, the decision to initiate those disciplinary proceedings is open to challenge as being incompatible with the petitioner's convention rights'.
- *Preiss v General Dental Council*: 'Since the decision of a majority of the European Court of Human Rights in *Le Compte, Van Leuven and De Meyere v Belgium* (1981) 4 EHRR 1 it has been accepted that a decision of a professional tribunal affecting the right to practise the profession is a determination of civil rights and obligations'.
- In *R (Johnson) v Nursing and Midwifery Council*[77] Beatson J approached the case from both the domestic and the ECHR viewpoints.

1.117 The principles as applied to regulatory proceedings have resulted in much the same conclusion. A registrant must show on a balance of probabilities that he or she will suffer or has suffered serious prejudice to the extent that no fair trial can be held.

1.118 Stays are thus to be granted:

i) in exceptional circumstances only;
ii) it will be even more rare where there is no fault on the part of the regulator or complainant;
iii) delay caused by the complexity of the case or by the registrant should never be the basis of a stay (see also *Haikel v General Medical Council*[78]).

1.119 In *Williams v General Medical Council*[79] W failed in his attempt to set aside a finding of serious professional misconduct on the basis of a 15-month delay between the matter being referred to the GMC and the hearing and, the failure by the GMC to serve a notice of inquiry on him expeditiously as required by the GMC (Fitness to Practise) Rules 2004. The panel finding that delay in service of the notice was 'not unreasonable' for the purposes of article 6 was not the same as a finding that the rule requiring service 'as soon as may be' had been met. However, a stay or dismissal of proceedings requires 'exceptional' circumstances and, without material prejudice a breach of the rule was of no practical significance.

---

77 [2008] EWHC 885 (Admin)
78 [2002] UKPC 37.
79 [2007] EWHC 2603 (Admin).

1.120   In *Varma v General Medical Council*[80] V was informed in April
2003 of the GMC's intention to take action over matters that occurred
in June 2002. The panel hearing did not begin until May 2006. The
GMC accepted that there had been unacceptable delay on their part.
V claimed that he could not attend through ill health (caused in part
by the delay) and that the case should be stayed at least until he was
well. The panel concluded his absence was voluntary and declined
to stay proceedings because the medical evidence indicated he was
able to attend, understand and participate. Forbes J ruled that in the
absence of serious prejudice such that no fair trial can be held, a stay
should not be granted in cases of delay.

1.121   While V did have health difficulties, Forbes J held that the panel
had balanced his rights against the public interest in investigating
and adjudicating upon serious matters and, since the decision was a
matter of judicial assessment rather than a conclusion based on facts
the court should be slow to interfere with an exercise of judgment by
a specialist panel – see *R v S*.[81]

1.122   Forbes J also referred to *R (TP) v West London Youth Court*[82] in
which it was said that, 'a trial should not be abandoned before all
practical steps to overcome the difficulties have been exhausted'.[83] V
received daily transcripts and was even permitted to communicate
directly with the panel by email. He was also granted a number of
adjournments to prepare his case. Collectively these measures were
sufficient to guarantee the fairness of the proceedings.

1.123   See also *R (Johnson) v Nursing and Midwifery Council*[84] (above) on
the particularity of charges – a stay is the exception, granted only if a
fair trial is not possible.

Delay as mitigation

1.124   Delay other than that caused by the registrant may give rise to matters
in mitigation. In *Selvarajan v General Medical Council*[85] S was erased
from the medical register after he admitted defrauding the local
authority of £150,000 between March 1994 and November 1996. He
argued that unreasonable delay was relevant to mitigation, a point

---

80   [2008] EWHC 753 (Admin).
81   [2006] EWCA Crim 77.
82   [2005] EWHC 2583 (Admin).
83   At para [18].
84   [2008] EWHC 885 (Admin).
85   [2008] EWHC 182 (Admin).

Forbes J had no hesitation in accepting. He did so as a matter of common sense, practice, fairness and from the GMC's own *Indicative sanctions guidelines*. He stated that the longer the threat of erasure and loss of livelihood hung over a practitioner, the more severe and punitive the sanction would appear to be despite this not being their main purpose. This is particularly so if the practitioner has been the subject of an interim order. This latter point may well be of importance when considering sanction since hitherto the fact of an interim order has not been relevant to final hearings. However, despite the delay he upheld the sanction of erasure owing to the seriousness of the misconduct.

1.125 See also *R (Madan) v General Medical Council* under interim orders below.

1.126 Thus, while it may be possible to allege abuse of process through a breach of article 6, it will only succeed when a fair trial is not possible or it would be otherwise unfair to try the registrant. Mere delay, absent prejudice, is not sufficient.[86] The need to maintain public confidence in the regulation of the professions requires that a complaint should, in the absence of some special and sufficient reason be publicly investigated.

1.127 Some regulators place time-limits on the receipt and prosecution of complaints unless to proceed 'is in the public interest, in the exceptional circumstances of the case'[87] or, 'it is necessary for the protection of the public, or otherwise in the public interest'.[88] These rules and any permitted circumvention of the time-bar must be strictly applied.

1.128 The above rules concerning delay were considered in *R (Peacock) v General Medical Council*,[89] *R (Gwynn) v General Medical Council*[90] and *R (Rycroft) v Royal Pharmaceutical Society of Great Britain*[91] (RPS).

1.129 In *Peacock* Gibbs J held that the regulator's decision to permit an allegation that P's fitness is impaired to proceed, despite the lapse of some seven years since the most recent events giving rise to the

86 [2004] EWHC 2781 (Admin); see also *Attorney-General's Ref (No 2 of 2001)* [2003] UKHL 68.
87 GMC (Fitness to Practise) Rules 2004 r4(5).
88 General Pharmaceutical Council (Fitness to Practise and Disqualification etc) Rules 2010 r6(2). These rules are contained in the Schedule to General Pharmaceutical Council (Fitness to Practise and Disqualification etc Rules) Order of Council 2010 SI No 1615.
89 [2007] EWHC 585 (Admin).
90 [2007] EWHC 3145 (Admin).
91 [2010] EWCH 2832 (Admin).

allegation, was unlawful. Prescription of certain drugs to the complainant led to a series of cardiac arrests which had caused neurological brain injury in 1998. The regulator permitted the complaint to proceed because the case 'raise[d] serious allegations' into the prescribing habits of P. The judge held that the judicial review challenge was not premature. There was no need to wait until the substantive finding because there would be no satisfactory remedy later in the proceedings. He went on to hold that on the facts of the case, there were no exceptional circumstances rendering it in the public interest to take the complaint further. At its gravest, the complaint was of serious negligence relating to one patient and one example of prescribing or a series of prescriptions. There was no sensible explanation for the delay.

1.130   In *Gwynn* the GMC alleged that G's fitness to practise was impaired due to deficient professional performance regarding ten patients, and misconduct in relation to one other patient. Four of the complaints arose from procedures carried out more than five years earlier. G applied for the proceedings to be stayed on the basis that there were no exceptional circumstances as required by GMC (Fitness to Practise) Rules 2004 r4(5). Not surprisingly, Sullivan J found that the GMC was bound to have regard to rule 4(5) when deciding whether to pursue cases that were over five years old. However, it was plain that it had not, and the subsequent attempt to do so retrospectively did not cure the defect. Indeed the lateness of the attempt compounded the situation since the decisions were made close to or on the eve of proceedings. Sullivan J concluded that it would be very difficult for any decision-maker to exclude the imminent hearing from his mind and without any identification of the required 'exceptional circumstances' or any express application of the rule 4(5) test, there was the very real possibility that undue weight was given to the imminence of the hearing.

1.131   The case against *Gwynn* also raised the spectre of re-opening a case closed by a caseworker four-and-a-half years previously as disclosing no professional misconduct or impairment. G argued that the GMC could not re-open a previously rejected complaint, and even if it could, it was unfair and/or unreasonable to do. Sullivan J agreed stating that the only way the GMC could re-open such a case was if the complainant asked the GMC to re-consider its decision.

1.132   In *Rycroft*, R took over the role of superintendent pharmacist for a chain of pharmacies in May 2002. In May 2006 the RPS received an allegation that they were re-using medication returned by clients. In April 2009 the registrar referred the matter to the Investigating

Committee. Rule 9(1)(a) and (2)(a) of the Royal Pharmaceutical Society of Great Britain (Fitness to Practise and Disqualification etc) Rules 2007[92] provided that the registrar shall not refer a fitness to practise matter or any other matter respectively if the conduct alleged is more than five years old, unless he or she considers it to be necessary for the protection of the public or otherwise in the public interest.

1.133   R sought to rely on *Gwynn* when arguing that the registrar was under an implied duty to make a referral within a reasonable period, and that in order for proceedings to be quashed and stayed, it was *not* necessary for the claimant to demonstrate prejudice. In rejecting R's contention, Williams J took account of the earlier decision of *R (Gibson) v General Medical Council*[93] that a stay should not be imposed even when unjustifiable delay was established unless:

> The defendant shows on balance of probabilities that owing to the delay he will suffer serious prejudice to the extent that no fair trial can be held: in other words that the continuance of the prosecution amounts to a misuse of the process of the court.[94]

(See *Attorney-General's Ref (No 1 of 1990)* [1992] 1 QB 630 at p644B.)

1.134   He concluded that the registrar is under an implicit obligation to make a referral within a reasonable time but a failure to do so did not amount to a reason for quashing the referral and staying proceedings unless the delay caused prejudice to such an extent that no fair disciplinary process is possible or that it is unfair for the process to continue. Despite there being inordinate and unjustified delay it did not prevent a fair hearing or make it unfair to proceed.

1.135   Finally, in *Rycroft* Williams J stated that while the extent of reasons may depend upon the nature of the decision, in deciding to refer a case where the conduct had occurred more than five years previously, the registrar had to address the statutory criteria and provide sufficient reasons to support his conclusion. The registrar purported to do so by stating that the referral was necessary 'for the protection of the public of otherwise in the public interest ... because the allegations are of a serious nature and it is necessary ... to maintain public confidence in the profession'.[95] These reasons were wholly inadequate rendering the decision to refer unlawful. Ordinarily this would

---

92 Contained in the Schedule to the Royal Pharmaceutical Society of Great Britain (Fitness to Practise and Disqualification etc Rules) Order of Council 2007 SI 2007 No 442.

93 [2004] EWHC 2781 (Admin).

94 At para 20.

95 At para 48.

have resulted in the decision being quashed but that was unnecessary in the light of pre-trial correspondence.

1.136   The conclusions from the above are:

a) The courts and regulatory panels are willing to recognise an abuse of process and/or a breach of article 6 and/or breach of an implied statutory duty but this alone will not give rise to a stay. The circumstances must be exceptional and there must be incurable prejudice.

b) In referring cases after time-limits imposed by regulation, there must be clearly defined and exceptional circumstances. These may relate to the lapse of time.

c) That the allegation raises serious concern about a practitioner's fitness to practise is *not* an exceptional circumstance, since this is a necessary precursor to any referral to a panel. Joinder of similar allegations is not an exceptional circumstance save that similar fact issues may at least be arguable when considering the protections of the public. On this last point it is worth considering the question of the admissibility of bad character (see 'character' below). Delay may be raised in mitigation of the sanction in appropriate cases. These are likely to be cases where risk to the public (patients) is minimal.

Disclosure

> While there is a duty to prevent inequality of arms, there is no positive duty on a disciplinary body to gather evidence to assist the practitioner.
>
> To allege unfairness under ECHR article 6(3)(b) a complainant must demonstrate that a duty exists, that it has been breached and that this has caused an inequality of arms.
>
> Each case will depend on its own facts.

1.137   In *Rajan v General Medical Council*[96] it was held that the duty on a regulator is to disclose relevant and material evidence. This means not just information they do not use but evidence that might weaken the regulator's case or strengthen the registrant's. While there is no clear parallel with criminal procedures the regulator must assess material in light of the registrant's case and, demonstrate that it has done so.

---

96 [2000] UKPC 1.

1.138   While there are no absolute parallels with criminal or civil proceedings, most disciplinary proceedings tend to follow the rules of
disclosure in the criminal courts. The difficulty now is that disclosure
in criminal proceedings is a hugely complex topic hedged around
with legislation, codes, rules and the competing views of prosecution,
defence and the court acting in its case-management capacity. The
main principles are derived from the Police and Criminal Evidence
Act (PACE) 1984, the Criminal Procedure and Investigations Act
(CPIA) 1996, the CPIA 1996 codes of conduct, the Criminal Justice
Act 2003, the Criminal Justice and Investigations Act 2008, the Criminal Procedure Rules (CPR), the Crown Court Protocol and more.

1.139   In broad terms, the principles of disclosure are first that the
prosecution should disclose to the defence any prosecution material
which 'might reasonably be considered capable of undermining the
case for the prosecution ... or of assisting the case for the accused'
(CPIA 1996 s3), and second that this should be kept under review
up until the point of conviction or acquittal (CPIA 1996 s7A). In particular, disclosure should be reconsidered in the light of the defence
case statement and, if the defence feel that material is being with-
held they can apply under section 8 for further disclosure. Finally,
disclosure should be made as soon as is reasonably practicable (CPIA
1996 s13).

1.140   In *R v H*[97] the House of Lords held that 'The golden rule is that
full disclosure of [material that weakens the prosecution or strength-
ens the defence] should be made'.[98]

1.141   The CPIA 1996 codes of practice provide first that:

> ... material may be relevant to the investigation if it appears ... that it
> has some bearing on any offence ... or any person being investigated,
> or on the surrounding circumstances of the case, unless it is incap-
> able of having any impact on the case.[99]

And second that:

> In conducting an investigation, the investigator should pursue all rea-
> sonable lines of inquiry, whether these point towards or away from
> the suspect. What is reasonable in each case will depend on the par-
> ticular circumstances.[100]

1.142   From the above it is reasonable to expect, first, that the investigating
and prosecuting bodies should look into exculpatory matters just as

97 [2004] AC 134.
98 At para 14.
99 CPIA 1996 Codes of Practice r2.1.
100 CPIA 1996 Codes of Practice r3.5.

much as those that support their case; and second, that the exculpatory material is disclosed because it is material relevant to the case for the defendant. Unfortunately expectation is not always met with fulfilment.

1.143   As cases have become more complex and expensive and disclosure has become more burdensome, so the pressures to restrict disclosure have increased. The now defunct Attorney-General's 1981 *Guidelines on disclosure* envisaged that material 'having some bearing on the offence(s) charged and the surrounding circumstances of the case' would be disclosed. In *Rowe and Davis v UK*[101] the ECtHR emphasised that disclosure should include all material evidence in the possession of the crown whether for or against the accused.

1.144   Disclosure under the Criminal Procedure Rules and CPIA 1996 does not require the wide disclosure envisioned by *Rowe and Davis*. Rather it is supposed to focus on what will undermine the prosecution or assist the defence case. A principal way to restrict disclosure is to require the defence to declare its case in a defence case statement and thereafter for the prosecution to focus its investigation of unused material on matters impacting upon the defence disclosed therein. That is not unreasonable if done properly, however, investigators do not always look at all lines of inquiry but concentrate on those that inculpate. Investigators do not inform prosecutors of material and, frequently neither review material nor do they understand or disclose material helpful to the defence. Defence statements are now frequently used as pleadings against a defendant, shown to witnesses to comment upon or are used as tools to cross-examine if there is any deviation from the contents of the statement. This is a far cry from their original (supposed) purpose of disclosure.

1.145   Disclosure does not include an obligation to disclose neutral evidence or evidence adverse to the defence *R v H* (above), nor does it include a duty to assist the defence in investigating its own case *R v Khan*[102] (withholding of a witness statement subsequently used to cross-examine the defendant was upheld).

1.146   Non-disclosure may result in an application to stay proceedings as an abuse of process. This has been argued in cases too numerous to set out but, it is not sufficient just to prove non-disclosure – the defence must demonstrate prejudice. In *R v Hadley*[103] the crown declined to serve video evidence but instead relied upon summaries.

101 (2000) 30 EHRR 1.
102 [2007] EWCA Crim 2911.
103 [2006] EWCA Crim 2544.

In quashing the conviction Moore-Blick LJ said that the appellant had to demonstrate that the undisclosed material was capable of affecting the jury.

1.147   In *Brants v Director of Public Prosecutions*[104] there were 13 adjournments before the crown provided disclosure that had been ordered by the court! The Divisional Court rejected B's appeal against the magistrates' court refusing to stay proceedings. It held that delay alone will not warrant a stay since the public interest in prosecuting cases transcends the notion of punishing the crown for causing delay.

1.148   In civil proceedings a claimant must provide sufficient disclosure to enable a defendant to properly instruct his or her representatives and refute, insofar as he or she can, the case against him or her – see *AF (No 3)*.[105]

Third party disclosure

1.149   Disciplinary tribunals have tended to follow the criminal rules of disclosure which include the CPIA 1996 code of practice for investigators mentioned above (see para 1.141). This places a burden on the regulators to search for and consider all material both inculpatory and exculpatory. However, as with criminal proceedings, it is unlikely that merely asserting a lack of disclosure will avail the defence. The registrant will have to demonstrate that there has been prejudice and unfairness.

1.150   In *R (Johnson) v Nursing and Midwifery Council*,[106] J applied for judicial review of the Professional Conduct Committee's refusal to stay proceedings on grounds (among others) of a failure to obtain relevant documents and other evidence. The NMC had agreed to do what they considered reasonable to obtain various records but they refused to obtain those they regarded as irrelevant. Beatson J held that the article 6 right to adequate facilities to prepare and equality of arms was case/fact specific. There was a balance to be struck between the parties to ensure fairness. This did *not* include a positive duty on the part of the regulator to gather evidence for the defence, provided the registrant was not at a disadvantage in having to gather the evidence he or she wished to deploy.

1.151   The principle in *Jespers v Belgium*[107] that 'Article 6(3)(b) recognized the right of the accused to have at his disposal … *all* relevant elements

104 [2011] 175 JP 246.
105 [2009] 3 WLR 74, HL, reference to *A and others* (2009) 49 EHRR 29.
106 [2008] EWHC 885 (Admin).
107 (1983) 5 EHRR CD 305.

that have been or could be collected by the competent authorities [and] if the element in question is a document, access to that document is a necessary "facility"'[108] is *not* authority for a singular positive duty on regulators to gather evidence for the defence.

1.152   The result is that the registrant must go further than simply assert a breach of article 6. The registrant will have to establish that there is inequality or unfairness for him or her to obtain documentation before a duty may be placed upon the regulator. Since J had done little or nothing to obtain the documents required, a complaint could not be levelled against the regulator.

1.153   In *R (Phillips) v Nursing and Midwifery Council*[109] the court adopted a similar approach when considering P's appeal based on the NMC's failure to call the patient who was named in the charge and a psychiatrist. Lloyd-Jones J held that P could have taken steps to obtain evidence and call witnesses. There was thus no basis to challenge the NMC's decision.

Interim orders

> Interim orders may be imposed prior to the substantive hearing on fitness if they are necessary to protect the public, or are in the public interest or in the registrant's interest.
>
> The threshold for an interim order is a high one because a registrant may be temporarily suspended or subject to conditions that limit or prevent his or her practise.
>
> No judgment is made regarding the alleged facts, so evidence is not called but the panel must be satisfied that, on a fair analysis, there may be a prima facie case.
>
> A registrant should be given a full opportunity to make representations. However, an IOP may proceed without the registrant provided all reasonable effort has been made to inform him or her of the hearing.

Overview

1.154   Healthcare regulators have the power to suspend or temporarily restrict the activities of practitioners. Examples are to be found in Medical Act (MA) 1983 s41A and Dentists Act (DA) 1984 s32(4)

---

108 At para 55.
109 [2008] EWHC 1698 (Admin).

which were brought into force owing to the fact that the GMC was unable to remove Dr Shipman from practice until the conclusion of his trial for murder and the subsequent fitness to practise hearing.

1.155   In general terms, interim orders may be made in proceedings brought by a regulator when the Interim Orders Panel is *satisfied* that it is:

a) necessary for the protection of the public; or
b) is otherwise in the public interest; or
c) in the interests of the practitioner.

1.156   The public interest includes:

- preserving public confidence in the profession;
- maintaining and declaring proper standards of conduct and performance.

1.157   As well as the element of protecting the public, it is important to note that when considering risk to the public, the order that is imposed, if any, must be that which is *necessary* to meet the risk. The issue of proportionality is of equal importance here as it is in fitness to practise proceedings. Article 8 ECHR may also be engaged (see under sanctions below for more on proportionality).

1.158   An interim order may be up to 18 months in length, however the regulator may apply to the High Court[110] for an extension of up to 12 months. Repeat applications may be made.

1.159   To suspend someone from practice or impose conditions is a serious step. Provision is thus made by the GMC to review an interim order every six months unless the practitioner requests an earlier review which he or she may do after three months have elapsed from its imposition. The review should then take place as soon as practicable after the request. The six-monthly review is also reduced to three if:

a) an order for conditions is replaced by suspension;
b) an order for suspension is replaced by conditions;
c) the High Court extends an order.

1.160   Other regulators have similar provisions such as a first review at six months and then three-monthly thereafter.

1.161   An Interim Orders Panel hearing may proceed in the absence of the registrant and the Interim Orders Panel may impose an order provided he or she has been given the opportunity to attend and be

110 If the registered address is Scotland or Northern Ireland, the Court of Sessions and High Court of NI respectively.

heard. To proceed in absence, notice of the hearing must be served 'in such time before the hearing as is reasonable in the circumstances of the case'[111] however, as with fitness to practise hearings, service does not have to be effected on the individual or indeed effective. The rules require only that all reasonable effort is made to effect service. (This topic is dealt with in greater detail under the Fitness to Practise Panel and absence of the registrant.)

1.162   The registrar, appointed officer or, where there is no such person, the Investigating Committee, may refer a case to an Interim Orders Panel at any stage if he or she is of the opinion that the Interim Orders Panel should consider making an interim order.[112] Case examiners, Investigation Committees or their equivalent also have the power to direct the registrar to refer a case to the Interim Orders Panel.[113]

Guidance on referral to an Interim Orders Panel

1.163   The regulators provide guidance on the type of cases that suggest referral is appropriate. These include (but are not limited to) three broad categories:

1) *Risk from clinical practice.* If the allegations are substantiated, there is an ongoing risk to patients from the registrant's clinical practice. For example, allegations of a series of failures to provide a proper standard of care, or one particularly serious failure, or allegations that indicate a serious lack of basic medical knowledge or skills. This category includes cases where a registrant has appeared before the Fitness to Practise Panel and been subject to an order but has not been immediately suspended, however new information, not available at the time of the original determination, suggests that the registrant poses an immediate risk to patients.

2) *Risk from non-clinical issues.* If the allegations are substantiated, the registrant poses a risk to patients if allowed to continue in unrestricted practice. This category deals with cases where public confidence in the profession may be seriously damaged by the registrant concerned holding unrestricted registration. It includes cases where the registrant faces allegations of a nature so serious that it would not be in the public interest for the registrant to hold

---

111 GMC (Fitness to Practise) Rules 2004 r26(1) but of general application.
112 GMC (Fitness to Practise) Rules 2004 (as amended) r6.
113 GMC (Fitness to Practise) Rules 2004 r8(6) and MA 1983 s35C(8) (both as amended).

unrestricted registration pending their resolution even though there may be no evidence of a direct risk to patients. Such cases are likely to be under investigation by the police and include cases of homicide, sexual offences and abuse of children. The point at which registrants who are the subject of criminal investigations should be referred to an Interim Orders Panel is flexible and will depend on all the circumstances of the case

3) *Breaches of existing orders.* Where a registrant has breached restrictions imposed on his or her registration, broken undertakings to his or her regulator to limit his or her practice, refused to co-operate with a performance or health assessment or, prevaricates or falls ill temporarily so that completion of an assessment or medical examination is delayed.

Evidence

1.164   The Interim Orders Panel has a duty to act to protect members of the public and the wider public interest. Cases are referred as soon as information made available suggests that a registrant's registration needs to be restricted on an interim basis. Because of this, the information available to an Interim Orders Panel may be received rather late in the day and is likely to be less detailed than that available to the Fitness to Practise Panel. It is important to note on this issue that the Interim Orders Panel makes no findings of fact and does not usually hear evidence although it does receive submissions.

1.165   However, it is also important to note the comments of Collins J in *R (George) v General Medical Council*[114] relating to late service of bulky documentation which meant that G did not have his side of events fully and properly considered, particularly when it came to argue upon the proportionality of the order of suspension sought by the regulator and whether a lesser order of conditions would have met the perceived risk.

1.166   The principles regarding a regulator's duty to properly investigate, disclose and accurately articulate matters in fitness to practise hearings have equal application to Interim Orders Panel hearings. This is of particular importance since the registrant has no opportunity to call evidence in rebuttal and, interim orders may have far-reaching effects upon his or her ability to practise. The admission of hearsay is a matter of some difficulty since Interim Orders Panel hearings are principally based upon reports and not live evidence. It is very

114 [2003] EWHC 1124 (Admin).

important for the material to be accurately stated by the regulator and carefully weighed by the panel. The registrant must be given a proper opportunity to make representations upon the alleged facts, risks, order and timescale.

The test

1.167   The Interim Orders Panel will impose an order if it is satisfied that in all the circumstances of the case there *may* be impairment of the registrant's fitness to practise which poses a real risk to members of the public, or may adversely affect the public interest or the interests of the registrant.

1.168   In deciding whether and what order to make, the Interim Orders Panel should balance the interests of the registrant and the interests of the public. The appropriate order is that which is *necessary* to guard against the risk or, is otherwise in the public or the practitioner's interest.

1.169   In reaching a decision whether to impose an interim order an Interim Orders Panel should consider the following:

- the seriousness of risk to members of the public and, in assessing this, the panel should consider the seriousness of the allegation(s), the weight of the information and the risk of further incidents;
- whether public confidence in the profession is likely to be seriously damaged if the registrant continues to hold unrestricted registration;
- whether it is in the registrant's interests to hold unrestricted registration (eg the registrant may lack insight and need protection from himself or herself).

1.170   It is for the Interim Orders Panel to decide what weight to give to these factors, remembering its first duty is to protect the public and the public interest. It should not assume responsibility for the treatment or rehabilitation of a registrant, although it may impose interim conditions relating to ongoing treatment and supervision.

1.171   Whether an Interim Orders Panel is satisfied that there may or may not be impairment is a matter of professional judgment. (See under Fitness to Practise Panel for more on 'impairment'.)

Interim conditions or interim suspension?

1.172   Having concluded that an order is necessary, the Interim Orders Panel must first consider whether conditions are appropriate to meet the risk. If they are not, then the panel should consider suspension. The panel must balance the need to impose an order with the impact on the registrant, ie the panel must consider whether suspension or the imposition of conditions is a proportionate response to the possible risk to members of the public, the public interest or the registrant's own interests.

1.173   An interim suspension must be *necessary either for the protection of the public* or is *otherwise in the public interest*, although the latter is likely to be rare. The difference is that the former requires there to be a real risk to patients or the public, whereas the latter is more an issue of desirability and maintaining standards – see *R (Shiekh) v General Dental Council*[115] (see also under 'sanctions'). Where an Interim Orders Panel does impose an interim suspension order, while no judgment is made on the facts, it at least carries the implication that suspension or erasure is a real possibility following the full fitness to practise hearing.

1.174   The Interim Orders Panel is required to take into account the following factors:

- the seriousness of the allegation;
- the nature and strength of the evidence including any admissions (whether there is a prima facie case);
- the registrant's previous character and conduct including compliance with any previous orders or undertakings;
- the likelihood of repetition of the alleged conduct;
- any evidence of appropriate steps taken to address the concerns.

1.175   Where the registrant has been charged with a criminal offence, the panel is entitled to work on the basis that there is sufficient evidence to justify charges being brought by the CPS. It is not always necessary to hear evidence or submissions as to the strength or weaknesses of the case, but each case must be decided on its own facts: *Fallon v Horseracing Regulatory Authority*.[116]

1.176   The impact on the registrant's right to practise, finances and reputation must be properly considered, bearing in mind the principles

---

115 [2007] EWHC 2972 (Admin).
116 [2006] EWHC 2030 (QB).

of necessity and proportionality – see *R (Madan) v General Medical Council.*[117]

1.177   *Madan* also provides some guidance on the issue of necessity (also see below on non-clinical risks). M was employed as a medical officer in child health. There were no complaints about her medical practice. She also ran a slimming clinic and prescribed appetite suppressants. It is about this that complaints were made. The Interim Orders Panel concluded that there was 'prima-facie evidence of inappropriate and irresponsible prescribing which, if proved, posed a risk to patients'.[118] It rejected conditions and suspended M for 18 months. On appeal Richards J held that 'whether one agrees or disagrees with [the judgment] on the merits, [it] cannot be said to have been manifestly wrong'[119] and he declined to substitute conditions. He also stated that the reasons given were adequate, intelligible and sufficient.

1.178   If imposing conditions, the Interim Orders Panel must ensure that they are workable, enforceable and will protect the public, the wider public interest or the registrant's own interests. As with fitness to practise proceedings, the regulators provide guidance in various 'conditions banks'.

1.179   When considering whether or not to make an interim order, the panel cannot accept any undertakings or assurances given by the registrant.

Period of order

1.180   The maximum period for which an initial order may be imposed is 18 months, although as with any interim order this may be extended. In considering the period the Interim Orders Panel should bear in mind the time that is likely to be needed before the matter is resolved and the impact of the order upon the registrant.

Reasons for decisions

1.181   The Interim Orders Panel must provide reasons for its decisions both upon the imposition (or non-imposition) of an order and the initial period of time for which it is imposed. The courts do not expect a panel to give long detailed reasons, but the reasons given must be

117 [2001] EWHC 577 (Admin).
118 At para 18.
119 At para 10.

clear and explain how the decisions were reached, including identifying the interest(s) for which the order is considered necessary. In *R (Walker) v General Medical Council*[120] Stanley Burnton J said that:

> ... a lack of adequate reasons, or a decision which is disproportionate in its interference with the rights of the doctor in question will encourage the court to examine broadly the decision made by the committee and substitute its own in a way which it might be less willing to do where the decision appeared to be fully reasoned and proportional.

> ... the court will normally give broad credit to the appreciation by a professionally qualified Committee of the conduct of the accused doctor [and where] full and substantial reasons are given ... the court will give considerable weight to those and will be slow to interfere.[121]

1.182 It is worth noting here that the principle of giving weight to the decisions of a properly appointed panel in any profession is a theme running through many decisions in both interim order and fitness to practise cases.

Recent cases on risk from non-clinical issues

1.183 As stated above, the regulators provide guidance for the referral of serious cases such as homicide, assaults or sexual offences which fall into the first category of cases, where the issue is the necessity of protecting the public. However, guidance is lacking on matters of integrity or honesty where there is no such necessity and, matters are 'otherwise in the public interest'. This is somewhat surprising given the importance attached to matters of probity and the potential affect suspension may have on the registrant. The previously mentioned comments of Collins J in *R (George) v General Medical Council*[122] relating to late service of bulky documentation resulting in G not presenting his best arguments may well have relevance here.

1.184 Consideration has been given to the meaning of 'in the public interest' in a number of cases. In *R (Shiekh) v General Dental Council*,[123] S who had been given a suspended prison sentence for fraud, posed no direct risk to the safety of the public. The case concerned his character not his clinical ability. Davis J overturned the GDC's suspension, finding that:

---

120 [2003] EWHC 2308 (Admin) at paras 9 and 10.
121 At paras [9] and [10].
122 [2003] EWHC 1124 (Admin).
123 [2007] EWHC 2972 (Admin).

It is a very serious thing indeed for a dentist or a doctor to be suspended. It is serious in many cases just because of the impact on that person's right to earn a living. It is serious in all cases because of the detriment to him in reputational terms. Accordingly, it is ... likely to be a relatively rare case where a suspension order will be made on an interim basis on the ground that it is in the public interest.[124]

1.185   On the absence of 'necessity' when considering public interest Davis J commented that if public interest is to be raised it at least carried 'some implication of necessity and certainly ... of desirability'. He went on to say that 'the bar is set high' and 'in the ordinary case at least, necessity is an appropriate yardstick. That is so because of reasons of proportionality'.[125] There is also an interesting parallel to be drawn with the article 8 argument in *Bonhoeffer* at para 1.215 and the damage to a registrant's reputation caused by the commencement of proceedings.

1.186   In *R (Sosanya) v General Medical Council*[126] Davis J again overturned a suspension imposed on grounds of public protection. S's husband had been convicted of fraud and she awaited trial on charges of money laundering. He overturned the first because the charge did not relate to clinical practice and in respect of the public interest he observed that the charges the doctor was facing were denied and that she had been 'convicted of nothing'.[127] He framed two questions for the panel to ask itself – on the one hand, 'will it be acceptable for us not to suspend in a case of this kind [if the charges are eventually proved?' and, on the other hand, 'will it be acceptable for us to suspend an applicant in a case of this kind [if the charges are eventually dismissed]?'[128]

1.187   However, two more recent decisions suggest that the above approach of importing the element of necessity into the test for public interest may be short lived. In *R (Sandler) v General Medical Council*[129] and *Bradshaw v General Medical Council*[130] the court refused to overturn suspensions imposed by the Interim Orders Panel.

1.188   In *Sandler* the doctor was suspended for allegedly failing to carry out examinations before completing 116 cremation certificates which is a criminal offence. Nicol J agreed that there should be no

124 At para [16].
125 At para [16].
126 [2009] EWHC 2814 (Admin).
127 At para [17].
128 At para 29.
129 [2010] EWHC 1029 (Admin) Nicol J.
130 [2010] EWHC 1296 (Admin), Judge Kaye QC.

suspension unless it was proportional and at least 'desirable' in the public interest but he declined to go further adding 'the Court must be cautious about superimposing additional tests over and above those which Parliament has set'.[131]

1.189   In *Bradshaw*, a former Civil Aviation Authority medical officer was suspended on grounds of risk to the public, public interest and own interest. There was no criticism of his clinical competence, rather the case was one of dishonesty surrounding the investigation of an alleged affair with a colleague. While HHJ Kaye QC commented that absent any clinical or patient issues, suspension for an affair alone might well be disproportionate, here B had lied to an investigation, falsely accused a colleague and fabricated evidence. Despite there being no issues of clinical competence, the GMC was rightly concerned regarding the public perception of doctors and, of the risk that B may be persuaded to lie if he was accused of something by a patient.

1.190   The High Court has emphasised that each case turns on its facts. That a distinction is to be made between what is necessary to protect the public and what is otherwise in the public or individual interest seems clear from the relevant statutes and the regulators' own rules. However, the breadth of the distinction is not settled and it remains to be seen whether the 'necessity' test of *Shiekh* or the 'desirable' test of *Sandler* prevails when considering public interest. One thing is certain, an interim order must be a proportionate response to the material put before the Interim Orders Panel taking account of seriousness, strength of evidence and, the impact of the order upon the registrant who must be given the opportunity to properly argue against the alleged facts and/or risks.

Review of interim orders

1.191   Review hearings must take place at regular intervals, not least because the information first provided is likely to be incomplete, and because of the serious effect an interim order may have upon a registrant. The evidence, risk identified and the order must all be reassessed.

1.192   The hearing provides an opportunity to revisit the initial information and reconsider the matter in the light of any fresh material. New material should be given significant weight. In particular a registrant may be able to argue that recent material more accurately reflects his or her current skills as opposed to mere allegations of shortcomings

131 R *(Sandler) v General Dental Council* [2010] EWHC 1079 (Admin), Nicol J at para 14.

and, demonstrate that concerns raised at an earlier hearing have been understood and are being or have been addressed. Through this the registrant may be able to argue that an order for suspension should be replaced by conditions or, that conditions be relaxed, or that there be no order.

Extension of interim orders

1.193   Interim orders are intended to be of limited, though not necessarily short, duration. However, they can be extended following an application to the High Court. Since the regulator makes the application to extend, it is the regulator that bears the burden of proving the case for an extension, although a registrant may consent to such an extension. The latter course may well be in the registrant's own interests if a final hearing is imminent.

1.194   In considering whether to extend an interim order, the court should consider the same factors as when the order was first imposed. These include the gravity of the allegation(s), the risk of harm to patients and the seriousness of that risk, the reasons why a case has not been concluded and, the prejudice to the registrant caused by a continuation of the order: *General Medical Council v Hiew*.[132]

1.195   Two recent cases demonstrate the application of the balancing exercise albeit that both resulted in extension. In *General Medical Council v Razoq*[133] the GMC applied for an extension pending the outcome of criminal proceedings. They wished to place all matters before the Fitness to Practise Panel rather than deal with some before and some after the criminal trial. The criminal case was moving very slowly, however the allegations concerned probity and honesty, and were thus serious. The High Court expressed concern about the significant delay and the effect this would have in de-skilling R who may thereby only return to work with conditions. The court sought to protect R from such prejudice and only granted an extension of eight months during which time the criminal trial ought to conclude. Any further delay would require a fresh application to extend the interim order.

1.196   In *R (Nursing and Midwifery Council) v Fofanah*[134] the High Court granted an eight month extension to an interim order of suspension. There had already been considerable delay and two previous extensions but, the allegations were serious (and had now been proved),

132 [2007] 1 WLR 2007, CA.
133 [2010] EWHC 2258 (Admin).
134 [2011] EWHC 1346 (Admin).

the risk of harm to patients was thus considered to be serious, the delay was not entirely caused by the NMC and, the extension caused no additional prejudice to F.

Fitness to practise hearings

Evidence: absent witnesses and hearsay

> The Fitness to Practise Panel has the discretion to proceed in the absence of a witness and to admit hearsay evidence, but the decision to proceed must be taken with 'the utmost care and caution' and only after full consideration of the competing interests with emphasis on those of the registrant.
>
> There must be compelling reasons to deprive a registrant of the opportunity to cross-examine a witness – all the more so if the case or its consequences are serious.

1.197   Hearsay evidence is, by its very nature, not the best evidence, being second-hand or reported – however, it is admissible in civil proceedings pursuant to the Civil Evidence Act (CEA) 1995 and in criminal proceedings pursuant to the Criminal Justice Act (CJA) 2003. Since regulatory proceedings tend to be governed by the criminal rules of evidence, this section deals with how the CJA 2003 rules apply to regulatory proceedings.

1.198   The principle guide to admissibility is 'fairness', balancing the interests of the prosecution and the defence. This approach has led to the increased use of hearsay but it is by no means routine and, each case and each application to admit hearsay must be carefully considered on its own facts.

1.199   In the Appeal Court judgment in *Horncastle*[135] Thomas LJ stated that it is 'ordinarily essential that evidence of the truth of a matter be given in person by a witness who speaks from his own observation or knowledge'.[136]

1.200   However, in some cases it may be the only evidence on an issue or of particular importance. The admission of hearsay is thus capable of being prejudicial to the fairness of proceedings but, its exclusion may also cause prejudice. Since panels should not consider

135 [2009] EWCA Crim 964 – a judgment said to complement the Supreme Court's own.

136 At para [7].

prejudicial matters the admission of hearsay evidence must be carefully scrutinised.[137]

1.201   Rules for regulatory proceedings generally provide a wider remit to receive evidence that a panel considers to be relevant and fair bearing in mind its' purpose of protecting the public and upholding standards. By way of example, the GMC (Fitness to Practise) Rules 2004 allow for the admission of evidence that the panel considers to be:

(1) ... fair and relevant to the case before them whether or not such evidence would be admissible in a court of law.

(2) Where evidence would not be admissible in criminal proceedings in England ... the Panel shall not admit such evidence unless ... satisfied that their duty of making due inquiry into the case before them makes its admission desirable.[138]

1.202   The NMC panel has a similar remit to receive evidence that it considers to be 'relevant and fair'.[139]

1.203   While the above rules permit the admission of evidence that might not be admitted in criminal cases, they should not be regarded as an easy route to the admission of hearsay. The central requirement is 'fairness'. This was emphasised in *Ogbonna v Nursing and Midwifery Council*[140] in which Rimer LJ rejected the notion promoted by the NMC that the rule admitting evidence 'subject only to the requirements of relevance and fairness' establishes a general principle to admit hearsay evidence as a matter of course and then address the issue of fairness by determining the weight to attach to that evidence.

1.204   The determination of fairness is fact-sensitive and will depend on the nature of the evidence, the reason for the non-attendance of a witness, what steps were taken to secure the attendance of that witness and the problems admission may cause to the registrant. Where such evidence is admitted, it is likely to carry less weight by virtue of the fact that it has not been tested in cross-examination.

1.205   In *Ogbonna*, O faced three serious charges all of which were found proved and she was struck off the register. On count one, the NMC placed sole reliance upon the statement of O's line manager P, with whom she was not on good terms. P did not give evidence rather her

---

137 See, for example, *Chauhan v General Medical Council* [2010] EWHC 2093 (Admin); *Roomi v General Medical Council* [2009] EWHC 2188 (Admin).

138 GMC (Fitness to Practise) Rules 2004 r34(1) and (2) but of general application.

139 NMC (Fitness to Practise) Rules 2004 r31(1).

140 [2010] EWCA Civ 1216.

statement was adduced as hearsay despite O's wish to cross-examine her. P had moved to the Caribbean. The NMC said that P was not available even though they had made no inquiry regarding her availability and said that no video-link was available at the panel hearing. On appeal Davies J found that the panel had misdirected itself in finding that P was not available since no inquiry had been made. The NMC (Fitness to Practise) Rules 2004 required the panel to consider the overall fairness of the hearing before admitting hearsay and, given the misdirection the test had not been met.

1.206   In her judgment on the first appeal, Davies J stated that:

> The evidence of the sole witness of fact was critical. That fact together with the evidence of bad feeling between the two women meant that every effort should have been made to secure Ms Pilgrim's attendance. Fairness required that the appellant was entitled to test the evidence of Ms Pilgrim by way of cross-examination unless good and cogent reasons could be given for non-attendance.[141]

1.207   The NMC challenged her judgment on the basis that it curtailed the admissibility of hearsay statements. However, the Court of Appeal upheld Davies J's decision 'in the particular circumstances' of the case. Her judgment was 'focused on the particular facts of the case and did not purport to lay down any more general principle than the need for a proper consideration to be given to the criterion of fairness when the question of [admitting hearsay arises]'.[142]

1.208   Rimer LJ stated that:

> ... decisions as to the admission or exclusion of a hearsay statement [are] to be governed by considerations, *inter alia*, of fairness ... [Here the NMC was seeking to adduce P's] statement as the sole evidence supporting the material parts of Charge 1 when it knew that that evidence was roundly disputed and could not be tested by cross-examination. It was [doing so in support of a case whose outcome could be and in the event was] the wrecking of [O's] career as a midwife, a career which had lasted over 20 years. I should have thought it was obvious that, in the circumstances, fairness to [O] demanded that in principle the statement ought only to be admitted if she had the opportunity of cross-examining [P] upon it.
>
> ... it should have been obvious to the NMC that it could and should have sought to make arrangements to enable such cross-examination to take place ... either by flying [P] to the UK at its expense, or else by setting up a video link.[143]

---

141 At p154.
142 At para 25.
143 At paras 23 and 24 of the judgment.

1.209 As for balancing fairness to the GMC he said:

> If ... despite reasonable efforts the NMC could not [arrange for P] to be available for cross-examination then the case for admitting her hearsay statement might well have been strong. But the NMC made no such efforts at all.[144]

1.210 The latter comment accords with the general principal that fairness means fairness to both sides. The danger when annunciating this principle is that fairness to the prosecution is frequently deployed as a reason to admit matters that plainly should not be admitted. This is precisely what happened in *Ogbonna*.

1.211 While no general principle was established other than to re-affirm the need to consider fairness before admitting hearsay, the circumstance bear repeating since they may be persuasive in any given case:

a) the witness was the sole and critical witness;

b) there was a history of animosity between the registrant and the witness;

c) there was a factual conflict between the registrant and the witness;

d) the consequence to the registrant could be (and was) the destruction of her career.

1.212 Although there is no absolute right to cross-examine a witness, there must be compelling reasons to deprive a registrant of this opportunity. This is all the more important if the case is serious and would have serious consequences if proved. Until recently, consequence has ordinarily meant sanction but, following *R (Bonhoeffer) v General Medical Council*[145] serious damage to reputation or standing should now be considered. Furthermore, it may no longer be sufficient to argue that an adverse finding based on hearsay can simply be challenged on appeal. The fact that the damage to the registrant will already have been done by then must be considered *before* the case proceeds further.

1.213 Professor Bonhoeffer faced several allegations of sexual misconduct while practising in Kenya. The GMC's case relied principally upon evidence from X who was willing to travel to London to give evidence. However, the police advised the GMC that he risked reprisals if he did so (not from B) and the GMC applied to admit X's evidence as hearsay. The panel found that the police assessment of risk was wrong and that the evidence would not have been admissible in a criminal trial, but nonetheless admitted the evidence on the basis

144 At para 24.
145 [2011] EWHC 1585 (Admin).

that it was appropriate given their remit of making 'due enquiry'[146] and, it was not unfair to B to do so. B challenged the decision (by way of judicial review) as irrational, unlawful, a misapplication of the rules and in breach of ECHR article 6 (right to a fair trial). The GMC argued that B had misconstrued the rules, the decision was reasonable and it was in the public interest to enquire into such serious allegations. The GMC also argued that B's challenge was premature, should only succeed if he could demonstrate that a fair hearing was not possible and, his rights were guaranteed by the panel's duty to properly assess evidence and his ability to appeal if convicted.

1.214   The court (Laws LJ, Stadlen J) upheld B's challenge concluding that:

a) The admission of hearsay was not necessarily unfair. Evidence that would not be admitted in a criminal trial may be fairly and properly admitted under the panel's own rules of practice. The key issue was whether admitting important evidence with no opportunity to cross-examine a witness was fair at common law and/or under article 6 given the seriousness of the case and any safeguards.

b) There is no absolute rule that a registrant must be afforded the opportunity to cross-examine a witness even where the witness provides the sole or decisive evidence. However, B's case was not argued upon whether such a rule existed but, was based on the facts. A key point was the serious (criminal) nature of the allegations and the very serious consequences if proved. As a general rule, the more serious the charges or consequences the greater the need for procedural safeguards to ensure a fair hearing. Labelling the proceedings as quasi-criminal or civil was not helpful. The main issues were seriousness and consequences. B's right to cross-examine a critical witness with whom his case conflicted could only be countered by *compelling* factors.

c) The panel did not find that X would be at any greater risk by giving live evidence than from reading his statement, nor had it considered the absence of the safeguards provided in criminal trials. The CJA 2003 curtails the routes and reasons by which hearsay is admitted. The court concluded that there were no compelling factors outweighing B's right to cross-examine X. The case was very serious both in terms of the allegation and any consequences. Finally, X had repeatedly said he was prepared to give live evidence and the panel's decision was, on the facts, irrational.

146 GMC (Fitness to Practise) Rules 2004 r34.

1.215   Interestingly, the challenge occurred before the substantive hearing rather than the usual process of alleging unfairness post conviction. The court took specific account of B's reputation and the damage to it if he were convicted, even if he later succeeded on appeal. This is an interesting extension/importation of what are normally regarded as ECHR article 8 rights (to respect for a private and family life) into matters usually falling to be decided under article 6 namely procedural and trial fairness.

1.216   It is also important to consider the position in criminal proceedings, since there has been a considerable amount of to and fro between the domestic courts and ECtHR.

1.217   In its initial decision on *Al-Khawaja and Tahery*[147] the ECtHR concluded that a conviction based 'solely or decisively' on the statement of a witness whom the defendant had no opportunity to convict was incompatible with article 6. This was rejected by the Supreme Court in *Horncastle*,[148] setting the Supreme Court and the European Court at odds. The Supreme Court concluded that the safeguards in the CJA 2003, H's ability to challenge the credibility of the principle witness, other evidence of his presence at the scene and, a full and clear judicial direction were sufficient safeguards and, evidence of a proper balance. Following this, the UK government referred the initial judgment in *Al-Khawaja and Tahery* to the Grand Chamber of the ECtHR.

1.218   The Grand Chamber decision in *Al-Khawaja and Tahery v UK*[149] effectively reversed the earlier decision. It concluded that an inability to cross-examine did not *automatically* result in unfairness or mean that article 6 was breached however there must be strong procedural safeguards to alleviate the difficulties caused to the defence.

1.219   The facts of each case are quite instructive and demonstrate the balance between fairness and unfairness. Al-Khawaja, a consultant physician, faced two counts of indecent assault on female patients under hypnosis. One patient (S) committed suicide before the trial, but a statement given to the police was admitted. The second complainant gave evidence and was cross-examined, as were two of S's friends in whom S had confided soon after the alleged incident. The trial judge cautioned the jury regarding S's untested evidence. Tahery allegedly stabbed someone during a fight. The only direct witness

147 (2009) 49 EHRR 1.
148 [2010] UKHRR 1, [2009] UKSC 14.
149 [2011] ECHR 2127 (Grand Chamber).

was too frightened to give evidence. The jury were likewise cautioned regarding the dangers of relying upon his untested statement.

1.220 The ECtHR reaffirmed the principles that: a) evidence must ordinarily be presented live at a hearing to enable the defendant to challenge it; b) there must be a good reason for non-attendance of a witness; and c) a conviction based solely or decisively on the statement of an absent witness was likely to be incompatible with the requirements of fairness under article 6. However, the court went on to say that the last principle was not absolute and inflexible. Account should be taken of the safeguards in the particular legal system and, the court should weigh the competing interests of the defendant, the complainant and the public interest in the proper administration of justice. Applying these rules, regarding *Al-Khawaja* although S was the only witness, her story could only be told through her statement. There was strong evidence to corroborate her account (both a 'recent complaint' and another similar incident) and, the jury had been properly directed. These provided sufficient safeguards or counterbalancing factors. In *Tahery*, the fact that T could challenge the prosecution case by giving evidence himself and the judge could and did give a strong warning to the jury were insufficient to counter the unfairness caused by reading the statement of the only witness against him.

1.221 In conclusion, hearsay is admissible in regulatory proceedings subject to the safeguards provided by the regulator's own rules (if any) and provided there has been:

a) appropriate and proportionate enquiry into the reasons why a witness is absent together with any supporting evidence;

b) appropriate and proportionate enquiry into alternatives means of facilitating live evidence (video-link, recorded interviews, alternative premises for hearings etc);

c) proper consideration of the competing interests of the parties;

d) proper consideration of whether it is the sole or decisive evidence or there is any supporting material;

e) a proper appraisal of the overall fairness of proceedings in the light of all the above.

1.222 Two further recent cases demonstrating the above process in action are *R (Thompson) v General Chiropractic Council*[150] and *Khan v General Teaching Council for England*.[151]

---

150 [2008] EWHC 2499 (Admin).
151 [2010] EWHC 3404 (Admin).

1.223　　In *Thompson*, T wished to call an expert witness but the panel took the view that his evidence was not relevant and set a hearing date when he was unavailable. The panel further considered that the hearing date was appropriate considering the interests of all parties and the need to avoid unnecessary delay. Lloyd Jones J concluded that while the court would normally be reluctant to interfere with the judgment of a professional panel it had a supervisory jurisdiction to ensure that parties are given a fair hearing. A short adjournment would cause no substantial prejudice. The expert evidence was crucial to the defence and, having concluded it was relevant, T should have been permitted to argue the point (irrespective of its merits on which his Lordship made no comment).

1.224　　In *Khan* two matters were in issue. The first was the panel's decision to proceed in K's absence rather than to adjourn. The second was that the panel relied upon transcripts of the students' complaints. Ouseley J dismissed K's appeal on both grounds. As to the adjournment his Lordship held that K had to show that the panel had acted outside its proper discretion, was wrong in principle, unfair or unreasonable or, that they had ignored relevant facts or considered irrelevant ones. K could not do so and the panel was right to proceed. As to the facts, again K had to show that the factual decision was wrong. Given that there was no reason to doubt the transcripts (K's representatives had the opportunity to check their accuracy) sight of the originals would not disclose collusion, manipulation, or other such matters which could be addressed by cross-examination on when, how and by whom statements were taken.

Character evidence

> Character is an integral part of the fitness to practise process. It is equally important when considering credibility and propensity, whether at the fact-finding stage, when judging the issue of impairment or when considering sanction.

1.225　In regulatory proceedings as in criminal proceedings, the character of the registrant is an important factor to be taken into account. There are three levels of character to consider – good, intermediate and bad.

1.226　　Although good character does not provide a defence to or excuse for any forms of misconduct, it has always been recognised as an important factor in criminal cases. The change in regulatory proceedings from an isolative consideration of a registrants alleged misconduct and impairment, to consideration of these matters in the context of his or her character (past, present *and likely future conduct*) brings regulatory proceedings in line with the established model in criminal trials. It accords with common sense and is fairer for reasons which become obvious when one considers the forward-looking approach to impairment propounded by the cases of *Cohen, Zygmunt* and *Cheatle* (see the discussion on impairment at para 1.393ff). Character should now be considered by the panel at *all* stages of the fitness to practise process – namely facts, impairment, sanction and even immediacy of order.

How should character be considered?

Good character

1.227 The following is adapted from the type of direction given in criminal proceedings. There are two distinct parts, known as first limb and second limb. They deal with credibility and propensity respectively. This or advice in similar terms adapted to the facts of the case must now be given by the legal assessor. A failure properly to consider character may be fatal to a finding adverse to the registrant.

1.228 In criminal proceedings good character means the defendant has no previous convictions or cautions. Reference might also be made to not being the subject of any other court order such as bind-overs and ASBOs if relevant. For regulatory proceedings this would mean an absence of previous penalties such as erasure or suspension, findings of impairment, misconduct, deficient professional performance, warnings, undertakings that recognise failures in conduct or performance short of misconduct, internal disciplinary proceedings as the case may be. In short, good character may (a) support a registrant's credibility – when he/she says that he did (or did not do) something he/she is entitled to expect weight to be given to his/her word and, (b) it may impact upon the issue of propensity and support the argument that he/she is less likely to act in the way alleged than a person who is not of good character. The direction should be as follows:[152]

- X is a person of good character. He/she has no previous (disciplinary matters to his/her name). Good character does not provide a defence but it is an important factor capable of assisting a registrant. It is relevant to your considerations in two ways.
- First, he/she has given evidence. His/her good character is a positive feature of the registrant which you should take into account when considering whether you accept what he/she told you.

152 Adapted from the Judicial Studies Board, *Crown Court Bench Book 2010* (Chapter 10).

- Second, the fact that the registrant has no previous disciplinary matters to his/her name may make it less likely that he/she acted as is now alleged. It has been submitted on behalf of the registrant that for the first time in his/her life he/she has been accused of misconduct (or deficient performance as the case may be). He/she is not the sort of person who would be likely to cast his/her good character aside in this way. That is a matter to which you should pay particular attention.
- However, judging what weight should be given to the registrant's good character and the extent to which it assists on the facts of this particular case is a matter for you. In making that assessment you are entitled to take account of everything you have heard about him/her.

1.229   As with all matters of weighing evidence, how important it is and how much it assists on any topic is a matter for the panel.

1.230   When a registrant gives evidence, he or she is entitled to a 'first-limb' character-direction regarding his or her credibility. Failure to do so may be fatal to the eventual decision of the panel – see *R v Berrada*[153] If the registrant does not give evidence but relies on other exculpatory statements by him or her as recounted by others (eg in police interviews), the registrant is entitled to a direction but modified in regard to the weight to be given to such comments because they are not made on oath – see *R v Vye*.[154] If the registrant has made no comments and does not give evidence, then a first-limb direction is not required.

1.231   In *Vye* the court of appeal held that the second limb direction should always be given regardless of whether an accused gives evidence. Such a policy decision was approved by the House of Lords in *R v Aziz*.[155]

1.232   Where matters occurred many years ago, the good character of the registrant in the intervening years may have particular significance – see *R v Small*.[156] In *GJB v R*[157] reference was made to this intervening time being a 'third limb' of the direction. The Court of Appeal rejected this, saying it is merely an appropriate adaptation of the propensity limb but, it illustrates how the legal assessor's advice should be properly crafted. This may be of particular significance given the lengthy delays before cases are heard by regulatory panels

153 (1989) 91 Cr App R 131.
154 [1993] 1 WLR 471.
155 [1996] AC 41.
156 [2008] EWCA Crim 2788.
157 [2011] EWCA Crim 867.

– two or more years is not uncommon. A careful assessment of character and its impact on a decision may be of particular importance.

1.233   If appropriate, reference should be made to the length and breadth of experience any witnesses (written or oral) have of the registrant. These are factors that the panel should consider when determining weight. Clearly if experienced reliable professionals have known a registrant for many years then he or she is entitled to expect considerable weight to be attached to their evidence (always remembering that character is not in itself a defence).

Intermediate character

1.234   In criminal proceedings it is often argued that a person who has old, spent or irrelevant convictions should benefit from a good character direction. It may be that the convictions are not mentioned in evidence or, they are mentioned to give a full picture and the jury is told to ignore them because they are old or spent, etc. Examples might be an old incident of speeding, a minor matter of disorder or similar – these would probably be irrelevant on a charge of dishonesty and vice-versa. The principle rule is that the jury must not be misled – likewise the panel should not be misled, nor should it mislead itself.[158]

1.235   Cautions involve an admission of guilt and may be evidence of bad character. Fixed penalty notices (even those for disorder) do not and are not. While convictions may, after a period of time become spent under the Rehabilitation of Offenders Act (ROA) 1974, this is relevant to civil matters and does not necessarily affect their relevance in criminal proceedings. The ROA 1974 does not apply to disciplinary proceedings against any registrants working in healthcare. Age is only one factor to consider in deciding whether a registrant may have regained his or her character.

1.236   As for incidents of previous misconduct or deficient performance, different considerations apply. If a registrant has a previous 'incident' on either his professional or personal record, it is a matter for the panel to consider its age, nature and intervening events before deciding whether having balanced the interests of both parties and the interests of justice, it is fair and reasonable to treat the registrant as someone who has regained his or her good character. This is a matter of discretion for the panel.[159] Of course if the previous incident is relevant to an issue the panel has to decide then it

158 *R v Gray* [2004] 2 Cr App R 498 and *R v Martin* [2000] 2 Cr App R 42.
159 *R v S* [2008] All ER (D) 295 (Nov).

may be impossible to disregard despite the passage of time – see *R v Rackham*[160] in which a sexual preference for young girls was in issue. An old conviction for unlawful (ie under-age) sexual intercourse was clearly relevant to character.

1.237   In regulatory proceedings, offences or previous misconduct involving dishonesty, sexual matters or pornographic material will almost always be relevant since these have a direct impact upon the safety of patients and the interests of the profession and, in particular, how the public (and the profession) must be able to place absolute trust in registrants. However, once again the panel should consider matters of time elapsed and similarity or otherwise when deciding what weight to apply to this evidence.

Bad character

1.238   The time-honoured approach to exclude bad character in criminal proceedings was swept away by the CJA 2003. The general exclusion was replaced by a complex set of rules the interpretation and application of which is still evolving. Whether this was a political decision or one based on evidence is moot but, the effect of the CJA 2003 is to bring bad character to centre-stage in criminal trials. Given that regulatory proceedings frequently take their lead from criminal proceedings, bad character is of importance in fitness to practise hearings. In addition, as outlined earlier in this section, matters of character are relevant at all stages of the case, not just sanction.

1.239   Bad character may be defined as 'evidence of or a disposition towards misconduct which is not to do with the alleged facts before the panel or in connection with the investigation or prosecution thereof.'[161] Misconduct is defined as an offence or other 'reprehensible behaviour'[162] which must itself have an element of culpability or blameworthiness as distinct from conduct that is irritating, inconvenient or merely upsetting to others.[163]

1.240   Given the wide ambit of the definition, even allegations of which a defendant has been acquitted are admissible to establish past misconduct if the prosecution can show it is relevant to an important issues and the defence do not succeed in excluding it (see CJA 2003 s101 below). This accords with the House of Lords decision in

---

160 [1997] 2 Cr App R 222.
161 Adapted from CJA 2003 s98.
162 CJA 2003 s112.
163 *R v Renda* [2006] 1 WLR 2948.

R v Z[164] in which multiple allegations of rape successfully defended on the basis of consent, were deployed by the prosecution to prove a further alleged offence where again the defence was consent. The relevance was that the previous matters demonstrated the improbability of his being so unlucky as to mistakenly believe a woman was consenting and be accused of rape for the fifth or sixth time.

1.241　While one talks in terms of 'previous convictions' matters occurring after the incident with which the panel is concerned may be admissible and, may be of particular relevance – see *R v Adenusi*[165] (and see the above discussion on good character post the alleged misconduct).

1.242　Bad character is now admissible in criminal proceedings under seven 'gateways' pursuant to CJA 2003 s101. In short these are as follows:

a) all parties agree to its admission;
b) the evidence is given by the defendant;
c) it is important explanatory evidence;
d) it is relevant to an important matter in issue between the defendant and the prosecution;
e) it has substantial probative value in relation to an important matter in issue between one defendant and another;
f) it corrects a false impression given by the defendant;
g) the defendant has attacked the character of another person.

1.243　It is important that the panel consider evidence of bad character in a proper staged process. The stages are (adapted from criminal procedure):

1) the panel determines admissibility;
2) the panel determines any application to exclude;
3) the weight to be given to the admitted evidence is a matter for the panel subject to appropriate advice as to the use(s) to which the evidence may be put;
4) the reasons for admission must be kept under review. If the ground of the hearing has shifted, the significance of the evidence may also have changed.

The panel should apply its mind to matters in this way and deal with these issues in its reasons.

1.244　The panel should also be warned a) not to place undue reliance on previous matters; b) that bad character cannot bolster a weak case;

164　[2000] 2 AC 483.
165　(2007) 171 JP 169.

and c) that current misconduct should not be inferred from past misdemeanours – see *R v Hanson*.[166]

1.245   Because the panel is judge of both law and fact, there is always the danger that it will hear an application that discloses bad character material but then, following advice, it decides to disregard it. While it is always to be remembered that a panel is comprised of professionals whose ability to sit upon panels has been assessed and affirmed by the regulatory body, to expect it to ignore irrelevant or marginally relevant previous misconduct may be a tall order. This is particularly so given that once character evidence is adduced its' application is not limited to the matters pertinent to the gateway by which it was admitted. It is in evidence generally and may be applied as the panel thinks appropriate.[167] This is subject only to a requirement for caution if evidence admissible and intended as background evidence might also go to propensity.[168]

1.246   Given the above, if possible and without misleading the panel, it is preferable for the parties to arrive at an agreed position to preserve both fairness and the appearance of fairness in fitness to practise proceedings. Issues of character should always be discussed with the legal assessor beforehand.

1.247   Gateways a) and b) require no elaboration save to say that it is preferable for counsel to obtain the registrant's agreement in writing before admitting previous matters or eliciting them voluntarily.

1.248   Evidence admissible under gateways d) and g) must be excluded on a defence application if its admission would have 'such an adverse effect on proceedings that the court ought not to admit it – see CJA 2003 s101(3). (See also the Police and Criminal Evidence Act 1984 s78 which gives the court power to exclude evidence that has such an adverse effect on proceedings. It applies to all gateways.)

1.249   Important explanatory evidence in c) means essential background evidence without which it would be 'impossible or difficult to properly understand other evidence in the case and its value for understanding the case as a whole is substantial'.[169] As stated above, this gateway should not be used slide in propensity evidence that would not otherwise be admitted. Where explanatory evidence is

---

166 [2005] 1 WLR 3169.
167 *R v Highton* [2005] 1 WLR 3472 (and several subsequent cases dealing with each of the gateways).
168 *R v Davis* (2008) 172 JP 358.
169 CJA 2003 s102(a) and (b).

admitted the better practice is to deal with it by way of agreement thus avoiding distraction and prejudice.[170]

1.250   In respect of d), important matters in issue are defined in the rather clumsy language of section 103. In essence they encompass whether the defendant has i) a propensity to commit the offences of the kind charged or ii) a propensity to be untruthful. Offences are of the same kind if they are of the same description, type or category. The only caveats to admission are that evidence of propensity under i), loosely akin to similar-fact evidence as opposed to untruthfulness, should not be admitted if the fact of the propensity makes it no more likely that he or she is guilty of the offence or, that the lapse of time since the earlier incident would make its admission unjust. 'Important matters' are yet further defined in section 112 as being 'of substantial importance in the context of the case as a whole'.

1.251   Gateway d) is not qualified by the old rule as regards similar fact evidence that its probative value is outweighed by its prejudicial effect. It need only be 'relevant'.[171] This is of particular importance as regards propensity since this is now a matter specifically in issue between prosecution and defence.[172]

1.252   The panel ought to apply its mind to propensity evidence in the following manner:

i)   Does the history establish a propensity to commit offences of the kind charged?

ii) Does that propensity make it more likely that he or she committed the offence?

iii) If the offence is of the same category or description (as opposed to type), is it just to rely upon it?

iv) Is it otherwise unfair to admit the evidence?

1.253   Propensity can be established by one previous event if it is of sufficient probative value – see *Hanson* (above). Whether the evidence is relevant, probative or ought to be excluded involves consideration of matters such as similarity of fact, the gravity and age of the previous conduct. The age of the conduct is particularly important since old events may simply be prejudicial without establishing any propensity.

---

170 *R v Cundell* [2009] EWCA Crim 2072 (a case on gateway a) but where the evidence would otherwise have been admitted under c)).

171 *Weir and others* [2006] 1 WLR 1885 (see the judgment in the case of the appellant *Somanathan*).

172 CJA 2003 s103.

1.254   Propensity to untruthfulness is distinct from mere dishonesty which may or may not involve lying.

1.255   Gateway e) is concerned with cut-throat defences. If the matter in issue is propensity to commit the type of offence then there is no limitation as between defendants save that it must be of substantial probative value. However, if the matter concerns a propensity to untruthfulness then under section 104, evidence as to a co-defendant's propensity to be untruthful is admissible only if one defendant has undermined the case for the other.

1.256   Gateway f) is essentially concerned with calling evidence in rebuttal of good character evidence led by the defence where such evidence is apt to mislead the jury.

1.257   Gateway g) is concerned with the position where an "imputation" has been cast upon another meaning that the other has committed an offence or is otherwise of bad character as defined by CJA 2003 s98.

Cross-admissibility in cases involving multiple charges

1.258   Section 112 provides that where a defendant faces multiple charges in the same case, the bad-character provisions apply as if the charges were in separate proceedings. Thus each count is cross-admissible against the other(s) pursuant to a gateway of admissibility. The intention is that if D faces several similar charges or, several similar accusations are brought in support of one charge, one accuser may support evidence from another. The rational, absent collusion between witnesses, is that there may be probative value in a multiplicity of similar allegations or, in the unlikelihood of multiple false allegations by independent witnesses.

1.259   In *R v Chopra*[173] it was considered more likely that a dentist had assaulted three complainants who made individual and independent complaint rather than if it was just one complainant. The court clearly took a holistic approach considering the evidence in the round when looking at cross-admissibility. However, in *R v Norris*[174] it was necessary for the jury to be sure that N had deliberately killed one patient by fatal injection before using that as evidence when considering other patient deaths.

1.260   The risk of collusion goes to the weight to be applied to evidence and not to its cross-admissibility since admissibility is approached on the basis that evidence is true unless it is patently obvious no jury

173 [2007] 1 Cr App R 225.
174 [2009] EWCA Crim 2697.

could find it so – see H^{175} a pre-CJA case but which was followed in *Weir and others* (see para 1.251 above). The caveat to admissibility is now in CJA 2003 s109, from which a panel need not assume evidence is true if 'no reasonable court or jury could reasonably find it to be true'. In addition, under section 107 if it becomes clear that evidence admitted as genuine is in fact contaminated by collusion or otherwise, the judge should direct an acquittal or a retrial if, bearing in mind the importance of the contaminated evidence, a conviction would be unsafe. In *Bhatt v GMC*[176] Langstaff J commented that section 107 applies only to criminal proceedings and 'not obviously' to disciplinary hearings. However, if collusion or the risk of collusion is established then a conviction may well be regarded as unsafe.[177]

1.261   A panel should be alive to the issue of contamination and deal with it as a matter of fairness and the weight to be applied to the evidence generally. If there is clear evidence of contamination, or the risk thereof, then doubtless the panel will apply less or even no weight to the particular evidence.

1.262   In considering cross-admissibility of allegations and/or other alleged misconduct, it is important to remember the message from *Chauhan v General Medical Council*[178] referred to previously (at para 1.59) that the panel should confine itself to the proper ambit of the disciplinary charges and should not consider prejudicial factual matters out-with the notice of hearing. The panel made findings of fact adverse to the registrant which could have been the subject of professional misconduct but were not within the charges as formulated. King J ruled that the findings of fact could not be properly or fairly used by the panel to support its decision. He further concluded that the panel had considered evidence of behaviour not the subject of a charge when determining the issue of dishonesty. He quoted Silber J from *Cohen v General Medical Council* (see para 1.57 above) that the process must focus solely on the heads of charge and rejected the GMC's submission that the extraneous material, even if strictly outside the ambit of the charges, could nonetheless be introduced as evidence of C's propensity to dishonestly exaggerate his expertise.

---

175 [1995] AC 596, HL.
176 [2011] EWHC 783 (Admin).
177 *R v Pepperrell* [2009] EWCA Crim 1209.
178 [2010] EWHC 2093 (Admin).

When should character be considered?

Facts

1.263 At the fact-finding stage, if some or all of the alleged conduct is disputed by a registrant, character is relevant to the weight to be applied to his or her evidence and to the cogency of his or her denials. It is also relevant when assessing propensity, that is the likelihood or otherwise of the registrant doing a specific act given that he or she has or has not previously committed the act complained of or anything else. How much weight is applied to character under each limb is a matter for the panel, but each limb must be considered.

Impairment

1.264 Character is now of considerable importance at the impairment stage. The cases of *Cohen, Zygmunt* and *Cheatle* (see under impairment at para 1.393ff) all require consideration of impairment in the light of all the facts and not just the misconduct admitted or found proved. A panel is to judge whether, given the facts admitted or proved, a registrant's fitness *is* impaired. In doing so the panel must judge matters now and look forward to consider how the registrant will behave in the future. The panel is making a judgment on risk to the profession, the public and the practitioner. These decisions can in part be explained as an assessment of the facts and risks in light of the registrant's character.

1.265 As stated above, good character is not a defence, conversely bad character is not always a signpost to future misconduct or risk. These should be weighed in the balance and may play an important role albeit subordinate to the risks implicit in the facts found proved.

1.266 Good character may play an important role when considering undertakings offered by a registrant or, when he or she asserts that a lesson has been learned following an admission of misconduct (a guilty plea). Clearly if the registrant has been disbelieved on oath that is not the case. The second limb of character (propensity) is likely to be of considerable importance, the more so because of the approach required by *Cohen, Zygmunt* and *Cheatle.*

Sanctions

1.267 While impairment involves a risk-assessment, the sanction stage involves the assessment of a *proportionate* response. Emphasis is rightly placed upon the public interest in declaring and upholding standards but, this does not preclude the consideration of character in appropriate cases.

1.268   If impairment stems from such gross misconduct that it is necessary to impose an immediate and lengthy order of suspension or order erasure to protect the profession or the public (eg sexual misconduct, dishonesty etc), then good character will play a much lesser role in determining sanction.

1.269   However, if the interests of the profession are less prominent and there is a greater public interest in returning the registrant to safe practice, character may play an important role in assessing the type or length of sanction. This is applicable in two instances:

a) where a short period of suspension is required to 'send a message' or uphold standards the panel will have to consider whether a shorter period is appropriate for a registrant with an otherwise unblemished record. A long order may not be necessary and may be disproportionate in the circumstances of such a case;

b) where the seriousness of the misconduct places the registrant on the cusp of one sanction or another, his or her good character may again play an important role in deciding whether to apply a greater sanction or, to mitigate the sanction from potential erasure to suspension or from suspension to conditions etc.

1.270   The above are all part and parcel of balancing the public and registrant's interests, protecting the profession but, allowing an otherwise good registrant to return to safe practice. To what extent character affects the type or length of sanction is a matter for the panel's professional judgment.

Immediate orders

1.271   Finally the panel should consider whether a registrant's good character affects the decision to impose an immediate order of conditions or of suspension. There may be occasions when an immediate order is not *necessary* to protect the public or in the practitioner's own interests but, a short suspension is otherwise required to uphold and declare standards.

1.272   The imposition of an immediate order, pending the expiry of the 28-day period during which a registrant may appeal, has the effect of lengthening the term of a suspension. If a suspension is short (eg two to three months) the effect of an immediate order is a 30–50 per cent increase in the suspension beyond that deemed appropriate. Despite the tenet that sanctions are not intended to be punitive, this may clearly have a punitive effect and be unfair and/or disproportionate. A registrant may ask for time to arrange his or her professional affairs before the sanction is invoked. While such applications are not to be encouraged, it is not necessarily an unreasonable request to make. A registrant's previous good character and clinical ability may be relevant in determining whether it is in the public interest to permit him or her to remain in unrestricted practice for a short period before the sanction bites so that they are not deprived of an otherwise competent practitioner longer than is necessary.

The tribunal and the hearing

Impartiality and independence of the tribunal

> The question is whether the fair-minded and informed observer, having considered the facts, would conclude that there was a real possibility that the tribunal was biased.[179]

1.273   Article 6 ECHR provides for the right to adjudication by an independent and impartial tribunal. Independence means separated from the executive and from the parties. Impartial means lacking in both bias and/or the appearance of bias.

1.274   Currently the regulators draw up the rules, and appoint both the prosecutors and the adjudicating panels to judge cases so they are not off to a good start. However, the mere fact that disciplinary proceedings against registrants are determined by a body which includes members of the same profession does not itself offend the requirement of independence and, it accords with the principle that a governing body is best placed to judge what is right for its profession – see *Stefan v UK*.[180] However, there is a clear potential conflict of interest. To address this, the Office of the Health Professions Adjudicator (OHPA) was established by the Health and Social Care Act (HSCA) 2008. The original plan was for the OHPA to take over proceedings at the GMC before rolling out to the other regulators however, it was abolished. A separate Medical Practitioners Tribunal Service has now taken over management of GMC proceedings. It remains to be seen whether it will take over other healthcare regulators' cases.

1.275   *Porter v Magill* provides the definitive statement on apparent bias as set out in the head-note. In addition, *R v Bow Street Metropolitan Stipendiary Magistrate ex p Pinochet*[181] makes clear the doctrine of automatic disqualification namely that no one should be a judge

---

179   *Porter v Magill* [2001] UKHL 67, [2002] 2 AC 357, at para 103, per Lord Hope.
180   (1998) 25 EHRR CD 130.
181   [2000] 1 AC 119 – *Pinochet No 2.*

in his or her own cause. The case revolved around the appearance of bias through Lord Hoffmann being a member of the House of Lords panel that gave judgment against Senator Pinochet in *Pinochet No 1*. Lord Hoffmann was at the time a director of, and raised funds for, Amnesty International Charity Ltd. This company is part of Amnesty International whose antipathetic views of Pinochet and the human-rights abuses in Chile were well known. Amnesty International was a party to the proceedings and supported the deportation and prosecution of Pinochet.

1.276   It was not suggested that Lord Hoffmann had any pecuniary interest in the decision rather it was an interest in a cause supported by a party. This led Lord Browne-Wilkinson to conclude that Lord Hoffmann should have automatically disqualified himself. His Lordship stated that there was no reason to limit the ambit of interests to pecuniary, proprietary or economic ones. Here the decision impacted upon a cause the judge promoted with others. While there was no suggestion of financial gain, his Lordship said 'there is no room for fine distinctions [if justice is done and seen to be done]'.[182] His Lordship emphasised the very unusual nature of the case including the fact that Amnesty International was a party to the proceedings and argued for a specific result.

1.277   Lord Nolan's admirably short comment at page 14 sums up the matter nicely 'where the impartiality of a judge is in question the appearance of the matter is just as important as the reality'.

1.278   In *Langborger v Sweden*[183] it was stated that in assessing independence and impartiality regard must be had to:

a) the manner in which panel members are appointed;
b) their term of office;
c) the existence of guarantees against outside pressure;
d) whether the regulator has the appearance of independence.

1.279   In *R v UKCC for Nursing, Midwifery and Health Visiting ex p Tehrani*[184] approved in *Preiss v General Dental Council*,[185] it was held that the fact that a member of the General Council could move between panels was sufficient to raise a real risk that the panels did not meet the requirements of independence and impartiality. There was also the added difficulty of the lack of an appeal.

182 At page 11.
183 (1990) 12 EHRR 416.
184 [2001] 1 IRLR 208.
185 [2001] UKPC 36, [2001] 1 WLR 1926 PC.

1.280   The Bar Council's own Disciplinary Tribunal failed to satisfy ECHR article 6 in *P (a barrister) v General Council of the Bar*.[186] The tribunal comprised members nominated by the President of the Council of the Inns of Court, some of whom came from a pool of names put forward by the Bar Council. One such member was also a member of the Bar Council's own Professional Conduct and Complaints Committee. The court held that i) there was a breach of article 6; ii) there was apparent bias satisfying the test in *Porter v Magill*; and iii) the committee and the Bar Council had a common interest in convictions. The member should have been disqualified at common law, under the *Pinochet* principle. In *Holder v Law Society*[187] the Divisional Court held the Solicitors Disciplinary Tribunal to be an independent and impartial tribunal that complied with article 6.

1.281   Evidence as to what actually happens generally and what happened in a specific instance may satisfy a criticism raised but, this is not a course to be recommended. In *National Greyhound Racing Club Ltd v Flaherty*[188] the Court of Appeal rejected an allegation of apparent bias against a steward. While the court was critical of the fact that the chief executive retired with the stewards on the panel, their clear evidence was that he did not take part in deliberations. The court commented that sporting bodies should be permitted to deal with disciplinary matters without the courts intervening provided their proceedings were consistent with the fundamental requirement of fairness. With respect to the National Greyhound Racing Club, when it comes to public safety, there is a distinction to be made between procedures that govern professional sporting complaints and professional healthcare complaints.

1.282   In *Kaur v ILEX*[189] K, a student member of the Institute of Legal Executives (ILEX), was accused of cheating in two examinations. One charge was found proved by a panel consisting of two lay members and a serving ILEX council member. Her appeal was dismissed by a tribunal consisting of two lay members and the vice-president of ILEX. She appealed on grounds of both apparent bias and automatic disqualification. Rix LJ concluded that the two doctrines were really part of 'a single overarching requirement: that judges should not sit [on cases] ... where there is a real possibility on the objective appearance of things, assessed by the fair-minded and informed observer

---

186 [2005] 1 WLR 3019.
187 [2005] EWHC 2023 (Admin).
188 [2005] EWCA Civ 1117.
189 [2011] EWCA Civ 1168.

... that the tribunal could be biased'.[190] He reiterated that any personal interest upon which this may be argued had to be more than negligible and concluded that by either test the vice-president was disqualified because of her senior role in ILEX and her consequent interest in its disciplinary policy.

1.283   From the above it can be concluded that panels should be, and be seen to be, divorced from any interest in the allegations, proceedings or result. Interest includes an intellectual or social concern or any other concern that is more than just passing.

Legal assessors

1.284   The role of the legal assessor is to advise the panel on matters of law, evidence, procedure and on its powers. The legal assessor has no part to play in respect of fact-finding, decisions or on the weight or cogency to be attached to evidence. The legal assessor may only advise upon its admissibility and, outline such factors as may impact upon matters of weight and cogency (eg time-lapse may affect memory, an honest witness may be mistaken etc) but he or she should be careful not to express or be seen to express an opinion on the evidence and what impact those factors have, if any – see *Walker v General Medical Council*.[191]

1.285   Likewise the legal assessor has no part to play in the decisions on impairment or sanction other than to advise upon the legal parameters and/or upon the legal accuracy of arguments deployed without giving a personal opinion on their veracity:

> The legal assessor is not a judge and his advice ... is not a summing up ... The legal assessor simply advises the [panel] on points of law ... The [panel is master] of both law and fact ...[192]

1.286   It is an advisory role, not a decision-making one. Any advice by a legal assessor should be given in open session with the parties afforded the opportunity to comment upon it – see *Nwabueze v General Medical Council*.[193] The panel are not bound to accept the legal advice given but, if they do not, they must clearly state this and, give full reasons.

1.287   If a registrant is represented, then the legal assessor may be invited to discuss matters with counsel for the registrant and the regulator in

190 At para 45.
191 [2002] UKPC 57.
192 *Libman v General Medical Council* [1971] UKPC 1 (per Lord Hailsham at page 3, numbered point 4).
193 [2000] 1 WLR 1760 PC.

order to clarify or reduce areas of conflict or, to determine disputes on admissibility of evidence to prevent a panel from becoming contaminated by inadmissible evidence.

1.288   If a registrant is not represented, then the legal assessor may do the above but, he or she should only do so with counsel for the regulator present to prevent a possible perception of bias and/or allegations of erroneous or biased advice. The legal assessor should never see the registrant alone. In the hearing, the legal assessor may assist by explaining procedure and/or rules of practice and evidence to the registrant, and explain what areas of evidence should be focused upon bearing in mind the decision(s) that the panel has to make. However, the legal assessor may not represent the registrant by putting questions or making submissions on his or her behalf.

Specialist advisers

> Specialist advisers are present to assist in the interpretation and/or significance of expert evidence. They should not give an opinion or comment upon the issue of fitness to practise. An adviser is not part of the panel, and as such he or she should not retire with the panel.
>
> Any advice must be given publicly, affording the parties an opportunity to challenge it including calling evidence if necessary.

1.289   If a registrant's fitness to practise is allegedly impaired by reason of adverse physical or mental health, a panel may direct that a specialist health or performance adviser be appointed to assist the panel, or that a health or performance assessment be carried out and a report provided. Medical assessors are distinct from legal assessors in that they are there to comment upon the evidence whereas legal assessors are not.

1.290   The case of *Watson v General Medical Council*[194] provides assistance on the role of such assessors. Stanley Burnton J reviewed both domestic and European cases when making his decisions. These included *Richardson v Redpath Brown and Co Ltd*[195] in which Viscount Simon LC said:

> [T]o treat a medical assessor, or indeed any assessor, as though he were an unsworn witness in the special confidence of the judge, whose testimony cannot be challenged by cross-examination and perhaps cannot even be fully appreciated by the parties until judgment is

194 [2005] EWHC 1896 (Admin).
195 [1944] AC 62.

given, is to misunderstand what the true functions of an assessor are. He is an expert available for the judge to consult if the judge requires assistance in understanding the effect and meaning of technical evidence. He may in proper cases suggest to the judge questions which the judge himself might put to an expert witness with a view to testing the witness's view or to making plain his meaning. The judge may consult him in cases if need as to the proper technical inferences to be drawn from the proved facts, or as to the extent of the difference between apparently contradictory conclusions in the expert field ... but I cannot agree that [giving evidence] is within the scope of an assessor's legitimate contribution.[196]

1.291   His Lordship also considered the position of similar independent advisers in European jurisdictions, the magistrates' clerk in the UK and a legal assessor in *Nwabueze v General Medical Council*.[197]

1.292   His Lordship concluded that:

> The role of a medical assessor is not the same as a legal assessor to a tribunal ... legal advisors do not in general give their personal views on the facts ...[198]

> ... those who advise a tribunal on issues of fact, whether as its experts or as assessors, should do so openly, in the presence of the parties [giving them an opportunity] to make submissions on that advise before the tribunal makes its decision [and to call experts in response if the advice is 'controversial'].[199]

> The medical assessors' special relationship with a tribunal makes it the more important that all their advice is given in the presence of the parties. The assessors are not parties to the case. Nor are they members of the panel. Where their advice may be adverse to the practitioner's case, it is particularly important that it is given in the presence of the parties [and that they be given] an opportunity to address that advice. Otherwise, the suspicion may be created that the advice given in private [is different] or that the assessors have exercised influence on the decision of the tribunal]. A perception of unfairness and of bias on the part of the tribunal is liable to be created.[200]

1.293   Specialist advisers should thus give advice in the presence of the parties, this being limited to the significance of the information before the panel. They are not entitled to express an opinion on the registrant's fitness to practise.

196   At pages 770–771.
197   [2000] 1 WLR 1760.
198   At [56].
199   At [60].
200   At [61].

Legal representation

> A registrant is entitled and best advised to be represented by
> counsel in regulatory proceedings before a panel determining
> fitness to practise (including Interim Orders Panels) since they have
> the potential substantially to affect his or her right to practise.
>
> A registrant *may* be entitled to representation in disciplinary
> proceedings if these have the potential substantially to affect his or
> her right to practise, or are likely to influence other proceedings that
> may themselves have such an impact. The risk should be closely
> considered since it may be indirect and not immediately apparent.
> If in doubt, it would be wise for the registrant to seek, and the
> regulator to permit, legal representation.

1.294   As noted previously, ECHR article 6 guarantees certain minimum
rights when facing a trial upon civil and/or criminal matters. These
rights include:

a) a fair and public hearing in the determination of civil or criminal
matters and, when charged with a criminal offence;

b) to have adequate time and facility to prepare; and

c) to defend himself or herself in person or through legal assistance of his or her own choosing or, if he or she has not sufficient
means to pay for legal assistance, to be given it free when the
interests of justice so require.

1.295   However, as we have seen from the above section on the ECHR (see
paras 1.25 and 1.26), it is not always clear that it applies to regulatory
proceedings. On the one hand they may determine the right to practise
a profession, and the ECHR is then engaged; on the other, if proceedings are unlikely to affect the right to practise then arguably the ECHR
will not apply. The uncertainty is an unfortunate state of affairs.

1.296   In criminal proceedings a defendant is entitled to be represented
by a properly qualified representative of his or her choice, however
in publicly funded matters this does not mean quite what it says.
There are two aspects – first in choosing a representative, and second
hearing dates being fixed so that a chosen representative can attend.
If a representation order is held by one firm, transferring to another
is extremely difficult and may only occur in limited circumstances
with the leave of the court. Despite the fact that counsel's availability
should be considered, it is rarely a determining factor. In civil proceedings, public funding for representation is severely curtailed if
not entirely extinguished.

1.297 In disciplinary proceedings, the registrant is frequently represented or seeks to be represented by someone chosen, appointed or paid for through a professional or union defence fund. It is important for the registrant to understand that, subject to the availability of funding, he or she has the right to choose an advocate for the hearing. The union or defence fund cannot dictate who this is.

1.298 Whether a registrant is entitled to be represented depends on the type of proceedings and the affect they may have on the registrant's career. Interim order hearings and fitness to practise hearings before regulatory panels require access to representation at the very least. Internal disciplinary proceedings are less likely to merit representation, particularly if the proceedings are not determinative of a registrant's right to practice. The fact that both High and Appeal Court rulings have been reversed suggests this is and will remain a thorny issue.

1.299 In *Kulkarni v Milton Keynes Hospital NHS Foundation Trust*[201] the purported contractual restrictions upon the right to representation were examined. K a trainee doctor was accused of misconduct (a sexual assault) and a Medical Protection Society (MPS) representative was assigned to his case. The representative was not legally qualified. The trust argued that based on Department of Health policy, K could be accompanied by a representative *not* acting in a legal capacity during the disciplinary proceedings. The MPS suggested that the trust had the discretion to allow legal representation and, since the case was complex and serious it should be exercised in favour of proper representation. The trust refused arguing that there were no exceptional circumstances to deviate from normal procedure. K sought a declaration that the trust had acted unlawfully and in breach of contract in their refusal to allow legal representation. The High Court dismissed K's application on the basis that the express contractual term did not permit legal representation so one could not be implied. Even if there was such a discretion the case was not exceptional. The court held that the refusal of legal representation was not a denial of natural justice and, queried whether article 6 applied to disciplinary proceedings. K appealed and the Court of Appeal held that, given the terms of K's employment contract, he was entitled to be represented at his disciplinary hearing by a lawyer instructed by the MPS.

1.300 In his judgment Smith LJ states that:

> ... the distinction which the [ECtHR made in *Le Compte v Belgium*] was that in ordinary disciplinary proceedings, where all that could be

at stake was the loss of a specific job, Article 6 would not be engaged. However, where the effect of the proceedings could be far more serious and could, as in this case, deprive the employee of the right to practice his or her profession, the article would be engaged.[202]

Since this was a sexual allegation there would undoubtedly be alert-letters warning others not to employ K if the matters were found proved. This would effectively end K's NHS practice.

1.301   From *Kulkarni*, article 6 appears to be engaged when a registrant faces grave and/or quasi-criminal charges that, if proved, will have a severe impact on his or her ability to work. This clearly reflects the discussion on the applicability of the ECHR (see *Ghosh v General Medical Council*[203] above). The decision was doubtless welcome to those accused of misconduct, but was met with less enthusiasm by NHS bodies.

1.302   In *Hameed v Central Manchester University Hospitals NHS Foundation Trust*[204] H argued that disciplinary proceedings which resulted in her dismissal for gross misconduct were not article 6 compliant. H used surgical scissors in an operation when they were no longer sterile having been used previously, and sought to persuade others to lie in a subsequent investigation. Swift J distinguished *Kulkarni* on the facts since although H's dismissal would make employment difficult, it was not impossible. Nor were there exceptional circumstances justifying departure from the normal procedures of the disciplinary process.

1.303   Swift J accepted the submission that it is:

> ... unsatisfactory for the decision as to whether article 6 applies to disciplinary proceedings against hospital practitioners to be taken on a case by case basis, depending on the gravity of the charge, the prospect of proceedings resulting in dismissal and/or the evidence about the ... chances of obtaining alternative employment in the event of dismissal.[205]

Not surprisingly Her Ladyship agreed such an approach caused uncertainty in the application of article 6, but opined that given the wide range of circumstances in which disciplinary proceedings may be brought pursuant to the 'Maintaining high professional standards in the modern NHS framework' (MHPS)[206] it was arguable that article 6 did not apply.

---

202 At para 65.
203 [2000] 1 WLR 1915.
204 [2010] EWHC 2009 (QB).
205 At para 89.
206 'Maintaining high professional standards in the modern NHS' framework. A Department of Health publication from 2003 reflecting the procedures agreed

1.304   In *R (G) v Governors of X School and Y City Council* [207] G faced the school's disciplinary procedures for allegedly kissing a pupil and was dismissed for abuse of trust and misconduct. This meant he would be reported to the Secretary of State for Children, Schools and Families as possibly unsuited to work with children and could be placed on the 'children's barred list' by the Independent Safeguarding Authority (ISA). G sought a declaration that the denial of a lawyer was in breach of his article 6 right to representation. The High Court and the Appeal Court agreed. The latter reasoned that G's right to practise his profession was at stake in the barring procedure before the ISA and this was likely to be 'profoundly' affected by the disciplinary proceedings. These in turn might well be affected by a professional advocate. Article 6 was engaged and G should have been afforded the opportunity to have a legal representatives present.

1.305   The Supreme Court disagreed (4:1) and held that the facts of each case must be considered on its merits taking account of: whether or not the first proceedings are determinative of the second; how closely linked the proceedings really are; whether the proceedings have the same object; and any policy reasons for dis-applying article 6. The majority judgment given by Lord Dyson was that article 6 undoubtedly applied to the ISA proceedings because these directly affected G's right to practise his profession as a teaching assistant and to continue to work with children. However, the disciplinary proceedings did not determine this but were merely concerned with whether G should be employed by the school. The disciplinary proceedings did not directly determine or substantially influence the ISA proceedings which were entirely independent. A judgment by the ISA would only be made after a full and independent assessment of the facts and merits of the case. Article 6 was thus not engaged at the stage of the disciplinary process.

1.306   Lord Kerr dissented, suggesting that the different stages could not be looked at in isolation. He thought the ISA would be substantially influenced by the school's disciplinary proceedings because this was where the evidence had been tested and was where G's rights should be protected.

1.307   With respect to the majority, while it may be correct to assert that the ISA *should* not be affected by the disciplinary proceedings, the idea that the views of the school governors will have 'receded far into

between the DoH, NHS, BMA and BDA regarding the resolution of conduct issues.
207 [2011] UKSC 30.

the background' risks overstating the point. Lord Kerr's view that the ISA is likely to pay 'close attention' to what was said, done, proved or disproved in live evidence before the governors is far more realistic.

1.308   The regulators have their own rules, investigations, fact-finding panels and appeals. They ought to be independent of and not influenced by internal disciplinary proceedings. However, a number of residual concerns remain. Disciplinary proceedings differ as between workplaces, and the reliability and fairness of some may be in question. What is clear is that when disciplinary proceedings have the potential substantially to affect a registrant's right to practise, or are likely to influence other proceedings that may themselves have such an impact, it is important that the registrant is properly represented in those disciplinary proceedings. This will protect the integrity of those proceedings and may affect the admissibility of any matters found proved.

1.309   The above concerns relate to the question of whether a regulator seeks to refer to disciplinary proceedings or findings at any subsequent regulatory hearing. They could only do so on the basis that the information is relevant and probative. If the registrant was not represented at the earlier disciplinary proceedings and matters went against him or her, it may well be argued that to introduce the material is unfair and/or prejudicial, particularly if it is capable of being described as of profound importance. The propriety and fairness of the earlier proceedings may then require examination. This risk is avoided if registrants are afforded access to appropriate assistance and representation from the outset. A little flexibility at the early stages may prevent a whole raft of problems later on.

1.310   A final matter relating to healthcare professionals is the system of alert letters regarding patient, public or staff safety, or other publicity within the health service itself. These may broadcast decisions or allegations leading to damage to reputation and make work within the public sector and/or the private sector impossible. If that happens or if there is a risk of this, then it remains arguable that a registrant should be represented (see *Bonhoeffer* discussed above under hearsay and under article 8 at para 1.39).

1.311   The emphasis on each case being decided on its own facts is of course the reason why this problem will not go away particularly when decisions may turn on very fine distinctions of fact and degree. If there is any doubt then it would behove the registrant to be represented and the regulator to permit representation whether the proceedings are internal disciplinary proceedings or not. The alternative is the risk of further lengthy, expensive and stressful litigation which benefits no one.

Absence of the practitioner

> The panel has the discretion to proceed in the absence of the practitioner but:
>
> a) there must be strict adherence to the requirement that all reasonable effort to effect service has been made; and
>
> b) the decision to proceed must be taken with 'the utmost care and caution' and only after full consideration of the competing interests with emphasis on those of the practitioner.

1.312   In broad terms, proceedings may continue in the absence of a practitioner, however this is subject to compliance with the appropriate rules of process and the general rule that all participants – complainant, accused and witnesses should normally be present.

1.313   When a registrant is neither present nor represented before the Fitness to Practise Panel, a panel may nevertheless proceed to consider and determine the allegation or adjourn and issue directions if they are satisfied that 'all reasonable efforts' have been made to serve the practitioner with notice of the hearing.[208]

1.314   The equivalent of this rule applies to interim order cases before most regulators. In GMC proceedings notice (whether effective or not) must be served in 'such time as is reasonable in the circumstances of the case'. Ordinarily this will be at least seven days, but it may be shorter in exceptional circumstances.[209]

1.315   It is incumbent upon all practitioners to maintain a professional or other address for service of documentation. If they change this address it is their responsibility to notify their regulator. Because the onus is on the practitioner to maintain lines of communication, it is not unusual for proceedings to go ahead in his or her absence once the safeguards provided by the rules have been met.

1.316   The rules do *not* require actual service to be made upon the registrant. The panel may proceed if satisfied that 'all reasonable effort/ steps have been made to serve [in accordance with the rules]'. This is because it is the practitioner's duty to be contactable, and when the regulator has done all it reasonably can, the paramount principles of protecting the public and the public interest come into play. Neither is served by delay.

---

208 GMC (Fitness to Practise) Rules 2004 r31; NMC (Fitness to Practise) Rules 2004 r21.

209 GMC (Fitness to Practise) Rules 2004 r26.

1.317   To be satisfied that all reasonable effort or steps have been made or taken, the panel must receive evidence. This is explicit in the case of the NMC Rules and implicit (but settled law) in respect of the GMC Rules. It is not sufficient for the panel simply to be told that service has been attempted. However, meeting the above criterion is not particularly difficult and in practice is usually settled by the regulator proving service by way of reference to recorded delivery documentation, email receipts or preferably both.

Service of notices and documents

1.318   Each regulator's rules of practice provide that once a matter has been referred to a panel, a notice giving details of the allegation and the date of any panel hearing should be served upon the registrant as soon as reasonably practicable. Generally there will be at least 28 days' notice.[210] The notice should include reference to the fact that a panel may proceed in the absence of the registrant provided 'all reasonable effort' has been used to effect service.[211] Some regulators require more than one notice with a general 28-day notice giving details of the allegation and hearing and, a further notice with precise details of time and place seven days before the hearing. Notice may be shortened by consent or if the registrar, case-manager or investigating committee, as the case may be, considers it reasonable, in the public interest and in the exceptional circumstances of the case.

1.319   Each regulator has its own rules on service. They should be rigorously adhered to and will be strictly construed both to prove service and in deciding whether to continue in absence or adjourn. In general, service may be by post to a registrant's professional address, or to the address of his or her solicitor, trade union or defence organisation, or email to his or her previously notified e-mail address or that of his or her representative. Service may be proved by evidence of confirmation of registered posting or recorded delivery, receipt of email or a signed statement of delivery to the registrant's proper address/email address or that of his or her representative. Notice does not actually have to reach the registrant it is enough to ensure that the rules have been adhered to.[212] (Note that the NMC Rules do not permit service of notice of hearings on the registrant. They do

---

210 GMC (Fitness to Practise) Rules 2004 r15; NMC (Fitness to Practise) Rules 2004 r11.

211 GMC (Fitness to Practise) Rules 2004 r31.

212 See as an example, GMC (Fitness to Practise) Rules 2004 r40 as amended to allow service by email; and MA 1983 Sch 4 para 8.

allow for serving notice on representatives and also the service of other documents.)

1.320   While a panel may proceed in absence, it should carefully consider whether it is fair and in the interests of justice so to do.

1.321   In *R v Hayward*[213] the Court of Appeal summarised the principles to be applied when dealing with an absent defendant as follows:

(a) An accused has, in general, a right to be present and represented at his trial.

(b) The above rights can be waived by the accused:
   (i) they may be wholly waived if, knowing or having the means of knowledge of his trial he deliberately and voluntarily absents himself and/or withdraws instructions from those representing him;
   (ii) they may be partly waived if, being present and represented at the outset, the accused behaves in such a way as to obstruct the proceedings and/or withdraws his instructions from those representing him.

(c) The trial judge has a discretion to permit a trial to take place or continue in the absence of an accused and/or his legal representatives.

(d) That discretion must be exercised with great care and it is only in rare and exceptional cases that it should be exercised in favour of a trial taking place or continuing, particularly if the accused is unrepresented.

(e) In exercising that discretion, fairness to the defence is of prime importance but fairness to the prosecution must also be taken into account. The judge must have regard to all the circumstances of the case including, in particular:
   (i)   the nature and circumstances of the accused's behaviour in absenting himself from or disrupting the trial and, in particular, whether his behaviour was deliberate, voluntary and such as plainly waives his right to appear;
   (ii)   whether an adjournment might result in his attending voluntarily and/or not disrupting proceedings;
   (iii) the likely length of such an adjournment;
   (iv)   whether though absent, he is, or wishes to be, legally represented at the trial or has waived his right to representation;
   (v)   the extent to which his legal representatives are able to present his defence;
   (vi)   the extent of the disadvantage to him in not being able to give his account of events, having regard to the nature of the evidence against him;
   (vii) the risk of the jury reaching an improper conclusion about his absence (but see (f) below);

213 [2001] 2 Cr App R 11.

(viii) the seriousness of the offence to the accused, victim and public;

(ix) the general public interest and the particular interest of victims and witnesses that a trial should take place within a reasonable time of the alleged events;

(x) the effect of delay on the memories of witnesses;

(xi) where there are co-defendants, the undesirability of separate trials, and the prospects of a fair trial for those who are present.

(f) If the judge decides that a trial should take place or continue in the absence of an unrepresented accused, he must ensure that the trial is as fair as the circumstances permit. He must, in particular, take reasonable steps, both during the giving of evidence and in the summing up, to expose weaknesses in the prosecution case and to make such points on behalf of the accused as the evidence permits. In summing up he must warn the jury that absence is not an admission of guilt and adds nothing to the prosecution case.[214]

1.322   *Hayward* was considered and approved by the House of Lords in *R v Jones*,[215] Lord Bingham making the following important observations:

> ... the discretion to commence a trial in the absence of a defendant should be exercised with the utmost care and caution ... If the absence of the defendant is attributable to involuntary illness or incapacity it would very rarely, if ever, be right to exercise the discretion in favour of commencing the trial, at any rate unless the defendant is represented and asks that the trial should begin.[216]

> ... the European Court of Human Rights has never found a breach of the Convention where a defendant, fully informed of a forthcoming trial, has voluntarily chosen not to attend and the trial has continued.[217]

1.323   Lord Hoffmann pointed out the principle repeatedly emphasised in the Strasbourg jurisprudence, that:

> The question ... is not whether the defendants waived the right to a fair trial but whether in all the circumstances they got one. It is whether on the particular facts of the case the proceedings, taken as a whole and including the appellate process, satisfied the requirements of the Convention.[218]

---

214 At para 22.
215 [2002] UKHL 5.
216 At para [6].
217 At para [9].
218 At para [20].

Lord Bingham added two caveats to the *Hayward* principles. First, the seriousness of the offence should not be considered, the principles would be the same whether the offence was serious or minor. Second, even if the accused absconded voluntarily, it would generally be desirable that he or she be represented.

1.324 Mr Jones took the matter to the ECtHR, arguing that the case had been a breach of his article 6 right to a fair trial. However, the ECtHR declined to admit his complaint, ruling that the proceedings were fair since he had deliberately absented himself and, when he subsequently appealed, he could have called fresh evidence. His complaint was thus 'manifestly ill founded'.[219]

1.325 While the above principles emanate from the criminal jurisdiction, the judgment of the Privy Council in *Tait v Royal College of Veterinary Surgeons*[220] makes it clear they have equal application to professional disciplinary hearings.

1.326 The clear message is that absence is not a bar to proceeding, but great caution should be exercised. In view of the need to ensure compliance with article 6 rights, that caution is entirely appropriate as is the focus on the practitioner's rights albeit taking account of other competing interests. However, if a panel proceeds with due care and diligence, voluntary absence will not avail the registrant on appeal.

1.327 In the criminal jurisdiction, if a defendant is absent from court for reasons beyond his or her control, such as illness, the trial may not continue in the defendant's absence unless he or she consents.[221] If the defendant becomes ill during his or her trial, the judge must either adjourn the case until the defendant recovers or discharge the jury.[222] Again these criminal principles have equal application in regulatory proceedings.

1.328 A number of recent cases illustrate the rather slavish application of the above principles of service, but also the caution with which the discretion to proceed must be exercised.

1.329 In *Jatta v Nursing and Midwifery Council*[223] the panel continued with disciplinary proceedings in the absence of the practitioner. Notice had been properly served at his registered address although the council was aware that he was travelling abroad and no longer lived there. While the panel could have adjourned for a message to be

---

sent to J's email address (which was known and would probably have resulted in contact and attendance), the rules only required all reasonable efforts be made to comply with the rules. Since they provided for postal service not email service the Court of Appeal held that there had been no procedural irregularity in proceeding in absence.

1.330   The above rather mechanical adherence to procedure proves the point that absence is no bar to proceedings once the rules have been complied with. However, unlike the NMC, the GMC (Fitness to Practise) (Amendment) Rules 2009,[224] which came into force on 7 August 2009, amended rule 40(2) to allow for service of notices and documents by email.

1.331   In *R (Raheem) v Nursing and Midwifery Council*[225] Holman J held that the NMC's Conduct and Competence Committee had not exercised its discretion properly when proceeding on an allegation of misconduct in the absence of the practitioner. Notice had been properly served even though R had not received the recorded delivery envelope and was unaware of the hearing. However, the legal assessor did not give any or any sufficient advice to the panel as to the separate exercise of the discretion to proceed in absence. The panel did not give any detailed consideration of the matter rather it went straight to its ruling. Holman J concluded that since the decision to continue in absence must be taken with the utmost care and caution, the legal assessor's advice was significantly flawed. Furthermore it was important for the panel to demonstrate its application of the care and caution required.

1.332   While *Raheem* may arguably be an appeal allowed in part upon defective reasons, the message is clear. There must be a demonstrably careful and reasoned approach to the issue. Despite the ruling in *Jatta* and, in light of *Raheem*, it is submitted that the increased reliance upon e-mail now means that it would be unwise to proceed without clear evidence covering both traditional and electronic methods of service. The optional methods of service provided by the GMC Rules make this a necessity. While the NMC rules may only require service by letter, it is not unreasonable to expect communication by email and, failure to do so will only lead to further challenge and wasted costs.

---

224 Schedule to the General Medical Council (Fitness to Practise) (Amendment) Rules Order of Council 2009 SI No 1913.
225 [2010] EWHC 2549 (Admin).

1.333   Recent examples of good practice are *Yusuf v Royal Pharmaceut-ical Society of Great Britain*[226] and *Varma v General Medical Council*.[227] In *Yusuf*, Munby J approved the council's staged approach of iden-tifying the key issue in the case (in this instance whether Y had vol-untarily absented himself) then assessing the evidence in a fair and measured way before concluding that he had. It then separately con-sidered whether to proceed doing so with the 'utmost caution'. This approach was said to be unassailable. In *Varma*, the practitioner had been granted short stays on medical grounds but, the evidence did not justify a complete stay since he was capable of participating in the pro-ceedings. The panel proceeded having properly balanced the compet-ing interests of the practitioner against the public interest of dealing with serious allegations. In fact V was able to attend some parts of the hearing. Forbes J approved the separation of the decision to refuse an application to stay from the decision whether to proceed in absence.

1.334   In contrast, the case of *R (Al-Zayyat) v General Medical Council*[228] is an example of poor practice. AZ had been involved in a high-profile criminal trial at which she had given evidence for the prosecution. She was later subjected to fitness to practise proceedings, however medical evidence confirmed that she was too ill to attend and likely to suffer a mental breakdown if she did. The panel concluded that it had to decide whether the illness was genuine or fake, and not being satisfied that the illness was genuine, it determined to proceed in absence. Mitting J reiterated that to proceed when a registrant was absent involuntarily was unusual and potentially unfair. He con-cluded that the decision to proceed was perverse in the absence of evidence showing the illness was not genuine and involuntary. It would also seem that the panel reversed the burden of proof (in not being satisfied the illness was genuine).

1.335   A word of caution for practitioners is added by *Abdalla v Health Professions Council*[229] in which A sought to argue that proceeding in her absence was in breach of her article 6(1) rights and/or it was a breach of natural justice. Sullivan J rejected this argument. Hav-ing failed to produce medical evidence to support her claim that she could not attend, he stated that A:

> ... was certainly entitled – whether under Article 6(1) or as a matter of fairness or natural justice – to an opportunity to attend the hearing.

226 [2009] EWHC 867 (Admin).
227 [2008] EWHC 753 (Admin).
228 [2010] EWHC 3213 (Admin).
229 [2009] EWHC 3498 (Admin).

But if she chose not to avail herself of that opportunity then the committee was entitled to proceed in her absence.[230]

1.336 The word of caution stems from the court concluding that the lack of funds to pay for legal representation which resulted in solicitors declining to act would not justify further adjournment when there was no realistic prospect of that situation changing in the reasonably near future. Ms A could have appeared and explained the position to the panel herself, although whether this would have made any difference is debateable given the public (and personal) interest in resolving allegations which were by then at least two-and-a-half years old.

1.337 The importance of providing medical evidence to support an application to adjourn on health grounds was demonstrated in *Faulkner v Nursing and Midwifery Council*.[231] The decision to proceed in the absence of the registrant who failed to provide such evidence was upheld. Although F later gave evidence via a telephone link, he was restricted to addressing sanctions since the decisions on misconduct and impairment had already been made in his absence. Similarly, in *R (Tinsa) v General Medical Council*[232] T had been convicted of public order offences and failing to surrender to bail. On appeal following disciplinary proceedings he submitted that he was unable to represent himself through mental illness, and the panel should have adjourned to obtain psychiatric evidence to assist on sanction. Underhill J concluded that there was no evidence before the panel to support T's claim that he was suffering from mental illness at the time or in difficulty defending himself or that he wanted an adjournment.

1.338 The court acknowledged that an appeal may be allowed if subsequent new or fresh evidence (ie not before the panel) demonstrates that an appellant was not in a fit state to defend himself at the time. However, the fresh evidence provided did not establish that T was unfit to defend himself. Finally, he stated that there was no basis to suggest that the panel had erred in law by failing to adjourn and obtain medical evidence of its own motion.

1.339 Clearly, as with so many issues, each decision is likely to be fact/case specific but, unless there is evidence before the panel to raise a concern, there is no requirement to adjourn on grounds of health. There may of course be rare cases where subsequent evidence comes to light and doubtless these can be considered on their merits when they arise.

230 At para [6].
231 [2009] EWHC 3349 (Admin).
232 [2008] EWHC 1284 (Admin).

The burden and standard of proof

> The burden of proving disputed facts is on the prosecuting authority.
>
> The standard required is 'on the balance of probabilities'.
>
> The standard does not change with the seriousness of the allegation.
>
> Serious allegations do not require better evidence.
>
> It is common sense that to prove that an unlikely event occurred may require persuasive evidence.
>
> Similarly the consequences of a finding do not alter the standard.

1.340   In all healthcare disciplinary proceedings the burden of proving allegations against a practitioner rests with the prosecuting council.[233] As with all fitness to practise proceedings, this relates only to the facts to be proved and the statutory ground, ie misconduct, lack of competence or health. Any issue of impairment flowing from facts found proved are a matter of 'judgment' to be made by the panel. (Whether or not proved facts amount to grounds for finding impairment are matters of 'judgment' not proof – see below under 'impairment'.)

1.341   The standard required to prove factual allegations is now settled in fitness to practise proceedings as being to the civil standard, or the 'balance of probabilities'. The GMC Rules[234] provide that the standard of proof applicable in any proceedings:

(a) before a FTP Panel where the allegation and the alleged facts are read out by the [panel secretary] on or after 31st May 2008; and

(b) before the Investigation Committee where the Presenting Officer begins to outline the allegation and the facts ... on or after 31st May 2008,

is that applicable to civil proceedings.

1.342   The only exception to the above is in NMC cases where the facts pre-date their 2004 change in rules from the criminal to the civil standard. In these very few historic cases the test is still 'beyond reasonable doubt'.

1.343   Despite the apparent simplicity in meaning of 'on the balance of probabilities', there has been debate on whether the seriousness of an allegation affects the threshold of the test. The starting point of this is

233 While this is recognised by all, only NMC (Fitness to Practise) Rules 2004 r30 makes it explicit thus 'where facts relating to an allegation are in dispute, the burden of proving such facts shall rest on the Council'.

234 GMC (Fitness to Practise) Rules 2004 r34(12).

Re H (Minors)[235] in which Lord Nicholls of Birkenhead expressed the opinion that the balance of probabilities test is satisfied if 'the court considers that, on the evidence, the occurrence of the event was more likely than not'.[236]His Lordship continued:

> When assessing the probabilities the court will have in mind as a factor, to whatever extent is appropriate in the particular case, that the more serious the allegation the less likely it is that the event occurred and, hence, the stronger should be the evidence before the court concludes that the allegation is established on the balance of probability. Fraud is usually less likely than negligence. Deliberate physical injury is usually less likely than accidental physical injury. A stepfather is usually less likely to have repeatedly raped and had non-consensual oral sex with his under age stepdaughter than on some occasion to have lost his temper and slapped her. Built into the preponderance of probability standard is a generous degree of flexibility in respect of the seriousness of the allegation.

> Although the result is much the same, this does not mean that where a serious allegation is in issue the standard of proof required is higher. It means only that the inherent probability or improbability of an event is itself a matter to be taken into account when weighing the probabilities and deciding whether, on balance, the event occurred. The more improbable the event, the stronger must be the evidence that it did occur before, on the balance of probability, its occurrence will be established. Ungoed-Thomas J. expressed this neatly in *In re Dellow's Will Trusts*[237] 'The more serious the allegation the more cogent is the evidence required to overcome the unlikelihood of what is alleged and thus to prove it.'[238]

1.344   Some of the above was seized upon as suggesting that a higher threshold needs to be attained when matters are serious and/or have serious consequences. However, in *Re B (children)*[239] and *Re D (Secretary of State for Northern Ireland intervening)*[240] the House of Lords made clear that while the seriousness of an allegation or its consequences may necessitate more careful consideration of the evidence, it did *not* affect the test to be applied.

1.345   In *Re D* the court stated that the civil standard of proof on the balance of probabilities was *'finite and unvarying'*. The speeches reflected

235 [1995] UKHL 16.
236 At para 73.
237 *In re Dellow's Will Trusts* [1964] 1 WLR 451.
238 At paras 73–74.
239 [2008] UKHL 35.
240 [2008] UKHL 33.

comments in *R (N) v Mental Health Review Tribunal*[241] that while a court or tribunal might have to look at facts more critically or more anxiously because of the inherent unlikelihood of an occurrence, the seriousness of an allegation, or, in some cases, the consequences which could follow, those were all matters of ordinary experience, requiring the application of good sense by the court or tribunal. They did *not* require a different standard of proof or an especially cogent standard of evidence.

1.346   In *Re B (children)* Lord Hoffmann commented that:

> There is only one rule of law, namely that the occurrence of the fact in issue must be proved to have been more probable than not. Common sense, not law, requires that in deciding this question, regard should be had, to whatever extent appropriate, to inherent probabilities ... it is common sense to start with the assumption that most parents do not abuse their children. But this assumption may be swiftly dispelled by other compelling evidence ... It would be absurd to suggest that the tribunal must in all cases assume that serious conduct is unlikely to have occurred. In many cases, the other evidence will show that it was all too likely.[242]

And Baroness Hale of Richmond:

> ... [announced loud and clear that there is one test]. The inherent probabilities were simply something to be taken into account, where relevant, in deciding where the truth lay ... there is no logical or necessary connection between seriousness and probability.[243]

1.347   Thus *Re B (children)* and *Re D* endorse the general approach that a serious allegation will require careful analysis of the evidence taking account of inherent probabilities and other matters requiring the application of good sense, but neither the probability, seriousness nor its consequences require a different standard of proof or an especially cogent type of evidence. *Re B* and *Re H* are quoted in the recent judgment of Judge Behrens in *Hosny v General Medical Council*.[244] While there is no further comment, it is submitted that this is, at least for the time being, the last word on the matter.

---

241 [2005] EWCA Civ 1605.
242 Para 15.
243 Paras 70 and 73.
244 [2011] EWHC 1355 (Admin).

Is there a case to answer? Half-time submissions

> Submissions of no case to answer may be made in respect of a case or a specific allegation.
>
> They may be made where a) there is no evidence or b) there is some evidence but it is weak, vague or inconsistent and, looked at 'in the round', a panel could not properly find the case (or fact) proved.

1.348   The rules of the healthcare regulators make different provision regarding the approach to submissions at the close of the prosecution case. Some have specific rules, others do not, but it is accepted practice to make a submission in appropriate cases. Submissions are made only on the evidence and information furnished by the prosecution. It is worth noting that the rules provide for submissions regarding whether there is *sufficient* evidence. This highlights the issues set out in *R v Galbraith*[245] below and particularly that a submission may still be made when there is some evidence on a particular matter as opposed to none at all. It is therefore very important to analyse the quality of the evidence at the close of the prosecution case to see whether it merits the epithet of sufficient or not.

1.349   Half-time submissions may be made in relation to the entire case or against discrete allegations. The latter is particularly important in complex cases with lengthy particulars where there may be some evidence regarding various allegations but little or none regarding others. This is a key opportunity to challenge the case as a whole or, to reduce its scope and/or gravity. To this end, the advocate should make separate submissions where appropriate as well as any global one(s) and the panel should look at them separately. Not only does this provide clarity and the opportunity for each submission to be given the attention it deserves, it also reflects the staged approach set out in *Cohen v General Medical Council*[246] to first make findings of fact, then consider impairment and finally decide sanctions.

1.350   Some regulators make express provision for submissions on the sufficiency of the evidence to a) find a fact proved or b) support a finding of impairment. They are worded slightly differently (eg the GMC rule makes reference to whether submissions should be upheld, while the NMC rule refers to determining whether there is a case to answer) but the meaning is the same.[247] The HPC rules (now HCPC)

245   (1981) 73 Cr App R 124.
246   [2008] EWHC 581 (Admin).
247   GMC (Fitness to Practise) Rules 2004 r17(2)(g); NMC (Fitness to Practise) Rules 2004 r24(7) and (8).

make no specific provision but submissions are usually made in accordance with those for the GMC.

1.351   Half-time submissions are based upon the test laid down by Lord Lane LCJ in the case of *R v Galbraith* as follows:

> (1) If there is no evidence that the crime alleged has been committed by the defendant, there is no difficulty. The judge will of course stop the case.
>
> (2) The difficulty arises where there is some evidence but it is of a tenuous character, for example because of inherent weakness or vagueness or because it is inconsistent with other evidence:
>
> (a) where the judge comes to the conclusion that the prosecution evidence, taken at its highest, is such that a jury properly directed could not properly convict upon it, it is his duty, upon submission being made, to stop the case,
>
> (b) where however the prosecution evidence is such that its strength or weakness depends on the view to be taken of a witness's reliability or other matters which are generally speaking within the province of the jury and where on one possible view of the facts there is evidence upon which a jury could properly come to the conclusion that the defendant is guilty, then the judge should allow the matter to be tried by the jury ... There will of course, as always in this branch of the law, be borderline cases. They can safely be left to the discretion of the judge.[248]

1.352   As His Lordship states, the first part of the test (where there is no evidence) is straightforward – it is the second part, and particularly the caveat regarding borderline cases, that causes the most difficulty. Various re-statements or commentaries have provided some assistance, but the question remains to some extent a matter of art rather than science.

1.353   As to the second limb, the problem in criminal cases is that the trial judge should not usurp the function of the jury. While His Lordship states that a case may also be stopped where there is some evidence but it is of a tenuous character because of inherent weakness, vagueness or inconsistency, those are matters usually left to a jury.

1.354   In regulatory proceedings the same effect is obtained by the panel asking itself the question, 'is there any evidence upon which *a properly directed panel could* find the alleged facts proved?'. If the answer is 'yes it could' (not that it would), then the panel should proceed to hear the defence case receiving evidence from the registrant and any supporting witnesses or material.

---

248 Per Lord Lane at p127.

1.355   Assistance, often referred to as a 'gloss', was provided by Turner J in *R v Shippey*[249] who said that the requirement to take the prosecution evidence at its highest did not mean 'picking out all the plums and leaving the duff behind'. Just because some parts of the evidence supported the prosecution case did not mean that a case should inevitably go to the jury. The judge should assess the evidence and, if it is self-contradictory and out of reason or common sense then it was tenuous and suffered from inherent weakness. In *R v Pryor, Sparkes and Walker*[250] a case from the Northern Ireland Court of Appeal it was said that *R v Shippey* was a case on its own facts that did not establish any new principles. This was further explained in *R v Alobaydi*[251] in which it was said that the inconsistencies between the witnesses in *Shippey* were so substantial as to render the complainant's whole evidence incredible. It was thus no more than an application of the principles in *Galbraith*.

1.356   Three further cases in point are:

- *R v P*,[252] a case involving circumstantial evidence where the court stated that the correct approach is to look at the evidence in the round, treat it with appropriate care and scrutiny and ask whether there is evidence upon which a properly directed jury could convict;
- *R v Jabber*[253] – where a case rested upon the drawing of an inference it does not have to be an inference that only an unreasonable person would fail to draw;
- *R v Gian and Mohd-Yusoff*,[254] in which it was said that the fact that a proposition consistent with innocence could not be scientifically excluded did not justify stopping the case. Juries assess all evidence, including expert evidence to make realistic judgments, not ones based on fanciful possibilities.

The same may be said of regulators' panels.

1.357   The application of the principle is well stated in *R v Hassan*,[255] where Lord Lowry LCJ said:

> I entirely accept the principles as stated by Lord Lane, always remembering that no evidence does not mean literally no evidence, but rather

249 [1988] Crim LR 767 (Crown Court).
250 [2004] EWCA Crim 1163.
251 [2007] EWCA Crim 145.
252 [2008] 2 Cr App R 6 CA.
253 [2006] 10 *Archbold News* 3.
254 [2010] Crim LR 409, CA.
255 [1981] 9 NIJB.

no evidence on which a reasonable jury properly directed *could* (and I emphasise that word) return a verdict of guilty.

1.358   The principles to be drawn from the above are:

- If there is no evidence, a half-time submission should be made and the panel should stop the case or dismiss a particular allegation.
- Where there is some evidence, a registrant will need to assess the *quality* of the evidence to see whether a submission can be made or not. To succeed a registrant must persuade the panel that the council has failed to present evidence capable of supporting the particular(s), or that such fact(s) about which there is evidence are themselves incapable of supporting a case of impairment.
- The quality of the evidence must be tested *holistically* looking at its strengths (eg clarity, any supporting evidence, what reasonable inferences may be drawn etc) *and* at its weakness (eg lack of reliability, inconsistency with other evidence, vagueness, lacking common-sense, unable to meet a reasoned as opposed to fanciful argument etc).

1.359   If following this exercise, the panel finds no evidence to support the case or the relevant particular(s), it has an obligation to stop the case. However, if on one possible view of the fact(s) there is evidence on which the panel could properly come to the conclusion that the allegation is well founded (ie there is evidence capable of founding a case), then the proceedings should continue. This does not mean that there will necessarily be sufficient information to find the facts proved to the required standard at the close of the evidence, only that there is a case to answer.

1.360   One final matter is the argument raised by the NMC regarding whether the *Galbraith* definition of no case to answer applies following the change from the criminal burden of proof to the civil burden of proof in disciplinary proceedings. The NMC has suggested that the half-time approach of the civil courts propounded in *Benham Ltd v Kythira Investments Ltd*[256] should be followed namely that the regulator need only produce a 'scintilla' of evidence.

1.361   With respect to the NMC, this ignores the type of proceedings and thus the context of Simon Brown LJ's comment. In *Benham*, pursuant to the Civil Procedure Rules, the question was 'what is the test for a submission of no case when the defendant has *not* been 'put to his election' before making submissions? That is if, contrary to the general rule, he or she has not been asked to indicate whether or not he

256 [2003] EWCA Civ 1794.

or she will give evidence if he or she loses the submission. In those circumstances alone the question should be:

> Have the claimants advanced a prima facie case, a case to answer, a scintilla of evidence, to support the inference for which they contend, sufficient to call for an explanation from the defendants? That it may be a weak case and unlikely to succeed unless assisted, rather than contradicted, by the defendant's evidence, or by adverse inferences to be drawn from the defendant's not calling any evidence, would not allow it to be dismissed on a no case submission.[257]

1.362   This is an unusual situation even for civil proceedings. Furthermore there is no such election before submissions in regulatory proceedings triggering an altered test. Regulatory proceedings are on all fours with criminal trials at this point where evidence and witnesses are being assessed, rather than issues of contract or tort. It is noteworthy that although Simon Brown LJ used three phrases all required the evidence called to be 'sufficient to call for an explanation'. There is also the clear wording of the NMC Rules which refer to 'a case to answer' and nothing more. The meaning of this phrase has been made clear in *Galbraith* and even in *Benham* is arguably more than just a scintilla.

1.363   In conclusion there appears to be little benefit to a new approach since if there is only a scintilla of evidence, there is the clear prospect of the case falling foul of the principles of proportionality and public interest in continuing a weak prosecution.

Findings

Impairment

There is no burden or standard of proof – it is a question of 'judgment' by the panel.

Impairment may be based upon historical matters or a continuing state of affairs, but it is to be judged at the time of the hearing. To do this, the panel must look forward taking account of any reparation, changes in practice, conduct or attitude since the matter(s) found proved actually occurred.

Personal mitigation is less relevant, but effort to accept and correct remediable errors should be taken into account.

---

257 At para 39.

1.364   All regulators take action when a registrant's fitness to practise is called into question. Each will inquire into whether a registrant's fitness is 'impaired'. The term impaired is an ordinary word in common usage. It is not defined in the MA 1983 or its equivalents, and there has been argument on its meaning and effect in matters of professional discipline.

1.365   The HPC publication *Managing fitness to practise*[258] states:

> When we say that someone is fit to practise, we mean that they have the skills, knowledge, character and health to practise their profession safely and effectively. We also mean that we trust them to act legally.[259]

1.366   It is important to recall the staged process that the panel *must* follow in regulatory hearings: first to make findings of fact, then to consider misconduct, then impairment and finally to decide sanctions. This is made clear by cases such as *Cohen v General Medical Council*[260] and *Cheatle v General Medical Council*[261] with which the panel will be familiar. The stages give the practitioner several chances to challenge the case – first on the facts, second on what conclusions can be drawn from the facts found proved and finally what sanctions may be imposed thereafter. Even if misconduct or poor performance is proved, that does not mean that impairment necessarily follows, or if it does, that sanctions are necessarily burdensome to the individual.

1.367   The case of *Saha v General Medical Council*[262] is not authority for an alternative proposition. In that case, one issue to be determined was the separate consideration of misconduct and impairment. Stephen Morris QC sitting as a Deputy High Court Judge held that while it would be better if the panel clearly indicated distinct consideration of the two issues it was not fatal in *all* cases if it did not. The rules require two steps but where misconduct inevitably or necessarily leads to a finding of impairment it may be that the reasoning for misconduct and impairment cannot be distinguished. While this may be correct as a matter of logic it is submitted that the staged process should be adopted with the panel giving clear and separate judgment upon each issue.

---

258 HPC, *Managing fitness to practise*. A guide for employers and registrars. July 2006. Available at www.hcpc-uk-org.

259 *Managing fitness to practise*, 2006, page 2.

260 [2008] EWHC 581 (Admin).

261 [2009] EWHC 645 (Admin).

262 [2009] EWHC 1907 (Admin).

1.368   Unlike matters of fact which are to be decided on balance of probabilities, whether or not proven facts amount to impairment are matters of judgment not proof – *Council for the Regulation of Healthcare
Professionals v General Medical Council and Biswas.*[263]

1.369   Where a panel finds some charges proved, but others not, it may
still reach the view that a registrant's fitness to practise is impaired.
In *Ndisang v Nursing and Midwifery Council*[264] N faced four charges.
The first charge was not proved, the second was proved and the third
and fourth were admitted. N appealed and was successful in respect
of the third charge only on a technical matter. The court held that
this had no effect on the panel's finding of fitness to practise or the
sanction imposed.

1.370   The GMC's authority to take action regarding a practitioner stems
from section 35C of the MA 1983. Other regulators act upon similar
authority so it is set out below as of general application.

- Section 35C(1) says that the section applies when an allegation is
made that a practitioner's 'fitness to practise *is* impaired' (emphasis added).
- Section 35C(2) provides that a person's fitness to practise *shall be
regarded as impaired* by reason only of the following five factors:
  a) misconduct;
  b) deficient professional performance;
  c) a criminal conviction or caution in the British Islands for a
  criminal offence, or a conviction elsewhere for an offence
  which, if committed in England and Wales, would constitute
  a criminal offence;
  d) adverse physical or mental health;
  e) a determination by a body in the UK responsible under any
  enactment for the regulation of a health or social care profession to the effect that his fitness to practise as a member of
  that profession is impaired, or a determination by a regulatory
  body elsewhere to the same effect.
- Section 35(3) makes it clear that the section applies even if the
matter(s) complained of occurred abroad, or before the practitioner was in fact registered.

1.371   While there is no definition, the above factors – misconduct, poor
performance, health, conviction or other censure – provide a fairly
broad idea of what is likely to be regarded as impairment; whether it

263 [2006] EWHC 464 (Admin).
264 [2009] EWHC 2487 (Admin).

is, is of course fact-specific. Further help is gleaned from *The meaning of fitness to practise*[265] provided by the GMC and summarised below. This illustrates the sort of behaviour that could call registration into question. It should be read in conjunction with the GMC's *Good medical practice*[266] but, is a sensible starting point. Similar publications by other regulators give equally clear guidance.

1.372   As a general principle, it is accepted and acceptable that everyone sometimes makes mistakes. One-off incidents will need to be investigated and any harm put right but, unless very serious or with very serious consequences, they are unlikely in themselves to indicate a fitness to practise problem. *Good medical practice* puts it this way:

> Serious or persistent failures to meet the standards in this booklet will put your registration at risk.[267]

1.373   However, queries regarding fitness to practise are likely to arise if a registrant has acted or failed to act with the following result(s):

- *The registrant's performance has harmed patients or put patients at risk of harm.* This might be indicated by a series of incidents, persistent technical failures or repeated departures from good practice.
- *The registrant shows a deliberate or reckless disregard of clinical responsibility towards patients.* This may manifest itself in an unwillingness to practise ethically or responsibly or a serious lack of insight into obvious problems of poor practice; it need not be criminal, but may indicate a lack of integrity;
- *The registrant's health is compromising patient safety.* A serious medical condition (including an addiction to drugs or alcohol) and a failure (or inability) to follow appropriate medical advice about modifying practise to minimise the risk to patients would meet this test.
- *The registrant has abused a patient's trust, violated a patient's autonomy or other fundamental right.* Acting without regard for patients' rights or feelings, or abusing his professional position as a doctor, will usually give rise to questions about a doctor's fitness to practise.
- *The registrant has behaved dishonestly, fraudulently or in a way designed to mislead or harm others.* This behaviour is such that public confidence in the profession generally might be undermined if the regulator did not take action.

265   GMC, *The meaning of fitness to practise*. A GMC policy statement approved in 2001.
266   GMC, *Good medical practice*. (Current edition is 2006.)
267   GMC, *Good medical practice*, page 5.

1.374   The above advice is illustrative of the behaviour or circumstances which could call registration into question. Guidance published by the individual regulators (eg the GMC's *Good medical practice*) provides a more complete picture but it is not exhaustive. It is always most important to remember that, while other cases are illustrative, the outcome of any case depends on its own particular facts.

Misconduct

1.375   Until recently a finding of misconduct on the facts was likely to result in a judgment of impairment. However, consistent with the words '*is impaired*' and with the oft-stated intent to regulate rather than punish, panels must now look forward and not just look back over past events. Cases of misconduct, particularly ones concerning errors in professional judgment, will have to be considered in the light of surrounding events including those that have occurred since the incident(s) complained of and any subsequent efforts at rectification. This is important because registrants may find themselves before a panel for one or two errors of judgment in patient management or professional conduct that fall short of deficient professional performance which covers a range of errors over a range of patients.

1.376   If a panel has made a judgment of misconduct based upon the facts found proved, it must now receive evidence on matters that might previously be regarded as mitigation – other competent work, pressures on the hospital of overwork, understaffing etc and, crucially, evidence on whether the misconduct is capable of remedy, and has since been or is being remediated by the registrant. The panel must thus consider what has occurred in the light of the registrant's professional record and both personal and professional character, before and after the event.

1.377   While each case is dealt with on its own facts, it may be that the above is unlikely to assist a registrant accused of gross personal misconduct such as dishonesty, sexual impropriety or other similarly reprehensible acts. It can and may make all the difference where the misconduct is relatively minor, or the care of or attitude toward an individual patient has been poor, but it has been acknowledged and practices or attitudes have been modified appropriately.

1.378   It may be suggested that this makes it more difficult for the regulator to sustain allegations of impairment due to misconduct when a registrant has made a serious mistake. However, this is in accordance with the policy of enabling an otherwise competent registrant's return to safe practice as opposed to merely dolling out punishment.

It was also not the intention of the legislature, As Silber J stated in *Cohen v General Medical Council* 'the fact that stage 2 is separate from stage 1 shows that it was not intended that every case of misconduct found at stage 1 must automatically mean that the practitioner's fitness to practise is impaired'.[268]

1.379 Having outlined the principles it is helpful to consider some of the cases in which this line of reasoning has now been made clear.

What is misconduct?

1.380 Misconduct and/or lack of competence are not defined by the regulators. They are potentially wide concepts and may include some though not all departures from good practice. Additionally not all misconduct will be so serious or beyond remedy to impair current fitness to practise. Whether there is actually a reference to 'serious' or 'gross' misconduct or not, a degree of gravity is required since matters must be reasonably serious to go up to the Interim Orders Panel or Fitness to Practise Panels. There is also a distinction to be made between misconduct and lack of competence. This may have an important effect on sanction and the public or professional perception or stigma attached to proceedings.[269] On the facts of a case, it may be beneficial and possible to argue that neither misconduct nor lack of competence are made out, or that it is only the latter.

1.381 Misconduct has been described and defined in several cases, the following being the most important.

1.382 In *Nandi v General Medical Council*[270] Collins J adopted the observation of Lord Clyde in *Rylands v General Medical Council*[271] that:

> ... professional misconduct is 'a falling short by omission or commission of the standards of conduct expected among medical practitioners, and such falling short must be serious'. The adjective 'serious' must be given its proper weight, and in other contexts there has been reference to conduct which would be regarded as deplorable by fellow practitioners. It is of course possible for negligent conduct to amount to serious professional misconduct, but the negligence must be to a high degree.[272]

1.383 His lordship stated that it is not restricted to conduct which is morally blameworthy. It could include seriously negligent treatment

---

268 [2008] EWHC 581 (Admin) para 63.
269 *Remedy UK Ltd v General Medical Council* [2010] EWHC 1245 (Admin).
270 [2004] EWHC 2317 (Admin) per Collins J, paras 31–33.
271 [1999] Lloyd's Rep Med 139.
272 At 149.

or a failure to provide treatment measured by objective professional standards. Obviously, dishonest conduct can very easily be regarded as serious professional misconduct, but conduct which does not amount in any way to dishonesty can constitute serious professional misconduct if it falls far short of the standard that is considered appropriate by the profession.

1.384   Lord Cooke of Thorndon in the Privy Council case of *Preiss v General Dental Council*[273] said:

> It is settled that serious professional misconduct does not require moral turpitude. Gross professional negligence can fall within it. Something more is required than a degree of professional negligence enough to give rise to civil liability but not calling for the opprobrium that inevitably attaches to the disciplinary offence.[274]

1.385   In *R (Calhaem) v General Medical Council*[275] Jackson J stated that:

> The word 'misconduct' in [MA 1983] section 35C(2)(a) does not mean any breach of the duty owed by a doctor to his patient: it connotes a serious breach which indicates that the doctor's fitness to practise is impaired.

1.386   Following a review of the authorities, His Lordship derived five principles relevant to that case which involved failures by a consultant anesthetist and departure from *Good medical practice* in the context of a serious operation. These are:

1) Mere negligence does not constitute 'misconduct' within the meaning of section 35C(2)(a) of the MA 1983. Nevertheless, and depending upon the circumstances, negligent acts or omissions which are particularly serious may amount to 'misconduct'.

2) A single negligent act or omission is less likely to cross the threshold of 'misconduct' than multiple acts or omissions. Nevertheless, and depending upon the circumstances, a single negligent act or omission, if particularly grave, could be characterised as 'misconduct'.

3) 'Deficient professional performance' within the meaning of section 35C(2)(b) is conceptually separate both from negligence and from misconduct. It does not mean any instance of sub-standard work. It connotes a level of professional performance which indicates that the doctor's fitness to practise is impaired. It is unacceptably low which (save in exceptional circumstances) has been demonstrated by reference to a fair sample of the doctor's work.

273 [2001] UKPC 36.
274 At para 28.
275 [2007] EWHC 2606 (Admin) at para 26.

4) A single instance of negligent treatment, unless very serious indeed, would be unlikely to constitute 'deficient professional performance'.

5) It is neither necessary nor appropriate to extend the interpretation of 'deficient professional performance' in order to encompass matters which constitute 'misconduct'. (See para 39 of the judgment.)

1.387 In *Mallon v General Medical Council*[276] Clarke LJ poured a little cold water on attempts to refine the meaning of misconduct or serious professional misconduct. He described misconduct as a 'wrongful or inadequate mode of performance of professional duty'. However, he regarded descriptions of 'serious' or 'would be regarded as deplorable by fellow practitioners' (per Collins J in *Nandi*) as 'tending to obscure rather than assist'. He said that it was better to leave such matters to the skilled judgment of the panel rather than pursue a 'definitional chimera'.

1.388 The above outline the limits of misconduct. This is important since a registrant may face a hearing not because of personal impropriety but because he or she has mismanaged or been negligent in a specific case. Previously, little account was taken of other positive factors. Now, it is important to set the matters complained of in the context of his or her whole practice. This is further apparent from a review of the facts and outcome of *Calhaem* (para 1.385 above).

1.389 C, an anaesthetist, made a number of mistakes while treating one patient. These resulted in the patient being taken to intensive care, although she eventually made a full recovery. The panel found that C's actions did amount to misconduct and deficient professional performance such that his fitness to practise was impaired. C was suspended for three months. Jackson J held that although all C's mistakes related to just one patient they did cross the line between negligence and misconduct. However, he quashed the finding of deficient professional performance because the legal assessor failed to advise the panel that this could only result from one episode of treatment in 'exceptional circumstances'. As a result, the sanction was downgraded, although the finding of impairment itself remained.

1.390 In *Williams v General Medical Council*[277] disciplinary action was taken on the basis of W's allegedly negligent conduct. He failed to disclose material based on an honest belief that it had no forensic value. W argued he had not acted in bad faith and a finding of serious

276 [2007] CSIH 17, 2007 SC 426.
277 [2007] EWHC 2603 (Admin).

professional misconduct was not justified. Davies J dismissed the appeal, citing *Preiss* (above) stating that gross or culpable negligence can constitute serious professional misconduct. Davies J concluded that the panel was entitled to take account of the fact that W had the highest responsibility, his evidence could be pivotal in criminal trials and the serious consequences of his actions. A finding of serious professional misconduct was justified given W's 'uncorrected' and 'formidable' errors over a three-year period.

1.391   In *Remedy UK Ltd v General Medical Council* (see para 1.380 above) the court reviewed several authorities in relation to the meaning of misconduct, including *Roylance v General Medical Council*,[278] *Allinson v General Medical Council*,[279] *Marten v Royal College of Veterinary Surgeons Disciplinary Committee*[280] and *Meadow v General Medical Council*[281] and derived the following principles regarding misconduct and fitness to practise:

(1) Misconduct is of two principal kinds. First, it may involve sufficiently serious misconduct in the exercise of professional practice such that it can properly be described as misconduct going to fitness to practise. Second, it can involve conduct of a morally culpable or otherwise disgraceful kind which may, and often will, occur outwith the course of professional practice itself, but which brings disgrace upon the doctor and thereby prejudices the reputation of the profession.

(2) Misconduct falling within the first limb need not arise in the context of a doctor exercising his clinical practice, but it must be in the exercise of the doctor's medical calling. There is no single or simple test for defining when that condition is satisfied.

(3) Conduct can properly be described as linked to the practice of medicine, even though it involves the exercise of administrative or managerial functions, where they are part of the day to day practice of a professional doctor. These functions include the matters identified in *Sadler*, such as proper record-keeping, adequate patient communication, proper courtesy shown to patients and so forth. Usually a failure adequately to perform these functions will fall within the scope of deficient performance rather than misconduct, but in a sufficiently grave case, where the negligence is gross, there is no reason in principle why a misconduct charge should not be sustained.

(4) Misconduct may also fall within the scope of a medical calling where it has no direct link with clinical practice at all. *Meadow*

278 [2000] 1 AC 311.
279 [1894] 1 QB 750.
280 [1966] 1 QB 462.
281 [2007] QB 462.

provides an example, where the activity in question was acting as an expert witness. It was an unusual case in the sense that Professor Meadow's error was to fail to recognise the limit of his skill and expertise. But he failed to do so in a context where he was being asked for his professional opinion as an expert paediatrician. Other examples may be someone who is involved in medical education or research when their medical skills are directly engaged.

(5) *Roylance* demonstrates that the obligation to take responsibility for the care of patients does not cease simply because a doctor is exercising managerial or administrative functions one step removed from direct patient care. Depending upon the nature of the duties being exercised, a continuing obligation to focus on patient care may co-exist with a range of distinct administrative duties, even where other doctors with a different specialty have primary responsibility for the patients concerned.

(6) Conduct falls into the second limb if it is dishonourable or disgraceful or attracts some kind of opprobrium; that fact may be sufficient to bring the profession of medicine into disrepute. It matters not whether such conduct is directly related to the exercise of professional skills.

(7) Deficient performance or incompetence, like misconduct falling within the first limb, it may in principle arise from the inadequate performance of any function which is part of a medical calling. Which charge is appropriate depends on the gravity of the alleged incompetence. Incompetence falling short of gross negligence but which is still seriously deficient will fall under [MA 1983] section 35C(2)(b) [deficient professional performance] rather than (a) [misconduct].

(8) Poor judgment could not of itself constitute gross negligence or negligence of a high degree but it may in an appropriate case, and particularly if exercised over a period of time, constitute seriously deficient performance.

(9) Unlike the concept of misconduct, conduct unrelated to the profession of medicine could not amount to deficient performance putting fitness to practise in question. Even where deficient performance leads to a lack of confidence and trust in the medical profession, as it well might – not least in the eyes of those patients adversely affected by the incompetent doctor's treatment – this will not of itself suffice to justify a finding of gross misconduct. The conduct must be at least disreputable before it can fall into the second misconduct limb.

(10) Accordingly, action taken in good faith and for legitimate reasons, however inefficient or ill-judged, is not capable of constituting misconduct within the meaning of section 35C(2)(a) [misconduct] merely because it might damage the reputation of the profession. Were that not the position then Professor Meadow would have

been guilty of misconduct on this basis alone. But that was never how the case was treated.[282]

1.392   The court commented that there was no clear boundary between conduct capable of rendering a doctor unfit to practise and conduct which is not. Fitness to practise is not solely limited to clinical practise alone. It may include other aspects of a doctor's calling 'sufficiently closely linked to the practise of medicine' (eg deficient research, incompetent teaching).

Is the misconduct capable of remedy?

1.393   This was outlined in *Cohen v General Medical Council*[283] in which Silber J said:

> Any approach to the issue of whether a doctor's fitness to practise should be regarded as 'impaired' must take account of 'the need to protect the individual patient, and the collective need to maintain confidence [in the] profession as well as declaring and upholding proper standards of conduct and behaviour of the public in their doctors and that public interest includes amongst other things the protection of patients, maintenance of public confidence in the' (sic). In my view, at stage 2 when fitness to practise is being considered, the task of the Panel is to take account of the misconduct of the practitioner and then to consider it in the light of all the other relevant factors known to them in answering whether by reason of the doctor's misconduct, his or her fitness to practise has been impaired. It must not be forgotten that a finding in respect of fitness to practise determines whether sanctions can be imposed: s 35D of the [MA 1983].[284]

> There must always be situations in which a Panel can properly conclude that the act of misconduct was an isolated error on the part of a medical practitioner and that the chance of it being repeated in the future is so remote that his or her fitness to practise has not been impaired. Indeed the Rules have been drafted on the basis that the once the Panel has found misconduct, it has to consider as a separate and discreet (sic) exercise whether the practitioner's fitness to practise has been impaired ...[285]

> ... It must be highly relevant in determining if a doctor's fitness to practise is impaired that first his or her conduct which led to the charge is easily remediable, second that it has been remedied and third that it is highly unlikely to be repeated.[286]

282   At para 37.
283   [2008] EWHC 581 (Admin) paras 62–63.
284   At para 62.
285   At para 64.
286   At para 65.

1.394   In *Zygmunt v General Medical Council*[287] Mitting J ruled that evidence
that Z was a safe doctor, given by many colleagues, should have been
adduced at the second (impairment) stage rather than when deciding on sanction as had hitherto been the case. He noted that even if
a panel found that a practitioner was guilty of misconduct it may yet
conclude that his fitness to practise is not impaired. It is an issue to
be addressed separately. He noted that Dame Janet Smith in the Fifth
Shipman Inquiry Report (2004) recognised that present impairment
must be gauged partly by his or her past conduct or performance but
also by reference to how he or she is likely to behave or perform in
the future. He said:

> In a misconduct or deficient performance case ... It may well be, espe-
> cially in circumstances in which the practitioner does acknowledge
> his deficiencies and takes prompt and sufficient steps to remedy
> them, that there will be cases in which a practitioner is no longer any
> less fit to practise than colleagues with an unblemished record.[288]

1.395   Mitting J adopted the approach of Silber J in *Cohen* that when fitness
to practise is being considered, the task of the panel is to take account
of the misconduct of the registrant and then to consider in the light
of all the other relevant factors known to them whether his or her fitness to practise *is* (rather than *has been*) impaired.

1.396   The correct approach is to focus on the registrant's fitness to practise as at the date of the hearing. In *Sarkodie-Gyan v Nursing and
Midwifery Council*,[289] a health case, the issue of present impairment
and looking forward (see the next section) was considered. Unfortunately, looking forward turned into speculation. S had a history of
addiction and depression. She had recently recovered but this had
not been tested in stressful situations at work. HHJ Grenfell held
that the panel had been wrong to speculate on whether S was susceptible to depression in the future. In the absence of evidence that there
was a real risk of relapse in S's case which could amount to present
impairment, there was nothing to suggest that she was more susceptible to further episodes than any other nurse in a similar situation.
By speculating that she might be susceptible to future impairment,
the panel had effectively reversed the burden of proof.

---

287 [2008] EWHC 2643 (Admin).
288 At [31].
289 [2009] EWHC 2131 (Admin).

Looking forward

1.397   That the panel must look to the future (but not speculate) was made plain in *Meadow v General Medical Council*[290] in which it was said that:

> ... the purpose of FTP proceedings is not to punish the practitioner for past misdoings but to protect the public against the acts and omissions of those who are not fit to practise. The FTP thus looks forward not back. However, in order to form a view as to the fitness of a person to practise today, it is evident that it will have to take account of the way in which the person concerned has acted or failed to act in the past.[291]

1.398   This was reiterated in *Azzam v General Medical Council*:[292]

> [The Fitness to Practise Panel should] ... consider facts material to the practitioner's fitness to practise looking forward and for that purpose to take into account evidence as to his present skills or lack of them and any steps taken, since the conduct criticised, to remedy any defects in skill ... [S]ome elements of reputation and character may well be matters of pure mitigation, not to be taken into account at the 'impairment' stage ... However, the line is a fine one and it is clear to me that evidence of a doctor's overall ability is relevant to the question of fitness to practise ... The panel must consider that evidence (in the same manner as any other evidence received) and weigh it up, decide whether to accept it and then to determine whether, in the light of the further evidence that it does accept and the facts found proved at stage 1, the practitioner's fitness to practise is impaired.

1.399   Finally, Cranston J provided guidance in *Cheatle v General Medical Council*:[293]

> ... a panel must engage in a two-step process. First, it must decide whether there has been misconduct, deficient professional performance or whether the other circumstances set out in the section are present. Then it must go on to determine whether, as a result, fitness to practise is impaired. Thus it may be that despite a doctor having been guilty of misconduct, for example, a Fitness to Practise Panel may decide that his or her fitness to practise is not impaired.
> ... the issue becomes whether that misconduct, in the context of the doctor's behaviour both before the misconduct and to the present time is such as to mean that his or her fitness to practise is impaired ... Seen within the context of an otherwise unblemished record a Panel

290 [2006] EWCA Civ 1390, per Sir Anthony Clarke, MR.
291 At para 32.
292 [2008] EWHC 2711 (Admin) para 44, per McCombe J.
293 [2009] EWHC 645 (Admin) paras 19 and 22.

could conclude that, looking forward, his or her FTP is not impaired, despite the misconduct.

1.400 In *Cheatle* the panel was criticised for declining to hear evidence of C's heavy workload, the pressure created by the absence of a colleague or other evidence regarding C's ability. It was further criticised for not considering the effect of MA 1983 s47 which meant that suspending C ended his NHS contract which may have been disproportionate.

Deficient professional performance

1.401 In essence, this encompasses conduct that has fallen far short of the standards expected of a reasonably competent practitioner and done so on more than one occasion. It need not be a repeat of the same conduct. One exceptionally serious event may also amount to deficient professional performance. Conduct occurring outside the UK and/or before the registrant was in fact registered may still found a case on deficient professional performance, the reason of course being risk to the public and profession.

1.402   In *Holton v General Medical Council*[294] the point was clarified that performance is to be measured as against that expected of a reasonably competent practitioner of the same grade (nurse against nurse, surgeon against surgeon, specialist against specialist) in the job the registrant is actually doing. Deficient professional performance may also stem from one aspect of the registrant's work provided it is a significant aspect, notwithstanding that their other work is of an acceptable standard.

1.403   Performance issues may be worded slightly differently – for the nurse, impairment may be evident through a 'lack of competence'; for the pharmacist deficient professional performance specifically includes incompetence. What is plain is that the standard required for both conduct and performance cases is the same, and that is a standard falling *well below* the expected norm. It should be a 'serious lapse' – see *Vranicki v Architects Registration Board*[295] (a case on the parallel issue of serious professional incompetence and unacceptable professional conduct in architects). As Jackson J put it in *R (Calhaem) v General Medical Council* (see para 1.407 below) it must be 'unacceptably low' and demonstrated across a range of work albeit that one incident that is 'very serious indeed' may suffice.

---

294 [2006] EWHC 2960 (Admin).
295 [2007] EWHC 1644 (Admin) Collins J.

1.404   In *Krippendorf v General Medical Council*[296] the Privy Council quashed a finding of seriously deficient professional performance on the basis that the right approach, at least in this case, was to assess the appellant's past performance over a significant period of time.

1.405   In *Sadler v General Medical Council*[297] the Privy Council approved the following definition provided by the GMC while emphasising that it was not exhaustive:

> Seriously deficient performance is ... 'a departure from good professional practice, whether or not it is covered by specific GMC guidance, sufficiently serious to call into question a doctor's registration.' This means that we will question your registration if we believe that you have been, repeatedly or persistently, not meeting the professional standards appropriate to the work you have been doing – especially if you might be putting patients at risk.[298]

1.406   The Privy Council dealt with a finding of seriously deficient professional misconduct based upon a detailed assessment of S's work as a surgeon over a lengthy period. This included a detailed review of six separate operations four of which were found to be unsatisfactory. Lord Walker said at paras 62 and 63 of the judgment that:

> [62] Although in *Krippendorf* the Board did not criticise the phrase 'repeatedly or persistently' in the GMC's guidance, it is important to bear in mind that that guidance is a generalisation seeking to cover a very wide range of professional performance. The professional demands made on a general practitioner are very different from those made on a consultant surgeon. A continuing failure to organise the efficient management of a general practice may (in a sufficiently bad case) amount to seriously deficient performance, but in the nature of things it must be assessed on very different evidence from that relating to shortcomings of technique in major surgery. It would plainly be contrary to the public interest if a sub-standard surgeon could not be dealt with by the CPP unless and until he had repeatedly made the same error in the course of similar operations. But as a general rule the GMC should not (and their Lordships have no reason to suppose they would) seek to aggregate a number of totally dissimilar incidents and alleged shortcomings in order to make out a case of seriously deficient performance against any practitioner.

> [63] ... Their Lordships do not consider negligence to be a relevant or useful concept at a performance hearing before the CPP. Negligence is concerned with compensating loss ... Seriously deficient perform-

ance is a much wider concept since (as already mentioned) it can extend to such matters as poor record-keeping, poor maintenance of professional obligations of confidentiality, or even deficiencies (if serious and persistent) in consideration and courtesy towards patients. It does not depend on proof of causation of actionable loss. (On the other hand one isolated error of judgment by a surgeon might give rise to liability in negligence but would be unlikely, unless very serious indeed, to amount by itself to seriously deficient performance.)

1.407   Jackson J in *R (Calhaem) v General Medical Council*[299] further defined deficient professional performance, having conducted a review of several cases:

> From this review of the authorities, I derive five principles which are relevant to the present case:
> (1) & (2) see under misconduct (Mere negligence is not misconduct unless 'particularly serious'; multiple acts/omissions are more likely to be misconduct; a single particularly grave act could be misconduct)
> (3) 'Deficient professional performance' within the meaning of 35C(2)(b) is conceptually separate both from negligence and from misconduct. It connotes a standard of professional performance which is unacceptably low and which (save in exceptional circumstances) has been demonstrated by reference to a fair sample of the doctor's work.
> (4) A single instance of negligent treatment, unless very serious indeed, would be unlikely to constitute 'deficient professional performance'.
> (5) It is neither necessary nor appropriate to extend the interpretation of 'deficient professional performance' in order to encompass matters which constitute 'misconduct'.

1.408   C made a number of negligent errors regarding one patient. The finding of misconduct was upheld. The finding of deficient professional performance was quashed since the panel had not properly considered the issue of exceptionality when there was only one incident.

1.409   In *Rao v General Medical Council*[300] the Privy Council quashed a finding of serious professional misconduct noting that only one instance of clinical failure was alleged. That incident undoubtedly amounted to negligence, but it was only a 'borderline case' of serious professional misconduct.

1.410   From the above it is clear that deficient professional performance may involve one very serious clinical error but is more frequently associated with poor treatment or other conduct associated with

299 [2007] EWHC 2606 (Admin) para 39.
300 [2002] UKPC 65.

practice measured over a lengthy period or a number of instances. Terms such as negligence do not assist in judging the issue. The conduct must itself relate directly to the registrant's work or, be closely connected to his or her practice. The latter includes important ancillary matters such as practice-management, deficiency in records and paperwork and deficiency in patient-relations.

1.411   At a fitness to practise hearing, performance related issues clinical or otherwise will almost certainly be addressed by experts. The regulator will call an expert in the appropriate area of practice to provide evidence upon what is the accepted norm and to advise upon whether the conduct complained of falls below or falls well below that expected of a competent practitioner. The registrant may either accept his or her opinion in whole or in part or, contest the opinion in which case an expert is likely to be needed to provide an alternative opinion. In *Uruakpa v General Medical Council*[301] the point was reiterated that it is for the regulator to set the standard of medical competence and the assessment thereof. If a registrant fails to submit to an assessment set by the regulator then a panel is quite entitled to find the registrant impaired by reason of having insufficient up-to-date information to meet the panel's duty to protect the public.

1.412   As with misconduct, matters addressing the issues of insight, remedy and future performance will all be of vital importance in addressing the issue of current impairment and sanction. (See above under 'misconduct'.)

1.413   Where the registrant has not acted in the patient's best interests, and has failed to provide an adequate level of care, falling well below the professional standards expected of a registrant and where a persistent failure to provide clinical care is apparent, erasure may be considered to be the only appropriate sanction. An important factor in such cases is whether the registrant has, or has the potential to develop, insight into these failures. Where there is no evidence of this, other forms of sanction may be insufficient – see *Garfoot v General Medical Council.*[302]

1.414   The distinction to be made between misconduct and lack of competence is important because lack of competence may invoke a lesser range of sanction and to some, a remediable lack of competence carries less stigma. It may be possible to argue that facts found proved amount to lack of competence but not misconduct. The professional and/or personal circumstances of a registrant may

301 [2010] EWCA Civ 1508, Saunders J.
302 [2002] UKPC 35.

provide mitigation upon the level of culpability and thus be relevant to the issue of whether the facts amount to misconduct and/or lack of competence.[303] However, issues such as a high caseload or personal trauma should be reported, discussed with a superior or result in requests for help. They may explain, but do not excuse, poor performance or conduct since registrants are expected to take personal responsibility for their actions or omissions. Evidence of past or subsequent good practice is important, although more general character evidence is unlikely to be relevant. Somewhat perversely, emphasising mitigating factors could undermine a registrant's ability to demonstrate insight (see below), and a case-by-case approach should be adopted.

Criminal convictions, discharges and cautions (in the UK or elsewhere)

1.415   Most regulators have specific rules for dealing with conviction or caution cases, which provide that the production of a certified copy of a notice of conviction is conclusive evidence of the offence committed and the facts thereof. The only challenge a registrant may make is that he or she is not the person who is referred to in the notice,[304] the registrant may not re-open and contest the facts behind the conviction – see *R (Trivedi) v General Medical Council*[305] and *Shepherd v Law Society*.[306]

1.416   In cases of criminal conduct, the interests of the profession always come first and impairment is a frequent result.

1.417   A distinction is sometime argued between a conviction that attracts a sentence and one that attracts a conditional or absolute discharge. This argument was rejected in *R v Patel*.[307] Hughes LJ noted that while section 14 of the Powers of Criminal Courts (Sentencing) Act 2000 prevents the discharge from ranking as a conviction, 'it does not enable any person to assert that they have never committed the offence or for that matter that they have never been found guilty of it. [One must look to the Rehabilitation of Offenders Act 1974 for that]'.[308] However,

---

303 *Campbell v General Medical Council* [2005] EWCA Civ 250; *Cohen v General Medical Council* [2008] EWHC 581 (Admin).

304 See, eg GMC (Fitness to Practise) Rules 2004 r34(3); NMC (Fitness to Practise) Rules 2004 r31(3).

305 [1996] EWCA Civ 503 (PC).

306 [1996] EWCA Civ 977.

307 [2006] EWCA Crim 2689.

308 At para 7.

the ROA 1974 does not apply to healthcare registrants. Thus convictions do not become spent as regards registrants regardless of the time elapsed and, if a conviction from which a discharge resulted is deployed as a basis for impairment, a registrant may not deny commission or conviction. The elapse of time since a conviction will be a factor the panel takes into account in deciding whether a registrant's fitness is *currently* impaired but it is not determinative.

1.418   A caution is administered only when there is an admission of guilt, the fact of the caution and the underlying events may be used to found a basis for impairment.

1.419   As regards a case upon which a registrant was acquitted, acquittal is not the same as never having done the act. Acquittal merely means that a jury could not be sure (beyond reasonable doubt) that the registrant committed the act/omission alleged. In *Bhatt v General Medical Council*[309] the court held that the GMC was entitled to bring a case against B based upon seven allegations of indecent assault of which he had been acquitted. The principal reasons were that the proceedings are of a different nature with a different purpose (upholding professional standards etc) and a different burden of proof. Furthermore, the plea of autrefois acquit (meaning 'previously acquitted of the same offence') does not apply to regulatory proceedings – see also *R (Redgrave) v Metropolitan Police Commissioner.*[310]

1.420   The position is different in respect of civil proceedings against a registrant. The findings of a civil court provide prima-facie evidence of the facts alleged and may found a case of misconduct etc but, the registrant may challenge the correctness of that prima-facie case – see *General Medical Council v Spackman.*[311]

1.421   In cases involving convictions or cautions for offences involving dishonesty, sexual offences, child pornography, drug misuse or other serious criminal offences, the wider public interest issues of upholding the reputation of the profession and maintaining confidence in the regulatory process will be of the greatest significance. It is highly likely to outweigh any argument concerning the registrant's risk or lack of risk to potential service users.

309 [2011] EWHC 783 (Admin).
310 [2003] 1 WLR 1136.
311 [1943] AC 627.

Adverse physical or mental health issues

1.422   While registrants do not necessarily have to be in the best health to practice safely, regulators will investigate a registrants physical and/or mental health status in circumstances where it may affect his or her ability to practise safely. Frequent problems include mental health issues, depression and alcohol or substance dependency. Recurrent illness is also an issue.

1.423   Registrants may be required to undergo physical or psychiatric assessment, including substance dependence, to assess their ability to continue in practise, whether restricted or otherwise. A report will be provided to the panel and the expert assessor will usually be called to give evidence. Refusal to undergo such an assessment will almost certainly result in suspension or erasure. Health matters are dealt with in private session.

1.424   The important point is again whether the health issues are adversely affecting the registrant's ability to practise safely or are otherwise adversely impacting upon the profession (or the registrant):

> If a doctor is suffering from ill health (for example, severe depression), one might say that s/he is not fit to practise because his/her concentration is so affected that s/he cannot make effective decisions on diagnosis and treatment; s/he presents a risk to patients.[312]

1.425   Some regulators do not consider erasure as appropriate if impairment results *only* through adverse health issues. However, where those or coincident issues also amount to misconduct no such limitation applies. In *Crabbie v General Medical Council*[313] (a case decided under the old GMC regime) the Privy Council held that the Conduct Committee should not refer a case to the Health Committee (which cannot strike off) unless and until it is satisfied that striking off would not be the right order to make. These committees have now been replaced by the single Fitness to Practise Panel but the principle remains the same such that if there are other concerns that contribute to the registrant's unfitness (ie unless health is the only relevant issue) all sanctions remain available including erasure.

1.426   In *Sarkodie-Gyan v Nursing and Midwifery Council*[314] (discussed at para 1.396 above) the issue of *present* impairment and looking forward was not properly considered. SG's history of addiction and depression (now in remission) was quite capable of amounting to

---

312 *Fifth Shipman Report* at 25.44 (on issues of what amounts to impairment).
313 Privy Council appeal 7 of 2002.
314 [2009] EWHC 2131 (Admin).

impairment but, in light of her remission it was wrong to speculate on her susceptibility to depression in the future. In the absence of evidence of a risk of relapse which could amount to present impairment there was nothing to suggest that she was more susceptible to further episodes than any other nurse in a similar situation.

A determination by another healthcare body

1.427   This heading needs no elaboration. The criterion is self-explanatory and the issues of public interest etc are the same as those involving convictions or other misconduct or deficient performance.

Decisions of the panel

> Reasons do not have to cover every aspect of the case but should be sufficient in breadth and detail to ensure that a party is able fully to understand the decision, why it has been made and on what evidence. The panel must clearly set out how the law or rules have been applied to the evidence and, what evidence is accepted and what rejected with reasons.

Reasons for decisions – Interim Orders Panel

1.428   The Interim Orders Panel must provide reasons for its decisions both upon the imposition (or non-imposition) of an order and the initial period of time for which it is imposed. The courts do not expect an Interim Orders Panel to give long detailed reasons, but the reasons given must be clear and explain how the decisions were reached, including identifying the interest(s) for which the order is considered necessary.

1.429   In *R (Walker) v General Medical Council*[315] Stanley Burnton J said that:

> ... a lack of adequate reasons, or a decision which is disproportionate in its interference with the rights of the doctor in question will encourage the court to examine broadly the decision made by the committee and substitute its own in a way which it might be less willing to do where the decision appeared to be fully reasoned and proportional.
>
> ... the court will normally give broad credit to the appreciation by a professionally qualified Committee of the conduct of the accused

315 [2003] EWHC 2308 (Admin) (at paras 9 and 10).

doctor [and where] full and substantial reasons are given ... the court will give considerable weight to those and will be slow to interfere.

1.430 The following comments regarding fitness to practise hearings also apply.

Reasons for decisions – Fitness to Practise Panel

1.431 In *English v Reimbold*[316] the comment was made that 'justice will not be done if it is not apparent to the parties why one has won and the other has lost'. Panels must provide sufficient reasons for their decisions to be clear and understandable. This is important both from the public perspective and from the registrant's. The Fifth Shipman Inquiry Report recommended that Fitness to Practise Panels should give reasons for their main findings of fact.[317]

1.432 As to the facts, in *Gupta v General Medical Council*[318] the Privy Council stated that, save in exceptional cases there is no general duty on the panel to give reasons for its decisions on matters of fact, particularly when the central issue is the credibility or reliability of a witness or evidence. However, the panel may give reasons if it considers it appropriate. This would be so when without reasons, the losing party will not know why it has lost. If the reasons for winning or losing are obvious then reasons do not need to be given.

1.433 In *Phipps v General Medical Council*[319] this area of law including *Gupta* and *English v Reimbold* (above) was re-analysed by Wall LJ who observed that 'what was exceptional in 2001 may well have become commonplace in 2006'.

1.434 Finally on facts, in *Southall v General Medical Council*[320] Leveson LJ expressing the view that:

> ... in straightforward cases, setting out the facts to be proved (as is the present practice of the GMC) and finding them proved or not proved will generally be sufficient both to demonstrate to the parties why they won or lost and to explain to any appellate tribunal the facts found. In most cases, particularly those concerned with comparatively simple conflicts of factual evidence, it will be obvious whose evidence has been rejected and why.[321]

316 [2002] 1 WLR 2409.
317 *The Shipman Inquiry 2004, Fifth Report – Safeguarding patients: lessons from the past – proposals for the future*, Cm 6394, published 9 December 2004.
318 [2001] UKPC 61.
319 [2006] EWCA Civ 397.
320 [2010] EWCA Civ 407.
321 At para 55.

Unfortunately the case was not straightforward and the panel's reasons were inadequate in particular because they failed to explain why S's evidence was rejected on a key point.

1.435   Leveson LJ queried the idea propounded in *Gupta* based upon the decision of *Wickramsinghe v UK*[322] that a registrant can study a transcript of the hearing, to see what evidence was accepted/rejected and why since this assumes that the panel will deal with and give full reasons on all issues. That assumption cannot be safely made as it might be in a criminal trial where a judge's summing is expected to provide an impartial analysis of fact and argument.

1.436   While not every issue needs to be decided and written up in lengthy judgment, the better approach to reasons on all aspects of a regulatory case is to be found in the cases of *Selvanathan v General Medical Council*[323] and *Needham v Nursing and Midwifery Council*.[324]

1.437   In *Selvanathan* the purely factual allegations were not in dispute, and S accepted that he had been clumsy but he denied dishonesty. He gave evidence and called two character witnesses. Lord Hope said that reasons should always be given by the panel on the issue of misconduct and penalty so that the registrant can make an informed decision to accept or appeal the decision. On the issue of facts, where the dispute was a relatively simple one, the registrant only needed to know whether the decision was for or against him or her.

1.438   In *Council for the Regulation of Healthcare Professionals v General Dental Council and Marshall*[325] the court held that panels must give reasons for imposing particular sanctions and why in the opinion of the panel the chosen sanction protects the public. In addition, while the indicative sanction guidelines referred to previously are guidelines and not tariffs, the panel's reasons must demonstrate that it has paid due regard to the guidelines. This is particularly important since it will inform any appellate court or review panel that account has been taken of the regulator's opinion on sanction and what is or may be necessary to protect the public and the profession – see *Salha and another v General Medical Council*.[326]

1.439   In *Needham v Nursing and Midwifery Council* the additional point was made that reasons should be sufficiently clear for any appellate court or review panel to understand exactly why a particular decision

---

322 Application no 31503/96, [1998] EHRLR 338.
323 (2000) 59 BMRL 96.
324 [2003] EWHC 1141 (Admin).
325 [2006] EWHC 1870 (Admin).
326 [2003] UKPC 80.

has been made. Thus panels should formulate their reasons by 'reference to the degree of illumination which a subsequent Committee might require'.[327]

1.440   When conflicting expert evidence is received, the panel should give cogent reasons for its decision – see *English v Reimbold* (para 1.431 above).

1.441   The rule to be drawn from the above is that if a case is straightforward then reasons on the facts need not be given if what is accepted or rejected and the reasons why are clear. When the case is not straightforward and can properly be described as exceptional, the position is different. In such cases sufficient reasons should be given to inform the parties what findings have been made, what evidence has been accepted or rejected and why. At all other stages of the hearing, the panel should give reasons in accordance with the judgments of *Selvanathan* and *Needham*.

Sanctions

> The principal aims of sanctions are to protect the public, uphold the standards and reputation of the profession and maintain public confidence therein.
>
> The punitive effect of sanctions is only one (and not the most important) factor to be borne in mind when assessing whether a sanction is proportional to the matters found proved against a practitioner.

General principles

Objectives and proportionality

1.442   The starting point for sanctions is the *Merrison report*[328] in which it was said that 'the GMC should be able to take action in relation to the registration of a doctor ... in the interests of the public' which had 'two closely woven strands', the need to protect the individual patient and the need to maintain the confidence of the public in their doctors.

1.443   All healthcare regulators state their main objectives to be protecting patients and the public, declaring and upholding standards of

---

327 At para 14.
328 *Report of the Committee of Inquiry into the Regulation of the Medical Profession* (1975).

conduct, promoting good practice and maintaining public confidence in their respective professions. These are expressed as follows:

- The GMC:

    ... to protect, promote and maintain the health and safety of the public[329]

    ... to deliver regulation that:
    - raises standards and enhances patient safety
    - fosters the professionalism of doctors
    - is independent, fair, efficient and effective
    - encourages early and effective local action
    - commands the confidence and support of all our key interest groups[330]

- The NMC:

    ... to establish from time to time standards of education and training, conduct and performance for nurses and midwives and to ensure the maintenance of those standards

    ... safeguard the health and well-being of persons using or needing the services of practitioners[331]

1.444   Each body also produces a code of practice and/or guidance such as the GMC's *Good medical practice* which 'sets out the principles and values on which good medical practice is founded, and the standards which society and the profession expects of all doctors (irrespective of their area of practice) throughout their careers'.[332] These standards and objectives include behaviour and governance as well as patient care and similar matters fundamental to healthcare professionals. The NMC's code – *The code: standards of conduct, Performance and ethics for nurses and midwives* – similarly deals with all aspects of patient care, dignity, confidentiality, consent, boundaries, working with others maintaining standards, integrity and the reputation of the profession.

1.445   A failure to follow published guidance such as *Good medical practice* or the NMC code may well found a case against a practitioner, although it does not by itself necessarily establish impairment.

1.446   Where the misconduct is grave or there has been a serious departure from professional standards, erasure from the register may be the only means of protecting patients and/or maintaining public

---

329 MA 1983 s1A.
330 GMC, *Annual Report 2010*, 31 July 2011 – First Objective.
331 The Nursing and Midwifery Order 2001 Part 2 article 3(2) and (4) respectively.
332 GMC, *Indicative sanctions guidance for Fitness to Practise Panels*, April 2009, revised August 2009, Introduction, para 4.

confidence in the profession. If possible a balance may be struck between the individual interest and the public interest but, this cannot always be achieved.

1.447　The importance of the above objectives and guidance is that the public interests and standing of the profession comes before the interests or rehabilitation of the practitioner appearing before the panel. As Lord Millett said in *Ghosh v General Medical Council*:[333]

> ... the primary considerations on the question of penalty are the maintenance of professional standards and the public interest, which includes not only the protection of the public but also the preservation of public confidence in the medical profession.

1.448　*Raschid and Fatnani v General Medical Council*[334] makes it plain that the panel 'is centrally concerned with the reputation or standing of the profession rather than the punishment of the doctor' this is despite the fact that sanctions may have a punitive, even a devastating effect. While a balance is to be struck between the necessity of imposing a sanction and the effect that sanction has on the individual, in *Bolton v Law Society*[335] (a case concerning a solicitor, but of general importance) Sir Thomas Bingham MR remarked that:

> ... A profession's most valuable asset is its collective reputation and the confidence which that inspires.
>
> ... the reputation of the profession is more important than the fortunes of an individual member. Membership of a profession brings many benefits but that is part of the price.

1.449　Further comment upon the primary importance of the profession rather than the individual is to be found in the judgment of Sir Anthony Clarke MR in *Meadow v General Medical Council*:[336]

> ... the purpose of [fitness to practise] proceedings is not to punish the practitioner for past misdoings but to protect the public against the acts and omissions of those who are not fit to practise.

1.450　By way of contrast in *Bijl v General Medical Council*[337] it was said that:

> [A panel should not feel obliged to erase] an otherwise competent and useful doctor who presents no danger to the public in order to satisfy [public] demand for blame and punishment.

333　[2000] 1 WLR 1915 at para 34.
334　[2007] 1 WLR 1460 at para 16.
335　[1993] EWCA Civ 32 per Lord Bingham MR at paras 15 and 16 (also *Gupta v General Medical Council* [2002] 1 WLR 1691).
336　[2006] EWCA Civ 1390 at para 32.
337　[2001] UKPC 42.

1.451   However, in this context it is to be noted that *Bijl* was a case concerning clinical errors of judgement during an operation and did not involve allegations such as dishonesty or inappropriate sexual behaviour which are in themselves serious and are most damaging to the profession.

1.452   The regulators each produce indicative guidelines on sanctions. The purpose is not to set out what a panel must do but, to advise the panel what, in the opinion of the regulator, may be appropriate or should at least be considered. The regulators regard their indicative sanctions guidance as providing a crucial link between the two key regulatory roles of setting standards for the profession and of taking action when a registrant's fitness to practise is called into question because those standards have not been met.

1.453   The aim of the guidance is to promote consistency and transparency in decisions. All parties are aware from the outset of the approach that may be expected of the panel. As Mr Justice Collins said in *Council for the Regulation of Healthcare Professionals v (1) General Medical Council (2) Leeper.*[338] In relation to the GMC's guidance:

> It helps to achieve a consistent approach to the imposition of penalties where serious professional misconduct is established. The [panel] must have regard to it although obviously each case will depend on its own facts and guidance is what it says and must not be regarded as laying down a rigid tariff.

1.454   In *R (Abrahaem) v General Medical Council*[339] Mr Justice Newman, described the Indicative Sanctions Guidance as:

> ... very useful guidelines and they form a framework which enables any tribunal, including this court, to focus its attention on the relevant issues. But one has to come back to the essential exercise which the law now requires in what lies behind the purpose of sanctions, which, as I have already pointed out, is not to be punitive but to protect the public interest; public interest is a label which gives rise to separate areas of consideration.

See also *Hazelhurst v Solicitors Regulation Authority.*[340]

1.455   The panel's decision on sanction is a matter of discretion and judgment, but it should take into consideration the standards of good practice established by the regulator and the sanctions guidance. Departure from the guidance must be explained.

---

338   [2004] EWHC 1850 (Admin).
339   [2004] EWHC 279 (Admin) para [36].
340   [2010] EWHC 462 (Admin).

1.456   That the profession is of primary importance, and not the registrant, may well have an effect upon the validity of some mitigation. In *Gupta v General Medical Council*[341] the Privy Council declared that:

> ... the relevant committee is not concerned exclusively, or even primarily, with the punishment of the practitioner concerned. Their Lordships refer, for example, to the judgment of Sir Thomas Bingham MR in *Bolton v Law Society* [1994] 1 WLR 512, 517-519 where his Lordship set out the general approach that has to be adopted. In particular he pointed out that, since the professional body is not primarily concerned with matters of punishment, considerations which would normally weigh in mitigation of punishment have less effect on the exercise of this kind of jurisdiction. And he observed that it can never be an objection to an order for suspension that the practitioner may be unable to re-establish his practice when the period has passed.

1.457   This means that a careful assessment is required as to what mitigation is available to the registrant and how it is to be presented.

1.458   In deciding what sanction to impose, if any, the panel should have regard to the principle of proportionality, weighing the interests of the public against those of the practitioner. Any sanction and the period for which it is imposed must be *necessary* to protect the public interest. The panel should consider the sanctions available starting with the least restrictive.

1.459   The indicative sanctions guidance sets out the criteria to take into account when considering which sanction to impose. These include the seriousness of the conduct found proved, early admissions, evidence of insight and reparation or retraining, references and testimonials. If the panel deals with matters in this way and, provided the sanction is not unreasonable or disproportionate, the higher courts are unlikely to interfere having repeatedly held that the regulator is best placed to decide what level of sanction is necessary and proportionate in its own professional field.[342]

1.460   While there may be a public interest in enabling a registrant's return to *safe* practice and the panel should facilitate this where appropriate, the protection of patients and the wider public interest remain the primary concern. The fact that a registrant has been subjected to an interim order for conditions or suspension carries little if any weight since the interim order panel makes no findings of fact. It also applies a different test when considering whether or not

341 [2002] 1 WLR 1691 para [18].
342 *Fouche v Nursing and Midwifery Council* [2011] EWHC 133 (Admin); *Raschid and Fatnani v General Medical Council* [2007] EWCA Civ 46.

to impose an interim order to that applied by the panel considering final sanctions.

1.461   The passage of time and the fact that there has been unreasonable delay may be mitigation as discussed under delay above – see *Selvarajan v General Medical Council.*[343]

1.462   The panel should be alive to the issue of unintended consequences and seek appropriate guidance from the legal assessor. In *Cheatle* (above) the panel was criticised for not considering the effect of MA 1983 s47 which meant that suspending C ended his NHS contract which may have been disproportionate.

1.463   The panel should not confuse suspension and the imposition of conditions. The latter must be reasonable and workable. In *Udom v General Medical Council*[344] the panel found U's fitness to practise impaired by reason of health and competence. It imposed a sanction which purported to be conditions that he was not to practise unsupervised for a period of nine months and was, during that period, to undergo a series of clinical attachments. The effect of the order was to suspend U from practise. Suspension and conditions of practise are separate mutually exclusive sanctions. Accordingly, the panel had been wrong to impose conditions which had the effect of suspending the registrant.

1.464   In *S v General Medical Council*[345] S was erased from the register following proof of charges relating to performance and misconduct including harassment of a former patient. Both were linked to S's alcoholism. Sullivan J upheld erasure largely because S had persistently failed to make any attempt to address his alcoholism and attendant problems. He was thus largely responsible for them. A health issue might otherwise be dealt with by suspension.

1.465   Sullivan J summarised the issues regarding sanction as follows:

> [13] Sanctions are not a punishment. They are imposed in order to protect patients and to ensure that doctors who are not properly capable of acting as such, and treating patients competently, should not be able to do so. If a doctor has been guilty of misconduct, whether or not directly connected with his activities as a doctor (for example, he has been convicted of a criminal offence, which is not directly related to his practice as a doctor) that can inevitably reduce public confidence in the profession. It is also a breach of the proper standards of conduct and behaviour to be expected of a doctor, thus a sanction of

---

343 [2008] EWHC 182 (Admin).
344 [2009] EWHC 3242 (Admin).
345 [2007] EWHC 3257 (Admin) at para 13ff.

lesser or greater seriousness, depending on the nature of the misconduct, can be imposed.

[14] In imposing sanctions the Panel must apply the principle of proportionality weighing the public interest against the interest of the
practitioner. If a practitioner can, through treatment or training, or
the imposition of conditions of one sort or another, be brought back
to be trusted as a competent doctor, or if guilty of a form of misconduct, but a highly competent practitioner, the public interest may
indicate that in such a case it would be wrong to deprive the public of
his services for any longer than is strictly necessary.

[15] Suspension is intended to send out a signal that the behaviour is
regarded as unacceptable, but is not so serious as to justify erasure.
That may arise not only because of the nature of the conduct in question, but also where there has been an acknowledgment of fault and
where the Panel is satisfied that there is unlikely to be any repetition.

[16] So far as erasure is concerned, it is to be noted that there is a
distinction drawn, which has always been drawn, albeit now they are
dealt with by the same Fitness to Practise Panel, between cases which
are regarded as health cases and cases regarded as conduct cases.
There used, until recently, to be a division between the two, but it
must be borne in mind that the division cannot necessarily be strictly
applied because health issues may be material where there has been
misconduct. However, the misconduct may be so serious that notwithstanding that it was caused by what might be regarded as health
problems, it has to result in erasure, particularly if it appears to the
Panel that there is a lack of insight and so a real risk of repetition of
such sort of conduct.

[17 In setting out the factors which are material in deciding upon suspension, as opposed to erasure, the guidance notes that no evidence
of repetition is a factor. The Panel may be satisfied that the doctor has
insight and does not pose a significant risk of repeating and, in cases
where the only issue relates to the doctor's health, there is a risk to
the patient's safety if the doctor is allowed to continue to practise even
under conditions. That means that in a pure health case it may well be
appropriate to impose suspension rather than merely conditions.

[18] Erasure is likely to be appropriate where there is a serious departure from professional standards, where serious harm is done to others,
where there is a continuing risk and where there is a persistent lack
of insight into the seriousness of actions or their consequences. It is
noted that erasure is not available in cases where the only issue relates
to the doctor's health. That then is the guidance that the Panel has to
apply and in this case they clearly considered the guidance and took it
properly into account.

1.466   *Brennan v Health Professions Council*[346] provides useful guidance in cases where a penalty is imposed solely on grounds of the reputation of the profession. Ouseley J suggested that maintenance of public confidence in the profession was achieved by the finding that the registrant's fitness to practise was impaired. When imposing sanction, the starting point and the fundamental factor was public safety. If a sanction is imposed in order to uphold the reputation of the profession, careful consideration would be needed as to whether the most severe sanction of striking off is necessary and proportionate, particularly where the registrant had demonstrated insight and such conduct was unlikely to be repeated. This suggests that there would have to be some evidence that the reputation of the profession would be harmed if a lesser sanction than strike off was imposed.

1.467   In *Brennan* a physiotherapist employed by a rugby team, on instruction from his coach, provided a player with a blood capsule in order for him to fake an injury during a match so that he could be substituted. B then assisted his employer in covering up the incident by provided false evidence at the subsequent investigation. B's conduct was dishonest, premeditated and continued over a period of time. However it involved no deception of his employer and no patient harm. There was evidence that B was an 'excellent physiotherapist' and he made full admissions before the HPC. The High Court quashed the striking off order imposed by the HPC and remitted the case back to the regulator to re-determine. The court indicated that a suspension order would have been sufficient but declined to substitute such an order since it was accepted that a striking off order may be appropriate if the registrant lacked insight, or it was necessary as a deterrent to address a real problem in the profession concerning this type of conduct.

Insight

1.468   Examining the extent of the registrant's insight is as essential to the panel's task in assessing sanction as it is to the issue of current impairment. In *Council for Healthcare Regulatory Excellence v Nursing and Midwifery Council and Grant*[347] the point was made that 'When considering whether fitness to practise is currently impaired, the level of insight shown by the practitioner is central to a proper determination ...'.

346 [2011] EWHC 41 (Admin).
347 [2011] EWHC 927 (Admin) at para 116.

1.469   Establishing insight is relevant when assessing risk. The panel will look for evidence of remorse, apology, understanding impact and remediation of conduct. This includes looking for such evidence during the hearing itself. The level of a registrant's insight may be critical to the question of current impairment and thus to sanction.

Examples and guidance on sanction in particular categories of cases

1.470   Decisions of healthcare regulators tend to be fact-specific and are therefore not regarded as forming a coherent body of jurisprudence[348]. Further the appellate courts often accord special respect to the judgment of the professional decision-making body in the shape of the panel *Ghosh v General Medical Council*[349] recognising that it is in the best position to judge what is best for the profession. They will frequently uphold a panel decision on sanction even if the court itself considers the decision to be lenient or harsh. Accordingly it is not possible to rely on any one case as a *firm* indicator of the appropriate outcome in another. However, particular features are regarded as significant by regulators and panels alike and, will be of assistance in advising a registrant as to the range of likely sanctions and in deciding how to pitch submissions on mitigation.

1.471   All panels will first consider the regulator's indicative sanctions guidance. Mitigation is frequently a case of arguing why a panel should follow or may depart from the guidance. The guidance is of considerable importance designed to promote consistency in similar cases but, it is guidance and not intended to be a rigid tariff (see *Council for the Regulation of Healthcare Professionals v (1) General Medical Council (2) Leeper* at para 1.453 above).

Drug and alcohol misuse

1.472   Many cases where the registrant's fitness to practise is said to be impaired by reason of drug or alcohol dependency but which do not involve other criminal misconduct (eg drink-driving, assault or possession offences) will be dealt with as a health issue. Some regulators have specific Health Committees for such cases. Being treated as a health issue will affect the range of sanctions available. While the panel is not responsible for the care or rehabilitation of any

348 *Shah v General Pharmaceutical Council* [2011] EWHC 73 (Admin).
349 [2001] UKPC 29, [2001] 1 WLR 1915.

registrant, the continued or return to *safe* practice of an otherwise competent registrant is in the public interest. A panel may endeavour to facilitate the registrant's safe practice if this outweighs the public and professional interest of upholding standards etc (see the chapters dealing with specific regulators for details of the powers of sanction).

1.473   Referral to a Health Committee will not be appropriate in all cases. A convictions case will almost certainly be dealt with as a conduct matter or mixed conduct and health. In *Crabbie v General Medical Council*[350] there was medical evidence that C suffered from alcohol dependency at the time of the matters that brought her before the panel. She had been convicted of causing death by dangerous driving and driving with excess alcohol and sentenced to five years' imprisonment and disqualified from driving for ten years. The matter was reported to the GMC as a conviction case. The Professional Conduct Committee refused C's application to transfer the case to the Health Committee. On appeal the court upheld the principle that if the case is one where erasure is a serious possibility, it should not be referred to the Health Committee.

1.474   In other, less serious cases, conditions of practice may be an appropriate disposal. This is where a requirement to co-operate with a treatment regime and provide reports periodically from a supervising medical practitioner (or, for example, a counsellor) arguably provides the requisite level of protection to the public. Representatives of registrants will need to ensure in such cases that there is supporting documentation from the medical practitioner or counsellor indicating a willingness to co-operate with the conditions and provide the information specified in any order. It will frequently be appropriate to call the existing or proposed supervisor to advise the panel as to his or her attitude to public protection and registrant rehabilitation.

1.475   It is open to a Health Committee to conclude that a registrant is suffering from alcohol dependency in cases where there is evidence from medical assessors, whether or not the specific diagnosis has been canvassed with the registrant. In *Boodoo v General Medical Council*[351] the court noted that the evidence contained clear reference to the attributes of the condition, accordingly the conclusion was neither wrong nor unjust.

1.476   The important features to consider are the attitude of the registrant to rehabilitation and, whether the public interest (risk to patients and

350 [2002] UKPC 45.
351 [2004] EWHC 2712 (Admin).

professional standards etc) outweighs or is itself outweighed by the prospect of a registrant's return to safe practice.

Convictions and cautions

1.477   Most regulators have specific rules for dealing with conviction or caution cases, which provide that the fact of conviction or caution is taken as proof of the facts of the offence (see chapters dealing with specific regulators for the applicable rule). It is not the function of a panel considering such a case to go behind the facts of the conviction or caution, or re-try the criminal case. Having decided that the registrant's fitness to practise is impaired by virtue of the conviction or caution, the panel then adopts the same approach to sanction as in other cases.

1.478   The interests of the profession will necessarily be treated as of paramount importance in any case involving criminal misconduct. Because of this conviction cases are frequently met with suspension or erasure. Where a case does not involve dishonesty, sexual or pornographic offences and/or any risk to patients or the profession can be properly addressed, erasure or suspension do not always result. Alternatively, if suspension is the result, in deciding the term of the suspension, the panel may take account of the registrant's possible return to safe practice in the future.

1.479   Convictions or cautions for offences involving dishonesty are likely to be regarded as particularly serious, especially if the offence was committed in the course of the registrant's professional practice. In *R (Rogers) v General Medical Council*[352] R received a suspended sentence having pleaded guilty to many offences of obtaining prescription drugs by deception and possession of controlled drugs. The conviction was reported to the GMC and R was erased from the register. On appeal, the court held that the sanction was appropriate in the light of various aggravating factors which included the repetition of the offence and the use of prescription forms to obtain the drugs.

1.480   In conviction cases, particularly for serious criminal offences, the wider public interest issues of upholding the reputation of the profession and maintaining confidence in the regulatory process will be of the greatest significance. It is highly likely to outweigh any argument concerning the registrant's risk or lack of risk to potential service users.

352 [2004] EWHC 424 (Admin).

1.481   In *Chanderaskera v Nursing and Midwifery Council*[353] the registrant pleaded guilty to manslaughter of her husband on grounds of diminished responsibility. She suffered from depression and anxiety at the time. There was no suggestion of any criticism of her professional performance. C was initially suspended from practice by the Interim Orders Panel. On review this was replaced with interim conditions, and subsequently even this was revoked allowing her to return to unrestricted practice pending conclusion of her case. She was later struck off by the Conduct and Competence Committee and appealed. The court upheld the decision to strike her off, notwithstanding the earlier decision to allow her to return to unrestricted practice. The committee's view that the conviction (or the behaviour that led to it) was fundamentally incompatible with remaining on the register was one that it was entitled to reach.

1.482   Cases involving conviction or caution for the possession of or other involvement with indecent images of children will focus on the wider public interest in determining sanction. They are almost inevitably dealt with by suspension or erasure (see below).

1.483   Perhaps obviously, a decision of a regulatory body based upon a conviction that is subsequently overturned, may also be quashed. In *R (Jenkinson) v Nursing and Midwifery Council*[354] the registrant had been convicted of causing grievous bodily harm to a patient in her care who had died. At trial evidence was given by an expert as to the functioning of a ventilator that had been operative in the patient's death. The expert's evidence was subsequently discredited and the criminal conviction overturned. The court held that once the conviction had been quashed the finding of misconduct and the decision on sanction 'fell away'.

1.484   In *Council for the Regulation of Healthcare Professionals v General Dental Council (Fleischmann)*[355] it was observed that if a registrant has been convicted of a serious criminal offence and is still serving his or her sentence at the time the matter comes before a panel, normally the registrant should not be permitted to resume practice until the criminal sentence has been satisfactorily completed. In such cases, therefore, representatives may need to consider requesting postponement of the hearing until after completion of the sentence.

353 [2009] EWHC 144 (Admin).
354 [2009] EWHC 1111 (Admin).
355 [2005] EWHC 87 (Admin).

Sexual offences and pornography

1.485 Cases involving sexual offences and/or sexual impropriety with a patient and/or cases involving pornography, particularly child pornography, are treated with the utmost seriousness. They will almost inevitably be met with an order of suspension or erasure, this being necessary to protect patients, promote trust in the professions and uphold standards.

1.486 Conduct involving sexual assault and/or sexual abuse of children and/or child pornography is an abuse of trust and fundamentally incompatible with the role of a health professional. An example of the approach adopted by the courts to such conduct is provided in the Privy Council case of *Haikel v General Medical Council*.[356] This concerned a GP who conducted intimate examinations of female patients which was not clinically appropriate and without offering chaperones to those patients. Upholding the sanction of erasure, their Lordships stated that:

> The public, and in particular female patients, must have confidence in the medical profession whatever their state of health might be. The conduct as found proved against Dr Haikel undoubtedly undermines such confidence and a severe sanction was inevitable. Their Lordships are satisfied that erasure was neither unreasonable, excessive nor disproportionate but necessary in the public interest.[357]

1.487 Two scales have been used to measure the seriousness of images. The ten-point Copine scale ('Combating Paedophile Information Networks in Europe') was originally developed for therapeutic purposes. This was adapted to a five-point scale in *R v Oliver*.[358] The Sentencing Council has now produced guidelines on cases involving indecent photographs, pseudo photographs and similar material. The latter guidelines are now of most importance. There is further Sentencing Council guidance on pseudo-imagery and related matters such as proximity to abuse, taking photographs or making images, commercial activity or swapping images. The Sentencing Council guideline is as follows:

- Level 1 – Nudity or erotic posing with no sexual activity
- Level 2 – Sexual activity between children, or solo masturbation by a child

356 [2002] UKPC 37.
357 At para 29.
358 [2003] 1 Cr App R 463.

- Level 3 – Non-penetrative sexual activity between adult(s) and child(ren)
- Level 4 – Penetrative sexual activity between child(ren) and adult(s)
- Level 5 – Sadism or bestiality

For further guidelines see the council's website: www.sentencing council.judiciary.org.uk.

1.488   Child pornography is illegal and even when accessed outside the workplace it will usually result in erasure there being no other way of maintaining public confidence in the profession.

1.489   In *Council for the Regulation of Healthcare Professionals v General Dental Council (Fleischmann)* (above) the CRHP challenged as 'unduly lenient' one year's suspension of a dentist convicted of several counts of possession of indecent photographs of children. The images included some level 5 images. The registrant pleaded guilty and was sentenced to a community rehabilitation order for three years and banned from unsupervised access to children under 16. The court upheld the CRHP's challenge, describing it as 'manifest' that a 12-month suspension in such a case could not protect the reputation of the profession or maintain standards. The court issued some guidance on cases of internet child pornography.

1.490   In essence, *any* involvement with child-pornography is illegal and morally unacceptable. While the criminal courts distinguish between degrees of seriousness, they do so for sentencing purposes. All regulators regard any conviction for child pornography as grave being a fundamental breach of trust and inevitably brings the profession into disrepute. Erasure will almost certainly result.

1.491   If an exceptional course is taken and erasure does not result, the panel must provide particularly careful and clear reasons to protect public confidence in the profession. Anything less will reflect badly upon the profession, and will doubtless result in further litigation at appellate level.

1.492   The position in relation to lawful adult pornography is more complex. The issue is likely to arise where pornographic material has been accessed at work. In *Council for the Regulation of Healthcare Professionals v Nursing and Midwifery Council (Truscott)*[359] the high court declined to overturn a 'lenient' five-year caution order imposed by the NMC on a nurse for accessing adult pornographic material while working in an adolescent hospital. The court deferred to the NMC panel's view that his conduct was not incompatible with his role as a nurse. On the other hand, in *R (Harry) v General Medical*

359 [2004] EWCA Civ 1356.

Council,[360] a six-month suspension order imposed by the GMC on a doctor who accessed adult pornographic material while working in a single-handed practice, when no patients were present, was not considered to be too severe, despite full admissions, no repetition and good testimonials. In the recent HPC panel decision of *Nolan*,[361] N fully admitted accessing adult websites while at work. The panel balanced the public interest, breach of trust upholding standards against N's immediate admission, clearly expressed remorse and evidence of remedial action both as to the offending conduct and health matters. The panel was able to conclude that there was no risk of repetition and so may impose a five-year caution (the maximum). While this is not authority upon sanction, it illustrates how carefully cases should be prepared and considered in order to permit a panel to consider what is an exceptional course.

1.493 Registrants who enter into a consensual sexual relationship with a patient also risk being struck off the register, since it is viewed as a breach of one of the fundamental tenets of the relationship of a health professional with their patients. This is particularly the case where the registrant is a psychiatrist or the patient is vulnerable. (Arguably all patients are vulnerable to some extent.)

1.494 Examples are *Dare v General Medical Council*[362] and *Wentzel v General Medical Council*.[363] In *Dare*, D, a psychiatrist, was struck off following use of 'his position of trust to establish an improper relationship'. In *Wentzel* the court reiterated the tenet that the reputation of the profession was more important than the fortunes of any individual member. W was erased from the medical register despite being an able practitioner having been found guilty of sexually exploiting a vulnerable patient and then lying to his superiors.

1.495 A slightly more lenient approach was adopted by Collins J in *Bevan v General Medical Council*,[364] commenting on the sanction of erasure imposed on a GP for having a 14-month sexual relationship with a patient whose marriage was breaking up:

> Every medical practitioner must know that a sexual relationship with a patient will almost inevitably be regarded as serious professional misconduct and will court erasure. There is always the element of a breach of trust and a concern that advantage is being taken of a vulnerable individual. This is particularly the case where a patient has

360 *R (Omboye Pax Harry) v General Medical Council* [2006] EWHC 3050 (Admin).
361 March 2012.
362 [2002] UKPC 54.
363 [2004] EWHC 381 (Admin).
364 [2005] EWHC 174 (Admin).

any psychiatric problems and it is not in those circumstances surprising that erasure has been upheld, however harsh the penalty might seem, where a psychiatrist has entered into such a relationship with one of his patients.[365]

1.496   However, striking off is not inevitable:

... sexual relations with a patient do not in my judgment automatically mean that there must be erasure, albeit they may mean that erasure will be considered as an option, and indeed perhaps even as the most probable option in most cases. But it is also in the public interest that good doctors should be able to continue in practice if that can be done consistently with the sending out of the message that particular forms of conduct will not be tolerated and the public can be satisfied that serious penalties will result.[366]

1.497   In *Bevan*, Collins J considered that testimonials, particularly from patients, were both material and important considerations in determining sanction, and indicated that a suspension order could have been imposed, although he declined to allow the appeal on this basis. By way of contrast, in *Council for the Regulation of Healthcare Professionals v General Medical Council (Leeper)*,[367] a case involving similar facts, an order of conditions on L's practice was considered to be too lenient.

1.498   Although in both cases the patients were considered to be vulnerable because they were going through marital breakdowns, the registrants were GPs not psychiatrists. The distinction drawn from the relative positions of power and vulnerability is a fine one and needs careful consideration by the panel.

1.499   In *Giele v General Medical Council*[368] Collins J replaced erasure with suspension of a surgeon who had entered into a sexual relationship with a patient, who he later became aware was vulnerable. Once the relationship had started, the patient received no further treatment from G although he remained on the record as her consultant. Collins J reiterated the need to maintain public confidence by:

... imposing such sanction as is in all the circumstances appropriate [which included] not ending the career of a competent doctor .... the fact that many patients and colleagues have, in the knowledge of the misconduct found, clearly indicated their views that erasure was not

365 At para 19.
366 At para 49.
367 [2004] EWHC 1850 (Admin).
368 [2005] EWHC 2143 (Admin).

needed is a matter which can carry some weight in deciding how confidence can properly be maintained.[369]

1.500　In *Raschid and Fatnani v General Medical Council*[370] Laws LJ reiterated that the two principles that are especially important in cases of this kind were the preservation of public confidence in the profession and the need to give special place to the judgment of regulatory bodies. The impact on the individual can only ever be of secondary importance.

1.501　　In *Yeong v General Medical Council*[371] Y challenged his 12-month suspension for impairment by way of misconduct following a sexual relationship with a former patient. He sought to rely on psychiatric evidence to suggest he was a low risk not having any disposition to engage in such relationships. Sales J dismissed the psychiatric evidence stating that:

> The question of the possibility of a recurrence of such misconduct ... was a matter of the ordinary assessment of likely human behaviour ... [and] ... is the sort of task which courts and tribunals regularly perform without needing to refer to expert psychiatric evidence.[372]

He distinguished *Cohen*, *Meadow* and *Azzam* because they concerned misconduct by way of clinical errors and stated that:

> ... the general public interest in clearly marking proper standards of behaviour for doctors in respect of relationships with their patients so as to uphold public confidence in the medical profession was by far the weightiest factor pointing in favour of the finding of impairment of fitness to practise and the sanction which was imposed.[373]

1.502　Y's conduct had breached the fundamental rule of the doctor–patient relationship and had undermined confidence in the profession as a whole. This required a firm mark of disapproval and a declaration of the proper standards to be adhered to in order to promote public confidence.

1.503　　Sales J made the point that this type of conduct is not easily remediable and the weight to be attached to remedial effort is less in this type of case:

> ... where the conduct consists of violating such a fundamental rule of the professional relationship between medical practitioner and patient and thereby undermining public confidence in the medical profession, a finding of impairment of fitness to practise may be justified on

369　At para 29.
370　[2007] EWCA Civ 46, [2007] 1 WLR 1460.
371　[2009] EWHC 1923 (Admin).
372　At [38].
373　At [40].

the grounds that it is necessary to reaffirm clear standards of professional conduct so as to maintain public confidence in the practitioner and in the profession. In such a case, the efforts made by the medical practitioner in question to address his behaviour for the future may carry very much less weight than in a case where the misconduct consists of clinical errors or incompetence.[374]

...

The [Fitness to Practise Panel] was entitled to conclude that Dr Yeong's case was one in which the question of remedial steps and compliance with improved practising standards for the future was of less importance than the imposition of a sanction which would convey a clear public statement of the importance with which the fundamental standard of professional conduct in relation to relationships between medical practitioners and patients is to be regarded.[375]

1.504   Contrast *Razza v General Medical Council*[376] in which R was suspended for 12 months for impairment by way of misconduct. R allegedly conducted himself inappropriately in a consultation, behaving in a sexually motivated way and abusing his position. It was submitted that the incident was in fact entirely innocent, he was of good character and there was no suggestion of predatory behaviour. The panel found that he had an 'underlying attitude' but did not expand upon this. HHJ Pelling QC concluded that the panel had not taken proper account of R's good character and record, this being a single isolated event, and the panel had misjudged his remedial action (ensuring that a chaperone is always present when examining female patients) in concluding it was for his benefit and not that of patients. He concluded that the panel had not approached its task of considering current impairment by reason of past misconduct in a proper fashion nor had it provided adequate reasons.

1.505   The conclusion to draw is that cases of sexual misconduct will always attract the prospect of suspension or erasure. If there is a *particular* relationship of trust such as that between a psychiatrist and a vulnerable patient, erasure will almost certainly result. Erasure or lengthy suspension is only likely to be prevented where there is no such particular relationship and, there is very strong evidence that the public interest is better served by keeping an otherwise excellent registrant in practice. Such cases are likely to be rare and evidence from colleagues and from patients will assist the panel on a matter of such close judgment.

374   At [48].
375   At [58].
376   [2011] EWHC 790 (Admin).

Dishonesty

1.506   All the regulators covered in this book require registrants to be 'honest and trustworthy'. Any matter of dishonesty is regarded as particularly serious since it is seen to undermine trust in the profession concerned, regardless of whether or not it leads to direct patient harm This was made clear in *Dey v General Medical Council*:[377]

> ... health authorities must be able to place complete reliance on the integrity of practitioners; and the Committee is entitled to regard conduct which undermines that confidence as calculated to reflect on the standards and reputation of the profession as a whole.

See also *R (Rogers) v General Medical Council*[378] above.

1.507   Regulators have adopted the two-stage test of dishonesty from *R v Ghosh*.[379] In determining whether a registrant had acted dishonestly, the panel will ask itself:

1) Was what the registrant did dishonest by the ordinary standards of reasonable and honest people? It is for you to decide what those standards are and to apply them to this question.

   If you are not satisfied on the balance of probabilities that reasonable and honest people would consider the registrant's actions to have been dishonest then that is an end to the issue. If, however, you are satisfied on the balance of probabilities that reasonable and honest people would consider the registrant's actions to have been dishonest you should move to the second question.

2) Must the registrant have realised that what he was doing would be considered dishonest by those standards? You are, in other words, drawing an inference as to what was the registrant's own state of mind.

   If you are satisfied on the balance of probabilities that the registrant knew that what he was doing was dishonest by the ordinary standards of reasonable and honest people then you will find that he was dishonest, whether he personally regarded it as dishonest or not.

Thus it is dishonest for a registrant to act in a way which he knows ordinary people consider being dishonest, even if he or she asserts or genuinely believes that he or she is morally justified in acting as he or she did.

---

377 [2001] UKPC 44 at para 13.
378 [2004] EWHC 424 (Admin).
379 [1982] QB 1053.

1.508   Dishonesty cases are wide-ranging and include conduct both inside and outside the workplace, such as:

- conviction for an offence of dishonesty such as theft;
- defrauding a regulator, employer, colleague, patient or other person. Examples include working in two jobs without declaring this, working while on sick leave, or seeing patients privately without informing the employer / service provider;
- submitting a false reference or including false information on a CV or application form;
- plagiarism or cheating in order to obtain a qualification;
- research misconduct such as presenting misleading information in publications and dishonesty in clinical drug trials;
- failure to disclose to the regulatory body or an employer criminal convictions or cautions; and
- improperly amending or changing the details on patient records.

1.509   *Bolton v Law Society*[380] is the starting-point in any case of dishonesty. B, a newly qualified solicitor, mishandled money in a client account. He admitted his misconduct and the money was repaid. The Solicitors Disciplinary Tribunal found that B was 'an honest man' and that his conduct was naïve and foolish rather than premeditated or deliberate. Although such conduct would normally be regarded as so very serious as to merit being struck off, in the circumstances the appropriate penalty was the more lenient order of suspension. In the leading judgment Lord Bingham, stated that:

> Any solicitor who is shown to have discharged his professional duties with anything less than complete integrity, probity and trustworthiness must expect severe sanctions to be imposed upon him ... Lapses from the required high standard may of course take different forms and be of varying degrees. The most serious involves proven dishonesty, whether or not leading to criminal proceedings or penalties. In such cases the Tribunal has almost invariably, no matter how strong the mitigation advanced by the solicitor, order that he be struck off the role of solicitors ... If a solicitor is not shown to have acted dishonestly, but is shown to have fallen below the required standards of integrity, probity and trustworthiness, his lapse is less serious but it remains very serious indeed in a member of a profession whose reputation depends upon trust. A striking off order will not necessarily follow in such a case, but it may well. The decision whether to strike off or to suspend will often involve a fine and difficult exercise of judgment, to be made by the tribunal as an informed and expert body on all the facts of the case. Only in a very unusual and venial case of this kind

380 [1994] 1 WLR 512, [1993] EWCA Civ 32.

would the tribunal be likely to regard as appropriate any order less severe than one of suspension.[381]

1.510   As is stated elsewhere, the comment is made in *Bolton* that the profession is more important than the individual.

1.511   The approach in *Bolton* means that insight, mitigating evidence, testimonials, evidence that the registrant has learned his or her lesson and the consequences of a sanction on the registrant, are considered to be of limited weight in cases involving integrity. (The same reasoning applies to cases of sexual misconduct.)

1.512   This was affirmed in *Law Society v Salsbury*,[382] albeit with the qualification that the human rights of the registrant under articles 6 and 8 of the ECHR must also be taken into account. See also the recent Court of Appeal case of *Solicitors Regulation Authority v Dennison*.[383]

1.513   The Law Society cases have been repeatedly applied to health professionals – see, for example, *Gupta v General Medical Council*[384] in which the Privy Council upheld the GMC's decision to strike off G who had permitted her husband to continue to practise despite his being struck off at an earlier date. There was no concern about G's clinical practice and it was accepted that she was doing important work in her community and had support from her patients. Referring to *Bolton*, the Privy Council considered that upholding the reputation of the profession was more important than the consequences for the individual.

1.514   While erasure is not necessary and/or inevitable in every case of dishonesty, a lesser sanction is only likely to be imposed where there is compelling evidence of insight, that the dishonesty in question was out of character or isolated in its duration or range and that permitting the registrant to return to practice would not damage the reputation of the profession: see *Atkinson v General Medical Council*.[385] In addition, there is merit in not depriving the public of an otherwise honest and competent practitioner – an argument highlighted previously and below.

1.515   If a registrant fails to attend the hearing or demonstrate insight and remorse or assure the panel that there will be no repetition, then

---

381 At p518B–E.
382 [2008] EWCA Civ 1285, [2009] 1 WLR 1286.
383 [2012] EWCA Civ 421.
384 [2001] UKPC 61, [2002] 1 WLR 1691.
385 [2009] EWHC 3636 (Admin), para 13.

he or she forfeits the small chance of persuading the panel to adopt a more lenient sanction: *Parkinson v Nursing and Midwifery Council*.[386]

1.516   That should be balanced with the following comments by Collins J in *Council for the Regulation of Healthcare Professionals v General Medical Council (Southall)*:[387]

> Absence of remorse and contrition is likely to be indicative of a lack of insight or of maintenance of unreasonable views. In either event, it may show that a risk of repetition exists. This is clearly relevant in deciding on the appropriate sanction. But lack of remorse should not result in a higher sanction as punishment. Punishment may be an inevitable effect of whatever sanction is imposed but it must not be an element in deciding what is the appropriate sanction.

1.517   In non-dishonesty cases, different considerations may apply between health professionals and solicitors. The loss to the profession of a competent and well respected professional who presents no danger to the public is a factor that can be taken into account – see *Bijl v General Medical Council*.[388] In *Southall*[389] it was stated that:

> It is clearly in the public interest that doctors who are competent and for whose skills many patients and colleagues have nothing but praise should not be precluded from practice altogether if that can be achieved with no danger to the public and with no damage to the reputation of the profession. So much was made clear by the Privy Council in *Bijl v General Medical Council* ...

> It follows that in my view testimonials can in the case of doctors be accorded greater weight than in the case of solicitors. The requirement of absolute honesty so that there can be absolute trust in a solicitor is obviously of paramount importance. That he may be a good solicitor is obviously something to be taken into account, but the public interest in him being able to continue to practise is not so important. Thus testimonials which establish that a doctor is, in the view of eminent colleagues and of nursing staff who have worked with him, one who is not only competent but whose loss to the profession and to his potential patients would be serious indeed can, in my opinion, be accorded substantial weight.

1.518   The *Southall* case arguably included elements of dishonesty since S, an eminent paediatrician, provided a misleading and incomplete report, including statistical evidence upon sudden cot-deaths, in a murder trial based on inadequate material and without himself being

---

386 [2010] EWHC 1898 (Admin), per Mitting J at para 18.
387 [2005] EWHC 579 (Admin) at para 30.
388 [2001] UKPC 42.
389 [2005] EWHC 579 (Admin) at para 13.

a statistician. He was found to have been guilty of serious professional misconduct including irresponsible and misleading conduct. The panel found that although he had not intended to mislead, his misguided insistence as to the correctness of his statistical evidence was 'disturbing and serious'.

1.519 See also similar comments by Collins J in *Giele v General Medical Council* (at para 1.499 above), a case involving an inappropriate sexual relationship.

1.520 In *Brennan v Health Professions Council* (at para 1.466 above) Ouseley J provided useful guidance on cases where the principal reason for sanction is the reputation of the profession. A very careful balancing exercise is required, and careful consideration would be needed regarding necessity and proportionality.

1.521 From the above it is clear that in appropriate cases a lesser sanction may be imposed. *James v Nursing and Midwifery Council*[390] is a rare example of the courts accepting that cautioning a registrant can be an appropriate sanction in some dishonesty cases. J pleaded guilty to possession of criminal property obtained by her husband (a non-work related dishonesty offence). Despite evidence that J had excellent nursing qualities and capabilities, the NMC struck her off. The High Court granted her appeal and remitted the case back to the NMC due to inadequate reasoning. In so doing, the High Court noted that the NMC appeared not to have taken into account character and mitigation evidence. In relation to sanction Holman J stated that while there were considerable arguments both for and against striking off, 'it seems to me that this is a case that required very definite step by step consideration of the sanction of caution and suspension', and furthermore that there were 'considerable arguments in favour of each of the alternative lesser penalties of caution or suspension'.

1.522 In *Nicholas-Pillai v General Medical Council*,[391] a case in which NP contested critical allegations of dishonest note-keeping, Mitting J made the important point that:

> In the ordinary case such as this, the attitude of the practitioner to the events which give rise to the specific allegations against him is, in principle, something which can be taken into account either in his favour or against him by the panel, both at the stage when it considers whether his fitness to practise is impaired, and at the stage of determining what sanction should be imposed upon him.[392]

390 [2008] EWHC 365 (Admin).
391 [2009] EWHC 1048 (Admin).
392 At para 19.

From this it is plain that an early plea and acceptance of a case may precipitate a reduced sanction. Contesting a matter throughout may result in a higher sanction since the panel may conclude that there is no insight, no remorse and no room for leniency.

1.523   The indicative sanctions guidelines do not set specific tariffs to be imposed in dishonesty cases. Panels have the full range of sanctions available to them. The need to distinguish between serious and less serious cases, the emphasis on early admissions and insight, the public interest in retaining good and competent health professionals where there is no likelihood of repetition suggests that erasure should not just become the norm for dishonesty.

1.524   Each case must be very carefully considered and panels may, and in appropriate cases should, consider and impose lesser sanctions. That such a course may be exceptional is no reason to do otherwise when the case requires it.

Deficient performance

1.525   Cases fall into this category where a registrant has failed to act in the best interests of a patient or provided inadequate care falling *well* below the expected standard of a competent practitioner. The range of cases in this category is necessarily wide, however of particular importance is the issue of patient protection. This is best served by considering whether the registrant has developed, or has the potential to develop, insight into his or her failures. Has the registrant altered his or her practices as a result of matters, sought assistance from a mentor or senior practitioner? Has the registrant sought to improve his or her knowledge base – be it clinical, practical, social, business etc – to prevent such occurrences? If the registrant has done none of the above, then is he or she open to suggestion, or is the failure indicative of an inability to gain insight?

1.526   In *Ghosh v General Medical Council*[393] the Privy Council provided guidance on such cases. G was found guilty of two matters of serious professional misconduct. One concerned the inaccurate and false completion of a cremation form. The second concerned a failure to visit a patient but nonetheless providing a prescription without assessing the condition of the patient or his treatment needs. G prescribed antibiotics to the second patient who was in fact suffering from life-threatening illnesses. G was placed under conditions including that she undertake supervised re-training to remedy her

393 [2001] UKPC 29.

clinical deficiencies, at the next hearing provide evidence that she had done so, not engage in locum posts, not engage in any unsupervised or single-handed practice and advise any prospective employer and any agency of the conditions. G singularly failed to meet the above conditions, indeed her conduct worsened with further complaints and a period of unexplained absence when seconded to a practice. She also failed to give adequate reasons for any these failings. She was subsequently erased from the register.

1.527 In its decision to uphold erasure their Lordships commented that:

> ... conditional registration, while in itself a lesser penalty than suspension in that the practitioner is permitted to continue in practice for the time being, is potentially more severe in that failure to comply with the conditions is likely to lead to erasure. The nature of the conditions imposed on Dr Ghosh indicated that she was regarded as unfit to practise unless she successfully completed a programme of supervised retraining. The original Committee did not decide that conditional registration was a sufficient penalty, but that Dr Ghosh needed to undergo retraining if the public was to be adequately protected. The logical response to her failure to complete such a programme was erasure, not suspension.

> Their Lordships have themselves reviewed the evidence, and are satisfied that this was a bad case. Dr Ghosh never acknowledged the seriousness of her original misconduct, and patently failed to attend, let alone successfully complete, the programme that had been arranged for her. Her conduct in leaving the country for 2 months without prior warning or subsequent explanation was unprofessional and in the highest degree irresponsible. On the evidence before it and without seeing Dr Ghosh and hearing her in person the Committee had no material on which it could be satisfied that Dr Ghosh would be any more likely to comply with the terms of a further period of conditional registration than she had in the past. Their Lordships recognise, as the Committee must have done, that erasure will effectively bring Dr Ghosh's career as a doctor to an end. But they consider that, in all the circumstances, the Committee had no real alternative but to order her name to be erased from the register.[394]

1.528 It is quite plain that the Privy Council regarded conditions as potentially burdensome but that they provide the registrant with the opportunity to prove that he or she has rectified the errors complained of. If a registrant does demonstrate insight, then he or she may well save his or her career, but if there is no evidence of rectification there is in their Lordships' words 'no material ... [and thus] ... no alternative but [erasure]'.

394 At paras 39–40.

1.529   In *Garfoot v General Medical Council*[395] G was erased from the medical register for the repeated 'irresponsible and/or inappropriate prescribing' of controlled drugs to addicts. G had little or no learning in this field and the panel found that G essentially provided addicts/patients what they requested. Some patients became addicted to the drugs with which they were being treated.

1.530   The panel found that numerous standards of practice were breached in the important area of creating a therapeutic relationship with the patient, thus:

> The Committee had to conclude that, by and large, patients dictated their own prescriptions. The Committee were reinforced in this view by your dismissive attitude to written agreements and to sanctions. The Committee concluded that the battle for medical intervention for change was lost before it had begun.[396]

1.531   Negotiation and agreement is key to treating addiction. The important point is thus G's 'dismissive attitude' toward the therapeutic norms.

1.532   The panel also found that despite some two-and-a-half years elapsing between the first letter from the GMC and the panel hearing, there was little evidence of concrete change in attitude or practice concluding that G still has 'difficulty in accepting the need for radical change in your prescribing and doubt that you are capable of achieving such change'. The Privy Council upheld the order of erasure on the basis of the seriousness of the conduct and the fact that no conditions could be devised in order to enable G to continue to practise.

1.533   In *Jalloh v Nursing and Midwifery Council*[397] J was found to have committed a series of mistakes, repeatedly failing to follow procedures and disregarding the interests of a vulnerable patient. The mistakes were serious, and despite her experience and mitigation including her excellent character and record, the risk of repetition remained. She was thus impaired and placed under conditions for 18 months. Silber J endorsed the oft-stated approach that the judgment and sanction of the committee, comprising members of the profession, deserved respect, it being the body best qualified to judge what the profession expects of its members and the measures necessary to maintain appropriate standards. J's appeal against the finding of impairment and the sanction were dismissed.

---

395 [2002] UKPC 35.

396 Quoting the findings of the Professional Conduct Committee at para 7 which are adopted as accurate and requiring the sanction of erasure – see paras 14–16.

397 [2009] EWHC 1697 (Admin).

1.534   From the above it is clear that in some very serious cases no amount of mitigation will prevent erasure of suspension from practice. However, where there is insight and a will to change or the potential for both to develop, the public may be better served by the registrant's return to practice if and when it is safe so to do.

Double jeopardy

> Regulatory proceedings need not be stayed pending the outcome of criminal proceedings unless there are exceptional circumstances such as an impossible workload from which the defendant can demonstrate serious prejudice or injustice. Arguments regarding double jeopardy, privilege and publicity are otherwise unlikely to succeed.

1.535   The interplay between civil and criminal proceedings has been and remains a contentious area, all the more so as the boundaries between these two strands of process blur through greater regulation, and simultaneous actions brought by claimants. The argument has usually been that civil proceedings should await the outcome of a criminal trial so that matters disclosed by the defence in civil proceedings do not compromise the defendant in his or her trial. However, criminal trials have changed markedly and the advent of defence disclosure means that the arguments deployed to stay or postpone civil or regulatory proceedings are less likely to prevail. A defendant must now disclose not only his or her defence and the details of witnesses relied upon, but must set out where he or she takes issue with the prosecution case and why. All parties, including defendants and their advocates, are expected to comply with the Criminal Procedure Rules designed to assist the trial process the effects of which are most keenly felt by the defence.

Is the principle of parallel proceedings acceptable?

1.536   The answer to this fundamental question is – yes. In *Jefferson Ltd v Bhetcha*[398] the plaintiff company J brought a claim to recover monies appropriated by its former employee B, who also faced criminal prosecution in connection with this. The Court of Appeal confirmed that the court had the discretion to stay or adjourn the civil proceedings having regard to the concurrent criminal proceedings, but the

398 [1979] 1 WLR 898.

defendant would have to persuade the court why this should happen. As Megaw J stated:

> ... while each case must be judged on its own facts, the burden is on the defendant in the civil action to show that it is just and convenient that the plaintiff's ordinary rights of having his claim processed and heard and decided should be interfered with ... one factor to be taken into account, and it may well be a very important factor, is whether there is a real danger of the causing of injustice in the criminal proceedings ... [399]

1.537 The arguments deployed to prevent parallel proceedings are that information necessarily disclosed in one hearing could be used in the other when it would not otherwise be available. The information may be statements that incriminate the witness/defendant or documents that are probative in the criminal hearing or, it may be that witnesses are rehearsed in their evidence. Alternatively there may be argument regarding prejudicial publicity or that parallel proceedings place an unfair burden on one party.

1.538 None of the arguments are received with enthusiasm by the higher courts. With the move towards swifter justice and more case management the emphasis is on continuing proceedings unless the court is persuaded otherwise by the risk of serious prejudice or injustice.

1.539 In *Mote v Secretary of State for Work and Pensions and another*[400] the Court of Appeal reviewed the matter of concurrent proceedings and reaffirmed that the civil court continues to enjoy the discretion to adjourn but that civil proceedings could frequently continue *without* prejudicing the criminal trial. The criminal courts have the power to stay proceedings as an abuse of process and, to control the admission of evidence. The fact that D may have to disclose his or her criminal defence during civil proceedings causes no prejudice since he or she is expected to disclose this in any event.

Privilege against self-incrimination – statements by the defendant

1.540 The privilege against self-incrimination prohibits a witness from being compelled to answer questions or produce documents if the answers or material might incriminate him or her in criminal proceedings. The fact that the exercise of that right means that someone may lose in civil proceedings does not provide a defence although it may in exceptional circumstances provide grounds for postponement.

399 At p905.
400 [2007] EWCA Civ 1324.

1.541   In *V v C*[401] the company V sought £11.3m and damages against C for misappropriation of funds. C said he could not respond to the particulars of claim for fear of self-incrimination. V sought summary judgment against him. The Court of Appeal confirmed that privilege arose when a person was being compelled on 'pain of punishment' to answer questions and held that pleadings in defence of an application for summary judgment did not involve compulsion. C could choose to plead his case or not, although the result might be that judgment is entered against him.

1.542   It is plain from *V v C* that the right to privilege against self-incrimination does not provide a 'right to silence' in civil cases, nor does the threat of criminal proceedings provide a defence. Civil claims are not prevented because the defendant may have to disclose his or her defence to criminal proceedings, not least because it is reasonable to proceed on the basis that a defence is deployed to exculpate. Finally, the introduction of defence case statements in criminal trials means that a defence should now be disclosed and, although the 'right to silence' exists it has been emasculated by adverse inferences being drawn when it is relied upon.

1.543   C could have applied to postpone the civil proceedings pending the outcome of the criminal trial, however following *Jefferson Ltd v Bhetcha*[402] above, the burden would be upon him to persuade the court that the civil proceedings could not be tried fairly, or trying them might affect the fairness of a criminal trial.

1.544   As alternatives, a defendant might try to argue that any civil court order should contain a clause preventing the use of disclosed material in other proceedings or, seek to agree such issues with the Crown Prosecution Service, however absent exceptional circumstances both are unlikely to succeed.

1.545   On the other side of the coin, there may be merit in a claimant deferring civil proceedings until the outcome of a criminal trial since a conviction will undoubtedly make it more difficult for the defendant's civil case to succeed. This may reduce costs and improve the claimant's prospects, particularly if the defendant's assets are restrained.

Privilege against self-incrimination – statements by lawyers

1.546   Statements made by a defendant's lawyer, while not strictly *self-incrimination*, may provide admissible evidence in subsequent proceedings since they are usually deemed to be made on authority.

401 [2001] EWCA Civ 1509.
402 [1979] 1 WLR 898.

In *R v Turner*,[403] pre-trial representations by an advocate at an early hearing were deployed. In *R v Hayes*[404] pre-trial negotiations on pleas contained in correspondence were deemed admissible. In *R (Firth) v Epping Magistrates' Court*[405] the pre-trial case-management form produced by F's advocate citing a defence of self-defence was used in committal proceedings to prove his presence at the scene of the crime when the evidence did not otherwise identify him. This caused considerable consternation given that defence representatives are obliged to fill in a form that could be used against their own client. It led to suggestions of simply marking the form 'privileged'. Thankfully common-sense appears to have prevailed in the subsequent case of *R v Newell*[406] in which the contents of a 'plea and case-management form' were deployed against N when the prosecution perceived a difference between what he said in evidence and what his lawyer had placed on the form.

1.547   On appeal the court held that a form filled in by an advocate was filled in with implied if not express authority. Alternatively the advocate had ostensible authority to do so. In addition the form was spoken to by counsel in court in N's presence so was again admissible but, the principle object of the form is to assist the court in the management of cases. The defence case is more readily to be observed in the defence case statement. For these reasons the form should have been excluded by the trial judge under PACE 1984 s78 as being unfair in all the circumstances. While each case should be decided on its own facts, an example of the appropriate use of such a form may be where the defence seek to ambush the Crown while they are in breach of their obligations under the Criminal Procedure Rules by failing to provide a defence case statement.

1.548   From this it may be concluded that statements made by lawyers, whether in writing or orally, are admissible against a defendant, but that they should only be deployed in exceptional circumstances such as correcting unfairness to the prosecution caused by a deliberate and inappropriate conduct of the defence case.

1.549   There is no reason to exclude statements made by a defendant's lawyers in civil or disciplinary proceedings from subsequent criminal proceedings or vice versa. This would include comments made during cross-examination and/or legal or factual argument.

403 (1975) 61 Cr App R 67.
404 [2004] EWCA Crim 2844.
405 [2011] EWHC 388 (Admin).
406 [2012] EWCA Crim 650.

Privilege against self-incrimination – documents

1.550 In *C plc v P and Attorney-General (Intervenor)*[407] the Court of Appeal held that the privilege against self-incrimination is no basis for withholding incriminating material (child pornography on a computer) found during the execution of a civil search order. The privilege against self-incrimination does not apply to material that exists independent of answers from compulsory questions. Furthermore, even if material is ruled inadmissible under PACE 1984 s78 (as having an adverse/unfair effect on the proceedings) if that material leads to further evidence, there is no basis to exclude the latter. Subject to section 78 and overriding issues such as the prohibition on the use of evidence tainted by torture, the central principle of admissibility in criminal proceedings is relevance and not how or why the material was obtained.

Adverse publicity

1.551 Adverse publicity as a ground for staying criminal proceedings, while still available in principle, is now all but defunct. Much of the case-law revolves around the freedom of the press to report matters, and the need for justice to be both open and public. The pendulum has swung against the idea that a jury could not ignore prejudicial material and the courts are far more willing to trust jurors and their oath. The deluge of prejudicial comment or other material surrounding recent terrorist cases or high profile murders (the Heathrow liquid bombs plot, Harold Shipman, Fred West, Ian Huntley and Maxine Carr etc) have not prevented trials.

1.552 Furthermore, regulatory proceedings are intended to be public, albeit with a discretion to exclude the public in certain circumstances. These include considerations of an interim order and/or when the physical or mental health of a registrant may be in question. There is a balance to be met between the interests of the maker of the allegation, any patient(s) concerned, whether a public hearing would adversely affect the health of the practitioner, the public interest. The latter point of public interest is accorded great weight since the primary function of the regulators is to protect public interest and uphold standards. This requires application of the old adage that justice must be seen to be done.

1.553 As a ground for staying regulatory proceedings the position is even more remote than in criminal trials since the panels consist of

407 [2007] EWCA Civ 493.

professional people guided by a legal assessor. However, cases such as *Roomi v General Medical Council*[408] (see para 1.58 above under charging protocols) show that mistakes can be made, and if a panel has demonstrably taken account of inappropriate material the decision may be open to challenge.

Double jeopardy

1.554   Double jeopardy is when a defendant repeatedly faces criminal proceedings for the same offence. It finds its origins in the doctrine of abuse of process – see *Connelly v Director of Public Prosecutions*.[409] The rule has always been tightly restricted, and on serious cases where fresh compelling evidence is available, it has now been entirely abrogated by Part 10 of the CJA 2003. In any event, it is limited to previous consideration by the criminal courts. Attempts to extend the principle to prevent the criminal trial of matters litigated in a civil court have failed. In *R v L*[410] L's conviction of the manslaughter of his child was upheld despite the previous finding by the judge in care proceedings that he could not determine whether it was the mother or father who was responsible.

1.555   In *Bhatt v General Medical Council*[411] the court held that the GMC was entitled to bring a case against B based upon seven allegations of indecent assault of which he had been acquitted in the criminal court. The principal reasons were that the proceedings are of a different nature with a different purpose (upholding professional standards etc) and a different burden of proof. Furthermore, the plea of autrefois acquit did not apply to regulatory proceedings – see also *R (Redgrave) v Metropolitan Police Commissioner*.[412]

Rehearsal of evidence

1.556   The fact that civil proceedings provide an opportunity for the rehearsal of witnesses, argument or unfair tailoring of cross-examination in criminal proceedings is no reason to stay the civil case. The argument was soundly rejected by the Court of Appeal in *Mote v Secretary of State for Work and Pensions and another*.[413] It was also rejected

408 [2009] EWHC 2188 (Admin).
409 [1964] AC 1245.
410 [2006] 1 WLR 3092.
411 [2011] EWHC 783 (Admin).
412 [2003] 1 WLR 1136.
413 [2007] EWCA Civ 1324.

in *Bhatt* (above) given that the panel were informed of the previous court case and were alert to the issue of contamination and rehearsal. Any such issue could in any event be explored in cross-examination.

Conducting concurrent litigation

1.557 The burden of conducting concurrent litigation may lead to the postponement of civil proceedings but only in exceptional circumstances. In *R v Institute of Chartered Accountants in England ex p Brindle*[414] the Court of Appeal stayed disciplinary proceedings principally on grounds of the volume of work in litigating on separate fronts. The case concerned the collapse of the Bank of Credit and Commerce International (BCCI) and was colossal. Contrast *R v Chance ex p Smith*[415] in which the Divisional Court refused an application by Robert Maxwell's accountants for judicial review of a refusal to stay civil proceedings on the grounds of the volume and number of enquiries (Serious Fraud Office, Department of Trade and Industry, Parliamentary Committee, civil and disciplinary hearings). Henry LJ said that *Ex p Brindle* was 'decided on its own facts', which is frequently taken to mean a judge disagrees with and seeks to limit application of a decision. He concluded that the overlap in preparation was useful to the defence since work in one case could be deployed in another and, if conflicting demands were made the tribunals should sort these out for or among themselves.

1.558 In *R (Land and others) v Executive Counsel of the Joint Disciplinary Scheme*[416] Stanley Burnton J clearly preferred the approach taken in *Ex p Smith*, suggesting that regulatory proceedings were capable of dealing with such issues and it was in accordance with the Court of Appeal's judgment in *R v Panel on Takeovers and Mergers ex p Fayed.*[417]

1.559 Finally, in *R (Ranson) v Institute of Actuaries*[418] Moses J stayed civil proceedings largely on the basis that the case placed a huge burden on litigants in person. He confirmed that this was a power to be exercised sparingly and that considerable weight was due to the decision of the regulatory body.

1.560 The contrasting cases do provide a glimmer of hope but make it plain that a stay will only be granted in exceptional circumstance

---

414 [1994] BCC 297.
415 [1995] BCC 1095.
416 [2002] EWHC 2086 (Admin).
417 [1992] BCC 524.
418 [2004] EWHC 3087 (Admin).

where the burden of preparation is intolerable and will lead to injustice. This is only likely to succeed where preparation in one case does not assist preparation in the other.

The jurisdiction of regulatory bodies

> The fact that matters complained of occurred outside the UK and/or before a practitioner was registered with a regulatory body is no bar to proceedings.
>
> The fact that the matters may have already been adjudicated upon in another jurisdiction is also no bar to proceedings.

1.561   The regulators have the power to consider acts that occurred outside the UK whether or not they have been adjudicated upon elsewhere and, they may consider acts that occurred before the registrant became a registered practitioner.

1.562   In *Mohammed v General Medical Council*[419] M was suspended for six months following disciplinary proceedings brought by the Irish Medical Council. Subsequently the GMC brought proceedings relating to the same misconduct and he was suspended for a further three months. In rejecting his appeal, the High Court referred to MA 1983 s35C(2) which permitted a finding of impairment based on the determination of a regulatory body in the UK or elsewhere, and under section 35C(3) was not prevented from doing so on the basis that the acts occurred outside the UK or prior to registration. The court held that since the panel could base a finding of impairment on another regulatory body's decision it, by implication, had the power to take such action as it considered appropriate.

1.563   In *Swanney v General Medical Council*[420] S admitted disciplinary charges relating to misconduct that occurred in Canada in 1999–2000. At that time S was not registered in the UK. By the time he pleaded (in 2003) S had dual registration in the UK and British Columbia, Canada. In 2007 the GMC brought charges in relation to the same misconduct. S argued that the GMC had no jurisdiction since at the time he was not registered or practising in the UK, the matter occurred abroad and he was at risk of double jeopardy The Court of Session rejected each of his contentions. It noted that MA 1983 s36(1)(b) authorises the GMC to take action against a registrant 'whether while so registered or not' which made it 'completely

---

419 [2007] EWHC 2728 (Admin).
420 2008 SLT 646.

clear that the committee was being given authority by Parliament to explore an issue of serious professional misconduct in relation to actions which may have occurred while the subject of the inquiry was not a registered person in the United Kingdom'. The court was concerned that the public would be at risk if a registrant found guilty of serious professional misconduct in some other jurisdiction could come to the UK and practice with impunity. The geographical location of the conduct was irrelevant given the legislative purpose of public protection. The court also dismissed the argument on double jeopardy on the basis that the purpose of each set of proceedings was to determine whether S ought to practice without restriction in each specific jurisdiction. The purposes were thus different and there was no prejudice or double jeopardy.

Voluntary erasure

A process permitting registrants to withdraw from their profession provided it is in the public interest for this to be permitted. It is only likely to be permitted if there are no FTP issues or no serious FTP issues. The registrant should genuinely be leaving practice. There must be no question of sweeping matters under the carpet.

1.564 Some regulators permit the removal of a registrant's name from the register by consent however the process is by no means uniform. Broadly speaking 'voluntary erasure' or 'disposal by consent' requires the public interest to be best served by this process. That includes both the protection of patients and, upholding the good standing of the profession. The latter is particularly important. There should be no question of sweeping a difficult case under the carpet. Given the difference in each regulator's stance, they are dealt with separately however the principles governing erasure and restoration as set out for GMC registrants apply across the board.

GMC registrants

1.565 The GMC process is dealt with under regulation 3(1) of the GMC (Voluntary Erasure and Restoration following Voluntary Erasure) Regulations 2004. A doctor may apply to the registrar for voluntary erasure at any point in the fitness to practise process. The application must include:

a) Details of any current person, body or organisation to whom he or she supplies or has an agreement to provide medical services. If none is current, this should be the most recent person/body/ organisation in that position.

b) A statement by the practitioner and the person/body/organisation that he/she/it is not aware of any fitness to practise (FTP) proceedings or of any reason why he or she could be subject to such proceedings, or

c) A statement that he or she has not been employed or had an arrangement to provide medical services in the five years prior to the application.

The registrar may grant the application, refer it to a medical and lay case examiner, refer the application to an FTP panel or, reject it.

1.566   An application will be referred to case examiners where an allegation is being investigated, the doctor is liable to investigation, or a case has been referred to a FTP panel but has *not yet commenced*. Case examiners may also consider an application if the doctor is currently suspended or subject to conditions or undertakings. If they cannot agree upon the application it is referred to an Investigation Committee. If an application is received and a hearing before a FTP panel *has commenced*, the application will be determined by that panel.

1.567   To protect the public interest (patient protection, public confidence in the profession etc), decisions on voluntary erasure are normally only made once current or pending investigations have concluded. Nonetheless voluntary erasure may be appropriate if it is considered right in all the circumstances, including the public interest, the doctor's health and the likelihood of return to practise. A genuine desire to be removed from the register, demonstrated by for example steps taken to retire or stop practice, is a significant factor in favour of voluntary erasure. An application apparently triggered by FTP proceedings will be treated with some scepticism in which case the doctor's insight into issues and his or her record with the regulator will affect how his alleged desire to leave practice is viewed.

1.568   While it may be argued that voluntary erasure best protects the public because a doctor will not be entitled to practise, this may not be the case since he or she may apply for restoration to the register albeit that restoration is not automatic where FTP concerns were raised during the original voluntary erasure process. There may also be evidential problems if an application for restoration is made some time later. From the GMC's perspective it is preferable for all FTP concerns to be dealt with by admission (or dismissal) such that possible evidential concerns fall away.

1.569   Matters to consider in any application for voluntary erasure include the doctor's health, the time elapsed since he or she last practised, the genuineness of the desire to be erased from the register, the likelihood of a future application for restoration and, any evidence that he or she really has no intention to practise in the UK *or elsewhere.* Given the GMC's general duty to protect the public, no distinction is made between an intention to practice in the UK, abroad, privately or in public practice. An intention to practice in another allied field of practice may be of equal relevance. A genuine desire to stop practice altogether is a strong factor in favour of voluntary erasure. Conversely the likelihood of return is a factor against the process. The stage of the doctor's career may be significant since someone in the latter stages of their career is less likely to return to practice than someone at the start. However there is no hard and fast rule and each case must be decided on its own merits.

1.570   Although there will always be exceptions, voluntary erasure is inappropriate if there are concerns regarding probity, sexual misconduct, harm to patients through deficient performance or cases involving convictions. Confidence in the profession is likely to be harmed if the regulator is not seen to deal with these issues. Voluntary erasure would only be appropriate in exceptional circumstance such as a doctor who is seriously ill and/or unfit to participate in FTP proceedings.

1.571   Voluntary erasure is more likely to be appropriate if the allegations and evidence relate to a doctor's health even if he or she has indicated that improved health may result in an application to restore. Where health has impacted upon performance voluntary erasure may depend upon the doctor's ability to participate in any FTP process. A doctor with a chronic condition and remote prospect of return to practise may well be granted voluntary erasure whereas an acute or episodic condition from which recovery may well occur is unlikely to result in voluntary erasure, particularly if it has impacted upon performance.

1.572   A registrant may apply for restoration following voluntary erasure but the burden lies with him or her to demonstrate that he or she is fit to practise. Any new or outstanding FTP concerns will be referred to the case examiners. Health concerns and/or performance concerns whether arising from historic complaints, referrals, concerns from another jurisdiction or by reason of an extended break from practice, must be met with proof that he or she is fit to practice. Such cases may well require an assessment as part of the restoration process. Cases with multiple concerns, including new or outstanding allegations, are likely be refused by case examiners or referred to the panel particularly if a finding of impairment is likely.

1.573   If a doctor has been convicted of a criminal offence, particularly an offence of serious violence, sexual misconduct, or offences involving children and/or pornography such that he or she presents a risk to public confidence in the profession, an application to restore will almost certainly be referred to the FTP.

1.574   A registrant may re-apply for restoration at any time after he or she has been refused restoration by a case-examiner. However, repeated applications may to be referred to the FTP. If restoration is refused by the FTP, he or she may reapply but only if at least 12 months has elapsed since refusal.

HCPC registrants

1.575   The HCPC permits disposal of a case by consent provided they are satisfied that the 'appropriate level of public protection is secured and, doing so would not be detrimental to the wider public interest'.[421] The process is staged and requires (a) an investigating panel to find that there is a case to answer in order to ensure the allegation has been fully considered, (b) a full and insight-full admission of the case and a willingness to address failures and, (c) any agreed remedial action to be consistent with the likely/expected outcome were the case to be contested. The agreed position is then placed before a panel which has the full range of sanctions available to it. The panel will then consider whether on the evidence presented it is appropriate to deal with the matter by way of consent or, to reject the proposal and adjourn the case for a full hearing. Since a full hearing is always a possibility, any admissions made for the purpose of the voluntary approach are treated as being 'without prejudice'.

GDC registrants

1.576   Voluntary erasure is available in GDC proceedings but not if there are ongoing FTP concerns. Under R.1.4 of the 2003 Rules,[422] a registrant may apply in writing to the registrar for erasure from the register. The application must include a declaration that the registrant is 'not aware of any reason for the institution of proceedings which might affect [his or her] registration'. The registrar may grant the

---

421 Health Professions Council Practice Note on Disposal of Cases by Consent, March 2011.

422 R.1.4, General Dental Council (Administration of Core Functions) Rules 2003.

application or, if he or she has 'any doubt', refer the matter to the preliminary proceedings committee for determination.

NMC registrants

1.577 The NMC are currently consulting on the issue of 'consensual disposal' with a view to considering a regime similar to that of the HCPC namely agreeing a statement of facts, admitting that fitness is impaired and placing the matter before a panel with an agreed suggested sanction. To ensure the process is in the public interest, the admission of fact must be on a 'full-facts' basis, there can be no plea-bargaining. Furthermore the panel will retain full discretion on whether to accept or reject the agreed position and, a case can only be dealt with in this way if it is in the public interest so to do.

GOC registrants

1.578 Voluntary erasure is not available at GOC proceedings.

Costs

1.579 The various healthcare regulators bring proceedings in the public interest, to protect the public or to uphold standards etc, they are not in the position of an ordinary litigant prosecuting a claim. Unless a complaint is improperly brought no order for costs is normally made against the regulator. (See *Walker v Law Society*.[423])

423 [2007] EWCA Civ 233.

CHAPTER 2

The General Medical Council

continued

Key points

- *Regulator:* General Medical Council (GMC)
- *Professions regulated:* Doctors
- *Common sources of referral:* Patients, employers, police, other health professionals
- *Type of proceedings:* Fitness to practise
- *Relevant statute:* Medical Act (MA) 1983 (Part V and Sch 4)
- *Fitness to Practise Rules:* General Medical Council (Fitness to Practise) Rules 2004 (Schedule to SI 2004 No 2608)
- *Key document: Good medical practice,* current edition 2006 (new edition due 2012)
- *Two-stage process:* Investigation (GMC (Fitness to Practise) Rules 2004 Part 2) and adjudication (GMC (Fitness to Practise) Rules 2004 Part 8)
- *Investigation Committee:* Yes (GMC (Fitness to Practise) Rules 2004 r9)
- *Adjudication Committee:* Fitness to Practise Panels – run by Medical Practitioners Tribunal Service (MPTS) from summer 2012
- *Location:* Main hearing centre: Manchester. Some cases heard in London
- *Notice of hearing provision:* GMC (Fitness to Practise) Rules 2004 r15
- *Case management provisions:* GMC (Fitness to Practise) Rules 2004 r16
- *Procedure before a Fitness to Practise Panel:* GMC (Fitness to Practise) Rules 2004 r17
- *Test:* Whether fitness to practise is impaired by reason of (in summary): a) misconduct; b) deficient professional performance; c) a criminal conviction or caution; d) adverse physical or mental health; e) a determination by another regulator (MA 1983 s35(2))
- *Power to require a doctor to undergo health or performance assessment?* Yes – MA 1983 Sch 4 para 5A(1)
- *Interim order power:* Yes – interim conditions of practice or interim suspension (MA 1983 s41A), GMC (Fitness to Practise) Rules 2004 Part 7 rr25–27 heard by Interim Orders Panel
- *Interim order guidance: Guidance for the Interim Orders Panel and the Fitness to Practise Panel*
- *Limited protection for historic complaints:* GMC (Fitness to Practise) Rules 2004 r4(5)

- *General composition for final hearings:* Usually three GMC-appointed members, lay and professional (medical) – not legally qualified
- *Addressing the panel:* Generally seated and 'Sir'/'Madam'
- *Independent legal assessor:* Yes
- *Evidence:* GMC (Fitness to Practise) Rules 2004 r34 – 'may admit any evidence they consider fair and relevant to the case before them, whether or not such evidence would be admissible in a court of law'
- *Half-time submission provision:* GMC (Fitness to Practise) Rules 2004 r17(g) – 'whether sufficient evidence has been adduced to find the facts proved or to support a finding of impairment'
- *Sanction provisions:* MA 1983 s35D
- *Sanction documents: Indicative sanctions guidance for the Fitness to Practise Panel; Fitness to practise guidance: warnings; Good medical practice*
- *Review hearings:* MA 1983 s35D, GMC (Fitness to Practise) Rules 2004 r22
- *Restoration hearings:* GMC (Fitness to Practise) Rules 2004 Part 6 rr23 and 24
- *Appeal rule:* MA 1983 s40
- *Costs:* No general provision

Introduction

Overview

2.1 This chapter outlines the fitness to practise procedures of the General Medical Council (GMC) and provides advice on preparation and tactical considerations. In this chapter the terms 'doctor' and 'registrant' are used interchangeably to refer to an individual practitioner(s) facing proceedings before the GMC. There are two main stages to GMC fitness to practise proceedings – investigation and adjudication. The adjudication stage (the hearing) is, if necessary, a three-stage process of 1) fact-finding, 2) impairment and 3) sanction. The overriding concern of fitness to practise proceedings is to protect the public interest. 'Public interest' has been widely defined by the courts and includes protection of members of the public, maintaining public confidence in the professions, and declaring and upholding proper standards of conduct and performance. To meet this objective the GMC has the power to erase or suspend a doctor from the register, place restrictions on his or her practice (conditions of practice) or put a note on the register for a period of time (warning). The GMC also has the power to impose an interim order until such time as proceedings have been determined.

The General Medical Council

2.2   The GMC is the regulatory body governing registered medical practitioners. All doctors must be licensed to be able legally to practise medicine and undertake activities restricted by law to doctors, such as signing death certificates. The licence to practise which is issued by the GMC applies to all doctors in the UK regardless of whether they are working in the NHS or private sector, either on a full- or part-time, permanent or locum basis. It also applies to all levels of registration, whether provisional, full or on the specialist or general registrant register. All doctors intending to practise medicine in the UK are also required to be registered with the GMC, follow the GMC's *Good medical practice* and other guidance and be subject to the GMC fitness to practise actions. In 2010, the GMC had 239,309 registrants.[1] A 'List of registered medical registrants' is maintained on the GMC website and this allows any member of the public to check the registration status of a doctor and see whether they are currently subject to any restrictions.[2]

2.3   The GMC's powers derive from the Medical Act (MA) 1983, as amended. The main objective of the GMC in exercising their functions 'is to protect, promote and maintain the health and safety of the public'.[3] When exercising its functions under the MA 1983, the GMC is required to have proper regard for:

- the interests of persons using or needing the services of provisionally or fully registered medical registrants in the UK; and
- any differing interests of different categories of provisionally or fully registered medical registrants.[4]

---

1   *Enabling excellence – autonomy and accountability for healthcare workers, social workers and social care workers*, Command Paper, Department of Health, February 2011, Annexe A (available at www.official-documents.gov.uk/document/cm80/8008/8008.pdf).

2   See www.gmc-uk.org/doctors/register/LRMP.asp.

3   MA 1983 s1A.

4   MA 1983 Sch 1 Part 2.

The meaning of 'fitness to practise'

2.4   The GMC has adopted the following as a statement of policy:[5]

- To practise safely, doctors must be competent in what they do. They must establish and maintain effective relationships with patients, respect patients' autonomy and act responsibly and appropriately if they or a colleague fall ill and their performance suffers.
- But these attributes, while essential, are not enough. Doctors have a respected position in society and their work gives them privileged access to patients, some of whom may be very vulnerable. A doctor whose conduct has shown that he cannot justify the trust placed in him should not continue in unrestricted practice while that remains the case.
- In short, the public is entitled to expect that their doctor is fit to practise, and follows the GMC's principles of good practice described in Good Medical Practice. It sets out the standards of competence, care and conduct expected of doctors, under the following main headings:

  Good clinical care – doctors must provide good standards of clinical care, must practise within the limits of their competence, and must ensure that patients are not put at unnecessary risk.

  Maintaining good medical practice – doctors must keep up to date with developments in their field, maintain their skills and audit their performance.

  Relationships with patients – doctors must develop and maintain successful relationships with their patients, by respecting patients' autonomy and other rights.

  Working with colleagues – doctors must work effectively with their colleagues. Teaching and training – where doctors have teaching responsibilities they must develop the skills, attitudes and practices of a competent teacher.

  Probity – doctors must be honest and trustworthy.

  Health – doctors must not allow their own health condition to endanger patients.

The GMC's role in regulation

2.5   Fitness to practise proceedings are concerned with stepping in when there are concerns that the requirements of *Good medical practice*

---

5   *Good medical practice*, GMC, approved in 2001. The quotes from *Good medical practice* are from the 2006 edition.

are not being met by a doctor. A question of fitness to practise may arise if:[6]

- a doctor's performance has harmed patients or put patients at risk of harm;
- a doctor has shown a deliberate or reckless disregard of clinical responsibilities towards patients;
- a doctor's health is compromising patient safety;
- a doctor has abused a patient's trust or violated a patient's autonomy or other fundamental rights;
- a doctor has behaved dishonestly, fraudulently or in a way designed to mislead or harm others.

2.6   The advice above is only illustrative of the sort of behaviour which could call registration into question. *Good medical practice* and other published GMC guidance provide a more complete picture of behaviour that may result in action by the GMC but is not exhaustive. The outcome in any case will depend on its particular facts and any mitigating and aggravating facts.

Key fitness to practise procedure documents[7]

2.7   The key fitness to practise documents include the following:

1) MA 1983;
2) GMC (Fitness to Practise) Rules 2004;
3) *Good medical practice* (2006);[8]
4) *Guidance for the Interim Orders Panel and the Fitness to Practise Panel;*
5) *Indicative sanctions guidance for the Fitness to Practise Panel;*
6) *Fitness to practise guidance: warnings;*
7) *Guidance to the GMC's Fitness to Practise Rules 2004;*
8) Charging Protocol;
9) Guidance for case examiners and the Investigation Committee;
10) Guidance on convictions, cautions and determinations;
11) Guidance on single clinical incidents;
12) Guidance on Voluntary Erasure.

---

6   See chapter 1 for further details; list taken from GMC, *The meaning of fitness to practise* – see www.gmc-uk.org/the_meaning_of_fitness_to_practise.pdf_25416562.pdf.

7   This is a non exhaustive list of current guidance. All guidance is currently available at www.gmc-uk.org – readers should always check for updated, revised or additional guidance.

8   A new edition of *Good medical practice* is due in 2012.

Relevant legislation and rules

2.8 The MA 1983 provides the fitness to practise procedural framework (Part V and Schedule 4). Specific and detailed rules are provided by the General Medical Council (Fitness to Practise) Rules 2004[9] as amended. These procedural rules cover the GMC's Investigation Committee, Interim Orders Panels and Fitness to Practise Panels. These rules are made under MA 1983 s43 and Sch 4 para 1(1).

Relevant guidance

2.9 The GMC is empowered by MA 1983 s35 to provide advice for members of the medical profession on i) standards of professional conduct, ii) standards of professional performance and iii) medical ethics.

2.10 The GMC has published guidance pursuant to section 35, divided between 'standards guidance', 'licence guidance' and 'fitness to practise guidance'.[10] The standards/ethical guidance includes the seminal *Good medical practice* (see below) and the following current guidance:

- *0–18 years: guidance for all doctors* (2007);
- *Accountability in multi-disciplinary and multi-agency mental health teams* (2006);
- *Taking up and ending appointments* (2008);
- *Making and using visual and audio recordings of patients* (2011);
- *Confidentiality* (2009);
- *Conflicts of interest* (2008);
- *Consent: patients and doctors making decision together* (2008);
- *Duties of a doctor registered with the GMC*;
- *Treatment and care towards the end of life* (2010);
- *Acting as an expert witness* (2008);
- *Good medical practice – pandemic influenza* (2009);
- *Maintaining boundaries* (2006);
- *Management for doctors* (2006);
- *Personal beliefs and medical practice* (2008);
- *Good practice in prescribing medicines* (2008);
- *Raising concerns about patient safety* (2006);
- *Writing references* (2007);
- *Reporting criminal and regulatory proceedings within and outside the UK* (2008);
- *Good practice in research and consent to research* (2010).[11]

9 SI 2004 No 2608.
10 See www.gmc-uk.org/publications/guidance_for_doctors.asp.
11 See www.gmc-uk.org/guidance/ethical_guidance.asp.

These can be useful for understanding the GMC's expectations of doctors, where relevant to fitness to practise concerns.

Good medical practice

2.11   *Good medical practice* was first published in 1995 (replacing the Blue Book) and sought to set out standards rather than examples of misconduct. It has now been through several iterations. The current version was published in November 2006, although the GMC have recently consulted on the new version: *Good medical practice 2012*.[12] The GMC describe *Good medical practice* as setting out 'the principles and values on which good practice is founded; these principles together describe medical professionalism in action. The guidance is addressed to doctors, but it is also intended to let the public know what they can expect from doctors'.[13] *Good medical practice* and other guidance is frequently referred to in fitness to practise proceedings to illustrate which standards are alleged to have been breached. *Good medical practice* is clear: 'serious or persistent failure to follow this guidance will put your registration at risk'. There are currently seven sections: 1) good clinical care; 2) maintaining good medical practice; 3) teaching and training; 4) appraising and assessing; 5) relationships with patients; 6) working with colleagues; 7) probity and health.

Fitness to practise procedures

Background

2.12   Substantial changes were made to GMC fitness to practise proceedings in 2004 following extensive consultation in 2000. These changes, largely, unified the approach to fitness to practise proceedings by ensuring that whether an issue raised about a doctor concerned health, conduct or performance there would be a single set of procedures and rules, and a single committee to consider all aspects of concern raised about a doctor that, in the GMC's view, merit a hearing. Since these changes were implemented, the work of the GMC in fitness to practise proceedings has grown, and the number of doctors facing fitness to practise proceedings has increased significantly in the last decade, as has the cost associated with such activities. The

---

12   Good Medical Practice, Draft for consultation: www.gmc-uk.org/Good_
   Medical_Practice_2012___Draft_for_consultation.pdf_45081179.pdf
13   *Good medical practice*, GMC, November 2006, p4 (available at www.gmc-uk.org/
   static/documents/content/GMP_0910.pdf).

GMC spent over £43 million on fitness to practise 'activities' in 2010, compared with £14 million in 2000.[14]

Recent and current consultations

2.13 The GMC consulted in early 2011 on the possibility of further significant changes to fitness to practise proceedings in the light of the current work load and regulatory environment. The first consultation paper – *Reform of the fitness to practise procedures at the GMC: changes to the way we deal with cases at the end of the investigation* – considered how best to achieve/redress the balance between public protection and fairness for doctors, through fitness to practise proceedings. The number of complaints against doctors has risen by 35 per cent in the last three years and by 117 per cent for those from employers and the police.[15] In the same time frame the number of hearing days has increased by 66 per cent. The consultation sought views on, inter alia, how, if at all, the number of public hearings could be reduced by entering into discussions with doctors under investigation regarding what the GMC would consider appropriate sanctions to be in individual cases, at the end of the investigation stage to conclude proceedings at that stage without a final hearing. This would not be straightforward, there is always a risk that the GMC might, for example, suggest a higher sanction than a doctor may receive at a hearing following the testing of evidence etc which could lead to pressure on a doctor to accept a sanction without knowing the full case against him or her or having the opportunity to fully understand the prospects of meeting such a case. Equally, it may mean that some of the hard fought procedural safeguards provided by a public fitness to practise hearing are lost behind the potentially closed doors of sanction negotiations. Although, it may also mean that many individuals (doctors and witnesses alike) will be able to know an outcome of the proceedings early on without waiting (with all the consequent stress and potential financial impact) for a full hearing to be listed, which can (and often does) take a period of years. It is likely to be most useful in cases where the clear outcome to be expected following a hearing would be conditions of practice. If this approach is adopted it underlines

14 *Reform of the fitness to practise procedures at the GMC – Changes to the way we deal with cases at the end of an investigation – a paper for consultation*, GMC, January 2011, p17.
15 *Reform of the fitness to practise procedures at the GMC – Changes to the way we deal with cases at the end of an investigation – a paper for consultation*, GMC, January 2011, p4.

the importance of early and timely legal advice for a doctor before entering into any potential discussions with the GMC regarding any acceptance of an early sanction. If changes are made it could result in significant use of mediation between the GMC and the doctor. However, until any such changes are introduced, this issue is outside the scope of this edition.

2.14   The second consultation paper – *Reform of the fitness to practise procedures at the GMC, The future of adjudication and the establishment of the Medical Practitioners Tribunal Service* – considered 'proposals for repositioning and further modernising adjudication within the GMC'. The proposals 'aim to underline and reinforce the autonomy of the adjudication function and the clear separation between investigation and adjudication and also to modernise existing procedures'.[16] This consultation sought views on, among other things, the establishment of the Medical Practitioners Tribunal Service (MPTS), the governance of the MPTS, management and reporting arrangements to support separation between investigation and adjudication work, and the potential for a right of appeal for the GMC against tribunal decisions. By way of background, following the previous Labour government's 2007 white paper, *Trust, assurance and safety – the regulation of health professionals in the 21st century*, and subsequently the passing of the Health and Social Care Act (HSCA) 2008, the Office of the Health Professions Adjudicator (OHPA) was established with the aim of being an independent body that would take over the adjudication function from the GMC from April 2011 (and then in time other health regulators). This was the result of a key recommendation of the inquiry by Dame Janet Smith into the serial killer doctor Harold Shipman.[17] However, the Coalition government announced their intention not to continue with this approach and the relevant parts of the HSCA 2008[18] will be repealed by the HSCA 2012.[19] As such, the GMC consulted on what steps they can take to achieve some of the

16   *Reform of the fitness to practise procedures at the GMC, The future of adjudication and the establishment of the Medical Practitioners Tribunal Service – a paper for consultation*, GMC, January 2011, p3.

17   Dame Janet Smith, *The Shipman Enquiry, Fifth Report – Safeguarding patients: lessons from the past – proposals for the future*, 9 December 2004, Command Paper (Cm 6394) – see www.shipman-inquiry.org.uk/images/fifthreport/SHIP05_COMPLETE_NO_APPS.pdf.

18   Health and Social Care Act 2008 s98.

19   Health and Social Care Act 2012 s231.

formal separation between investigation and adjudication that was intended to be achieved through OHPA.

2.15 The GMC have now established the MPTS and appointed His Honour Judge David Pearl as the chair of the new service. The MPTS began the management of fitness to practise hearings on 11 June 2012. The role of His Honour Judge Pearl will be to appoint, train, appraise and mentor panel members and will require an annual report to parliament.[20] Once implemented, the MPTS could serve as an important step towards more rigorous training for panel members and most importantly a further step towards a separation of GMC being judge, jury and prosecutor. Many of the proposals consulted on in 2011 will require amendments to the MA 1983, which are unlikely to be effected before the end of 2013.[21] In light of this, a further consultation in May 2012 proposes changes to the fitness to practise rules and to the constitution of a panels and Investigation Committee rules, which can be effected without amendments to the statute.[22] The proposals are intended to 'make the pre-hearing and hearing procedure shorter' and include: improving witness scheduling, removing the need to read out the written allegations at the start of a hearing, routinely using written witness statements as evidence-in-chief, clarifying the process for use of video-link and telephone-link evidence at hearings, allowing case managers to make a broader range of decisions relating to preliminary issues and enabling panel chairs to be involved in pre-hearing case management.[23] The MPTS is already implementing 'cultural' changes that do not require rule or statute changes – including the configuration of the seating layout of the panel members and the legal assessor. There are also currently pilots running in relation to proactive case management changes. In terms of more substantive changes in the form of new statutory rules the Department of Health is expected to consult in late 2012 on issues

20 See www.gmc-uk.org/news/11346.asp.
21 *The future of adjudication: making changes to our fitness to practise rules and to our constitution of panels and Investigation Committee rules, A paper for consultation,* GMC, May 2012, p6: www.gmc-uk.org/The_future_of_adjudication___rules.pdf_48726068.pdf.
22 *The future of adjudication: making changes to our fitness to practise rules and to our constitution of panels and Investigation Committee rules, A paper for consultation,* GMC, May 2012: www.gmc-uk.org/The_future_of_adjudication___rules.pdf_48726068.pdf.
23 *The future of adjudication: making changes to our fitness to practise rules and to our constitution of panels and Investigation Committee rules, A paper for consultation,* GMC, May 2012, p1.

including legally qualified chairs and proposals for costs awards. As a result of the change to the MPTS, over time, there are likely to be significant changes to the adjudication process for doctors. Those working in this area would be well advised to keep a close eye on developments through the MPTS website and consultations.[24]

Fitness to practise – overview

2.16 There are two distinct stages to the GMC fitness to practise procedures:

1) *Investigation* – cases are investigated as to whether they need to be referred for adjudication.
2) *Adjudication* – hearing the cases that have been referred to the Fitness to Practise Panel.

Investigation – overview

Initial assessment

2.17 All complaints and queries are considered by GMC staff who have three options available: 1) close the case, 2) refer the case to the doctor's employer or 3) begin an investigation. A matter might be closed in cases where, even if the facts are found proved, no regulatory action would be required. A doctor's employer might be notified in cases where the issues complained of would not, in and of themselves, require action but might if they formed part of a wider pattern of behaviour. Where the complaint arose in a work context it is likely that the employer is already aware of the issue (and may already have undertaken their own investigation or disciplinary proceedings at the employer level – see chapter 7 for further information) but previous or additional employers may also be contacted.

Investigation stage

2.18 The investigation stage involves evidence-gathering, which could include the GMC obtaining information from employers, an independent assessment of the doctor's health or clinical performance, obtaining an expert opinion on a particular issue or gathering witness statements. There is also an opportunity for a registrant to engage

24 www.mpts-uk.org.uk

with the investigation. It is important that legal advice is sought at this stage, as any response given by a doctor to a complaint can potentially be used by the GMC against a registrant at a full hearing if what is later stated in any eventual hearing is inconsistent. *Good medical practice* places an obligation on registrants to co-operate with such formal inquiries,[25] however co-operation does not need to equate with full disclosure at such an early stage in proceedings, particularly when a registrant may not know exactly what allegations he or she is responding to. The principle of protection against self-incrimination is also relevant here (see chapter 7 for further information). However, the level of detailed response a registrant chooses to provide should be carefully considered, with the assistance of legal advice, if possible.

2.19   It is advisable to make written representations if i) the allegation is uncontested, ii) there is overwhelming evidence to rebut the allegation or iii) the allegation is so minor or trivial in nature that it would not support a finding of impairment at the hearing stage. Where a case involves a conflict of fact, the registrant will need to provide clear, corroborative evidence to support his or her account, such as contemporaneous records or a statement from a witness. It is important at this stage to exercise great caution with early disclosure of information, since factual inaccuracies or inconsistencies can be adduced at the main hearing. Similarly, care should be taken before suggesting that an allegation is minor or trivial in nature, since any statement to this effect could be used to demonstrate lack of insight or understanding of the seriousness of the allegation. To avoid any risk, the safest course would be to seek legal advice.

2.20   Once sufficient information has been obtained, two case examiners (one of whom is medically qualified) consider the information available and determine the next step. The GMC aim to complete an investigation within six months. If the evidence does not suggest a serious or persistent breach of the standards expected of a doctor as contained in *Good medical practice* and the doctor's fitness to practise could not be considered to be impaired, then the case examiners may:

a) conclude the case with no further action;
b) issue a warning;

---

25 *Good medical practice* para 68: 'You must co-operate fully with any formal inquiry into the treatment of a patient and with any complaints procedure that applies to your work. You must disclose to anyone entitled to ask for it any information relevant to an investigation into your own or a colleague's conduct, performance or health. In doing so you must follow the guidance in *Confidentiality*.'

c) refer the case to a Fitness to Practise to Panel; or

d) agree undertakings, for example to retrain or work under supervision.[26]

2.21   A referral to an Fitness to Practise to Panel can only occur with the agreement of both a medical and non-medical case examiner. If the two case examiners cannot agree, then the matter will be referred to the Investigation Committee of the GMC.

2.22   A case can be referred to an Interim Orders Panel at any time – the Interim Orders Panel can place restrictions on a doctor's practice, if required, to, among other things, protect patients while an investigation is being carried out or a case is being prepared for a hearing.

Adjudication stage – overview

Overview

2.23   This stage involves a case before a Fitness to Practise Panel. The panel is usually made up of three panellists – a chair and two members – one of whom must be medical and one non-medical. A legal assessor advises the panel.[27] The doctor may be represented by a solicitor, barrister, a representative from a professional organisation or, at the discretion of the panel, a member of his or her family or other person (see para 2.164).[28] The GMC will likely be represented by a solicitor or barrister ('the GMC presenting officer'). There are three stages to a hearing: 1) fact-finding, 2) impairment and 3) sanction. If no facts are found proved the matter concludes at stage 1. If no impairment is found at the end of stage two, then the panel may close the case with or without advice or issue a warning. If impairment is found at stage two, then the panel move to stage three and may agree undertakings, impose conditions, suspend or erase the doctor from the register. There is the potential for an appeal by the doctor or a review by the Council for Healthcare Regulatory Excellence (CHRE).[29]

---

26   *A guide to doctors referred to the GMC*, GMC, available at www.gmc-uk.org/ concerns/doctors_under_investigation/a_guide_for_referred_doctors.asp.

27   General Medical Council (Legal Assessors) Rules 2004 SI No 2625 – see para 2.115 below.

28   GMC (Fitness to Practise) Rules 2004 r33.

29   The Council of Healthcare Regulatory Excellence name will change (it is anticipated during the course of 2012) to the Professional Standards Authority for Health and Social Care (pursuant to Health and Social Care Act 2012 s222).

2.24   Before the MA 1983 was amended, a doctor, with sufficient allegations against him or her, could find himself or herself before one or more of the separate Professional Conduct, Health and Performance Committees, which could lead to duplication of hearings and inconsistent decisions. The amendment by the Medical Act 1983 (Amendment) Order 2002[30] created a single Fitness to Practise Panel to determine the all-encompassing issue of whether the doctor's fitness to practise is impaired, whatever the range and breadth of the allegations.

2.25   The GMC is entitled to restrict or remove the registration of a registrant whose fitness to practise is found to be impaired. Under MA 1983 s35C(2), a registrant's fitness to practise may be found to be impaired by reason of any or all of the following (known as the 'statutory grounds'):

1) misconduct;
2) deficient professional performance;
3) a criminal conviction or caution in the British Islands for a criminal offence, or a conviction elsewhere for an offence which, if committed in England and Wales, would constitute a criminal offence;
4) adverse physical or mental health;
5) a determination by a body in the UK responsible under any enactment for the regulation of a health or social care profession to the effect that his or her fitness to practise as a member of that profession is impaired, or a determination by a regulatory body elsewhere to the same effect.

Statutory grounds

2.26   The section below provides basic details relating to each of the five statutory grounds. A fuller exposition can be found in chapter 1 at paras 1.375–1.427.

Misconduct and deficient professional performance

2.27   'Misconduct' and/or 'deficient professional performance' are not defined by the regulators. They are potentially wide concepts and may include some though not all departures from good practice. Additionally not all misconduct will be so serious or beyond remedy to impair current fitness to practise. There is also a distinction to be made between misconduct and deficient professional performance. This may have an important effect on sanction and the public

---

30 SI No 3135.

or professional perception/stigma attached to proceedings.[31] On the facts of a case it may be beneficial and possible to argue that neither misconduct nor lack of competence are made out, or that it is only the latter.

2.28 'Misconduct' has, however, been described, and a definition attempted in a large number of cases, the following being the most oft-cited.

2.29 In *Nandi v General Medical Council*[32] Collins J adopted the observation of Lord Clyde in *Rylands v General Medical Council*[33] that:

> ... professional misconduct is 'a falling short by omission or commission of the standards of conduct expected among medical practitioners, and such falling short must be serious'. The adjective 'serious' must be given its proper weight, and in other contexts there has been reference to conduct which would be regarded as deplorable by fellow practitioners. It is of course possible for negligent conduct to amount to serious professional misconduct, but the negligence must be to a high degree.[34]

2.30 His Lordship stated that it is not restricted to conduct that is morally blameworthy. It could include seriously negligent treatment or a failure to provide treatment measured by objective professional standards. Obviously, dishonest conduct can very easily (although not always) be regarded as serious professional misconduct, but conduct that does not amount in any way to dishonesty can constitute serious professional misconduct if it falls far short of the standard that is considered appropriate by the profession.

2.31 Lord Cooke of Thorndon in the Privy Council case of *Preiss v General Dental Council*[35] said:

> It is settled that serious professional misconduct does not require moral turpitude. Gross professional negligence can fall within it. Something more is required than a degree of professional negligence enough to give rise to civil liability but not calling for the opprobrium that inevitably attaches to the disciplinary offence.[36]

---

31 *Remedy UK Ltd v General Medical Council* [2010] EWHC 1245 (Admin).
32 [2004] EWHC 2317 (Admin).
33 [1999] Lloyd's Rep Med 139 at 149.
34 *Nandi v General Medical Council* [2004] EWHC 2317 (Admin) per Collins J at paras 31–33.
35 [2001] UKPC 36.
36 At para 28.

2.32   In *R (Calhaem) v General Medical Council*[37] Jackson J stated that:

The word 'misconduct' in section 35C(2)(a) does not mean any breach of the duty owed by a doctor to his patient: it connotes a serious breach which indicates that the doctor's fitness to practise is impaired.[38]

2.33   Following a review of the authorities, His Lordship derived five principles relevant to that case which involved failures by a consultant anesthetist and departure from *Good medical practice* in the context of a serious operation. These are:

1) Mere negligence does not constitute 'misconduct' within the meaning of MA 1983 s35C(2)(a). Nevertheless, and depending upon the circumstances, negligent acts or omissions which are particularly serious may amount to 'misconduct'.

2) A single negligent act or omission is less likely to cross the threshold of 'misconduct' than multiple acts or omissions. Nevertheless, and depending upon the circumstances, a single negligent act or omission, if particularly grave, could be characterised as 'misconduct'.

3) 'Deficient professional performance' within the meaning of section 35C(2)(b) is conceptually separate both from negligence and from misconduct. It does not mean any instance of substandard work. It connotes a level of professional performance that indicates that the doctor's fitness to practise is impaired. It is unacceptably low which (save in exceptional circumstances) has been demonstrated by reference to a fair sample of the doctor's work.

4) A single instance of negligent treatment, unless very serious indeed, would be unlikely to constitute 'deficient professional performance'.

5) It is neither necessary nor appropriate to extend the interpretation of 'deficient professional performance' in order to encompass matters that constitute 'misconduct'.[39]

Deficient professional performance[40]

2.34   In essence this encompasses conduct that has fallen far short of the standards expected of a reasonably competent practitioner and done so on more than one occasion. It need not be a repeat of the same conduct. One exceptionally serious event may also amount to deficient professional performance. Conduct occurring outside the UK

37 [2007] EWHC 2606 (Admin); [2008] LS Law Medical 96.
38 At para 26.
39 At para 39.
40 Other regulators refer to this as 'lack of competence'.

and/or before the registrant was in fact registered may still found a case on deficient professional performance, the reason of course being risk to the public and profession (see also para 2.1 above and chapter 1).

Conviction cases

2.35   MA 1983 s35C(2)(c) provides that the GMC has jurisdiction to consider cases where it is alleged that a registrant's fitness to practise is impaired by reason of a conviction or caution in the British Islands for a criminal offence, or a conviction elsewhere for an offence, which, if committed in England and Wales, would constitute a criminal offence. The procedure for dealing with such cases is broadly the same as for those on the other statutory grounds.

2.36   The GMC Rules provide[41] that a certified copy of the certificate of conviction (or in Scotland an extract conviction) is proof of the conviction and of the fact upon which it was based. Accordingly in such cases, it will not be open to registrants to suggest that they did not commit the offence in question, and representations will need to focus on any mitigating circumstances, insight, remorse and reparation. The only permissible route for rebutting evidence would be in the rare circumstances where a registrant was able to adduce evidence for the purposes of proving that he is not the person referred to in the certificate or extract.[42] There is only a discretion to admit this evidence. See para 7.17 for a fuller discussion of this issue.

2.37   Community sentences can present particular problems in the light of the decision in *Council for the Regulation of Healthcare Professionals v General Dental Council and Fleischman*[43] as, if the conviction was for a serious offence and the sentence is still being served at the time of consideration by a fitness to practise panel, the registrant should not normally be permitted to resume practice until the sentence has been satisfactorily completed. In the light of this unhelpful principle, representatives may wish to seek an adjournment of cases where a community sentence is ongoing until such time as it has been completed.

Health

2.38   Where the allegation that fitness to practise is impaired due to physical or mental health, the factual background will be relevant but is likely to be largely admitted. Therefore the main focus will be on the

---

41   GMC (Fitness to Practise) Rules 2004 r34(3).
42   GMC (Fitness to Practise) Rules 2004 r34(5).
43   [2005] EWHC 87 (Admin).

particular health condition in question, and whether it caused or contributed to the alleged facts. If the expertise of an expert is required and the registrant has been assessed by a GMC medical assessor it is likely that he or she will be called to give evidence. The registrant may need to call his or her own medical expert if the GMC assessor's report is disputed.

2.39   If a medical expert is to be called, then the following evidence should be adduced:

- the expert's professional qualifications and area of specialisation;
- what documentation the expert has considered, whether the expert has personally assessed the registrant, and whether the expert has had any prior involvement with the registrant;
- diagnosis and prognosis, and whether the medical condition in question caused or contributed to the factual allegations; and
- whether a registrant's current fitness to practise is impaired by reason of ill health, and the likelihood and extent of recurrence of the medical condition, steps that the registrant has already taken to reduce recurrence, and any further steps that can be taken.

Determination by another regulator

> The fact that matters complained of occurred outside the UK and/or before a practitioner was registered with a regulatory body is no bar to proceedings. The fact that the matters may have already been adjudicated upon in another jurisdiction is also no bar to proceedings.

2.40   The GMC also has jurisdiction to consider allegations on the ground of a determination by a body responsible for the regulation of a health or social care profession that his or her fitness to practise is impaired. In practice the approach to dealing with such cases will be similar to that applying to conviction cases. Referral by another regulator does not infringe the principle of double jeopardy – see chapters 1 and 7 for a fuller discussion of the law. See also chapter 8 regarding the Independent Safeguarding Authority.

Key terms

What is 'impairment'?

2.41   'Impairment' is not defined by legislation, however there is considerable case-law on this issue (see para 1.364). Crucially, it is well-established that it is a present-day test. Therefore the purpose of fitness to practise proceedings is not to punish the registrant for past wrongdoings but to protect the public or profession where a registrant's current fitness to practise is impaired. In reaching this decision the panel can take into account the past wrongdoing, but it is also required to take into account other relevant factors such as whether the conduct in question is easily remediable, whether it has been remedied and the likelihood of repetition.[44] Therefore it is a forward-looking test.[45] Some conduct may be incapable of being easily remedied. In other cases, even if the conduct in question is capable of remedy, and has been remedied, the nature of the conduct may be such that such steps carry little weight. This is where the conduct involved a fundamental breach of professional standards, such that the need to maintain public confidence in the profession overrides the interests of the registrant.

2.42   Impairment is a vital concept to understand within this jurisdiction, because the issue of impairment is, arguably, the most crucial determination the Fitness to Practise Panel will have to make. While a finding of impairment does not automatically lead to the imposition of a sanction, it makes one much more likely. It is also a difficult determination for a registrant to have made against him or her (regardless of whether any sanction is eventually imposed): it is stating that an individual's fitness to practise *is* impaired – a difficult blow for any professional who has undertaken substantial training to get to that position (whether a junior doctor or consultant) and one that ultimately has to be declared to current and prospective employers for a considerable time period. The issue of impairment must necessarily be the focus of preparation for any eventual hearing – the way the facts are presented and challenged, and the decisions made upon them will likely have a significant impact on what determinations are made at both the impairment, and if required, the sanction stage.

What is 'insight'?

2.43   'Insight' is the expectation that a registrant will be able to stand back and accept that with hindsight, he or she should have behaved differently, and that it is expected that he or she will take steps to prevent a recurrence and learn from their mistakes. Factors which may assist

---

44 *Cohen v General Medical Council* [2008] EWHC 581 (Admin). See also *Zygmunt v General Medical Council* [2008] EWHC 2643 (Admin) and *Sarkodie-Gyan v Nursing and Midwifery Council* [2009] EWHC 2131 (Admin).

45 *Meadow v General Medical Council* [2007] QB 462; [2006] EWCA Civ 1390; *Cheatle v General Medical Council* [2009] EWHC 645 (Admin).

a committee when considering whether a registrant has the insight necessary to avoid or mitigate sanctions, and to accept and comply with proposed undertakings, include:

- demonstrating an understanding of the gravity of the conduct in question;
- being open and honest when things go wrong;
- showing a willingness to act differently in the future;
- offering an apology;
- the conduct and demeanour of the registrant at the hearing.

The investigation stage in detail

Investigation

2.44   Once the registrar of the GMC receives information about a regis-
trant which falls into any of the categories above, he or she may make appropriate enquiries. The investigation may include:

- obtaining medical records;
- obtaining documentary evidence from third parties;
- taking statements from witnesses;
- obtaining expert reports on clinical or other matters;
- directing the registrant to undergo an assessment of his or her health or performance. Assessments are carried out by one lay and two medical assessors, who will produce a report, which will be disclosed (GMC (Fitness to Practise) Rules 2004 r7(4) and (5)).

2.45   At the outcome of the investigation stage, the registrar may decide to conclude the case, issue a warning, or, if an issue is raised that the doctor's fitness is or may be impaired, refer the case forward to a Fitness to Practise Panel for adjudication.

2.46   As noted, above at paras 2.18 and 2.19, it is important to take great care from the earliest stage in corresponding with the regulator and disclosing further information. Any inconsistencies or inaccuracies can potentially be used to the doctor's detriment at the main hearing. Care should also be taken before suggesting that an allegation is minor or trivial in nature. On the one hand, it can be persuasive to emphasise that the matters alleged are too minor to amount to misconduct or lack of competence even if proven. On the other hand, this could be used by the GMC to demonstrate a lack of insight or understanding of the seriousness of the allegation. To minimise risk, the safest course of action is to take legal advice.

Referral of allegations and investigations – overview

2.47 This section outlines the key rules that apply when a complaint is first received. Complaints are usually received from employers, patients, police or other health professionals.

Initial referrals (rule 4)

2.48 The key rules are as follows:

a) Initial referral:
   – Rule 4: Initial consideration by registrar and referral of allegations if any of categories of impairment in MA 1983 s35C(2) may apply.

b) Registrar decision:
   – Case concluded if no question of impairment.
   – Conclude case if vexatious.
   – Advise maker of allegation of other means of resolution (eg NHS complaints procedure) or refer to another body.

c) If the allegation is more than five years old, refer only if in the public interest, in exceptional circumstances to do so (rule 4 (5)) (see para 2.124 below and chapter 1 at para 1.102).

d) Refer on for investigation or direct for adjudication.

Convictions, cautions and determinations (rule 5)

2.49 The key rules are as follows:

a) There is a presumption that if a doctor has been the subject of a criminal conviction or caution or a determination by another regulatory body, the matter will proceed directly to adjudication.

b) There is an irrebuttable presumption if an immediate or suspended sentence was imposed following criminal conviction that the matter will proceed directly to adjudication.

c) In other cases further investigation may occur before referral.

d) There is no requirement for the GMC to reprove matters proved in other proceedings (rule 34(3)–(5)).

Investigation (rule 7)

2.50 Investigative steps may include:

• obtaining medical records;
• obtaining other documentary evidence from third parties;
• taking witness statements;
• obtaining expert reports on clinical or other matters;

- directing the registrant to undergo an assessment of his or her health or performance.[46]

Case examiner decision or Investigation Committee (rules 8 and 9)

2.51 A decision is taken by two case examiners (one medical and one non-medical) as to the next step in the process. Before referral for adjudication or the issuing of a warning, the registrant will be informed of allegations and evidence and given at least 28 days to provide written comments.

2.52 Case examiners may decide to:

a) conclude case;
b) issue a warning;
c) refer for adjudication only if there is realistic prospect of establishing that the practitioner's fitness to practise is impaired to a degree justifying action on registration, can adjourn for further information if required;
d) if both case examiners agree, invite doctor to accept undertakings restricting relevant practice; if no agreement, referred to Investigation Committee.

Undertakings (rule 10)

2.53 Where fitness to practise is found to be impaired (or may become so on recurrence of a medical condition) the registrar may invite a registrant to make undertakings (eg to restrict his practice, undergo treatment or retraining). Undertakings can only be sought where to do so would provide sufficient protection to the public. (See *Crabbie v General Medical Council.*[47])

2.54 Where case examiners agree that a registrant's fitness to practise is impaired, they may invite a doctor to agree to undertakings, subject to the following caveats:

a) only if sufficient public protection is achieved through undertakings;
b) undertakings must be accepted, otherwise referred for adjudication;
c) undertakings are reviewed by the GMC Case Review Team.

46 Any decision for health/performance assessment must be agreed by medical case examiner.
47 [2002] All ER (D) 153 (Sep).

Warnings (rule 11)

Introduction

2.55   The GMC has produced *Guidance on warnings*.[48] As noted above, a warning is available at both the investigation and adjudication stage of fitness to practise proceedings, as paragraph 4 of the guidance indicates:

> At the investigation stage the case examiners or the Investigation Committee must first apply the investigation stage test and satisfy themselves that there is no realistic prospect of establishing that the doctor's fitness to practise is impaired to a degree requiring action on his or her registration. At the adjudication stage, the panel should only consider whether a warning is appropriate, once it has found that the doctor's fitness to practise is not impaired.

2.56   A warning will be issued where the evidence suggests that the registrant's behaviour or performance has fallen below acceptable standards to a degree warranting formal censure by the GMC, but which does not make referral to a Fitness to Practise Panel or action on registration necessary. The registrant will be asked to make comments, and he or she can require an oral hearing.

Warning hearing

2.57   If a registrant comments on a warning proposal or disputes the facts on which a warning is based, an oral hearing will be held to determine the issue. In such a hearing, written representations are permissible but the presumption is that oral evidence will not be received. The hearing will be a public hearing unless the circumstances of the case outweigh the public interest in the hearing being held in public. Where adjudication on the facts is required, this will be determined on the civil standard (see para 2.163 on the standard of proof, below). The options available to the committee will be to:

a) issue a warning;

b) conclude the case with or without letters of advice (where there are considered to be minor departures from *Good medical practice*); or

c) if there is new evidence and it is appropriate to do so, refer the matter for adjudication.

48   August 2010 – due for review August 2015. See www.gmc-uk.org/Guidance_on_Warnings.pdf_27286909.pdf.

The purpose of warnings

Warnings allow the GMC to indicate to a doctor that any given conduct, practice or behaviour represents a departure from the standards expected of members of the profession and should not be repeated. They are a formal response from the GMC in the interests of maintaining good professional standards and public confidence in doctors. The recording of warnings allows the GMC to identify any repetition of the particular conduct, practice or behaviour and to take appropriate action in that event. Breach of a warning may be taken into account by a Panel in relation to a future case against a doctor, or may itself comprise misconduct serious enough to lead to a finding of impaired fitness to practise.[49]

2.58   There is no difference in the 'significance attached to warnings issued at the investigation stage and warnings issued at the adjudication stage'.[50] Warnings are not available where allegations relate solely to a doctor's health – they are available where health is one factor of the case.

2.59   Warnings must be disclosed as per paragraph 8 of the Guidance:

They are disclosed to any enquirer and published via the GMC's website on the List of Registered Medical Registrants for a five-year period. After five years warnings cease to be published on [the List of Registered Medical Registrants] and are no longer disclosed to general enquirers. However, they are kept on record and disclosed to employers on request, indefinitely.

2.60   Perhaps most importantly, for the registrant, a 'warning does not prevent a doctor from holding a licence to practise and does not place any restrictions on their registration'.[51] However, that may be too simplistic approach to the matter because while registration is unrestricted, current and future employability may be significantly affected by the imposition of the warning and the requirement to disclose it.

2.61   Decision-makers are provided with factors to take into account when determining whether a warning would be an appropriate action.[52] These include:

- a clear and specific breach of guidance;
- the conduct approaches but falls short of the relevant test for impairment;

49 *Guidance on warnings*, GMC, August 2010 para 11.
50 *Guidance on warnings* para 6.
51 *Guidance on warnings* para 9.
52 *Guidance on warnings* para 20.

- concerns are sufficiently serious that repetition of them would likely result in an impairment finding;
- the need to formally record the particular concerns.

2.62   The guidance then provides specific advice in types of cases: treatment (para 21), convictions and cautions (para 22) and dishonesty (para 23). The need for a panel to take a proportionate approach is highlighted (para 25) as is the relevance (or otherwise) of mitigation (para 31). Personal mitigation cannot be used to reduce a sanction to a warning if fitness to practise has been found to be impaired. At para 33 a non-exhaustive list of aggravating or mitigating factors that might be relevant is provided:

a) insight;
b) apology;
c) previous good history;
d) risk of repetition;
e) remedial steps taken;
f) relevant and appropriate testimonials.

2.63   Reasons are required for a decision (para 34) and Annex A provides a warnings template, but in summary a warning will need to:

a) highlight the concerns requiring the warning;
b) make clear why the concerns impact on patient safety/public confidence in/reputation of the profession;
c) make clear what conduct led to warning, and why it should not be repeated; and
d) refer to any relevant GMC guidance or relevant sections of *Good medical practice*.

2.64   Where a registrant's conduct raises a minor cause for concern, but does not merit a formal warning, a letter of advice may be issued. (See GMC's guidance *Good medical practice*.)

Review of decisions (rule 12)

2.65   If the GMC conclude a case, issue a warning or accept undertakings, the registrar may review the decision on application of the registrant, complainant or of his or her own initiative if:

a) the decision in question may be materially flawed or there is new information which may have led to a different decision; and
b) the registrar considers a review is necessary for the protection of the public, the prevention of injustice to the registrant, or is otherwise necessary in the public interest.

2.66   There is a two-year limitation on such a review being undertaken unless there are exceptional circumstances.

2.67   The following options are available to the registrar on conclusion of the review:

a) uphold the previous decision;
b) quash the previous decision and substitute a fresh decision;
c) refer for reconsideration by case examiners.

2.68   Reasons for the decision must be provided to all parties.

Notifying employers (rule 13)

2.69   A doctor subject to investigation by the GMC must provide his or her employer's details to the GMC so that they may be notified of the investigation (MA 1983 ss35B(1)(b) and 35A(2)).

Appointment of specialist advisers (rule 14)

> Specialist advisers are present to assist on the interpretation and/or significance of expert evidence – including health and performance expertise. They should not give an opinion or comment upon the issue of fitness to practise. An adviser is not part of the panel and as such he or she should not retire with the panel. Any advice must be given publicly affording the parties an opportunity to challenge it including calling evidence if necessary.

2.70   If a registrant's fitness to practise is allegedly impaired by reason of adverse physical or mental health, a panel may direct that a specialist health adviser and/or a specialist performance adviser be appointed to assist the panel or, that a health or performance assessment be carried out and a report provided (rule 13A). Medical assessors are distinct from legal assessors in that they are there to comment upon the evidence whereas legal assessors are not. See chapter 1, para 1.289 for a fuller discussion.

Health or performance assessments

2.71   A recommendation for a health or performance assessment can be made by a medical case examiner, but in any event must be agreed by a medical case examiner. The power to require a doctor to undergo such an assessment derives from MA 1983 Sch 4 para 5A(1):

5A(1) The General Council may make rules –
  (a) authorising the giving of directions by any of –
     (i)   the Investigation Committee,
     (ii) a Fitness to Practise Panel,
     (iii) such other persons as may be specified in the rules, requiring an assessment of the standard of a registered person's professional performance to be carried out;
  (b) specifying circumstances in which such an assessment may be carried out otherwise than in accordance with a direction.

2.72   GMC (Fitness to Practise) Rules 2004 r7(3) indicates, together with Schedule 1 (for performance assessment) and Schedule 2 (for health assessment), further details on this process.

2.73   These assessments can be onerous – lasting a number of days. For a performance assessment, an assessment team is made up of at least one lay assessor and two medical assessors. One of the medical assessors will act as team leader. The elements of the assessment include a) peer review and b) a test of competence to assess knowledge and skills.[53] The peer review may include any of the following:

- a visit to the doctor's place of work;
- interviews with the doctor;
- interviews with third parties, including the complainant or complainants in the case;
- a review of a sample of the doctor's records and practice documents;
- a case based discussion using a selection of the above cases to explore the doctor's reasoning;
- observation of the doctor's interaction with patients (where this is practical and the doctor is working).

2.74   Any written advice or information the team choose to obtain is shared with the registrant for comment. A report is then produced, disclosed to the registrant and any employer. The scope and depth of a performance assessment is not to be underestimated and it is in the doctor's interests to take the test seriously and ensure that there is a medically qualified individual with experience within the particular area of practice under investigation. A performance assessment can sometimes result in further areas of concern (unrelated to the initial concerns that triggered the assessment) and therefore further allegations being potentially referred for adjudication – but areas of concern can only form part of formal consideration at a hearing if they

---

53 For more information see www.gmc-uk.org/concerns/doctors_under_
    investigation/undergoing_a_test_of_competence.asp.

are included in the notice of allegation (see *Roomi v General Medical Council*[54]). Any concerns with the performance assessment process (for example concern re conflict of interest of an assessor or concerns over fairness) should be raised at the time of assessment or recorded in writing directly after. Another consideration may be seeking confirmation of how patient records were selected for any audit undertaken to ensure a fair sample of work over a fair period of time. For a health assessment, the registrant's mental and/or physical health is examined by two separate doctors selected by the GMC. Each examiner then prepares a report.

2.75 Where a doctor refuses to undergo a health or performance assessment, as required, or fails to cooperate with the assessment process, the case will be referred to a Fitness to Practise Panel to consider whether the doctor's fitness to practise is impaired and if any action is required on his or her registration. A failure to co-operate could, in and of itself, be deemed a breach of *Good medical practice* para 68:

> You must co-operate fully with any formal inquiry into the treatment of a patient and with any complaints procedure that applies to your work.

Such a failure is specifically catered for within GMC (Fitness to Practise) Rules 2004 r17(7):

> Where a registrant has been referred under rule 7 (6) (ii) for failure to comply with reasonable requirements imposed by an Assessment Team, the FTP Panel may dispose of the case, where it considers it appropriate to do so, by suspending the registrant's name from the register or imposing conditions on his registration in accordance with section 35D of the Act.

Interim orders and Interim Orders Panels (rules 25–27)

> Interim orders may be made if they are necessary to protect the public or in the public interest or in the registrant's interest prior to the substantive hearing on fitness.
>
> The threshold for an interim order is a high one because a registrant may be temporarily suspended or be subject to temporary conditions that limit or prevent his or her practice.
>
> No judgment is made regarding the facts of the allegation but the panel must be satisfied that, on a fair analysis, there *may* be a prima facie case.

54 [2009] EWHC 2188 (Admin), per Collins J.

2.76   The GMC may suspend or impose conditions on a registrant's registration on an interim basis, pending investigation/adjudication of the case. The registrar may refer a case to an Interim Orders Panel to consider whether such an order should be made for the protection of patients, or in the interests of the public or the registrant. A decision to impose an interim order, particularly interim suspension can have a devastating impact on a registrant and make it much harder for a doctor to show how (if applicable) they have remediated any issues that may eventually be found proved at a full hearing because, if the interim suspension order remains in place, a registrant will not be able to work as a doctor at all for the duration of the interim suspension order. Referral can occur at any time following initial complaint and hearings can be listed quickly.

Medical Act 1983 s41A – interim orders

(1) Where an Interim Orders Panel or a Fitness to Practise Panel are satisfied that it is necessary *for the protection of members of the public or is otherwise in the public interest, or is in the interests of a fully registered person*, for the registration of that person to be suspended or to be made subject to conditions, the Panel may make an order –

(a) that his registration in the register shall be suspended (that is to say, shall not have effect) during such period *not exceeding eighteen months* as may be specified in the order (an 'interim suspension order'); or

(b) that his registration shall be conditional on his compliance, during such period not exceeding eighteen months as may be specified in the order, with such requirements so specified as the Panel think fit to impose (an 'order for interim conditional registration'). [Emphasis added.]

2.77   The following are key cases in relation to interim orders:

• *General Medical Council v Uruakpa*, 1 [2007] EWHC 1454 (Admin) (Collins J);

• *General Medical Council v Uruakpa*, 2 [2007] EWHC 2057 (Admin) (Beatson J).

2.78   The procedure governing referrals to an Interim Orders Panel and consideration of cases by such a panel is governed by Part 7 (rules 25–27).

2.79   The composition of a panel is governed by the GMC (Fitness to Practise) Rules 2004, consisting of a chair and a lay and a medical member, sitting with a legal assessor.

2.80   The registrant will be given reasonable notice of the hearing, and provided with a reasonable opportunity to make representations. The hearings will normally be held in private (rule 41).

2.81   This is likely to be the first hearing a doctor will be invited to attend and it can be at short notice and somewhat daunting (see below at paras 2.149–2.155 for practical information concerning venues). Again, as much evidence as possible should be gathered to make submissions against an order as persuasive as possible, or if, on advice, an order is likely, consideration should be given to making suggestions for conditions that are realistic, achievable and meet concerns raised and are manageable/the best outcome for the doctor. It is important to be realistic about conditions and there is absolutely no point in a registrant agreeing to conditions which cannot be met, as it is likely not only to add more stress but also to lead to more onerous conditions or even interim suspension if compliance with conditions cannot be shown at a subsequent review. At the final hearing a panel will not be informed whether a doctor been subject to an Interim Orders Panel (unless the time comes where it needs to be considered because a hearing needs to be adjourned part-heard). The GMC Guidance 'Imposing Interim Orders' is a very helpful starting point for advisers, see para 2.7 above.

2.82   At the first hearing, the panel may impose an interim order for a period of up to 18 months. It must be reviewed within six months of being made, and thereafter every six months.[55] A registrant can request an earlier review – which shall be heard as soon as practicable after three months from the date of the immediately preceding order. A review can also take place when new and relevant evidence emerges which could affect the order.

2.83   An Fitness to Practise Panel will generally revoke any interim order which is in place prior to its determination at the conclusion of a hearing, or to impose one where, eg it has decided to adjourn the case.

2.84   For an interim order to be extended beyond 18 months the GMC must apply to the High Court. At review hearings, interim orders can be revoked, modified or replaced or remain as before.

2.85   Before an interim order is imposed there must be a *real risk to patients, colleagues or other members of the public* – it is not enough to be merely desirable. Relevant considerations include the seriousness of the allegation, the nature of the evidence and the likelihood of repetition.

2.86   Interim orders should rarely be imposed merely to maintain public confidence in the profession/proper standards of conduct and

---

55 A review must take place within three months of the first or any subsequent order where a) interim conditions have been replaced with interim suspension, b) interim suspension has been relaced with interim conditions or c) the High Court has extended an order beyond the period initially set.

performance (*R (Sheikh) v General Dental Council*[56]). The panel must take into account the impact on the doctor's right to practise, their finances and reputation (*R (Madan) v General Medical Council*[57]). An allegation that is trivial should not be given weight (*General Medical Council v Sheill*[58]) – see chapter 1, para 1.154 for a fuller discussion.

2.87   The doctor has the opportunity to attend and be represented. The process at the hearing (which will be held in private in accordance with rule 41(3)(a) is that the GMC will make representations as to the need for an Interim Orders Panel, followed by the doctor's opportunity to make representations. Generally the panel do not receive oral evidence and are not required to adjudicate on the facts. This is difficult to understand for practitioners who may end up under an interim suspension order without having had the opportunity to challenge the allegations or facts behind them. Indeed at the point of an interim hearing the allegations may not yet have even been set out or particularised. The considerations at paras 2.18 and 2.19 are equally applicable to IOP hearings. The legal assessor gives advice to the panel and then the panel retire to consider their decision, returning to announce their decision and give reasons – it is likely that the doctor will be provided with a written decision there and then. It is important to take the time to consider this decision and ensure that the doctor fully understands what is required of him or her in order to comply with the order.

2.88   Review hearings will follow a similar format, but it will be expected that evidence can be provided to show compliance with the previously imposed order (more relevant where there is a conditions order). Particularly with interim conditions, at review hearings if non-repetition of a less serious issue can be shown it may be sufficient to persuade a panel to remove or vary conditions.

Fraud or error in relation to registration

2.89   Where the registrar is satisfied that any entry in the register has been fraudulently procured or incorrectly made, he or she may erase the entry from the register. MA 1983 s39 is the relevant provision, in relation to registration fraud. The appeal mechanism is contained within MA 1983 Sch 3A.

---

56 [2007] EWHC 2972 (Admin).
57 [2001] EWHC 577 (Admin).
58 [2006] EWHC 3025 (Admin).

Following a referral to a Fitness to Practise Panel

Service of notices and other documents

2.90   Rule 15 of the GMC (Fitness to Practise) Rules 2004 provides that:

> (1) Subject to rule 16, as soon as reasonably practicable after an allegation has been referred to a FTP Panel the Registrar shall serve a notice of hearing on the registrant.
> (2) The notice of hearing shall –
>   (a) particularise the allegation against the registrant and the facts upon which it is based ...

2.91   Rule 16 deals with case management issues and provides that when a case is referred to a case manager:

> (6) Directions issued by the Case Manager may include, but are not limited to, such of the following as he considers appropriate having regard to the nature of the allegation, any representations made by the parties and all other material factors:
> that each party disclose to or inform the other of:
>   (a) the material they intend to rely upon namely documentary evidence, details of the witnesses (this includes the registrant if giving evidence), signed witness statements, any expert report and skeleton arguments;
>   (b) time estimates;
>   (c) whether or not the health of the registrant is to be raised as an issue;
>   (d) that the registrant indicates, so far as is practicable –
>   (i)   whether the allegation is admitted,
>   (ii) which facts are admitted and which remain in dispute,
>   (iii) which witness evidence is admitted and which witnesses are required for cross-examination, and
>   (iv) whether any preliminary legal arguments are to be made;
>   (e) where the allegation is admitted, a direction that the parties produce a statement of agreed facts ...

2.93   In recent times the length and detail of notices has increased. This may reflect the requirement to provide sufficient particulars to the registrant so that he or she understands the case against him or her.

Allegations

> The particulars of the allegation and the facts upon which they are founded should be clear and settled in advance of any hearing.
>
> If in doubt, clarification and/or further and better particulars should be obtained.
>
> The panel may, having heard from both parties, amend either the allegation or the facts provided no injustice is caused but this should be the exception not the rule.

2.94   In fitness to practise cases the GMC's 'notice of proceedings' identifies both the case brought against a registrant and the alleged facts upon which it is based. It is one of the most important documents in the case and should be drafted with some care. Although amendments may be made, there are limitations. It is only fair and reasonable that both parties and the panel have a firm and settled idea of what the case is about before it is under way.

2.95   The particulars of the allegation and the facts upon which they are founded should be made clear in advance of any hearing. In *Gee v General Medical Council*[59] the court held it to be a requirement that the registrant had fair notice of the nature of the evidence to be led in support of the allegations, time to prepare for his defence and, that the panel should make plain which of the allegations of fact, if any, they had found proved. It is an aspect of European Convention on Human Rights (ECHR) article 6 (right to a fair trial) that an applicant should be made aware of the charges against him or her. Allegations should not be drafted in a vague or ambiguous manner. The case-law relating to the drafting of allegations is discussed in more detail in chapter 1.

2.96   The following is a summary of the GMC's general principles on drafting:

- The notice needs to be sufficiently particularised as to the basis of the alleged impairment, but without unnecessary detail. It is not a narrative of the case, a summary of the evidence, or an opening statement of case. It should set out the facts which the GMC says indicate impairment.
- Charges should be unambiguously drafted, using succinct plain language, concise and, sub-clauses should be avoided. They should say what is meant.
- A charge should be chronological.

59 [1987] 1 WLR 564.

- It should i) identify and describe the doctor's practice and location; ii) describe the key factual elements of what is alleged avoiding unnecessary narrative detail; iii) indicate what is being criticised and how it is being criticised. Guidance may be obtained from an expert report or from publications such as *Good medical practice* or other specific guidance. It is not, however, necessary for allegations to be tied to specific provisions in such guidance.
- It should allege that practice is impaired by reason of misconduct etc, as the case may be.
- Facts should only be alleged where they are provable through admissible evidence (GMC (Fitness to Practise) Rules 2004 r34(1) and (2)) – this should include consideration of the 'best evidence' rule – that is, where possible, the use direct evidence rather than hearsay and, reliance on evidence that is supported by another witness or by documentation.
- The use of 'failed' versus 'did not'. The term 'you failed' (eg 'you failed to examine Patient A') means that the GMC must prove two elements. First that the registrant did not examine Patient A and second that the registrant should have done so. This approach should only be adopted where the *failure to examine is core* to the allegation, otherwise the wording should be 'you did not examine Patient A'.

2.97   In most cases the drafting is sufficiently clear for the registrant to understand the allegation and be able to respond, but if not, this should be raised at the earliest opportunity with the case manager. Sometimes the matter can be easily rectified (for example, by providing the identity of particular patients/service users) but if not it should be pursued well in advance of the final hearing.

2.98   In *R (Wheeler) v Assistant Commissioner House of the Metropolitan Police*[60] it was alleged that W had failed to carry out duties 'to an acceptable standard' thereby breaching the code of conduct. Stanley Burnton J said:

> Vagueness is a ground for judicial review if it leads to unfairness in the proceedings, and the danger with a vague charge is that the parties, and in particular the respondent, do not know with some precision what is alleged against them, and therefore are not fully able to address those matters in the course of a hearing.

2.99   His Lordship commented that while the particulars of a charge may be refined following an initial draft, it should be sufficiently

60 [2008] EWHC 439 (Admin) para 6.

particularised well before the hearing for the respondent to disciplinary charges to know what it is alleged he failed to do and, in what respects he failed.

2.100   The application of article 6 may be relied upon if necessary to achieve the appropriate level of particularisation. Certain matters are required to be explicitly stated in the allegation, including dishonesty and sexual motivation. For a fuller discussion of the law relating to the drafting of allegations see chapter 1.

Absence of the registrant

The panel has the discretion to proceed in the absence of the registrant but,

(i) there must be strict adherence to the requirement that all reasonable effort at service has been met; and

(ii) the decision to proceed must be taken with 'the utmost care and caution' and only after full consideration of the competing interests with emphasis on those of the registrant.

2.101   Rule 15 of the GMC (Fitness to Practise) Rules 2004 provides that once a matter has been referred to a panel, a notice giving details of the allegation and any hearing should be served upon the registrant as soon as reasonably practicable. The notice must include reference to rule 31 which empowers the Fitness to Practise Panel to proceed in the absence of the registrant provided 'all reasonable efforts' have been made to effect service. A general notice should be served 28 days before the hearing and, this should be reiterated giving precise details of time and place seven days before the hearing. Notice may be shortened by consent or if the registrar considers it reasonable in the public interest in the exceptional circumstances of the case.

2.102   GMC (Fitness to Practise) Rules 2004 r40[61] provides that:

(1) Notice of any hearing required shall be served in accordance with Schedule 4 Para 8 to the Medical Act 1983.

(2) Notice may be served by (a) post or (b) email at an address that the registrant has notified to the Registrar as an address for communications.

(3) If the registrant is represented by a solicitor, trade union or defence organisation it may be served by post or email (at an email address notified as above).

(4) Service of any notice or document may be proved by –

(a) a confirmation of posting (by Post Office or other delivery service);

(b) a confirmation of receipt of the relevant electronic mail; or

---

61   As amended to allow service by email.

(c) a signed statement from any person serving the notice or document confirming that the notice or document was delivered to, sent to or left at –
  (i) the registrant's proper address;
  (ii) the solicitor's address or email; or
  (iii) the trade union or defence organisation's address or email.

2.103 MA 1983 Sch 4 para 8 provides that service of notification shall be made by:

a) delivering it to the registrant;
b) leaving it at the registrant's proper address;
c) sending it by registered post;
d) sending it by recorded delivery.

Further investigation of allegations (rule 13A)

2.104 Once a case has been referred to the Fitness to Practise Panel, the GMC will continue, with the assistance of its lawyers, to investigate in order to prepare the evidence to be presented at the hearing. This may include:

- obtaining further documentary evidence;
- taking statements from witnesses;
- obtaining expert reports on clinical and other matters;
- directing the registrant to undergo an assessment of his or her health performance.

GMC pre-adjudication case management procedure

Case management (rule 16)

2.105 The rules introduce a case management mechanism intended to reduce delays, narrow the issues before the Fitness to Practise Panel and minimise stress to witnesses at the hearing. The registrar may order case reviews if appropriate, and retains the discretion to review a cases relating to any kind of allegation of impairment.

2.106 A case review will normally be held by telephone conference, in the presence of the parties and a case manager, who must act independently of the parties. The case manager will issue directions. See rule 16(6) for a non-exhaustive list. Particularly important is rule 16(6)(d)(i) and (ii) requiring the registrant to indicate, so far as is practicable, whether the allegation is admitted and which facts are admitted and which remain in dispute. The term 'allegation' means the entirety of the sub-facts and particulars that cumulatively amount to the single global allegation that fitness to practise is impaired. Therefore, indications will be required to each particular not just the global allegation. Where a stage 1 and a stage 2 conference are required (there may be either or both depending on the complexity of the case, or a conference may be adjourned if limited or no progress can be made at that time) the following issues will likely be considered, so it is important to be ready to address them at the relevant time.

2.107   Stage 1:

- Date GMC will complete investigation (witness statements, expert reports, medical records etc).
- Date GMC to disclose evidence and draft allegations.
- Doctor to indicate time required to prepared defence from date of final disclosure.
- Will there be any preliminary legal arguments at the hearing, how long is it estimated that these will take?
- Will the doctor's health be raised as an issue at the hearing?
- Is a specialist adviser required (usually in cases where there is a performance or health assessment)?
- Estimated hearing length (to include estimate of cross-examination of witnesses, submissions on impairment and sanction and panel in camera time).
- Hearing location, provisional hearing date. Parties should have the availability of the main participants. Counsel availability cannot normally be taken into consideration.
- Are there any vulnerable witnesses? If so how will their evidence be obtained or presented?
- Other witnesses.
- Request, if any, for a case review.

2.108   At a stage 2 case review the following (among other things) will be considered:

- Are stage 1 actions complete? If not, what are amended timescales?
- Any outstanding procedural or legal issues?
- Any preliminary arguments to be made at the hearing? Time estimate?
- Health issues?
- Specialist advisers?
- Confirm hearing date.
- Confirm hearing estimate.
- Confirm location.

- Vulnerable witnesses?
- Other witnesses?
- Will any witnesses need to give evidence via video-link? If so, specify location.
- Are other facilities required – eg video player etc?
- Are daily transcripts required (for cases of six to ten days)?
- Is a follow-up stage 2 conference required?
- Is a stage 2 case review required?
- For unrepresented doctors, date and time of stage 3 conference.

Disclosure delays

2.109   It is important to note that there is no costs provision within the GMC (Fitness to Practise) Rules 2004 (see para 2.238) and if the GMC do deviate considerably on their timescales for disclosure then it is important to maintain pressure (and have concerns recorded in the minutes to the case conferences and recorded in writing to the GMC) to meet the deadlines and ensure that this does not prevent the doctor having sufficient time to consider GMC disclosure in detail and prepare his or her case fully for the hearing. However, rule 16(8) can be used against any defaulting party at an eventual hearing. Rule 16(8) provides that a Fitness to Practise Panel 'may draw such inferences as it considers appropriate in respect of a failure by a party to comply with directions issued by the Case Manager'. In practice, such inferences are rare, but clearly it is important to comply with the case manager's directions within timeframes and if this is not possible then to write in advance of the deadline to both the GMC and the case manager setting out the reasons why the deadline cannot be met and proposals for a new deadline.

2.110   Once a hearing date has been set and hearing days allocated, because of pressure on timetabling, there is often difficulty in seeking to postpone it on the basis of late disclosure which can mean that a party is left having to make an application to adjourn on the first day of a hearing – clearly less than ideal. If such an adjournment is required, it is sensible to try and seek agreement of the need for an adjournment and the length of time required with the GMC presenting officer and then give advance written notice to the panel (or contact the Adjudications Department) setting out the reasons why an adjournment is sought, how long is required and the next available hearing dates. It is likely then that the first preliminary issue dealt with will be the adjournment application.

Amending the allegation(s)

> The allegations/charges may be amended provided no injustice is caused.
>
> The later and/or more substantial the change the more likely it is to cause injustice.
>
> If the risk of injustice can be met then charges may be changed late in the proceedings. Some difficulties may be dealt with by adjourning to allow all parties time to prepare the newly altered case or, call or recall witnesses.

2.111   It is important to note that there is discretion for the panel to hear an application to amend particulars during the hearing. Rule 17(3) provides as follows:

> 17(3) Where it appears to the FTP Panel at any time that –
>   (a) the particulars of the allegation or the facts upon which it is based, of which notice has been given under rule 15, should be amended; and
>   (b) the amendment can be made without injustice,
> It may, after hearing the parties and consulting with the Legal assessor, amend the particulars on appropriate terms.

2.112   The parties are entitled to make representations prior to any decision. Where a charge has been poorly drafted, is duplicitous or otherwise wrong, it is advised that representations be first made to the GMC presenting officer either before or at the hearing, since an application to amend is more likely to succeed if the parties agree. Such representations can also be made prior to the hearing in the forum of a preliminary meeting. For a consideration of the case law on charging, see chapter 1.

Full hearings by the Fitness to Practise Panel

Procedure

Order of proceedings

2.113   GMC (Fitness to Practise) Rules 2004 r17(2) sets out the full and detailed procedure before a Fitness to Practise Panel, the order of proceedings is as follows (not all stages will be applicable to all hearings):

1) Preliminary legal arguments (rule 17(2)(a)).
2) Registrant, if present (or GMC presenting officer, if not present), confirms doctor's name and GMC reference number (rule 17(2)(b)(i) and (ii)).

3) The panel secretary reads out the allegation (rule 17(2)(c)).
4) The panel chair invites any admissions and where admissions are made these facts are announced as proved (rule 17(2)(d) and (e)).
5) For those facts in dispute, the presenting officer will open the case and call witnesses in support of their case (rule 17(2)(f)).
6) At the close of the GMC case the registrant may make submissions regarding whether sufficient evidence has been adduced to find the facts proved or to support a finding of impairment, and the panel shall consider and announce its decision as to whether any such submissions should be upheld (rule 17(2)(g) – see para 2.172 below).
7) The registrant may open his or her case and adduce evidence and call witnesses in support (rule 17(2)(h)).
8) The panel deliberate (in private) and then announce its findings of fact (rule 17(2)(i)).
9) Further evidence and any further submissions can then be provided as to whether, on the basis of any facts found proved, the registrant's fitness to practise is impaired (rule 17(2)(j)).
10) The panel deliberate (in private) and then announce any findings in relation to impairment, giving reasons (rule 17(2)(k)).
11) Further evidence and submissions from both parties as to the appropriate sanction, if any, are then heard, or if no impairment is found submissions are heard on the question of whether a warning should be imposed (rule 17(2)(l) and consider and announce its decision on sanction, giving reasons for the decision (rule 17(2)(n)).
12) The panel may agree written undertakings offered by the registrant as an alternative to imposing a sanction, provided that: a) the undertakings are sufficient to protect patients and protection the public interest; b) the registrant expressly agree to disclose the details of undertakings (unless they relate exclusively to health) to any employer, prospective employer or any enquirer (rule 17(2)(m)).
13) Any application for interim suspension or interim conditions should be made and responded to, if required. The panel will consider the application and announce its decision with reasons (rule 17(2)(o)).
14) The panel will then deal with any interim order in place against the registrant (rule 17(2)(p)).

General provisions applicable throughout the proceedings

2.114   The remainder of rule 17 addresses issues that may arise at any stage during the proceedings, as follows:

a) *Amendment applications:* At any time, after hearing from the parties and on advice from the legal assessor a panel can amend the particulars of the allegation or the facts upon which the allegation is based, if the amendment can be made without injustice (rule 17(3)).

b) *Specialist advisers:* At any time in the proceedings before a determination is made that the registrant's fitness to practise is impaired a panel, having regard to the nature of the allegation, may adjourn proceedings to appoint a specialist health or performance adviser to assist the panel or direct that a performance or health assessment of the registrant be carried out (rule 17(4)).

c) *Performance assessment:* Once the assessment report has been obtained the panel proceed to consider the allegation in accordance with usual procedure (rule 17(2), above) or refer the allegation to the registrar for consideration by the case examiners in accordance with rule 10(2) (which provides for the circumstances in which certain health issues may be dealt with by way of undertakings (rule 17(5)).

d) *Health:* When a panel are determining whether a registrant's fitness to practise is impaired by reason of adverse physical or mental health, the panel may take into account: a) the registrant's current physical or mental condition; b) any continuing or episodic condition suffered by the registrant; and c) a condition suffered by the registrant which, although currently in remission, may be expected to cause a recurrence of impairment of the registrant's fitness to practise (rule 17(6)).

e) *Failure to comply with reasonable requirements imposed by an assessment team:* The panel may, if appropriate, dispose of the case by suspending the registrant or imposing conditions (rule 17(7)).

f) *Failure to submit to, or comply with a performance assessment:* Where there is credible evidence before the panel that the registrant's fitness to practise is impaired and a reasonable request has been made of the registrant to submit to or comply with the assessment and no reasonable excuse for such failure has been provided the Fitness to Practise Panel may take such failure into account in determining the question of whether the registrant's fitness to practise is impaired. (rule 17(8)).

g) At any stage before making its decision as to sanction or warning, the Fitness to Practise Panel may adjourn for further information or reports to be obtained in order to assist it in exercising its functions (rule 17(9)).

Role of the legal assessor

2.115 The panel will sit with a legal assessor, a senior lawyer whose job is to advise the panel on points of law, and whose functions are set out in the GMC Legal Assessor Rules 2004 as amended.[62] An assessor may intervene in a hearing to correct legal or procedural errors. In the course of the hearing his advice will be communicated in the presence of the parties. Where the panel have begun their deliberations, requires advice, and considers that it would be prejudicial to the discharge of its functions to hear the advice in the presence of the parties or their representatives, it can take advice in their absence. Where this has occurred, the assessor shall, as soon as practicable after the completion of the panel's deliberations, inform the parties etc of the advice he or she gave along with the question which led to the advice.

2.116   It is customary to ensure that the GMC's representative is also present when a registrant's representative (and vice versa) wishes to speak with the legal assessor outside the hearing.

2.117   If any issues of admissibility of evidence cannot be resolved by agreement between the representatives a joint approach to the legal assessor prior to commencement of the hearing is advisable. Similarly legal assessors welcome advance notification (on the day of the hearing but before the panel has formally convened) of any applications (for example for the hearing to be held in private or for an adjournment) prior to the application being made.

2.118   For a fuller discussion of the role of the legal assessor see chapter 1 at para 1.284.

Preliminary legal arguments (rule 30)

2.119 This section addresses some (non-exhaustive) potential preliminary legal arguments which may be relevant to a doctor's case and may need to be raised as a preliminary matter prior to the substantive hearing. Usually preliminary legal arguments that need to be heard by a panel are heard at the start of the hearing and time estimates should take into account any time required for such arguments.

---

62 General Medical Council (Legal Assessors) Rules 2004 SI No 2625 (see in particular, rules 4 and 5 re the provision of advice).

Historic complaints (rule 4(5))

> ECHR article 6 and domestic case-law confer a right to a hearing within a reasonable time however to stay proceedings is an exceptional course and delay is not a ground unless there is material prejudice to the extent that no fair trial is possible.
>
> Where a regulatory body's rules impose a time bar preventing proceedings save in exceptional circumstances, an assessment of those circumstances must be fair, transparent and understandable – see GMC (Fitness to Practise) Rules 2004 r4(5).

2.120   While delay may, in certain circumstances constitute a breach of article 6 ECHR rights, mere delay is insufficient to stop proceedings.

2.121   In the case of *R (Gibson) v General Medical Council*[63] Elias J stated as follows:

> I bear in mind the observations of Lightman J in *R v General Medical Council ex p Toth* [2001] 1 WLR 2209, that both the legitimate expectation of complainants and the public confidence in the regulation of the medical profession require that the complainant should, in the absence of some special and sufficient reason, be publicly investigated. It would undermine that important principle if mere unreasonable delay, absent prejudice, were to require a stay to be granted.[64]

2.122   For the purposes of the ECHR, time runs from when a person is subjected to a 'charge', meaning that they are officially notified of or substantially affected by proceedings. In regulatory proceedings this is likely to be the date of the letter notifying the registrant of the allegations.

2.123   For a fuller discussion of the relevant authorities on this issue, and of the applicability of article 6 to regulatory proceedings see chapter 1.

GMC (Fitness to Practise) Rules 2004 r4(5)

2.124   This rule recognises the potential difficulty of historic complaints, in the following terms:

> No allegation shall proceed further if, at the time it is first made or first comes to the attention of the General Council, more than five years have elapsed since the most recent events giving rise to the allegation, unless the Registrar considers that is in the public interest, in the exceptional circumstances of the case, for it to proceed.

---

63   [2004] EWHC 2781 (Admin).
64   At para 36.

2.125 There is limited case-law on this issue, the following case addressed a case where the registrar failed to consider the rule 4(5) at all prior to a Fitness to Practise Panel referral occurring.

2.126 In *R (Peacock) v General Medical Council*[65] Gibbs J held that the regulator's decision to permit an allegation that P's fitness is impaired to proceed despite the lapse of some seven years since the most recent events giving rise to the allegation, was unlawful. Prescription of certain drugs to the complainant led to a series of cardiac arrests which had caused neurological brain injury in 1998. The regulator permitted the complaint to proceed because the case 'raise[d] serious allegations' into the prescribing habits of P. The judge held that the judicial review challenge was not premature. There was no need to wait until the substantive finding because there would be no satisfactory remedy later in the proceedings. He went on to hold that on the facts of the case, there were no exceptional circumstances rendering it in the public interest to take the complaint further. At its gravest the complaint was of serious negligence relating to one patient and one example of prescribing or a series of prescriptions of drugs. There was no sensible explanation for the delay.

2.127 In *R (Gwynn) v General Medical Council*[66] the GMC alleged G's fitness to practise was impaired due to deficient professional performance regarding ten patients and misconduct in relation to one other patient. Four of the complaints arose from procedures carried out over five years earlier. G applied for the proceedings to be stayed on the basis that there were no exceptional circumstances as required by rule 4(5). Not surprisingly, Sullivan J found that the GMC was bound to have regard to rule 4(5) when deciding whether to pursue cases that were over five years old. However, it was plain that it had not and the subsequent attempt to do so retrospectively did not cure the defect. Indeed the lateness of the attempt compounded the situation since the decisions were made close to or on the eve of proceedings. Sullivan J concluded that it would be very difficult for any decision-maker to exclude the imminent hearing from his mind and without any identification of the required 'exceptional circumstances' or any express application of the rule 4(5) test, there was the very real possibility that undue weight was given to the imminence of the hearing.

2.128 The case against *Gwynn* also raised the issue of reopening a case previously closed by a caseworker four-and-a-half years earlier as disclosing no professional misconduct or impairment. G argued that

65 [2007] EWHC 585 (Admin).
66 [2007] EWHC 3145 (Admin).

the GMC could not re-open a previously rejected complaint, and even if it could, it was unfair and/or unreasonable to do. Sullivan J agreed stating that the only way the GMC could re-open such a case was if the complainant asked the GMC to re-consider its decision.

2.129   In referring cases after time-limits imposed by regulation, there must be clearly defined and exceptional circumstances. These may relate to the lapse of time. That the allegation raises serious concern about a registrant's fitness to practise is not an exceptional circumstance, since this is a necessary precursor of any referral to a panel. Joinder of similar allegations is not an exceptional circumstance save that similar fact issues may at least be arguable when considering the protections of the public.

Media and public/private hearings

2.130   GMC (Fitness to Practise) Rules 2004 r41 provides as to when a committee or Fitness to Practise Panel will sit in public or in private. The starting point is that all hearings will be held in public (rule 41(1)), however there is a discretion for a panel to 'determine that the public shall be excluded from the proceedings or any part of the proceedings, where they consider that the particular circumstances of the case outweigh the public interest in holding the hearing in public' (rule 41(2)).

2.131   There is a presumption that hearings will be private when considering whether to make or review an interim order (rule 41(3)(a), unless the registrant requests it to sit in public. There is also a presumption that hearings will be held in private when considering the 'physical or mental health of the registrant' (rule 41(3)(b)). However, the panel do have a discretion to hold a hearing relating to either interim orders or health issues in public 'where they consider that to do so would be appropriate' having regard to the following factors:

- the interests of the maker of the allegation (if any);
- the interests of any patient concerned;
- whether a public hearing would adversely affect the health of the registrant;
- all the circumstances, including the public interest.

2.132   Clearly, consideration will need to be given to either making or defending an application in relation to the status of the proceedings. General consideration will have to be given to the practicalities of a hearing being in public – for example, patient information will need to be carefully and consistently redacted and anoymised as Patient 1, 2, 3 or A, B, C etc in a way that still ensures the documents make sense.

Preparing for the hearing

> While there is a duty to prevent inequality of arms, there is no positive duty on a disciplinary body to gather evidence to assist the registrant.
>
> To allege unfairness under ECHR article 6(3)(b) a complainant must demonstrate that a duty exists, that it has been breached and this has caused an inequality of arms.
>
> Each case will depend on its own facts.

Disclosure

2.133   Careful consideration should be given to all disclosure provided by the GMC. Disclosure can occur in a piecemeal way and it is important to be organised and stay on top of what has been disclosed. If it appears that there are any documents missing then consideration should be given to raising this with the GMC at the earliest opportunity to ensure the doctor has the benefit of the fullest disclosure. Witness statements tend to be served in draft and potentially in a number of iterations. It is important to carefully monitor the content of all witness statements and not just assume that a later draft will only contain slight amendments. It is imperative that a doctor, prior to the hearing, has, so far as possible all the witness statements that the GMC have obtained. Equally, it is important to ensure that the doctor has been provided with all the supporting documents exhibited by each witness statement.

2.134   Confirmation should be sought as to what documents the GMC intend to rely on to prove the allegations and which are served as unused. As soon as reasonably possible following complete disclosure (including witness statements), a view should be sought from the GMC as to what documents they may intend to place before the panel at the hearing. From the doctor's perspective, careful consideration needs to be given to these documents to ensure that they do not raise any potential concerns that are not the subject of the particulars the panel will be asked to adjudicate on (regardless of whether charges are accepted or not). Scrutiny should be given to potential issues of bad character (which may include suggestions of clinical incompetence when the particulars are only concerned with, for example, an alleged dishonest declaration on a form) and hearsay that may be raised within the documentation. A clear decision should be made as to what may need to be removed or redacted. Initial conversations should be had, ideally with the relevant presenting officer (this may need to happen relatively close to the hearing date), to see

212 *Professional discipline and healthcare regulators* / *chapter 2*

if agreement can be reached and an agreed bundle created. This is a preferable course than having to have arguments concerning particular documents or redactions (removal of a word, words, sentence, section, page or document(s)) before the panel that will then go on to consider the case, but only if the agreements with the relevant presenting officer are acceptable to the doctor or a sufficient compromise to decide not to then argue the issue before the panel. As with other courts and tribunals, the panellists may be given a direction that any extraneous/prejudicial material they may have heard for the purposes of determining its relevance which they subsequently exclude should be excluded from their mind. However, the tactics of presenting this information at the start of the hearing for adjudication and inviting close scrutiny of it, when the passages of concern may have simply been 'forgotten' in a large bundle of documents, should be carefully considered. If agreement cannot be reached and there is an argument why such information should be excluded, then the panel can be asked to adjudicate on this issue as a preliminary issue at the hearing. If redactions are too extensive, it may be possible to reduce issues to an agreed statement of fact to be presented to the panel. This may be a neater approach to contain factual concerns in some circumstances, however it may make issues that would have otherwise been contained diffusely in a large number of documents become more visible than they would have been if simply left within the documentation. It is a matter of judgment as to whether some issues which may not immediately appear to assist a doctor's case are best kept in if they can be used in cross-examination to show the unreasonabless of a witness – however this can be dangerous course. It is important to ensure that any redactions are as fair and balanced as possible but that also they don't render documentation unintelligible for the panel or witnesses who will be referred to them. GMC witnesses will be warned, once there is agreement on redactions that they are not to give evidence on these issues.

Witness statements

Live vs read witnesses

2.135   If agreement on redactions of GMC witness statements can be reached such that the whole statement can be agreed, then that means that the statement can simply be read without the witness being called to give live evidence. It is important to understand that if a doctor agrees to a witness statement being read (with or without redactions) that the totality of that witness statement is taken to have been agreed and has as much weight as oral evidence that the panel may hear from live witnesses. If there are only minor areas of disagreement in a witness statement and they are peripheral to the allegation then it may be possible to redact them so as to avoid a witness being called for insignificant factual discrepancies. Consideration will need to be given as to which witnesses are required for cross-examination and what if anything the doctor hopes to obtain/challenge from that questioning. Some witnesses will come across better than others and the doctor is likely to have the advantage of having some firsthand knowledge of that individual and how they might come across to the panel. It will be a matter of advice and judgment as to which witnesses are required, consideration must be given as to which charge they go to and how their evidence may assist or hinder the doctor's or GMC's case. It must be remembered at all times that these hearings are determined on the civil standard – the balance of probabilities and it is for the GMC to prove their case, not for the doctor to disprove it.[67] Equally, the test of insight is important if every minute detail of every witnesses factual account is challenged (without cause) then this may hinder issues relating to insight (see para 2.43).

Doctor's evidence

2.136 A doctor will also need to be advised upon, and at the relevant time, make a final decision about whether he or she will give evidence in his or her case and in so doing be subject to cross-examination and questioning by the Panel. A key consideration here is that while agreement can be reached between the GMC representative and the doctor's representative(s) outside the hearing room as to which if any issues will not be addressed during cross-examination, such agreement cannot be reached with the panel who regulate their own proceedings and often ask the most direct and probing questions of a doctor or indeed any other witness. If a doctor does not intend to give evidence then consideration must be given to how certain charges (if they require a positive answer or explanation at the end of the GMC case) can be challenged – either through cross-examination or through defence witnesses and/or testimonials (if these can be agreed with the GMC). Although, of course it is not for the doctor to disprove any allegations, it is for the GMC to prove them and therefore a doctor is perfectly entitled not to give evidence in his or her case. If a doctor does give evidence and is disbelieved or found to be evasive and the panel find the allegations proved, then this can

67 The GMC used to operate on the criminal standard of proof.

significantly impact the impairment decision and sanction because this provides current day concerns about fitness to practise and not just (often quite) historical concerns that are part of the allegations. In such circumstances it is harder to argue that the concerns only stem from the 'moment in time' of the allegations.

2.137   It is usually helpful if a doctor's witness statement addresses the following:

a) introductory paragraphs setting out experience/expertise;
b) paragraphs addressing the specific allegations, identifying which, if any, facts are admitted and which are denied;
c) all mitigating features.

Witness unable to attend

2.138   If witnesses are unable to attend in person (for particular reasons – such as surgical commitments etc) then an application can be made for their evidence to be given either via video-link or by phone. It should further be noted that witness statements are only provided to the panel when a witness does not give live evidence. If a witness statement is agreed, it goes before the panel in lieu of live evidence and if it is not agreed then a witness is either called or if they are not available then a party may have to abandon reliance on that evidence in its entirety. It can be useful preparation for a doctor to provide a full witness statement to his or her representatives but it should be remembered that if the doctor gives evidence that this will not be circulated and cannot stand instead of oral evidence (except in the rare circumstance that the doctor's witness statement can be agreed in its entirety). Equally, if a doctor does not give evidence, and the statement is not agreed then the witness statement cannot go before the panel. However, potentially useful documents, in lieu of a witness statement can go before the panel – such as any full response to the original rule 7 or 8 letter concerning the allegations, if they are likely to assist and are consistent with the doctor's defence at the hearing. If the doctor was not in receipt of legal advice at the point of responding to the original allegations then it may not be appropriate to use these responses – a decision will need to be made on the content.

Evidence

2.139   The rule relevant to evidence is rule 34, which states:

(1) Subject to paragraph (2), the Committee or Panel may admit any evidence they consider fair and relevant to the case before them, whether or not such evidence would be admissible in a court of law.

(2) Where evidence would not be admissible in criminal proceedings in England, the Committee or Panel shall not admit such evidence unless, on the advice of the Legal Assessor, they are satisfied that their duty of making due inquiry into the case before them makes its admission desirable.

Hearsay

> The panel has the discretion to proceed in the absence of a witness and to admit hearsay evidence but the decision to proceed must be taken with 'the utmost care and caution' and only after full consideration of the competing interests with emphasis on those of the registrant.
>
> There must be compelling reasons to deprive a registrant of the opportunity to cross-examine a witness – this all the more so if the case or its consequences are serious.

2.140   It is outside the scope of this book to provide a full account of hearsay evidence, however, hearsay can (unless challenged) be frequently found in GMC disclosure. It is therefore very important to be alert to hearsay, identifying it and determine whether its redaction can be agreed or whether its admissibility and the weight to be placed on it will need to be argued (for decision) before the panel and at what stage.

2.141   The rules of evidence in these proceedings do not require the exclusion of evidence merely on the ground that it is hearsay. In considering hearsay evidence, allowance needs to be made to the fact that the person who is the source of that evidence is not before the Fitness to Practise Panel and therefore the parties have not had the opportunity to question or assess their credibility. Equally, the evidence has not been tested by cross-examination and thus there is no opportunity to see how it withstood that form of challenge. Neither party can know how the person might have responded to cross-examination and it is inappropriate to speculate about such matters. Regard must be had to the circumstances in which the statement was made and the extent to which the hearsay is supported by, or is consistent with, other evidence, and the scope for error or the existence of a reason to be untruthful.

2.142   Although hearsay evidence must be treated with circumspection, there is no rule of law that prevents a prosecuting authority from relying upon hearsay solely or to a decisive degree to support a case where otherwise it would have none.

2.143   The most recent significant case on this issue as it relates to the GMC is *R (on the application of Bonhoeffer) v General Medical Council*[68] – see chapter 1, paras 1.197–1.224 for a full discussion of this case and the recent European Court of Human Rights cases on hearsay evidence.

The burden and standard of proof

> The burden of proving disputed facts is on the prosecuting authority.
>
> The standard required is 'on the balance of probabilities'.
>
> The standard does not change with the seriousness of the allegation.
>
> Serious allegations do not require better evidence.
>
> It is just common sense that to prove an unlikely event occurred may require persuasive evidence.
>
> The consequences of a finding are irrelevant.

Preparing a defence

2.144   Careful consideration needs to be given to how a doctor intends, if at all, to meet the case against him or her, although a registrant has no burden to discharge in these proceedings, the burden is on the GMC to prove the allegations on the civil standard of the balance of probabilities. Detailed consideration will need to be given to what are often complex and interrelated charges (even in relatively simple cases). Charges need to be understandable and capable of answer. The doctor will need to be clear on which charges, if any, a 'plea' will be entered to and which, if any, will be denied. This will require careful consideration, legal advice and an understanding of the proceedings, evidence and documentation as well as concepts of insight and impairment. Consideration should be given to preparing a signed schedule of admissions (a table or list indicating whether a charge, sub-part or stem are admitted or denied in whole or in part) prior to the hearing, which can be provided to the GMC presenting officer and the panel on day one of the hearing, or before if so agreed. If served prior to the hearing, or even on day one, it would be sensible to carefully note within that document that any admissions or otherwise are on the basis of the information/evidence served to date. There is no requirement for such a schedule but as the process of charging and answering charges can become somewhat complex, it

68 [2010] EWHC 1585 (Admin), [2011] ACD 104.

is often the most straightforward way.[69] The responses to the allegations will need to be made orally to the panel at the start of the hearing, in any event and so can simply be communicated purely orally if this is more convenient to the doctor (as per rule 17(2)(d)).

2.145 King J made the following observations in relation to the requirements for evidence only relating to particulars alleged to be relied upon in a fitness to practise case and, future, in relation to how charges should be clear and answerable, in the case of *Chauhan v General Medical Council*:[70]

> In so far as the Panel, at stage one of its decision process, makes material findings of fact adverse to the registrant which could themselves have been the subject of a charge of professional misconduct, which however are not within the charges as formulated and particularised in the Notice of Hearing, then those findings in my judgment cannot properly or fairly be used by the Panel to support its findings under the Notice and in so far as the Panel has so used them, then the Notice findings are liable to be held vitiated and set aside. I agree with Silber J in *Cohen v GMC* [2008] EWHC 581 (Admin) 581, paragraph 48 that findings in relation to any particular charge at stage one 'must be focussed solely on the heads of the charges themselves'. The observations of Pill LJ in *Strouthos v London Underground Ltd* [2004] EWCA Civ 402 at paragraph 12 that a 'it is a basic proposition, whether in criminal or disciplinary proceedings, that the charge against the defendant or the employee facing dismissal should be precisely framed and that the evidence should be confined to the particulars in the charge' must be equally apposite to hearings before the FTP of the Respondent. An associated principle relied upon by the Appellant is that rehearsed by the *Privy Council in Salha v GMC* [2003] UKPC 80 at paragraph 14, namely that 'it s a fundamental principle of fairness that a charge of dishonesty should be unambiguously formulated and adequately particularised'.

Defence documents and defence witnesses

2.146 Careful consideration will need to be given to what documents the doctor may need to provide to the panel in defending the case against him or her. Depending on the charges, this may include the need for expert evidence to rebut (or in the absence of) GMC expert evidence.

---

69 This may become less necessary as the GMC move to more streamlined charging more akin to a criminal indictment. The pilot scheme of a new approach to the 'notice of hearing' including a 'statement of case' is currently the subject of a judicial review challenge. The status of the 'statement of case' is not currently clear – particularly in relation to whether it can be the subject of half time submissions or whether it is more akin to an opening note.

70 [2010] EWHC 2093 (Admin) at [6].

This clearly needs to be obtained sufficiently early to enable the report to be served on all parties to see if the content can be agreed (with or without amendment/redaction) or to see if the GMC will require the expert for cross-examination – in which case the expert's availability will need to be known at the time the hearing date is set. An educated guess will need to be made as to what day/time of day the expert will need to attend on and this is likely to be subject to change so if possible it is best to have an expert available for several sessions of the hearing. If the expert can only attend at a specific time and this would put their evidence out of turn, provided the doctor would be content for this evidence to be heard out of turn (and where it was unlikely to impact other evidence that might need to be given) then the possibility of taking the expert (or indeed any other time-limited witness) out of turn can be canvassed with those acting for the GMC and if agreement can be reached, leave of the panel can be sought. If agreement cannot be reached, the matter can be raised with the panel – but clearly reasons will need to be given for the interposing of a witness out of turn and any objections to it met as far as possible. Such an application can be argued and may be acceded to provided it does not significantly inconvenience the proceedings, because it is likely to be in the interest of justice and fairness for the doctor to be able to present his or her expert evidence if that is the only time that the expert can attend.

2.147   If a registrant decides to disclose documents at any stage in the proceedings as part of his or her defence, then he or she is advised to ensure that any references to third parties are redacted, in particular references to patients. Particular caution should be exercised when disclosing, for example patient notes, supervision records and practice development reviews. Further registrants are advised to obtain their employer's permission in writing to use such records. Of course this does not apply to documents obtained by and disclosed by the GMC. For further information about the Data Protection Act 1998 see chapter 7.

Testimonials and character references

2.148   A doctor will also need to gather relevant and positive testimonials from (if possible and depending on the type of misconduct alleged) both before the time of the alleged misconduct, during it and after it. This is one advantage of how long proceedings can take to come to a full hearing, it gives a pro-active registrant (and one who is not limited through the restrictions of an Interim Orders Panel) the opportunity to ensure that by the date of the hearing they are in the best position possible to show that any concerns (that may or may not be found proved) have been remedied. Testimonials should be as full as possible, come from individuals who have first-hand knowledge of the doctor and be provided in writing (ideally witness statement format) and signed. The writer will need to make it clear in their testimonial that they are fully aware of the charges the doctor faces (it is often simplest to send the charges to a potential referee to avoid any concerns that they are not fully aware of all the details of the charges). These will need to be obtained sufficiently early in the process so that an informed decision can be made about which if any referees might be willing to attend the hearing to give oral evidence. Often it can be difficult for doctors to obtain such testimonials from other doctors, for a number of reasons – eg lack of time, lack of first-hand knowledge or a reluctance to become involved in GMC proceedings, particularly if they are still in the employ of the body where the alleged misconduct took place. Every effort should be made to gather as many positive testimonials as possible (although this can be more problematic for junior doctors). However, quality can often be better than pure quantity. It is very helpful if at least one individual can attend to speak to the doctor's ability/credibility/clinical competence (whichever is relevant to the charges faced) because oral evidence can have a much more powerful impact than a paper testimonial. However, an individual who does attend to give evidence as a character witness will, in the usual way, be subject to questioning by the GMC representatives and the panel and will be under oath. Therefore if an individual also has negative comments on the doctor concerned these may be elicited through such questioning. It is important to note that, with the exception of the doctor, witnesses are not permitted to sit in the hearing prior to their giving of evidence.

Day one of the hearing

Arrival and venue

General

2.149   The main hearing centre is in central Manchester. The geographical location and often lengthy hearings can cause significant financial and work pressures for a doctor.

2.150   On the day of the hearing, it is advisable to arrive at the relevant venue at least one hour before the hearing is scheduled to start. If there is sufficient space, each doctor will be allocated a private waiting room which can usually be used for the duration of the hearing, depending on demand. Rooms are normally allocated in advance so when you sign in the reception should be able to provide this information. Free hot and cold drinks are available and photocopying facilities are also available. Each of the waiting rooms has tables and chairs and space for papers. Many legal teams/doctors attending for longer hearings will consider bringing other essential office equipment with them – such as a laptop (there is wifi access), printer, hole-punch, stapler and other stationery.

2.151   It is also useful to bring a number of empty files and dividers so that a defence bundle can be created of ad hoc material, if required. This allows an empty file (labelled D) with numbered empty dividers to be handed to each panel member, the legal assessor and panel secretary and then as and when documents need to be handed in they can be labelled D1, D2, D3 etc and put behind the relevant divider 1, 2, 3 – this enables a 'tidy approach' to documentation and means that it is easy for all parties to refer to specific documents during the course of submissions and all parties will be able to find them easily.

2.152   It should be noted that at least 10 to 12 additional copies of each document intended for distribution will be required: three for the panel, two for the GMC if both solicitor and advocate are present, one for the legal assessor, one for the panel secretary, and one for the short hand writer (if applicable) and one for the witness table. It is much better to have too many, than too few. Remember that all patient identifying information will need to be fully redacted or anonymised in a way that is clear, consistent and meaningful.

The hearing

2.153   It is advisable on arrival to make contact with the presenting officer for the GMC, the legal assessor and the panel secretary in the case, and also locate the hearing room. If there is agreement between the parties that some time is required for final discussions/redactions/narrowing of issues/basis of pleas, then this can either be communicated prior to the hearing start time to the panel via the panel secretary (fairness requires that no party speaks with any of the panel members during any part of a hearing without the presence of both parties). The panel may agree or, more usually, they will wish to formally convene to be appraised of the situation and time frames and make a decision as to how much time, if any to provide. The panel may also seek some provisional reading so that any time can be used productively. If a short adjournment (to commence the hearing later that same day) is likely to shorten proceedings or has the potential to, or at least to make them more efficient then the adjournment application may be granted. Such an application can often be shortly and simply put (see para 2.156 below).

2.154　　When the hearing is to commence, all parties will be invited to enter the hearing room, name plates will indicate where parties and individuals should sit. The usual layout is a 'U' shaped series of tables, with the panel at the bottom of the U, along with the legal adviser, and the doctor and his or her representatives to the right of the panel and the GMC, short hand writer and clerk on the left hand side of the U. At the top of the U will be a witness table where all live witnesses will give evidence from when sworn (unless special measures are to be applied) and there are usually additional chairs behind the witness table for members of the public, interested individuals or journalists to observe the proceedings. No individual (with the exception of the doctor) who is an intended witness in the proceedings is entitled to sit in the hearing room as a member of the public until after they have given their evidence.

2.155　　On a practical note, there is no need to stand when a panel come into the hearing room, in fact, frequently, they will already be seated when the parties enter. Panellists are currently addressed as either 'Sir/Madam'. Most of the proceedings are conducted with all parties (including representatives and witnesses) seated, however counsel will often stand in a case alleging misconduct because this is seen to be similar to a criminal case, but this is not universal. A doctor may sometimes be asked to stand when confirming his or her name and GMC registration number, but again this is not universal and as with most procedural issues – a matter for the individual panel to regulate within the parameters of the MA 1983 and the GMC (Fitness to Practise) Rules 2004.

Postponements and adjournments

2.156　　GMC (Fitness to Practise) Rules 2004 r29 provides a discretion for a committee to postpone 'any hearing of which notice has been served on the practitioner' in accordance with the GMC (Fitness to Practise) Rules 2004, on application or of a committee's own motion. This is called a postponement application if the application is made before the opening of the hearing (rule 29(1)) and an adjournment application if made at any stage in the proceedings (rule 29(2)). Each party must be given a reasonable opportunity to make representations on the matter (rule 29(3)).

Stage 1: findings of fact

Overview

2.157   Having dealt with any preliminary arguments and other matters, such as admissions by the doctor, the panel hears evidence and submissions as to whether the facts are proved or whether they are capable of supporting a finding of impairment.

2.158   Evidence, as noted above, can also be received in a less formal way, eg where a witness cannot attend in person or give evidence via video link, evidence can be given over the telephone.

2.159   Submissions can be made to the panel to exclude and disregard inadmissible or unduly prejudicial material.

2.160   The 'presenting officer', ie counsel instructed by the GMC, will open the case, and then present the evidence through read or live witnesses. It is good practice to keep a full note of the opening because it is this case the GMC need to meet and it can be important if a half-time submission is being considered. GMC witnesses are called and then can be subject to cross-examination by the doctor's representative, followed by re-examination by the GMC, then questions by the panel, followed by any matters arising out of the panel's questioning being clarified by first the doctor's representative and then the GMC. Careful consideration needs to be given to what type of cross-examination is required. Clearly, sensitive but relevant and robust cross-examination will be required, if necessary, of a patient complainant. As with any hearing, preparation is the key to determining what if anything needs to be obtained, if possible, through questioning that witness. It is important that cross-examination achieves something. If it is a doctor's case that someone else (for example, another GMC witness) is to blame wholly or partly for the conduct they are charged with then this must be explored with care and with an evidence base because otherwise there is a risk that unsupported aspersions or suggestions could have a detrimental impact on any panel's later determination as to the doctor's insight into the issues he or she faces if they are subsequently found proved.

2.161   Once the GMC's evidence has been presented, the doctor may make submissions that insufficient evidence has been adduced to find the disputed facts proved. If this fails the doctor may give and call evidence on his or her behalf.

2.162   The panel then consider in camera (in private) whether the facts have been proved. This process can take quite some time and parties wait for the decision – although often parties will be released for a period of time (a day, an afternoon, an hour) once the panel have an idea of how long they might need to deliberate. This is often a lengthy process as the decision has to be reached and then typed up, read, agreed in written form and then finalised and printed. This can be an anxious wait for the registrant, and while it is often difficult to think in terms of the next stage, it can be a useful distraction to complete preparations for stage 2, in case they are required. If admissions have been made then it will be clearer that stage 2 is likely to be reached and therefore this preparation time is even more important.

2.163 The panel apply the civil standard of proof. It is now abundantly clear that there is only one civil standard of proof regardless of the seriousness of the allegations.[71] The panel's decision is announced in open session, and a written judgment is distributed. See para 1.431.

Witnesses

2.164 Witnesses attending the hearing will be required to take an oath or affirm before giving evidence.[72] Until the point when a witness is required to give evidence in the hearing, a witness of fact cannot be present in the hearing room, without leave of the panel[73] (this does not apply to the registrant), but can apply to a representative if they are a friend or colleague who intends to give evidence (character evidence would be permissible as this would not necessarily be a witness of fact), so thought needs to be given to this when deciding upon representation. Once a witness has given their evidence they are then permitted, if they so choose to remain for the duration of the hearing in their capacity as a member of the public. If a witness does not finish his or her evidence in one sitting and there are breaks or overnight adjournments during their evidence then they remain under oath for the duration of their evidence and are not permitted to discuss the case with anyone else while they are under oath. A reminder is usually given to each witness every time there is a break in their evidence. This is an important consideration for advisers in terms of the timing of cases, because this applies equally to a registrant who gives evidence. Care needs to be taken that a registrant does not go part-heard in their evidence at the point when proceedings need to be adjourned because the adviser and registrant will not be able to discuss the case until the registrant completes their evidence.

2.165 All witnesses (unless they are vulnerable witnesses) are first examined by the party calling them, and may then be cross-examined by

---

71 *Re B (Children)* [2008] UKHL 35.
72 GMC (Fitness to Practise) Rules 2004 r35(1).
73 GMC (Fitness to Practise) Rules 2004 r35(6).

the opposing party. The witness may then be re-examined. Finally, the witness may be questioned by the practice committee.[74]

Vulnerable witnesses

2.166　Witnesses, the quality of whose evidence is likely to be adversely affected by the proceedings, may be treated as vulnerable witnesses.[75] They are likely to include any witness under 17 years of age at the time of the hearing, witnesses with a mental disorder within the meaning of the Mental Health Act 1983, those with mental impairment, or physical disabilities that require assistance at the hearing. Also included is any witness making an allegation against the registrant is of a sexual nature, where the witness was the alleged victim, and any witness who complains of intimidation.[76] In such instances, the committee may decide to adopt special measures to help them give evidence.

Video-links and other measures

2.167　In certain cases, particularly cases involving vulnerable witnesses, the use of video-links may be permitted. Sometimes, the use of pre-recorded evidence will be approved, provided that the witness is available at the hearing to be cross-examined. Screens will be used where it is considered necessary to prevent the witness's identity being revealed to the press or the general public, or to prevent access to the witness by the registrant. Hearings may also, if necessary, be held in private. The GMC are consulting on the widening of the use of telephone and video evidence (see para 2.15).

Proceedings in the absence of a witness

2.168　The panel has a discretion to proceed in the absence of a witness, and to admit hearsay evidence, but the decision to do so must be taken with great care, and only after full consideration of the competing interests, with emphasis if those of the registrant.

2.169　There must be compelling reasons to deprive a registrant of the opportunity to cross-examine a witness, particularly if the case or its consequences are serious.

2.170　The committee may admit any evidence they consider fair and relevant to the case before them, whether or not such evidence would

---

74　GMC (Fitness to Practise) Rules 2004 r35(2).
75　GMC (Fitness to Practise) Rules 2004 r36(1).
76　GMC (Fitness to Practise) Rules 2004 r36(1).

be admissible in a court of law.[77] Subject to one proviso: where evidence would not be admissible in criminal proceedings the committee or panel shall not admit such evidence unless, on the advice of the legal assessor, they are satisfied that their duty of making due inquiry into the case before them make its admission desirable.

Proceeding in the absence of the registrant[78]

2.171   As discussed at para 2.312, where the registrant is neither present nor represented at a hearing, the committee may nevertheless proceed if:

1) they are satisfied that all reasonable efforts have been made to notify the registrant of the hearing; and
2) having regard to any reasons for absence which have been provided by the registrant, they are satisfied that it is in the public interest to proceed.[79]

77 GMC (Fitness to Practise) Rules 2004 r34(1).

78 GMC (Fitness to Practise) Rules 2004 r31.

79 In *Yusuf v The Royal Pharmaceutical Society of Great Britain* [2009] EWHC 867 (Admin), it was held that the disciplinary committee had correctly identified that the key issue was whether the registrant had voluntarily chosen not to attend. The committee had been properly alert to the need to exercise its discretion to proceed in his absence with absolute caution. A similar approach was taken in *Varma v General Medical Council* [2008] EWHC 753 (Admin), where the panel had properly reminded itself of the need to balance the registrant's private rights against the public interest of having serious allegations investigated and dealt with. In the circumstances it had been justified in treating the registrant's absence as a voluntary choice not to attend.

The importance of providing medical evidence to support an application to adjourn on health grounds was illustrated in *Faulkner v Nursing and Midwifery Council* [2009] EWHC 3349 (Admin), where the committee made a decision to proceed in the registrant's absence at a time when he had not provided any such evidence. Although he later gave evidence by way of telephone link, he was only able to do so in relation to sanction as decisions on misconduct and impairment had already been made in his absence.

In *Abdalla v Health Professions Council* [2009] EWHC 3498 (Admin), the registrant argued that the decision to proceed in her absence amounted to a breach of her rights under ECHR article 6(i), or alternatively a breach of natural justice. Her arguments were rejected on the grounds that she had voluntarily opted not to attend and further adjournment could not be justified on the basis that she lacked funds to pay for legal representation, since that position was unlikely to change.

Is there a case to answer? Half-time submissions

> Submissions of no case to answer may be made in respect of a
> case or a specific allegation. They may be made where a) there is
> no evidence or, b) there is some evidence but it is weak, vague or
> inconsistent and, looked at 'in the round', a panel *could* not properly
> find the case (or fact) proved (rule 17(g)).

2.172   GMC (Fitness to Practise) Rules 2004 r17(g) provides the mechanism
for a half-time submission to be made:

> ... the registrant may make submissions regarding *whether sufficient
> evidence has been adduced to find the facts proved or to support a find-
> ing of impairment*,[80] and the FTP Panel shall consider and announce
> its decision as to whether any such submissions should be upheld.
> [Emphasis added.]

2.173   Such submissions need to be made at the end of the GMC's case on
stage 1. At this stage the only information the panel can take into
account in reaching a decision, if asked to do so, under rule 17(g) is
the evidence adduced by the GMC. Therefore, if any defence documents have been handed out (for example documents handed to
GMC witnesses for the purpose of cross-examination) these cannot
be taken into account at this stage.

2.174   While it is likely to be acceptable to ask for a short amount of
time after the GMC have closed their case to decide whether such
a submission is required, the reality is that unless the evidence has
come out in an entirely different way than expected in the hearing, a
preliminary view will have been taken either prior to or during that
evidence that such an application will need to be made and therefore
can be prepared prior to the end of the GMC case, if possible.

2.175   An application should be as long as necessary, but often there is
only a limited amount that can be said, because the doctor's positive
case cannot be advanced at this stage. Set out the test relied upon
and then explain why the GMC's evidence as presented and tested by
cross-examination does not meet that test.

2.176   The half-time submission test effectively stems from the well-
known criminal case of *R v Galbraith*[81] in which, the test was laid
down by Lord Lane, the Chief Justice as follows:

---

80   See para 2.15 for details of consultation seeking views on removing 'or to
support a finding of impairment' from this rule.
81   [1981] 1 WLR 1039.

(1) If there is no evidence that the crime alleged has been committed by the defendant, there is no difficulty. The judge will of course stop the case.

(2) The difficulty arises where there is some evidence but it is of a tenuous character, for example because of inherent weakness or vagueness or because it is inconsistent with other evidence –

(a) where the judge comes to the conclusion that the prosecution evidence, taken at its highest, is such that a jury properly directed could not properly convict upon it, it is his duty, upon submission being made, to stop the case;

(b) where however the prosecution evidence is such that its strength or weakness depends on the view to be taken of a witness's reliability or other matters which are generally speaking within the province of the jury and where on one possible view of the facts there is evidence upon which a jury could properly come to the conclusion that the defendant is guilty, then the judge should allow the matter to be tried by the jury ... There will of course, as always in this branch of the law, be borderline cases. They can safely be left to the discretion of the judge.

2.177   In essence, his Lordship held that, first, if there is no evidence the case should be stopped. That is the first limb of the test. The second limb is set out in these terms, that the case should also be stopped where there is some evidence but it is of a tenuous character, for example because of inherent weakness or vagueness or because it is inconsistent with other evidence, and where that evidence, taken at its highest, is such that the panel could not properly conclude that a relevant fact is made out.

2.178   A further gloss was put on that test in *R v Shippey*[82] where Turner J said that the requirement to take the prosecution evidence at its highest did not mean 'picking out all the plums and leaving the duff behind'.

2.179   Therefore a doctor will need to persuade the panel that the GMC has failed to present any evidence to support the particulars, or evidence which is so tenuous, for example because it is inherently, vague, weak or inconsistent with other evidence, that taken at its highest the panel could not on the basis of it properly find the relevant particulars to be well founded, in which case the panel would have an obligation to stop the case.

2.180   However, if the panel are satisfied, following submissions, that on one possible view of the facts there is evidence on which they could properly come to the conclusion that the allegation is well

82 [1998] Crim LR 767.

founded, then the proceedings should continue. Ultimately, if there is some evidence, it is not difficult for a panel to determine that the case should continue, this does not, however, mean that there will necessarily be sufficient information to find the facts proved to the civil standard at the end of stage 1.

2.181   An application can be made in relation to all the allegations – globally; however, what is more likely is that an application will be made in relation to particular, discrete allegations. Particularly in complex cases with extensive charges, it is very important for those representing the doctor to monitor and analyse whether any or sufficient evidence has been adduced in relation to each particular, so that the opportunity to make a submission in relation to a particular is not missed.

2.182   This is a key (and first) opportunity to properly challenge whether the case should continue and therefore if there is a need for such an application, it can and should be made.

Stage 2: Findings of impairment

There is no burden or standard of proof it is a question of 'judgment' by the panel.

Impairment may be based upon historical matters or a continuing state of affairs but, it is to be judged at the time of the hearing. To do this the panel must look forward taking account of any reparation, changes in practice conduct or attitude since the matter(s) found proved actually occurred.

Personal mitigation is less relevant but effort to accept and correct remediable errors should be taken into account.

2.183   If some or all facts are found proved, then the panel will need to go on to consider the issue of impairment (stage 2). Once a decision has been read in relation to facts it is often sensible to ask for a period of time to fully absorb the decision and then to consider/re-consider the approach to stage 2, in the light of the findings of fact in stage 1 and what the panel have concluded to be important/material and what they have not and any comments they have made on the evidence of various witnesses.

2.184   It is perfectly permissible to ask for some time to consider the decision, even though the expectation may seem to be to move immediately to stage 2. Clearly, stage 2 must always be anticipated and prepared for, submissions and evidence should be ready prior to the determination of stage 1, however time should be taken, if necessary, to adapt the planned approach. For example, if a panel find a doctor who did give evidence in his or her defence to lack credibility or have been evasive in answering questions then this will have a significant impact on what might need to be said in stage 2 submissions and whether a doctor will need to be called again at stage 2. Such a finding at stage 1, could, arguably, for example, be used by the GMC as an illustration of a) lack of insight and b) why fitness to practise is still impaired at today's date.

2.185 The process for this stage, in terms of the hearing, is similar. The GMC will make submissions, followed by those acting for the doctor a) calling any further evidence in relation to impairment not adduced at stage 1 – including testimonials, documentary evidence and live witnesses (which may include recalling the doctor, if advisable – remember the doctor will once again be subjected to the possibility of cross-examination by the GMC and questioning by the panel) and b) making submissions in relation to impairment. The legal assessor will then advise the panel before they retire to deliberate, before announcing their decision in the reconvened hearing. Again the process of deliberations can take quite some time at the impairment stage, and there may be further significant periods of nervous waiting.

2.186 As described above, the term 'impairment' is somewhat elusive (see para 2.41) – it has not been defined and this is both a positive and a negative for registrants. It is a matter of judgment for the panel (with no burden or standard of proof attached to it) and therefore it is important that this issue is at the forefront, as noted above, of a doctor's defence preparation. How a doctor comes across (if he or she does or doesn't give evidence) can have a significant impact on views the panel will form when reaching a determination on impairment. The most important issue to grasp is that while the term is undefined, the panel, will, as a result of the extensive authorities (all of which add a particular consideration, nuance or gloss to the approach that can/should be taken by a Fitness to Practise Panel) be guided as to how to approach this stage of the proceedings, both by GMC counsel and the legal assessor. Submissions on behalf of the doctor are likely to be of most assistance to the panel where they are presented under headings/themes that foreshadow the approach that will be commended to the panel. Of particular importance are addressing: a) whether the misconduct alleged can be appropriately categorised as serious and if not why not; b) whether, on a forward-looking basis that still takes into account past conduct, public interest or patient safety (etc) are still at risk; c) what steps if any have been taken to address the concerns raised and meet them as far as possible; and d) what aspects, if any, of *Good medical practice* are said to be engaged and is this a fair categorisation of them on the basis of the findings of fact at stage 1.

Importance of testimonials about current performance at stage 2

2.187   In *Meadow v General Medical Council*,[83] Sir Anthony Clarke MR emphasised that the role of the Fitness to Practise Panel was not to punish the registrant for past wrongdoing, but to protect the public: to look forward, not back. Sir Anthony Clarke acknowledged, however, that the panel's view of a registrant's fitness to practise today would inevitably be influenced by how they had acted or failed to act in the past. In this connection, both judges in the Administrative Court held that the Fitness to Practise Panel's practice of not hearing evidence from testimonials about current performance until the stage of sanction was wrong. Such evidence may be highly relevant to the question of current impairment and should be considered before the panel reaches its conclusion on impairment.

2.188   It is important to consider carefully at what stage documentation, testimonials and character witnesses should be provided. The GMC tend to be quite strict as to what can be adduced at which stage. Positive general testimonials in a clinical competence case, that don't deal with the facts as alleged, are likely to have no place in proceedings until stage 2 or even 3. However, testimonials attesting to the credibility of the doctor are likely to be admissible at stage 1 if the allegations are of dishonesty and therefore an assessment of the doctor's credibility is central to a determination of the facts.

Insight

2.189   'Insight' is 'the expectation that a doctor will be able to stand back and accept that, with hindsight, they should have behaved differently, and that it is expected that he/she will take steps to prevent a recurrence' and learn from their mistakes (see *Indicative sanctions guidance* para 34). See para 2.43 above.

2.190   Factors that may assist a panel when considering whether a doctor has demonstrated the insight necessary to avoid or mitigate sanctions and to accept and comply with proposed undertakings include:

- being open and honest when things go wrong (see *Good medical practice* paras 30 and 31);

83 [2007] QB 462 at para 32.

- offering an apology, although not a prerequisite for insight. The *Indicative sanctions guidance* recognises that while the duty to 'offer an apology' where appropriate, reflects that, in our society, it almost always expected that a person will apologise when things go wrong, there can be different cultural factors which influence somebody's willingness to do so;
- conduct and demeanour at the hearing.

Stage 3: Sanctions

Objectives and proportionality: an overview

> The principal aims of sanctions are to protect the public, uphold the standards and reputation of the profession and maintain public confidence therein.
>
> The punitive effect of sanctions is only one (and not the most important) factor to be borne in mind when assessing whether a sanction is proportional to the matters found proved against a registrant.

2.191 The key provisions are:

- MA 1983 s35D;
- *Indicative sanctions guidance*;
- *Good medical practice*.

2.192 Once a decision has been announced in relation to stage 2 (impairment), a registrant will know whether stage 3 (sanction) is necessary. If no impairment is found then the GMC may still invite the panel to consider imposing a warning – in which case both the GMC and the doctor's representatives would make submissions to the panel, followed by advice from the legal assessor and the panel retiring once more to deliberate before announcing their decision.[84]

2.193 If impairment is found, then the approach to stage 3 is similar. The GMC will make any submissions in relation to sanction – usually this will not invite a particular sanction but simply draw relevant aspects of the case to the panel and make observations which may assist the panel in their consideration of sanction, if any. Sometimes the GMC will take a robust view on sanction and have instructions, for example, to seek erasure. It is important to have this conversation with the GMC presenting officer in advance so that the GMC posi-

---

84 See the section above on warnings and the GMC guidance on warnings.

tion is known (although often no final instructions are given until the decision on impairment has been considered). It is important to know in advance exactly what suggestions have to be rebutted in submissions on behalf of the doctor. Further evidence and submissions may then be made on the doctor's behalf in relation to sanction. It is important, at this stage to focus on issues particularly relevant to sanction. By stage 3 much of what can be said, will have already been said and while it is important not to miss key submissions at any stage, repeating previous submissions is unlikely to engage the panel fully at this stage. The advantage at this stage is that a doctor has the panel's determination on facts and impairment – the real concerns of the panel are known and it is important to acknowledge these and take the time to address these concerns and be realistic about what sanction may, if required, sufficiently address the concerns raised.

Mitigation

Personal mitigation

2.194   At this stage, personal mitigation also becomes very important and information as to this can and should be provided to the panel with other relevant documentation. However, because disciplinary sanctions are not punitive in nature, personal considerations that would ordinarily weigh in mitigation of punishment have less effect than they would on sentencing in the criminal context. The guidance provides that the risk of harm to the public or the need to protect the public may properly override persuasive mitigation. In performance cases, evidence that failure to meet the expected standards was associated with particular circumstances which no longer exist may give some degree of reassurance. However, the chance of those circumstances recurring may be relevant to the evaluation of risk and to the disposal of the case.

2.195   It is important to remember, that while it may not seem that way for a doctor facing stage 3 proceedings, the purpose of sanctions is not to punish, but to protect the public and maintain confidence in the profession.

Indicative sanctions guidance

2.196   The *Indicative sanctions guidance*, along with *Good medical practice*, are the key documents to consider for this stage of the proceedings. The *Indicative sanctions guidance* aims to promote consistency and transparency in decision-making. In *Council for the Regulation of Healthcare Professionals v (1) General Medical Council (2) Leeper*[85] Collins J stated:

> It helps to achieve a consistent approach to the imposition of penalties where serious professional misconduct is established. The [panel] must have regard to it, although obviously each case will depend on its own facts and guidance is what it says and must not be regarded as laying down a rigid tariff.[86]

2.197   Newman J, in *R (Abrahaem) v General Medical Council*[87] described the guidance thus:

> Those are very useful guidelines and they form a framework which enables any tribunal, including this court, to focus its attention on the relevant issues. But one has to come back to the essential exercise which the law now requires in what lies behind the purpose of sanctions, which is not to be punitive but to protect the public interest; public interest is a label which gives rise to separate areas of consideration.

2.198   The observation above reflects the fact that the purpose of sanctions is not punishment, but the protection of patients, the maintenance of public confidence in the profession and declaring and upholding proper standards of conduct and behaviour.

Sanctions should be proportionate

2.199   In *Cohen v General Medical Council* there were four significant factors that led individually and cumulatively to the conclusion that the panel had erred in finding C's fitness to practise had been impaired:

a) the panel was obliged to explain why it did not accept the expert anaesthetist's opinion in respect of C's misconduct;

b) having found misconduct proved against C the panel automatically concluded that his fitness to practise had been impaired without looking at all the other relevant factors, such as C's long and unblemished career record;

c) the panel had wrongly disregarded the expert anaesthetist's opinion that C's misconduct would have been easily remediable;

d) the very grave consequences of C's misconduct finding served as a salutary lesson which served to prevent recurrence.

---

85 [2004] EWHC 1850 (Admin).
86 [2004] EWHC 1850 (Admin) at para 24.
87 [2004] EWHC 279 (Admin) at para 36.

2.200   The court found that C's fitness to practise should not have been regarded as impaired and the sanction imposed by the panel was substituted for a warning.

Nature of sanctions

2.201   Where no impairment is found, the panel may:

* take no action (*Indicative sanctions guidance* para 38); or
* issue warnings or order the doctor.

2.202   Where impairment is found, the panel may:

* take no action (*Indicative sanctions guidance* paras 45 and 48);
* agree, as an alternative to sanctions, to written undertakings (para 49);
* impose conditional registration: maximum three years (paras 45 and 56–68);
* order suspension (paras 69–76);
* erase a doctor from the register (save in cases relating solely to a doctor's health) where this is the only means of protecting patients and the wider public interest, which includes maintaining public trust and confidence in the profession (paras 77–84).

For general guidance see the judgment of Lord Bingham (MR) in *Bolton v The Law Society*.[88]

Voluntary erasure is also a possibility but only if the registrant applies for it. A doctor may apply in writing to the Registrar for voluntary erasure – that is to have his or her name removed from the register. Regulations provide information on the process for applying for voluntary erasure, including what must be included with and in the written application and the decision-making process.[89] If there are any active fitness to practise proceedings against the doctor at the time of the application then the application will be referred either to case examiners – one lay and one medical (if no fitness to practise panel has commenced) for a determination as to whether to reject or grant the application for voluntary erasure. If it is granted no fitness to practise panel will follow. If a fitness to practise panel has already commenced then the application will be referred to the panel for determination, if they grant the application that will be the end of the proceedings. See para 1.564 for further information.

---

88 [1994] 1 WLR 512.
89 The General Medical Council (Voluntary Erasure and Restoration following Voluntary Erasure) Regulations Order of Council 2004 SI No 2609.

2.203   There is no provision for the fitness to practise panel to take no action or issue a warning within MA 1983 s35D(2), however the power to do so has been inferred from the word 'may' contained within this section.

2.204   A warning may be considered appropriate in circumstances where there is no risk to the public or to patients. It cannot be given in conjunction with another determination.

2.205   Conditions should be clear, relevant, addressed to the registrant (not to third parties), necessary in order to protect patients, the public or in the interests of the registrant, proportionate to the allegations, formulated so that the conditions are not in effect a suspension, and written in such a way that compliance can be easily verified.

2.206   The guidance provides that conditions can only be adequate when there is reasonable confidence of the registrant's capacity to comply with them. If there is an issue between imposing conditions and suspension, suspension may be necessary to give the public the protection expected. If circumstances prevent the registrant from complying with the conditions, then suspension should be chosen.

2.207   As a matter of good practice representatives may wish to propose suitable conditions (on instructions from the respondent) as an alternative to suspension or erasure. The GMC maintains a conditions bank which can be used as a source.

2.208   Suspension is suitable where a committee finds that the withdrawal of registration is necessary for public protection but does not need to last the five-year term that would be a minimum for erasure. Suspension will be for a given period of time not exceeding 12 months. The determination must make clear whether the suspension will be automatically lifted at the end of the stated period or whether it will be reviewed.

2.209   Erasure is obviously the most serious sanction. Following erasure a person cannot practise as a doctor. The person can, however, apply for the restoration of his or her name to the register after a minimum of five years. The Guidance states that erasure is imposed in order to protect the public and maintain its confidence in the profession as a whole. Prior to erasure being considered, all other available sanctions should be discussed to ensure that the case is being considered bearing in mind the principles of proportionality.

2.210   No committee may erase purely on health grounds. The *Indicative sanctions guidance* deals with health cases as follows:

> 72. As far as doctors with serious health problems are concerned, the option of erasure does not exist unless there are also other factors

(such as conviction, misconduct or deficient performance), which have resulted in the finding of impaired fitness to practise. In those cases, suspension is appropriate where the doctor's health is such that he/she cannot practise safely even under conditions. In such cases, the Panel may direction a review hearing to obtain further information as to whether the doctor is then fit to resume practice either under conditions or unrestricted.

73. In cases which relate solely to a doctor's health, it is open to the Panel, if the doctor's registration has been suspended for at least two years because of two or more successive periods of suspension, to suspend the doctor's registration indefinitely. If the Panel decides to direct indefinite suspension there is no automatic further hearing of the case, although it is open to the doctor to request a review hearing after a period of two years has elapsed from the date when the indefinite suspension took effect.

Relevant case-law on suspension and erasure

2.211   In *John v Rees*,[90] Megarry J said of suspension in disciplinary proceedings:

> ... *suspension is merely expulsion pro tanto*. Each is penal and each deprives the member concerned of the enjoyment of his rights of membership or office. Accordingly, in my judgment, the rules of natural justice prima facie apply to any such process in the same way that they apply to expulsion.[91]

2.212   Suspension from practice equates in seriousness with permanent exclusion. In the case of *Dad v General Dental Council*,[92] the Privy Council stated in relation to suspension that:

> Such consequences can properly be regarded as inevitable where the nature or gravity of the offence indicated that a dentist was unfit to practise, that rehabilitation was unlikely and that he had to be suspended or have his name erased from the register ... But, in the present case, where there is a real possibility of rehabilitation and there are no other grounds for doubting the appellant's fitness to practise as a dentist, the consequences were so far out of keeping with what was needed that it could be reasonably be said that the penalty of suspension from the register for 12 months was wrong and unjustified. [93]

90 [1969] 2 All ER 274.
91 [1969] 2 All ER 274 at 305E.
92 [2000] UKPC 17.
93 [2000] UKPC 17 at para 13.

2.213 In *Bijl v General Medical Council*[94] where a surgeon had committed serious errors of judgment which, however, did not involve his practical skills as a doctor and were unlikely to be repeated it was held to be inappropriate that his name should be removed from the medical register.

2.214 Further, per Collins J in *Giele v General Medical Council*:[95]

> I do not doubt that the maintenance of public confidence in the profession must outweigh the interests of the individual doctor. But that confidence will surely be maintained by imposing such sanction as is in all the circumstances appropriate. Thus, in considering the maintenance of confidence, the existence of a public interest in not ending the career of a competent doctor will play a part. Furthermore, the fact that many patients and colleagues have, in the knowledge of the misconduct found, clearly indicated their views that erasure was not needed is a matter which can carry some weight in deciding how confidence can properly be maintained.[96]

Interim orders following determination

2.215 Where a sanction has been imposed, that sanction will not take effect until after the end of the appeal period and therefore it may be that the GMC will make an application to the panel for an interim order to be imposed to cover the appeal period (interim suspension or interim conditions). Appeals are governed by MA 1983 s40, an appeal should be made to the High Court within 28 days 'beginning with the date on which notification of the decision was served'.[97] Therefore no sanction order will have effect until the end of the 28-day period, and if an appeal is lodged within that period until the appeal has been finally disposed of.

2.216 To cover the appeal period the panel has the power to impose an interim order which will take effect during the 28 days and during any further appeal period (as appeals can take some time to be heard by the High Court). It is for this reason that an interim order is usually imposed at this stage for a period of 18 months. In practice, if no appeal is made then once the appeal period has passed the interim order will cease and be replaced immediately with the full order imposed at the sanction stage by the panel.

---

94 [2000] UKPC 41.
95 [2006] 1 WLR 942.
96 At para 29.
97 MA 1983 s40(4).

2.217   Any interim order made is likely to be on the same terms as the substantive order, eg, if conditions are imposed they will be be interim conditions. The test is the same as that which applies to interim orders generally (see para 2.76) and an interim order may only be imposed where it is considered by the panel to be necessary for the protection of the public or is otherwise in the public interest or the interests of the person concerned.

2.218   An interim order application by the GMC at the end of a hearing can be a particularly difficult application for registrants to endure, who by this stage often simply want to leave the hearing to process the decisions made against them in the proceedings. Consideration will need to be given as to how, if at all, the application will be responded to. It should not be assumed to be automatic that simply because a sanction has been imposed that an interim order should be.

2.219   When a panel is considering imposing an interim order then it is required to invite representations from the parties and take such representations into account. The panel should be informed if there are any particular reasons why an interim order should not be imposed, for example, if the registrant has patients booked or needs a period of time to arrange cover for his or her practice. The panel will adjourn to deliberate in private and then announce its decision and the reasons for that decision.

Reviews and challenges

Review hearings (rule 22)

2.220 GMC (Fitness to Practise) Rules 2004 r22 sets out the procedure that a panel must follow at a review hearing. It will need to decide whether a doctor's fitness to practise is impaired or if the doctor has failed to comply with any conditions imposed at a previous hearing before determining whether to make a further order. The panel's powers are set out in MA 1983 s35D.

2.221   Where a panel, having ordered suspension or a period of conditional registration, directs a review hearing pursuant to section 35D, it will assist the registrant if it makes clear what it expects the doctor to do in the interim.

2.222   Under section 35D(12)(d), the panel may revoke or vary any of the conditions it has previously imposed, for the remainder of the current period of conditional registration, but shall not extend any period of conditional registration for more than three years at a time.

Restoration hearings (rules 23 and 24)

2.223 A restoration hearing will be held to consider an application to restore a registrant onto the register.[98] The procedure for such a hearing is set out at rule 24.

Judicial review

2.224 In appropriate circumstances consideration may be given to mounting a challenge to a decision (or omission) of the GMC by way of judicial review. Further consideration of when a judicial review may be appropriate in this context and the procedural and substantive requirements of making such an application are considered in chapter 7.

Appeals

2.225 The usual route for challenging a Fitness to Practise Panel decision is through the statutory appeal mechanism provided for by the MA 1983. Appeals are governed by section 40 of the MA 1983. Appeals should be made to the High Court within 28 days 'beginning with the date on which notification of the decision was served' (section 40(4)) and extend, among other things, to decisions in relation to:

- erasure, suspension, conditional registration or varying conditions;
- directions that the right to make applications for restoration of the doctor's name to the register if previously unsuccessful, be suspended indefinitely (section 41(9));
- refusal to restore a doctor's name to the register.

2.226 There is no statutory appeal available where a doctor has accepted undertakings. In accepting undertakings in response to the findings of the panel, a doctor forfeits any right to appeal, because there is no order made against the doctor that could be subject to an appeal (MA 1983 s40(1)).

2.227 It has been recognised by the High Court that judgment exercised by the High Court in such appeals is 'distinctly and firmly a secondary judgment' (per Laws LJ in *Raschid and Fatnani v General Medical Council*).[99]

---

98 GMC (Fitness to Practise) Rules 2004 r23.
99 [2007] 1 WLR 1460 at para 20.

2.228   For this reason, the High Court will be reluctant to interfere with findings of fact made by the specialist tribunal of the GMC, as enunciated in the case of *Nandi v General Medical Council*:[100]

> 27. So far as this court's approach is concerned, there is very little, if anything, between counsel. The Committee deals with the matter in stages. First of all, it finds the facts. It then goes on to consider whether, on those facts, it is appropriate to make a finding of serious professional misconduct, and then it considers also the question as to what penalties should be imposed if such a finding is made. So far as findings of fact are concerned, this is an appeal which is not limited but, in accordance with the general approach of the Court of Appeal, there will not be interference with findings of fact unless the court takes the view that they are clearly wrong. The Committee have heard the evidence, have seen the witnesses give that evidence and will be in the best position to judge what evidence they accept and what they reject. Of course, if this court is persuaded that a particular finding was one which was not appropriate, should not have been made and was clearly wrong, then it will interfere, but not otherwise.'

This was also considered in *Council for Healthcare Regulatory Excellence v Nursing and Midwifery Council and Grant*:[101]

> Courts considering challenges to decisions of this kind will therefore acknowledge the deference due to the specialist tribunal seized with the task of determining the nature or gravity of the misconduct, and the extent to which it is likely to undermine public confidence in the profession.

> Cases in this jurisdiction are, however, particularly fact-sensitive. The degree of deference is likely to be higher where issues of technical competence or clinical practice arise, in assessing how best the needs of the public and of the profession should be protected. It is likely to be lower, where the case concerns behavioural issues such as dishonesty or sexual misconduct; see for example the observations to this effect in *The Council for the Regulation of Health Care Professionals v General Dental Council and Fleischmann* [2005] EWHC 87 (Admin).[102]

Council for Healthcare Regulatory Excellence

2.229   The Council for Healthcare Regulatory Excellence (CHRE) (which following the Health and Social Care Act 2012 will become the Professional Standards Authority for Health and Social Care)[103] has an

100 [2004] EWHC 2317 (Admin) per Collins J at [27].
101 [2011] EWHC 927 (Admin).
102 [2011] EWHC 927 (Admin), Mrs Justice Cox DBE at paras 62–63.
103 Health and Social Care Act 2012 s222.

oversight function in relation to reviewing all decisions of healthcare regulators fitness to practise decisions, including those of the GMC.

2.230   This remit involves reporting annually on each regulator, initiating investigations if required and making a referral to the High Court in cases where decisions appear to the CHRE be unduly lenient or where a decision should not have been made.

2.231   This power derives from section 29(4) of the NHS Reform and Health Professions Act 2002.[104]

2.232   The authorities establish that section 29(4) is sufficiently broad to include both unduly lenient findings of fact and unduly lenient sanctions; see in particular *Council for the Regulation of Healthcare Professionals v General Medical Council and Basiouny.*[105] It appears that there is, as yet, no decided case concerning an unduly lenient failure to find impairment of fitness to practise.

2.233   A key case in this area is *Council for the Regulation of Healthcare Professionals v General Medical Council and Ruscillo,*[106] where the Court of Appeal considered in detail the relevant statutory framework and the purpose behind implementation of the NHS Reform and Healthcare Professions Act 2002.

2.234   Lord Phillips MR, giving the judgment of the court, stated as follows:

> 73 What are the criteria to be applied by the court when deciding whether a relevant decision was 'wrong'? The task of the disciplinary tribunal is to consider whether the relevant facts demonstrate that the registrant has been guilty of the defined professional misconduct that gives rise to the right or duty to impose a penalty and, where they do, to impose the penalty that is appropriate, having regard to the safety of the public and the reputation of the profession. The role of the court when a case is referred is to consider whether the disciplinary tribunal

104 Section 29 provides, so far as is material, as follows (the reference to 'relevant court' being a reference to the High Court): '(4) If the Council considers that –a relevant decision falling within subsection (1) has been unduly lenient, whether as to any finding of professional misconduct or fitness to practise on the part of the registrant concerned (or lack of such a finding), or as to any penalty imposed, or both, or a relevant decision falling within subsection (2) should not have been made, and that it would be desirable for the protection of members of the public for the Council to take action under this section, the Council may refer the case to the relevant court ... (8) The court may – dismiss the appeal, allow the appeal and quash the relevant decision, substitute for the relevant decision any other decision which could have been made by the committee or other person concerned, or remit the case to the committee or other person concerned to dispose of the case in accordance with the directions of the court, and make such order as to costs ... as it thinks fit.'

105 [2005] EWHC 68 (Admin).

106 [2005] 1 WLR 717.

has properly performed that task so as to reach a correct decision as to the imposition of a penalty. Is that any different from the role of the council in considering whether a relevant decision has been 'unduly lenient'? We do not consider that it is. The test of undue leniency in this context must we think, involve considering whether, having regard to the material facts, the decision reached has due regard for the safety of the public and the reputation of the profession.

77 ... In any particular case under section 29 the issue is likely to be whether the disciplinary tribunal has reached a decision as to penalty that is manifestly inappropriate having regard to the registrant's conduct and the interests of the public.

Further, at paragraph 78 in *Ruscillo* Lord Phillips said this:

78 The question was raised in argument as to the extent to which the council and the court should defer to the expertise of the disciplinary tribunal. That expertise is one of the most cogent arguments for self-regulation. At the same time, Part 2 of the Act has been introduced because of concern as to the reliability of self-regulation. Where all material evidence has been placed before the disciplinary tribunal and it has given due consideration to the relevant factors, the council and the court should place weight on the expertise brought to bear in evaluating how best the needs of the public and the profession should be protected.

The European Convention on Human Rights

It is undoubtedly the case that the European Convention on Human Rights (ECHR) applies to regulatory proceedings although there may be argument when there is no prospect of suspension or erasure.

The better approach to case preparation and presentation is to adopt the *spirit* of, in particular article 6 (right to a fair trial), the letter of which is frequently reflected in domestic case-law.

Article 6 and appeals

2.235   The issue of article 6 has yet to be finally and fully determined, however the current view is that any article 6 concerns there may be at the Fitness to Practise Panel level can be remedied by the access of a right to a review through the MA 1983 s40 appeal mechanism, as per Collins J in *Watson v General Medical Council*:[107]

107 [2006] EWHC 18 (Admin) at [11].

The Privy Council rarely if ever had witnesses give evidence before it. There is no reason to believe that when Parliament provided that appeals should come to this court instead it intended to widen the scope of those appeals. In *Nandi* ... I considered this question and observed that the Practice Direction 22.32, which disapplied CPR [Civil Procedure Rules 1998] r52.11(1), was inappropriate. It may be that it reflected a view that article 6 of the European Convention on Human Rights required fuller appeal rights since at that time there were doubts about the independence of the GMC committees. The reforms have established that the [Fitness to Practise Panels] now have sufficient independence to mean that an appeal which is in the form of a review is all that is needed to comply with article 6.

2.236 In the disciplinary context, see also the case of *R (on the application of G) v The Governors of X School*[108] (see chapter 7, para 7.55).

2.237 See chapter 1, para 1.19 for more detail on article 6 as it pertains to disciplinary proceedings.

Costs

2.238 The GMC bring proceedings in the public interest, to protect the public and uphold standards, therefore the GMC is not in the position of an ordinary litigant prosecuting a claim. Unless a complaint is improperly brought, no order for costs is normally made against the regulator.[109] The following case also emphasises this issue in relation to costs in disciplinary proceedings – Cranston J made the following remarks in *Levy v Solicitors Regulation Authority*:[110]

> It is clear that the ordinary rules of costs following the event does not apply in disciplinary proceedings. A disciplinary body is not in the same position as a party in ordinary civil litigation. It is acting in the public interest and should not be dissuaded from properly brought proceedings by an adverse costs order. However, it may be that it is appropriate to give a discount on the costs awarded to the disciplinary body when its success is only partial.

---

108 [2011] UKSC 30.
109 *Walker v Law Society* [2007] EWCA Civ 233.
110 [2011] EWHC 740 (Admin) at para 42.

The Nursing and
Midwifery Council

continued

Key points

- *Regulator:* Nursing and Midwifery Council (NMC)
- *Professions regulated:* Nurses and midwives
- *Type of proceedings:* Fitness to practise; and fraudulent or improper entry onto the register
- *Common sources of referral:* Patients, employers, police
- *Relevant statute:* Nursing and Midwifery Order (NMO) 2001 SI 2002 No 253
- *Fitness to Practise Rules:* Nursing and Midwifery Council (Fitness to Practise) Rules 2004 (Schedule to SI 2004 No 1761), as amended
- *Key document: The Code: standards of conduct, performance and ethics for nurses and midwives* (NMC Code)
- *Function:* To establish and keep under review standards of conduct, performance and ethics expected of registrants and prospective registrants and to give such guidance as it sees fit, and to make arrangements to protect the public from persons whose fitness to practise is impaired (NMO 2001 article 21)
- *Four-stage process:* Referral, investigation, adjudication and review
- *Three practice committees:* Investigating Committee (NMC (Fitness to Practise) Rules 2004 Part 2), Conduct and Competence Committee and Health Committee (Part 4)
- *Location:* The main hearing centres are in London, Cardiff, Edinburgh and Belfast
- *Fitness to practise test:* Whether fitness to practise is impaired by reason of (in summary) a) misconduct; b) lack of competence; c) a criminal conviction or caution; d) physical or mental health; e) a determination by another regulator or inclusion on a barred list
- *Notice of hearing provision:* Yes – usually 28 days
- *Case management provisions:* Yes, including power to hold preliminary meetings (NMC (Fitness to Practise) Rules 2004 r18), power to postpone and adjourn (rule 32) and power to continue in absence of registrant (rule 21)
- *Investigating Committee:* Yes (NMC (Fitness to Practise) Rules 2004 Part 2). The Investigating Committee has the power in relation to a fitness to practise allegation to close the case, investigate or refer the allegation to the Conduct and Competence Committee or Health Committee for adjudication. The

Investigating Committee also has the power to determine an allegation of fraudulent or improper entry onto the register
- *Interim order power:* Yes – all practice committees have the power to impose interim conditions of practice or interim suspension orders (NMO 2001 article 31; NMC (Fitness to Practise) Rules 2004 Part 3)
- *Interim order guidance:* Yes
- *Power to require a registrant to undergo health assessment?* Yes
- *Composition of practice committee panels:* Three persons, at least one will be a lay member and at least one will be from the relevant profession. A Health Committee panel will also include a registered medical practitioner. Address the panel as 'Sir'/'Madam', remain seated but stand on entry and exit
- *Independent legal assessor:* Yes
- *Fitness to practise hearing procedure:* Four stages – 1) preliminary stage; 2) factual stage; 3) impairment stage; and 4) sanction stage (NMC (Fitness to Practise) Rules 2004 r24)
- *Burden of proof:* Balance of probabilities (civil standard). Burden on NMC to prove the facts (NMC (Fitness to Practise) Rules 2004 r30)
- *Submission of no case to answer:* Yes – test is whether 'sufficient evidence' has been presented to find the facts proved or to support a finding of impairment (NMC (Fitness to Practise) Rules 2004 rr24(8) and 24(9))
- *Sanction provisions:* Power to take no further action or make a caution order of not less than one year and not more than five years; conditions of practice order of not more than three years; suspension order of up to one year; or striking off order (NMO 2001 article 29)
- *Sanction documents: Indicative sanctions guidance to panels: Guidance to Panels on conditions of practice orders* and NMC *Conditions of Practice library*
- *Review hearings:* Yes – to review a conditions of practice order or suspension order prior to expiry or otherwise (NMO 2001 article 30)
- *Restoration hearings:* Yes – to consider an application by a person who has been struck off to be restored to the register (NMO 2001 article 33)
- *Appeal:* Yes – to the High Court (NMO 2001 article 38)
- *Costs:* No general provision

Introduction

3.1   It is illegal to work as a nurse or midwife in UK without being on the register maintained by the Nursing and Midwifery Council (NMC). This is regardless of whether the position is temporary or permanent, paid or voluntary, within the NHS or private. In order to be on the register a nurse or midwife must:

- comply with NMC standards of education and training;
- pay an annual fee;
- undertake 450 hours of registered practice in the previous three years;
- undertake 35 hours of learning activity (continuing professional development (CPD)) in the previous three years (usually evidenced by production of a portfolio); and
- be fit to practise.

3.2   The NMC's principal function is to set standards of education and training, conduct and performance for nurses and midwives, and to ensure that the profession maintains those standards.[1] The NMC's main objective in exercising its functions is to 'safeguard the health and well-being of persons using or needing the services of registrants'.[2] The NMC is required to have in the exercise of its functions proper regard to the interests of all registrants as well as the interests of those using or needing the services of registrants. 'Public interest' has been widely defined by the courts and includes protection of members of the public, maintaining public confidence in the professions, and declaring and upholding proper standards of conduct and performance. In furtherance of this objective the NMC has the power to strike off or suspend a nurse or midwife from the register, place restrictions on his or her practice (conditions of practice),[3] or put a note on the register for a period of time (caution). The NMC also has the power to impose an interim order until such time as an allegation has been determined. These proceedings are known as 'fitness to practise proceedings' and are the subject matter of this chapter.

---

1   Nursing and Midwifery Order 2001 SI 2002 No 253 (NMO 2001) article 3(2).
2   NMO 2001 article 3(4).
3   See paras 3.185–3.189.

Background to regulation

3.3 Nurses and midwives have been subject to statutory regulation for approximately 100 years. The two professions were brought together in 1983 under the auspices of the UK Central Council which maintained the register and which primarily had a disciplinary role and four National Boards which primarily dealt with education and training. These functions were brought together with the creation of the NMC in 2002. The NMC is independent of government, and is paid for by the profession. However, over the years in order to maintain public confidence there has been an increase in the number of non-professional (lay) persons, who now make up 50 per cent of the NMC Board.

3.4 Currently the NMC, like other health regulatory bodies, conducts fitness to practise hearings as prosecutor, judge and jury. The NMC brings a case which is determined by an NMC committee, giving rise to a potential conflict of interest (see para 3.61). In order to address this concern the previous Labour government established the Office of the Health Professions Adjudicator (OHPA).[4] The OHPA was initially to take over the adjudication of fitness to practise cases from the General Medical Council (GMC), with the aim of extending its function to the other health professions. The OHPA has been abolished by the current coalition government, and instead the GMC have announced that it is to establish a separate Medical Practitioners Tribunal Service.[5] At the time of writing, it is not known if the NMC is likely to develop their own adjudication system. The NMC is consulting over a proposed change to their rules. On 16 February 2011, the government announced a review of the framework, referring the project to the Law Commission. It is thought that the outcome of this will be a recommendation to consolidate the rules of various regulators, to create a single system.

3.5 The NMC rules were changed in 2004, when the burden of proof was changed from the criminal standard of beyond reasonable doubt, to the civil standard of balance of probabilities. This rule change came into force on 3 November 2008. Despite the rule change, the burden of proof remains with the NMC to prove the allegations – there is no requirement on the registrant to disprove the allegations. The NMC often cites the change in the burden of proof as an indication that the NMC are moving from a criminal towards a civil system. However, the adoption to a civil burden of proof does not require the NMC to

4 Health and Social Care Act 2008.
5 See chapter 2.

adopt other civil tests and procedures, since its regulatory functions are a hybrid of criminal and civil functions.

Remit

3.6   The NMC regulates 670,000 nurses and midwives, across England, Wales, Scotland, Northern Ireland and the Islands. It also regulates health visitors who are viewed as specialist nurses. It does not regulate healthcare assistants (HCAs), who are increasingly taking on some of the traditional nursing roles. There is an ongoing debate as to whether HCAs should be regulated, but the government's decision not to include this in the Health and Social Care Act 2012 indicates that this is unlikely to occur in the foreseeable future.

3.7   The NMC has power to consider allegations against a registrant where either an entry onto the register has been fraudulently or incorrectly made,[6] or their fitness to practise is impaired for a specific reason which includes misconduct,[7] lack of competence,[8] a conviction or caution,[9] physical or mental health,[10] a finding of impairment by any other health or social care regulator,[11] or inclusion on a barred or other list.[12]

3.8   'Misconduct' is widely defined and includes not just clinical conduct but also managerial and administrative conduct, and can also include conduct unrelated to the performance of a professional role but which brings the profession into disrepute. A breach of the standards expected of a nurse or midwife may constitute misconduct.

Sources of law

3.9   The NMC derives its regulatory powers from NMO 2001. Article 21 requires the NMC to establish and keep under review standards of conduct, performance and ethics expected of registrants and prospective registrants and to give such guidance on these matters as it sees

---

6   NMO 2001 article 22(1)(b).
7   NMO 2001 article 22(1)(a)(i).
8   NMO 2001 article 22(1)(a)(ii).
9   NMO 2001 article 22(1)(a)(iii).
10   NMO 2001 article 22(1)(a)(iv).
11   NMO 2001 article 22(1)(a)(v).
12   NMO 2001 article 22(1)(a)(vi) and (vii). These are lists under the Safeguarding Vulnerable Groups Act 2006, Safeguarding Vulnerable Groups (Northern Ireland) Order 2007 SI No 1351 (NI 11) and the Protection of Vulnerable Groups (Scotland) Act 2007 is not yet in force.

fit,[13] and to make arrangements to protect the public from persons whose fitness to practise is impaired.[14]

3.10 The standards expected of nurses and midwives are set out in *The Code: Standards of conduct, performance and ethics for nurses and midwives* (NMC Code),[15] breach of which may bring a registrant's fitness to practise into question. The NMC Code covers:

- all aspects of patient care, including:
  - the need to treat people as individuals and with dignity;
  - the need for confidentiality;
  - the need for informed consent; and
  - maintenance of professional boundaries;
- working with other professionals, families and carers and the wider community;
- maintaining high standards of practice, including keeping skills and knowledge up to date, and clear and accurate record-keeping; and
- the requirement to be open and honest, act with integrity and uphold the reputation of the profession.

Midwives are also subject to separate 'Midwives rules and standards'. In addition, the NMC has produced standards and guidance on various aspects of nursing and midwifery practice as follows:

- *Standards for medicine management;*
- *Record keeping: guidance for nurses and midwives;*
- *Guidance for the care of older people;*
- *Raising and escalating concerns: guidance for nurses and midwives.*

3.11 A failure to comply with the standards of the NMC Code or other standards, guidance or advice produced by the NMC can be taken into account in any fitness to practise proceedings, although it does not of itself establish that a registrant's fitness to practise is impaired.[16] In practice the relevant breach of the NMC Code is almost always referred to during fitness to practise hearings, and the registrant will be judged against those standards.

3.12 Fitness to practise proceedings are governed both by the NMO 2001 and the Nursing and Midwifery Council (Fitness to Practise)

---

13 NMO 2001 article 21(1)(a).
14 NMO 2001 article 21(1)(b).
15 NMC, May 2008, available at www.nmc-uk.org/publications/standards.
16 NMO 2001 article 22(4).

Rules Order of Council 2004 (NMC Rules), as amended.[17] In accordance with NMO 2001 article 47(1), the NMC Rules 2004 have been approved by order of the Privy Council. These rules are explained in more detail below. In addition the NMC provides indicative guidance to panels on interim orders and sanctions. These are regularly referred to in hearings.

3.13   The NMO 2001, NMC (Fitness to Practise) Rules 2004 and NMC Code and other standards, as well as the NMC guidance and fitness to practise decisions, can be obtained from the NMC website: www. nmc-uk.org. Both the NMO 2001 and NMC Rules 2004 have been amended since their original enactment and the website provides a consolidated version – although it has no official statutory status, it is a useful working document. The website also provides advice to registrants, witnesses and members of the public who attend a hearing.

Case-law

3.14   There is a body of regulatory case-law that is developing through High Court, Court of Appeal and Supreme Court decisions. For older cases there are also Privy Council decisions. Regulatory cases relating to the NMC are binding and those relating to other health professions are highly persuasive and generally followed. In addition, other regulatory decisions and relevant decisions of the criminal courts are also relied upon.

3.15   The NMC is a public authority and it is well established that the European Convention of Human Rights (ECHR) applies, especially article 6 (right to a fair trial). Therefore decisions of the domestic and European Court of Human Rights on, for example, the right to a fair hearing, the right to a hearing within a reasonable period of time and the right to a public hearing are also relevant (see chapter 1).

17   Nursing and Midwifery Council (Fitness to Practise) Rules Order of Council 2004 SI No 1761 as amended by Nursing and Midwifery Council (Fitness to Practise) (Amendment) Rules 2007 SI No 893; Nursing and Midwifery Council (Midwifery and Practice Committees) (Constitution) Rules 2008 SI No 3148; Nursing and Midwifery Council (Fitness to Practise) (Amendment) Rules 2011 Order of Council 2012 SI No 17.

NMC decisions

3.16 NMC hearing decisions are published on the NMC website. These are not binding on any subsequent panel, and are generally not relied upon in hearings, however they can provide a useful indication of how the NMC panels treat certain evidence or view certain conduct.

Fitness to practise – overview

Three practice committees

3.17 In order to carry out its functions the NMC has three committees (practice committees):

- *Investigating Committee*: to investigate the complaint, determine interim orders and allegations about fraudulent / incorrect entries onto the register;
- *Conduct and Competence Committee*: to determine fitness to practise allegations other than by reason of health;
- *Health Committee*: to determine fitness to practise allegations by reason of health.

3.18 The constitution of the practice committees is determined by statute.[18] The panels of practice committees are usually made up of three persons and will always comprise at least one lay member and one member from the relevant profession. The chair will be a member of the NMC Board and could be either a lay or professional representative. A Health Committee panel (including panels considering interim orders) will also include a registered medical practitioner. The panel should be addressed as 'Sir'/'Madam'. All persons present should stand on entry or exit of the panel, otherwise they should remain seated.

Four stages

3.19 There are at least four stages to the current fitness to practise procedures:

1) *Initial referral to the Investigating Committee (sometimes referred to as a section 1 meeting, or ICs1)*. An allegation will be referred to the Investigating Committee for initial consideration. The Investigating Committee will send the registrant a notice of referral

---

18 Nursing and Midwifery Council (Midwifery and Practice Committees) (Constitution) Rules 2008 SI No 3148.

enclosing documentation, and providing 28 days to make representations. The notice may be accompanied by notice of hearing
for an interim order. Following receipt of any representations the
Investigating Committee will normally conduct an investigation
(this can take some time and involve several stages).

2) *Final Investigating Committee meeting (sometimes referred to as a
section 4 meeting or ICs4).* The Committee has the power to close
the case, refer it for further investigation or refer the matter to the
Conduct and Competence Committee or Health Committee. The
registrant will be provided with any additional documentation,
draft particulars of allegations and again provided with 28 days to
make any representations.

3) *An adjudication hearing before the Conduct and Competence Committee, or Health Committee.*

4) *Review Hearing before a Conduct and Competence Committee, or
Health Committee.*

Location of hearing centres

3.20   NMC hearing centres are located in London, Cardiff, Edinburgh and
Belfast, and other locations throughout the UK. The addresses can
be obtained from the NMC website. If a registrant has a particular
reason for wanting a different hearing centre to that proposed by
the NMC, then this should be raised with the NMC at the earliest
opportunity, providing full reasons. However, any amendment to the
venue is the exception to the rule. The NMC position is that NMC
hearings occur in the hearing centre applicable to the registrant's
address on the NMC register.

Assistance

3.21   NMC hearings have potentially serious consequences for a registrant
since they can prevent him or her from practising as a nurse or midwife. It is therefore vital that a registrant takes such hearings seriously and seeks assistance at the earliest possible opportunity; preferably
upon being advised by the referring party of a referral to the NMC or
upon receiving the initial NMC Notice of Referral letter. If the registrant is a member of a trade union or professional association the
registrant should seek assistance from his or her representative. If the
registrant is not a member of such body then the registrant should
contact his or her local Citizens Advice Bureau, Legal Advice Centre
or a solicitor or public access barrister specialising in regulatory

work. Some registrants represent themselves – if so, they are strongly advised to attend other NMC hearings to familiarise themselves with the process.[19] If the registrant has a query relating to his or her case then he or she or their representative should contact the NMC case officer identified on the correspondence.

Referral

3.22   Anyone can make an allegation about the fitness to practise of a nurse or midwife. There is no need for the conduct in question to have occurred in the UK or relate to a time when the nurse or midwife was registered.[20]

3.23   Most referrals will be made by an employer or service provider following an internal disciplinary procedure. However a referral may be made prior to such proceedings being completed in serious cases where the public is at risk. A member of the public may make a referral and sometimes a registrant will self-refer. A registrant is required to inform the NMC if he or she has been cautioned, charged or found guilty of a criminal offence.[21] The police are also under an obligation to inform the NMC in such circumstances. Finally, the NMC is permitted to make a referral where it appears to the NMC that there should be an investigation into fitness to practise.[22]

3.24   There is no time limit for a complaint to be made. It may be possible to challenge a long delay as an abuse of process or breach of article 6 where a fair trial would not be possible, or it would be otherwise unfair to try to registrant, for example due to bad faith, unlawfulness or executive manipulation. However mere delay, absent prejudice, is not sufficient. The need to maintain public confidence in the regulation of the medical profession requires that a complaint should, in the absence of some special and sufficient reason, be publicly investigated. See paras 3.107–3.108 and chapter 1.

3.25   Following a referral there is an initial screening by at least two NMC screeners (one lay and one from the profession), to ensure that the matter does concern fitness to practise.[23] In the year 2010–2011 over 4000 referrals were received by the NMC, an increase by 41

19 Booking to attend as an observer can be done on-line, see www.nmc-uk.org/hearings/attending-a-hearing.
20 NMO 2001 article 22(3).
21 NMC Code para 50.
22 NMO 2001 article 22(6).
23 NMO 2001 article 24.

per cent over the previous year.[24] Only those cases which fall within the NMC's remit will be forwarded for a hearing before a practice committee.

3.26   Following receipt of a referral it may take many months, even years, for a practice committee to hold a hearing to determine the matter. If possible registrants should take steps during this period to address any concerns and gather evidence in support of their case, so that they are fully prepared by the time any hearing takes place.

Concurrent criminal proceedings and double jeopardy

> Regulatory proceedings need not be stayed pending the outcome of criminal proceedings unless there are exceptional circumstances such as an impossible workload from which the defendant can demonstrate serious prejudice or injustice.
>
> Arguments regarding double jeopardy, privilege and publicity are otherwise unlikely to succeed.

3.27   Often a referral of an allegation that is subject to a criminal investigation will be adjourned pending the outcome of that criminal investigation and any trial. However, there is no requirement on regulators to adjourn. For a fuller discussion of the cases on this matter see chapters 1 and 7.

3.28   Regulators may continue to investigate an allegation that is criminal in nature even where criminal proceedings have not been pursued due to insufficient evidence or there has been an acquittal at trial. This is because the burden of proof in criminal proceedings is beyond reasonable doubt, as opposed to a balance of probabilities used in civil proceedings (see paras 3.158–3.159).

Preliminary issues applicable to all hearings

Service of documents and notice

3.29   The NMC is required to keep the registrant informed of the progress of the proceedings. It will send out notices informing the registrant of when a case has been referred from one body to another, notice of hearing, notice of decision and any other notice as from time to time may be required.

24   *NMC annual fitness to practise report 2010–2011* p10 (July 2011), see www.nmc-ik.org/Aboutus.

3.30   The NMC is required to send or deliver a notice of hearing by a postal or delivery service to the registrant's address on the register or last known address, if different.[25] If the registrant is represented then notice of hearing may also be sent, delivered or sent by email to the registrant's solicitor, his or her professional body or trade union.[26] Any other notice or document may be sent by ordinary post or email to a previously notified address.[27] Time limits run from the day after the notice was sent by delivery service, or the day on which it was left at the address or sent by email.[28]

3.31   To date, the courts have held that as long as the NMC has complied with the rules of service, the notice of hearing will be deemed to have been effectively served. This has been the case even where a registrant had requested that notice of hearing be served by email because he was going to be out of the country,[29] or where notice served by recorded delivery letter was returned unopened and undelivered.[30] For discussion of these cases see chapter 1. Since the rules still do not provide for a notice of hearing to be sent to a *registrant* by email, registrants who go abroad are advised to ensure that notice is provided to a legal or union representative.

Evidence gathering

> While there is a duty to prevent inequality of arms, there is no positive duty on a disciplinary body to gather evidence to assist the registrant.
>
> To allege unfairness under article 6(3)(b) ECHR a complainant must demonstrate that a duty exists, that it has been breached and this has caused an inequality of arms.
>
> Each case will depend on its own facts.

3.32   The NMC Rules do not impose on it a positive duty to gather evidence to assist a registrant,[31] however the NMC, along with other regulatory bodies, generally follow the rules of disclosure that exist in the criminal courts. These are explained in chapter 1. In general

---

25 NMC (Fitness to Practise) Rules 2004 r34(1).
26 NMC (Fitness to Practise) Rules 2004 r34(2).
27 NMC (Fitness to Practise) Rules 2004 r34(3).
28 NMC (Fitness to Practise) Rules 2004 r34(5).
29 *Jatta v Nursing and Midwifery Council* [2009] EWCA Civ 824.
30 *Raheem v Nursing and Midwifery Council* [2010] EWHC 2549 (Admin).
31 *R (Johnson) v Nursing and Midwifery Council* [2008] EWHC 885 (Admin).

terms, the NMC is required to disclose evidence that not only supports its case but which could undermine its case or assist the case of the registrant. A failure to disclose may lead to an application to stay proceeding on the grounds of an abuse of process. However, a regulator is only required to disclose that evidence which is considered to be relevant, and an abuse of process argument is only likely to succeed if the registrant is able to establish that the failure to disclose the evidence in question was unfair. Thus in *R (Johnson) v Nursing and Midwifery Council*,[32] the failure by the registrant to take steps to obtain the documentation meant that the regulator could not be blamed and therefore there was no unfairness. Similarly in *R (Phillips) v Nursing and Midwifery Council*[33] the failure of the NMC to call the patient named in the charge to give evidence was held not to be unfair because the registrant could have called the witness himself or herself.

Disclosure

3.33   The NMC council, practice committees or authorised person, may require any person, including a third party, to supply relevant information and/or produce relevant documentation[34]. The power is limited to that information and those documents that a party is required to disclose in civil proceedings,[35] and which is not otherwise prohibited by any enactment.[36] If there are particular documents or evidence relevant to the registrant's case held by a third party, then a request should be made initially to the NMC, and if refused, to the relevant committee to obtain that information. Preliminary meetings can also be requested by the registrant to request that the NMC be directed to obtain documentation (see paras 3.38–3.41).

3.34   The requirement to disclose does not apply to the registrant under investigation. However, once the matter has been referred to the Investigating Committee, there is a more limited requirement on the registrant to disclose to the NMC the identity of any person by whom he is employed to provide nursing or midwifery services, or with whom he or she has an arrangement to provide such services.[37] The NMC Code requires registrants to engage with internal

32   [2008] EWHC 885 (Admin).
33   [2008] EWHC 1698 (Admin).
34   NMO 2001 article 25(1).
35   NMO 2001 article 25(5).
36   NMO 2001 article 25(3).
37   NMO 2001 article 25(2)(a).

and external investigations. The registrant is also required to disclose details of any regulated body which authorises him or her to practise both in the UK and elsewhere.[38]

3.35   The registrant is under a strict duty to inform employers and potential employers of a referral to the NMC, the imposition of an interim order or substantive sanction. There is no obligation to inform an employer or potential employer if a case is subsequently closed either at the investigation stage or following a hearing if the facts are unfounded or there is no finding of current impairment.

Protection of third party information

3.36   NMO 2001 article 25 provides the NMC with the power to anonymise documentation, or other evidence, that may lead to the identification of any person during the proceedings.[39] During a hearing patients will be referred to in accordance to a key, rather than by name or even their initials. Further, NMC (Fitness to Practise) Rules 2004 r35 provides the NMC with the power to take 'such steps as it thinks fit' to prevent the disclosure of personal data which relates to individuals who are not a party to the proceedings, in breach of the Data Protection Act (DPA) 1998. One of the steps the NMC may take where a registrant discloses third party information is to consider the disclosure to be a breach of the provisions in the NMC Code on confidentiality, potentially resulting in further allegations and/or proceedings.

3.37   If a registrant decides to disclose documents at any stage in the proceedings as part of his or her defence, then he or she is advised to ensure that any references to third parties are redacted, in particular references to patients. Particular caution should be exercised when disclosing, for example, patient notes, supervision records and practice development reviews. Further registrants are advised to obtain their employer's permission in writing to use such records. Of course this does not apply to documents obtained by and disclosed by the NMC. For further information about DPA 1998 see chapter 7.

Preliminary meetings

3.38   NMC (Fitness to Practise) Rules 2004 r18 provides practice committees with the power to hold a preliminary meeting where such

---

38 NMO 2001 article 25(2)(b).
39 NMO 2001 article 25(4).

a meeting would assist in the performance of its functions.[40] The chair of the relevant committee will preside over the hearing, with the legal assessor in attendance together with the parties, their representatives, and any other appropriate persons.[41] The parties shall be given not less than 14 days' notice of the hearing,[42] though this notice period can be waived by the registrant.

3.39   Preliminary meetings are held in private and are administrative in nature. NMO 2001 article 32 permits the chair to issue case management directions and to impose sanctions on non-compliance. The NMC (Fitness to Practise) Rules 2004 set out a non-exhaustive list of directions.[43] The chair has power:

- to issue directions regarding the service of expert evidence;
- to consider an application for special measures for vulnerable witnesses under rule 23 (see paras 3.118–3.120);
- to consider an application for failure to comply with directions under rule 31(8); and
- to consider an application for adjournment under rule 32 (see paras 3.42–3.46).

3.40   Preliminary meetings are only likely to occur where the nature of the case requires a lengthy hearing or where there are particular evidential or legal issues that need to be resolved prior to the main hearing. If an issue arises that is likely to result in postponing or adjourning the main hearing, then it should usually be dealt with at a preliminary meeting in order to save costs and inconvenience for all concerned.

3.41   A preliminary meeting may occur at any stage in the proceedings including when a case is still under investigation.

Postponements and adjournments

3.42   NMC (Fitness to Practise) Rules 2004 r32 sets out the provisions for postponements and adjournments. Where notice of a hearing has been given, the chair of his or her own motion or by application of a party may postpone the hearing before the hearing begins.[44] Where a hearing has commenced the practice committee may of its own motion or by application by a party adjourn proceedings at any stage,

---

40 NMC (Fitness to Practise) Rules 2004 r18(1).
41 NMC (Fitness to Practise) Rules 2004 r18(2).
42 NMC (Fitness to Practise) Rules 2004 r18(4).
43 NMC (Fitness to Practise) Rules 2004 r18(5).
44 NMC (Fitness to Practise) Rules 2004 r32(1).

provided that no injustice is caused.[45] In considering whether or not to postpone or adjourn a hearing the chair or panel shall have regard to:

- the public interest in the expeditious disposal of the case;
- the potential inconvenience caused to a party or any witnesses to be called by that party; and
- the fairness to registrant.[46]

This is a non-exhaustive list.

3.43   Before adjourning proceedings, the chair or panel is required to consider whether or not to make an interim order.[47]

3.44   Whether or not to grant an adjournment is a discretionary decision and will only be interfered with by the appellate courts where there are very clear grounds for doing so. Factors to take into account include:

- the need for expedition in the prosecution of proceedings;
- where an adjournment is being sought by the NMC, the interests of the registrant;
- where the adjournment is being sought by the registrant, whether, if not granted, the registrant will be able fully to present a defence;
- the likely consequences of the adjournment, including the length and any impact a delay may have on a fair trial;
- the reason for the adjournment application and whether it arises out of the fault of the party applying for or opposing the adjournment;
- the history of the proceedings and any previous adjournments; and
- the need to ensure justice between the parties.

For a discussion on cases dealing with this issue see chapter 1.

3.45   A postponement or adjournment may be sought for a variety of reasons, for example to obtain certain evidence, to ensure a specified witness can attend, to ensure that the registrant can attend, to extend the length of the hearing, to put special measures in place, or to obtain or change legal representation. Whatever the reason it is important that the application is made without delay and supported by relevant evidence. An application is less likely to succeed if made at the commencement of a hearing, due to the added factor of the

---

45 NMC (Fitness to Practise) Rules 2004 r32(2).
46 NMC (Fitness to Practise) Rules 2004 r32(4).
47 NMC (Fitness to Practise) Rules 2004 r32(5).

inconvenience to any witness who has attended to give evidence. The
extent to which the registrant has co-operated with proceedings to
date and is engaged with the process will be a relevant factor.

3.46   An application to adjourn may be linked to submissions as
to whether to proceed in the absence of a registrant (see paras
3.49–3.55).

Cancellation of a hearing

3.47   NMC (Fitness to Practise) Rules 2004 r33 provides the panel with
the power to cancel a hearing and close a case on advice from a case
presenter.[48] If this is being proposed, a preliminary meeting will be
held and the complainant will be provided with the opportunity to
comment.[49] Where this occurs there will be no entry made on the
register.

Representation and entitlement to be heard

3.48   Both the NMC case presenter and the registrant have a right to be
heard in any hearing before a practice committee.[50] The registrant
also has the right to be represented by a solicitor or barrister, professional or trade union representative or any other person.[51] The
legal extent and limits of this entitlement is considered in chapter 1.
Where a registrant is not represented, he or she has the right to be
accompanied and advised by any person, save that such person is not
entitled to address the panel without permission.[52] Further, a person
who represents or accompanies a registrant shall not be called as a
witness to the hearing.[53] Therefore if the registrant is accompanied
by a supportive colleague or employer who is intending to provide
evidence, including character evidence, then that person may be
excluded until after he or she has given evidence. A representative
may also be excluded from all or part of the hearing if his or her conduct has disrupted or is likely to disrupt proceedings.[54]

48 NMC (Fitness to Practise) Rules 2004 r33(3).
49 NMC (Fitness to Practise) Rules 2004 r33(4).
50 NMC (Fitness to Practise) Rules 2004 r20(1).
51 NMC (Fitness to Practise) Rules 2004 r20(2).
52 NMC (Fitness to Practise) Rules 2004 r20(3).
53 NMC (Fitness to Practise) Rules 2004 r20(4).
54 NMC (Fitness to Practise) Rules 2004 r20(5).

Absence of registrant

> The panel has the discretion to proceed in the absence of the practitioner but: i) there must be strict adherence to the requirement that all reasonable effort at service has been met; and ii) the decision to proceed must be taken with 'the utmost care and caution' and only after full consideration of the competing interests, with emphasis on those of the practitioner.

3.49   NMC (Fitness to Practise) Rules 2004 r21 provides that where a registrant fails to attend and is not represented, the panel may proceed in his or her absence as long as it is satisfied that 'all reasonable effort' has been made to serve notice in accordance with the NMC Rules.[55] The rule explicitly requires the NMC case presenter to adduce evidence that all reasonable effort has been made such as evidence that notice has been posted, faxed or sent by recorded delivery, it is not sufficient for the panel to be informed that service has been attempted. Service may be proved by confirmation of posting issued by, for example, the post office, confirmation of receipt where notice was sent by email, or a signed statement from the sender or person delivering the notice.[56]

3.50   Even if the panel is satisfied that notice has been correctly served the power to proceed in a registrant's absence is a discretionary power, and should only be exercised in exceptional circumstances and with 'utmost caution and care'[57] (see chapter 1); the alternative is to adjourn and issue directions.[58] This rule does not apply to interim order hearings,[59] which are subject to separate albeit similar provisions under rule 8(6) (see para 3.81). Rule 8(6) also requires the panel to be satisfied that all reasonable efforts have been made to serve an interim order notice, or notice of meeting or hearing, unless the registrant has informed the NMC that he or she does not wish to appear or be heard at the interim order hearing.

3.51   In determining whether to proceed in the absence of a registrant a panel is required to take all the circumstances into account. Factors which should be drawn to the panel's attention include:

---

55 NMC (Fitness to Practise) Rules 2004 r21(2).
56 NMC (Fitness to Practise) Rules 2004 r34(4).
57 *R v Jones* [2002] 2 WLR 524; see also *Tait v Royal College of Vetinary Surgeons* [2003] UKPC 34 and *Raheem v Nursing and Midwifery Council* [2010] EWHC 2549 (Admin).
58 NMC (Fitness to Practise) Rules 2004 r21(2).
59 NMC (Fitness to Practise) Rules 2004 r21(1).

- the nature and circumstances of the absence in particular whether it was deliberate and voluntary;
- whether the adjournment may result in the registrant's attending on the next occasion;
- the likely length of an adjournment;
- whether the registrant is or wishes to be legally represented, or has by his or her conduct waived the right to be represented;
- whether the representative is able to receive instructions and the extent to which he or she is able to present the defence;
- the extent of the disadvantage to the registrant in not being able to give his or her account of events having regard to the nature of the evidence against him or her;
- the risk of reaching an improper conclusion about the absence of the registrant;
- the general public interest and particularly the interest of the complainant and witnesses that a trial should take place within a reasonable time of the events to which it relates; and
- the effect of the delay on the memories of witnesses.

3.52   The leading case is the House of Lords decision in *R v Jones*[60] which approved the factors set out in the Court of Appeal case of *R v Hayward*.[61] These were criminal cases but have been applied to regulator proceedings.[62] For a discussion of the case-law on absence see chapter 1.

3.53   Where a registrant has deliberately and voluntarily absented himself or herself from a hearing, or behaves in such a way as to obstruct the proper course of proceedings, it is likely that the panel will proceed in the registrant's absence. A more difficult question arises in relation to involuntary absence such as ill-health or incapacity. Generally if a registrant is unable to attend for an involuntary reason then the panel will agree to adjourn unless the defendant is represented and asks that the hearing continue. However, the mere fact that a registrant has claimed to be ill does not require an adjournment. If the registrant and his or her representative has failed to attend and the registrant has failed or refused to provide medical evidence, then the panel may conclude that the registrant had voluntarily chosen not

---

60 [2002] 2 WLR 524.
61 [2001] EWCA Crim 168, [2001] 1 QB 862.
62 *Tait v Royal College of Vetinary Surgeons* [2003] UKPC 34. See also *Raheem v Nursing and Midwifery Council* [2010] EWHC 2549 (Admin).

to attend or be represented and to proceed in his or her absence.[63] Therefore, it is always advisable, when applying to postpone or adjourn a hearing due to ill health, to support the application with medical evidence specifically addressing the registrant's fitness to attend the hearing (a medical certificate stating that a registrant is signed off work sick may be not be sufficient).

3.54　It is important to refer panels to the legal tests and emphasise that it is only in rare and exceptional circumstances that the panel may proceed in the absence of the registrant. Fitness to practise hearings are significant hearings, the outcome of which could affect the registrant's livelihood and career; a registrant has the right to be present and represented. Usually a panel will agree to adjourn where there is evidence that the registrant is engaged with the proceedings and there has been no previous application to adjourn.

3.55　Where a registrant is unable to attend a hearing in person (for example, he or she is in custody) then it may be possible to apply to admit evidence via video-link or telephone link either under the general discretion under rule 31(1) or by reference to ECHR article 6 (right to a fair trial).

Public and private hearings

3.56　Under both common law and the ECHR it is viewed as an important safeguard that regulatory hearings be held in public, in order to ensure proper public scrutiny and maintenance of public confidence in proceedings. However, the press and members of the public regularly attend fitness to practise hearings, so protecting the privacy of a registrant and their family can be an issue, and may affect the evidence that they are willing to give. The NMC (Fitness to Practise) Rules 2004 provide panels with express power to hold hearings in private, in certain circumstances. However, a registrant should be made aware that these rules only apply to the hearing; the registrant's name and allegations, decision and any sanctions will still be made publically available if there is a finding that fitness to practise is impaired. Private information such as health conditon will be redacted.

3.57　There is a rebuttable presumption that Conduct and Competence Committee and Investigating Committee hearings will be held in public under rule 19(1). However, rule 19(3) provides that a hearing in whole or in part may be held in private, where the panel is satisfied

---

63　*Yusuf v Royal Pharmaceutical Society of Great Britain* [2009] EWHC 867 (Admin); *Faulkner v Nursing and Midwifery Council* [2009] EWHC 3349 (Admin).

that it would be justified in the interests of any party or of any third party (including the complainant, witness or patient), or in the public interest. Conversely, there is a rebuttable presumption that Health Committee hearings will be held in private under rule 19(2), unless the public interest or interests of any third party outweigh the need to protect the privacy or confidentiality of the registrant. Additionally, more general case-law under ECHR article 6(1) may be relied upon where the interests of a child are at stake. In all cases the relevant panel is obliged to give the parties, and any third party, the opportunity to make representations, and may obtain advice from the legal assessor. The decision, with reasons, will be given in public, subject to private information being appropriately redacted.

3.58   The 'private life' exception enables the panel to take into account the interests of the registrant and their family, and is regularly used where it involved matters of a health or medical nature. The rules do not limit circumstances to ones of a medical nature; the only requirement is that of justification. The 'public interest' exception is likely to be more narrowly construed, and limited to matters such as public interest immunity, national security, witness whose identity needs protecting, and maintenance of public order.

3.59   The decision to hold a hearing in private must be consistent with ECHR article 6(1) and therefore it must be a proportionate response to a legitimate aim. Representatives are advised to consider if there are alternatives, such as anonymising witness evidence, redactions or an application to hold only part of the hearing in private. This may be the case where medical conditions or personal information, form part of the mitigating circumstances but do not relate to the facts of the allegation.

3.60   It may also be necessary to apply to have the rule 19 application in private; this is where the application would refer to the matter for which privacy is being sought.

Impartiality of the panel

The question is whether the fair-minded and informed observer, having considered the facts, would conclude that there was a real possibility that the tribunal was biased.[64]

3.61   Article 6 ECHR provides the right to adjudication by an independent and impartial tribunal. Independence means separated from the executive and from the parties. Impartiality means both subjective

64 *Porter v Magill* [2001] UKHL 67, [2002] 2 AC 357, at para 103, per Lord Hope.

impartiality (the lack of actual bias), and objective impartiality (the lack of the appearance of bias). The courts have accepted that the fact that disciplinary proceedings against registrants are determined by a body which includes members of the same profession does not of itself offend the requirement of 'independence' in article 6(1),[65] and accords with the principle that a governing body is best placed to judge what is right for its profession. For a fuller discussion of the applicable authorities on this point see chapter 1.

Decisions

3.62   The NMC is required to publish, as soon as reasonably practicable, its decision and any orders imposed.[66] Publication is usually done via the NMC website and the decision and any order will be will be linked to a registrant's PIN and therefore generally available to employers and the general public. Further the NMC may disclose to any person information relating to a registrant's fitness to practise which it considers to be in the public interest to disclose.[67]

3.63   Only decisions where fitness to practise has been found to be impaired will be published. If an allegation is dismissed either because the facts are not proved, or the facts as proved do not amount to a lack of competence or misconduct, or current impairment is not established, then no publication is required and all references will be immediately removed from the NMC website, unless the registrant requests otherwise. Once a decision has been made, the NMC does not have the power to rescind that decision unless it was an accidental mistake which did not substantially affect the rights of the parties or the decision arrived at, known as a 'slip'.[68]

Transcripts

3.64   NMC (Fitness to Practise) Rules 2004 r27 provides that all hearings and preliminary meetings shall be recorded in writing or electronic form.[69] Either party may apply to be furnished with a transcript of the

---

65   *Tehrani v United Kingdom Central Council for Nursing Midwifery and Health Visiting* [2001] SC 581. See also *Stefan v General Medical Council (No 1)* [1999] 1 WLR 1293.
66   NMO 2001 article 22(9).
67   NMO 2001 article 22(10).
68   *R (B) v Nursing and Midwifery Council* [2012] EWHC 1264 (Admin).
69   NMC Rules 2004 r27.

whole or part of any hearing that they were entitled to attend.[70] This is particularly useful where a case has gone part-heard, or at review and restoration hearings, since the transcript can be referred to in submissions to remind the panel of the evidence.

Legal assessors

3.65   All panels are advised by a legal assessor, who must be a qualified lawyer.[71] The function of the legal assessor is to advise the panel on questions of law, including procedural matters. Although often called upon to assist in the drafting of the panel's reasons for its decision, the legal assessor does not participate in the decision making itself. For a fuller discussion of the role of the legal assessor see chapter 1.

3.66   Legal assessors are a helpful source of information for the registrant and their advisers. The NMC case presenter should also be present (and vice versa) in any discussion with the legal assessor outside the hearing.

Medical assessors

3.67   The NMC has the power to appointed registered medical practitioners to be medical assessors.[72] The function of the medical assessor is to advise the panel on any matter within their professional competence.

Investigating Committee

Investigating Committee stages

3.68   All cases will initially be referred to the Investigating Committee. Upon receipt of a referral the Investigating Committee is required to serve a notice of referral on the registrant[73] without delay.[74] The notice shall be accompanied by any documents not previously disclosed to the registrant but will not at this stage particularise the allegation. The registrant may make written representations within 28 days of service of the notice of referral. The registrant has further opportuni-

---

70   NMC Rules 2004 r27(2).
71   NMO 2001 article 34.
72   NMO 2001 article 35.
73   NMC (Fitness to Practise) Rules 2004 r3(1).
74   NMO 2001 article 26(2)(a).

ties to make written representations in advance of any Investigating Committee meeting. The registrant will be notified of these meetings, provided with copies of any additional documentation obtained and given 28 days to make written representations. Any representations made by the registrant will be considered by the Investigating Committee. It may also be shown to the complainant for a response. The notices will be served in accordance with the service provisions under rule 34(3), since these are not notices of hearing (see paras 3.29–3.30).

3.69 There are two main Investigating Committee stages:

1) *The initial Investigating Committee meeting* (sometimes referred to as a section 1 meeting, or ICs1). It is following this initial meeting that the registrant will receive the notice of referral. The current practice of the NMC is to refer all matters received for further investigation, unless it involves a criminal conviction, in which case it may be referred directly to the Conduct and Competence Committee.

2) *The final Investigating Committee meeting* (sometimes referred to as a section 4 meeting, or ICs4). If the first Investigating Committee refers the matter for further investigation, further Investigating Committee meetings may occur to review progress of the investigation. After the completion of the investigation, a final Investigating Committee meeting will be held to consider whether there is sufficient evidence to refer the case to the Conduct and Competence Committee or Health Committee for determination. If there is no case to answer then the case will be closed. The registrant will be sent the documentation gathered during the investigation, particulars of the allegation setting out the exact charges alleged. The registrant will be provided with 28 day notice to provide written representations.

3.70 The primary role of the Investigating Committee is to determine whether there is a case to answer on the papers. These meetings are held in private; the registrant is not entitled to attend but is entitled to submit written representations.[75] Many cases are dismissed at this stage, so written representations are advised if there is uncontested or overwhelming evidence to rebut the allegation, or where the allegation is obviously minor or trivial in nature to such an extent that even if proven on the facts it would not support a finding of impairment at the hearing stage. Where a case involves a conflict of fact the

75 NMO 2001 article 26(2)(a); NMC (Fitness to Practise) Rules 2004 r4(1) and (2).

registrant will need to provide clear corroborative evidence to support his or her account, such as contemporaneous nursing records or
statement from a witness. In the absence of corroborative evidence
the case is likely to be referred to a full hearing for witnesses to be
heard and their credibility and reliability tested. Registrants may use
written representations to advise the NMC of evidence held by the
registrant or a third party which could corroborate their position.
Advising the NMC of the location of relevant evidence could allow
the registrant to influence the direction of the NMC investigation at
an early stage. However, caution should be exercised with disclosure
of any information to the NMC and legal advice should be sought
where possible. If written representations are made at this stage, care
must be taken to ensure they are factually accurate and consistent
with the registrant's case, since any inconsistencies may be adduced
at the main hearing. Great caution should be exercised before making submissions that an allegation is minor or trivial in nature since
it could demonstrate lack of insight or understanding of the seriousness of the allegation. Allegations which potentially put patients
at risk, or which involve dishonesty, are sexual in nature, or which
involve a criminal conviction or caution are likely to be viewed as sufficiently serious for a matter to proceed to a full hearing.

3.71   The panel is required to take such steps as are reasonably practicable to obtain as much information about the case prior to making
its decision.[76] The panel may require the registrant to submit to a
medical or professional assessment where the allegation is one of ill
health, drug- or alcohol-related or comprises lack of competence.[77]
The panel may adjourn to enable further information to be obtained
or an assessment / medical report to be provided[78]. Failure to submit
to medical assessment will be considered by the NMC to be a lack of
engagement on the part of the registrant.

3.72   In some circumstances the registrant may be in a position to
apply for a Preliminary Meeting to determine whether there is a case
to answer even before the investigation is completed. There would
need to be a strong basis for such an application. Investigations can
be lengthy and stressful for all concerned and preliminary meetings
may be used as a mechanism for dealing with cases which are obviously without merit.

---

76   NMO 2001 article 26(2)(c).
77   NMC (Fitness to Practise) Rules 2004 r4(2).
78   NMC (Fitness to Practise) Rules 2004 r4(3).

3.73   Following the panel's deliberations, the NMC is required to send the registrant a written notice of decision informing him or her of whether it has decided that there is a case to answer.[79] This will contain the panel's reasons[80] and be provided without delay.[81] The notice may enclose a case management form. Completion of case management forms is important to evidence engagement with the NMC process. The cautions expressed in para 3.70 also apply to written representations made at this stage – a registrant should therefore take advice before completing the case management form.

3.74   If the panel has decided that there is no case to answer, it has the power to take the allegation into account if a further allegation is received within three years of the date of the notice of decision,[82] and to refer both the new and the original complaint to the relevant practice committee for determination.[83] It should be noted that the NMC will often refer to allegations received which are more than three years old, specifically in situations where the referral related to matters found proved at a local level. A registrant in such circumstances should exercise caution in claiming an unblemished career or the absence of any previous concerns relating to misconduct or competence.

3.75   The NMO 2001 provides the Investigating Committee with the option to undertake mediation where there is a case to answer, as an alternative to a referral to a Health or Conduct and Competence Committee. This power is not currently used by the NMC.[84]

3.76   The Investigating Committee will hold a hearing in two defined circumstances: a) when considering whether there has been a fraudulent or improper entry onto the Register and b) when considering interim orders. These are subject to the same procedures as Conduct and Competence Committee and Health Committee hearings, unless otherwise specified.[85]

Fraudulent or improper entry onto the register

3.77   Following referral, the panel has the power to determine an allegation that an entry in the register has been fraudulently procured or

79 NMO 2001 article 26(5).
80 NMO 2001 article 26(5); NMC (Fitness to Practise) Rules 2004 r6(1).
81 NMC (Fitness to Practise) Rules 2004 r6(1).
82 NMC (Fitness to Practise) Rules 2004 r6(2).
83 NMC (Fitness to Practise) Rules 2004 r7.
84 See *NMC annual fitness to practise report 2010–2011* p7.
85 NMO 2001 article 26(4); NMC (Fitness to Practise) Rules 2004 Parts 5 and 6.

incorrectly made.[86] This usually involves an allegation that a registrant does not have the necessary qualification to support his or her inclusion on the register. The procedures are set out in NMC Rules 2004 r5. The panel will initially consider the allegation in private[87] and before making a decision will send any relevant information or document to the registrant and invite him or her to provide comments.[88] If there is a case to answer, the registrant shall be notified[89] and a differently constituted panel will hold a hearing, where a hearing has been requested by the registrant or is otherwise considered desirable.[90] The registrant will be sent a notice of hearing at least 28 days before the hearing and will be informed of the right to attend and be represented.[91] The Investigating Committee has the power to amend the charge on the same basis as the Conduct and Competence Committee[92] (see para 3.104). The NMC will inform the employer and other specified parties of the referral.[93]

3.78   If no hearing is requested or otherwise considered necessary, the panel will invite written representations[94] and meet in private.[95] The panel has the power to dispose of the matter in the absence of written representations from the registrant.[96]

3.79   If a hearing is arranged, then the procedure under NMC Rules 2004 Part 5 applies, in particular rule 22 (witnesses), rule 23 (vulnerable witnesses) and rule 24 (order of proceeding at initial hearing). The standard of proof is the civil standard (balance of probability) under rule 30. If the Investigating Committee is satisfied that an entry has been fraudulently procured or incorrectly made, the panel has the power to order that the registrant's record on the NMC register be removed or amended.[97] The order will not take effect during any appeals period,[98] and the panel may impose an interim order

86 NMO 2001 article 26(7).
87 NMC (Fitness to Practise) Rules 2004 r5(1).
88 NMC (Fitness to Practise) Rules 2004 r5(2).
89 NMC (Fitness to Practise) Rules 2004 r5(5).
90 NMC (Fitness to Practise) Rules 2004 r5(6).
91 NMC (Fitness to Practise) Rules 2004 r5(8) and (9).
92 NMC (Fitness to Practise) Rules 2004 r28.
93 NMC (Fitness to Practise) Rules 2004 r5(7).
94 NMC (Fitness to Practise) Rules 2004 r5(11)(a).
95 NMC (Fitness to Practise) Rules 2004 r5(11)(b).
96 NMC (Fitness to Practise) Rules 2004 r5(11)(b).
97 NMO 2001 article 26(7).
98 NMO 2001 article 26(10).

to cover this period.[99] The registrant will be sent a notice of decision, informing him or her of the decision and the reasons[100] and of his or her right to appeal to the High Court[101] (see para 3.208). If the panel concludes that there is no case to answer or no such entry has been made, it has the power to make a declaration and provide reasons with the consent of the person concerned.[102]

3.80   The panel has the power to review an order imposed by it on receipt of new evidence.[103] This is also subject to an appeals process.

Interim orders

> Interim orders may be made if they are necessary to protect the public or in the public interest or in the registrant's interest prior to the substantive hearing on fitness.
>
> The threshold for an interim order is a high one because a registrant may be temporarily suspended or be subject to temporary conditions that limit or prevent his or her practice.
>
> No judgment is made regarding the facts of the allegation but the panel must be satisfied that, on a fair analysis, there *may* be a prima facie case. The registrant should be given the opportunity to make representations and may adduce evidence.

3.81   Practice committees have the power to impose an interim suspension or conditions of practice order under NMO 2001 article 31, either prior to having reached a decision or at the point where a final disposal decision has been made and a relevant sanction imposed. Therefore an interim order may be imposed by an Investigating Committee on referral even before it has determined whether there is a case to answer, by a Health or Conduct and Competence Committee prior to reaching a decision on fitness to practise, or by any practice committee after reaching a decision and imposing a sanction to cover an appeal period. Where an interim order has been imposed, the review panel has the power to revoke, confirm or vary

---

99 NMO 2001 article 26(11).
100 NMO 2001 article 26(5).
101 NMO 2001 article 26(7).
102 NMO 2001 article 26(8) and (9).
103 NMO 2001 article 26(12).

any condition, and replace an interim suspension order with a conditions of practice order and vice versa.[104]

3.82   Interim orders can have serious consequences for a registrant's
livelihood and career and should only be imposed where the relevant
committee is satisfied that it is necessary for the protection of members of the public, or is otherwise in the public interest, or is in the
interests of the registrant.[105] An order on public protection grounds
requires that there is a real risk to patients, colleagues or other members of the public. The test is whether an order is necessary, not
merely that an order may be desirable. The courts have held that the
wider public interest such as maintaining public confidence in the
profession and upholding standards is only a sufficient reason for
imposing an order in rare circumstances.[106] Therefore in many cases
an interim order can be resisted on the grounds that it is not necessary in all the circumstances. However, registrants and representatives should note that it is the NMC's position that a strict reading of
the case-law suggests that the requirement of necessity only applies
to interim orders made solely on public protection grounds and not
interim orders made on public interest ground or in the interest of
the registrant. In fact the legal position is not currently clear: there
is one line of authority which suggests that necessity is required
(*R (Shiehk) v General Dental Council*[107]) and another which suggests
that desirability is sufficient (*Sandler v General Medical Council*[108]). It
is also unclear as to the extent that this distinction makes a difference
in practice, since there is still a requirement that any order imposed
on an as yet unfounded allegation must be proportionate. For a discussion of these cases see chapter 1.

3.83   Panels are required to take into account factors such as the impact
on the registrant's right to practise, finances and reputation, seriousness of the allegation, nature and strength of the evidence, and
likelihood of the alleged conduct being repeated. An allegation that
is trivial or clearly misconceived should not be given weight. The
approach to be adopted and the factors to take into account are set
out in the NMC *Guidance on interim orders*.[109] If the panel is considering imposing an interim conditions of practice order then it will also

104 NMO 2001 article 31(7).
105 NMO 2001 article 31(2).
106 *R (Shiekh) v General Dental Council* [2007] EWHC 2972 (Admin).
107 [2007] EWHC 2972 (Admin).
108 [2010] EWHC 1029 (Admin).
109 NMC *Guidance to panels considering whether to make an interim order* (adopted
       June 2010).

refer to the NMC *Guidance to panels on conditions of practice orders*[110] and the NMC *Conditions of practice library*.[111]

3.84   If possible, the registrant should provide a reference from his or her employer setting out any mitigating factors, the steps taken by the employer to address relevant concerns and the extent to which a registrant has addressed any acknowledged failure. In a health case it may also be appropriate to provide an up to date medical report confirming a registrant's state of health and any compliance with medication or treatment regimes. References from other professionals, and evidence of the consequences for the registrant were they to be suspended should also be adduced. Any testimonials should include a statement that the writer is aware of the NMC proceedings and the nature of the allegations.

3.85   A suspension order should only be imposed if a panel considers that a condition of practice order is not deemed sufficient and proportionate. If there is a risk that the panel will consider that an interim order is necessary, and the registrant is willing and able to comply with conditions, the registrant or his or her representative may tactically decide to propose suitable conditions. These should address the issues in question and be relevant, proportionate, workable and measurable.[112] Examples include training and supervision (either direct or indirect), auditing of patient records, an assessment of practice, temporary restrictions on an area or type of practice (eg not to administer medication), agreement to undergo a medical assessment, or to comply with suitable medical treatment or attend counselling. Conditions are most likely to be considered suitable where the registrant remains in employment as a nurse or midwife, or has identified such employment.

3.86   In cases where there is an employer or prospective employer, they should be asked to provide a supportive statement confirming that they are willing to put in place the suggested conditions. If the registrant is not in employment, then conditions which do not require third party engagement should be proposed. For example, a condition that the registrant only be permitted to practise in certain areas or roles, or until they have attended a suitable and accredited course. Any concern as to the lack of a named actual or prospective employer can be addressed by imposing a condition that the NMC be notified within a specified time period of employment being offered, and the

110 NMC *Guidance to panels on conditions of practice orders* (approved 18 May 2012).
111 NMC *Conditions of practice library* (approved 18 May 2012).
112 NMC *Guidance to panels on conditions of practice orders*, paras 11–15.

registrant consenting to the potential employer being contacted by the NMC. All conditions of practice orders include a condition that the registrant informs his or her employer or prospective employer of the order, and informs the NMC if he or she changes employer.

3.87   Where a condition requires support or input from a third party the *Guidance to panels on conditions of practice orders* suggests that the NMC should arrange for that third party to be available to comment and if necessary the panel should adjourn the case for up to one hour to enable contact to be made and comments sought. If no contact can be made during this time then the Guidance suggests that the panel may conclude that the condition is unworkable and impose a suspension order. In such circumstances the registrant can seek an early review once evidence of third party cooperation is available. The onus for compliance with any condition will be on the registrant not the third party. Prior to an interim condition of practice order being imposed the panel will provide the registrant and his or her representatives with the opportunity to comment on the draft wording.[113]

3.88   An interim order may be imposed for up to 18 months, and must be reviewed after the first six months then every three months thereafter, or if there is new evidence.[114] Therefore where new evidence comes to light, for example there is a change in employment, a registrant may apply for a review without waiting for the prescribed review hearing. In order to extend an interim order beyond 18 months, the NMC must apply to High Court. Unless revoked or varied by a practice committee or the High Court, the order shall cease to have effect where the relevant practice committee has reached a decision in relation to the allegation in question. Where an order has been made to cover an appeal period, it will cease to have effect when the period has expired or any appeal finally disposed of.[115]

3.89   A registrant has the right to attend an interim order hearing or review hearing[116] and to be represented.[117] The relevant committee is required to send the registrant an interim order notice in accordance with the service provisions under NMC Rules 2004 r34(1), unless the order is being proposed at a hearing where a decision to impose a sanction has been made[118] (see paras 3.198–3.200). The rules provide

---

113 NMC *Guidance to panels on conditions of practice orders* (approved 18 May 2012), paras 20–25.

114 NMO 2001 article 31(2) and (6).

115 NMO 2001 article 31(5).

116 NMO 2001 article 31(15).

117 NMO 2001 article 31(16).

118 NMC (Fitness to Practise) Rules 2004 r8(2).

that the registrant should be provided with such notice as soon as is reasonable in all the circumstances, but there is no specified notice period.[119] Due to the nature of interim orders, it is likely that only short notice will be given. The notice should state the reasons for the order and invite the registrant to attend the hearing or provide written representations.[120] The panel has the power to make or vary an interim order in the absence of a registrant, or any written representations from the registrant, where the panel is satisfied that all reasonable efforts have been made to serve the relevant notice or the registrant has informed the NMC that he or she does not wish to appear or be heard on the question of whether an interim order should be made.[121] There is no need for a registrant or his or her representative to attend a review hearing if the registrant is not contesting the order, and there is no other reason for them to attend. A registrant who has been suspended may find it unduly onerous to attend three monthly hearings merely to have that order confirmed. The registrant should notify the NMC in writing of his or her intentions, in order to demonstrate that he or she is engaging with the regulatory process. In the absence of any representations or communication from the registrant, panels are likely to express concern about the lack of engagement. Any evidence of non-engagement and therefore non-compliance with the Code of Conduct, during the NMC process can be considered by the committee at the substantive hearing.

3.90   The normal procedure[122] is that:

- The NMC case presenter will make representations as to why it may be necessary to impose, revoke, confirm, vary or replace an interim order and may adduce relevant evidence.
- The registrant may then make representations and adduce relevant evidence. The registrant may give oral testimony. Registrants should note that the interim order hearing is not a fact-finding forum, and any attempt by a registrant to adduce evidence is often halted by the panel.
- The legal assessor may provide advice on questions of law.
- The panel will adjourn to deliberate in private and announce its decision with reasons.[123]

---

119 NMC (Fitness to Practise) Rules 2004 r8(4).
120 NMC (Fitness to Practise) Rules 2004 r8(3).
121 NMC (Fitness to Practise) Rules 2004 r8(6).
122 A different procedure is applied whether the interim order is imposed following a decision on sanction pending appeal.
123 NMC (Fitness to Practise) Rules 2004 r26(2).

- Applications under NMC Rules 2004 r19 for hearings to be heard in private are also available to interim order hearings.

The procedures in NMC Rules 2004 Part 5 apply to interim order hearings.[124]

3.91   In considering whether to impose an interim order, the panel will take into account the strength of the evidence, admissions and subsequent steps taken by the registrant to address any concerns. Where the registrant has been charged with a criminal offence, a regulatory body is not 'always obliged' to hear evidence or submissions as to the weaknesses of the case, the panel may assume that there was sufficient evidence to justify charges being brought by the Crown Prosecution Service (CPS)[125] (see chapter 1).

3.92   The registrant must be notified of: the decision, the reasons for the order and the right of appeal to the High Court.[126]

Conduct and Competence Committee and Health Committee

Remit

3.93   Allegations that fitness to practise is impaired by reason of misconduct, lack of competence and/or criminal conviction are dealt with by the Competence and Conduct Committee. Allegations that a registrant's fitness to practise is impaired by reason of physical or mental health are dealt with by the Health Committee. Both committees will consider allegations referred by the council, screeners, Investigating Committee or one another.[127]

Initial referral

3.94   Upon receipt of a referral the Conduct and Competence Committee or Health Committee is required to send the registrant a notice of referral under NMC (Fitness to Practise) Rules 2004 r9. The notice of referral will be served in accordance with the service provisions under rule 34(3) since it is not a notice of hearing (see para 3.29). The notice will require the registrant to notify the NMC within 28 days

---

124 NMC (Fitness to Practise) Rules 2004 r16(a).
125 *Fallon v Horseracing Regulatory Authority* [2006] EWHC 2030 (QB).
126 NMO 2001 article 31(14).
127 NMO 2001 articles 27 and 28.

if he or she would like the allegation to be considered at a hearing. If the registrant does not respond within this time period, then the NMC have the power to determine the matter without a hearing, so it is essential that registrants do respond promptly.[128]

3.95   The notice should contain any further disclosure and invite the registrant to submit written representations within 28 days.[129] The Committee has the power to refer any representations received to the complainant for a response.[130] The Conduct and Competence Committee has the power to require the registrant to submit to an assessment and the Health Committee has the power to require a registrant to submit to a health assessment.[131] Failure to submit to an assessment will be considered as non-engagement. The notice of referral may be sent to the registrant's employer or any other person with whom he or she has arrangements to provide professional services, any other relevant regulatory body and the relevant secretary of state.[132]

3.96   Under rule 10 the Conduct and Competence Committee or Health Committee has the power to hold a hearing or meeting to consider a fitness to practise allegation (referred to in the rules as an initial hearing), or to review any order made by it (eg an interim order or sanction), or to consider an application for restoration to the register.[133] A registrant is entitled to attend a hearing but not a meeting. The committee is required to hold a hearing either where the registrant has requested a hearing within the specified 28-day limit or it considers a hearing to be desirable.[134] If no hearing is requested, or considered desirable, the committee has the power to consider the allegation, review any previous order made by it or consider an application for restoration to the register in the absence of the registrant or his or her legal representative.[135]

Notice of hearing or meeting

3.97   Where a hearing is to be held, the committee is required to send the registrant a notice of hearing not later than 28 days before the hear-

128 NMC (Fitness to Practise) Rules 2004 rr9(2)(d) and 10(2).
129 NMC (Fitness to Practise) Rules 2004 r9(2)(b).
130 NMC (Fitness to Practise) Rules 2004 r9(5).
131 NMC (Fitness to Practise) Rules 2004 r9(4).
132 NMC (Fitness to Practise) Rules 2004 r9(3).
133 NMC (Fitness to Practise) Rules 2004 r10(1).
134 NMC (Fitness to Practise) Rules 2004 r10(2).
135 NMC (Fitness to Practise) Rules 2004 r10(3).

ing.[136] The NMC is required under its rules to provide the registrant with a charge particularising the allegation,[137] although it is likely that this will have already been provided in an earlier notice following investigation stage. The notice should also inform the registrant of the date, time and venue of the hearing,[138] and provide any further relevant documentation or (if relevant) copies of any previous orders made.[139] The registrant should be informed of his or her right to be represented and that the committee has the power to proceed in the registrant's absence.[140] The registrant will be required to inform the NMC within 14 days of his or her intention to attend the hearing and/or be represented.[141] If the registrant is represented, then it is important that the NMC are informed as soon as possible so that the representative can be contacted by the NMC scheduling team to discuss the suitability of the proposed hearing dates. The registrant should also be provided with other information relating to their rights under the rules.

3.98   Where the hearing is a fitness to practise hearing, the notice will be accompanied with a notice to admit facts.[142] Any admissions can be taken into account at the main hearing.[143] Where the allegation, previous order or application for restoration is to be considered by the Health Committee, the registrant will also be asked if he or she wishes the hearing to be conducted in public.[144] Registrants are strongly advised to seek advice before responding. The status of admissions is dealt with at para 3.141.

3.99   Where a meeting is to be held, the registrant will receive a notice of meeting no later than 28 days before the date of the meeting. This will contain more limited information than a notice of hearing but will set out the particulars of the allegation plus a notice to admit facts, enclose any relevant documentation and inform the registrant of the committee's powers. A registrant is not entitled to attend a meeting.

---

136 NMC (Fitness to Practise) Rules 2004 r11(1) and (2).
137 NMC (Fitness to Practise) Rules 2004 r11(3)(b).
138 NMC (Fitness to Practise) Rules 2004 r11(3)(a).
139 NMC (Fitness to Practise) Rules 2004 r11(3)(c).
140 NMC (Fitness to Practise) Rules 2004 r11(3)(d) and (e).
141 NMC (Fitness to Practise) Rules 2004 r11(h).
142 NMC (Fitness to Practise) Rules 2004 r11(3)(l).
143 NMC (Fitness to Practise) Rules 2004 r11(3)(l).
144 NMC (Fitness to Practise) Rules 2004 r11(3)(m).

Reference between Conduct and Competence Committee and Health Committee

3.100   Under NMC (Fitness to Practise) Rules 2004 r14, the Conduct and Competence Committee has the power, at any stage during proceeding, to refer a matter to the Health Committee where it considers that a fitness to practise allegation 'would be better dealt with' by the Health Committee.[145] The test suggests that there is no need for the registrant's physical or mental health to have been the sole cause of the matters that gave rise to the allegations. However, a referral may only be made if the panel is satisfied that it would not make a striking off order in the event that the registrant's fitness to practise was found to be impaired.[146] If a referral is made, the panel will suspend its consideration of the allegation, and is required to resume its considerations only if the Health Committee subsequently certifies that a registrant's fitness to practise is not impaired by reason of his or her physical or mental health.[147] The rules therefore reflect the Privy Council judgment of *Crabbie v General Medical Council*[148] (see chapter 1).

3.101   Under NMC (Fitness to Practise) Rules 2004 r15, the Health Committee has the power, at any stage during proceeding, to refer a matter to the Conduct and Competence Committee where it considers that a fitness to practise allegation 'would be better dealt with' by the Conduct and Competence Committee.[149] The Health Committee will suspend its consideration of the allegation and may only resume consideration if the Conduct and Competence Committee subsequently determines that the allegation is not well founded or has not been proved to the requisite standard.[150] In other words, the matter cannot be considered by the Health Committee if there is a finding on impairment or a sanction is imposed.

3.102   Matters to take into account in considering whether to make an application to refer a matter to the Health Committee include:

- The hearings are usually held in private (see paras 3.56–3.60).
- The panel does not have the power to issue a strike off order unless the registrant has been continuously suspended or subject

---

145 NMC (Fitness to Practise) Rules 2004 r14(1); NMO 2001 article 32(2)(a).
146 NMC (Fitness to Practise) Rules 2004 r14(2).
147 NMC (Fitness to Practise) Rules 2004 r14(1), (3) and (4).
148 [2002] UKPC 45.
149 NMC (Fitness to Practise) Rules 2004 r15(1).
150 NMC (Fitness to Practise) Rules 2004 r15(2).

to a conditions of practice order for no less than two years[151] (see para 3.194).

- The focus will be on the registrant's health, both at the time of the incident and at the time of the hearing, rather than the incident itself. Therefore if there has been a significant improvement in the registrant's health by the time of the hearing, and the health condition is not likely to recur, then it can be argued that there is no current impairment (see paras 3.163–3.172).

- If current impairment is found, then the sanction imposed should be linked to the registrant's health. This makes it unlikely that no further action or a caution will be imposed, on the other hand conditions of practice or suspension orders may be reviewed early if the registrant's health improves (see paras 3.201–3.203).

- Arguably less stigma is attached to a finding that fitness to practise is impaired on grounds of health rather than on grounds of conduct or competence.

3.103   If a registrant does wish his or her case to be referred to the Health Committee, then such an application should be made early in the proceedings and well in advance of the hearing date, and should be supported by medical evidence (such as a letter or report from his or her GP, occupational health adviser or a medical expert). Preliminary meetings can be used to request a transfer to the Health Committee. A preliminary meeting can be requested at any stage in the proceedings up to the hearing date. The case management form contains a section in which it is possible to request a preliminary meeting to make submissions on a transfer to the Health Committee.

Charges

> The particulars of the allegation and the facts upon which they are founded should be clear and settled in advance of any hearing.
>
> If in doubt, clarification and/or further and better particulars should be obtained.
>
> The panel may, having heard from both parties, amend either the allegation or the facts provided no injustice is caused but this should be the exception not the rule.

3.104   The notice of hearing will contain the text of the charge which is in three parts:

---

151 NMO 2001 article 29(6).

1) The factual particulars, such as the date, the patient/person and the incident. Often a single incident will give rise to a number of particulars, for example 'on date X, when visiting patient A, the registrant failed to a) conduct a specified procedure; b) make a record of that procedure; c) notify the appropriate person'. In responding to a charge, the registrant will therefore need to consider each separate particular.
2) Whether the factual particulars constitute lack of competence, misconduct, physical or mental health, police caution or conviction (the statutory ground).
3) Whether as a result of the statutory ground the registrant's fitness to practise is impaired.

3.105   NMC (Fitness to Practise) Rules 2004 r28 provides the panel with the power to amend a charge set out in the notice of hearing any time prior to the findings of fact stage, unless having regard to the merits of the case and the fairness of proceedings the amendment would be unjust.[152] The parties are entitled to make representations prior to any decision.[153] Where a charge has been poorly drafted, is duplicitous or otherwise wrong, it is advised that representations be first made to the NMC case presenter either before or at the hearing, since an application to amend is more likely to succeed if the parties agree. Such representations can also be made prior to the hearing at a preliminary meeting. For a consideration of the case law on charging see chapter 1.

3.106   Rule 29 provides the panel with the power to join allegations. It permits allegations against two or more registrants to be joined unless there is a risk of prejudice to the fairness of the proceedings. Joinder is permitted where the allegation against each registrant arises out of the same circumstances or a joint hearing is otherwise necessary.[154] It permits more than one category of allegation to be heard in a single hearing, with the exception of allegations of a conviction or caution which should only be heard after any allegation of misconduct has been determined.[155] New allegations of a similar kind, or founded on the same facts, may be considered by the panel even if it is not included in the notice of hearing.[156] For a consideration of the case-law on amendment of the charge see chapter 1.

---

152 NMC (Fitness to Practise) Rules 2004 r28(1).
153 NMC (Fitness to Practise) Rules 2004 r28(2).
154 NMC (Fitness to Practise) Rules 2004 r29(1).
155 NMC (Fitness to Practise) Rules 2004 r29(2).
156 NMC (Fitness to Practise) Rules 2004 r29(3).

Delay

> ECHR article 6 and domestic case-law confer a right to a hearing within a reasonable time, however to stay proceedings is an exceptional course and delay is not a ground unless there is material prejudice to the extent that no fair trial is possible.

3.107   There is no requirement under the NMC rules for a hearing to be held within a specified timescale. In the case of *Toth v General Medical Council*[157] the court held that both the legitimate expectation of complainants and the public confidence in the regulation of the medical profession require that the complaint should, in the absence of some special and sufficient reason, be publicly investigated. It would undermine that important principle if mere unreasonable delay, absent prejudice, were to require a stay to be granted.

3.108   It may take months or even years for a case to be heard. However the NMC, like other regulatory bodies, is subject to domestic and European case-law which confers the right to a hearing within a reasonable time. Where the delay becomes unreasonable, then a registrant may be able to apply for a stay of the proceedings on grounds of an abuse of process. In order to succeed in such an application the delay must be not merely unreasonable but also prejudicial.[158] A stay of process will only be granted in exceptional circumstances where a fair trial is not possible.[159] Where the regulator or complainant is not responsible for the delay then it is highly unlikely that such an application will succeed. However, delay may be taken into account as mitigation at the sanction stage. For a consideration of the case-law on delay see chapter 1.

Exclusion of evidence

3.109   Panels should not consider prejudicial matters which have not been charged[160] (for a consideration of case-law on charging see chapter 1). Therefore a registrant will be entitled to request that unrelated prejudicial evidence be redacted. The NMC will usually agree to redact references to interim orders and disciplinary decisions by employers,

---

157   [2001] 1 WLR 2209.
158   *R (Toth) v General Medical Council* [2000] EWHC 361 (Admin).
159   *R (Johnson) v Professional Conduct Committee of the Nursing and Midwifery Council* [2008] EWHC 885 (Admin).
160   *Chauhan v General Medical Council* [2010] EWHC 2093 (Admin); *Roomi v General Medical Council* [2009] EWHC 2188 (Admin).

but representations may need to be made in relation to other prejudicial matters. However, if there is an acceptable explanation for what would otherwise be prejudicial or irrelevant material, it may be preferable to adduce that explanation rather than seek redactions. This is a matter of judgment, but sometimes having large sections of a document banked out, or witnesses alluding to other matters, can cause more prejudice since the panel may form the view that registrant has something to hide.

3.110   Ideally any disputes over admissibility of evidence should be resolved prior to the hearing (if need be at a preliminary meeting), otherwise an application to exclude evidence will need to be made before the very panel which the registrant wishes to exclude the evidence from. In some circumstances this may result in the panel that has seen the prejudicial evidence having to recuse itself resulting in the hearing being adjourned, sometimes for several months to another date.

3.111   The panel is permitted to refuse to admit evidence from a registrant where there has been a failure to comply with directions issued at a preliminary meeting and there is no good cause for the failure to comply.[161] Therefore if the registrant is seeking to adduce evidence which is subject to a direction then any reason for the non-compliance should be provided along with evidence.

Witnesses

3.112   Except in relation to the author of an expert report, the NMC does not have power under its rules to require the attendance of a witness.[162] This is in contrast to other regulatory bodies. The NMC can apply to the High Court for a witness summons.

3.113   Witnesses attending a hearing will be required to take an oath or affirm before giving evidence.[163] A witness will be examined by the calling party, cross-examined, re-examined and questioned by the panel.[164] Any further questioning is at the discretion of the panel.[165] The panel may of its own motion require a witness to attend or produce relevant documents.[166] The NMC rules have recently been amended to include a greater discretion for panels prior to the

---

161 NMC (Fitness to Practise) Rules 2004 r31(8).
162 NMC (Fitness to Practise) Rules 2004 r18(5)(e).
163 NMC (Fitness to Practise) Rules 2004 r22(1).
164 NMC (Fitness to Practise) Rules 2004 r22(3).
165 NMC (Fitness to Practise) Rules 2004 r22(4).
166 NMC (Fitness to Practise) Rules 2004 r22(5).

determination of sanction to request evidence from third parties as to the impact which a registrant's alleged actions had on them.[167] This amendment appears to be similar to victim impact statements used in criminal proceedings, however it is too early to tell how, or if, these powers will be used by panels.

3.114   There is no express provision under the NMC (Fitness to Practise) Rules 2004 as to how witness evidence is to be adduced. The NMC is not bound by the Civil Procedure Rules which provide for statements to be tendered as evidence in chief, and arguably rule 31(1) only applies to the admission of evidence not the means by which it may be adduced (see para 3.116). In the past, when the criminal burden of proof applied, it was accepted that the criminal rules of evidence also applied. With the change in the burden of proof, some NMC case presenters have attempted to argue that panels should now follow civil rules of evidence. Whatever approach is adopted, it should be agreed between the parties in advance of the hearing. There are considerable benefits in insisting that evidence be adduced orally since it ensures that evidence is given in the witness' own words and that the questions asked are not leading, enabling the panel to assess the quality of the evidence given. The giving of evidence should not be a memory test and a witness can always refer to their statement to refresh their memory. On the other hand, a registrant or representative may be prepared to agree that a witness read their statement, for example where there is no significant dispute of fact and it would save time.

3.115   Witnesses are not permitted to attend the hearing until they have completed the evidence.[168] The panel may direct, on application by a party, that details that may identify a witness should not be revealed in public.[169] This is regularly used to protect the identity of patients.

Proceeding the absence of a witness

> The panel has the discretion to proceed in the absence of a witness and to admit hearsay evidence, but the decision to proceed must be taken with 'the utmost care and caution' and only after full consideration of the competing interests with emphasis on those of the registrant.
>
> There must be compelling reasons to deprive a registrant of the opportunity to cross-examine a witness – this all the more so if the case or its consequences are serious.

167 NMC (Fitness to Practise) Rules 2004 r24(13).
168 NMC (Fitness to Practise) Rules 2004 r22(6).
169 NMC (Fitness to Practise) Rules 2004 r22(2).

3.116 Under NMC (Fitness to Practise) Rules 2004 r31(1) oral, documentary or other evidence is admissible as long as it is 'relevant and fair'. This includes evidence that would not otherwise be admissible in civil proceedings, and permits the panel to admit hearsay evidence and to allow witness statements to be read where a witness is unable to attend. The central requirement of 'fairness' in determining whether to admit evidence in such circumstances was emphasised in the Court of Appeal case of *Ogbonna v Nursing and Midwifery Council*.[170] It was held that rule 31(1) does not establish a more general principle to admit hearsay evidence, and that the determination of fairness is fact-sensitive. It will depend on the nature of the evidence and considerations such as the reason for the non-attendance of a witness and what steps were taken to secure the attendance of a witness.

3.117 Although there is no absolute right under ECHR article 6 or common law to cross-examine a witness, there would need to be compelling reasons to deprive a registrant of the opportunity to cross-examine a witness whose evidence was central to the issues to be determined.[171] Where such evidence is admitted, it is likely to carry less weight by virtue of the fact that it has not been tested in cross-examination. For a consideration of the case-law on absent witnesses and hearsay see chapter 1.

Vulnerable witnesses

3.118 Special measures may be made where a witness is vulnerable. NMC Rules 2004 r23 defines a 'vulnerable witness' as:

- any witness under the age of 18;
- a witness with a mental disorder or who is significantly impaired in relation to intelligence or social functioning;
- a witness with physical disabilities who requires assistance to give evidence;
- a witness who is the alleged victim where an allegation is sexual in nature; and/or
- a witness who complains of intimidation.[172]

---

170 [2010] EWCA Civ 1216.
171 *R (Bonhoeffer) v General Medical Council* [2011] EWHC 1585 (Admin).
172 NMC (Fitness to Practise) Rules 2004 r23(1).

3.119   The panel has the power to adopt such measure as it considers necessary to enable it to receive the evidence.[173] Such measures may include:[174]

- the use of video links;
- pre-recorded evidence in chief, provided the witness attends for cross-examination and questioning (note: an un-represented registrant is not permitted to cross-examine the alleged victim where the allegation is sexual in nature.[175] In such circumstances the panel will appoint an appropriate person.[176] There is no provision for the alleged victim to provide written consent to be cross-examined by the registrant);
- the use of interpreters including signers; and
- the hearing of evidence in private, albeit in the presence of the parties and their representatives.[177]

This is a non-exhaustive list.

3.120   It is likely that vulnerable witness measures will be determined at a preliminary meeting. It is a discretionary power, and legal principles established by criminal cases are likely to be relevant to decisions on special measures, since the legal provisions are similar, see chapter 1.

Expert evidence

3.121   A party may seek to adduce evidence from a medical or professional assessor, or other expert evidence. The panel is not obliged to admit this evidence and an expert's opinion is only admissible where the opinion is likely to furnish information that is outside the panel's experience and knowledge.

3.122   An expert should be provided with the hearing bundles and, if relevant, the registrant's medical records. If required, the expert should arrange for a consultation with the registrant.

3.123   An expert should be reminded of his or her duty to provide independent evidence irrespective of the party that calls them. Further, that the expert is only entitled to give opinion evidence within the expert's area of expertise.

173 NMC (Fitness to Practise) Rules 2004 r23(2).
174 NMC (Fitness to Practise) Rules 2004 r23(3).
175 NMC (Fitness to Practise) Rules 2004 r23(4).
176 NMC (Fitness to Practise) Rules 2004 r23(5).
177 NMC (Fitness to Practise) Rules 2004 r23(6).

Preparation

3.124   NMC fitness to practise hearings are public hearings, and if a registrant is representing himself or herself it is advisable for the registrant to attend another hearing to become familiar with the layout of the room and the process.

3.125   Prior to a hearing the registrant will receive the Investigating Committee bundle containing witness statements and documentation (referred to as exhibits). If a registrant does not dispute the evidence provided by a witness, then the NMC should be notified that their statement can be agreed. If a statement or exhibit contains irrelevant or prejudicial material, then the NMC should be requested to redact that evidence. The NMC should be asked to confirm that the redactions apply to not just the factual stage but also the impairment and sanction stages. The case management form identifies the name of a case presenter who will be presenting the case for the NMC. While the named individual is often not the case presenter who appears at the hearing, registrants or their representatives may wish to contact the case presenter to discuss issues identified in the NMC documentation. Early discussions about evidence and documentation can prevent the need to have such discussions on the day of the hearing, and can therefore reduce inefficiency in the proceedings.

3.126   A registrant should draft a witness statement or proof of evidence. These are important hearings that could affect the registrant's livelihood and reputation. The statement should have an introductory paragraph setting out his or her experience and/or expertise, the statement should then address the allegations, in particular identifying which, if any, facts are admitted and those that are denied, and setting out any mitigating circumstances. Where an allegation is admitted on the facts, the statement should include evidence of insight (see para 3.168). Even where evidence in chief is to be given orally, it will assist the registrant if they have already set down their thoughts in writing.

3.127   In addition to a witness statement, registrants are advised to produce their own bundle of exhibits which should include any additional documentation relevant to the allegations, documentation of subsequent employment, relevant training certificates, testimonials and any other relevant documentation. Unless subject to a direction at a preliminary meeting, there is no requirement on a registrant to have served on the NMC evidence in advance of the hearing, and NMC panels do not currently receive documents in advance of a hearing.

3.128   If a registrant is represented a pre-hearing conference should be arranged to take full instructions and to ensure that he or she is fully prepared for the hearing.

Fitness to practise hearings

Pre-hearing and housekeeping matters

3.129   It is always advisable to get to a hearing at least 30 minutes before commencement. The first day is often a frustrating and bewildering experience. There will usually be housekeeping and documentary issues to resolve. Some hearing centres have no dedicated waiting room for registrants or their witnesses, so it is advisable to meet in advance in order to confirm instructions and provide advice. Coffee, tea and lunch should be provided.

3.130   Currently there is no agreed hearing bundle (although the NMC is moving towards this). A registrant will often be served with a differently paginated hearing bundle on the first day of the hearing, this should contain only those documents previously disclosed, but the registrant may need to ask for extra time to check the bundle before the hearing commences. If there are redactions, then these should be checked to ensure that the changes are agreed. If the registrant objects to any documents within the bundle, the NMC cannot put the document before the panel but must first make an application to the panel for the document to be submitted. The registrant will be provided with an opportunity to explain their objections to the panel prior to a decision being made.

3.131   The registrant or his or her representative should introduce himself or herself to the NMC case presenter, who is the person who will be prosecuting the case on behalf of the NMC. They should provide him or her with copies of any additional documentation to be relied upon, and if appropriate inform him or her of the registrant's response to the allegations or any change in position to the allegations. This provides an opportunity for the NMC to indicate its position – eg any intention to offer no evidence, or a view that a particular allegation will be put on the grounds of lack of competence rather than misconduct. It may be that the parties can reach agreement on certain procedural issues, such as the wording of proposed amendments to the charges, an application to hold the hearing in private, or an application to adjourn.

3.132   The registrant or his or her representative should also introduce himself or herself to the NMC council officer, sometimes known as the panel secretary, who is the person responsible for the administration of the hearing, and may assist with reasonable requests to photocopy last minute documents.

3.133   Finally, the registrant or his or her representative should also introduce himself or herself to the legal assessor. Any legal issues should be discussed with the assessor in the presence of the NMC case presenter. The legal assessor is often influential in the legal advice that they provide to hearings and can provide invaluable assistance to representatives and registrants in resolving legal issues. However, there is no requirement for a representative to agree or accept the legal advice of an assessor. If the case raises a legal issue, it is always advisable to bring to the hearing copies of any case to be relied upon and it is good practice to provide a copy to the legal assessor and NMC case presenter prior to addressing the panel.

3.134   If the registrant or representative has failed to attend on time, or more time is needed to take instructions or to sort out documentary or other preliminary issues before the hearing commences, then the NMC council officer should be informed. The panel may require the parties to appear in front of him or her and explain the reason for the delay.

3.135   If the registrant or representative wishes to leave the hearing centre during an adjournment it is always advisable to inform the NMC council officer in case the matter is called on.

Overview of the procedure

3.136   Fitness to practise hearings should be conducted in accordance with the NMC's primary function which is to safeguard the health and well-being of persons using or needing the services of the registrant. In exercising its function the panel is required to have proper regard to both the interests of service users and those of the registrant.[178]

3.137   Present at a fitness to practise hearing will be:

- the committee panel, which will be made up of at least one registrant (a nurse or midwife), one non-registrant (lay person) and the chair who may also count as either the registrant or non-registrant. A Health Committee panel will also include a registered medical practitioner;

178 NMO 2001 article 3.

- the legal assessor;
- the registrant and his or her representative;
- the NMC case presenter;
- the NMC council officer;
- the transcriber.

3.138   Under NMC Rules (Fitness to Practise) 2004 r24(1), the hearing shall be conducted in the following stages:

1) the preliminary stage;
2) the factual stage;

and, if one or more of the facts are found proved:

3) the impairment stage;

and, if the registrant is found to be currently impaired:

4) the sanction stage.

The preliminary stage

3.139   Following introductions, the registrant will be asked to confirm his or her name and personal identification number. The panel will then ask if there has been correct service of the notice (usually demonstrated by the fact that the registrant and/or representative has attended).

3.140   The charges will then be read out and the registrant will be asked if there is any objection to the charge on a point of law.[179] Normally there will be no objection, however this is the point at which arguments over the wording of a charge or an application to amend a charge may be made. The case presenter and the registrant or his or her representative may be asked to make representations and the legal assessor may be asked for advice. Unless the application is unopposed and straightforward, the panel will adjourn to deliberate in private and will then announce its decision and give reasons.[180]

3.141   Once the wording of the charge has been resolved, the registrant will be asked to indicate if he or she is making any admissions as to the alleged facts, whether it is accepted that any admitted facts amount to misconduct, lack of competence or ill health, and whether it is accepted that his or her fitness to practise is impaired.[181] If the facts are partially admitted, then this should be stated at the outset.

179 NMC (Fitness to Practise) Rules 2004 r24(2).
180 NMC (Fitness to Practise) Rules 2004 r24(3).
181 NMC (Fitness to Practise) Rules 2004 r24(4).

While partial admissions will not be recorded as an admission, it helps to identify which matters are in dispute and require the panel to resolve them. In many cases there will be mixed admissions and denials, not just in relation to the factual particulars but also lack of competence may be admitted but misconduct denied, or the particulars may be admitted but impairment denied. Admissions are often taken as an indication of insight (see para 3.168), however a registrant should only admit those matters that he or she accepts. Where facts are admitted, the chair shall announce that such facts have been found proved.[182]

3.142   Other matters that may need to be raised at the preliminary stage are applications to hold the hearing in private, to adjourn, that the proceedings are an abuse of process or on other evidential matters.

The factual stage

3.143   The NMC case presenter will open the NMC's case and present evidence in support of the allegations including those admitted by the registrant.[183] The panel does not see witness statements or documentation in advance of the hearing. Documents will be given exhibit numbers as they are adduced. The first exhibit is likely to be a document identifying any patients who are referred to in the evidence, by reference to a letter of the alphabet.

3.144   Unless there is a submission of no case to answer (see paras 3.161–3.162) the registrant will then present his or her case and present evidence in support.[184] There is no requirement on a registrant to give evidence on his or her own behalf at a hearing; the burden is on the NMC at all times to prove its case. If a registrant does give evidence, then he or she will be subject to cross-examination and questions from the panel, which may result in prejudicial evidence being adduced. Whether the registrant gives evidence is a matter of judgment, and in most cases a registrant will be advised to do so, particularly where there are disputes of fact which the panel will need to resolve. Further, a registrant is advised to give evidence where there is mitigating and explanatory evidence which the registrant can provide, or where the registrant is able to demonstrate insight and understanding. If the registrant does give evidence, then this should

---

182 NMC (Fitness to Practise) Rules 2004 r24(5).
183 NMC (Fitness to Practise) Rules 2004 r24(6).
184 NMC (Fitness to Practise) Rules 2004 r24(9).

be as full as possible – bare denials without explanation or insight are unlikely to be viewed positively by the panel.

3.145   Where a registrant does decide to provide evidence, his or her evidence in chief may be adduced either by oral questions or reading out the registrant's statement. The registrant will then be cross-examined by the NMC case presenter and usually there will be questions from the panel. Sometimes the panel will adjourn in order to decide what questions to ask and it is likely that the member of the panel from the profession will ask questions about the registrant's practice. The registrant may then call any additional witnesses of fact to give evidence on the registrant's behalf.

3.146   Following completion of the evidence on the facts, the panel may invite both parties to make final submissions.[185] Such submissions may be oral and/or in writing. Written submissions are not expected but are useful where there is a point of law that the panel need to consider, or where a case has gone part-heard. The panel, NMC case presenter and legal assessor should be provided with a copy of any cases referred to. If a case has gone part-heard and the panel are referred to evidence contained in the transcript, then the relevant page and line number should be referred to. In general the purpose of a closing submission is to persuade the panel to draw certain conclusions from the evidence they have heard by identifying consistencies in the registrant's case and inconsistencies in the NMC's case. The panel should also be addressed on any evidential issues such as hearsay, witness credibility and relevance, along with any other legal points. There is no need to refer to cases where a legal principle or test is well-established. The fact-finding stage does not usually involve much law, and un-represented registrants will not be expected to have a detailed knowledge of legal issues (the legal assessor will usually inform the panel of any legal issues that they need to consider).

3.147   Usually closing submissions will address both the facts as set out in the particulars of the allegation and whether they amount to a NMO 2001 reason. However, sometimes tactically it may be advisable to separate these processes, since submissions on the reasons may depend on what disputed facts are found proven. This is most likely to occur where a registrant accepts lack of competence but denies misconduct. The panel should be informed of this approach at the outset and why it may be in the interests of justice to depart from the norm.

185 NMC (Fitness to Practise) Rules 2004 r24(10).

3.148   In all cases the panel will invite the legal assessor to advise on any question of law.[186] The legal assessor will usually remind the panel of the burden and standard of proof, identify any evidential issues that need to be resolved and identify the key legal authorities on the reasons, such as misconduct or lack of competence, and any other issue. The parties will then be given the opportunity to indicate if they agree with the advice of the legal assessor and to make further representations if they disagree.

3.149   In all cases the panel will adjourn to deliberate in private, and then announce their decision with reasons.[187] The legal assessor sits in on these deliberations but plays no part in the decision-making. The legal assessor may at the request of the panel assist in drafting any decision. The legal assessor will inform the parties in open session of any advice given during these private deliberations.

3.150   The fact-finding stage is likely to be the lengthiest part of the hearing and will deal with whether the facts which make up the allegation are proven to the required standard, determine background facts and determine whether the facts as found amount to misconduct and/or lack of competence. The focus should be on the facts of the allegation. Even where the facts are admitted the registrant should adduce at this stage mitigating evidence which limits the degree of seriousness of an allegation or culpability. If facts are denied, the registrant should be clear about what is denied particularly where there are mixed admissions and denials. The registrant should also be clear as to whether they are admitting misconduct or lack of competence and why.

3.151   'Misconduct' and 'lack of competence' are not defined by the NMC Rules, and they are potentially very wide concepts comprising any departure from good professional practice whether or not it is covered by the NMC standards. However, not all breaches of NMC standards necessarily constitute misconduct and/or lack of competence. Further, not all misconduct or lack of competence will be of the level of seriousness to impair fitness to practise, ie to warrant action on the register that could affect a registrant's future practice and/or livelihood. Therefore, although the test does not refer to 'serious' conduct, a level of seriousness is required and the GMC cases in this area are persuasive[188] (see chapter 1). Further, there is

---

186 NMO 2001 article 34(2).
187 NMC (Fitness to Practise) Rules 2004 r24(11).
188 *Nandi v General Medical Council* [2004] EWHC 2317 (Admin); *R (Calhaem) v General Medical Council* [2007] EWHC 2606 (Admin).

a distinction to be made between misconduct and lack of competence.[189] This is important not only because lack of competence carries a lesser range of sanctions, but also because there is slightly less
stigma attached to lack of competence. For a consideration of the
case-law on the distinction between misconduct and competence see
chapter 1. It is therefore possible in suitable cases to argue that the
facts as found were either not sufficiently serious to constitute misconduct or lack of competence, or that they amount to lack of competence but not misconduct.

3.152   Mitigation arising from the circumstances in which the practitioner found himself or herself may be relevant to the level of culpability,[190] and therefore could be relevant to the issue as to whether
the facts amount to misconduct and/or lack of competence. Evidence
of past or subsequent good practice may also be relevant, although
more general character evidence is unlikely to be relevant at this
stage. Circumstances such as high workload or personal difficulties may explain why the conduct in question arose, but will seldom
excuse the conduct due to the requirement under the NMC Code that
registrants be 'personally accountable for actions and omissions' in
their practice and must always be able to justify their decision.[191] A
registrant whose workload was too high would be expected to have
raised this with his or her superiors and to have refused to do anything that could call the registrant's fitness to practise into question.
A registrant experiencing difficult personal circumstances would be
expected to have sought appropriate help or taken time off. Further,
too much emphasis on mitigating factors could undermine a registrant's ability to demonstrate insight. The approach to be adopted
will depend on the facts of the case against the registrant.

3.153   In almost all cases, complaints about the way the employer or
service provider may have investigated an allegation will be of little
relevance. The panel will not be interested in whether a fair investigation was conducted unless it affects the quality of the evidence that
they are being invited to consider. For example, if the NMC seeks to
draw inferences from certain evidence provided during an investigatory interview the way the interview was conducted may be relevant
to explain why that evidence is unreliable. Another area may be the

---

189 *Priess v General Dental Council* [2001] UKPC 36; *R (on the application of
    Calhaem) v General Medical Council* [2007] EWHC 2606 (Admin); *Remedy UK
    Ltd v General Medical Council* [2010] EWHC 1245 (Admin).
190 *Campbell v General Medical Council* [2005] EWCA Civ 250.
191 NMC Code, page 2.

failure of an investigator to pursue an obvious line of enquiry, which therefore undermines the conclusion that the investigator came to.

Conviction cases and determinations by another regulator

3.154   Convictions include those that occur in a court outside the UK, but where the offence is recognised as a crime in the UK,[192] as well as convictions by a Court Martial.[193] Where a registrant has been convicted of a criminal offence, a copy of the certificate of conviction shall be conclusive proof of the conviction and findings of facts upon which the conviction is based and is admissible as proof of those facts.[194] The only evidence that a registrant may adduce in rebuttal is that they were not the person referred to in the certificate.[195]

3.155   A similar approach is adopted in relation to placement on a barred list[196] (see chapter 1), and determinations by another UK regulatory health or social care body or licensing body elsewhere.[197]

Health cases

3.156   Where the allegation that fitness to practise was impaired due to physical or mental health, the factual background will be relevant but is likely to be largely admitted. Therefore the main focus will be on the particular health condition in question, and whether it caused or contributed to the alleged facts. If the expertise of an expert is required and the registrant has been assessed by an NMC medical assessor it is likely that he or she will be called to give evidence. The registrant may need to call their own medical expert if the NMC assessor's report is disputed.

3.157   If a medical expert is to be called then the following evidence should be adduced:

- the expert's professional qualifications and area of specialisation;
- what documentation the expert has considered, whether the expert has personally assessed the registrant, and whether the expert has had any prior involvement with the registrant;
- diagnosis and prognosis, and whether the medical condition in question caused or contributed to the factual allegations; and

---

192 NMO 2001 article 22(1)(iii).
193 NMO 2001 article 22(2).
194 NMC (Fitness to Practise) Rules 2004 r31(2).
195 NMC (Fitness to Practise) Rules 2004 r31(3).
196 NMC (Fitness to Practise) Rules 2004 r31(3A) and (3B).
197 NMC (Fitness to Practise) Rules 2004 r31(4).

- whether a registrant's current fitness to practise is impaired by reason of ill health, and the likelihood and extent of recurrence of the medical condition, steps that the registrant has already taken to reduce recurrence, and any further steps that can be taken.

Burden of proof

3.158 According to NMC Rules 2004 r30, the NMC has the burden of proving any facts relating to an allegation which is in dispute. The NMC Rules make this explicit, whereas for other regulators this is implicit. The rule relates only to 'facts' of an allegation. The decision as to whether those facts amount to misconduct or lack of competence, and whether a registrant's fitness to practise has been impaired, is a matter for the panel's judgment.

3.159 The standard is the civil standard of balance of probabilities, ie whether the fact in issue more probably occurred than not. The approach to be adopted in applying the civil standard has been set out in the House of Lords decisions of *Re B (children)*[198] and *Re D (Secretary of State for Northern Ireland intervening)*[199] and has been quoted with approval in the regulatory context in *Hosny v General Medical Council.*[200] It is a single standard and does not change with the seriousness of the allegation. These cases are considered in chapter 1. There is an exception to the above in that there remains a very small number of 'legacy cases', ie cases which pre-date the change in the NMC Rules in 2004 where the criminal burden of proof (beyond reasonable doubt) continues to apply.

Good character

3.160 Good character evidence (ie whether or not the registrant has been subjected to previous regulatory proceedings or criminal proceedings) is relevant to the issue of credibility and whether, where there is a dispute of fact, the registrant is to be believed (see chapter 1). If the registrant is of good character then this evidence should be adduced.

198 [2008] UKHL 35.
199 [2008] UKHL 33.
200 [2011] EWHC 1355 (Admin).

No case to answer

> Submissions of no case to answer may be made in respect of a case or a specific allegation. They may be made where a) there is no evidence, or b) there is some evidence but it is weak, vague or inconsistent and, looked at 'in the round', a panel *could* not properly find the case (or fact) proved.

3.161 At the conclusion of the NMC's case, the registrant, or the panel on its own volition, may indicate that there is no case to answer either on the basis of whether 'sufficient evidence' has been presented to find the facts of an allegation proved,[201] and/or to support a finding of impairment.[202] The panel will hear submissions from both parties and the legal assessor may give advice as to the appropriate test to be applied.

3.162 Prior to the change in the burden of proof from the criminal to the civil standard, it was well established that the test to be applied was that set out in the criminal case of *R v Galbraith*.[203] This is whether a) there was any evidence upon which a panel could find matters proved, or b) whether there was some evidence, but of such an unsatisfactory nature that the panel properly directed could not find the matter proved. This is still the test applied by the other regulators however the NMC has sought to argue that the *Galbraith* test no longer applies following the change to the civil burden of proof and suggests that the approach of the civil courts in *Benham*[204] should be adopted. This merely requires that there be established a prima facie case, a case to answer, a 'scintilla' of evidence from which an adverse inference could be drawn and/or sufficient evidence to call for an explanation.[205] It is respectfully suggested that this ignores the disciplinary nature of NMC proceedings which are more akin to criminal cases than civil disputes of a contractual or tortious nature. It also ignores the requirement under the NMC's own rules for there to be 'sufficient evidence' (for further consideration of these cases see chapter 1).

---

201 NMC (Fitness to Practise) Rules 2004 r24(7).

202 NMC (Fitness to Practise) Rules 2004 r24(8).

203 [1981] 1 WLR 1039, [1981] 2 All ER 1060. See also *Tutin v General Medical Council* [2009] EWHC 553 (Admin). The test in the GMC rules was 'sufficient evidence'.

204 *Benham Ltd v Kythira Investments Ltd* [2003] EWCA Civ 1794, [2004] CP Rep 17.

205 *Benham Ltd v Kythira Investments Ltd* [2003] EWCA Civ 1794 at para 39.

The impairment stage

3.163   The panel will only consider impairment where the facts of one or more allegations were held to be well-founded. Even where impairment is admitted by the registrant the panel is still required to reach its own determination, since this is a matter of judgment rather than fact. The panel can of course take into account the admission. The panel is also entitled to take into account a breach of the standards set out in the NMC Code or other standards, guidance or advice produced by the NMC.[206] While a breach of standards does not in itself establish that a registrant's fitness to practise is impaired, it is persuasive and registrants are advised specifically to address in evidence any breach of NMC standards.

3.164   Impairment is not defined by legislation or the NMC Code, however there is considerable case-law on this issue (see chapter 1). Crucially it is well-established that it is a present-day test, since the wording of the NMO 2001 only provides powers to investigate an allegation that the registrant's fitness to practise '*is* impaired'.[207] Therefore the purpose of fitness to practise proceedings is not to punish the registrant for past wrongdoings but to protect the public or profession where a registrant's current fitness to practise is impaired. In reaching this decision the panel can take into account the past wrongdoing, but it is also required to take into account other relevant factors such as whether the conduct in question is easily remediable, whether it has been remedied and the likelihood of repetition.[208] Therefore it is a forward-looking test.[209] Some conduct may be incapable of being easily remedied. In other cases, even if the conduct in question is capable of remedy, and has been remedied, the nature of the conduct may be such that such steps carry little weight. This is where the conduct involved a fundamental breach of professional standards, such that the need to maintain public confidence in the profession overrides the interests of the registrant[210] (see chapter 1).

206 NMO 2001 article 22(4); NMC Rules 2004 r31(7).

207 NMO 2001 article 22(1)(a).

208 *Cohen v General Medical Council* [2008] EWHC 581 (Admin). See also *Zygmunt v General Medical Council* [2008] EWHC 2643 (Admin) and *Sarkodie-Gyan v Nursing and Midwifery Council* [2009] EWHC 2131 (Admin).

209 *Meadow v General Medical Council* [2006] EWCA Civ 1390; *Cheatle v General Medical Council* [2009] EWHC 645 (Admin).

210 *Council for Healthcare Regulatory Excellence v Nursing and Midwifery Council* [2011] EWHC 927 (Admin).

3.165   Under NMC (Fitness to Practise) Rules 2004 r24(12) the parties are given the opportunity to call evidence in relation to whether a registrant's fitness to practise is impaired and make further representations. It is unlikely at this stage that the NMC will call further witnesses. Whether the registrant wishes to adduce further evidence may be a tactical decision. It will depend on whether or not the registrant has any insight into their conduct and/or is able to give evidence that his or her current fitness to practise is not impaired. It may also depend on whether sufficient insight has already been demonstrated at the fact-finding stage, or the findings of fact identify issues that the registrant now needs to address.

3.166   Again the parties may be invited to make closing submissions and the legal assessor will be invited to advise on legal matters. There are a large number of legal authorities dealing with impairment (see chapter 1) and it is more likely at this stage that there will be some reference to the legal tests and case-law by both the NMC case presenter and the legal assessor. Representatives and registrants who are representing themselves should familiarise themselves with the key legal issues. The panel will adjourn to deliberate in private and will announce its decision and give reasons.[211]

3.167   Relevant evidence that the registrant may seek to adduce at this stage includes:

- written or oral evidence that explains the registrant's thought processes at the relevant time, and demonstrates an understanding of why the conduct constituted misconduct and/or lack of competence;
- what the registrant would do differently if in the same position again, including any evidence that the registrant has found himself or herself in a similar position and acted differently;
- what, if any, steps the registrant has subsequently taken to change his or her practice or behaviour. This may include seeking medical assistance, attending counselling, direct or indirect supervision, audits/assessment of work, mentoring, self-reflection, personal research and/or training. If possible, provide documentary evidence in support, such as medical records, reports from counsellors, supervisors, mentors, appraisals and supervision sessions, training certificates and relevant documentation, evidence of research conducted and reflection pieces;
- character evidence relevant to the conduct in question, such as evidence that the registrant acted out of character or to demonstrate

211 NMC (Fitness to Practise) Rules 2004 r24(12)(b) and (c).

that the registrant is capable of learning from his or her mistakes (although more general character evidence is only relevant to the sanctions stage);

- relevant evidence of surrounding circumstances and mitigation, if not already adduced at the fact-finding stage; and
- oral or written evidence from other health professionals, supervisors, managers or other appropriate persons which confirms steps taken and that the registrant has insight.

Insight

3.168   An important consideration at this stage in the proceedings (and also at the sanction stage) is the issue of 'insight'. A minor matter may become more serious in the eye of the panel if the registrant fails to demonstrate insight, by repeated denials or trivialising, whereas a serious matter may be made less serious if a registrant demonstrates insight. This is basically an understanding of the gravity of the conduct in question, an appreciation of what caused the registrant to act as he or she did, and a willingness to act differently in future. Where factual matters have been denied it may be difficult for a registrant to demonstrate insight and therefore it is important that the basis of any denial is made clear and whether the registrant, despite the factual denials, accepts the findings that have been made against him or her. If there are mitigating factors then these should be presented along with an understanding of the personal responsibility of the registrant for ensuring that such factors do not affect their practice in future.

Competence cases – additional considerations

3.169   NMC (Fitness to Practise) Rules 2004 r31(6) provides that in determining whether fitness to practise is impaired by reason of lack of competence, the panel may take into account any refusal by a registrant to submit to a professional assessment of his or her practice. If there has been such a refusal the registrant should explain the registrant's reasons.

Health cases – additional considerations

3.170   NMC (Fitness to Practise) Rules 2004 r31(5) provides that in determining whether fitness to practise is impaired, a panel of the Health Committee may take into account:

- a refusal by a registrant to submit to medical examination;
- the registrant's current physical or mental condition, any continuing or episodic condition suffered by the registrant; and

- a condition suffered by the registrant which although currently in remission may be expected to recur to the impairment of the registrant's fitness to practise.

This is a non-exhaustive list and other health matters may be taken into account, for example the reason why the registrant refused to submit to medical examination, the extent to which a registrant is complying with medical or professional practitioners, the nature of the condition and the registrant's insight into that condition, the steps taken by the registrant to limit the impact of that condition on his or her work, the registrant's relationship with other health professionals and patient care.

3.171 If the registrant has a long-term or recurring condition, then it is likely that he or she will fall within the definition of disability under the Equality Act 2010.[212] The mere fact of having a disability does not mean that a registrant's fitness to practise as a midwife or nurse is impaired, and if possible registrants and their representatives should adduce medical evidence to this effect. The tricky area is where a registrant with a disability is perfectly fit to practise but only where reasonable adjustments are made by the employer or service provider. If the registrant is in employment, then evidence from an employer that they are willing to make such adjustments would be helpful. The registrant may be in a more difficult position where either an employer is not prepared to make the necessary reasonable adjustments or where the registrant is not in employment. In the past, the emphasis by health regulators on a registrant's health and fitness, without regard to the need for reasonable adjustments, has been criticised by the former Disability Rights Commission.[213]

3.172 On a separate point, in some cases it may be necessary for the NMC to make reasonable adjustments to enable the registrant to fully participate in the process. If a registrant does require any special arrangement to be made, they or their representative should inform the NMC case officer.

---

212 Discrimination law is outside the scope of this work.
213 Council's response to the former Disability Rights Commission's *Formal investigation into the regulation of professionals' health in nursing, teaching and social work, maintaining standards: promoting equality* published in September 2007.

The sanction stage

> The principal aims of sanctions are to protect the public, uphold the standards and reputation of the profession and to maintain public confidence therein.
>
> The punitive effect of sanctions is only one (and not the most important) factor to be borne in mind when assessing whether a sanction is proportionate to the matters found proved against a registrant.

Process

3.173   Where a panel has concluded that a registrant's fitness to practise is impaired, the panel will proceed to consider what, if any, sanction to impose. The panel may decide that it is not appropriate to take any further action.[214] Alternatively if further action is required the panel must make one of the following orders:

- a caution order;
- conditions of practice order;
- suspension order; or
- striking-off order.[215]

3.174   In imposing an order the panel may specify a period of time within which an application to vary, replace or revoke the order may not be made.[216] The panel shall direct the registrar to record the decision on the register.[217]

Key principles

3.175   Panels are required to consider the least restrictive sanction first.[218] In considering which if any sanction to impose the panel must have regard to the public interest. Public interest is defined as:

- protecting members of the public;
- maintaining public confidence in the professions and the NMC; and
- declaring and upholding proper standards of conduct and behaviour.

---

214   NMO 2001 article 29(4)(b).
215   NMO 2001 article 29(5).
216   NMO 2001 article 29(7).
217   NMO 2001 article 29(8).
218   *Giele v General Medical Council* [2005] EWHC 2143 (Admin).

Since the principle function of sanctions is not punitive but to protect the public interest, mitigation evidence carries less weight than in other jurisdictions. However, the public interest may include consideration of the skills of the registrant.[219] The NMC Indicative Sanctions Guidance to Panels acknowledges this but states that its main objective is public protection and maintaining public confidence and professional standards.[220]

3.176   While a sanction should not be punitive, it undoubtedly has that effect. Panels are required to have regard to the interests of the registrant and act proportionately. This requires panels to balance the interests of the public against those of the registrant . Thus any interference with a registrant's practice should be no more than is necessary in the public interest. The courts generally accept that the regulator is best placed to decide what level of sanction is necessary and proportionate in all the circumstances. Case-law from other regulatory bodies will be relevant to the issue of sanction (see chapter 1).

3.177   In considering sanction, the panel should generally take into account the NMC *Indicative sanctions guidance.*[221] The *Indicative sanctions guidance* requires panels to refer to it in every case after having found impairment. This has been accepted by the courts as a valuable reference point, and registrants and their representatives are advised to read it prior to making submissions. It emphasises that the panel must always exercise its own personal judgment when making a decision. The guidance sets out criteria to take into account in considering which, if any, sanction to impose, including the seriousness of the allegations, early admissions, insight, relevant references and testimonials. Specific guidance is provided in relation to cases involving dishonesty, sexual misconduct and/or criminal conviction, (for a discussion of the case law in this area, see chapter 1). In addition, in every case panels are required to take into account the extent to which a registrant has departed from the NMC standards and other guidance (see para 3.10).

Process

3.178   The panel has the power to invite any person who has an interest in the proceedings to submit written representations.[222] This permits the panel to receive 'victim impact statements'. The panel may

219 *Giele v General Medical Council* [2005] EWHC 2143 (Admin).
220 NMC *Indicative Sanctions Guidance to Panels*, para 23.
221 *Indicative sanctions guidance for panels*, NMC, approved 18 May 2012.
222 NMC (Fitness to Practise) Rules 2004 r24(13)(a).

hear further evidence from the parties as to previous history (including previous findings of impairment) or mitigating circumstances
or other relevant factors.[223] Unless the evidence is contentious, it is
usually sufficient for it to be adduced by means of representations.
Testimonials and character evidence should be adduced either in
documentary form or by live evidence from witnesses.

3.179   There is no limit to the character evidence that may be adduced
at this stage, but the most compelling will be that from other health
and social care professionals with whom the registrant has worked.
Other appropriate persons may be managers, patients, local dignitar-
ies, other employers and neighbours. If the registrant is involved in
charitable work, a reference from that charity. Referees should state
that they are aware of the allegations, set out their relationship to the
registrant, and state how long they have known the registrant. An
appropriate witness attending a hearing in order to show support
for the registrant can be powerful evidence. The indicative guidance
suggests that panels should take into account of how recent the testimonials are, the expertise of the writers, whether the writers are
aware of the allegations and how their letters are to be used. In addition to character references, other evidence of character is also useful,
such as 'thank you' letters from patients, or expressions of gratitude
from colleagues. The absence of references or testimonials should
not, however, count against a registrant.

3.180   The panel is required to provide the parties with the opportunity
to make submissions identifying relevant factors which may affect
the panel's decision.[224] Currently NMC case presenters take a neutral
stance and do not seek to persuade the panel to adopt a particular
sanction, although they may comment on the appropriateness of
sanctions proposed by or on behalf of the registrant, and will remind
the panel of the sanctions available and of any aggravating and mitigating circumstances. The legal assessor will then be invited to advise
the panel on any legal issues. The panel will adjourn to deliberate in
private and announce its decision and give reasons.

3.181   In all cases, a finding of impairment may be taken into account in
any subsequent proceedings, even if no further action is taken or any
order imposed has lapsed. Moreover NMC case presenters will ask
panels to take into account any other relevant background matters
such as allegations found proven at local disciplinary level, even if

---

223 NMC (Fitness to Practise) Rules 2004 r24(13)(c).
224 NMC (Fitness to Practise) Rules 2004 r24(13)(b).

not referred to the NMC or which had been dismissed by the NMC following a submission of no case to answer.

No further action

3.182 Panels are not required to impose a sanction in every case. No further action may be decided where there is a relatively minor breach of the code of conduct, which has been fully admitted and remedied. It is only in rare cases where taking no action will be appropriate, and in general registrants whose fitness to practise has been found to be impaired should be warned to expect a sanction of some sort to be applied.

Caution order

3.183 A caution order may be imposed for not less than one year and not more than five years.[225] The length will reflect the seriousness of the allegation. It has serious consequences for a registrant since any current or prospective employer will need to be informed of its existence, and the order will be recorded on the register and therefore in the public domain. The advantage of a caution order over a conditions of practice or suspension order is that it does not place any other restrictions on a registrant's practice and does not require a review (see paras 3.196–3.198). Once the period has passed, the order lapses and no other action is required.

3.184 The *Indicative sanctions guidance* suggests that a caution order may be appropriate where the case is at the lower end of the spectrum and there is no risk to the public or patients.[226]

Conditions of practice order

3.185 A conditions of practice order may be imposed for not more than three years at a time.[227] There is no restriction on what constitutes a condition but it should address the panel's concerns about the registrant's practice. It can be restrictive, or remedial, or both. Conditions must be relevant, proportionate, workable and measurable. The NMC has produced *Guidance to panels on conditions of practice orders.*[228] Suitable conditions may include a requirement to undertake further training, to be subject to supervision and reports, to comply with medical or

---

225 NMO 2001 article 29(5)(d).
226 NMC *Indicative sanctions guidance to panels*, para 64.
227 NMO 2001 article 29(5)(c).
228 NMC *Guidance to panels on conditions of practice orders* (approved 18 May 2012)

professional assistance, or place a restriction on an area of practice. A list of commonly used conditions can be found in the NMC *Conditions of practice library* document.[229] Both these documents are available from the NMC website.[230]

3.186   The *Indicative sanctions guidance* states that the key consideration is whether imposing conditions is sufficient to protect patients and the public interest. A conditions of practice order may be appropriate where:

- there is no evidence of harmful deep-seated personality or attitudinal problems;
- there are identifiable areas of practise in need of assessment and/ or retraining;
- there is no evidence of general incompetence;
- there is potential and willingness to respond positively to retraining;
- there is insight;
- there is no direct or indirect risk to patients;
- patients will be protected for the duration of the order;
- it is possible to formulate and monitor the conditions.

This list is non-exhaustive and not all factors have to be present.[231]

3.187   Where conditions of practice are being sought by a registrant (as the most appropriate or favourable outcome), it is advisable to adduce evidence from the registrant that they are willing to comply with any proposed conditions. Further evidence from his or her employer, line manager or other appropriate professional should be provided confirming that they are aware of the proposed conditions and willing and able to provide the necessary support or facilities to enable a registrant to comply with those conditions. Examples may include agreeing to provide a regular audit of patient notes done by a registrant or provide mentoring, supervision or training. In many cases the employer or professional will be asked to provide a report to the NMC at appropriate intervals confirming the registrant's compliance and progress.

3.188   Where a registrant has been subjected to an interim conditions of practice order, the operation of that order and compliance may be relevant evidence. Unless the registrant has adduced this evidence at

---

229 NMC *Conditions of practice library* (approved 18 May 2012).
230 www.nmc-uk/hearing/How-the-process-works/sanctions.
231 NMC *Indicative sanction guidance to panels*, paras 66–67.

an earlier stage in the proceedings the panel will be unaware of any such order.

3.189   Conditions of practice orders are subject to review and can be revoked, modified or replaced. The panel has the power to specify a period of time of up to two years within which no application to vary, replace or revoke may be made.[232] This power is rarely exercised. If for any reason the registrant is unable to comply with the conditions of practice order, the NMC should be informed as soon as possible. Unless the panel has imposed a restriction, an early review should be sought with an application to vary the terms of the order. A registrant who simply fails to comply with an order runs the risk that the order will be extended or replaced by a more severe sanction.

Suspension order

3.190   A suspension order is an order removing the registrant's name from the register for a specified period of time of up to one year at any one time.[233] The panel has the power to specify a period of time of up to ten months within which no application to vary, replace or revoke the order may be made.[234]

3.191   The *Indicative sanctions guidance* states that key considerations are whether imposing a suspension order is required due to the seriousness of the case and sufficient to protect patients and the public interest. The guidance suggests that a suspension order may be justified for the purposes of conveying a clear public message of the importance of fundamental standards of professional conduct.[235] A suspension order may be appropriate where:

- there has been a single instance of misconduct but where a lesser sanction is not sufficient;
- the misconduct is not fundamentally incompatible with continuing to be a registered nurse or midwife, and that the public interest can be satisfied by a less severe outcome than striking off;
- there is no evidence of harmful deep-seated personality or attitudinal problems;
- there is no evidence of repetition of behaviour since the incident;
- there is insight and no significant risk of repetition of behaviour;
- in health cases and competence there would be a risk to patients were the registrant to continue to practise even with conditions;

232 NMO 2001 article 29(7)(c).
233 NMO 2001 article 29(5)(b).
234 NMO 2001 article 29(7)(b).
235 NMC *Indicative sanctions guidance to panels*, para 73.

This list is non-exhaustive and not all factors have to be present.[236]

3.192   A suspension order is often imposed where striking off is too harsh but no condition of practice can be devised or is appropriate. If a registrant is not working as a nurse or midwife, either because he or she has been subjected to an interim suspension order or for other reasons, then conditions of practice which require a supportive employer will often not be deemed suitable. Therefore there is a risk that if a caution order is not appropriate then the only realistic alternative is a suspension order. Short suspension orders are designed to punish and should generally be resisted, however sometimes a short suspension order may be preferable to a lengthy conditions of practice order. Representatives should always discuss with registrants the approach to be adopted in relation to sanctions.

3.193   A panel is not permitted to impose conditions of practice alongside a suspension order. However, often the panel will provide guidance on any expectations or actions that may be taken that may assist a future panel in any subsequent review. While a registrant is not required to comply with this guidance it is strongly suggested that they do in order to achieve the most favourable outcome to the review, bearing in mind that the panel at any review will have the power to impose a further sanction, including a further period of suspension.

Striking-off order

3.194   A striking-off order is an order removing the registrant from the register for an indefinite period, preventing them from working as a nurse or midwife. Under NMO 2001 article 33(2) the registrant may not apply for restoration for a period of five years, unless new evidence comes to light. The panel may specify a longer period of time within which no application to vary, replace or revoke the order may be made.[237]

3.195   A striking-off order may not be imposed where fitness to practise is impaired by reason of lack of competence or mental or physical health, unless the registrant has been continuously suspended or subject to a conditions of practice order for no less than two years.[238] Therefore, earlier in the proceedings, there may be tactical advantages to an application to transfer a matter to the Health Committee or admitting lack of competence but denying misconduct. The *Indicative sanctions guidance* suggests that the two-year period under article

236 NMC *Indicative sanctions guidance to panels*, paras 74–75.
237 NMO 2001 article 29(7)(a).
238 NMO 2001 article 29(6).

29(6) includes time that a registrant has been subjected to an interim order, however it is highly unlikely that this interpretation is correct. Registrants and their representatives should argue that the two-year period only runs from the date that the substantive sanction order was imposed.

3.196 Striking-off orders should be reserved for the most serious cases. The *Indicative sanctions guidance* states that key considerations are whether it is the only sanction sufficient to protect the public interest, whether the seriousness of the case is incompatible with ongoing registration and whether public confidence in the profession can be sustained if the registrant is not struck off the register. A striking-off order is likely to be appropriate when the conduct is fundamentally incompatible with being a nurse or midwife. The guidance suggests that this may occur where the conduct involves any of the following:

- a serious departure from the relevant professional standards, guidance and advice;
- doing harm (physical, emotional or financial) to others or behaving in a way that could foreseeably result in harm to others particularly patients and other professionals;
- an abuse of a position of trust or violation of the rights of a patient particularly vulnerable patients;
- serious misconduct of a sexual nature including involvement in child pornography;
- any violent conduct whether towards members of the public or patients, where the public interests can only be satisfied by removal;
- dishonesty, especially where persistent or covered up;
- persistent lack of insight into seriousness of their actions or consequences; and/or
- criminal convictions or cautions involving any of the conduct set out above

This list is a non-exhaustive list.[239]

3.197 The *Indicative sanctions guidance* states that there is case-law that supports the removal of health professionals from the register where there has been a lack of probity, honesty or trustworthiness even where there are no concerns about their clinical skills or risk of harm to patients.[240] For a consideration of the case law in this area see chapter 1.

---

239 NMC *Indicative sanctions guidance to panels*, paras 74–75.
240 NMC *Indicative sanctions guidance to panels*, para 76.

Interim orders during the appeal period

3.198   The registrant has the right to appeal against any sanction order imposed within 28 days of the date that the notice of the order or decision is served.[241] Service is deemed to be the date that the letter arrives at the registrant's address. It is important that a registrant considering appeal makes a note of the date that they receive the letter confirming the outcome of the hearing. Therefore no sanction order will have effect until the end of the 28-day appeal period, and if an appeal is lodged within that period until the appeal has been finally disposed of. To cover this period the panel has the power to impose an interim order which will take effect during the 28 days and any further appeal period. The interim order is likely to be on the same terms as the substantive order. The test is the same as that which applies to interim orders generally (see paras 3.81–3.92), and an interim order may only be imposed where it is considered by the panel to be necessary for the protection of the public or is otherwise in the public interest or in the interests of the person concerned.

3.199   In practice, an interim suspension order is likely to be imposed where a suspension or striking off order has been made. It is separate from, and additional to, the substantive order. Therefore where a short suspension order has been made this may result in the interim order being longer than the suspension and in such cases it may be possible to argue that an interim order is unnecessary. Whether an interim conditions of practice order is considered necessary where a substantive conditions of practice order has been imposed will often depend on the particular circumstances and terms of the order. The terms of an interim conditions of practice order are likely to be the same as the substantive order, although representations should be made if such terms are not appropriate for an interim order.

3.200   Where a panel is considering imposing an interim order then it is required to invite representations from the parties and take such representations into account. The panel should be informed if there are any particular reasons why an interim order should not be imposed, for example if the registrant has patients booked or needs a period of time to arrange cover for his or her practice. The panel will adjourn to deliberate in private and then announce its decision and the reasons for that decision.

241 NMO 2001 article 29(10).

Review hearings and restoration hearings

Review hearings

3.201　NMO 2001 article 30 provides that a review hearing will be held to review a conditions of practice order or suspension order prior to the end of the specified time period,[242] or on application by the registrant, or otherwise, may set the matter down for a review.[243] Thus a review hearing is mandatory prior to an order expiring and may occur in other circumstances such as where a registrant applies for a variation to a conditions of practice order or the NMC requests a review due to any non-compliance by the registrant. At a review hearing the panel has the power under article 30(4) to:

- confirm the current order;
- extend or further extend the period of the current order;
- reduced the period of the current order, save that a caution order may not be reduced to less than one year beginning on the date that the order was made;
- replace the order with any order that it could have made at the initial hearing;
- vary any condition imposed by the current order; or
- revoke either the order or any condition imposed by the order, save that the panel may make revocation of a suspension order subject to the registrant satisfying the NMC standards on additional education, training or experience.[244] This arises because the registrant will have had a period of non-practice, and therefore may be in breach of the NMC standards were he or she to resume practice without undergoing additional education or training. If a registrant is in the position to comply with such education, training or experience requirements during the period of suspension then the registrant should do so in order to avoid further delay at the end of the suspension period. This could include ensuring that his or her portfolio is up-to-date. Where a registrant cannot afford to attend training courses, online training may be freely available.

3.202　The panel may not extend a conditions of practice order for more than three years at a time, or a suspension order for more than one

242　NMO 2001 article 30(1).
243　NMO 2001 article 30(2).
244　NMO 2001 article 30(6).

year at the time.[245] Therefore the power to extend an existing order could result in the overall period being for longer than the period stated when the order was imposed. However, it is submitted that the panel must have an evidential basis for repeated extensions and such extensions should not amount to the equivalent of a striking-off order or semi-permanent restriction on a registrant's practice.

3.203　　In order to avoid an unfavourable outcome to the review hearing, registrants should adduce evidence of compliance with NMC orders, such as a report from their employer, further testimonials from colleagues and health professionals, or other steps taken to address the issues in question. If a registrant was able to continue to work as a practitioner then clearly evidence as to his or her conduct since the NMC proceedings and further references and testimonials from health professionals and colleagues will be helpful. Even where a registrant has not been able to work as a health professional, a letter or statement from a current employer is still useful character evidence, particularly where the area of concern is not specific to their practice. Therefore, if the registrant had been found to be dishonest, evidence as to their honesty will be relevant along with evidence as to their general approach to the NMC proceedings and lessons learnt. Where the registrant was found to be lacking in competence due to finding themselves in a stressful situation or with too much work, evidence of dealing with stressful situations or managing workload will be relevant.

Restoration hearings

3.204　A restoration hearing will be held to consider an application to restore a registrant onto the register. In considering whether to grant an application to restore, the panel will have to satisfy itself that the registrant:

a) holds an approved qualification as is required under NMO 2001 article 9(2)(a);

b) is capable of safe and effective practice as required by article 9(2)(b); and

c) having regard to the circumstances that led to the registrant's removal, is a fit and proper person to practise in the relevant profession.[246]

---

245 NMO 2001 article 30(5).
246 NMO 2001 article 33(5).

The panel also has the power to require that the registrant satisfies any additional post-registration education and training requirements imposed under article 19(3),[247] and has the power to impose a conditions of practice order.[248]

3.205 Where an application for restoration to the register has been rejected at a review hearing, a further application may not be made for the next 12 months.[249]

3.206 The normal procedure at a review or restoration hearing is that:

1) the NMC case presenter will inform the panel of the background to the case, the sanctions previously imposed, and refer to relevant evidence including transcripts from previous hearings;
2) the registrant or their representative may then make representations and adduce relevant evidence; the registrant may give oral testimony;
3) the legal assessor may provide advice on questions of law; and
4) the panel will adjourn to deliberate in private and announce its decision with reasons.[250]

The provisions of Part 5 of the NMC rules apply to review and restoration hearings.[251]

Notice of decision

3.207 The Conduct and Competence Committee or Health Committee is required to give the registrant and the complainant a notice of the decision setting out reasoning and informing the registrant of his or her rights to appeal.[252] This notice is usually sent out within seven days of a hearing.

Appeals

3.208 A registrant has the right of appeal to the High Court against any order or decision of the panel.[253] The time limit is 28 days from the

247 NMO 2001 article 33(6).
248 NMO 2001 article 33(7)(b).
249 NMO 2001 article 33(2)(b).
250 NMC (Fitness to Practise) Rules 2004 r25(2).
251 NMC (Fitness to Practise) Rules 2004 r12(2).
252 NMC (Fitness to Practise) Rules 2004 r13.
253 NMO 2001 article 38(1) and (4).

date of the notice of decision. Alternatively the Council for Healthcare Regulatory Excellence (CHRE), soon to be renamed the Professional Standards Authority for Health and Social Care,[254] may appeal an 'unduly lenient' decision. The appellate court has the power to allow or dismiss the appeal, remit the appeal back to the appropriate NMC Committee or to substitute the decision by one that could have been made.[255] Therefore there is a risk that an appeal against a sanction could result in a harsher sanction being imposed.

Costs

3.209   Since the various healthcare regulators bring proceedings in the public interest, to protect the public or to uphold standards etc, they are not in the position of an ordinary litigant prosecuting a claim. Unless a complaint is improperly brought, no order for costs is normally made against the regulator.[256]

254 Health and Social Care Act 2012 s222.
255 NMC 2001 article 38(3).
256 *Walker v Law Society* [2007] EWCA Civ 233.

The Health and Care Professions Council

continued

Key points

- *Regulator:* Health and Care Professions Council (HCPC)
- *Professions regulated:* 15 (plus social workers from August 2012) including physiotherapists, paramedics and radiographers
- *Common sources of referral:* Patients, employers, police
- *Type of proceedings:* Fitness to practise
- *Relevant legislation:* Health Professions Order (HPO) 2001 SI 2002 No 254
- *Fitness to Practise Rules:* Health Professions Council (Investigating Committee) (Procedure) Rules 2003 (Schedule to SI No 1574); Health Professions Council (Conduct and Competence Committee) (Procedure) Rules 2003 (Schedule to SI 2003 No 1575); Health Professions Council (Health Committee) (Procedure) Rules 2003 (Schedule to SI 2003 No 1576)
- *Two-stage process:* Investigation and hearing
- *Investigating Committee:* Yes (HPC (Investigating Committee) Rules 2003)
- *Hearing panels:* Conduct and Competence Committee or Health Committee
- *Key documents: Standards of performance, conduct and ethics* (2008) (apply to all registrants); *Standards of proficiency* (specific to each profession)
- *Location:* Main hearing centre: HCPC offices Kennington, London. Panels also sit outside London
- *Notice of hearing provision:* HPC (Investigating Committee) Rules 2003 r5
- *Case management provisions:* HPC (Investigating Committee) Rules 2003 r7
- *Procedure before a Fitness to Practise Panel:* HPC (Investigating Committee) Rules 2003 r8; HPC (Conduct and Competence Committee) Rules 2003 r10; and HPC (Health Committee) Rules 2003 r10
- *Test:* Whether fitness to practise is impaired by reason of (in summary) a) misconduct; b) lack of competence; c) a criminal conviction or caution; d) physical or mental health; e) a determination by another regulator (HPO 2001 article 22(1)(a))
- *Interim order power:* Yes – interim conditions of practice or interim suspension (HPO 2001 article 31) heard by Interim Orders Panel
- *Interim order guidance:* Practice note on interim orders

- *General composition for final hearings:* Three-member panels, minimum one lay partner and one from the relevant profession
- *How to address panel:* Generally seated and 'Sir'/'Madam'
- *Independent legal assessor:* Yes
- *Evidence:* HPC (Investigating Committee) (Procedure) Rules 2003 r8; HPC (Conduct and Competence Committee) (Procedure) Rules 2003 r10; and HPC (Health Committee) (Procedure) Rules 2003 r10; civil admissibility plus other evidence where necessary to protect the public
- *Half-time submission provision:* None specific, but permitted
- Sanction provisions: HPO 2001 article 29
- *Sanction documents: Indicative sanctions policy*
- *Review hearings:* HPO 2001 article 30
- *Restoration hearings:* HPO 2001 article 33
- *Appeal rule:* HPO 2001 article 38
- *Costs:* No general provision

Introduction

Establishment

4.1   The Health Professions Council (HPC) was established in April 2002[1] as a successor to the Council for the Professions Supplementary to Medicine (CPSM). The CPSM had been established in 1960 and by the time of its demise was responsible for regulating 12 different professions. As of 1 August 2012 the HPC became the Health and Care Professions Council (HCPC) and regulates 16 professions, including all of those that previously came under the jurisdiction of the CPSM (albeit with a name change in one case).

Current issues

4.2   As of 1 August 2012 social workers will come under the remit of the HCPC. In 2010 the government published *Liberating the NHS: report of the arm's length bodies review*,[2] which recommended the transfer of the regulatory functions of the General Social Care Council (GSCC) to the HCPC (with an appropriate name change to reflect the widening

---

1   Under the Health Professions Order 2001 (HPO 2001) 2002 SI No 254.
2   Department of Health, 26 July 2010.

of the scope of its jurisdiction). The Health and Social Care Act 2012 contains the relevant provisions relating to the abolition of the GSCC and the broadening of the remit of the renamed Health and Care Professions Council (HCPC). The register transferred on 1 August 2012.

4.3　　　Any references to HPC in this chapter should accordingly be read to cover the HCPC.

4.4　　　The Law Commission consultation on changes to the statutory framework for healthcare regulators closed on 31 May 2012. The outcome is unknown (report not anticipated until February 2014) but it seems likely that in future there will be more consistency between regulators operating under a single statutory regime.

Jurisdictional reach

4.5　　　The 15 professions currently regulated by the HCPC are:

1) arts therapists;
2) biomedical scientists;
3) chiropodists/podiatrists;
4) clinical scientists;
5) dieticians;
6) hearing aid dispensers;
7) occupational therapists;
8) operating department practitioners;
9) orthoptists;
10) paramedics;
11) physiotherapists;
12) practitioner psychologists;
13) prosthetists/orthotists;
14) radiographers;
15) speech and language therapists.

Social workers will be added from August 2012.

4.6　　　The total number of professionals who come under the jurisdiction of the HCPC is in excess of 215,000 (which will increase significantly when social workers are added) and the size of the individual professions ranges from the relatively niche such as hearing aid dispensers (1,587 as at March 2012) and prosthetists/orthotists (901) to the much more familiar physiotherapists (the largest numerically at 45,002) and paramedics (16,782). All of the professions have at least one legally protected title, and the HCPC regards it as part of its remit to prosecute cases of individuals infringing the relevant provisions.

4.7   In common with many of the other healthcare regulators, the HCPC's primary function is protection of the public and it fulfils this by setting and publishing standards of proficiency for each of the registered professions as well as standards of conduct, performance and ethics that apply to all registrants, and by considering complaints against registrants.

4.8   As with other healthcare regulators, the HCPC's regulatory work is overseen by the Council for Healthcare Regulatory Excellence (CHRE).[3] In summary, the CHRE has the power to challenge any of the HCPC's fitness to practise decisions that it considers to be unduly lenient in the High Court or Court of Session.[4] The role of the CHRE is also subject to the Law Commission's review of health-care regulators referred to in para 4.4 above.

4.9   Complaints against registrants fall within the HCPC's jurisdic-tion notwithstanding that the matters giving rise to the complaint occurred outside the UK, or that they pre-dated the registrant's registration.[5]

Approach to regulation

4.10   In its fitness to practise function, the HCPC adopts the same test as most other healthcare regulators: that a registrant's fitness to practise is impaired. Impairment can be alleged on the grounds of miscon-duct, lack of competence, physical or mental health, criminal convic-tion or caution or a determination of impairment by another health or social care regulator. The HCPC also has powers to investigate allegations of fraudulent or incorrect entry on the register.[6] For a full discussion of each of these terms see chapter 1. Case-law from other regulatory bodies including the General Medical Council (GMC) and Nursing and Midwifery Council (NMC) is applicable to decisions of the HCPC.

4.11   Again, in line with most of the other healthcare regulators, the regime followed by the HCPC involves complaints from whatever source (usually either patients or service users, or employers or former employers of the registrant in question) being initially referred to an Investigating Committee Panel which will consider, on the basis of

---

3   The CHRE will be renamed the Professional Standards Authority for Health and Social Care pursuant to Health and Social Care Act 2012 s222.

4   NHS Reform and Health Care Professions Act 2002 s29.

5   HPO 2001 article 22(3).

6   HPO 2001 article 22(1) and (2).

the written complaint and any written response from the registrant, whether there is a case to answer. If there is, the case is referred to either the Conduct and Competence Committee or the Health Committee, depending on the nature of the allegation.

4.12 After investigation (which can take many months and in some cases years) a panel of the relevant committee will be convened to hear the complaint. It is upon this stage of the process that this chapter will primarily focus.

4.13 The matters covered in para 4.93 and onwards apply to health and conviction cases as well as to misconduct and competence cases. Matters specific to health and conviction cases are covered at paras 4.98–4.91 and 4.84–4.88 respectively.

Sources of law

4.14 The HPC was established by the Health Professions Order 2001 (HPO 2001) 2002 SI No 254, which was made under the Health Act 1999 s60. HPO 2001 has been amended since its original enactment and, helpfully, the HCPC website[7] contains a link to a consolidated version which includes all amendments up to January 2012. Although the website warns that this version is an internal working document and has no official status, it is plainly an extremely useful resource for registrants and representatives.

4.15 HPO 2001 covers all matters relating to the establishment of the HCPC, including the establishment and maintenance of the register and the HCPC's educational functions. The main provisions relating to fitness to practise are contained in Part V.

4.16 The specific rules governing the relevant committees are contained in:

- Health Professions Council (Practice Committees and Miscellaneous Amendments) Rules 2009;[8]
- Health Professions Council (Investigating Committee) (Procedure) Rules 2003;[9]
- Health Professions Council (Conduct and Competence Committee) (Procedure) Rules 2003;[10] and

---

7 See www.hcpc-uk.org.
8 Schedule to Health Professions Council (Practice Committees and Miscellaneous Amendments) Rules Order of Council 2009 SI No 1355.
9 Schedule to Health Professions Council (Investigating Committee) (Procedure) Rules Order of Council 2003 SI No 1574.
10 Schedule to Health Professions Council (Conduct and Competence Committee) (Procedure) Rules Order of Council 2003 SI No 1575.

- Health Professions Council (Health Committee) (Procedure) Rules 2003.[11]

Again there is a consolidated version on the HCPC's website which includes amendments to the rules up to January 2012.[12]

4.17   In addition to the statutory provisions set out above, the HCPC publishes a number of practice notes on matters of particular interest (for example, on making a finding of impairment and its indicative sanctions policy). Many of these contain references to relevant authorities and are a helpful starting point for registrants facing proceedings and representatives. All current practice notes are available on the HCPC website.[13]

Fitness to practise – general and pre-hearing matters

Referrals

4.18   As indicated earlier, referrals to the HCPC can come from any source, but in the main come from individual patients or service users or their families, and from employers or former employers of the registrant in question. The HPC annual report 2012 shows that 33.6 per cent of complaints came from members of the public and 28.59 per cent from employers (presumably including former employers).[14]

4.19   Standard 4 of the standards of conduct, performance and ethics,[15] which apply to all registrants, provides that they are under a duty to provide to the HCPC and any other relevant regulators any important information about their conduct and competence. The HCPC has powers under HPO 2001 article 22(6) to investigate a matter even if a complaint has not been raised in the usual way and these powers may be used in cases of self referral and also where information has come from other sources, such as media reports.

---

11   Schedule to Health Professions Council (Health Committee) (Procedure) Rules Order of Council 2003 SI No 1576.

12   See www.hcpc-uk.org/assets/documents/100038F0HPC-practicecommitteerules-2012consolidation.pdf.

13   See www.hcpc-uk.org.

14   HPC, *Annual report 2011*.

15   HPC, *Standards of conduct, performance and ethics* (2008).

4.20 No particular form is required for a complaint to be made to the HCPC, but it has standards of acceptance that require the complaint to:

- be in writing;
- identify the registrant concerned;
- provide as much information as possible about the incident.

4.21 The HCPC states that it will not normally act on complaints that are made anonymously given its commitment to openness and transparency, but indicates that it may do so where information provided anonymously relates to 'serious and credible' concerns about a registrant it may consider taking further action.

Historic complaints

> Article 6 (right to fair trial) of the European Convention on Human Rights (ECHR) and domestic case-law confer a right to a hearing within a reasonable time, however to stay proceedings is an exceptional course and delay is not a ground unless there is material prejudice to the extent that no fair trial is possible.

4.22 Unlike some other regulators, the HCPC's rules do not impose any time limit for the bringing of complaints, but both domestic case-law and the ECHR confer a right to the speedy and just resolution of disputes. While delay may, in certain circumstances, constitute a breach of article 6 rights, mere delay is insufficient to stop proceedings. In the case of *R (Gibson) v General Medical Council*,[16] the court held that:

> ... both the legitimate expectation of complainants and the public confidence in the regulation of the medical profession require that the complaint should, in the absence of some special and sufficient reason, be publicly investigated. It would undermine that important principle if mere unreasonable delay, absent prejudice, were to require a stay to be granted.

4.23 For the purposes of the ECHR, time runs from when a person is subjected to a 'charge', meaning that they are officially notified of or substantially affected by proceedings. In regulatory proceedings this is likely to be the date of the letter notifying the registrant of the allegations.

16 [2004] EWHC 2781 (Admin).

4.24   For a fuller discussion of the relevant authorities on this issue, and of the applicability of article 6 to regulatory proceedings, see chapter 1.

Double jeopardy

> Regulatory proceedings need not be stayed pending the outcome of criminal proceedings unless there are exceptional circumstances such as an impossible workload from which the defendant can demonstrate serious prejudice or injustice. Arguments regarding double jeopardy, privilege and publicity are otherwise unlikely to succeed.

4.25   In *Mote v Secretary of State for Work and Pensions and another*[17] the Court of Appeal reviewed the matter of concurrent proceedings and reaffirmed that the civil court continues to enjoy the discretion to adjourn but that civil proceedings could frequently continue *without* prejudicing the criminal trial. The criminal courts have the power to stay proceedings as an abuse of process and to control the admission of evidence. The fact that D may have to disclose his or her criminal defence during civil proceedings causes no prejudice since he or she is expected to disclose this in any event. For a fuller discussion of the authorities on this matter see chapters 1 and 8.

Legal representation

4.26   A registrant is entitled to be represented by counsel, solicitor or other representative of his or her choice. In practice many registrants before the HCPC are have legal representation provided through their trade union or professional body.

4.27   Once a representative has notified the HCPC that he or she is 'on the record', the case manager assigned to the case will normally be accommodating about arranging hearing dates to suit the representative's availability.

4.28   For a fuller discussion of the legal issues relating to representation see chapter 1.

17 [2008] CP Rep 13.

Impartiality of the panel

> The question is whether the fair-minded and informed observer, having considered the facts, would conclude that there was a real possibility that the tribunal was biased.[18]

4.29   Article 6 ECHR provides the right to adjudication by an independent and impartial tribunal. Independence means separated from the executive and from the parties. Impartiality means both subjective impartiality (the lack of actual bias) and objective impartiality (the lack of the appearance of bias).

4.30   Currently the HCPC, like most healthcare regulators, appoints both the prosecutors and the adjudicating panels to judge cases. The fact that disciplinary proceedings against registrants are determined by a body which includes members of the same profession does not of itself offend the requirement of 'independence' in article 6(1): see *Stefan v UK*[19] and accords with the principle that a governing body is best placed to judge what is right for its profession.

4.31   For a fuller discussion of the applicable authorities on this point see chapter 1.

The role of the legal assessor

4.32   Panels of both the Conduct and Competence Committee and the Health Committee sit with a legal assessor, who must be a qualified lawyer.[20] The function of the legal assessor is to advise the panel on matters of law and procedure. Although often called upon to assist in the drafting of the panel's reasons for its decision, the legal assessor does not participate in the decision making itself. Legal assessors at the HCPC are experienced in regulatory law (many also sit as legal assessors on other regulatory bodies such as the NMC and GMC) and are a helpful source of information for the novice representative.

4.33   It is customary to ensure that the HCPC's representative is also present when a registrant's representative (and vice versa) wishes to speak with the legal assessor outside the hearing.

4.34   If any issues of admissibility of evidence cannot be resolved by agreement between the representatives a joint approach to the legal assessor prior to commencement of the hearing is advisable. Similarly, legal assessors welcome advance notification (on the day

---

18 *Porter v Magill* [2001] UKHL 67, [2002] 2 AC 357, at para 103, per Lord Hope.

19 [1998] EHRR CD 130.

20 Health Professions Council (Functions of Assessors) Rules Order of Council 2003 Sch 1

of the hearing but before the panel has formally convened) of any applications (for example, for the hearing to be held in private or for an adjournment) prior to the application being made.

4.35   For a fuller discussion of the role of the legal assessor see chapter 1.

Investigating Committee

Procedure

4.36   Once a complaint has been made to the fitness to practise department, if it meets the standards of acceptance, it will be allocated to a case manager. The case manager will notify the registrant that concerns have been raised and may indicate that further investigations are to be carried out. Further investigation at this stage normally involves contacting the original complainant to seek further details or documentation.

4.37   Once this process is complete the registrant will be notified of the allegation and provided with copies of all supporting documents. The registrant is invited to respond in writing and will normally have 28 days to do so, although this is often extended at the request of the registrant.

4.38   The original complaint, together with any other material obtained in the course of investigation and the registrant's response are then considered by a panel of the Investigating Committee. Panels comprise three members including one from the same profession as the registrant. Panels meet in private and consider whether, if the matter were to proceed to a hearing, the allegations would be likely to be proven. The test applied by panels is whether there is a 'realistic prospect' of establishing that the registrant's fitness to practise is impaired.

4.39   The panel can decide that there is a case to answer, in which case the matter is referred forward for a hearing, either to the Conduct and Competency Committee or the Health Committee, or that there is no case to answer, in which case no further action is taken other than to notify the registrant and complainant. Alternatively the panel may decide that more investigation is required.

4.40   From September 2010 panels have also had the option of issuing 'learning points' to a registrant in cases where there is a realistic prospect of proving facts and misconduct or lack of competence but not of establishing current impairment. The annual report states that this power has been used on 16 occasions in 2010/2011.

4.41   The 'realistic prospect test' is applied to all three parts of the allegation: facts, statutory ground (eg misconduct, lack of competence, health or conviction/determination of another regulator) and current impairment. For the most part panels do not regard it as possible to resolve conflicts of fact on the basis of the written complaint and submissions so cases that turn on substantial conflicts of fact tend to be referred forward to a hearing in order that witnesses can be heard and their reliability and credibility tested.

Register entry allegations

4.42   The Investigating Committee has jurisdiction to consider allegations that an entry in the register has been fraudulently procured or incorrectly made.[21]

4.43   Such cases normally relate to whether a registrant has the appropriate qualifications to entitle him or her to be a registered practitioner of the profession in question. In such cases the Investigating Committee will send a notice to the registrant who may request that the matter be considered at a hearing. If the registrant does not request a hearing the committee may hold one of its own volition.[22]

4.44   If a hearing is to be held, the registrant will be provided with a minimum of 28 days' notice, and has the right to attend and be represented as in other fitness to practise hearings.

Interim orders

Interim orders may be made if they are necessary to protect the public or in the public interest or in the registrant's interest prior to the substantive hearing on fitness.

The threshold for an interim order is a high one because a registrant may be temporarily suspended or be subject to temporary conditions that limit or prevent his or her practice.

No judgment is made regarding the facts of the allegation but the panel must be satisfied that, on a fair analysis, there *may* be a prima facie case. The registrant should be given the opportunity to make representations and may adduce evidence.

4.45   Under HPO 2001 article 31 the Investigating Committee and the practice committees have the power to apply to a panel of the relevant committee for an interim order. Such applications are made in cases

21   HPO 2001 article 22(1)(b).
22   HPC (Investigating Committee) Rules 2003 r6(1)(a)(ii).

where the severity of the allegations is such that the registrant may pose a risk to the public if permitted to continue to practise without restriction pending final disposal.

4.46   Interim orders fall into two categories: interim conditions of practice and interim suspension orders, and in either case may be made for a maximum period of 18 months. If the case has still not been disposed of within that period the HCPC may apply to the High Court to extend the order.[23]

4.47   The test that a panel will consider in cases where an interim order is applied for is a high one: it must be necessary for the protection of the public, otherwise in the public interest or in the interests of the registrant.

4.48   The courts have considered the issue of wider public interest in this context. In *R (Shiekh) v General Dental Council*[24] S who had been given a suspended prison sentence for fraud posed no direct risk to the safety of the public. The case concerned his character not his clinical ability. Davis J overturned the GDC's suspension, finding that:

> It is a very serious thing indeed for a dentist or a doctor to be suspended. It is serious in many cases just because of the impact on that person's right to earn a living. It is serious in all cases because of the detriment to him in reputational terms. Accordingly, it is ... likely to be a relatively rare case where a suspension order will be made on an interim basis on the ground that it is in the public interest.

4.49   The fact that the allegations do not raise issues of clinical competence does not mean that an interim order will never be required. In *Bradshaw v General Medical Council*[25] a former Civil Aviation Authority medical officer was suspended on grounds of risk to the public, public interest and in his own interest. There was no criticism of his clinical competence, rather the case was one of dishonesty surrounding the investigation of an alleged affair with a colleague. While HHJ Kaye QC commented that absent any clinical or patient issues, suspension for an affair alone might well be disproportionate, here B had lied to an investigation, falsely accused a colleague and fabricated evidence. Despite there being no issues of clinical competence, the GMC was rightly concerned regarding the public perception of doctors and, of the risk that B may be persuaded to lie if he was accused of something by a patient.

23   HPO 2001 article 31(8).
24   [2007] EWHC 2972 (Admin).
25   [2010] EWHC 1296 (Admin).

4.50 For a fuller discussion of the authorities on interim orders see chapter 1.

4.51 In cases where the application is made on grounds of protection of the public, it may be possible to oppose the application on the basis that an interim order is not necessary. Such arguments are most likely to succeed where, for example, the allegation relates to issues of competence and the registrant remains employed by an employer who is aware of the HCPC proceedings and who has in place measures to monitor the registrant's performance.

4.52 HPO 2001 article 31(5) requires that a registrant be given the opportunity to appear and be heard before any interim order is made, but no specific timescale is set out for notification to the registrant. Due to the nature of interim orders, applications tend to be made at short notice, but it is essential that a registrant attends to give evidence and make submissions if an order is to be avoided or any restrictions on his or her practice to be minimised. There are no specific provisions relating to notification to the registrant, but normal practice is around seven days. If a registrant wishes to attend a hearing but is unable to do so on the date specified, an application to adjourn may be made under the applicable rule,[26] but it must be borne in mind that the nature of interim orders is such that repeated or lengthy adjournments are unlikely to be granted.

4.53 If an adjournment application is to be made it will be important to do so as soon as possible after notification is received and to provide as much information as possible about the reason why the adjournment is sought. Specific issues, such as the registrant's line manager being on leave for a period of days or weeks, from whom evidence about current supervision arrangements will be provided, are likely to be more persuasive than a vague reference to the registrant needing more time to gather evidence.

4.54 Supporting evidence from an employer in cases where the allegation relates to competence, confirming knowledge of the HCPC proceedings and setting out monitoring mechanisms, may also be determinative.

4.55 In health cases, an up-to-date report from a relevant medical practitioner may well be of assistance if it confirms good compliance with a medication regime or other forms of treatment so as to indicate that the health condition is sufficiently controlled.

---

26 HPC (Investigating Committee) Rules 2003 r8(f); HPC (Conduct and Competence Committee) Rules 2003 and HPC (Health Committee) Rules 2003 r10(f).

334 Professional discipline and healthcare regulators / chapter 4

4.56   Panels are required to consider conditions of practice before resorting to a suspension order, so if an order seems likely to be imposed it is worth considering what kind of conditions might be suggested that would adequately protect the public. The kind of interim conditions that may be considered include:

- not to practise a particular form of treatment;
- not to practise on a particular group of patients or service users;
- not to practise a particular form of treatment without a chaperone;
- not to practise above a given level of seniority;
- not to practise without a specified level of supervision (this is often tied to a requirement for the registrant to provided evidence or reports periodically to the HCPC);
- to notify the HCPC if changing employers.

4.57   Representatives will need to give considerable thought to the kind of conditions that might be suggested in the alternative to submissions opposing the application for a suspension order. Supporting evidence to show willingness to comply on the part of the registrant and any other party (for example, an employer) must also be adduced.

4.58   A 'bank' of draft conditions is annexed to the HCPC's practice note on drafting fitness to practise decisions, which is a useful resource for representatives and is available on the HCPC website.[27]

4.59   Interim orders must be reviewed within six months of being made and every three months thereafter.[28] Once an interim order is in place, if the registrant does not require any change to conditions, or if there are no good grounds to apply for the removal of a suspension order, it is not necessary for the registrant to attend all review hearings. It is important, however that registrants are seen to be engaging with the regulatory process and accordingly in most cases it will be appropriate for a letter to be sent to the HCPC prior to the review confirming compliance and that the registrant does not oppose the continuation of the existing order.

4.60   A registrant who is subject to an interim order may make an application for it to be reviewed where new evidence has become available which is relevant to the order.[29] This provision is particularly useful in cases where the registrant's employment status has changed during the currency of the interim order (for example, by the receipt of an offer of new employment or on the conclusion of an employer's

---

27 See www.hcpc-uk.org/assets/documents/10002B35PRACTICENOTE_
    draftingFTPdecisions.pdf.
28 HPO 2001 article 31(6).
29 HPO 2001 article 31(6)(b).

investigation under its own disciplinary procedure into substantially the same matters as are before the HCPC and where the registrant has been mainly or wholly exonerated of any wrongdoing). As with initial interim order hearings, a registrant seeking to vary conditions of practice or to have a suspension order replaced with conditions should ensure that he or she provides as much supporting evidence as possible demonstrating how any risk to the public will be managed by the proposed conditions.

4.61   In all hearings relating to interim orders, the panel will not consider whether the allegations are proven, but plainly if there is good evidence that this is unlikely (for example, where an employer's disciplinary investigation has exonerated the registrant on substantially the same matters) this should be put before the panel.

4.62   The HCPC's *Fitness to Practise annual report 2011*[30] shows that interim orders were applied for in 48 cases, and granted in 44 of those, out of a total of 759 cases received in the same period. It appears from these figures that the HCPC uses these powers sparingly and the majority of cases do not require an interim order.

Responding to the Investigating Committee Panel

4.63   If assisting a registrant to draft a response to an allegation at this stage, it is important to address the specific allegations directly. If the matters alleged are so minor that even if proven they are unlikely to amount to misconduct or lack of competence, this should be strongly emphasised from the outset as this will be a key consideration for the panel. The best chance for a registrant at this stage lies in responding in such way as to indicate that no finding of impairment at a full hearing would be likely because of the minor nature of the matter(s) alleged.

4.64   Of course in many cases it is not possible to make such an argument with credibility. It should also be borne in mind that, although a registrant's written representations to the Investigating Committee are not as a matter of course put before a Conduct and Competence Committee or Health Committee panel at a full hearing, they can be in the event that the registrant gives evidence at the hearing that is inconsistent with the contents of the earlier submissions. Great care needs therefore to be taken that any factual assertions set out in the submissions are correct. Similarly it is unhelpful to express patently unrealistic views: for example that an allegation of serious

30 HPC, *Fitness to Practise annual report 2011*.

dishonesty is unlikely, even if proven to lead to a finding of misconduct or impairment.

4.65   In cases where there are conflicts of fact between the complainant and registrant it is important to refer to and provide copies of any documents that support the registrant's account. Often this will be contemporaneous records such as treatment notes, but could also include written statements from witnesses. In deciding whether the allegations can be proven, the panel must consider significant persuasive evidence that would be likely to undermine the complainant's account.

4.66   In many cases, however, where allegations of a serious nature are raised it is highly likely that the Investigating Committee Panel will refer the matter on to the Conduct and Competence Committee or the Health Committee as appropriate. Registrants should be made aware of this likelihood at an early stage and also that the timescale for completion of the process can be extremely protracted. The relevant case manager should be able to give some idea of timescales in any given case but most take more than a year from referral to final disposal.

Mediation

4.67   There is provision under HPO 2001 article 26(6) for the Investigating Committee, having decided that there is a case to answer, to refer a case for mediation. This can either be undertaken by the committee itself[31] or be referred to screeners for the mediation.[32] Given the consensual nature of disposal by mediation, panels will only refer cases where they are satisfied that, whatever the outcome, no other steps are necessary to protect the public.

4.68   The powers to refer cases for mediation are not currently used, but the issue is under active consideration by the HPC at the time of writing (April 2012).

---

31 HPO 2001 article 26(6)(a).
32 HPO 2001 article 26(6)(b).

Allegations

> The particulars of the allegation and the facts upon which they are founded should be clear and settled in advance of any hearing.
>
> If in doubt, clarification and/or further and better particulars should be obtained.
>
> The panel may, having heard from both parties, amend either the allegation or the facts provided no injustice is caused but this should be the exception not the rule.

Procedure

4.69   When an Investigating Committee Panel finds that there is a case to answer and refers it to either the Conduct and Competence Committee or the Health Committee, the registrant will be informed and will be provided with brief reasons as to why the panel reached its decision.

4.70   At this point the allegation will be in draft form, but is likely to be sufficiently close to the final version that the registrant can begin to prepare his or her response to it.

4.71   The allegation is set out in three parts:

1) first, the factual particulars (eg on a specified date the registrant failed to provide adequate care to patient A in that he or she failed to record the findings of his or her assessment and treatment);
2) second, the statutory ground (eg that the conduct set out above amounted to misconduct and/or lack of competence); and
3) third, that, by reason of the misconduct or lack of competence set out, the registrant's fitness to practise is impaired.

4.72   The HCPC's practice note on the standard of acceptance for allegations requires the nature of the impairment alleged to be stated (presumably a reference to the need to identify the statutory ground) and the events and circumstances giving rise to the allegation in sufficient detail for that registrant to be able to understand and respond to that allegation.

4.73   In most cases the drafting is sufficiently clear for the registrant to understand the allegation and be able to respond, but if not, this should be raised at the earliest opportunity with the case manager. Sometimes the matter can be easily rectified (for example, by providing the identity of particular patients/service users) but if not it should be pursued well in advance of the final hearing.

4.74   In *R (Wheeler) v Assistant Commissioner House of the Metropolitan Police*[33] it was alleged that W had failed to carry out duties 'to an acceptable standard' thereby breaching the code of conduct. Stanley Burnton J said:

> Vagueness is a ground for judicial review if it leads to unfairness in the proceedings, and the danger with a vague charge is that the parties, and in particular the respondent, do not know with some precision what is alleged against them, and therefore are not fully able to address those matters in the course of a hearing.[34]

4.75   His Lordship commented that while the particulars of a charge may be refined following an initial draft, it should be sufficiently particularised well before the hearing for the respondent to disciplinary charges to know what it is alleged he failed to do and, in what respects he failed.

4.76   In *Roomi v General Medical Council*[35] Collins J allowed R's appeal against a finding of impairment by reason of deficient professional performance (ie lack of competence) on the grounds that the finding by the panel went beyond the allegations contained in the notice of hearing. During the case, R called evidence to show that he had taken steps to improve his skills which led the panel to conclude that the deficiencies identified in the notice had been remedied. However, the panel still made an adverse finding relying on managerial matters out-with the original allegations. His Lordship was critical both of the panel for going beyond the matters alleged and of the assessor for failing to advise them of their error.

4.77   The application of ECHR article 6 may be relied upon if necessary to achieve the appropriate level of particularisation. Certain matters are required to be explicitly stated in the allegation, including dishonesty and sexual motivation. For a fuller discussion of the law relating to the drafting of allegations see chapter 1.

4.78   The practice committee rules[36] allow for allegations to be joined where it would be just to do so. Joinder can apply to allegations against a single registrant or multiple registrants. Joinder is usually considered where there is a connection between the allegations (and the registrants) as hearing them together can save time, costs

33   [2008] EWHC 439 (Admin).
34   [2008] EWHC 439 (Admin) para 6.
35   [2009] EWHC 2188 (Admin).
36   HPC (Investigating Committee) Rules 2003 rr4(8) and 6(7); HPC (Health Committee) Rules 2003 and HPC (Conduct and Competence Committee) Rules 2003 r5(4).

and the need for prosecution witnesses to attend on more than one occasion.

4.79 Allegations against a single registrant will normally only be joined where they are:

- of the same or similar character;
- based on the same acts, events or course of dealing; or
- based on connected or related acts, events or courses of dealing.

4.80 Allegations against more than one registrant will only be joined where:

- the registrants are subject to the same allegation;
- there is evidence that the registrants acted in concert; or
- the allegations against the registrants are linked in time or by other factors, for example where:
  - the allegations concern participation in the same act, event or course of dealing (or any series of them);
  - the allegations are based upon connected or related acts, events or courses of dealing; or
  - the allegations relate to actions taken in furtherance of a common enterprise.

4.81 Even where joinder appears to be appropriate based on the nature of the allegations, there may be other reasons why the discretion to do so should not be exercised. For example, where one registrant has failed to respond and joinder might cause delay or unfairness in dealing with another registrant or where it is apparent that registrants will present antagonistic or mutually exclusive defences.

4.82 In practice registrants are given the opportunity to oppose or consent to a proposal to join one or more allegations and representatives will need to give active consideration to what, if any, prejudice the registrant may suffer as a result. Many registrants find the lengthy period of uncertainty awaiting resolution of allegations to be particularly stressful and the desirability of a quicker outcome is one of the factors to be taken into consideration.

4.83 If allegations are joined however this is not necessarily the end of the matter as panels have a similar discretion to sever in appropriate cases.

4.84 There is a practice note on joinder (also dealing with severance) available on the HCPC's website.[37]

---

37 See www.hcpc-uk.org/assets/documents/100028AOJoinder.

Conviction cases

4.85   HPO 2001 article 22(1)(a)(iii) provides that the HCPC has jurisdiction to consider cases where it is alleged that a registrant's fitness to practise is impaired by reason of a criminal conviction or caution. The procedure for dealing with such cases is broadly the same as for those on the other statutory grounds.

4.86   Conviction includes those which occur in a court outside the UK, but where the offence is recognised as a crime in the UK, as well as convictions by a court martial.[38] Binding over and discharge do not amount to convictions, but the HCPC may in any event investigate the circumstances that led to the bind-over or discharge and deal with it as an allegation of misconduct.

4.87   The practice committee rules provide[39] that a certified copy of the certificate of conviction (or in Scotland, an extract conviction) is proof of the conviction and of the fact upon which it was based. Accordingly, in such cases it will not be open to registrants to suggest that they did not commit the offence in question, and representations will need to focus on any mitigating circumstances, insight, remorse and reparation.

4.88   Community sentences can present particular problems in light of the decision in *Council for the Regulation of Healthcare Professionals v General Dental Council and Fleischman*[40] as, if the conviction was for a serious offence and the sentence is still being served at the time of consideration by a fitness to practise panel, the registrant should not normally be permitted to resume practice until the sentence has been satisfactorily completed. In light of this unhelpful principle, representatives may wish to seek an adjournment of cases where a community sentence is ongoing until such time as it has been completed.

4.89   There is a practice note on conviction and caution allegations which contains helpful information and which is available on the HCPC website.[41]

---

38   HPO 2001 article 22(2).
39   HPC (Investigating Committee) Rules 2003 r8((1)(d); HPC (Conduct and Competence Committee) Rules 2003 and HPC (Health Committee) Rules 2003 r10(1)(d).
40   [2005] EWHC 87 (Admin).
41   See www.hcpc-uk.org/assets/documents/10002B34PRACTICENOTE/ convictionandcautionallegations.pdf.

Health cases

4.90   One of the statutory grounds under the HPO 2001[42] is impairment by reason of the registrant's physical or mental health. Such cases will be considered by the Investigating Committee initially and will, if there is a case to answer, then normally be referred to the Health Committee. The Health Committee rules and hearings are broadly similar to those of the Conduct and Competence Committee, however panels must include at least one registered medical practitioner[43] and may receive advice from a medical assessor.

4.91   Cases can be referred by the Health Committee to the Conduct and Competence Committee[44] where it appears that the allegation would be better dealt with by the Conduct and Competence Committee. The Health Committee's consideration is then suspended pending consideration by the Conduct and Competence Committee. Similarly the Conduct and Competence Committee can refer cases to the Health Committee where it appears that it would be better dealt with by the Health Committee[45] and parallel provisions apply regarding suspension of consideration by the Conduct and Competence Committee.

4.92   A significant matter for representatives to consider in cases where referral to the Health Committee may be appropriate is that in health cases a striking-off order is not available as a sanction until the registrant has been suspended or subject to a conditions of practice order for a period of two years preceding the date of the decision to strike off.[46] An application for a case to be referred to the Health Committee should be made at an early stage in proceedings and well in advance of any hearing date being fixed, and should be supported by evidence from a medical practitioner.

Determination by another regulator

4.93   The HCPC also has jurisdiction to consider allegations on the ground of a determination by a body responsible for the regulation of a health or social care profession that his or her fitness to practise is impaired.[47] In practice, the approach to dealing with such cases will

---

42   HPO 2001 article 22(1)(a)(iv).
43   HPO 2001 Sch 1 para 19(6)(b).
44   HPC (Health Committee) Rules 2003 r4(1).
45   HPC (Conduct and Competence Committee) Rules 2003 r4(1).
46   HPO 2001 article 29(6).
47   HPO 2001 article 22(1)(a)(v).

be similar to that applying to conviction cases. Referral by another regulator does not infringe the principle of double jeopardy – see chapters 1 and 7 for a fuller discussion of the law. See also chapter 8 regarding the Independent Safeguarding Authority.

Disposal by consent

4.94   The HCPC has discretion to deal with certain cases by consent. Its practice note (available on the website) indicates three criteria which must be met before this will be considered:

a) after an Investigating Committee Panel has found that there is a 'case to answer', so that a proper assessment has been made of the nature, extent and viability of the allegation;

b) where the registrant is willing to admit the allegation in full. A registrant's insight into, and willingness to address, failings are key elements in the fitness to practise process and it would be inappropriate to dispose of a case by consent where the registrant denies liability; and

c) where any remedial action agreed between the registrant and the HCPC is consistent with the expected outcome if the case was to proceed to a contested hearing.

4.95   The practice note goes on to clarify that the decision as to whether a case may be disposed of by consent will be a matter for the panel, and if an application by a registrant is rejected the case will then be listed before a different panel for hearing in the usual way.

4.96   A registrant is not permitted to resign from the register while subject to an allegation or to a conditions of practice or suspension order,[48] but the HCPC can enter into a voluntary removal agreement allowing him or her to do so if it is satisfied that doing so will adequately protect the public. The terms of such an agreement will be similar to those applying had the registrant been struck off.

---

48   HPO 2001 article 11(3).

Evidence

> While there is a duty to prevent inequality of arms, there is no positive duty on a disciplinary body to gather evidence to assist the registrant.
>
> To allege unfairness under HPO 2001 article 6(3)(b) a complainant must demonstrate that a duty exists, that it has been breached and this has caused an inequality of arms.
>
> Each case will depend on its own facts.

4.97 The HCPC has standard directions for case management which provide that it will serve a copy of documents it intends to rely upon at the final hearing at least 42 days before the date of the hearing.

4.98 The HCPC bundles of documents for hearings are now separated into two sections, one containing witness statements (core bundle) and the other (exhibits bundle) containing other documents which are exhibited by the witnesses.

4.99 The HCPC standard directions require the registrant to provide any documents he or she intends to rely upon 28 days before the date of the hearing.

4.100 In practice, many registrants are unable to comply with the 28-day rule, and extensions of time are frequently given. In cases where a significant number of further documents are to be relied upon by the registrant, however, it is important to provide them sufficiently far in advance for them to be sent out to panel members in good time before the hearing, particularly where the volume of documents is large.

4.101 In *R (Johnson) v Professional Conduct Committee of the Nursing and Midwifery Council*,[49] J applied for judicial review of the Professional Conduct Committee's refusal to stay proceedings on grounds (among others) of a failure to obtain relevant documents and other evidence. The NMC had agreed to do what they considered reasonable to obtain various records but they refused to obtain those they regarded them as irrelevant. Beatson J held that the ECHR article 6 right to adequate facilities to prepare and equality of arms was case/fact specific. There was a balance to be struck between the parties to ensure fairness. This did not include a positive duty on the part of the regulator to gather evidence for the defence, provided the registrant was not at a disadvantage in having to gather the evidence he or she wished to deploy.

49 [2008] EWHC 885 (Admin).

4.102   For a fuller discussion of the law relating to regulators' duty to disclose evidence see chapter 1.

4.103   Character references do not need to be provided in advance of the hearing as they only become relevant at the sanctions stage of proceedings, if a finding of impairment is made. Professional testimonials, however, should be provided if possible before the hearing as this evidence is considered at the misconduct/impairment stage. In practice, panels do not decline to consider evidence of this nature even if it is provided on the day of the hearing, but representatives should remember that this may delay proceedings, irritate the panel and generally not set the case off on a good footing, so should be avoided if at all possible. Clearly how much importance to place on this depends on the number and nature of the documents involved and any reasons why it has not been possible to provide them in advance, which should be brought to the panel's attention.

4.104   The standard directions also provide for a notice to admit facts to be served on the registrant at any time up until 21 days before the hearing. The practice note specifies that if a notice to admit facts is not responded to within 14 days indicating that the specified facts are disputed, the registrant will be taken to admit the facts set out in the notice. Care must therefore be taken to ensure that any such notice is responded to within the timescale.

4.105   Similarly, a notice to admit documents or witness statement(s) may also be served by the HCPC and must be responded to by the registrant in the same terms. It should be noted, however, that any admissions made through this process may be permitted to be amended or withdrawn where it is just to do so. This provision should not be relied upon though as if a registrant has inadvertently admitted witness statements witnesses may have been de-warned in light of the registrant's admissions and late withdrawal may jeopardise the hearing date (or, potentially may lead to a refusal of the request to withdraw).

4.106   Generally registrants find the protracted timescale these cases take to reach a final hearing extremely stressful and accordingly are keen for the matter to be progressed as speedily as possible so it is important to avoid any action or omission that could inadvertently delay the final hearing.

Pleas

4.107   Irrespective of the notice to admit facts procedure, registrants are invariably asked at the outset of the final hearing to indicate their response to the allegation. In practice, the panel is likely to have prior indication from the registrant's witness statement that will have been provided together with documents in advance of the hearing. Admissions can be made in respect of any or all of the factual particulars, to the statutory grounds and to impairment.

4.108   In some cases the registrant's position may be that while the factual particulars are not substantially disputed, there is a part of the wording that they object to. The most common circumstance is where particulars are drafted as 'on a specified date you failed to ...'. The registrant may accept that he or she did not do the act in question, but not that it amounted to any failure on his or her part. In these circumstances panels are usually receptive to an indication of the position in precise terms at the start of the hearing. While any objection to the wording of a factual particular will prevent its being formally recorded as an admission, panels nevertheless find it helpful to have such matters clarified at the outset as it assists them in judging where best to focus their attention on the evidence.

4.109   In practice, admitting to a particular that states that a registrant failed to take the specified action is not prejudicial to his or her position as the issue of failure is really best addressed at the next stage of misconduct or lack of competence.

4.110   It is common practice for admissions to be partial – for example, some factual particulars but not others and that some of those admitted particulars amount to misconduct and/or lack of competence but that others do not.

4.111   If significant factual admissions are to be made, it is helpful if this can be indicated to the HCPC at an early stage as it will ensure that witnesses are not required to attend unnecessarily, which can reduce the overall time estimate for the hearing. More importantly though, registrants may gain credit in the later stages of the process if they have made admissions. Of course this does not suggest that registrants should admit to something they do not agree with, but careful scrutiny of the factual particulars will often reveal some that can without any difficulty be admitted, even if misconduct and/or lack of competence is not.

4.112   Pragmatism is appreciated by HCPC panels and if the factual particulars that are to be admitted are of a serious and/or widespread nature then admissions in relation to misconduct/lack of competence and impairment should be considered. At sanctions stage, strike-off is not initially available in cases of lack of competence so if, as is often the case, an allegation is put on the alternative grounds of misconduct and/or lack of competence it is open to a registrant (and

346 Professional discipline and healthcare regulators / chapter 4

may be beneficial) to admit lack of competence but not misconduct in respect of the same factual particulars.

4.113   In common with the other main healthcare regulators, impairment is to be judged as at the time of the hearing (not at the time of the matters giving rise to the allegations) so in some cases it is possible to argue persuasively that, even thought standards of conduct or competence were breached at the time in question, those deficiencies have since been rectified. This is most commonly seen in lack of competence cases where the registrant has subsequently undertaken further training or had supervision such that the level of competence has in the meantime reached the requisite standard. It may also succeed in cases of misconduct where the conduct in question was a one-off in an otherwise distinguished professional career, particularly where accompanied by expressions of remorse and insight.

4.114   For a full discussion of the law on misconduct, lack of competence and impairment see chapter 1.

Witnesses

> The panel has the discretion to proceed in the absence of a witness and to admit hearsay evidence but the decision to proceed must be taken with 'the utmost care and caution' and only after full consideration of the competing interests with emphasis on those of the registrant.
>
> There must be compelling reasons to deprive a registrant of the opportunity to cross-examine a witness – this all the more so if the case or its consequences are serious.

General rules and procedures

4.115   The HCPC will call whichever witnesses it considers necessary to prove the case (taking account of any prior notification from the registrant of facts or statements that will be admitted). Where a statement is agreed by the registrant it will often, though not always, not be considered necessary to call the witness but simply to rely on the written statement. In some cases where the witness in question is key to the matter (for example, a manager who has conducted an investigation under an employer's own disciplinary procedure) they will be required to attend the hearing and give live evidence notwithstanding admissions by the registrant.

4.116   Hearsay evidence can be adduced at hearings,[50] and as in other courts, if statements are not agreed but the witness still does not appear in person the panel will be advised by the legal assessor about the weight it can place upon their evidence given that it has not been tested in cross-examination, a matter the registrant's representative will need to address in submissions at the facts stage.

4.117   In *Nursing and Midwifery Council v Ogbonna*,[51] O faced three serious charges all of which were found proved and she was struck off the register. On count one, the NMC placed sole reliance upon the statement of O's line manager P, with whom she was not on good terms. P did not give evidence, rather her statement was adduced as hearsay despite O's wish to cross-examine her. P had moved to the Caribbean. The NMC said that P was not available even though they had made no inquiry regarding her availability and said that no video-link was available at the panel hearing. On appeal, Davis J found that the panel had misdirected itself in finding that P was not available since no inquiry had been. The NMC rules required the panel to consider the overall fairness of the hearing before admitting hearsay and, given the misdirection the test had not been met. The NMC appealed on the basis that his judgment curtailed the admissibility of hearsay statements. However, the Court of Appeal upheld Davis J's decision on the facts. No general principle was established other than to reaffirm the need to consider fairness before admitting hearsay. Fairness is required on both sides and it was commented that if, despite reasonable efforts the NMC could not arrange for P to be available for cross-examination, then the case for admitting her hearsay statement might well have been strong.

4.118   More recently in *R (Bonhoeffer) v General Medical Council*[52] B faced several allegations of sexual misconduct while practising in Kenya. See chapter 1 for a summary of the facts and fuller discussion of this decision and others on the admissibility of evidence. In that case, the court upheld B's challenge and concluded, in essence that:

> The admission of hearsay was not necessarily unfair. The key issue was whether admitting important evidence with no opportunity to cross-examine a witness was fair at common law and/or under Art 6 given the seriousness of the case and any safeguards.

---

50 HPC (Investigating Committee) Rules 2003 r8(1)(b) and (c); HPC (Health Committee) Rules 2003 and HPC (Conduct and Competence Committee) Rules 2003 r10(1)(b) and (c).

51 [2010] EWCA Civ 1216.

52 [2011] EWHC 1585 (Admin).

4.119   There is no absolute rule that a registrant must be afforded the opportunity to cross-examine a witness even where the witness provides the sole or decisive evidence. However a key point was the serious (criminal) nature of the allegations and the very serious consequences if proved. As a general rule the more serious the charges or consequences the greater the need for procedural safeguards to ensure a fair hearing. B's right to cross-examine a central witness could only be countered by *compelling* factors.

4.120   Registrants are of course entitled to call witnesses in support of their own case. Witnesses of fact will be called at the first stage of the hearing whereas those providing evidence of professional standing or purely in relation to character will be called at misconduct/lack of competence or impairment stage and sanctions stage respectively.

4.121   It is worth giving careful consideration as to the most beneficial stage at which to call a supporting witness. In practice, at the hearing panels often agree to hear a single witness's evidence in one go (rather than splitting it into separate parts going to facts, misconduct/ health/lack of competence and impairment) for reasons of convenience. There is rarely any disadvantage to the registrant of taking this approach – generally the earlier a panel hears evidence of a registrant's good standard of practice the better.

4.122   Generally the HCPC and those who prosecute cases on its behalf are helpful to accommodating witness availability, so if there are constraints for a particular witness it is advisable to flag this up with the case manager in advance of the hearing and to seek to agree a provisional timetable.

4.123   Where a potential witness is unwilling to co-operate with an HCPC investigation, investigators have powers[53] to require any person to supply information or provide any document which appears to be relevant to the discharge of the practice committees' fitness to practise functions. In practice the power is rarely used as such information is usually in the possession either of the complainant or a current or former employer and such parties are usually willing to co-operate. The power is exercised through service of a requirement notice, which indicates that failure to comply without reasonable excuse amounts to a criminal offence punishable on summary conviction by a fine not exceeding level five on the standard scale.[54]

---

53   HPO 2001 article 25(1).
54   HPO 2001 article 39(5).

4.124　　The power does not apply to the registrant who is the subject of the proceedings however, although there is a more limited power[55] to require him or her to provide details of his or her employer, of any person with whom he or she has an arrangement to provide services and any other healthcare regulator by which he or she is authorised to practise. The enforcement provisions are the same as those set out in the previous paragraph applying to third parties.

4.125　　In addition to the above, which apply during the investigation stage, practice committee panels have the power[56] to require any person (other than the registrant) to attend and give evidence at hearings or to produce documents. The power can be exercised by the panel of its own volition or on application by the parties.

4.126　　Cases where the registrant may wish to use this provision are relatively rare, but may be appropriate in circumstances where, for example, only partial documentation has been provided to the HCPC by an employer and the registrant is aware of other documents in existence that would assist in his or her defence.

4.127　　An application for such an order must be made in writing and must contain the following information:

- the name and address of the person concerned;
- the terms of the order sought;
- details of any information being sought;
- any steps the applicant has taken to secure the attendance of (or production by) that person on a voluntary basis; and
- evidence to show why the attendance of (or production by) that person is likely to support the case of the applicant.

4.128　　In addition, a panel will normally require the party applying to indicate that they will meet the reasonable costs of the party providing/attending, accordingly an undertaking to this effect should be included in the application. Where the application is for documents to be produced, they must be identified individually or by reference to a class of documents, and must contain sufficient detail that the recipient is able to understand the obligation the order places upon them.

4.129　　A copy of the application and any evidence in support of it should normally be sent to the person concerned. The panel may hold a hearing to consider the application or simply deal with the matter on paper if the parties agree or if a hearing is considered unnecessary.

55　HPO 2001 article 25(2).
56　HPO 2001 article 32(2)(m).

4.130   If a witness order is granted, in order to be binding on the recipient, it must be served at least seven days before the hearing, so this timescale should be borne in mind when making any application for such an order.

4.131   The use of expert witnesses in fitness to practise proceedings is relatively rare but may be necessary in certain cases. The need for expert evidence is most likely to arise in competency cases where the registrant wishes to defend his or her practice on the matter under scrutiny as being of an acceptable standard. There is a practice note on the use of expert witnesses which is available on the HCPC website. The practice note sets out detailed requirements to be observed if expert evidence is to be relied upon, which broadly mirror those applicable in the civil courts.

4.132   Panels have discretion as to whether expert evidence is required in a particular case, the overriding principle being that it will assist the panel in dealing with the case.

Video-link

4.133   Video-links are used on occasion for convenience (eg where a key witness is out of the country for a prolonged period) as in other courts. From a registrant's perspective there is rarely any objection to the practice in these circumstances. Provided facilities can be accessed, the same can apply to witnesses in support of a registrant's case and can be helpful in overcoming limitations on availability. There are particular provisions in relation to the use of video-link and other measures for vulnerable witnesses, which are covered in paras 4.159–4.163 below.

Location

4.134   The HCPC's office in Kennington, London[57] is the venue for most fitness to practise hearings, although the volume of cases means that on occasions hotels or other business meeting venues in London are used. Panels also sit outside London in major cities such as Cardiff, Manchester, Leeds and Glasgow on which occasions hotels are normally used for the purpose. The HCPC offices can accommodate more than one hearing at a time (although availability of private meeting rooms for registrants is limited – early arrival to stake a claim is highly recommended), but only one hearing room has a video-link facility which sometimes necessitates juggling the listings.

57 184 Kennington Park Road, London SE11 4BU.

Lunch and tea and coffee is provided for registrants and representatives. The HCPC staff are generally very helpful, including about occasional requests for last-minute photocopying (although of course this should not be relied upon and documents and statements should be provided within the stipulated timescales wherever possible).

4.135　If a registrant has a particular reason for wanting the hearing held outside London this should be raised at an early stage with the case manager and full reasons given for the request.

Preliminary meetings

4.136　The Investigating Committee and the practice committees, or their chair, may hold preliminary meetings in private with the parties, their representatives and any other person the committee or chair considers appropriate where such a meeting will assist the committee to perform its functions.[58]

4.137　At such meetings the chair may make directions[59] and with the agreement of the parties, take any action the committee could take at such a meeting. In practice, preliminary meetings are usually held where the nature of the case is such that it is likely to require a lengthy hearing or where issues such as expert evidence need to be considered. Directions will be made to clarify the steps necessary prior to the final hearing. Such meetings often also deal with applications for witness orders, the joinder of allegations or vulnerable witness measures (on which see paras 4.159–4.163 below).

4.138　It is important to seek to resolve any preliminary issues prior to the final disposal hearing wherever possible, otherwise time taken to do so on the first day of the hearing can jeopardise the prospect of completing the case within the time allocated. Preliminary meetings are also a good opportunity to seek clarification of any issues relating to the drafting of the allegations.

Main hearings

Preparing for the main hearing

4.139　For all final disposal hearings it is advisable to prepare a full witness statement for a registrant, and for any other witness who intends to

---

58　HPC (Investigating Committee) Rules 2003, HPC (Health Committee) Rules 2003 and HPC (Conduct and Competence Committee) Rules 2003 r7.
59　HPO 2001 article 32(3).

give evidence. Statements are drafted in the usual form and documentary evidence can either be exhibited and attached thereto or set out in a separate bundle with reference to the bundle pagination in the statement (remembering to distinguish the registrant's bundle from the HCPC bundle).

4.140   As in all civil proceedings, statements should be full and set out all matters upon which the registrant seeks to rely. The form is a matter for the individual representative, but generally it will be helpful if the statement contains some introductory paragraphs setting out the registrant's route to qualification and a brief summary of the registrant's career to date. If appropriate, it would be helpful if it contains some general information about the surrounding circumstances in the course of the employment giving rise to the allegation (this is particularly important in cases where the registrant is asserting excessive workload, for example, or inadequate supervision). Each factual particular can then be set out with the registrant's response, then dealing with the issues of misconduct and/or lack of competence, impairment and finally issues going to mitigation.

4.141   The occasions when it is not beneficial to call the registrant to give evidence on his or her own behalf will be very rare indeed (this is most likely to arise in health cases, on which see paras 4.89–4.91 above) but in many cases the registrant is the only witness at the facts stage and others are called to give evidence more generally about the standards of the registrant's practice, hence their relevance tends to relate to misconduct/lack of competence or impairment. Full witness statements should be provided for all witnesses, although the formalities are often relaxed in the case of professional witnesses at sanctions stage and often these are accepted in the form of a testimonial or letter addressed to the relevant committee.

Admissibility of evidence

4.142   The practice committee rules[60] provide that the civil rules of admissibility apply, although rules 8(c)[61] and 10(c)[62] provide that the committee may hear or receive evidence which would not be admissible in such proceedings if it is satisfied that admission of that evidence

---

60 HPC (Investigating Committee) Rules 2003 r8(1)(b), HPC (Health Committee) Rules 2003 and HPC (Conduct and Competence Committee) Rules 2003 r10(1)(b).

61 Of the HPC (Investigating Committee) Rules 2003.

62 Of the HPC (Health Committee) Rules 2003 and HPC (Conduct and Competence Committee) Rules 2003.

is necessary in order to protect members of the public. Accordingly, panels have wide discretion to admit evidence, though plainly any that is not relevant to the matters under consideration will not fall within the scope of the discretion. See paras 4.115–4.119 regarding the admissibility of hearsay evidence.

4.143   Any issues about admissibility of evidence must be raised with the case manager at an early stage in proceedings and resolved well before the final hearing. Alternatively it may prove possible to resolve by approaching the legal assessor jointly with the HCPC's representative on the day of the hearing but before it has commenced.

4.144   If the matter is not resolved prior to the hearing, the registrant's representative will be faced with the dilemma of making an application to exclude the evidence in question from the very panel from which he or she wishes to keep it. This may ultimately result in an application for a panel to recuse itself (if it has seen evidence that is prejudicial to the registrant and not properly admissible in the course of the application being made), resulting in adjournment of the hearing to another date. As most registrants have already waited many months and seek resolution to the uncertainty of facing proceedings, this is to be avoided, which reinforces the importance of resolving such issues at an early stage.

Public hearings

4.145   Under the practice committee rules[63] the presumption is that hearings are held in public. The rationale for this is clear: the importance of transparency and openness in regulatory proceedings to maintain public confidence in the process. There will however be occasions when evidence to be adduced will contain reference to intensely personal matters which are not appropriate to be heard in public.

4.146   The rules make provision for the presumption of a public hearing to be disapplied where a panel is satisfied that it is in the interests of justice or for the protection of the private life of the health professional, the complainant, any person giving evidence or of any patient or client. On such occasions the public will be excluded from all or part of the hearing. Such applications are frequently granted where the evidence in question deals with matters such as the physical or mental health of the registrant. If an application is to be made on behalf of a registrant, the nature of the evidence should be made

63   HPC (Investigating Committee) Rules 2003 r8(1)(a), and HPC (Conduct and Competence Committee) Rules 2003 r10(1)(a).

known to the panel and the particular ground relied upon (eg inter-ests of justice or protection of private life). There is a practice note on conducting hearings in private which contains useful information for representatives which is available on the HCPC website.[64]

4.147   Representatives should clarify to the registrant however that if the application is granted (and often they are only granted in relation to a specific witness or part of a witness' testimony) this does not mean that all publicity will be avoided. The registrant's name and the allegation will already have been placed on the HCPC website and the final decision and any sanction will also be posted on the HCPC website in most cases.

4.148   In exceptional cases the HCPC may agree to limit the detail of alle-gations to be posted on the website. If agreement to such an approach is to be sought, an application must be made to the case manager at the earliest opportunity and supported by as much evidence as pos-sible. Cases where such an approach may receive sympathetic con-sideration include allegations of child abuse or child pornography, where there may be fears of repercussions for the family of the reg-istrant if details of the offence are made public. Such a request is unlikely to be granted however if the information is already in the public domain (for example, as a consequence of criminal proceed-ings being reported in the press).

4.149   Registrants frequently find this aspect of the process particularly unpalatable and make comparisons with the treatment of complain-ants who are often anonymised for the whole of the proceedings, so care must be taken to explain the position at the outset.

4.150   If at the final hearing the panel finds that the allegation not well founded, the registrant will be given the choice of having the decision posted on the website or all reference to the case removed immedi-ately. Most registrants opt for the latter, taking the view that they will inform anyone with a proper interest in the outcome and the less time their name remains publicly associated with proceedings the better.

64   See www.hcpc-uk.org/assets/documents/1000289EConductingHearingsin private.pdf.

Postponements, adjournments and absent registrants

> The panel has the discretion to proceed in the absence of
> the practitioner but a) there must be strict adherence to the
> requirement that all reasonable effort at service has been met and
> b) the decision to proceed must be taken with 'the utmost care and
> caution' and only after full consideration of the competing interests
> with emphasis on those of the practitioner.

4.151 A registrant facing an allegation has the right to attend the hearing
and be represented, but in some cases the registrant does not wish
to do so, or may be unable to do so on the dates fixed for the hearing. In the latter case, of course a postponement should be requested
as soon as it becomes apparent that one is needed, giving full and
detailed reasons as to why the postponement is needed. If the reason
is related to the registrant's health, it is important to include supporting evidence from a medical practitioner.

4.152   There is a practice note, available on the HCPC website,[65]
which clarifies the distinction it draws between adjournments and
postponements:

• postponement is an administrative action which may be taken on
behalf of a practice committee by the HCPC's Head of Adjudication at any time up to 14 days before the date on which a hearing
is due to begin; and

• adjournment is a decision for the panel or the panel chair, taken
at any time after that 14-day limit has passed or once the proceedings have begun or are part heard.

4.153 An application to postpone or adjourn for more time to prepare the
registrant's case is more likely to be granted if specific reasons can
be given as to the further additional evidence needed and reasons
why it has not been possible to obtain it within the usual timescales.
Article 6 ECHR arguments can of course be used in support of such
an application, on which see chapter 1.

4.154   *Faulkner v Nursing and Midwifery Council*[66] demonstrated the
importance of providing medical evidence to support an application to adjourn on health grounds. The decision to proceed in the
absence of the registrant who failed to provide such evidence was
upheld. Although F later gave evidence via a telephone link, he was

65 See www.hcpc-uk.org/assets/documents/10001DD7PRACTICE_NOTE_
Adjournment_of_proceedings.pdf.
66 [2009] EWHC 3349 (Admin).

restricted to addressing sanctions since the decisions on misconduct and impairment had already been made in his absence.

4.155   Panels have discretion to proceed in the absence of the registrant.[67] The discretion must be exercised with the utmost care and caution, given the potentially disastrous consequences for the registrant of an adverse finding in his or her absence. In exercising the discretion, panels are required to have regard to all of the circumstances known to them, including whether the absence is voluntary and amounting to a waiver of the right to attend. This underlines the importance of registrants engaging with the process at an early stage and making any application to adjourn at the earliest possible opportunity and supported by as much detail as is available.

4.156   In *R v Jones (Anthony)*[68] the following important observations were made:

> ... the discretion to commence a trial in the absence of a defendant should be exercised with the utmost care and caution ... If the absence of the defendant is attributable to involuntary illness or incapacity it would very rarely, if ever, be right to exercise the discretion in favour of commencing the trial, at any rate unless the defendant is represented and asks that the trial should begin.[69]

4.157   The applicability of these principles to regulatory proceedings was confirmed in *Tait v Royal College of Veterinary Surgeons*.[70]

4.158   There is a practice note, available on the HCPC website, for panels considering proceeding in the absence of the registrant which sets out all of the factors to be considered, and provides a useful checklist as to matters to include in any application to adjourn.[71]

Vulnerable witnesses

4.159   Witness statements will have been provided by the HCPC along with the bundle of documents it proposes to rely upon and, unless agreed by the registrant, will normally be called to give evidence at the hearing. In some cases, where the evidence given by a witness is not central to the HCPC case or the person is unavailable, the written statement will be relied upon alone. See paras 4.115–4.119 on

---

67 HPC (Investigating Committee) Rules 2003 r9, HPC (Health Committee) Rules 2003 and HPC (Conduct and Competence Committee) Rules 2003 r11.

68 [2002] UKHL 5.

69 [2002] UKHL 5 para 13.

70 [2003] UKPC 34.

71 See www.hcpc-uk.org/assets/documents/100028A1ProceedingsintheAbsenceof theRegistrant.pdf.

the admissibility of hearsay evidence to which the registrant has not agreed.

4.160   There are particular considerations regarding witnesses in cases where the allegations are of a sexual nature. Where the witness is the complainant, and where the registrant is representing him/herself the registrant is prevented from cross-examining the witness unless the witness has provided written consent. Where written consent is not given, the registrant must appoint a legally qualified person to cross-examine the witness on his or her behalf. If the registrant does not do so seven days before the hearing date, the HCPC will appoint a legally qualified person to do so.[72] This measure reflects similar provisions that have been adopted in relation to criminal cases.

4.161   There are also provisions under rules 8A and 10A for panels to adopt such measures as it considers desirable in relation to vulnerable witnesses. 'Vulnerable witnesses' are defined as:

- aged under 17;
- having a mental disorder;
- having an impairment of intelligence and social functioning;
- having physical disabilities;
- where the allegation against the registrant is of a sexual nature; and
- where the witness complains of intimidation.

4.162   A number of possible measures are set out in the rule, including video-links, pre-recorded evidence in chief, interpreters, screens and private hearings. In practice, the most commonly adopted measures are screens and video-links. Again, these measures reflect similar provisions adopted by the criminal courts. Applications for such measures are usually made at preliminary meetings, but may on occasion be made on the first day of the final disposal hearing. The test as to whether such an application should be granted is that the quality of the witness's evidence is likely to be adversely affected as a result of his or her vulnerability.

4.163   A registrant or his or her representative may object to the use of such measures, but clear reasons need to be stated in support of the objection. It may be argued for example that where a case turns on a conflict of fact between the complainant and the registrant (as is often the case where the complaint is of a sexual nature) it is necessary for the panel to observe as closely as possible the demeanour

---

72   HCP (Investigating Committee) Rules 2003 r8A(4) and (5); HCP (Health Committee) Rules 2003 and HCP (Conduct and Competence Committee) Rules 2003 r10A(4) and (5).

of the witness in cross-examination and this is not possible through a video-link. Such an argument will not, of course, necessarily succeed, but on occasions panels may be persuaded to opt for screens rather than video-link. The registrant should be advised that requests for such measures in appropriate cases are often granted.

Cross-examination

4.164   As referred to in para 4.114 above, it is possible in many cases for the statements of some of the HCPC witnesses to be agreed. Where they are not, witnesses will be called to give evidence live, or via video-link.

4.165   The usual rules apply in cross-examination of witnesses, so the registrant's case must be put and any factual conflicts challenged. There are tactical considerations in putting the registrant's case depending on the type of witness. For example, while robust cross-examination of a manager who has failed adequately to support a registrant facing allegations of unsatisfactory professional practice may be perfectly appropriate, such an approach might be less productive where the witness in question is a patient or service user, particularly if they are elderly, injured or otherwise vulnerable.

No case to answer

> Submissions of no case to answer may be made in respect of a case or a specific allegation.
>
> They may be made where a) there is no evidence or b) there is some evidence but it is weak, vague or inconsistent and, looked at 'in the round', a panel *could* not properly find the case (or fact) proved.

4.166   Although the HCPC's rules do not make specific provision for a submission of no case to answer at the conclusion of the HCPC's case (unlike, for example, those of the NMC), there is the opportunity to do so in appropriate cases.

4.167   Such a submission is most likely to be considered appropriate in cases where either the factual basis has been significantly undermined in the course of cross-examination (for example where a witness has retracted previous assertions, or otherwise shown to lack credibility or reliability) or where the facts set out in the particulars are of a low level of seriousness such that it is possible to argue that even if the HCPC's case is accepted in its entirety it will not amount either to the statutory ground (misconduct, lack of competence or health) or to impairment. A submission of no case to answer can also be appropriate where a key witness for the HCPC has failed to attend, although it should be borne in mind that his or her witness statement may in any event be admissible as hearsay evidence, so in the absence of any conflicting evidence from another witness (or contradictory documentary evidence) it may nevertheless be accepted.

4.168   There are tactical considerations to making such a submission, in particular if it is to be on the second basis. It must be borne in mind that, if the submission is not accepted and the case continues, it may affect the panel's willingness to accept that the registrant has insight into his or her failings or a full appreciation of the need to adhere to the requisite standards.

4.169   If such a submission is to be made the *Galbraith*[73] test is the relevant basis, being applicable in regulatory proceedings, on which see chapter 1.

Evidence-in-chief

4.170   As previously stated, it will be necessary to have drafted and submitted a full witness statement setting out the registrant's response to the allegations, together with other information that is relevant to consideration of the statutory ground and impairment. The usual practice is for the panel members to read the registrant's statement before the start of the hearing (although for certainty it is appropriate for a representative to check that they have done so) and in many cases now panels are content to take the statement as read. This means that having read it to themselves, it is unnecessary for the registrant to read the statement aloud. It should be explained to the registrant that his or her evidence will carry the same weight as if the registrant had read it aloud. There may be some supplementary questions from the registrant's representative to cover additional matters that have arisen in the course of evidence from the HCPC witnesses, and of course it may be necessary to take the panel to documents referred to in the statement, either in the HCPC bundle or in the registrant's if he or she has provided one.

4.171   The advantage of taking statements as read is that it saves time, and many registrants are keen to minimise the time they have to spend on the witness stand. Taking this approach can, however, feel to some registrants as though they have not told their side of the story to the panel, so in particular cases it may still be appropriate to ask the registrant to read the statement aloud. Panel chairs are usually

73   *R v Galbraith* (1981) 73 Cr App R 124, CA.

content to take evidence-in-chief in whatever manner the registrant's representative suggests.

4.172   At the conclusion of evidence-in-chief (however taken) the registrant will be cross-examined in the usual way by the HCPC's representative and usually there will be questions from the members of the panel. In cases concerned with aspects of professional practice it is likely that the majority of questions will be asked by the registrant member of the panel.

4.173   In cases where a supporting witness is being called on behalf of the registrant to give evidence either on issues of fact or of good professional performance, which is relevant to impairment, that witness will usually be called at this point. As with the registrant it is essential to have a full witness statement which can be taken as read. In most cases, unless the registrant's representative objects, the HCPC's practice is for the panel to withdraw to deliberate only once to decide on facts, statutory ground and impairment. Evidence given by witnesses which goes to both impairment and mitigation need not be called twice, panels are familiar with the overlap between the two and are content to be reminded at sanction stage of the evidence previously given which remains relevant.

Submissions

4.174   As previously indicated , the usual practice at the HCPC is to take submissions on facts, statutory ground and impairment all together and for the panel to withdraw to deliberate just once, albeit that the decision is taken in the three stages and separate reasons are given.

4.175   In most cases this practice has no particular disadvantage to the registrant, but occasionally there may be good reason for objecting. Any objection to the usual practice should be made known to the legal assessor and the HCPC advocate at the earliest opportunity.

4.176   The circumstances in which this can arise are where the registrant faces a number of allegations, where the facts of which are denied and where there is a significantly varying degree of seriousness in the factual particulars. In such cases it may be helpful for the registrant's representative to know which of the factual particulars are proven before making submissions on statutory ground and impairment. So, for example, if the most serious factual particulars are found proven, the representative may wish to take a different approach in submissions on the remaining stages (or even take instructions as to whether admissions may be made).

4.177   In all cases it will be helpful to keep submissions focused on the three stages of the exercise and deal with each in turn. While it is common practice to refer to fundamental issues such as the burden and standard of proof, these will be covered by the legal assessor and referred to by the HCPC advocate in his or her opening statement. Written submissions or skeleton arguments are rarely necessary, but can be of assistance in cases where, for example, an unusual point of law is to be argued, or if a case has gone part heard, when it may be helpful to remind the panel of the evidence heard on the earlier occasion.

4.178   The panel will be taken through the key authorities on the statutory ground and impairment by the legal assessor. There is a practice note on impairment available on the HCPC's website to which panels are always urged to have regard.[74] Accordingly, it will not be necessary for the registrant's representative to set out the law on these matters (unless intending to rely upon an authority that is not referred to in the practice note) but simply to apply the tests derived from them to the facts of the case in hand.

4.179   See chapter 1 for a full discussion of the key authorities on impairment and the statutory grounds.

Mitigation and sanctions

> The principal aims of sanctions are to protect the public, uphold the standards and reputation of the profession and to maintain public confidence therein.
>
> The punitive effect of sanctions is only one (and not the most important) factor to be borne in mind when assessing whether a sanction is proportional to the matters found proved against a practitioner.

4.180   The panel will give its decision on facts, statutory ground and impairment with reasons for the decision reached at each stage. At the conclusion of the decision and reasons, further evidence and submissions will be invited from the HCPC's and the registrant's representatives.

4.181   In cases of misconduct the panel may apply any of the sanctions set out in HPO 2001 article 29(4) and (5) which are:

• refer to screeners or undertake mediation;

74 See www.hcpc-uk.org/assets/documents/10000A9CPractice_Note_Sanctions.pdf.

- take no action;
- impose a caution order of between one and five years;
- impose a conditions of practice order up to a maximum of three years;
- impose a suspension order for a maximum period of one year; or
- make a striking-off order.

4.182   In cases of lack of competence and health, the same sanctions are available with the exception of a striking-off order, which may only be imposed after a registrant has already been suspended or subject to a conditions of practice order for a minimum period of two years preceding the date of the striking off order.[75]

4.183   This distinction in powers of sanction is an important consideration at earlier stages in the proceedings – for example, when deciding whether to make an application for a case to be referred to the Health Committee rather than to the Conduct and Competence Committee. Similarly there may be a tactical advantage to making admissions of lack of competence (but not misconduct) where allegations are put in the alternative, as is often the case.

4.184   The HCPC's advocates normally take a neutral stance on sanction and do not seek to persuade the panel that a particular sanction is appropriate in a given case. Usually he or she will simply bring the disposals available (depending on the statutory ground upon which impairment has been found) to the panel's attention and refer to mitigating and aggravating features.

4.185   Further evidence may be called by the registrant at the mitigation stage, although as referred to above, testimonials going to professional practice will have been adduced at impairment stage. Purely personal character references are only relevant at sanctions stage. In many cases where the registrant is not practising their profession at the time of the hearing it will not be possible to obtain current professional testimonials, but panels are generally open to receiving relevant material in other forms such as 'thank you' letters or cards from former patients, or expressions of gratitude from colleagues.

4.186   The HCPC has an indicative sanctions policy (updated in July 2011) which is available on its website[76] and which helpfully sets out the purpose of sanction, the key principles of proportionality, equality and diversity issues, the procedure to be adopted by panels in deciding on sanction and an indication of the kind of factors that

75 HPO 2001 article 29(6).
76 See www.hcpc-uk.org.

are likely to make a case suitable for each of the given sanctions. The policy is essential reading for any representative, and will be of great assistance in deciding how to pitch submissions at the final stage of the process.

4.187   Panels are invariably reminded that the purpose of sanctions is to protect the public, not to punish the registrant (although it is recognised that some, notably caution orders and suspension orders, will have a punitive effect). Protection of the public includes consideration of the deterrent effect, the reputation of the profession and public confidence in the regulatory process.

4.188   In addition to the factors set out in the policy, it will be necessary to give consideration to the impact of a particular sanction to the registrant in question.

4.189   A finding of impairment will not invariably lead to a sanction; there is an express power[77] for a panel to take no further action. Such disposals are rare, but arguments in support may be made in cases where the allegations raise low levels of concern and there has been full remediation of any deficiencies by the registrant prior to the hearing.

4.190   Mediation is rarely used and is only appropriate in cases where both parties (ie registrant and complainant) agree to its use and where the panel is satisfied that no other action is appropriate.

4.191   Caution orders are used in cases where the allegation represents an isolated lapse by the registrant or is of a minor nature. The advantage of a caution order over conditions of practice (apart from the obvious absence of any restriction on the registrant's ability to practise) is that there is no requirement for review. Once the period has passed, the order lapses and no other action is required. Registrants should however be advised that even once lapsed a caution may be taken into account if a further allegation is made against the same registrant.

4.192   Conditions of practice are often imposed in cases of lack of competence and health and may be restrictive or remedial or both. If conditions appear to be the appropriate (or most favourable) disposal it will be important to provide evidence to the panel of the registrant's willingness and ability to comply. If available, supporting evidence from another professional (for example, a manager or potential mentor) of their willingness to provide a particular form of support to the registrant will be very helpful.

---

77   HPO 2001 article 29(4)(b).

4.193   Representatives should give careful consideration as to the kind of conditions that will be appropriate (in the sense of meeting the particular concerns) and workable in a given case. Such orders must be reviewed before the expiry of the original term[78] and registrants must be made aware that if, following imposition of such an order, there is any difficulty in complying with the specified conditions, the HCPC should be informed as soon as possible. In such cases, an early review should be sought to request a variation of the terms. A registrant who has simply failed to comply and not raised the matter before expiry will be viewed much less sympathetically by any reviewing panel and will risk an extension of the order.

4.194   Panels should not confuse suspension and the imposition of conditions and if imposing the latter, they must be reasonable and workable. In *Udom v General Medical Council*[79] the panel found U's fitness to practise impaired by reason of health and competence. It imposed a sanction which purported to be conditions that he was not to practise unsupervised for a period of nine months and was, during that period, to undergo a series of clinical attachments. The effect of the order was to suspend U from practice. Suspension and conditions of practice are separate mutually exclusive sanctions. Accordingly, the panel had been wrong to impose conditions which had the effect of suspending the registrant.

4.195   Suspension orders are used for cases where no conditions can be devised that will protect the public, but where repetition is unlikely and therefore striking off is not appropriate. Although the powers of sanction under HPO 2001 article 29 are alternatives and a combination (for example, of suspension with conditions) may not be imposed, in many cases a panel will, when suspending a registrant, provide an indication of the kind of steps that may be taken during the period of suspension that would assist a panel on review. Registrants who are subject to such an order should be made aware that compliance with the suggested steps is highly advisable in order to achieve a successful outcome to the review.

4.196   Striking-off orders are reserved for the most serious cases, and registrants who are struck off may not apply to be restored to the register for a period of five years following the order being made, unless new evidence relevant to the order has become available since the order was made.[80]

---

78 HPO 2001 article 30(1).
79 [2009] EWHC 3242 (Admin).
80 HPO 2001 articles 33(2)(a) and 29(7)(a).

4.197   Cases that may merit a striking-off order include those that involve repeated and/or very serious allegations of abuse of trust or dishonesty, or ongoing persistent failures.

4.198   In some cases of conditions – and whenever suspension or strike-off orders have been made – after the panel gives its decision on sanction, the HCPC's advocate will make an application for an interim order to cover the period of 28 days (or longer if an appeal is lodged) during which the substantive order does not take effect. In cases of strike-off and suspension, the application will be for an interim suspension order, while in conditions cases the application will normally be for conditions replicating those in the substantive order, although this may not be necessary where conditions are purely remedial and have no restrictive effect.

4.199   Representatives will need to take instructions from the registrant if there are particular reasons for opposing the imposition of an interim order, for example if the registrant has patients booked in for the following days and needs time to arrange cover for his or her practice. Such a reason may, however, not find favour with a panel as the failure to make suitable alternative arrangements prior to the hearing may be regarded as indicative of a lack of appreciation of the seriousness of the allegations the registrant faces and the likelihood of strike-off. Although the panel will be advised that the making of an order in these circumstances is not automatic, realistically in many cases panels will feel that the public needs to be protected during the appeal period.

4.200   For a full discussion of authorities on sanction and guideline cases see chapter 1.

Reviews and challenges

Reviews

4.201   Conditions of practice and suspension orders must be reviewed before expiry.[81] In either case, the reviewing panel may extend the period of the order for a maximum period of three years for conditions and one year for suspension, or may replace with a different order of a kind that would have been available to the panel imposing the original order, or may make a conditions of practice order to take effect following expiry of a suspension order.

81 HPO 2001 article 30(1).

4.202   The importance of complying fully with conditions of practice has been referred to at para 4.193 above, and where recommended steps are brought to the registrant's attention by a panel imposing a suspension order, the importance of having followed them by the time of any review is clear if a subsequent conditions of practice order is to be avoided.

4.203   In addition to the mandatory review provided for under HPO 2001 article 30(1), a registrant subject to a caution, conditions or suspension is entitled to seek a review at any time.[82] Upon such a review, the panel is able to confirm the original order, extend or reduce the period for which it has effect, replace it with another order of a kind that would have been available to the original panel, revoke any condition imposed by the order or revoke the order itself.

4.204   The most common circumstances in which a registrant will wish to take advantage of this provision is where remedial conditions have been imposed which have been complied with well in advance of the normal expiry date of the order, or where there has been a material change to the registrant's status (for example a change in employment). An application for such a review should be made in writing at the earliest opportunity setting out the reason why it is sought and supporting evidence of compliance with the conditions or the changed circumstances will need to be adduced at the review hearing.

Restoration

4.205   A registrant who is subject to a striking-off order may apply for restoration to the register, and there is a practice note that contains useful information for potential applicants and their representatives.[83]

4.206   The application must be made in writing to the registrar, although it will be referred for consideration to a panel of the practice committee that made the original order. No such application may be made for a period of five years following imposition of the original order unless new evidence that is relevant to the order becomes available. No further application may be made within a period of 12 months from a previous unsuccessful application for restoration.

4.207   The applicant must be given an opportunity to appear before a panel of the appropriate practice committee to argue his or her case. Restoration hearings follow a similar procedure as other fitness to

82 HPO 2001 article 30(2).
83 See www.hcpc-uk.org/publications/practicenotes.

practise hearings except that the applicant bears the burden of proof and therefore presents his or her case before any submissions are made by the HCPC's representative.

4.208   Panels in restoration hearings must ensure that the applicant has the requisite qualifications to be registered in the applicable profession and also that he or she is a fit and proper person to practise that profession. In applying the second requirement the panel is to have regard in particular to the circumstances that led to the making of the striking off order.

4.209   In presenting an application for restoration it will be important to address matters such as the applicant's insight into the matters that led to the striking-off order and any remedial steps that have been taken in the interim as well as action taken to ensure his or her professional skills and knowledge have been kept up-to-date.

4.210   Panels may restore an applicant to the register with conditions or unconditionally. In order to avoid conditions therefore it is important to adduce as much evidence as possible of updated skills and knowledge at the restoration hearing.

4.211   If an application for restoration is unsuccessful on two or more occasions, the relevant practice committee may suspend the applicant's right to make further applications indefinitely. Where such a direction is made, the prospective applicant may apply for it to be reviewed after a period of three years has elapsed.

Appeals

4.212   Any order (other than an interim order) of the practice committees is subject to a right of appeal to the appropriate court, which is the High Court (England and Wales), the Court of Session (Scotland) or the High Court of Justice of Northern Ireland. The time limit for lodging and appeal is 28 days from the date when the notice of order or decision was served on the registrant.[84]

4.213   Where an appeal is lodged within the appropriate period, the order appealed does not take effect until the appeal is disposed of (hence the practice of imposing an interim order at the conclusion of a final disposal hearing as referred to in para 4.198 above) and the HCPC will be the respondent in the appeal proceedings.

4.214   The most likely grounds of appeal will be where the panel has imposed a sanction that is not within its powers (for example, conditions and suspension combined), otherwise made an error of law,

84 HPO 2001 articles 29(9) and 38.

failed to give adequate reasons for the decision or that the sanction imposed is too severe in the circumstances. Case-law from other regulatory bodies is of course applicable to appeals against decisions of the HCPC.

Challenge by the Council for Healthcare Regulatory Excellence

4.215 As referred to at para 4.8 above, fitness to practise decisions by the HCPC are subject to scrutiny by the Council for Healthcare Regulatory Excellence[85] (CHRE) where they are considered by the CHRE to be 'unduly lenient'. The CHRE has four weeks from the last day of the appeal period (ie 28th day from service of the notice of order) to bring such a challenge. The CHRE uses alternative dispute resolution (ADR) on occasions to dispose of such cases, others go to a full hearing in the appropriate court. The prospect of challenge by the CHRE of course takes some of the pleasure out of obtaining a good outcome for a registrant, but representatives should inform the registrant of the possibility.

Costs

4.216 Since the various healthcare regulators bring proceedings in the public interest, to protect the public or to uphold standards etc, they are not in the position of an ordinary litigant prosecuting a claim. Unless a complaint is improperly brought, no order for costs is normally made against the regulator (see *Walker v Law Society*[86]).

---

85 Soon to be renamed the Professional Standards Authority for Health and Social Care: Health and Social Care Act 2012 s222.

86 [2007] EWCA Civ 233.

The General Dental Council

Key points

- *Regulator:* General Dental Council (GDC)
- *Professions regulated:* Dentists, clinical dental technicians, dental nurses, dental technicians, orthodontic therapists, dental hygienists
- *Type of proceedings:* Fitness to practise, fraudulent register entry hearings, restoration hearings, registration appeals
- *Relevant statute:* Dentists Act (DA) 1984
- *Fitness to Practise Rules:* General Dental Council (Fitness to Practise) Rules 2006 (Schedule to SI 2006 No 1663)
- *Two-stage process (for fitness to practise):* Yes
- *Investigation Committee:* Yes (GDC (Fitness to Practise) Rules 2006 r5)
- *Notification of hearing:* Yes (GDC (Fitness to Practise) Rules 2006 r13)
- *Interim Orders Committee (IOC):* Yes (GDC (Fitness to Practise) Rules 2006 r36)
- *Practice committees (for fitness to practise):* The Professional Performance Committee, the Professional Conduct Committee and the Health Committee. The Professional Performance Committee also hears fraudulent register entry hearings and restoration hearings
- *Registration appeals:* Heard by the Registration Appeals Committee
- *Key documents: GDC standards for dental professionals*
- *Location:* 37 Wimpole Street, London W1G 8DQ
- *Case management provisions:* GDC (Fitness to Practise) Rules 2006 r51
- *Procedure before a Fitness to Practise Panel:* GDC (Fitness to Practise) Rules 2006 r14
- *Test:* Whether fitness to practise is impaired by reason of (in summary): a) misconduct; b) deficient professional performance; c) adverse physical or mental health; d) a conviction or caution for a criminal offence; e) determination by a regulator or by the Office of the Health Professions Adjudicator (OHPA) that fitness to practise is impaired; f) inclusion in an Independent Safeguarding Authority barred list (DA 1984 s27(2))
- *Interim order power:* Yes – interim conditions of practice or interim suspension (DA 1984 s32)
- *Interim order guidance: Interim Orders Committee guidance*

- *General composition for final hearings:* At least three persons, to include at least one registered dentist, one lay person and (in any case concerning the registration of a dental care profession-al) one registered dental care professional
- *How address panel:* Generally seated and 'Sir'/'Madam'
- *Advisers to the panel:* The panel is assisted by a legal adviser. The panel may also be advised by professional and medical advisers
- *Sanction provisions:* DA 1984 s27B
- *Sanction documents: Guidance, Professional Conduct Committee, Professional Performance Committee and Health Committee; GDC conditions bank* (precedent for earlier conditions of practice)
- *Resumed hearings:* GDC (Fitness to Practise) Rules 2006 r29. The purpose of a resumed hearing is to review conditions of prac-tice or suspension orders which have been imposed at an earlier hearing (these hearings are known as 'review hearings' before other regulatory bodies)
- *Restoration hearings:* DA 1984 s28
- *Appeal rule:* DA 1984 s29

Introduction

Background

5.1   The GDC is the regulatory body which governs the dental profession and professions complementary to dentistry. It was originally created by the Dentists Act 1956. Its present powers derive from the Dentists Act (DA) 1984.

5.2   When exercising its functions the GDC is required:

- to have regard for the interests of persons using or needing the services of registered dentists or registered dental care profes-sionals in the UK (ie protection of the public);
- to have regard for any differing interests of different categories of registered dentists or registered dental care professionals;
- to promote high standards of education at all its stages in all aspects of dentistry;
- to promote high standards of professional conduct, performance and practice among persons registered under the DA 1984.[1]

---

1   DA 1984 ss1A, 2.

5.3 The DA 1984 established six statutory committees to carry out the principal regulatory and disciplinary functions of the GDC. Three of these committees are collectively described as 'Practice Committees', namely the Health Committee, the Professional Conduct Committee and the Professional Performance Committee. The other three committees are the Investigating Committee, the Interim Orders Committee and the Registration Appeals Committee. The work of the statutory committees will be considered in more detail later in this chapter.

5.4 The GDC's other functions (such as education, financial and business planning and policy) are carried out by non-statutory committees. An Appointments Committee exists to appoint members to the six statutory committees.

5.5 The GDC's regulatory work is overseen by the Council for Healthcare Regulatory Excellence (CHRE).[2] As for other regulators, the CHRE has the power to challenge any fitness to practise decisions that it considers to be unduly lenient in the High Court or Court of Session. The quorum for each panel of a committee is three, of which there must be at least one registered dentist, one lay person and (in any case concerning a person's registration in the dental care professionals register), one registered dental care professional. Any of the three members can act as the chair of the committee.

5.6 The committee is advised on questions of law by a legal adviser and may be advised by professional and medical advisers. Legal advisers must have a ten-year general qualification.[3] The role of the legal adviser (known in other areas of regulatory law as the legal assessor) is discussed in more detail in chapter 1.

Current issues

5.7 An issue which has recently emerged is whether tooth whitening treatments such as laser whitening and bleach whitening amount to the practice of dentistry and are therefore reserved for dentists or dental care professionals. At present, these treatments are offered by a number of unqualified and unregulated bodies and agencies. The popularity of tooth whitening treatments was not envisaged at the time of the DA 1984. The GDC's position is that these treatments do amount to the practice of dentistry.

---

2 The CHRE is to be renamed the Professional Standards Authority for Health and Social Care pursuant to Health and Social Care Act 2012 s222.

3 DA 1984 Sch 4C Part 1(5).

5.8   In March 2011 the GDC successfully prosecuted Paul William Hill of Warrington, Director of PW Healthcare Consulting Ltd (trading nationally as 'Style Smile Clinics'), at City of Westminster magistrates' court. He pleaded guilty to four offences including practising dentistry while not registered as a dentist or dental care professional.[4]

5.9   At the time of writing, the tooth whitening issue has not been considered by the higher courts.

Jurisdictional reach

5.10   The GDC regulates dentists and professions complementary to dentistry.

Dentists

5.11   Any person who is a graduate or licentiate in dentistry of a UK dental authority and who satisfies the registrar of his or her identity, good character and good physical and mental health is entitled to be included in the register of dentists.[5]

5.12   Any 'exempt person' who holds an appropriate European diploma or who is a person to whom certain provisions of the European Communities (Recognition of Professional Qualifications) Regulations 2007[6] apply, and who is permitted to pursue the profession of dentistry in the UK by virtue of these regulations and who has passed any aptitude test or completed any adaptation period which is required, is entitled to be included in the register. Again, these persons must satisfy the registrar of their identity, good character and good physical and mental health.

5.13   An 'exempt person', for these purposes, means a national of a relevant European state other than the UK, a national of the UK who is seeking access to, or is pursuing, the profession by virtue of an enforceable EU right or a person who is not a national of a relevant European state but who is, by virtue of an enforceable EU right, entitled to be treated, for the purposes of access to and pursuit of the profession, no less favourably than a national of a relevant European state.[7]

---

4   GDC Press Release 25 March 2011.
5   DA 1984 s15.
6   SI 2007 No 2781.
7   DA 1984 s53(1) (definition added by the European Qualifications (Health and Social Care Professions) Regulations 2007 SI No 3101).

5.14   Any person who holds a recognised overseas diploma and who satisfies the GDC of his or her requisite knowledge and skill, knowledge of English (except in the case of an exempt person), good character and good physical and mental health is entitled to be included in the register.[8] There are also provisions for the inclusion of visiting dentists and temporary registrants.[9]

5.15   Under the DA 1984, the practice of dentistry includes the performance of any operation, treatment, advice or attendance as is usually performed or given by dentists. This includes operations, treatment, advice or attendance on persons in connection with the fitting, insertion or fixing of dentures, artificial teeth or other dental appliances.[10]

5.16   'Operation' means a surgical operation on the mouth of the patient.[11] 'Treatment, advice or attendance' includes taking an impression of the mouth for the purpose of repairing a denture.[12] It does not include the alteration of an existing denture that is unconnected with the fitting to the mouth itself.[13]

5.17   The performance of any medical task by a person who is qualified to carry out the task and is a member of any of the other regulatory bodies which are subject to the CHRE is not deemed to amount to the practice of dentistry.[14] This work, therefore, falls outside the ambit of the GDC and is instead supervised by the appropriate regulatory body.

5.18   Appropriately supervised work undertaken by dental students, medical students or dental care professional students is not deemed to amount to the practice of dentistry.[15] Accordingly, this work also falls outside the ambit of the GDC (although the supervisor would be subject to the GDC's jurisdiction in his or her own right).

Professions complementary to dentistry

5.19   The DA 1984 defines professions complementary to dentistry as professions where the majority of members work in connection with the provision of dental care. This can either mean that they work with

8   DA 1984 s15.
9   DA 1984 s14.
10   DA 1984 s37.
11   *Hennan and Co Ltd v Duckworth* [1904–1907] All ER Rep 862.
12   *Almy v Thomas* [1953] 2 All ER 1050, [1953] 1 WLR 1296.
13   *Twyford v Puntschart* [1947] 1 All ER 773.
14   DA 1984 s37(1A).
15   DA 1984 s37(2).

persons receiving dental care (ie patients), or with dentists or other dental care professionals.[16]

5.20   The definition of 'professions complementary to dentistry' *excludes* professions that are regulated by bodies other than the GDC that are themselves regulated by the CHRE.[17]

5.21   The following professions and job titles currently fall within the category of professions complementary to dentistry and are regulated by the GDC:[18]

Profession	Job titles
Clinical dental technicians	Clinical dental technician, clinical dental technologist, denturist
Dental nurses	Dental nurse, dental surgery assistant
Dental technicians	Dental technician, dental technologist
Orthodontic therapists	Orthodontic therapist, orthodontic auxiliary
Dental hygienists	Dental hygienist

5.22   It is a criminal offence for a person who is not listed in the Dental Care Professionals Register to use any of the titles specified by regulations (as set out in the list of professions complementary to dentistry above). The offence is punishable on summary conviction by a fine up to the level five on the standard scale.[19]

5.23   The practice of dentistry is reserved to registered dentists and dental care professionals. It is illegal for persons who are not registered dentists or registered dental care professionals to hold themselves out, either directly or by implication, as practising or being prepared to practise dentistry. This is a criminal offence punishable on summary conviction to a fine not exceeding the level five on the standard scale.[20]

---

16 DA 1984 s36A.
17 Under the Health and Social Care Act 2012 the CHRE is to become the Professional Standards Authority for Health and Social Care.
18 General Dental Council (Professions Complementary to Dentistry) Regulations Order of Council 2006 SI No 1440 made under DA 1984 s36A(2) and (3) and s52(1A) and (1B); General Dental Council (Professions Complementary to Dentistry) (Dental Hygienists and Dental Therapists) Regulations Order of Council 2006 SI No 1667 made under DA 1984 s36A(2) and (3).
19 DA 1984 s39.
20 DA1984 s38.

Approach to regulation

5.24   In assessing fitness to practise the GDC adopts the same test as other healthcare regulators: that a registrant's fitness to practise is impaired. Impairment can be alleged by reason of (in summary):

a) misconduct;
b) deficient professional performance;
c) adverse physical or mental health;
d) a conviction or caution for a criminal offence;
e) determination by a regulator that fitness to practise is impaired;
f) inclusion in an Independent Safeguarding Authority (ISA) barred list.[21]

For full discussion of each of these issues see chapters 1 and 8. The case-law from other regulatory bodies, including the GMC, Health and Care Professions Council (HCPC) and Nursing and Midwifery Council (NMC) is applicable to decisions of the GDC.

5.25   Complaints against registrants will be considered even where the matter giving rise to the complaint occurred outside the UK or at a time when the registrant was not included on the register.[22]

5.26   A registrant who is the subject of an allegation and/or of proceedings before one of the committees is known as a respondent. At hearings before a committee, respondents have the right to be legally represented or represented by a friend, family member or member of an organisation of which the respondent is a member.[23] For a fuller discussion of the legal issues relating to representation see para 1.294.

5.27   In line with many of the other healthcare regulators, fitness to practise proceedings typically begin with a complaint from sources such as the registrant's patients or employers made to the GDC. The GDC caseworkers consider whether the allegation appears to raise a question that needs to be looked into.[24] Any allegation that appears to raise a question that needs to be looked into is referred to the Investigating Committee. The role of the Investigating Committee is to determine which allegations should be passed to a practice committee.

---

21   DA 1984 s27(2).
22   DA 1984 s27(3).
23   General Dental Council (Fitness to Practise) Rules 2006 (Schedule 1 to the General Dental Council (Fitness to Practise) Rules Order of Council 2006 SI No 1663) r52.
24   'How we Investigate' available at www.gdc-uk.org/membersofpublic/raisingaconcern/pages.

5.28   The GDC has three separate practice committees dealing with different types of fitness to practise issues: the Professional Conduct Committee, the Professional Performance Committee and the Health Committee.

5.29   All hearings before the statutory committees, including the Interim Orders Committee, are to be conducted in public except:

- where the interests of the parties or the protection of the private and family life of the respondent or any other person so requires; or
- to the extent that a committee are of the opinion that, in the special circumstances of the case, it is strictly necessary to do so as publicity would prejudice the interests of justice.

5.30   Before deciding whether or not to conduct a hearing (or part of a hearing) in private, the committee must invite representations from the parties and any other party whom a committee considers it appropriate to hear, and obtain the advice of the legal adviser.[25] There seems no reason why 'any other party' should not include the media.

5.31   Article 8 (right to a fair trial) of the European Convention on Human Rights (ECHR) may be engaged by the decision as to whether or not to conduct a hearing in private. Most hearings are held in public as weight is typically given to the regulator's purpose of acting in the public interest and protecting the public. The case-law on human rights and regulatory law is discussed in more detail in chapter 1.

5.32   The practice committee may take any steps which they regard as necessary to protect vulnerable witnesses. Vulnerable witnesses may include:

- any witness under the age of 18;
- any witness with a mental disorder;
- any witness who is significantly impaired in relation to intelligence or social functioning;
- any witness with physical disabilities who requires assistance to give evidence;
- any witness where the subject matter of the hearing is of a sexual nature and the witness was the alleged victim; or
- any witness who complains of intimidation.[26]

Where appropriate, evidence can be given by video-link and/or pre-recorded evidence can be used as evidence-in-chief. Where proceedings concern a sexual allegation, respondents acting in

25 GDC (Fitness to Practise) Rules 2006 r53.
26 GDC (Fitness to Practise) Rules 2006 r56.

person are not permitted to cross-examine the alleged victim directly in person.[27]

5.33   The three practice committees – the Professional Performance Committee, the Professional Conduct Committee and the Health Committee – may refer cases to each other or take advice from each other where appropriate.[28]

5.34   The practice committees must apply the civil standard of proof. The case-law relating to the standard of proof is discussed in more detail in chapter 1 (see para 1.340).

Sources of law

5.35   The GDC's powers derive from the DA 1984, which covers matters such as registration, the functions of the various committees, interim orders, sanction and appeals, and which empowers the GDC to make orders, rules and regulations in relevant areas.

5.36   The procedure followed in fitness to practise matters from the complaint stage onwards is governed by the GDC (Fitness to Practise) Rules 2006.[29] The Registration Appeals Committee has its own procedure rules: the GDC (Registration Appeals) Rules 2006.[30]

5.37   The GDC publishes useful guidance documents for the various committees, including the *Interim Orders Committee guidance*, *Professional Conduct Committee guidance*, *Professional Performance Committee guidance* and *Health Committee guidance*. These documents are available from the GDC website.[31]

Proceedings

Referrals

5.38   Disciplinary proceedings against dentists and dental care professionals begin with a complaint or other information alerting the GDC to a potential issue. The complaint can come from any source, including

---

27 GDC (Fitness to Practise) Rules 2006 r56.
28 GDC (Fitness to Practise) Rules 2006 r26.
29 Schedule to the General Dental Council (Fitness to Practise) Rules Order of Council 2006 No 1663.
30 Schedule to the General Dental Council (Registration Appeals) Rules Order of Council 2006 SI No 1668.
31 See www.gdc-uk.org – the guidance documents are accessed via the pages for the individual committees.

other dental professionals, other professionals and members of the public.

5.39   A complaint or other information about a registrant (including a registrant whose registration is suspended) is initially passed to the registrar. The registrar determines whether a complaint or information amounts to an allegation.[32] Allegations are passed to the Investigating Committee.

5.40   Where the registrar determines that a complaint or information amounts to an allegation, he or she must send a notification to the respondent and any maker of the allegation accordingly. The notification must:

- contain a summary of the allegation;
- be accompanied by a copy of the documents in the registrar's possession which relate to the allegation (however, the registrar shall not disclose to the maker of the allegation any evidence relating to the health or private and family life of the respondent or a third party, which has been provided by the respondent or a third party);
- invite the respondent to respond to the allegation with written representations addressed to the Investigating Committee within a period which the registrar shall specify in the notification; and
- where the allegation has been made by a person, inform the respondent that representations received from him or her may be disclosed to that person for comment.[33]

5.41   It is important to take great care from the earliest stage in corresponding with the regulator and disclosing further information. Any inconsistencies or inaccuracies can be used at the main hearing. Care should also be taken before suggesting that an allegation is minor or trivial in nature. On the one hand, it can be persuasive to emphasise that the matters alleged are too minor to amount to misconduct or lack of competence even if proven. On the other hand, this could be used to demonstrate a lack of insight or understanding of the seriousness of the allegation. To minimise risk, the safest course of action is to take legal advice.

5.42   *Standards for dental professionals, principles of raising concerns,*[34] provides that dental professionals have a duty to co-operate fully with

---

32 GDC (Fitness to Practise) Rules 2006 r3.
33 GDC (Fitness to Practise) Rules 2006 r4.
34 Available from www.gdc-uk.org/Newsandpublications/Publications/RaisingConcerns[1].pdf.

any procedure for bringing concerns which applies to their work.[35] They have a duty to approach the GDC in relation to concerns about other dental professionals if taking action at a local level would not be practical or has failed, or if the problem is so severe that the GDC genuinely needs to be involved, or if there is a genuine fear of victimisation or a cover-up.[36]

5.43   Although the GDC does not impose any time limit for the bringing of complaints, both domestic law and the ECHR confer a right to the speedy and just resolution of disputes. However, unreasonable delay in itself is insufficient to stay proceedings against a respondent. The law on delay is discussed in more detail in chapter 1 (see paras 1.19 and 1.102).

5.44   Regulatory proceedings do not need to be stayed pending the outcome of criminal proceedings unless there are exceptional circumstances from which the defendant can demonstrate serious prejudice or injustice. The law relating to concurrent proceedings is discussed in more detail in chapters 1 and 7.

Investigating Committee

> The Investigating Committee determines whether or not to make further enquiries into allegations and determines whether or not allegations should be passed to a practice committee.

5.45   The Investigating Committee's role is to determine which allegations should be passed to a practice committee. The Investigating Committee is empowered to issue advice or warnings in appropriate cases rather than passing the matter to a practice committee, or to take no action where appropriate.

5.46   After an allegation has been referred to the Investigating Committee, the Investigating Committee is required to hold a meeting in the presence of the registrar but in the absence of the parties.[37]

5.47   The Investigating Committee may, subject only to the requirements of relevance and fairness, admit any documentary evidence, whether or not that evidence would be admissible in any proceedings in a court.[38]

---

35 www.gdc-uk.org/Newsandpublications/Publications/RaisingConcerns[1].pdf, para 1.3.

36 www.gdc-uk.org/Newsandpublications/Publications/RaisingConcerns[1].pdf, para 3.6.

37 GDC (Fitness to Practise) Rules 2006 r5.

38 GDC (Fitness to Practise) Rules 2006 r6.

5.48   After considering the allegation, the Investigating Committee can determine as follows:[39]

- to adjourn consideration of the allegation and direct the registrar to carry out such enquiries as the Investigating Committee shall specify;
- that the allegation ought not to be considered by a practice committee but no warning or advice ought to be given;
- that the allegation ought not to be considered by a practice committee and that the matter should be closed by the communication to the respondent or to any other person involved in the investigation of such advice as the Investigating Committee may issue.[40]
- that the allegation ought not to be considered by a practice committee and that the matter should be closed by the communication to the respondent of such warning as the Investigating Committee may issue;[41] or
- that the allegation ought to be considered by a practice committee.

5.49   In considering a case, the Investigating Committee determines whether there is a real prospect of the facts, as alleged, being found proved and if so whether or not there is a real prospect of a finding of current impairment being made. The Investigating Committee does *not* decide whether an allegation is true or untrue, although it is entitled to take a view on the evidence presented to it.[42]

5.50   Although the GDC (Fitness to Practise) Rules 2006 do not specifically provide for this, the Investigating Committee will in certain circumstances direct that any letter of advice issued to a registrant should be published on the GDC website.[43]

5.51   Further enquiries may include specific factual enquiries, the commissioning of medical or other expert reports or the commissioning of an assessment of the respondent's professional performance.[44].In performance cases the GDC makes use of assessments provided by the National Clinical Assessment Service (NCAS). NCAS is a division of the National Patient Safety Agency (NPSA). Assessments are commissioned by the Investigating Committee.

---

39 GDC (Fitness to Practise) Rules 2006 r7.
40 DA 1984 ss27A(2) and 36O(2).
41 DA 1984 ss27A(2)(a) and 36O(2)(a).
42 Investigating Committee Guidance para 6, www.gdc-uk.org/ governanceandcorporate/Committees/Documents/ICGuidance.pdf.
43 www.gdc-uk.org/governanceandcorporate/Committees/Documents/ ICGuidance.pdf.
44 GDC (Fitness to Practise) Rules 2006 r8.

5.52   If the allegation proceeds to a practice committee, the respondent and the maker of the allegation must be given a reasonable opportunity to submit written representations commenting upon the allegation and upon the evidence (except evidence relating to the health or private and family life of the respondent or a third party which has been provided by the respondent or a third party).[45]

5.53   The particulars of the allegation and the facts upon which they are founded should be made clear in advance of any hearing. In *Gee v General Medical Council*[46] the court held it to be a requirement that the registrant had fair notice of the nature of the evidence to be led in support of the allegations, time to prepare for his defence and, that the panel should make plain which of the allegations of fact, if any, they had found proved. It is an aspect of ECHR article 6 that an applicant should be made aware of the charges against him or her. Allegations should not be drafted in a vague or ambiguous manner. The case-law relating to the drafting of allegations is discussed in more detail in chapter 1 (para 1.43).

Interim Orders Committee

> The Interim Orders Committee has the power to make an interim order for conditions of practice or for suspension. Weight is given to any risk to the public.

5.54   The Interim Orders Committee has the power to impose an interim order upon a respondent pending a hearing before one of the practice committees.[47] The Interim Orders Committee does not make findings of fact and does not make substantive decisions upon alleged impairment of fitness to practise.

5.55   The threshold for making an interim order is a high one, because no findings of fact have been made and the consequences for the respondent can be grave. Interim orders may only be made in the following circumstances:[48]

- where the Interim Orders Committee is satisfied that the order is necessary for the protection of the public;
- where it is otherwise in the public interest;
- where it is in the interests of the respondent.

---

45 GDC (Fitness to Practise) Rules 2006 r7(2).
46 [1987] 1 WLR 564.
47 DA 1984 s32(4).
48 Interim Orders Committee Guidance para 12, www.gdc-uk.org/governance andcorporate/GuidancefortheIOC.pdf.

5.56 In R (*Shiekh*) v *General Dental Council*,[49] a case where there was no direct risk to the safety of the public, an interim suspension order made by the GDC was overturned because of the serious impact upon the respondent's ability to make a living. Davis J observed that it was 'likely to be a relatively rare case' where an interim suspension order would be made on the grounds of public interest alone. However, the fact that the allegations do not raise issues of clinical competence does not mean that an interim order will never be required.[50] In all cases the committee must have regard for the principle of proportionality. The authorities on interim orders are discussed in more detail in chapter 1.

5.57 Respondents have the right to attend an interim orders hearing and to be legally represented. They must receive notice of the reason why it may be necessary to impose an interim order in the notification of interim orders hearing.[51]

5.58 Evidence in an interim orders hearing is admissible whether or not that evidence would be admissible in any proceedings in a court, subject to the requirements of relevance and fairness.[52]

5.59 At the interim orders hearing, unless the committee determines otherwise, the GDC presenter makes submissions and presents evidence as to why it may be necessary to make, revoke, confirm or replace an interim order. After this the respondent, or his or her representative, may make submissions and present evidence. With the chair's permission, legal or professional advisers may question a witness. Those present at the hearing will be informed of any advice given to the committee, even if it was given during private deliberations.

5.60 After hearing the evidence, the Interim Orders Committee deliberates in private. A decision is then made in public.[53] Reasons must be given. Chapter 1 contains a discussion on the requirement to give reasons (see paras 1.181 and 1.428).

5.61 The principal basis upon which the Interim Orders Committee assesses whether or not to exercise its powers is by looking at the risks (actual or potential) to the public if the registrant is permitted to continue to practise prior to a practice committee hearing. Although each case is decided on its merits, the *Interim Orders Committee*

49 [2007] EWHC 2972 (Admin).
50 See *Bradshaw v General Medical Council* [2010] EWHC 1296 (Admin).
51 GDC (Fitness to Practise) Rules 2006 r35.
52 GDC (Fitness to Practise) Rules 2006 r38.
53 GDC (Fitness to Practise) Rules 2006 r36.

guidance provides that particular regard may be had to the following matters:

- the serious abuse of a clinical relationship;
- a sexual or violent offence or indecency;
- undertaking treatment or procedures beyond competence;
- other serious abuse of the privileged position enjoyed by registered professionals;
- lack of evidence of appropriate indemnity cover;
- risk of patient harm due to the registrant's alcohol or drug abuse;
- dishonesty.

5.62   In relation to risks to the respondent, the *Interim Orders Committee guidance* provides that the following matters are usually considered:

- impact on the registrant's physical or mental health;
- risk to financial commitments and dependencies;
- loss of reputation and good standing.

5.63   The Interim Orders Committee has the power to make the following orders:

- *Suspension:* Suspending a respondent's registration for a period not exceeding 18 months.
- *Conditions:* Subjecting a respondent's registration to compliance with such conditions as the Interim Orders Committee may impose for a period not exceeding 18 months.

5.64   The guidance provides the following (non-exhaustive) examples of conditions which might be considered for inclusion in an order:

- limiting patient contact (either undertaking consultations only with chaperones, not treating patients at all or not treating certain kinds of patients);
- requiring a registrant to keep the GDC informed as to where he or she is or might be working;
- ensuring that any employer, partner, director or healthcare colleague (current or potential) is informed of pending fitness to practise proceedings and of the existence of any interim order, as appropriate;
- limiting the types of treatment that can be undertaken or the number of hours that may be worked.

5.65   Conditions should be clear; relevant; addressed to the registrant (not to third parties); necessary in order to protect patients, the public or in the interests of the registrant; proportionate to the allegations;

formulated so that the conditions are not in effect a suspension; and written in such a way that compliance can be easily verified. The law relating to conditions of practice is discussed in detail in chapter 1 (see para 1.442).

5.66 The guidance provides that conditions can only be adequate when there is reasonable confidence in the registrant's capacity to comply with them. If there is an issue between imposing conditions and suspension, suspension may be necessary to protect the public interest. If circumstances prevent the registrant from complying with the conditions, then suspension might be required.

5.67 It is important to obtain clear instructions from the client before proposing conditions to the Interim Orders Committee as an alternative to suspension. The GDC maintains a 'conditions bank' of standard conditions applicable in various types of interim orders cases. These are downloadable from the GDC website[54] and can be used as a template where appropriate.

5.68 Interim orders may be reviewed at any time. An order must be reviewed if new evidence comes to light at any time, or if the registrant requests it. Review of an order by the request of the registrant can only apply after three months from the date of the order. The order must be reviewed every six months while it is in force as a minimum.[55]

5.69 Decisions of the Interim Orders Committee are published on the GDC website, with the exception of any confidential details relating to the respondent's physical or mental health. Where a hearing has been held in private, parties or witnesses who took part in the private hearing (or part of hearing) must not be identified.[56] The circumstances in which hearings are to be held in private are discussed at paras 5.31–5.33 above.

5.70 The three practice committees – the Professional Performance Committee, the Professional Conduct Committee and the Health Committee – are themselves empowered to conduct interim orders hearings. This can be upon the committee's own motion or upon the application of a party. The respondent has the right to appear and to be heard.[57] The practice committees will hear the matter themselves rather than referring the matter back to the Interim Orders

---

54 See www.gdc-uk.org/Membersofpublic/Hearings/Documents/IOCConditions HE.pdf.

55 See *Interim Orders Committee guidance*, www.gdc-uk.org/Membersofpublic/ Hearings/Documents/IOCConditionsHE.pdf, para 22

56 GDC (Fitness to Practise) Rules 2006 r39.

57 GDC (Fitness to Practise) Rules 2006 r15.

Committee in circumstances where, for example, the matter is urgent. The *Interim Orders Committee guidance* also applies to interim orders hearings before practice committees.

Preliminary meetings

5.71   Before the substantive hearing a preliminary meeting may be held if the committee members regard it as appropriate. A preliminary meeting is for case management purposes, and if necessary, the giving of directions. The parties attend the meeting, and a legal adviser is present. The preliminary meeting may also be attended by any person the committee thinks is appropriate – this can include a professional or medical adviser if the committee thinks this necessary.[58] The preliminary meeting may be held by the chairman of a practice committee.

5.72   Directions may include:[59]

- time limits for the service of evidence and disclosure of expert evidence (if any);
- a requirement that each party provide an estimate of the length of the hearing and any dates on which they or any witnesses would not be able to attend the hearing;
- where the facts are not in dispute a requirement that the parties produce a statement of agreed facts;
- mutual disclosure of documents;
- the preparation of agreed bundles of documents to be distributed to the chair of a practice committee, members of a practice committee and the legal adviser in advance of the hearing;
- issues of joinder;
- the preparation of skeleton arguments where the parties are legally represented;
- a requirement that a party call the author of any expert report;
- where agreed between the parties, a direction that the witness statement of a witness shall stand as the evidence-in-chief of that witness;
- whether the hearing or part of it should be held in public or in private;

---

58   See *Guidance for handling cases at preliminary meetings*, available at www.gdc-uk.org/Membersofpublic/Hearings/Documents/Guidanceforhandlingcases atpreliminarymeetings.pdf, para 9.

59   GDC (Fitness to Practise) Rules 2006 r51.

- special measures to be put in place at the hearing for vulnerable witnesses;
- a direction for an adjournment of the preliminary meeting or that a further preliminary meeting should be held; and
- the date of any hearing or part of a hearing.

The fitness to practise hearing

> Fitness to practise is assessed looking forward from the date of the hearing. Much weight is given to the respondent's level of insight.

5.73   There are three practice committees: the Professional Conduct Committee, the Professional Performance Committee and the Health Committee.

5.74   The Professional Conduct Committee deals with cases where it is alleged that a registrant's fitness to practise has been impaired by his or her conduct (eg cases of alleged assault, dishonesty or abuse of position). 'Misconduct' is not defined in the statutory materials. The case-law provides that it is conceptually separate from inadequate professional performance (*R (Calhaem) v General Medical Council*[60]). In *Remedy UK Ltd v General Medical Council*[61] the court identified two kinds of misconduct: a) sufficiently serious misconduct within the exercise of professional practice and b) morally culpable or disgraceful conduct outside the course of professional practice. Ultimately the decision as to whether a respondent's actions amount to misconduct in a particular case is a question for the panel (*Mallon v General Medical Council*[62]).

5.75   The Professional Performance Committee deals with cases where it is alleged that a registrant's fitness to practise has been impaired by his or her inadequate professional performance (ie poor standard of work). 'Lack of competence', like misconduct, has not been defined by the regulators. In *R (Calhaem) v General Medical Council* Jackson J observed that it connotes an 'unacceptably low' standard of professional performance which (save in exceptional circumstances) has been demonstrated by reference to a fair sample of work. It goes beyond mere negligence; however, particularly serious negligence may amount to misconduct.

60   [2007] EWHC 2606 (Admin).
61   [2010] EWHC 1245 (Admin).
62   [2007] EWHC 2602 (Admin).

5.76   The Health Committee deals with cases where it is alleged that a registrant's fitness to practise may be impaired due to his or her own physical or mental health. The sanction of erasure from the register may not be imposed if the finding is one of impairment solely on health grounds.[63]

5.77   In all cases the panel must look to the future and focus upon the respondent's fitness to practise from the date of the hearing onwards (*Meadow v General Medical Council*[64]). Much weight is given to the insight or remorse demonstrated by the respondent in determining whether fitness to practise is likely to be impaired in the future. For a fuller discussion of the law relating to fitness to practise, see chapter 1 (para 1.364).

5.78   The basic procedure at the hearing[65] is common to all three practice committees. The hearing begins with the preliminary stage (reading out the notification of hearing and amendment of the charge if appropriate). After this there is a factual enquiry. The parties then make submissions. The panel then makes a determination.

5.79   At the preliminary stage the notification of hearing is read out (unless both parties state that they do not desire it to be read out). The notification of hearing contains the charge or charges against the respondent. At any stage before making findings of fact, the practice committee may amend the charge set out in the notification of hearing unless, having regard to the merits of the case and the fairness of the proceedings, the required amendment cannot be made without injustice. The later the amendment, the more likely it is that injustice may be caused. Before making any amendment to the charge, the practice committee must consider any representations from the parties.[66] The case-law on allegations, charges and amendment applications is discussed in detail in chapter 1 (see para 1.89).

5.80   The factual inquiry begins with the GDC presenter opening the case and presenting evidence. The respondent or the respondent's representative has the right to cross-examine any witness called by the presenter.

5.81   When the presenter has finished presenting the GDC case, the respondent or the respondent's representative may open the case for the respondent. This may commence with a submission that there is no case to answer.

---

63 DA 1984 s27B.
64 *Meadow v General Medical Council* [2007] QB 462.
65 GDC (Fitness to Practise) Rules 2006 r14.
66 GDC (Fitness to Practise) Rules 2006 rr17 and 18.

5.82   In relation to submissions of no case to answer, it appears that the test set out in the criminal case of *R v Galbraith*[67] applies to submissions of no case to answer in regulatory law. The test in *R v Galbraith* is whether 1) there was any evidence upon which a panel could find matters proved, or 2) whether there was some evidence, but it was of such an unsatisfactory nature that the panel, properly directed, could not find the matter proved. The relevant law is discussed in more detail at chapter 1.

5.83   Where the respondent or the respondent's representative makes a submission that there is no case to answer, the practice committee must adjourn the hearing and deliberate in private for the purpose of determining whether to accept the submission. The chair of the practice committee shall announce whether the submission that there is no case to answer has been accepted. Where the practice committee has accepted the submission, they may make such orders as to costs and other matters as they consider necessary.[68]

5.84   If the hearing proceeds, the respondent or the respondent's representative shall present evidence. The GDC presenter may cross-examine any witness called by the respondent or the respondent's representative. The respondent or the respondent's representative shall set out or conclude the case for the respondent after the evidence has been set out.

5.85   At this stage the evidence that may be presented should not include any evidence as to mitigation, but should be restricted to evidence relating to the facts alleged in the notification of hearing.

5.86   All witnesses are first examined by the party calling them, and may then be cross-examined by the opposing party. The witness may then be re-examined. Finally, the witness may be questioned by the practice committee.[69]

5.87   After the case for the respondent concludes, the practice committee must adjourn the hearing to deliberate in private as to their findings of fact. The practice committee must announce their findings of fact, by reference to the matters mentioned in the notification of hearing, in the presence of the parties.

5.88   Where a practice committee determines that none of the facts alleged in the notification of hearing have been proved against the respondent, they shall make the determination that the respondent's

67 [1981] 1 WLR 1039, [1981] 2 All ER 1060.
68 GDC (Fitness to Practise) Rules 2006 r19.
69 GDC (Fitness to Practise) Rules 2006 r55.

fitness to practise as a dentist or as a member of a profession complementary to dentistry is not impaired.[70]

5.89   Where a practice committee determines that some or all of the facts alleged in the notification of hearing have been proved against the respondent, submissions will be made by both the GDC representative and the respondent or respondent's representative. The submissions *must* cover the following matters:[71]

- the respondent's history;
- the question of whether, in the light of the facts found, the respondent's fitness to practise as a dentist or as a member of a profession complementary to dentistry is impaired; and
- where the GDC presenter's submission is that the respondent's fitness to practise as a dentist or as a member of a profession complementary to dentistry is impaired, what action should be taken (ie sanction).

5.90   The respondent or representative may also make submissions on mitigation by reference to the respondent's personal circumstances.

5.91   Following the submissions the practice committee will withdraw to deliberate in private. The determination, together with reasons, is then given in public (except in the case of a private hearing as set out above). The practice committee must determine whether the respondent's fitness to practise is impaired and, if so, whether to impose any sanction against the respondent and what sanction to impose.

Sanctions

> The sanctions available to the GDC are: a reprimand, conditions of practice, suspension and erasure from the register.

5.92   The purpose of sanctions is to protect the public, not to punish the registrant. However, the protection of the public includes consideration of the deterrent effect, the reputation of the profession and public confidence in the regulatory process. Even if fitness to practise has been proved, it is not mandatory to impose a sanction.[72]

---

70 GDC (Fitness to Practise) Rules 2006 r19.
71 GDC (Fitness to Practise) Rules 2006 r20.
72 GDC (Fitness to Practise) Rules 2006 r21(1)(b).

Sanctions available

5.93   The sanctions available to the practice committees are as follows (in ascending order of gravity)[73]:

- *Reprimand:* This is a statement of the committee's disapproval, but the registrant is still fit to practise with no restrictions.
- *Conditions:* Requirements (of a restrictive or a rehabilitative nature) are placed on the registrant's work for a set amount of time. The period will not exceed three years. The conditions usually have to be reviewed within a set period.
- *Suspension:* The committee can suspend the dental professional's registration. This means that the registrant cannot work as a dental professional for that set period of time.
- *Erasure:* This is the most serious sanction as it removes a registrant's name from the register. This means that the registrant can no longer work in dentistry in the UK (unless and until he or she applies for re-inclusion).

5.94   A reprimand may be considered appropriate in circumstances where there is no risk to the public or to patients. It cannot be given in conjunction with another determination.[74]

5.95   Conditions should be clear; relevant; addressed to the registrant (not to third parties); necessary in order to protect patients, the public or in the interests of the registrant; proportionate to the allegations; formulated so that the conditions are not in effect a suspension; and written in such a way that compliance can be easily verified.

5.96   The guidance provides that conditions can only be adequate when there is reasonable confidence in the registrant's capacity to comply with them. If there is an issue between imposing conditions and suspension, suspension may be necessary to give the public the protection expected. If circumstances prevent the registrant from complying with the conditions, then suspension might be required. The law relating to conditions of practice is discussed in detail in chapter 1 (see para 1.442).

5.97   Representatives may wish to propose suitable conditions (on instructions from the respondent) as an alternative to suspension or erasure. The GDC maintains a conditions bank (separate from

---

73 DA 1984 s27B.
74 *Guidance, Professional Conduct Committee, Professional Performance Committee and Health Committee.*

the interim orders conditions bank) which can be used as a source.[75] Providing supporting evidence (eg a statement from a person who is willing to mentor the respondent) can be important in appropriate cases.

5.98　Suspension is suitable where a committee finds that the withdrawal of registration is necessary for public protection but does not need to last the five-year term that would be the minimum with erasure. Suspension will be for a given period of time not exceeding 12 months. The determination must make clear whether the suspension will be automatically lifted at the end of the stated period or whether it will be reviewed.[76] Review hearings will be dealt with below.

5.99　Erasure from the register is obviously the most serious sanction. Following erasure a person cannot practise as a dentist or dental professional. The person can, however, apply for the restoration of his or her name to the register after a minimum of five years.[77] The guidance states that erasure is imposed in order to protect the public and maintain its confidence in the profession as a whole. Prior to erasure being considered, all other available sanctions should be considered in ascending order of seriousness to ensure that the case is being considered bearing in mind the principle of proportionality. No committee may erase purely on health grounds.[78]

Mitigation

5.100　Because disciplinary sanctions are not punitive in nature, personal considerations that would ordinarily weigh in mitigation of punishment have less effect than they would on sentencing in the criminal context. The guidance provides that in some situations the risk of harm to the public or the need to protect the public may properly override persuasive mitigation. In performance cases, evidence that failure to meet the expected standards was associated with particular circumstances which no longer exist may give some degree of reassurance. However, the chance of those circumstances recurring may be relevant to the evaluation of risk and to the disposal of the case.

75　See www.gdc-uk.org/Membersofpublic/Hearings/Documents/PCConditions BankHE.pdf.

76　*Guidance, Professional Conduct Committee, Professional Performance Committee and Health Committee.*

77　DA 1984 s28.

78　DA 1984 s27B(7).

5.101   Commonly, respondents before the committees provide testimonials in support of their character. The guidance deals with the
approach which the committee will take to such testimonials:

> Testimonials prepared in advance of a hearing need to be considered
> in the light of the factual findings made at the hearing. For example, if
> findings of serious and persistent dishonesty have been made against
> a registrant, as opposed to a single 'heat of the moment' action, testi-
> monials vouching for their honesty and trustworthiness might be
> given relatively little weight. The referees may not have known or
> taken full account of the factual background to the case.[79]

5.102   It can consequently be useful to make referees aware of the factual
background to the case prior to giving a testimonial. Care should,
however, be taken to ensure that evidence is not provided which
amounts to an admission contrary to the respondent's instructions.

5.103   The guidance also provides that if a registrant's conduct shows
that he or she is fundamentally unsuited for registration as a dental
professional, no amount of remorse, apologies or positive personal
qualities can mitigate the seriousness of that conclusion and its
impact on registration.

5.104   The guidance provides that in conduct cases a decision *not* to
erase would require careful justification in the following circumstances – however, each case must be considered on its own merits:

- serious abuse of the clinical relationship (eg abuse of patients for
  sexual gratification or profit);
- other serious abuse of the privileged position enjoyed by registered professionals (eg abuse of the privilege to prescribe controlled drugs);
- deliberately or recklessly causing serious avoidable harm to
  patients. This is distinguished from a poor judgment call and
  relates to situations where a patient suffers serious harm which
  could and should have been avoided, and the registrant knew
  better or ought to have known better;
- failing to maintain safe standards of premises, equipment and
  other aspects of the clinical environment. The guidance envisages
  that erasure would be appropriate in the case of *serious* failings in
  this regard;
- dishonesty (particularly where associated with professional
  practice);

---

79 *Guidance for the Professional Conduct Committee*, www.gdc-uk.org/Governance
andcorporate/Documents/GuidanceforthePCC/pdffinal.pdf, para 22.

- failure to maintain professional knowledge and competence in areas relevant to the registrant's practice. The guidance envisages that erasure may be appropriate where a registrant is proven to have *neglected* this responsibility;
- undertaking treatment or procedures beyond one's competence. This does not include situations where a task is more challenging than expected, provided that the registrant behaves appropriately;
- patterns of behaviour which are incompatible with professional registration, eg serious criminality or serious or persistent contempt for the safety, rights or dignity of others;
- failure to maintain appropriate indemnity or otherwise ensure adequate protection for patients;
- personal behaviour (eg violence, indecency or encouraging other registrants to indulge in inappropriate behaviour).

Appeals from fitness to practise decisions

5.105   A right of appeal to the High Court lies from decisions of practice committees giving directions for erasure, suspension or conditional registration. An appeal must be lodged within 28 days of the day that the decision was served.[80]

5.106   The CHRE can challenge decisions that they regard as unduly lenient.

Resumed hearings

5.107   A resumed hearing takes place when a direction for conditions or for suspension has previously been made. It usually takes place towards the end of the period of conditions or suspension.

5.108   At a resumed hearing the GDC presenter will inform the practice committee of the background to the case and the sanctions previously imposed on the respondent, direct the attention of the practice committee to any relevant evidence previously considered by the practice committee including transcripts of previous hearings, present any relevant evidence not previously considered by the practice committee, and make submissions as to the matters being considered by the practice committee. The respondent or representative may present

80   DA 1984 s29.

evidence and make submissions.[81] The committee retires to deliberate and then gives the decision in public.[82]

5.109   As a matter of good practice it is important to provide evidence of compliance with conditions and of other steps taken to address the concerns raised at the earlier hearing (for example, any relevant continuing professional development). The committee will look for evidence of insight and for willingness to take on board lessons learnt from the original proceedings. They will ask what has changed since the date of the original proceedings. A resumed hearing should not be seen as an opportunity to challenge the original decision.

5.110   At a resumed hearing the practice committee has the following powers if a suspension order was originally imposed:[83]

- to terminate the suspension;
- to extend the suspension for a period not exceeding 12 months from the expiry of the original suspension;
- to replace the suspension with conditions of practice for a period of up to three years;
- to suspend registration indefinitely, provided that the registrant will have been suspended for at least two years on the date on which the direction takes effect, and the direction is made not more than two months before the date on which the period of suspension would otherwise expire. (In practice, this order will only be made at a second or subsequent resumed hearing, as DA 1984 s27B provides that practice committees are only able to impose a suspension order of up to 12 months.) If this order is imposed, there is a provision for a review at the registrant's request after at least two years of the date of the order.[84]

5.111   If conditions of practice were originally imposed, the practice committee has the following powers at a resumed hearing:[85]

- to remove the conditions;
- to extend the conditions for a period of not more than three years;
- to vary, revoke or add to any of the conditions; or
- to suspend registration for not more than 12 months. Suspension of registration can also be imposed where a practice committee determines that a person has failed to comply with any condition.

81   GDC (Fitness to Practise) Rules 2006 r29.
82   GDC (Fitness to Practise) Rules 2006 r29.
83   DA 1984 s27C.
84   DA 1984 s27C(4).
85   DA 1984 s27C.

5.112   There is the right of appeal to the High Court against resumed hearing decisions which result in conditions or suspension.[86] The appeal must be lodged within 28 days of the date of the decision.

Fraudulent register entry hearings before the Professional Conduct Committee

5.113   In addition to fitness to practise hearings, the DA 1984 provides that the Professional Conduct Committee hears cases where the registrar has reason to believe that an entry on the register has been procured by fraud.[87] The procedure is essentially the same as the fitness to practise procedure.[88]

5.114   If the Professional Conduct Committee determines that an entry has been fraudulently procured, it shall direct that that person's name be erased.[89]

5.115   There is a right of appeal to the High Court against fraudulent register entry decisions.[90] Appeals must be lodged within 28 days of service of the decision.

Restoration hearings before the Professional Conduct Committee

5.116   A dental professional whose name has been erased from the register following a practice committee hearing may apply for restoration to the register.[91] The Professional Conduct Committee also hears applications for restoration to the register following a determination that an entry on the register has been procured by fraud.[92] If the original complaint was made before 31 July 2006 when the DA 1984 was amended, the application can be made ten months following erasure. If the complaint was made after 31 July 2006, the application can be made five years after erasure. No application may be made within 12 months of an earlier unsuccessful application. Where a second or

---

86   DA 1984 s29.
87   DA 1984 s24.
88   GDC (Fitness to Practise) Rules 2006 r48.
89   DA 1984 s24.
90   DA 1984 s29.
91   DA 1984 s28.
92   DA 1984 s24.

subsequent application is unsuccessful during the same period of erasure, the Professional Conduct Committee may indefinitely suspend the right to make further applications.[93]

5.117   The application for restoration is dealt with by the Professional Conduct Committee. The evidence relating to the original erasure is considered. The applicant may address the committee and call witnesses. He or she may be legally represented. An applicant may be required to provide specific evidence as to fitness to practise and to undergo further requirements including education and training. Where an application is granted, the Professional Conduct Committee may impose conditions for a period of up to three years.[94]

5.118   There is a right of appeal to the High Court against a decision to refuse to restore a person's name to the register. There is also a right of appeal to the High Court against the decision to suspend the right to make further applications. Appeals must be lodged within 28 days of service of the decision.[95]

Registration Appeals Committee

5.119   The Registration Appeals Committee considers appeals from dental professionals made against the registrar in the following circumstances:

- where registration has been refused;
- where a person has been removed from the register (*except* by a practice committee);
- where a person has not been restored to the register (*except* by a practice committee).

5.120   If a decision is taken solely on the grounds that a person has failed to pay an appropriate fee or has failed to make the required application, this is not appealable.[96]

5.121   The Registration Appeals Committee is governed by its own rules of procedure, the General Dental Council (Registration Appeals) Rules 2006. Under these rules, appeals are initiated by the registrant or would-be registrant. Appeals do not automatically proceed to a

93   DA 1984 s28.
94   DA 1984 s28.
95   DA 1984 s29.
96   DA 1984 Schs 2A Part 2 and 4A Part 2.

hearing unless either the appellant requests it or the GDC regards it as appropriate.[97]

5.122   If the matter proceeds to a hearing, a directions hearing may be scheduled for the purpose of case management.[98] Appeals are held in public unless the committee is satisfied that, in the interests of justice or for the protection of the private or family life of the appellant or of any other person, the public should be excluded from all or part of the hearing. Appellants may be legally represented or represented by a professional colleague, officer or member of organisation or family member.[99]

5.123   At the hearing, the parties and their representative may address the committee, give evidence, call and examine witnesses and cross-examine witnesses called by the other party or their representative. The committee may also examine witnesses. The committee may admit any evidence which they consider fair and relevant to the case before them, whether or not this evidence was available to the registrar at the time of the appealable registration decision at issue or would be admissible in a court of law. The appellant has the right to address the committee last.[100]

5.124   The committee's determination is given in the presence of the parties, together with reasons.[101]

5.125   There is a right of appeal from decisions of the Registration Appeals Committee. Appeals are heard in the county court.[102] This is in contrast with appeals from the other committees, which are heard in the High Court.

Costs

5.126   There is a provision for costs orders to be made by a practice committee where a submission of no case to answer has been accepted.[103] In general, as for other regulators, costs orders are not typically made unless a complaint is improperly brought, as the regulators act in the public interest and are not in the position of the ordinary litigant (*Walker v Law Society*[104]).

97 GDC (Registration Appeals) Rules 2006 r4.
98 GDC (Registration Appeals) Rules 2006 r9.
99 GDC (Registration Appeals) Rules 2006 r14.
100 GDC (Registration Appeals) Rules 2006 r15.
101 GDC (Registration Appeals) Rules 2006 r16.
102 DA 1984 Schs 2A and 4A Part 6.
103 GDC (Fitness to Practise) Rules 2006 r19(6).
104 [2007] EWCA Civ 233.

The General Optical Council

continued

Key points

- *Regulator:* General Optical Council (GOC)
- *Professions regulated:* Optometrists, dispensing opticians, student opticians and optical businesses
- *Common sources of referral:* Registrant's employer, primary care organisations, professional or educational body, patients, members of the public, fellow registrants
- *Relevant statute:* Opticians Act (OA) 1989
- *Fitness to Practise Rules:* General Optical Council (Fitness to Practise) Rules 2005 (Schedule to SI 2005 No 1475)
- *Type of proceedings:* Fitness to practise
- *Two-stage process:* Investigation (GOC (Fitness to Practise) Rules 2005 Part 2) and Adjudication (Part 8)
- *Investigation Committee:* Yes (GOC (Fitness to Practise) Rules 2005 r6)
- *Adjudication Committee:* Fitness to Practise Panels
- *Location:* General Optical Council, 41 Harley Street, London, W1G 8DJ
- *Notice of hearing provision:* GOC (Fitness to Practise) Rules 2005 Part 6
- *Procedure before a Fitness to Practise Panel:* GOC (Fitness to Practise) Rules 2005 Part 17
- *Test:* Whether fitness to practise is impaired by reason of (in summary): a) misconduct; b) deficient professional performance; c) a criminal conviction or caution; d) adverse physical or mental health (OA 1989 ss7, 8A and 9)
- *Power to require a practitioner to undergo health or performance assessment?* Yes – GOC (Fitness to Practise) Rules 2005 r8
- *Interim order power:* Yes – interim conditions of practice or interim suspension (GOC (Fitness to Practise) Rules 2005 Part 7 rr25–27) heard by Interim Orders Panel
- *Interim order guidance: Guidance for the Interim Orders Panel and the Fitness to Practise Panel*
- *General composition for final hearings:* Five GOC-appointed members, lay and professional (at least one medical) – not legally qualified, plus chair
- *How to address panel:* Generally seated and 'Sir'/'Madam'
- *Independent legal adviser:* Yes

- *Evidence:* GOC (Fitness to Practise) Rules 2005 r38(1) 'may admit any evidence they consider fair and relevant to the case before them, whether or not such evidence would be admissible in a court of law'
- *Sanction provisions:* OA 1989
- *Review hearings:* GOC (Fitness to Practise) Rules 2005 Part 9

Introduction

Establishment

6.1 The General Optical Council (GOC) was established by the Opticians Act (OA) 1958 to regulate the optical professions in the UK. The GOC currently registers around 24,000 optometrists and dispensing opticians, approximately 4,000 students and approximately 1,500 optical businesses.

Core functions

6.2 The GOC has four core functions:

1) setting standards for optical education and training, performance and conduct;
2) approving qualifications leading to registration;
3) maintaining a register of individuals who are qualified and fit to practise, train or carry on business as optometrists and dispensing opticians;
4) investigating and acting where registrants' fitness to practise, train or carry on business is impaired.

Future reform

6.3 Council members recently considered the Law Commission's review of the legal framework for UK healthcare regulators. The review, commissioned by the government in the command paper *Enabling excellence,*[1] intends to introduce a single overarching statute allowing each of the healthcare regulators – including the GOC – to decide for themselves how they deliver their core functions. On 1 March 2012,

---

1 *Enabling Excellence: autonomy and accountability for healthcare workers, social workers and social care workers,* February 2011.

the Law Commission published its consultation paper *Regulation of healthcare professionals,* and asked the GOC and other regulators to submit responses by 31 May 2012. The consultation document includes almost 200 questions and proposals, affecting the full range of regulators' functions overall governance, including a single statute that would govern all the health professional regulators, replacing current individual statutes. The GOC has already indicated that it will review student registration, body corporate registration (optical businesses) and the statutory basis of advisory committees (such as Registration and Companies Committees).

6.4   The timetable for the Law Commission's work remains uncertain. Although the new legislation is planned to be passed by 2015, there appears to be no confirmed place in the parliamentary timetable for this work. As such, there is a risk that the legislation may not be able to be considered in the current session of parliament, before the next election. This raises uncertainty as to when or if it will happen.[2] At the time of writing, GOC members have agreed new rules that will underpin the GOC's fitness to practise proceedings, designed to make the process faster, fairer and reflect legal developments and any changes to best practice over the last five years. The rules are to be sent to the Department of Health, and laid before the Privy Council for approval. The proposed changes will be referred to in the relevant sections of this chapter.

Jurisdictional reach

6.5   The GOC regulates and maintains registers of all fully trained optometrists and dispensing opticians who practise or intend to practise in the UK, and any students who are undertaking training, examination or study towards a qualification in these areas of practice.

6.6   It also regulates and maintains registers of corporate bodies carrying on business as a registered optometrist or a dispensing optician or both, and companies who trade using the protected titles ophthalmic optician, optometrist or dispensing optician, or whose names imply as much.[3]

6.7   The GOC's primary function is to protect the public by promoting high standards of education and conduct among optometrists and opticians. This is achieved by setting and publishing standards of

2 Updates on the consultation process can be found on the GOC website at www.optical.org.

3 Opticians Act (OA) 1989 ss7, 8A and 9.

professional proficiency, as well as standards of conduct, performance and ethics that apply to all registrants, and by considering complaints against registrants. The GOC publishes a code of conduct for individual registrants (optometrists, dispensing opticians and optical students) and a code of conduct for business registrants (companies and their employees).

Approach to regulation: the statutory grounds

> In order to promote safe and competent practice and to maintain public confidence in the profession, the GOC has the powers to take action where there is an impairment of an optometrist's or dispensing optician's fitness to practise, and it is for the Fitness to Practise Committee to determine the appropriate sanction. Impairment of registered individuals can be based on numerous grounds, known as 'statutory grounds'.

6.8   The statutory grounds cover allegations of misconduct, instances of deficient professional performance (although not in the case of a registered student), a previous conviction or caution, issues arising from adverse physical or mental health, or a determination by any other UK healthcare body[4] that fitness to practise is impaired. A finding of impaired fitness to practise against a business registrant can be based, among other things, on practices or patterns of behaviour within the business amounting to misconduct or deficient professional performance.

Sources of law

6.9   The OA 1958, under which the GOC was established, was consolidated and amended by the OA 1989 and the Opticians Act 1989 (Amendment) Order 2005.[5] Part 2A of the order governs fitness to practise issues.

6.10   The OA 1989 gives the GOC powers to make orders, rules and regulations in relevant areas, subject to approval by the Privy Council. These include the General Optical Council (Registration Rules) Order of Council 2005,[6] the General Optical Council (Registration Appeals Rules) Order of Council 2005[7] and the General Optical

---

4   In Scotland only, an absolute discharge or a specified statutory penalty.
5   SI 2005 No 848.
6   SI 2005 No 1478.
7   SI 2005 No 1477.

Council (Fitness to Practise Rules) Order of Council 2005,[8] on which this chapter will largely focus.

6.11 In addition to the statutory provisions and rules and codes of practice referred to above, the GOC publishes on its website a number of regularly updated notes of guidance, such as the *Fitness to practise hearings guidance and indicative sanctions, Protocol for the investigation and prosecution of criminal offences* and *Guidance regarding warnings issued by the Investigation Committee.*[9]

Starting the process

6.12 As with other healthcare regulators, the investigative and disciplinary process may be triggered by a written complaint from a patient, service user, employer or former employer of the registrant. It is initially referred to an Investigating Committee, comprising GOC registrants and lay members, which will consider the evidence and any written response from the registrant in private, before deciding whether there is a case to answer. If there is, the Investigating Committee must decide whether to take no further action, advise the registrant as to his or her future practice or conduct, issue a warning, invite the registrant to attend a voluntary performance review, or to refer the allegation to a Fitness to Practise Committee, which will usually hold a public hearing to decide what action to take.

Referrals

6.13 Referrals to the GOC come from many sources, including a registrant's employer, a primary care organisation, the registrant's professional or educational body, or even, on occasions, self-declarations by the registrant. The majority, however, come from individual patients or members of the public, or a fellow GOC registrant. Between 1 April 2009 and 31 March 2010, the GOC received 160 complaints, 82 of which came from patients or members of the public.[10]

6.14 The GOC also has powers, seldom exercised, to initiate its own investigation where a fitness to practise issue arises in respect of a registrant, even where no complaint has been made.[11]

8 SI 2005 No 1475.
9 See www.optical.org.
10 *GOC annual report 2009–2010.*
11 OA 1989 s13E(3).

6.15   Complaints must be made in writing. The registrant must be identified, and as much information as possible about the incident should be provided. Once received by the GOC, the completed investigation form will be acknowledged, and the registrant involved will be notified that a complaint against him or her is being investigated.

Gathering the evidence

6.16   Evidence will then be gathered, which may include obtaining copies of clinical records from optical practices or hospitals. When this occurs, the person making the complaint ('the complainant') will be required to sign a consent form. Witness statements may be taken from the complainant or other witnesses.

6.17   Once the evidence is gathered it is sent to the registrant who is provided with an opportunity to make written representations about the complaint within 28 days.[12] The Investigation Committee will then meet in private to consider the complaint and any statements and additional supporting evidence, including written representations.[13] It is advisable to make written representations if the allegation is uncontested, where there is overwhelming evidence to rebut the allegation, or where the allegation is so minor or trivial in nature that it would not support a finding of impairment at the hearing stage. Where a case involves a conflict of fact, the registrant will need to provide clear, corroborative evidence to support his or her account, such as contemporaneous records or a statement from a witness. It is important at this stage to exercise great caution with early disclosure of information, since factual inaccuracies or inconsistencies can be adduced at the main hearing. Similarly, care should be taken before suggesting that an allegation is minor or trivial in nature, since any statement to this effect could be used to demonstrate lack of insight or understanding of the seriousness of the allegation. To avoid any risk, the safest course would be to seek legal advice.

---

12 GOC (Fitness to Practise) Rules 2005 r5.
13 GOC (Fitness to Practise) Rules 2005 r6(a).

The Investigation Committee

> The Investigation Committee will consist of a panel of nine members, of whom three must be registered optometrists, two must be registered dispensing opticians, three must be lay persons and one must be a medical practitioner.

6.18   The procedures and powers of the Investigation Committee are set out in the OA 1989.

6.19   When considering the complaint, the Investigation Committee may appoint one or more expert assessors to assess and report to them on the registrant's health,[14] or on the standard and quality of the work done or being done by the registrant.[15] It may decide to gather further information or evidence. This can be carried out without informing either the complainant or the registrant of the nature of the further investigation to be undertaken. The committee may also direct the registrant to be examined by the appointed assessor or assessors, for the purpose of their assessment and report on the registrant's health and/or the standard or quality of the work done or being done by the registrant.[16] Similarly, the committee has the same powers where it has referred a registrant to the Fitness to Practise Committee.[17]

6.20   Where the committee considers an assessment is necessary, it must notify the registrant, and inform him or her of the date of any meeting and any directions it has made.[18] Such meetings cannot take place earlier than 28 days after notification.[19] Once the assessment report has been prepared, it must be sent to both the registrar and the registrant.[20] If the registrant fails to comply with any of these directions, or is unco-operative, the committee will draw such inferences as they think appropriate.[21]

14 GOC (Fitness to Practise) Rules 2005 r7(1)(a)(i).
15 GOC (Fitness to Practise) Rules 2005 r7(1)(a)(ii).
16 GOC (Fitness to Practise) Rules 2005 r7(1)(b).
17 GOC (Fitness to Practise) Rules 2005 r8(1)(a) and (b).
18 GOC (Fitness to Practise) Rules 2005 r9(a), (b) and (c).
19 GOC (Fitness to Practise) Rules 2005 r10.
20 GOC (Fitness to Practise) Rules 2005 r11(a) and (b).
21 GOC (Fitness to Practise) Rules 2005 r12.

Referral to the Fitness to Practise Committee

6.21   The Investigation Committee must, having taken into account any report, decide whether the complaint should be referred to the independent Fitness to Practise Committee,[22] although one of the proposed changes to the rules is that in future, a layer of decision-making will take place prior to a case being considered by the Investigation Committee, whereby two individual case examiners will decide whether to refer a complaint for a Fitness to Practise hearing.[23]

6.22   The Investigation Committee must also consider whether an application should be made to the Fitness to Practise Committee for the imposition of an interim order suspending or placing conditions upon the registrant's registration. Further information about the circumstances in which interim orders can be imposed is dealt with later in this chapter.[24]

6.23   When considering whether to refer a complaint to the Fitness to Practise Committee, the test to be applied is known as 'the realistic prospect test', namely whether there is a realistic prospect of establishing that the registrant's fitness to practise is impaired to a degree that justifies action being taken against his or her registration. It involves consideration of two issues:

a)   Is there a realistic prospect of being able to prove the facts alleged against the registrant, if the complaint is referred to the Fitness to Practise Committee?

b)   If the alleged facts are proved, are they so significant as to indicate that the registrant's fitness to practise is or may be impaired to a degree that justifies action being taken against his or her registration?

Role of the Investigation Committee

> Complaints must be supported by credible evidence. If not, there is no case to be answered.

6.24   It is not the role of the Investigation Committee to refer to the Fitness to Practise Committee complaints that are not supported by any

---

22   OA 1989 s13D(5) and GOC (Fitness to Practise) Rules 2005 r13.

23   The Commission contemplate an overarching statute which will consolidate the availability of decisions and outcomes at the investigation stage. This would give regulators powers to issue or agree at the investigation stage warnings, interim orders, undertakings, voluntary erasure and advice. The power to introduce mediation is also proposed.

24   See paras 6.35–6.45.

credible evidence. In such circumstances, the Investigation Committee will decide that there is no case to be answered, and notify the registrant accordingly. A decision not to refer an allegation to the Fitness to Practise Committee may be reviewed by the Investigation Committee only if they consider that there is new evidence or information which makes such a review necessary for the protection of the public, or to prevent injustice to the registrant, or because it is necessary in the public interest, or because the GOC has erred in the administrative handling of the case.[25]

Options following decision not to refer

6.25 If the Investigation Committee decides that a particular complaint ought not to be referred to the Fitness to Practise Committee, it must then consider the following options:

- take no further action;
- ask for further investigations to be carried out;
- issue a warning to the registrant;
- send a letter of advice to the registrant;
- invite the registrant to a voluntary performance review;
- refer the allegation to a Fitness to Practise Committee.

Take no further action

6.26 A decision to close a case and take no further action will only be taken if:

- the complaint demonstrates no issue that could call into question the registrant's fitness to practise; or
- the alleged facts, if proved, may demonstrate a shortcoming on the part of the registrant, but not one serious enough to result in the registrant's fitness to practise being impaired to the extent that would justify action being taken with regard to the registrant's registration; or
- the alleged facts, once proved, may demonstrate that the registrant's fitness to practise is impaired, but there is no realistic prospect of being able to prove the alleged facts for evidential reasons.

Ask for further investigations to be carried out

6.27 Such investigations could be undertaking an assessment of the registrant's health or performance. The case is returned to the Investigation Committee once this information has been gathered.

---

25 GOC (Fitness to Practise) Rules 2005 r15.

Issue a warning to the registrant

6.28   When the Investigation Committee considers whether a warning should be given, it will direct the registrar to write to the registrant, to inform him that he or she is entitled to make written representations within 28 days of the notice.[26] The Investigation Committee must then take into account any representations which the registrant has made.[27] Since a warning is a record of concern on the part of the Investigation Committee which, while not requiring referral to the Fitness to Practise Committee, is potentially significant. A warning is not shown on the publicly available GOC register, but is recorded by the GOC for a period of four years. Warnings given by the Fitness to Practise Committee do appear on the public record.

Send a letter of advice to the registrant

6.29   Such a letter may contain (but will not be limited to) advice about future conduct, including advice about the appropriate handling of dissatisfied patients.

Invite the registrant to a voluntary performance review

6.30   The registrant may be invited to attend a voluntary performance review with the College of Optometrists or the Association of British Dispensing Opticians. Such an invitation will only be issued where no public safety issues have arisen, and will involve an informal discussion about standards of practice between the registrant and a representative of his or her professional body.

Refer the allegation to a Fitness to Practise Committee

6.31   The Fitness to Practise Committee will usually hold a public hearing to decide what action to take.

Review of decision not to refer[28]

6.32   Once a decision has been made not to refer an allegation to the Fitness to Practise Committee, the Investigation Committee may not review it unless new evidence or information comes to light which makes a review necessary for the protection of the public, to prevent

---

26   GOC (Fitness to Practise) Rules 2005 r14(2).

27   GOC (Fitness to Practise) Rules 2005 r14(3).

28   It is proposed in the new rules that the decision not to refer a complaint to the Fitness to Practise Committee can be reviewed by the case examiners at any time within five years, or within a longer period where it is considered that the circumstances are exceptional.

injustice to the registrant, or in the public interest.[29] A review may also take place if the Committee receives information that the GOC has mishandled the administration of the complaint and that it is in the public interest to conduct such a review.[30]

6.33 Where the Investigation Committee does decide to review a decision, the registrar must inform both the registrant and the complainant, if any, of the decision.[31] The registrar must also provide them with any evidence or information[32] and seek their views.[33] Once a review has taken place, the Investigation Committee may decide that the original decision should stand,[34] or to refer the matter to the Fitness to Practise Committee.[35] After the review has been concluded, the registrar must as soon as possible notify the parties, and anyone else with an interest in the matter, of its decision and the reasons for it.[36]

6.34 A referral may be reviewed by the Investigation Committee even after it has been referred to the Fitness to Practise Committee, if it is believed that the allegation should no longer be considered.[37] When this occurs, the registrar must inform all the interested parties in writing of the decision and the reasons for it.[38]

Interim orders

Interim orders may be made if they are necessary to protect the public, or in the public interest, or in the registrant's interest, prior to the substantive hearing on fitness. An interim order can either suspend a registrant from the register or place conditions on his or her registration. Interim orders take effect immediately.

6.35 Interim orders are reviewed every six months, and usually remain in place until the investigation has been completed and the substantive

29 GOC (Fitness to Practise) Rules 2005 r15(2)(a)–(c).
30 GOC (Fitness to Practise) Rules 2005 r15(3).
31 GOC (Fitness to Practise) Rules 2005 r15 (4)(a).
32 GOC (Fitness to Practise) Rules 2005 r15 (4)(b).
33 GOC (Fitness to Practise) Rules 2005 r15 (4)(c).
34 GOC (Fitness to Practise) Rules 2005 r15 (5)(a).
35 GOC (Fitness to Practise) Rules 2005 r15(5)(b).
36 GOC (Fitness to Practise) Rules 2005 r15(6) (a)–(c).
37 GOC (Fitness to Practise) Rules 2005 r16(2).
38 GOC (Fitness to Practise) Rules 2005 r16(3)(a) –(c).

Fitness to Practise Committee hearing has finished.[39] The threshold for an interim order is a high one. No judgment is made regarding the facts of the allegation, but the panel must be satisfied that on a fair analysis, there *may* be a prima facie case. The registrant should be given the opportunity to make representations, and may adduce evidence.

6.36　　This type of hearing takes place if the Fitness to Practise Committee feels that the severity of the allegations is such that a registrant poses an immediate risk to the public and/or himself or herself if permitted to practise without restriction pending final disposal.[40]

The registrar's duties

6.37　Where a complaint has been referred to the Fitness to Practise Committee to consider whether to make an interim order, the registrar must, as soon as is practicable, notify the registrant of the fact that such an application is to be made, the hearing date, and a statement of facts constituting the basis of the application.[41] The registrar must also provide the names of any witnesses on whom it is intended to rely, copies of any statements or reports made by witnesses or other documents. Lastly, the registrar is required to provide the registrant with written notification of the charges, a copy of the hearing questionnaire completed by the presenting officer, and a hearing questionnaire for the registrant to complete.[42]

Timing

6.38　Due to the nature of interim orders, it is likely that only short notice will be given. An interim order hearing will take place no earlier than seven days after service of the notification, unless the Fitness to Practise Committee feels that an earlier hearing is required.[43]

6.39　　The Fitness to Practise Committee decides whether an immediate suspension order or conditions placed on the registrant's registration should be imposed while the GOC's solicitors obtain evidence for the matter to be heard at a substantive hearing.

39　OA 1989 s13L(2). There is provision for six-monthly reviews, starting with the date when the order was made (s13L(3)).
40　OA1989 s13L.
41　GOC (Fitness to Practise) Rules 2005 r17(a) and (b).
42　GOC (Fitness to Practise) Rules 2005 r17(c)–(e).
43　GOC (Fitness to Practise) Rules 2005 r18.

Criteria for making the order

6.40 In deciding whether or not to take this step, the Fitness to Practise Committee must have particular regard to:

- the effect which any order may have on the registrant;
- the requirement on the Fitness to Practise Committee to balance the need for an order against the consequences which an order would have for the registrant, in order to satisfy themselves that the consequences are not disproportionate to the risk to the public.

6.41 Interim orders can have serious consequences for the registrant's livelihood and career and the Fitness to Practise Committee should only make such an order where they are satisfied that it is necessary to do so:

- for the protection of members of the public;
- otherwise in the public interest; or
- in the interests of the registrant.[44]

The nature of an interim order

6.42 An interim order may be an order for suspension, or for conditions to be imposed on registration, or for an entry relating to a specialty or proficiency to be removed temporarily or made subject to conditions. The period of an order may not exceed 18 months,[45] and there is provision for six-monthly reviews, starting with the date when the order was made.[46] At the end of the first six-monthly review, the suspended registrant may request a further review any time after three months, which must take place as soon as practicable. The GOC may apply to the High Court (or in Scotland, the Court of Sessions) for an extension of the interim order for a further period of 12 months.[47]

6.43 An interim suspension must be 'necessary' either for the protection of the public or otherwise in the public interest, although the latter is likely to be rare. The difference is that the former requires there to be a real risk to patients or the public whereas the latter is more an issue of desirability and maintaining standards –see *R (Shiekh) v General Dental Council*.[48] Where an interim suspension

44 OA 1989 s13L(1)
45 OA 1989 s13L(2).
46 OA 1989 s13L(3).
47 OA 1989 s13L(6).
48 [2007] EWHC 2972 (Admin).

order is imposed, while no judgment is made on the facts, it carries the implication that suspension or erasure is a real possibility following the full fitness to practise hearing.

6.44   The committee is required to take into account factors such as the impact on a registrant's right to practice, finances and reputation, the seriousness of the allegation, the nature of the evidence and whether it amounts to a prima facie case, and the likelihood of the alleged conduct being repeated.

Terminating an interim order

6.45   A registrant wishing to terminate the interim order or to revoke or vary a condition may apply to the same court. It is important that the registrant should, if possible, provide a reference from his or her employer setting out any mitigating factors, the steps taken by the employer to address relevant concerns if relevant, and the extent to which a registrant has addressed and acknowledged failure. Where the registrant's state of health is an issue, an up-to-date medical report should be sought. Any testimonials should include a statement that the writer is aware of the GOC proceedings and the nature of the allegations.

Interim order hearings

Location of hearings

6.46   Like other hearings, interim order hearings are normally conducted at the General Optical Council, 41 Harley Street, London W1G 8DJ. On occasions, proceedings will take place at the Royal Institute of British Architects, 66 Portland Place, London W1B 1AD. (See too para 6.139.)

Claimant's right to attend and to representation

6.47   A registrant has the right to attend an interim order or review hearing and to be represented[49] by:

- a barrister;
- a solicitor;
- a representative of the registrant's professional organisation;
- an officer of the company if the registrant is a business; or
- any other suitable person (subject to the agreement of the Fitness to Practise Committee).

49   GOC (Fitness to Practise) Rules 2005 r20(1) –(4).

6.48 Proceedings may be conducted in the absence of the registrant or his or her representative if the Fitness to Practise Committee is satisfied that all reasonable efforts have been made to notify the registrant of the hearing, and that having considered any reasons for the registrant's absence, it is in the public interest to proceed.[50]

Conduct of interim order hearings

6.49 The conduct of interim order hearings is governed by the GOC (Fitness to Practise) Rules 2005.[51] The normal procedure is that:

- the GOC case presenter will make representations as to why it may be necessary to impose, revoke, confirm, vary or replace an interim order and may adduce relevant evidence;
- the registrant may then make representations and adduce relevant evidence;
- the registrant may give oral testimony, however an interim order hearing is not a fact-finding process;
- the GOC's case presenter may provide advice on questions of law;
- the panel will adjourn to deliberate in private and announce its decision with reasons;
- the hearing shall be held in public unless the Fitness to Practise Committee considers that the proceedings, or part of the proceedings, should be held in private.[52] In making this decision, the committee will consider:
  - the interests of the complainant;
  - the interests of any patient or witness;
  - the interests of the registrant (particularly where issues of his or her mental or physical health arise);
  - all relevant circumstances, including the public interest.

6.50 In considering whether to impose an interim order, the committee will take into account the strength of the evidence, admissions and any steps taken by the registrant to address any concerns. Where the registrant has been charged with a criminal offence, a regulatory body is not 'always obliged' to hear evidence or submissions as to the weakness of the case. The committee may assume that there was

50 GOC (Fitness to Practise) Rules 2005 r21(a) and (b).
51 GOC (Fitness to Practise) Rules 2005 r19(1).
52 GOC (Fitness to Practise) Rules 2005 r23(1)–(5).

sufficient evidence to justify charges being brought by the Crown Prosecution Service[53] (see para 1.175).

Reviewing an interim order

6.51   The Fitness to Practise Committee should direct that there be a review of an interim order[54] which should be treated as a substantive hearing.

Timing

6.52   The review hearing will take place:

* within the first six months of an interim suspension order, and every six months thereafter for as long as the registrant is suspended from the register; or
* at the end of a registrant's suspension period, if a substantive hearing has not yet taken place.

Decision

6.53   The panel will decide if new sanctions should be imposed on the registrant, or if the current sanction is adequate, or if all sanctions should be lifted.

Mediation

6.54   Under OA 1989, the GOC has no power to mediate between registrants and members of the public who are dissatisfied with the services they have received. The GOC has, however, entered into a contract with the Optical Consumer Complaints Service (OCCS), to which it refers appropriate complaints. The OCCS is an independent body which attempts to settle a wide variety of disputes, ranging from refunds and faulty glasses to issues of customer service.

---

53 *Fallon v Horseracing Regulatory Authority* [2006] EWHC 2030 (QB).
54 GOC (Fitness to Practise) Rules 2005 Part 9.

Fitness to practise hearings

Notice of hearing

6.55   The rules state that once an allegation is referred to the Fitness to Practise Committee, the registrant must be served 'as soon as reasonably practicable', with a notification setting out each allegation to be determined, along with a hearing questionnaire duly completed by the registrar and a hearing questionnaire for the registrant to complete.[55]

6.56   The notice of the hearing will contain the text of the charge which is in three parts:

1) The factual particulars including the date, the patient or person and the incident. Often a single incident will give rise to a number of particulars.
2) Whether the factual particulars constitute a lack of competence, misconduct, etc.
3) Whether, as a result, the registrant's fitness to practise is impaired.

Allegations and approach to charging

6.57   The particulars of the allegation and the facts upon which they are founded should be clear and settled in advance of any hearing. If in doubt, clarification and/or further and better particulars should be obtained. The committee may, having heard from both parties, amend either the allegation or the facts provided no injustice is caused, but this should be the exception, not the rule.

6.58   Rule 34 of the GOC (Fitness to Practise) Rules 2005 permit the committee to amend the particulars of the allegation provided it is satisfied that it would be just to do so. If a decision is made to amend, the registrar must notify the registrant accordingly. Allegations must be clearly particularised in the notice of hearing and accurately reflect the facts on which they are based.[56]

Delay

6.59   Article 6 (right to a fair trial) of the European Convention on Human Rights (ECHR) and domestic case-law confer a right to a hearing within a reasonable time. To stay proceedings is an exceptional

---

55 GOC (Fitness to Practise) Rules 2005 r26.
56 See, for example, *Roomi v General Medical Council* [2009] EWHC 2188 (Admin).

course, and delay is not a ground unless the registrant is materially prejudiced and a fair trial is no longer possible.[57] It may take many months for a case to be heard. However, the GOC, like other regulatory bodies, is subject to domestic and European case-law which confers the right to a hearing within a reasonable time. Where the delay becomes unreasonable, the registrant may be able to apply for a stay of the proceedings on grounds of an abuse of process. For a consideration of the case-law on delay, see paras 1.102–1.136.

Evidence and disclosure

6.60   The Fitness to Practise Committee may admit any evidence that they consider fair and relevant to the case before them, whether or not such evidence would be admissible in a court of law. They can receive oral, documentary or other evidence provided it is relevant to the charge or charges under consideration. It is not permissible, however, to introduce evidence that would not be admissible in criminal proceedings unless the committee is satisfied it would be in the interests of justice to do so.[58]

Excluding evidence

6.61   Panels should not consider prejudicial matters that have not been charged. Likewise, evidence which is irrelevant to the charges, or has been unfairly obtained, or which is of a tenuous or unreliable character, or which would otherwise be unfair to admit, should be excluded.[59]

6.62   A registrant will therefore be entitled to request that such material be redacted or removed. Attempts should first be made to reach agreement with the GOC's presenting officer about any disputed part of a witness's statement or report. Exhibit bundles should be edited by agreement. Occasionally, if agreement between the parties cannot be reached, the legal assessor should be asked for a preliminary view before the hearing begins.

6.63   Failure to resolve disputes will lead to an application to the committee to exclude the evidence. This can be prejudicial to the registrant's case, since the panel hearing the application and considering the material will be the same panel who will be considering the case.

57 *R (Toth) v General Medical Council* [2000] EWHC 261 (Admin).
58 GOC (Fitness to Practise) Rules 2005 r38(1).
59 *R v (Johnson) v Professional Conduct Committee of the Nursing and Midwifery Council* [2008] EWHC 885 (Admin).

It may be necessary to invite the members of the panel to recuse themselves if, having seen the prejudicial material, they decide to exclude it.

6.64   Evidence that is relied on by either the presenting officer or the registrant and which has not been disclosed in advance,[60] can, if one of the parties objects to its admission, only be admitted with the permission of the Fitness to Practise Committee at the substantive hearing.[61] Alternatively, where a matter arises unexpectedly in the registrant's case, the Presenting Officer may apply to the committee to call evidence in rebuttal. (See para 6.101.)

Witnesses

6.65   Witnesses attending the hearing will be required to take an oath or affirm before giving evidence.[62]

Proceedings in the absence of a witness

6.66   The panel has a discretion to proceed in the absence of a witness, and to admit hearsay evidence, but the decision to do so must be taken with great care, and only after full consideration of the competing interests, with emphasis if those of the registrant.

6.67   There must be compelling reasons to deprive a registrant of the opportunity to cross-examine a witness, particularly if the case or its consequences are serious.

6.68   The committee may admit any evidence they consider fair and relevant to the case before them, whether or not such evidence would be admissible in a court of law.[63] This is subject to two provisos:

a) that evidence which would be inadmissible in criminal proceedings[64] should not be admitted unless the committee is satisfied that its duty of making due inquiry makes the admission of such evidence desirable;[65]

b) that evidence disclosed late can only be admitted with the committee's permission.[66]

60 The timetable for the advance provision of information is set out in GOC (Fitness to Practise) Rules 2005 r32(1) and (2).
61 GOC (Fitness to Practise) Rules 2005 r38(3).
62 GOC (Fitness to Practise) Rules 2005 r40.
63 GOC (Fitness to Practise) Rules 2005 r38(1).
64 *Al-Khawaja and Tahery v UK* [2011] ECHR 2127 (Grand Chamber).
65 GOC (Fitness to Practise) Rules 2005 r38(2).
66 GOC (Fitness to Practise) Rules 2005 r38(3).

Proceeding in the absence of the registrant[67]

6.69   As already stated at para 6.48 above, where the registrant is neither present nor represented at a hearing, the Fitness to Practise Committee may nevertheless proceed if:

- they are satisfied that all reasonable efforts have been made to notify the registrant of the hearing; and
- having regard to any reasons for absence which have been provided by the registrant, they are satisfied that it is in the public interest to proceed.[68]

Vulnerable witnesses

6.70   Witnesses, the quality of whose evidence is likely to be adversely affected by the proceedings, may be treated as vulnerable witnesses. They are likely to include:

- any witness under 17 years of age at the time of the hearing;[69]
- witnesses with a mental disorder within the meaning of the Mental Health Act 1983;[70]

67 GOC (Fitness to Practise) Rules 2005 r21.
68 In *Yusuf v Royal Pharmaceutical Society of Great Britain* [2009] EWHC 867 (Admin), it was held that the disciplinary committee had correctly identified that the key issue was whether the registrant had voluntarily chosen not to attend. The committee had been properly alert to the need to exercise its discretion to proceed in his absence with absolute caution. A similar approach was taken in *Varma v General Medical Council* [2008] EWHC 753 (Admin), where the panel had properly reminded itself of the need to balance the registrant's private rights against the public interest of having serious allegations investigated and dealt with. In the circumstances it had been justified in treating the registrant's absence as a voluntary choice not to attend.
      The importance of providing medical evidence to support an application to adjourn on health grounds was illustrated in *Faulkner v Nursing and Midwifery Council* [2009] EWHC 3349 (Admin), where the committee made a decision to proceed in the registrant's absence at a time when he had not provided any such evidence. Although he later gave evidence by way of telephone link, he was only able to do so in relation to sanction as decisions on misconduct and impairment had already been made in his absence.
      In *Abdalla v Health Professions Council* [2009] EWHC 3498 (Admin), the registrant argued that the decision to proceed in her absence amounted to a breach of her rights under ECHR article 6(1), or alternatively a breach of natural justice. Her arguments were rejected on the grounds that she had voluntarily opted not to attend and further adjournment could not be justified on the basis that she lacked funds to pay for legal representation, since that position was unlikely to change.
69 GOC (Fitness to Practise) Rules 2005 r39(1)(a).
70 GOC (Fitness to Practise) Rules 2005 r39(1)(b).

- witnesses with mental impairment[71]or physical disabilities that require assistance at the hearing.[72]

Also included is any witness making allegation against the registrant is of a sexual nature,[73] where the witness was the alleged victim, and any witness who complains of intimidation.[74] In such instances, the committee may decide to adopt special measures (discussed below) to help them give evidence.

Video-links and other measures

6.71   In certain cases, particularly cases involving vulnerable witnesses, the use of video links may be permitted. Sometimes, the use of pre-recorded evidence will be approved, provided that the witness is available at the hearing to be cross-examined. Screens will be used where it is considered necessary to prevent the witness's identity being revealed to the press or the general public, or to prevent access to the witness by the applicant. Hearings may also, if necessary, be held in private.

The Fitness to Practise Committee, personnel and representation

The Fitness to Practise Committee

6.72   The Fitness to Practise Committee will comprise medical and non-medical people appointed by the GOC to inquire into allegations of impaired fitness to practise. The panellists, who are not members of the GOC, are appointed through open competition against agreed competencies. The pool of panellists is large, but panels considering individual cases normally comprise five panellists. In addition to the chair, who may be medical or non-medical, there must be at least one medical and one non-medical panellist on each panel.

Hearings manager

6.73   A hearings manager attends every hearing to provide administrative support to the committee. He or she is also the person who is

71   GOC (Fitness to Practise) Rules 2005 r39(1)(c).
72   GOC (Fitness to Practise) Rules 2005 r39(1)(d).
73   GOC (Fitness to Practise) Rules 2005 r39(1)(e).
74   GOC (Fitness to Practise) Rules 2005 r39(1)(f).

responsible for arranging hearing dates. The hearings manager is not involved in the committee's decision-making.

Legal advisers

6.74   The Fitness to Practise Panel will sit with a legal adviser, who must be a trained barrister or solicitor. He or she will advise the committee on all matters of law, including procedural matters. Although often called on to assist in the drafting of the panel's reasons for its decision, the legal adviser does not participate in the decision-making itself.

6.75   Legal advisers are a helpful source of information for registrants and their advisers. The GOC presenting officer (see para 6.78 below) should be present (and vice versa) in any discussion with the legal adviser outside the hearing.

6.76   For a fuller discussion of the role of a disciplinary panel's legal adviser or assessor, see paras 1.284–1.288.

6.77   Additionally, the Fitness to Practise Panel may appoint a clinical adviser where the registrant's physical or mental health is in issue,[75] and/or a specialist adviser[76] who may be present at the proceedings, and advise the committee on any matter within their professional competence.

Presenting officer

6.78   The GOC will be represented by a presenting officer, who will be a trained barrister or solicitor. He or she is responsible for presenting the evidence which has been gathered about the complaint or allegation.

The registrant

6.79   A registrant's entitlement to representation is dealt with at para 6.47 above.

The transcriber

6.80   A transcriber will take notes of the hearing so that a full record is retained.

---

75 GOC (Fitness to Practise) Rules 2005 r42.
76 GOC (Fitness to Practise) Rules 2005 r43.

Procedural or case management hearings

> Proceedings before a Fitness to Practise Committee are divided
> into two stages. The first stage consists of procedural or case
> management hearings.[77] The second stage is the substantive
> hearing.

6.81   At the procedural hearing both parties agree dates for exchanging
witness and expert evidence. As soon as is practicably possible, the
registrant must be served with a notification setting out the allegation, a copy of the hearing questionnaire completed by the presenting officer, a hearing questionnaire for the registrant to complete,
and copies of all statements and documents which the presenting
officer intends to rely on.[78] The hearing questionnaire must be completed by the registrant and served on the presenting officer within
28 days.[79] At least seven days must pass thereafter before a procedural hearing can be held.[80]

6.82   At a procedural hearing, the Fitness to Practise Committee:

- may consider the completed hearing questionnaires;
- may invite representations from the parties (if present);
- may establish a timetable for the disclosure of evidence by each
  party; and
- shall make directions for the further conduct of the matter.

Public and private hearings

6.83   GOC hearings are generally held in public, but where it is felt necessary to hold a hearing or part of a hearing in private, an application
can be made to the panel to do so. This might arise, for example,
where a vulnerable witness is to give evidence. If a registrant is
unrepresented, it is advisable that he or she should attend another
hearing to familiarise himself or herself with the layout of the room
or process. The press frequently attend.

Preparation for hearings

6.84   Prior to the hearing, the registrant will receive the Investigation Committee bundle containing witness statements and documentation

77 GOC (Fitness to Practise) Rules 2005 rr28–30.
78 GOC (Fitness to Practise) Rules 2005 r26(a)–(e).
79 GOC (Fitness to Practise) Rules 2005 r27.
80 GOC (Fitness to Practise) Rules 2005 r29.

(referred to as exhibits) on which the presenting officer intends to rely. If a registrant does not dispute the evidence provided by the witness, then the GOC should be notified that their statement can be agreed. If a statement or exhibit contains irrelevant or inadmissible material, then the GOC should be requested to redact the evidence. Early discussions about evidence and documentation enable agreed and properly paginated hearing bundles to be prepared well in advance of the hearing.

6.85   A registrant should draft a witness statement or proof of evidence. It should contain:

- an introductory paragraph setting out experience/expertise;
- a paragraph dealing with the allegations, identifying which, if any, facts are admitted and those which are denied;
- all mitigating factors.

6.86   Where an allegation is admitted on the facts, the statement should include evidence of insight (see para 6.120). Even where evidence-in-chief is to be given orally, it will assist the registrant if he or she can refresh his or her memory beforehand.

6.87   Registrants are well advised to produce their own bundle of exhibits which should include any additional documentation relevant to the allegations, reports, documents relating to subsequent employment, training certificates, evidence of continuing education and training, testimonials and other relevant documentation. If the registrant wishes to rely on these documents at the hearing, he or she should, subject to any timetable for the disclosure of evidence, provide copies to the presenter no later than 14 days before the date fixed for the substantive hearing.[81]

6.88   If a registrant is represented, a pre-hearing conference should be arranged to take full instructions and to ensure that he or she is fully prepared for the hearing.

6.89   On the day of the hearing, it is advisable to arrive at least one hour before the commencement in order to confirm instructions and provide advice. A check should be made of the bundle of exhibits to be put before the committee. Any documents that have been inserted but which cannot be agreed should be removed or redacted. If the GOC wish to place a disputed document before the panel, the presenting officer will make an application. The registrant will be provided with an opportunity to explain their objections to the panel

---

81   GOC (Fitness to Practise) Rules 2005 r32(1) and (2).

prior to the decision being made. Late commencement of hearings causes scheduling problems and inconvenience.

6.90   The registrant, or his or her representative, should introduce himself or herself to the case presenter who will be prosecuting the case on behalf of the GOC. The case presenter should be provided with copies of any additional documentation to be relied on, and if appropriate, he or she should be informed of the registrant's response to the allegations, or any change in position to the allegations. This provides an opportunity for the GOC to indicate whether, eg it will offer no evidence on a particular charge or reduce it. It may be that the parties can reach agreement on certain procedural issues, eg the wording of proposed amendments to the charges, an application to hold the hearing in private, or an application to adjourn. As far as possible these matters should be dealt with in pre-hearing correspondence.

6.91   The registrant, or his or her representative, should also ensure that he or she meets the panel's legal adviser who advises the committee on any matters of law, evidence or procedure. Any legal issues should be discussed with the legal adviser in the presence of the GOC case presenter. The legal adviser is often influential in the legal advice that he or she provides to hearings, and can provide invaluable assistance to representatives and registrants in resolving legal issues. There is, however, no requirement for a representative to agree or accept the legal advice of the panel's adviser. If the case raises a legal issue, it is always advisable to bring to the hearing copies of any case to be relied upon, and it is good practice to provide a copy to the legal assessor and the GOC case presenter and the transcriber prior to addressing the panel.

The substantive hearing

6.92   The registrar must serve copies of the documents, including statements on the registrant, after which, but no later than 14 days before the hearing, each party must serve on the other copies of any documents, statements or reports made by witnesses upon whose oral evidence the parties intend to rely and which they agree may be disclosed to each other.[82] Evidence that has not been disclosed in accordance with the timetable, or some other preliminary direction, may not be given without the permission of the Fitness to Practise Committee.

82 GOC (Fitness to Practise) Rules 2005 r32.

6.93   The substantive hearing may, if the parties agree, follow on immediately from a procedural hearing. If not, the registrar must notify
the parties in writing of the date of the substantive hearing, which
may not be held earlier than 28 days after notification.

6.94   Following introductions, the registrant will be asked to confirm
his or her name and correct service of the notice. The charges will
then be read out. Application by the presenting officer may be
made to amend the charges. If the registrant is present at the hearing, the committee asks whether the registrant wishes to make any
admissions.[83]

Presentation of the presenting officer's case

6.95   After addressing the Fitness to Practise Committee in relation to
each allegation, the presenting officer will call his or her witnesses
and adduce documentary and other evidence in support of the case
against the registrant.[84] The committee does not see witness statements or documentation in advance of the hearing. Witnesses will be
required to take the oath or to affirm before giving oral evidence.[85]
Evidence given by a witness at this stage is referred to as exami-
nation-in-chief. Any witness who gives oral evidence may then be
cross-examined by the registrant and re-examined by the presenting
officer.[86]

No case to answer

6.96   If a charge is unsupported by the evidence, or the evidence that supports it is tenuous or contradictory, then at the close of the presenting
officer's case, the registrant or the registrant's legal representative
may submit that that the allegation has not been proved, and invite
the committee to dismiss the charge.

6.97   Submissions are based on the test laid down by Lord Lane LCJ in
R v Galbraith,[87] and may be made where there is a) no evidence or b)
some evidence but it is weak, vague or inconsistent, and looked at 'in

---

83   GOC (Fitness to Practise) Rules 2005 r44.
84   GOC (Fitness to Practise) Rules 2005 r45(1).
85   GOC (Fitness to Practise) Rules 2005 r40.
86   GOC (Fitness to Practise) Rules 2005 r45(1). However, rule 39(4) prohibits
cross-examination by a registrant in person where the allegation is one of a
sexual nature and where the witness is an alleged victim, unless the victim
agrees in writing to be cross-examined by the registrant.
87   [1981] 1 WLR 1039, [1981] 2 All ER 1060; *Tutin v General Medical Council* [2009]
EWHC 553 (Admin).

the round' a panel could not properly find the case (or fact) proved. The committee will hear arguments from both parties, and the legal adviser will give advice as to the appropriate test to be applied.

6.98   A full discussion of the case-law and principles relating to half-time submissions is to be found at paras 1.355–1.363.

Presentation of the registrant's case

6.100   Following the presentation of the evidence by the presenting officer, the registrant may also address the committee, give evidence, call witnesses and adduce documentary or other evidence in support.[88] The registrant and his witnesses may also be cross-examined by the presenting officer and re-examined by the registrant.[89]

6.101   If a matter is raised unexpectedly in the course of the registrant's case, the presenting officer may apply to the committee to call evidence in rebuttal. (See para 6.64 above.)

6.102   If a matter is raised in evidence by the registrant or his or her witnesses which the presenting officer wishes to rebut, he or she may, with the committee's permission, call witnesses or introduce documentary or other evidence in rebuttal.[90]

6.103   Witnesses can be asked questions by members of the committee or, with the permission of the chair of the committee, the legal adviser or any clinical adviser or specialist adviser appointed by the committee.[91]

Closing submissions

6.104   At the conclusion of all the evidence, the presenting officer is entitled to address the committee, followed by an address by or on behalf of the registrant.[92] Usually closing submissions will address both the facts as set out in the particulars of the allegation and whether they amount to a statutory ground. Sometimes, however, it may be tactically advisable to separate these processes, since submissions on the statutory grounds[93] may depend on what disputed facts are found proven. This is most likely to occur where a registrant accepts lack of competence but denies misconduct. The panel should be informed

---

88   GOC (Fitness to Practise) Rules 2005 r46(1).
89   GOC (Fitness to Practise) Rules 2005 r46(2).
90   GOC (Fitness to Practise) Rules 2005 r47(1).
91   GOC (Fitness to Practise) Rules 2005 r48.
92   GOC (Fitness to Practise) Rules 2005 r49.
93   Referred to in para 6.7 above.

of this approach at the outset, and the reasons why it may be in the interests of justice to depart from the norm.

6.105   In all cases, the panel will invite the legal adviser to advise it on any question of law. The legal adviser will usually remind the panel of the burden and standard of proof, identify any legal issues that need to be resolved, and identify the key legal authorities on the statutory ground and on any other issue. The parties will then be given the opportunity to indicate if they agree with the advice of the legal adviser, and to make further representations if they disagree.

Findings

6.106   The committee then adjourns to determine their findings on the facts and decide whether or not the allegation is proved.[94] The legal adviser sits in on these deliberations but plays no part in the decision making. The legal adviser may, at the request of the committee, assist in the drafting of any decision.

6.107   The legal adviser will inform the parties in open session of any advice that he or she is given during these private deliberations. The committee will then return and the chair will announce whether such facts have been found proved.

Burden and standard of proof

> The burden of proving its case is on the GOC, and the facts of the case must be proved according to the civil standard of proof on the balance of probabilities; a fact will be established if it is more likely than not to have happened.[95]

6.108   Questions as to whether or not, in the light of the findings, the registrant has acted in a way which amounts to misconduct or deficient personal performance, or that he or she has adverse physical or mental health, are a matter of judgment in respect of which the standard of proof is not relevant. Nor is it relevant for interim orders to take place where no findings of fact are made.

6.109   The standard of proof, although finite and unvarying, must be applied flexibly: As stated in *In Re Doherty*[96] the more serious the allegation or the more serious the consequences to the registrant if

---

94 GOC (Fitness to Practise) Rules 2005 r50.
95 GOC (Fitness to Practise) Rules 2005 r50A.
96 [2008] UKHL 33.

the allegation is proven, the stronger must be the evidence. See also *R (Bonhoeffer) v General Medical Council.*[97]

The impairment stage

6.110   If the charge or charges against the registrant are proved, the committee will go on to consider the issue of impairment. As indicated at para 6.108 below, a finding of impaired fitness to practise against a registered individual can be based on any of the following:

- misconduct;
- deficient professional performance (although not in the case of a registered student);
- a conviction or caution in the British Isles for a criminal offence, or a conviction elsewhere for an offence, which, if committed in England and Wales, would constitute a criminal offence;
- the registrant having accepted a conditional offer under section 302 of the Criminal Procedure (Scotland) Act 1995 (fixed penalty: conditional offer by procurator fiscal) or agreed to pay a penalty under section 246(2) or (3) of the Criminal Procedure (Scotland) Act discharging him or her absolutely;
- adverse physical or mental health; or
- a determination by any other UK health regulatory body that fitness to practise is impaired.

6.111   A finding of impaired fitness to practise against a business registrant can be based on any of the following:

- misconduct (by the business registrant or a director);
- practices or patterns of behaviour occurring within the business which:
  - the registrant knew or ought reasonably to have known of; and
  - amount to misconduct or deficient personal performance;
- the instigations by the business registrant of practices or patterns of behaviour within the business where the practice or behaviour amounts to, or would if implemented amount to, misconduct or deficient personal performance;
- a conviction or caution in the British Isles of the business registrant or one of its directors for a criminal defence, or a conviction elsewhere for an offence which, if committed in England and Wales, would constitute a criminal offence;

- the registrant or one of its directors having accepted a conditional offer under section 302 of the Criminal Procedure (Scotland) Act 1995, or agreed to pay a penalty under section 246(2) or (3) of the Criminal Procedure (Scotland) Act discharging it or him absolutely;
- a determination by any other UK health regulatory body that:
  - the business registrant's fitness to carry on business as a member of that profession is impaired; or
  - the fitness of a director of the business registrant to practise that profession is impaired.

6.112   There is no statutory definition of impairment of fitness to practise. It is, however, not to be equated with misconduct, and must become the subject of a separate decision. A two-stage test must be adopted. It may be decided by the Fitness to Practise Committee that, in the case of a registrant found guilty of misconduct his or her fitness to practise is not impaired.[98] Where a committee finds some charges proven, but others unproven, it may still reach the view that a registrant's fitness to practise is impaired.[99]

6.113   In coming to a conclusion on impairment, the committee must look forward, not back. The committee may decide that what a registrant has done is so bad that looking forward, he or she is simply not fit to practise without restrictions or at all. Alternatively, the committee may conclude, looking forward, that what the misconduct, put in the context of the registrant's previous good record, has not impaired fitness to practise. In reaching this decision, the committee will take into account any insight the registrant has demonstrated, and any remedial steps he or she may have taken.

6.114   The committee must apply a two-stage process. First, there must be a finding of serious misconduct and second, the committee must conclude as a result of its finding that the registrant's fitness to practise is impaired. In reaching a conclusion on impairment, the committee must consider evidence of the registrant's conduct and ability demonstrated both before and after the misconduct in question.[100]

6.115   When considering the issue of impairment, the correct approach is to focus on the registrant's fitness to practise as at the date of the hearing. Speculation as to whether a registrant might become unfit to practise in the future due, for example, to the recurrence

---

98 R *(Zygmunt) v General Medical Council* [2008] EWHC 2643 (Admin).
99 *Ndisang v Nursing and Midwifery Council* [2009] EWHC 2487 (Admin).
100 *Cheatle v General Medical Council* [2009] EWHC 645 (Admin).

of some condition from which the registrant has recovered, is not permitted.[101]

6.116   Submissions directed to the issue of impairment should emphasise the following matters, if applicable:

- that the finding of misconduct, etc, is not so bad as to lead the committee, looking forward, logically to conclude that the registrant's conduct is impaired;
- that the registrant's previous record of good and safe practice is unblemished;
- that the registrant has demonstrated insight into his or her conduct;
- that the conduct which led to the allegation is capable of being remedied; or
- that the conduct which led to the allegation has been remedied.

6.117   It will be important to provide evidence which focuses on these points. Relevant evidence which could be adduced at this stage includes:

- written or oral evidence that explains the registrant's thought processes at the relevant time and demonstrates an understanding of why the conduct constituted missed conduct or lack of competence;
- what the registrant would do differently if in the same position again, including any evidence of an occasion when the registrant was in a similar position and did act differently;
- what, if any, steps the registrant has subsequently taken to change his or her practice or behaviour – this may include seeking medical assistance, attending counselling, direct or indirect supervision, audits or assessments of work, mentoring, self-reflection, personal research and/or training. If possible, documentary evidence should be supplied in support;
- character evidence relevant to the conduct in question to demonstrate, for example, that the registrant acted out of character or is capable of learning from his or her mistakes;
- oral or written evidence from other health professionals, supervisors, managers or other appropriate persons which confirms the steps the registrant has taken and that he or she has insight.

Future developments

6.118   Currently, the commission is seeking views on the definition of 'impairment' in relation to registrants' fitness to practise. They are

---

101 *Sarkodie-Gyan v Nursing and Midwifery Council* [2009] EWHC 2131 (Admin).

asking whether the current investigative approach should be retained, based on investigating complaints against set categories of impairment such as misconduct and poor professional performance. As an alternative, the commission sets out the approach recommended in the *Shipman Inquiry report,* in which impairment is considered specifically in terms of whether the practitioner has caused risk of harm to the public or might in the future, or acted dishonestly, or might in the future. It is argued that this would introduce more objective criteria.

6.119   The commission also sets out a third, more open approach. Under this model, impairment would be considered against a very general analysis of whether a registrant poses a risk to the health and safety of the public (and whether confidence in the profession has or will be undermined).

Insight

6.120   'Insight' is the expectation that a registrant will be able to stand back and accept that with hindsight, he or she should have behaved differently, and that it is expected that he or she will take steps to prevent a recurrence and learn from their mistakes. Factors that may assist a committee when considering whether a registrant has the insight necessary to avoid or mitigate sanctions, and to accept and comply with proposed undertakings, include:

- demonstrating an understanding of the gravity of the conduct in question;
- being open and honest when things go wrong;
- showing a willingness to act differently in the future;
- offering an apology;
- the conduct and demeanour of the registrant at the hearing.

Sanctions

6.121   The principle aims of sanctions are to protect the public, uphold the standards and reputation of the profession and maintain public confidence in the profession. The punitive effect of sanctions is only one, and not necessarily the most important, factor to be borne in mind.

6.122   If the panel concludes that the doctor's fitness to practise is impaired, it will go on to consider what if any sanctions to impose. The purpose of any sanction is not to punish the registrant, but to protect patients and the wider public interest. The sanction should therefore be proportionate, and balance the interests of the registrant with the interests of the public and the seriousness of the allegations found proven.

6.123   The following sanctions are available:

- to take no action;
- to accept undertakings offered by the registrant, provided the panel is satisfied that such undertakings protect patients and the wider public interest;
- to place conditions on the registrant's registration for up to three years. This will ordinarily be followed by a review (see para 6.136 below);
- to suspend the registrant's registration for up to 12 months. This will ordinarily be followed by a review;
- financial penalty (see paras 6.129–6.131 below). This will not be applicable in a health case;
- to erase the registrant's name from the register, so that he or she can no longer practise. This will not be applicable in a case which involves the physical or mental health of the registrant (see paras 6.132–6.134 below).

Conditional registration (maximum three years)

6.124   The aim of imposing conditions is to protect the public, and the test is whether such conditions are sufficient to protect patients and the public interest. The conditions must impose a requirement for the registrant to be under strict supervision either in his or her current or future practice or places of work.

6.125   Conditions can be imposed on a registrant's registration for up to three years. These can be ordered to take effect immediately or deferred, and should be appropriate, proportionate, workable and measurable. Conditional registration allows a registrant to return to practice under certain conditions, and include, for example, no longer being able to carry out certain procedures. In some cases further education or training may be required, where the committee are satisfied on the evidence that the registrant would respond positively and remedy any deficiencies of practise.[102] Evidence will be required that he or she has insight into any health problems, and has the potential and willingness to respond positively to retraining.

---

102 GOC, *Fitness to Practise Panels hearings guidance and indicative sanctions*, revised 18 January 2011.

Suspension (maximum 12 months)[103]

6.126   Suspension, which involves a temporary removal from the register, may be imposed in certain circumstances, including:

- where a serious instance of misconduct has occurred where a lesser sanction is insufficient;
- where there is no evidence of repetition;
- where the committee is satisfied that the registrant has insight, and there is no risk of repetition.

6.127   An order for suspension and the imposition of conditions of practice are separate and should not be confused.[104]

6.128   When imposing a period of suspension, it is normally appropriate to direct a review hearing (see para 6.136 below).

Financial penalty orders[105]

6.129   The committee has the power to impose a financial penalty order of any sum not exceeding £50,000. The order may be made in addition to, or instead of, an erasure order, suspension or a conditional registration order. However, for a case where the events occurred before 1 July 2005, the penalty must not exceed £1,600 (this being the maximum penalty then available to the Disciplinary Committee.

6.130   When making a financial penalty order, the committee must specify the period or date within which the sum is to be paid.

6.131   Where the committee is considering making such an award against an individual registrant, his or her ability to pay must be taken into account.

103 Opticians Act 1989 s13F.
104 In *Udom v General Medical Council* [2009] EWHC 3242 (Admin), a panel had, on finding the registrant's fitness to practise impaired both by reason of his health and competence, imposed a sanction which purported to be conditions but in fact amounted to a suspension. The panel had ordered that the registrant was not to practise unsupervised for a period of nine months and was, during that period, to undergo a series of clinical attachments. It was confirmed that the impact of a sanction on the practitioner is a relevant consideration, although in the exercise of proportionality, it is not the primary consideration. In the present case, the effect of the order was to suspend the registrant from practice, given that the clinical attachments were to be purely observational. Suspension and conditions of practice were entirely separate sanctions under the applicable rules and were mutually exclusive. Accordingly, the panel had been wrong to impose conditions which had the effect of suspending the registrant.
105 Section 13H.

Erasure

6.132 Where the misconduct is grave, or there has been a serious departure from the relevant professional standards, erasure from the register may be the only means of protecting patients and/or maintaining public confidence in the optical profession. A balance must be struck, however, between an individualised approach to sanctions and the need for deterrence. In *Bijl v General Medical Council*,[106] it was held that a committee should not feel it necessary to remove 'an otherwise competent and useful [registrant] who presents no danger to the public in order to satisfy [public] demand for blame and punishment'.[107] Whereas in *Bolton v Law Society*,[108] considered in *Gupta v General Medical Council*,[109] it was held that 'the reputation of the profession is more important than the fortunes of any individual member. Membership of a profession brings many benefits but that is part of the price'.[110]

6.133 Erasure is likely when the behaviour is fundamentally incompatible with being a registered professional, such as doing serious harm to individuals, abuse of a position of trust, the commission of criminal offences such as those involving sexual misconduct, child pornography and dishonesty, or a persistent lack of insight into the seriousness of actions or consequences.

6.134 Where the registrant has not acted in the patient's best interests, and has failed to provide an adequate level of care, falling well below the professional standards expected of a registered optometrist or dispensing optician, and where a persistent failure to provide clinical care is apparent, erasure may be considered to be the only appropriate sanction. An important factor in such cases is whether the registrant has, or has the potential to develop, insight into these failures. Where there is no evidence of this, other forms of sanction may be insufficient (*Garfoot v General Medical Council*[111]).

No further action

6.135 Where a registrant's fitness to practise is impaired, there may be exceptional circumstances which would justify the committee in taking no further action. Such cases are rare, but might be appropriate

---

106 Privy Council Appeal no 78 of 2000.
107 Privy Council appeal no 78 of 2000, para 13.
108 [1994] 1 WLR 512.
109 [2002] 1 WLR 1691.
110 *Bolton v Law Society* [1994] 1 WLR 512 at 519E.
111 [2002] UKPC 35.

where the registrant has demonstrated considerable insight into his or her behaviour and has already embarked on, and completed, any remedial action which the committee might require him or her to undertake. It will be important for the registrant to produce evidence to show that the registrant has taken steps to mitigate his or her actions.

Review hearings

6.136   As with interim orders, the committee should also normally direct that there be a review of a conditional order or a suspension order before they expire, so that the committee can be reassured that the registrant is fit to resume practice unrestricted, or with the same or further conditions, such as educational or training conditions.

6.137   The registrant will need to provide objective evidence to satisfy the committee that he or she has fully appreciated the gravity of the offence, has not re-offended and has maintained his or her skills and knowledge, and that the registrant's patients will not be placed at risk by resumption of practice or by the imposition of conditional registration.

6.138   At a review hearing, further educational or training conditions may be imposed, if it is thought that the registrant may not improve his or her performance through existing conditions.

Location

6.139   Hearings are normally conducted at the General Optical Council, 41 Harley Street, London W1G 8DJ. On occasions, proceedings will take place at the Royal Institute of British Architects, 66 Portland Place, London W1B 1AD. Other locations may also be used.

Registration appeals and applications for restoration hearing

6.140   A registration appeal hearing is held if an individual is refused entry to the register and he or she wishes to appeal against the registrar's decision.

6.141   A restoration application hearing is held when a practitioner has been erased from the register for disciplinary reasons and he or she wants to apply to rejoin the register.

6.142   Appeals from the Fitness to Practise Committee in relation to an erasure from the register for fraudulent or incorrect register entries lie to the county court (or in Scotland, to the sheriff).

Appeals to the High Court

6.143 Appeals against the Fitness to Practise Committee in respect of disciplinary orders lie to the High Court (or in Scotland, to the Court of Session) within 28 days beginning with the date on which notification was served.

6.144   Fresh evidence may be considered on appeal, if it was not available at the time of the original hearing (*Chandraseka v Nursing and Midwifery Council*[112]). However, the significance of fresh evidence is best considered by a Review Panel, and will not be considered by the court if a review has not taken place (*Muscat v Health Professions Council*[113]).

Costs and expenses

6.145 The Fitness to Practise Committee has the power summarily to assess the costs of any party to the proceedings, and can order the GOC or registrant to pay part or all of their costs (in both a substantive and review hearing).

6.146   An order for costs against the GOC by a successful registrant is rare. Since the GOC, as with any regulatory body, is in a wholly different position from an ordinary litigant, the general rule in litigation that 'costs follow the event' has no application. The GOC brings proceedings in the public interest and to maintain proper professional standards, so unless a complaint is improperly brought, no order for costs is normally made against the GOC (*Walker v Law Society*[114]). The GOC policy is currently under review.

6.147   As far as costs against an unsuccessful registrant are concerned, the GOC will in future only request this if it considers that the defence's conduct of the case had led to unnecessary expense – for example, failing to comply with directions issues by the Fitness to Practise Committee. This change will not apply to interim order hearings.

112 [2008] EWHC 3528 (Admin).
113 [2009] EWCA Civ 1090.
114 [2007] EWCA Civ 233.

CHAPTER 7

Linked litigation and other cross-cutting issues

continued

Key points

- Concurrent litigation can have a significant impact upon the regulatory process; advisers and registrants should always consider the impact that the conduct of on-going litigation can have on the regulatory process.
- Concurrent criminal proceedings can cause significant delays to the regulatory process, sometimes stretching to years. Despite the potential for prejudice that this may cause, it will only be in 'exceptional circumstances' that proceedings may be stayed on the basis of delay.
- A registrant must consider the impact of the regulatory process on the registrant's employment. If the registrant is given a suspension order, even on an interim basis, this is likely to jeopardise his or her job security. Further, if a registrant losses his or her employment, it may significantly affect a registrant's ability to argue that his or her fitness to practise is not impaired.
- Decisions of regulatory bodies can be subject to both statutory appeals and judicial reviews. Often the types of arguments deployed in both types of challenge will overlap. If the procedure of the Fitness to Practise Panel is unfair etc, it may be challenged by way of judicial review.
- Mediation may be a possibility before the stage of a referral to a regulatory body. If a registrant receives a complaint, mediation is often a sensible step to prevent the matter escalating. The Health and Care Professions Council (HCPC) has an official mediation process and other regulators are considering developing this approach.
- Advisers and registrants should be aware of the need carefully to uphold the principles set out under the Data Protection Act 1998 and when appropriate redact evidence that is provided to a regulator to protect patients' personal information.

Introduction

7.1   During the process of a regulatory body undertaking a conduct or competency hearing, there may be a wide range of linked litigation and legal issues which, if they arise, can significantly affect the fitness to practise proceedings. It is often the case that while regulatory proceedings are ongoing there are concurrent legal proceedings taking place in different forums. For example, in cases involving alleged misconduct there may be ongoing criminal proceedings as well as employment tribunal proceedings or internal disciplinary proceedings within the registrant's employer.

7.2   When advising on or conducting a professional disciplinary matter before one of the five councils, the impact of such linked litigation must be carefully considered. Proceedings in other areas may have a significant impact on how a registrant should conduct himself or herself once a referral to a regulator has been made.

7.3   This chapter examines the effects of litigation in other forums on the regulatory process and considers the potential ramifications for registrants. The most significant concurrent legal proceedings are those within the criminal and employment context.

7.4   The impact of criminal proceedings is far-reaching. Convictions may instigate a referral to a regulator; a criminal trial may significantly delay fitness to practise hearings; or evidence from a criminal trial may be used by a regulator against a registrant. A registrant's employment will also significantly affect the regulatory process; whether a registrant remains in employment is crucial to the issue of impairment and in turn, if a regulator imposes an interim suspension order, this will seriously jeopardise a registrant's security of employment.

7.5   It is not just concurrent litigation that can influence regulatory proceedings. A range of other legal issues might also affect a registrant who is subject to a referral. Registrants may wish to consider the possibility of mediation; the role of judicial review; making a subject access request under the Freedom of Information Act (FOIA) 2000 and the importance of understanding the principles of the Data Protection Act (DPA) 1998.

7.6   In addition, many registrants will also face a referral to the Independent Safeguarding Authority (ISA) with respect to potential inclusion on the children's and/or adults' barred lists. This subject is dealt with in detail in chapter 8.

Criminal investigations and proceedings

7.7   A registrant who has been referred to his or her regulatory body may well face concurrent criminal proceedings – alternatively, a criminal conviction can trigger a referral to a regulatory body itself. An ongoing criminal process and its outcome impact upon the regulatory process in a variety of ways. Primarily, a conviction can in and of itself be treated as misconduct. Generally, regulators either treat a conviction in one of two ways: it is either evidence of serious professional misconduct, or alternatively, being convicted is seen as misconduct in its own right.

Health and Care Professions Council and convictions

7.8 Health Professions Order (HPO) 2001[1] article 22(1)(a)(ii) provides that one of the grounds upon which an allegation may be made is that a registrant's fitness to practise is impaired by reason of: '(iii) a conviction or caution in the United Kingdom for a criminal offence, or a conviction elsewhere for an offence which, if committed in England and Wales, would constitute a criminal offence'.

General Medical Council and convictions

7.9 Under the General Medical Council (GMC) regime, rule 5 of the General Medical Council (Fitness to Practise) Rules 2004[2] states as follows:

> 5.(1) Subject to rule 4(5), the Registrar shall refer an allegation falling within section 35C(2)(c) of the Act relating to a conviction resulting in the imposition of a custodial sentence, whether immediate or suspended, directly to a FTP Panel.

> (2) Subject to rule 4(5), the Registrar shall refer any other allegation falling within section 35C(2)(c) or (e) of the Act directly to a FTP Panel, unless he is of the opinion that it ought to be referred to a medical and a lay Case Examiner for consideration under rule 8.

7.10 This means that any conviction resulting in a custodial sentence must be referred to a Fitness to Practise Panel, however the GMC has some discretion when a referral is received concerning a conviction that results in a non-custodial sentence. The GMC have issued guidance as to how convictions are to be treated.[3] The rules explain that whether a conviction resulting in a non-custodial sentence requires a referral to a Fitness to Practise Panel will entirely be determined by the seriousness of the conviction. In particular, the GMC guidance suggests that certain 'low level' crimes will not need to go before

---

1 SI 2002 No 254.
2 Schedule to the General Medical Council (Fitness to Practise) Rules Order of Council 2004 SI No 2608.
3 GMC, *Guidance on convictions, cautions, and determinations*, available at www.gmc-uk.org/guidance_convictions_cautions_and_determinations.pdf_25416518.pdf

a Fitness to Practise Panel as they set out at paragraph 14 of the guidance:

> 14. The following types of conviction can (unless there are any exceptional aggravating factors) normally be concluded by the Registrar – as they are extremely unlikely to raise any issues which might impact on the doctor's registration:
>
> a. Any offence committed in the UK which is a fixed penalty offence for the purposes of the Road Traffic Offenders Act 1988 or any statutory modification or replacement thereof for the time being in force.
>
> b. An offence committed in the UK or abroad which is dealt with by a procedure substantially similar to that applicable to such a fixed penalty offence.
>
> c. An offence the main ingredient of which is the unlawful parking of a motor vehicle.[4]

However, it should be noted that this is subject to the caveat at paragraph 15 that 'the Registrar will only conclude these cases where there are no other matters requiring investigation'.

Nursing and Midwifery Council and convictions

7.11   The Nursing and Midwifery Council (NMC) have issued separate guidance as to where a referral is necessary if the conviction relates to drug or alcohol offences.[5] The NMC treat convictions in general as character offences, their guidance stating that:

> Only **serious** criminal convictions or cautions should be referred to the NMC. A minor fixed penalty traffic offence, for example a speeding fine or parking ticket, is unlikely to be a case for us.[6]

However the standards code[7] at paragraph 50 states: 'you must inform the NMC if you have been cautioned, charged or found guilty

---

4   In 2011 the GMC opened a consultation process which proposes that there be an automatic erasure for conviction for certain criminal convictions. At the time of writing, the outcome of this consultation was unknown. See GMC, *Reform of the fitness to practise procedures at the GMC. Changes to the way we deal with cases at the end of an investigation. A paper for consultation*, 2011, available at www.gmc-uk.org/FTP_reforms_consultation_paper.pdf_38085201.pdf.

5   NMC, *Policy for nurses and midwives who have received a caution or conviction for an alcohol or drug related offence*, July 2010, available at www.nmc-uk.org/ Documents/Registration/Drugs-and-alcohol/drug_and_alcohol_policy.pdf.

6   See www.nmc-uk.org/Employers-and-managers/Fitness-to-practise/Character-issues/.

7   NMC, *The code: Standards of conduct, performance and ethics for nurses and midwives*, May 2008: www.nmc-uk.org/Nurses-and-midwives/Thecode/the-code-in-full.

of a criminal offence' and at paragraph 61: 'You must uphold the reputation of your profession at all times'. As a breach of the standards code can amount to misconduct, a conviction could also be characterised as misconduct.

7.12   In all three UK jurisdictions, evidence that a person has been convicted of an offence is generally admissible in civil proceedings as proof that the person concerned committed that offence, regardless of whether or not the person pleaded guilty.[8]

7.13   In addition, the existence of a criminal conviction may result in the instigation of a referral to the regulator by the police and be the beginning of disciplinary proceedings. Home Office Circular 6/2006[9] (Annex D) requests police to refer matters to the relevant regulatory body, in particularly where the registrant is involved in the protection of the vulnerable, including children; this is likely to include a wide number of health care professionals.

Evidence in criminal trials

7.14   The registrant's behaviour during the criminal proceedings may be taken into account by a regulator. For example, the HCPC's guidance suggests that Fitness to Practise Panels should have regard to whether the registrant pleaded guilty to the offence and, if so, at what stage in the proceedings. They suggest that:

> ... a guilty plea entered at the first reasonable opportunity is indicative of a greater insight on the part of the registrant than one entered at the last moment. A registrant who is convicted of an offence but maintains that the conviction was wrong may be deemed as lacking insight into their offending behaviour and this may have a significant bearing upon the sanction which a panel should impose in order to protect the public.[10]

7.15   Therefore, practitioners should ensure that they are aware of the registrant's conduct during the criminal case and consider the impact that defending any criminal charges may have upon the regulatory process and how this should be approached. If, for example, the registrant has entered a not guilty plea, this may not be on a denial of the facts, but on the basis of the lack of criminal culpability or for legal reasons, and arguably this would not necessarily show a lack

8 Civil Evidence Act 1968 s11.
9 GMC, *The notifiable occupations scheme: revised guidance for police forces*, April 2006, available at www.gmc-uk.org/ACPO_MoU_Annex_D.pdf_29141718.pdf.
10 HPC, *Convictions and cautions practice note*, October 2009.

of insight as it may be that the registrant has accepted his or her culpability for the acts but does not necessarily accept one element of the criminal offence, for example, intentionality, dishonesty etc.

Privilege against self-incrimination

7.16   Legally there is a right not to self-incriminate yourself when answering questions as a witness. This means that you cannot be compelled to answer questions or produce documents if the answers or material might incriminate a witness. This right may be exercised in regulatory proceedings and advisers should be alert to it when a registrant is giving evidence. The legal principles of privilege against self-incrimination are discussed at para 1.540.

Challenging the judgment of a criminal trial

7.17   The registrant may not agree with the outcome of a criminal case against him or her. However, the general rule is that a challenge to a criminal conviction should not be entertained by a regulatory body. This principle was approved by the Court of Appeal in *Shepherd v The Law Society*,[11] where Lord Taylor LCJ considered the matter carefully and referred in his judgment to *Smith v Linkskill*[12] where Sir Thomas Bingham MR set out three public policy considerations underlying the rules to challenging a conviction:

a) that it was an affront to any coherent system of justice stemming from inconsistent final decisions of courts of competent jurisdiction;

b) the impossibility of retrying the issues which was before the court on an earlier occasion;

c) the importance of the finality of litigation.

7.18   Advisers should therefore be aware that it is only in exceptional circumstances that a challenge to a criminal conviction would be entertained by one of the Councils and if a registrant wishes to challenge the findings of a criminal court, the registrant should be aware of the high threshold he or she will need to surmount in order to be able to succeed in this argument before the regulator. If a registrant does

---

11   [1996] EWCA Civ 977.
12   (1996) *Times* 7 February.

want to challenge a conviction, then the appropriate route is through a criminal appeal.[13]

7.19   If an appeal to a criminal conviction is ongoing, advisers may want to consider applying for a stay of the disciplinary proceedings as a conviction will impact on the regulatory process significantly and would undoubtedly cause prejudice to the registrant. Advisers making such applications for a stay on this ground should consider addressing the prejudice the registrant would suffer by reference to the charges he or she faces, the evidence against him or her and its impact on findings regarding the registrant's own insight and potential sanction (see para 1.535).

Delay

7.20   Procedurally, concurrent criminal investigations arising out of the same factual background may delay the regulatory proceedings. Whether the regulatory proceedings should be adjourned is ultimately a matter for the regulatory body to decide. When making such a decision they should take into account competing considerations. Advisers may feel that it is advantageous to a registrant to seek postponement of the regulatory case until the criminal matter is finished, for example in order to preserve his or her defence.[14] However, this may cause significant delays to the process and if there is an interim suspension order in place this may have significant professional and financial implications.

7.21   If the registrant does want to delay the process, the registrant is likely to have to show that there are exceptional circumstances in order for the regulator to exercise their discretion favourably and it is likely to be rare that such an argument is allowed. In *Jefferson v Bhetcha*,[15] the court of appeal held that there was no general principle of law that, if criminal proceedings are pending against a defendant in respect of the same subject matter as the concurrent civil proceedings that the defendant is entitled to delay or be excused the civil proceedings and that:

> ... while each case must be judged on its own facts, the burden is on the defendant in the civil action to show that it is just and convenient that the plaintiff's ordinary rights of having his claim processed and heard and decided should be interfered with....one factor to be taken

13 However, the correctness of a finding in civil proceedings against a registrant can be challenged, see para 1.420.

14 See chapter 1, paras 1.102 and 1.535.

15 [1979] 1 WLR 898.

into account, and it may well be a very important factor, is whether there is a real danger of the causing of injustice in the criminal proceedings ...[16]

The legal principles concerning delaying civil proceedings are discussed in full at paras 1.102 and 1.537.

7.22   However, some regulatory bodies may be more willing than others to extend that discretion in the favour of postponement. For example, the HCPC has issued a practice note on concurrent proceedings which advises that HCPC hearings may be postponed as:

> A potential injustice may arise if regulatory proceedings are conducted at the same time as a related criminal trial. As more restrictive rules of evidence will apply in criminal proceedings, there is a risk that evidence which has not been admitted at that trial may enter the public domain by being admitted in the course of the regulatory proceedings.[17]

7.23   Conversely, a regulatory body may not wish to hear a case until the criminal case is over, since a conviction can impact on which charges are brought against a registrant, and whether the regulatory body needs to prove that the charge is misconduct (see para 1.415). It may also reduce the regulator's costs and give the regulatory body access to a wider range of evidence. If a case is delayed until the criminal process is complete, it can cause significant delays, which can stretch over a number of years, particularly if the criminal process is delayed by adjournments. Such delays may either be characterised as an abuse of process or a breach of article 6 (right to fair trial) of the European Convention on Human Rights,[18] which it has been established confers a right to be tried within a reasonable time-frame.[19] If such delays occur, an adviser may want to consider arguing at an interim stage that the hearing should be expedited as the delay is causing the registrant prejudice and is an abuse of process or a breach of article 6. If a significant delay has already occurred, advisers may argue that a fair trial is no longer possible and that the matter should be stayed as an abuse of process, however for this argument to succeed a registrant must show on a balance of probabilities that he or she will suffer or has suffered serious prejudice to the extent that no fair trial can be held in order to succeed. Although the courts and regulatory

---

16   *Jefferson v Bhetcha* [1979] 1 WLR 898 para 905.
17   See www.hcpc-uk.org/assets/documents/ 1000289DConcurrentCourtProceedings.pdf.
18   See para 1.19 for discussion of the application of article 6 to disciplinary proceedings.
19   See para 1.19.

panels have been willing to recognise an abuse of process and/or a breach of article 6(1), case-law has made it clear that this alone will not give rise to a stay. The circumstances must be exceptional and there must be incurable prejudice. The legal principles concerning the delay of proceedings are discussed in detail at para 1.102.

Double jeopardy

7.24   The doctrine of double jeopardy has no application to disciplinary proceedings insofar as a registrant cannot rely on criminal proceedings to prevent the continuance of disciplinary proceedings against him or her. Lord Diplock has explained the principle as follows:

> The purpose of disciplinary proceedings against a person convicted of crime is not to punish him a second time for the same offence by to protect the public who come to him as patients and to maintain the high standard and good reputation of an honourable profession.[20]

7.25   The point was conceded in the cases of *R v Pharmaceutical Society of Great Britain ex p Pharmaceutical Society of Great Britain*.[21] This means that if the criminal proceedings have already taken place the registrant cannot rely upon them in order to prevent the regulatory proceedings continuing and nor can he prevent an ensuing criminal trial on the basis that the matter has already litigated in the civil court. See para 1.535 for a further discussion on the legal principle of double jeopardy.

Sentencing and sanctions

7.26   Following the case of *Council for the Regulation of Healthcare Professionals v General Dental Council and Fleischman*[22] if a registrant has been convicted of a serious criminal offence and is still serving his or her sentence at the time the matter comes before a fitness to practise panel, normally the panel will not permit the registrant to resume his or her practise until that sentence has been satisfactorily completed; it will only be allowed in exceptional circumstances.

---

20   *Ziderman v General Dental Council* [1976] 2 All ER 334.
21   [1981] 2 All ER 805.
22   [2005] EWHC 87 (Admin).

Employment tribunals and internal disciplinary proceedings

Postponements and delay

7.27   If there are any ongoing civil proceedings, such as an employment tribunal, there may be a case for the regulator voluntarily deferring the investigation pending the outcome of the civil litigation, this can be advantageous as other legal forums may have greater evidential powers – for example, to order disclosure against the parties. However, awaiting the decision of a separate legal forum will cause delay to the disciplinary process, which may in turn cause evidential difficulties and ultimately could be an infringement upon the registrant's right to a fair trial. In particular, if the regulator awaits the outcome of the civil proceedings it may not provide any factual findings, whether helpful or otherwise, in particular as such claims regularly settle out of court. In addition, delay can make investigating matters more difficult as the passage of time elapses memories fade and documentation can prove more difficult to obtain.

7.28   Registrants may wish to postpone a disciplinary hearing pending a civil action. When faced with such an application the most obvious starting point is for the regulator to ask itself whether the two matters concern overlapping issues. If this is the case, then there may be good reason to postpone and the regulator should consider the matter further. If the civil action and disciplinary proceedings deal with entirely separate points, it is far less likely that there be good reasons to postpone. However, as Steyn J stated in *Archer v South West Thames Regional Health Authority*,[23] the issues in civil and disciplinary proceedings are seldom the same.

Bringing a claim in an employment tribunal

7.29   The subject of a referral to a regulatory body also being the subject of proceedings within the employment tribunal is most likely to occur in the case of misconduct referrals, but may occur if there are health concerns that have resulted in a referral. It will of course be the registrant who has initiated the proceedings in the employment tribunal, and the way in which an employment claim is pursued can be tactically important in terms of the regulatory process.

23   See Harris QC, *Disciplinary and regulatory proceedings*, 5th edn, Jordans, 2009 p107.

7.30   The obvious and immediate impact may be that the evidence for both hearings is likely to overlap and duplicate itself. Litigants going through the employment tribunal process may deny various allegations of misconduct against them, if they are found proven at the stage of an employment tribunal it may be used as evidence against a registrant in the regulatory hearing. Furthermore a denial of misconduct at the stage of the employment tribunal may impact upon the ability of the registrant to show that she or he has insight into the conduct that has brought him before a regulator. Evidentially, the consistency of the registrant's evidence is an important consideration. That does not mean that such claims will inevitably have a negative impact upon the outcome of the regulatory process; the facts of the charge against a registrant may not be proven in either forum or alternatively the facts of misconduct could be admitted in an employment tribunal but the fairness of a resulting dismissal may still be challenged under Employment Rights Act 1996 s98. In the same way, a disciplinary process could be discriminatory, without there being any need to deny the facts underpinning the disciplinary process. Advisers should establish whether a registrant has brought any other proceedings or is receiving separate advice about doing so, and if so, ensure that copies of any judgments and evidence that was put before any alternative forum are, where possible, obtained. Once these have been obtained, the impact of any statements of findings should carefully be considered in terms of its impact upon the regulatory process. Registrants may feel that delaying civil proceedings would be preferable, as then they can argue about their 'insight' in the disciplinary hearing without being constrained by any evidence they have given previously. Practitioners should be aware when advising on this issue, of the limitation periods for employment tribunal claims, where the majority of all claims have a limitation period of three months.[24]

7.31   Unlike in criminal proceedings, it is notable that findings made in civil proceedings are not conclusive in disciplinary proceedings. In *R v Council for License Conveyancers ex p Watson*,[25] the investigating committees of the Council for Licensed Conveyancers was entitled to consider a complaint by a purchaser of land, based on an allegation

---

24 Employment Rights Act 1996 s111 deals with the limitation period for unfair dismissal claims, while Equality Act 2010 s123 deals with limitation claims for all discrimination claims in the field of employment from the 1 October 2010 going forward.

25 (2000) *Times* 16 June.

of a lack of quality of service from a conveyancer, despite the fact a county court had dismissed a claim in negligence.

Dismissal

7.32 If the registrant has been dismissed from his or her role, this will have a very significant impact on the regulatory process when applying any test of 'impairment', as any registrant who is the subject of a hearing will need to demonstrate that the registrant is currently fit to practise if the misconduct is made out against him or her. If the registrant has been dismissed and is consequently not working, this will inevitably be harder evidentially, as the registrant will not be able to show current examples of his or her work and will be unable to bring testimonials from current workplace supervisors or managers. If the registrant has been out of work for a long period before the case is heard, then this could mean that it would be sensible to admit impairment as this will enable a registrant to from an argument that the registrant has insight into both his or her conduct and his or her current capabilities.

7.33 The regulatory process may impact upon the registrant's employment status prior to any disciplinary hearing – for example a registrant may be vulnerable to dismissal if they are suspended due to an interim order for a long period of time and therefore are unable to fulfil his or her work duties. In such a circumstance, it is highly likely that a dismissal will be seen as being fair by an employment tribunal. Employers may make references to a regulator where there are allegations of misconduct against an employee who is a health care professional and then use an interim suspension order, if imposed, as a reason to dismiss an employee. Practitioners should be aware that this is a potential consequence of an interim suspension order. In addition, if a registrant is struck off the register, then his or her contract of employment will be frustrated as the employee will no longer be able to undertake the duties of his or her employment – again, this is highly unlikely to be open to challenge in the employment tribunal.

7.34 Dismissal may have far-reaching consequences, as not only will a registrant lose his or her current employment, but if, after such a dismissal, the registrant applies for a new job, he or she will need to disclose to the new employer the existence of the disciplinary proceedings. This in turn may impact upon the likelihood of the registrant obtaining a new position. In nearly all regulatory proceedings the registrant will be professionally obliged to inform a new employer of the referral and the regulatory procedures that are ongoing. Any failure to do so (for example, by not ticking the relevant box on a declaration form) could result in a further allegation of dishonesty being brought against the registrant by the regulator.

7.35   For example, paragraph 59 of the GMC's *Good medical practice* requires doctors to do as follows:

> If you are suspended by an organisation from a medical post, or have restrictions placed on your practise you must, without delay, inform any other organisations for which you undertake medical work and any patients you see independently.

The NMC's code, *Standards of conduct, performance and ethics for nurses and midwives*, requires registrants to act with integrity, and includes at paragraph 51:

> You must inform any employers you work for if your fitness to practise is called into question.[26]

Judicial review

7.36   The decisions of the various regulatory bodies may be the subject of a judicial review, which can, in certain circumstances, provide an alternative method to challenge the decisions of a regulator. However, the question of which decisions can be the subject of a judicial review can be a very difficult one to answer.

7.37   Judicial review is not an appeal from a decision, but a review of the manner in which the decision was carried out. A judicial review is heard by the administrative court of the Queen's Bench Division of the High Court and an application for review is started by issuing a claim form (see Civil Procedure Rules (CPR) r54.6).[27] It is only those exercising public powers performing public duties bodies who can be the subject of a judicial review. In *R v Insurance Ombudsman Bureau ex p Aegon Life Insurance Ltd*[28] the court's approach to this question was said to be that judicial review would not lie against a body whose 'constitution owed nothing to any exercise of government power', a body could only be classed a public if it 'had been woven into the fabric of public regulation or into a system of government control'.

---

26 See www.nmc-uk.org/Publications/Standards/The-code/Be-open-and-honest-act-with-integrity-and-uphold-the-reputation-of-your-profession/.

27 In addition to the Royal Courts of Justice, the administrative court now sits in the regional centres of the High Court including Manchester, Cardiff and Birmingham.

28 (1994) *Times* 7 January, QB.

Generally it is highly likely that a decision made by the health care regulatory bodies while carrying out their regulatory functions could be the subject of a review.

7.38   There are various hurdles an application for judicial review must meet before it will be allowed to proceed by the court.

7.39   First, it is necessary to apply and obtain permission from the court before a judicial review can proceed to a full hearing (see CPR r54.9). The reason permission is required is to prevent the time of the court being 'wasted by busy bodies with misguided tor trivial complaints'.[29]

7.40   Additionally, a judicial review must be brought before the court within three months of the decision under review being made, however advisers should be aware that any such claim must additionally be brought promptly and an application could be refused by the court if there has been delay even if the applicant is still within the three months of the decision under challenge (CPR r54.5). The court does have discretion under CPR r54.5 to allow a review after the three-month time period, but only if there is considered to be good reason for such an extension.

7.41   If these hurdles are surmountable, then an adviser must consider on what grounds a decision is going to be challenged. There are only certain grounds upon which a decision can be challenged by way of judicial review. A full discussion of the grounds of judicial review is outside of the scope of this work and therefore the following is only meant to provide an introduction.[30]

7.42   If a decision-maker fails to follow the law that regulates them their decision-making will be 'illegal' or 'ultra vires'.[31] Thus, a decision may be challenged on the basis it is illegal as the public body has no power to take a particular action or decision, or has acted beyond its powers. This arises, for example, when the legislation relating to a public body does not include the necessary power or has precise limits on when the power can be used. Where a regulator has power to exercise a discretion, the courts have developed a range of principles in order to ensure its decision is not 'illegal' – for example, a regulator must take into account relevant information; it must ignore irrelevant information; it must not delegate a decision for which it is exclusively responsible; and it must ensure that it has not fettered its discretion by, for example, applying a very rigid policy. In addition,

29 *R v Land Revenue Commissioner ex p National Federation of Self-employed and Small Businesses Ltd* [1982] AC 617.

30 For a comprehensive view of the law pertaining to judicial review see Michael Fordham QC, *Judicial review handbook*, 5th edn, Hart Publishing, 2008.

31 Meaning a public body has acted unlawfully as it has gone beyond its powers.

by virtue of section 6 of the Human Rights Act 1998, a public authority that fails to act in accordance with rights set out in the ECHR is acting unlawfully, which brings challenges made under article 6 (right to a fair trial) and article 8 (right to privacy) within the ambit of illegality. See paras 1.94 and 1.30 for a discussion of the application of articles 6 and 8 in the regulatory context.

7.43   A decision may also be challenged on the basis that it is considered by the courts to be so demonstrably unreasonable as to constitute 'irrationality' or 'perversity' on the part of the decision-maker. Lord Greene stated that:

> If a decision on a competent matter is so unreasonable that no reasonable authority could ever have come to it, then the courts can interfere ... but to prove a case of that kind would require something overwhelming ...[32]

7.44   A further ground of challenge is that a decision is not proportionate, which means that it went further than was necessary to achieve the aims of the decision-maker. In general terms, the concept of proportionality requires a balancing exercise between, on the one hand, the general interests of society and the legitimate aims of the regulator and, on the other, the protection of the individual's rights and interests. The general approach to the question of proportionality is to ask the following three questions:

a) Is the public body's objective legitimate?
b) Is the measure suitable for achieving it?
c) Is it necessary, in the sense of being the least intrusive means of achieving the aim?

7.45   The House of Lords and the Supreme Court have repeatedly stated that the question of whether a decision is proportionate is one that the court must take for itself, particularly when ECHR article 8 is engaged, which it will be in regulatory cases – see, for example, *Belfast City Council v Miss Behavin' Ltd*[33] and *R (Quila and another) v Secretary of State for the Home Department.*[34]

7.46   Finally, there is a requirement that a public body should never act so unfairly that it amounts to an abuse of power. This means that regulators must follow proper procedure when reaching decisions – for example, they must follow any express procedures laid down

---

32 *Associated Provincial Picture Houses Ltd v Wednesbury Corporation* [1948] 1 KB 223, HL.
33 [2007] UKHL 19.
34 [2011] 3 WLR 836.

by legislation in reaching their decisions and in addition, they must not breach the rules of natural justice. One of the key issues here is the rule against bias, which requires the public body to be impartial and to be seen to be so. There must also be a 'fair hearing' before a decision is reached. What constitutes a fair hearing will depend on the circumstances of the case and there is no set list of requirements; however, in the case of regulatory bodies it is suggested that it would require that:

a) a registrant knows the case against him or her in advance of any hearing and has the opportunity to put his or her case properly;

b) the decision-maker does not take into account evidence or factors which he or she was not aware, or does not refuse to hear evidence which might have led to a different decision;

c) a registrant is not denied access to relevant documents and nor is a hearing held in the absence of the registrant when the registrant had a good reason for not being able to attend;

d) finally, fairness may also demand that a regulator give reasons for their decision.

7.47   The Councils have their own procedural rules, which follow these principles – therefore if there is a failure of the part of the regulatory to uphold their own procedures, it could be challenged on both the grounds of illegality and a breach of the rules of natural justice.

7.48   The cases set out below are examples of recent judicial reviews[35] which demonstrate the type of decisions made by regulators that might be subject to judicial review and where such action is likely to succeed.

Witness evidence

R (Bonhoeffer) v General Medical Council[36]

7.49   *Bonhoeffer* concerned a decision by the GMC to admit the hearsay evidence of witness A in fitness to practise proceedings brought against the claimant by the GMC. The decision not to call the witness in question to give oral evidence was made on the basis of concern for his safety. The allegations against the doctor involved allegations of sexual misconduct, the abuse of young boys and young men and the abuse of a position of trust in Kenya. The evidence of the witness in

---

35   *Ogbonna* was a statutory appeal where the arguments overlapped with those that can be raised in a judicial review application, see para 7.49.

36   [2011] EWHC 1585 (Admin).

question was the sole evidence against the claimant in support of most of the allegations against him, but insofar as those allegations involve alleged misconduct towards other victims, those victims were interviewed by the Metropolitan Police and denied that the allegations were true (see chapter 1, para 1.213 for a fuller discussion).

7.50   The court found that:

> ... the Fitness to Practise Panel's decision that it would be 'desirable' to admit the hearsay evidence pursuant to Rule 34(2) was irrational, (2) that its decision that it would be 'fair' to admit the hearsay evidence pursuant to Rule 34(1) was irrational and (3) that the decision amounted to a breach Article 6(1) of the European Convention on Human Rights (ECHR) in that (a) the Claimant's right to a fair hearing as protected by Article 6(1) requires in the particular circumstances of this case that he be given the opportunity to cross-examine his accuser and (b) that the fitness to practise panel acted unlawfully in subordinating the Claimant's rights to a fair hearing, as protected by Article 6(1) to the public interest in 'protecting patients, maintaining public confidence in the profession, and declaring and upholding proper standards of behavior.[37]

Ogbonna v Nursing and Midwifery Council[38]

7.51   The High Court allowed an appeal against a decision of the conduct and competence committee of the NMC to permit the NMC to adduce hearsay evidence by way of the written statement of a key witness who had moved to live abroad in support of misconduct proceedings. The panel had admitted the statement pursuant to rule 31(1) of the Nursing and Midwifery Council (Fitness to Practise) Rules Order 2004,[39] which provides:

> Upon receiving the advice of the Legal Assessor, and subject only to the requirements of relevance and fairness, a fitness to practise committee considering an allegation may admit oral, documentary or other evidence, whether or not such evidence would be admissible in civil proceedings (in the appropriate court in that part of the United Kingdom in which the hearing takes place).

7.52   The witness whose hearsay statement was admitted was the sole witness of fact in support of one of the charges against the appellant nurse. The NMC had made no effort to secure the attendance of the witness at the hearing either in person or by way of video-link. The court found that the admission of the hearsay statement was unfair.

---

37 At para 25.
38 [2010] EWHC 272 Admin.
39 SI No 1761.

7.53   The NMC appealed to the court of appeal on the basis that the high court had laid down general principles for the admission of hearsay evidence. The court of appeal, in refusing permission, stated:

> ... the judge laid down no general rule, and certainly not a new rule, but examined the issue of fairness in the context of the particular facts ... Those were essentially matters for the judge, and she did not stray into a more general operation of laying down rules.[40]

7.54   Advisers should be aware that despite both of these cases reinforcing that the right to cross-examine witnesses is a fundamental tenant of natural justice, the admission of hearsay evidence is not automatically a breach of natural justice. Stadlen J's judgment in *Bonhoeffer* said, when discussing the decision in *Ogbonna*: 'The resolution of the "fairness" arising under Rule 31(1) will necessarily be fact-sensitive'.[41] It is also important to note the overlap between the process of judicial review and an appeal. The issues before the High Court in both cases were very similar, albeit the first case had been taken on the basis of a judicial review and the second as a statutory appeal. The principles and arguments that can be made in an application for judicial review often are equally appropriate being raised in a statutory appeal. Therefore, if a registrant does not meet the necessary requirements to be able to bring a judicial review, then advisers may consider raising the same points by way of an appeal.

Legal representation

R (G) v Governors of X School[42]

7.55   The claimant, a music assistant at a primary school, was denied permission by the defendant school governors for his solicitor to represent him at disciplinary proceedings for alleged sexual impropriety.

7.56   A claim for judicial review was allowed on the ground that, although the proceedings were civil not criminal in nature such that the procedural safeguards contained in ECHR article 6(3) did not apply, he was entitled, given the severity of the consequences of an adverse finding, to an enhanced measure of procedural protection under article 6(1) and was entitled to legal representation at both the disciplinary and appeal committee hearings. Dismissing the defendant's appeal, the court of appeal held that since an adverse outcome

---

40   [2010] EWCA Civ 1216 para 25.
41   At para 25.
42   [2011] UKSC 30.

of the disciplinary proceedings would have a substantial effect on the outcome of barred list procedures, which would then be applied to him, and since his right to practise his profession was directly at stake in the barred list procedure, the right to legal representation was a civil right for the purposes of article 6 and might be irretrievably prejudiced at disciplinary proceedings, article 6 was engaged by the disciplinary proceedings. In the light of what was at stake in the disciplinary proceedings and since an advocate might have a significant effect on the outcome of those proceedings, article 6 required that the claimant be afforded the opportunity to arrange for legal representation for them should he so choose.

7.57   Laws LJ said:

> The next question is whether, in the context of civil proceedings, Article 6 implies a right to legal representation. In my view, in circumstances of this kind, it should imply such a right because the doctor is facing what is in effect a criminal charge although it is being dealt with by disciplinary proceedings. The issues are virtually the same and, although the consequences of a finding of guilt cannot be the deprivation of liberty, they can be very serious.[43]

7.58   Overturning the Court of Appeal,[44] the Supreme Court held that there was no ECHR article 6(1) right to legal representation at the school's disciplinary hearing.

7.59   The leading judgment was given by Lord Dyson, who primarily agreed with the Court of Appeal that the question whether proceedings are directly decisive of the right in question, where they are related to a second set of proceedings which are themselves directly decisive, should be assessed by reference to whether those proceedings have a substantial influence on the second proceedings.

7.60   However, in applying that test, the majority of the Supreme Court came to a different outcome to the courts below. It had been agreed between the parties that any decision taken by the ISA to place G on the barred list – and any appeal from the ISA[45] to the Upper Tribunal – was directly decisive of G's right to practise his profession. However, the majority saw the decision of the school only to go to G's employment with that school and not any wider right. There was undoubtedly a link between the school hearing and any ISA decision, but the ISA is required to take its own decision and is not bound by

43 [2010] 1 WLR 2218 at para 68.
44 [2010] EWCA Civ 1.
45 For a full discussion of the role of the ISA and its interplay with the regulatory process, see chapter 8.

any previous findings of fact. The refusal of the school to permit legal representation at its disciplinary hearing was therefore not a breach of ECHR article 6(1). It lacked a substantial influence over the decisive proceedings. Lord Kerr dissented, holding that it was artificial to separate out the two stages of the proceedings.

Quorum of panel

R (Michalak) v General Medial Council[46]

7.61   A lengthy hearing (34 days were taken up and 28 witnesses were heard) of a Fitness to Practise Panel was adjourned on the basis that the medical member of the panel became ill and it was clear that he would not be able to resume participation in any resumed hearing in the foreseeable future. The GMC's registrar decided to substitute another medical member so as to bring the panel back to three members, which would be sufficient for the panel to be quorate, and believed that it was in the interests of justice to make such substitution.

7.62   The panel itself reviewed the substitution decision by the registrar and concluded that the substitution was proper and that it would be in the interests of justice to allow the substitution. However, the issue remained as to how the panel should proceed. One procedure contemplated was for the new member simply to read the transcripts so as, colloquially, to bring himself up to speed and be on the same footing as the other two members, and then the hearing could simply proceed from the point at which it had terminated.

7.63   However, the panel took the view that that would not be conducive to the promotion of justice. Having regard to the nature of the case and the evidence that had been presented, the panel believed that it was necessary that the third member, in order to be put in the same position as the two original members of the panel, needed to hear the witnesses live and therefore the decision was that the reconstituted panel should hear all the witnesses again, that was the 28 witnesses, over what would be a very similar if not exactly the same timescale.

7.64   The judicial review application challenged both whether or not the GMC registrar had the power to make a substitution for a panel member, and in addition that the proposed procedure going forward was neither fair nor rational.

46 [2011] EWHC 2307 (Admin).

7.65   The court held that it was:

> ... not at all persuaded that there is any advantage whatsoever in the course proposed by the panel in comparison to an alternative by which a fresh panel entirely would be constituted to hear the case again. It has been suggested on behalf of the defendant that there would be advantages in terms of firstly the opening for example having already been heard by two members of the panel and therefore proceedings could be shortened by the course adopted and secondly that the two existing original panel ...[47]

and to:

> ... quash the decision that has been made. I have held that in principle there is power to make a substitution and therefore the matter needs to be remitted to the defendant for the defendant to consider what action should be taken as a matter of law and as a matter of correct policy to allow, if that be the case, the proceedings to continue.[48]

Delay

R (Whitehead) v Nursing and Midwifery Council[49]

7.66   A nurse was refused permission to bring judicial review proceedings against the NMC for excessive delay in the prosecution of fitness to practise proceedings. It had taken the NMC more than four years to investigate the allegations, after which the Investigating Committee decided that there was no case to answer in either case. The claimant's claim was that the NMC had breached article 32(3) of the Nursing and Midwifery Order (NMO) 2001[50] and ECHR articles 6(1) and 8.

R (Rycroft) v Royal Pharmaceutical Society of Great Britain[51]

7.67   This case concerned a delay in the Royal Society's registrar referral of allegations made against the claimant to the Royal Society's investigation committee. In approximately September 2006 the claimant first became aware of the allegations against him, and it was only on 30 April 2009 (ie about two years and eight months later) that the defendant's registrar referred a fitness to practise allegation against the claimant to the defendant's investigation committee.

47   [2011] EWHC 2307 (Admin) para 20.
48   [2011] EWHC 2307 (Admin) para 25.
49   (2011) 4 October, unreported.
50   SI 2002 No 253.
51   [2010] EWHC 2832 (Admin).

7.68   The Royal Pharmaceutical Society of Great Britain (Fitness to Practise and Disqualification etc) Rules 2007[52] contain detailed provisions relating to the process by which an allegation may be brought, ultimately, before a Disciplinary Committee or a Health Committee. They include that a registrar must refer any allegation to the Investigating Committee unless one of the subparagraphs in rule 9 are satisfied. One of the subsections of rule 9 was that the registrar must refer to the committee unless more than five years have elapsed since the circumstances giving rise to the allegation.

7.69   Wyn Williams J held that the:

> Defendant's Registrar is under an implicit obligation to make a referral within a reasonable time. However, I do not accept that a failure to make a referral within a reasonable time amounts to a reason to quash the referral and stay the proceedings unless it is also established that the failure to act within a reasonable time has caused prejudice to such an extent that no fair disciplinary process is possible or that it is unfair for the process to continue.[53]

7.70   The court held that there was no prejudice; it would therefore not quash the decision.

Mediation

7.71   Many allegations that form the substance of referrals may be more suited to mediation, either because they are not sufficiently serious to warrant action on registration, or because they concern contractual disputes in private practise, that do not imply any impediment on the registrant's fitness to practise. Often regulatory bodies, upon receipt of a referral from a patient or a member of the public, will track the complaint and assess first whether they require taking action and second whether the complaint calls into question a registrant's fitness to practise. For those complaints that do not meet this level of seriousness, the matter if often referred to the NHS trust who is the employer, or advice is given to attempt to mediate the matter if a dispute concerns a private practitioner.

7.72   Within the NHS there are a number of routes that can assist with mediation and may be able to prevent the matter from either being referred to a regulator or alternatively from the referral progressing

---

52   Schedule to the Royal Pharmaceutical Society of Great Britain (Fitness to Practise and Disqualification etc Rules) Order of Council 2007 SI No 442.

53   [2010] EWHC 2832 (Admin) para 38.

to a full investigation. Where there is an immediate problem, patients who are concerned with a registrant's behaviour can refer the problem to Patient Advisory Liaison Service (PALS) who can negotiate and mediate the problem on the patient's behalf; this may prevent the situation arising where a referral is made. Once a referral has been made, National Clinical Assessment Service (NCAS) may be involved.[54] NCAS is a body within the NHS which provides case management services in connection with the practise of doctors, dentists and pharmacists endeavoring to bring disputes to a resolution reducing the need to use disciplinary procedures, they employ trained mediators who are able to help resolve disputes without the need for the regulator to be involved.[55]

7.73 Some regulatory bodies provide mediation as an alternative to a hearing. The HCPC[56] offers a mediation service, which it encourages registrants and those making referrals to use if the matter relates to a private dispute. The Health Professions Order 2001 provides that, in relation to a fitness to practise allegation, if an investigating committee panel concludes that there is a case to answer, it may undertake mediation instead of referring the allegation to another practise committee; a panel of the Conduct and Competence Committee or Health Committee finds that the allegation is well founded, it may undertake mediation if it satisfied that it does not need to impose any further sanction on the registrant.[57]

7.74 However, as the HCPC practice note on mediation states, 'As mediation is essentially a consensual process, any decision to mediate will fail unless it is supported by both the registrant concerned and the other party',[58] and mediation will not be pursued if the panel is not satisfied that, irrespective of the outcome of the mediation, it does not need to take any further steps to protect the public.

7.75 There are signs that the other regulatory bodies may consider taking a similar approach. The GMC opened a consultation in April 2011 concerning how to refine its procedures to reduce the need for public hearings.[59] However, they state that:

54 See www.ncas.npsa.nhs.uk/home/.
55 See www.ncas.npsa.nhs.uk/accessing-case-services/case-services-overview/.
56 HPO 2001 SI 2002 No 254 states that council is obliged to have a mediation scheme in place (relevant sections: articles 24(3)(d); 26(6)(a) and (b)(i)).
57 HPO 2001 article 26(6) and article 29(4).
58 See www.hcpc-uk.org/assets/documents/10001DDCPRACTICE_NOTE_Mediation.pdf.
59 See www.gmc-uk.org/FTP_reforms_consultation_paper.pdf_38085201.pdf.

... mediation is designed primarily for situations where the outcome is open to negotiation. We do not believe mediation is appropriate in meetings with doctors facing allegations that their fitness to practise is impaired. The sanction appropriate to protect the public should not be open to negotiation and it would be wrong for the GMC to agree a lesser sanction in exchange for a consensual outcome.[60]

They do suggest that a different approach is taken to investigating complaints, including opening a dialogue with doctors about complaints, and go on to state that:

... given the nature of our discussions with doctors, where the focus will be the exchange of information and a discussion about the appropriate sanction to protect the public, we believe that facilitation rather than mediation skills would be most appropriate and effective.[61]

Freedom of Information Act 2000

7.76   The Freedom of Information Act (FOIA) 2000 came into force on 1 January 2005. The Act provides that anyone may request information from a public authority in England, Wales and/or Northern Ireland (separate legislation applies to Scotland). Prospective applicants for information under the Act have a right:

1) to be told whether or not the public authority holds that information, and if so,
2) to have that information communicated to them.

7.77   Any person may request information under the Act,[62] regardless of their age, nationality or location. A full list of public authorities subject to the Act is contained in Schedule 1 to the Act. Generally speaking, all government departments are included as public authorities and also those working within the health sector, thus all the healthcare regulators are prescribed public bodies for the purposes of the Act; other regulators, such as the Financial Services Authority, are listed specifically by name.

7.78   There are a number of exemptions within the statute that operate to protect information which is permitted to be kept confidential. The exemptions most likely to relate to the regulatory process are:

• personal information (section 40), which is subject to a separate regime under the Data Protection Act (DPA) 1998;

60 GMC Consultation, pages 18 and 19.
61 GMC Consultation, pages 18 and 19.
62 FOIA 2000 s1(1).

- information provided in confidence (section 41) – this exemption applies where the disclosure of information would constitute a breach of confidence actionable at common law; and
- legal professional privilege (section 42) where information between lawyers or their clients for the purpose of giving or receiving legal advice or in contemplation of prosecuting or defending legal proceedings.

7.79   A request made to a public authority must be made in writing. On receiving a request, the public authority must respond as soon as possible and no later than 20 working days after receipt of the request (section 10). The public authority's response should confirm or deny whether or not such information is held and either provide the information or state why it is not being provided and what provisions of the Act they rely on to withhold the information requested. The duties of public authorities also extend to advising and assisting requesters in their pursuit of information. If a refusal to provide information is made by a public authority relying on one of the exemptions specified in the Act, the public authority must identify which exemption it relies upon giving details to the applicant of how to apply for an internal review of the decision to refuse (section 17). If after this the public authority still refuses the applicant's request, an applicant may seek a review of that decision by the Information Commissioner.[63]

7.80   'Personal data' is exempt information under FOIA 2000. If an individual makes a request for access to information held by a public authority about himself or herself, it will generally be dealt with under the provisions of the DPA 1998. If the information, however, is of a more general nature, then the FOIA 2000 may be more appropriate. Regulatory bodies who are, or may be, public bodies may find themselves the subject of dual applications under both the FOIA 2000 and the DPA 1998. An applicant may wish to elicit information which may both be specific to that individual as well as information of concern to that individual but not within the category of personal data to which the DPA 1998 applies. The Information Commissioner is the last adjudicator and if necessary enforcer of both these statutes. The following decisions of the Information Commissioner give an idea of the type of freedom of information requests that have been made concerning regulatory bodies.[64]

---

63   See www.ico.gov.uk.
64   Taken from the Information Commissioner's website at www.ico.gov.uk/tools_ and_resources/decision_notices.aspx.

Case Ref: FS50276047
Date: 18/10/2010
Public Authority: Nursing and Midwifery Council
Summary: The complainant requested copies of information provided to the Nursing and Midwifery Council (the NMC) by the Brighton and Sussex University Hospitals Trust (the Trust) in relation to a fitness to practise complaint she made in 2007. The NMC refused disclosure on the grounds of section 40(2) of the Act. The Commissioner has investigated and finds that the public authority was excluded from its duty to respond to the request under section 1(1)(a) of the Act by virtue of the provision of section 40(5)(b)(i). The public authority also failed to issue a valid refusal notice under section 17(1) of the Act. He does not require the NMC to take any remedial steps in relation to the request.

Case Ref: FS50064698
Date: 15/12/2006
Public Authority: General Medical Council
Summary: The complainant requested details of the complaints histories of six named doctors from the General Medical Council (the 'GMC'). The GMC refused this request under section 40 of the Freedom of Information Act 2000 on the basis that it constituted the personal data of the doctors in question and that to release the information would breach the data protection principles. It further argued that it would also breach their human rights and therefore a statutory prohibition applied under section 44 of the Act. During the course of the investigation the GMC also submitted that it owed a duty of confidence to the doctors involved and that, as a result, an exemption under section 41 of the Act applied. It also submitted that a section 31 exemption may be applicable as disclosure of the requested information could harm the GMC's ability to effectively regulate doctors. Having considered both parties submissions and conducted a thorough investigation, the Commissioner found that the exemption under section 40 of the Act was applicable and that the GMC had therefore been right to withhold the information.

Case Ref: FS50277585
Date: 25/05/2010
Public Authority: General Medical Council
Summary: The complainant asked for documentation relating to a complaint she made about two specified doctors. Some information was her personal data and was provided under the Data Protection Act (the 'DPA'). In relation to the remainder, after carefully considering the case, the Commissioner finds that the public authority was excluded from its duty to respond to the request under section 1(1)(a) of the Freedom of Information Act (the 'Act') by virtue of the provision of section 40(5)(b)(i) (exclusion from the duty to confirm or deny

a public authority holds third party personal information) because in confirming or denying it held information, it would have to disclose to the public, information which would constitute third party personal data the release of which would breach the first data protection principle. He does find a breach of sections 17(1)(a) and 17(1)(b) because the public authority failed to specify that it was relying on the exclusion in relation to any information it may hold until the time of his investigation. He requires no remedial steps to be taken in this case.
Section of Act/EIR & Finding: FOI 17 – Complaint Upheld , FOI 40 – Complaint Not upheld

Case Ref: FS50372823
Date: 08/09/2011
Public Authority: Health Professions Council
Summary: The complainant requested information relating to a complaint made against a health professional. Specifically, he asked for a copy of the health professional's response in regard to the complaint. The public authority refused to disclose this information under sections 30, 31, 40 and 41 of the Act. After investigating the case the Commissioner decided that section 40(5)(b)(i) applied, and the public authority was therefore excluded from its duty to confirm or deny whether the information was held. The Commissioner does not require the public authority to take any steps.
Section of Act/EIR & Finding: FOI 40 – Complaint Not upheld.

Data Protection Act 1998

7.81   The DPA 1998 is built around a set of enforceable principles intended to protect personal privacy, to encourage good practice in the handling of personal information and to give individuals a right of access to information about themselves (eg financial or health information). The DPA 1998 is not limited to the retention of data by public authorities. It applies to all bodies that process personal information. Therefore its implications are far more wide ranging than the FOIA 2000.

7.82   The DPA 1998 requires 'data controllers' to handle personal data in accordance with a series of principles set out in DPA 1998.[65] The DPA 1998 defines 'personal data' as that which relates to a living individual who can be identified from that data, or from that data and any other information that is in the possession of the data controller, and includes any expression of opinion about the individual.

---

65 As set out at DPA 1998 Sch 1.

7.83   The definition of 'data' in DPA 1998 includes information that is contained in a health, educational or social services record.[66] A health record for the purposes of DPA 1998 is one which relates to the physical or mental health of an individual that has been made by or on behalf of a health professional in connection with the care of that individual. All processing of data to which DPA 1998 applies must comply with eight principles set out in Schedule 1 to the Act.[67] The first principle is particularly important as it emphasises that processing must be fair and lawful in the context of the common law and other UK legislation. Generally, there will be compliance if all of the following conditions are met:

a) the law of confidentiality[68] and any other applicable statutory restrictions on the use of information are complied with;
b) the data subject was not misled or deceived into giving the data;
c) the data subject is given basic information about who will process the data and or what purpose.

7.84   As health data is defined as sensitive data by DPA 1998, it is subject to additional requirements set out in both Schedules 2 and 3 to the Act. There is, however, an exemption for regulatory activity at section 31(1) of the Act, to the extent to which 'the application of those provisions to the data would be likely to prejudice the proper discharge of those functions'. 'Subject provisions' refers to the first of the data protections principles set out above that requires the lawful processing of personal data.

Subject access rights

7.85   The DPA 1998 also creates 'subject access rights' under section 7. These allow individuals to access the data held about them. There are various exceptions to this rule, including under the Data Protection

---

66   DPA 1998 s68.
67   The eight principles are that personal data must be: 1) processed fairly and lawfully; 2) obtained for specified and lawful purposes; 3) adequate, relevant and not excessive; 4) accurate and up-to-date; 5) not kept any longer than necessary; 6) processed in accordance with the 'data subject's' (the individual's) rights; 7) securely kept; and 8) not transferred to any other country without adequate protection in place.
68   Breach of confidence is a common law tort that protects private information that is conveyed in confidence. A claim for breach of confidence typically requires the information to be of a confidential nature, which was communicated in confidence, and was disclosed to the detriment of the claimant.

(Subject Access Modification) (Health) Order 2000[69] Part 3, which allows healthcare professionals to restrict access to information they hold on a person in their care, if that information is likely to cause serious harm to the individual or another person. In addition, under DPA 1998 s31(1) there is an exemption where the application of the access provisions would be likely to prejudice the proper discharge of regulatory functions. To be exempt, the function must be statutory, governmental or exercised in the public interest. This will therefore apply to all healthcare regulatory bodies.

Patient confidentiality

7.86   The NHS is under a duty to keep patient records confidential; this arises from both the DPA 1998 and under common law.[70] This right to privacy has also been recognised under article 8 of the ECHR by European Court of Human Rights, where it was stated, in *Z v Finland*,[71] that:

> Respecting the confidentiality of health data is a vital principle in the legal system of all the contracting parties to the Convention. It is crucial not only to respect the sense of privacy of the patient but also to preserve his or her confidence in the medical profession and in the health services in general.[72]

7.87   The best practice on maintaining the confidentiality of patient records is set out in the *NHS Confidentiality code of practice*[73] and the *NHS Code of practice: records management*.[74] However, the privacy of medical records is not absolute and, for example, records will normally be disclosed for the purposes of the proper regulation of healthcare professionals. This includes professional disciplinary proceedings, as most of the healthcare regulators have statutory powers for each of the regulatory bodies to access patient records.[75] Where there is a statutory duty to disclose private information this will not be a

---

69   SI 2000 No 413.
70   See, for example, *X v Y* [1988] 2 All ER 648.
71   (1997) 25 EHRR 371.
72   *Z v Finland* (1997) 25 EHRR 371 para 95.
73   Department of Health, November 2003.
74   Department of Health, 2006, available at www.dh.gov.uk/en/
     Publicationsandstatistics/Publications/PublicationsPolicyAndGuidance/DH_
     4069253.
75   The GMC has such powers under the Medical Act 1983; HPO 2001 article 25(1)
     gives such powers to the HPC; and Nursing and Midwifery Order 2001 SI 2002
     No 253 article 25 gives such powers to the NMC.

breach of the DPA 1998 as section 35(1) provides an exemption for disclosures 'required by law'.

7.88   The importance of regulatory bodies having access to medical records to be able to carry out their regulatory functions was emphasised in the *General Dental Council v Rimmer*[76] where a dentist argued that he wouldn't disclosure patient's records to the General Dental Council (GDC) in order to investigate a complaint about him as he was under a duty of confidentiality. In deciding the case Lloyd Jones J quoted Thorpe LJ in *A Health Authority v X*.[77] Thorpe LJ said:

> There is obviously a high public interest, analogous to the public interest in the due administration of criminal justice, in the proper administration of professional disciplinary hearings, particularly in the field of medicine.[78]

He continued:

> A balance still had to be struck between competing interests. The balance came down in favour of production as it invariably does, save in exceptional circumstances.[79]

Anonymity of patients' details

7.89   If a regulator has to use a patient's details in a hearing, it would be normal practice to anonymise the details of the patient in order to protect his or her privacy. Often the rules governing procedure in relation to disciplinary proceedings expressly provide for hearings before the committee or Fitness to Practise Panel to be held in public, but that the committee or panel may determine that the public shall be excluded from the proceedings for any part of the proceedings 'where they consider that the particular circumstances of the case outweigh the public interest in holding the hearing in public': see, for example, rule 41(2) of the General Medical Council (Fitness to Practise) Rules Order of Council 2004 and rule 42(4) of the Royal Pharmaceutical Society of Great Britain (Fitness to Practise and Disqualification etc Rules) Order of Council 2007. The NMC will normally hold their Health Committees in private, and if part of a Conduct and Competence Committee relates to a health matter, this part of the proceedings will normally be heard in private.[80]

---

76 [2010] EWHC 1049 (Admin) (15 April 2010).
77 [2010] EWCA Civ 2014.
78 *General Dental Council v Rimmer* [2010] EWHC 1049 (Admin).
79 *General Dental Council v Rimmer* [2010] EWHC 1049 (Admin).
80 Nursing and Midwifery Council (Fitness to Practise) Rules Order 2004 r19.

7.90   The need to hold hearings in private when they concern sensitive information, such as patient data, was recognised in *Diennet v France*[81] which concerned a doctor who had been disqualified by the French Ordre des Medicins from practising medicine for three years for undertaking consultations by correspondence. He complained to the European Court of Human Rights that the hearings before the disciplinary bodies had not been conducted in public. The French government argued that the power of the tribunal to decide facts, possibly including medically confidential information about patients, was good reason to exclude the public. The court rejected that defence because there was no reason to suppose that confidential information would be relevant in an accusation such as the appellant faced, however it recognised the necessity of such measures in other circumstances.

Obligations on practitioners

7.91   There are obligations on all healthcare practitioners to keep personal information confidential. Not only is this set out in the DPA 1998, it is reinforced by the standards expected by professional regulators of their members. A breach of confidentiality will be deemed to be misconduct by all healthcare regulatory bodies.

7.92   The NMC's code, *Standards of conduct, performance and ethics for nurses and midwives*, requires registrants to respect people's confidentiality.[82] The GMC's *Good medical practice* states at paragraph 37:

> Patients have a right to expect that information about them will be held in confidence by their doctors. You must treat information about patients as confidential, including after a patient has died. If you are considering disclosing confidential information without a patient's consent, you must follow the guidance in with confidentiality.

The GMC also have published additional confidentiality guidance[83] to assist doctors in making decisions about how to deal with confidentiality and when they may need to breach it. The third of the six main principles of the GDC's standards of dental professionals is to maintain patient confidentiality. The GDC have also published additional guidance for dentists on how to deal with issues of

---

81   (1995) 21 EHRR 554.
82   NMC, *Standards of conduct, performance and ethics for nurses and midwives*, 2008 para 5.
83   See www.gmc-uk.org/guidance/ethical_guidance/confidentiality_contents.asp.

confidentiality.[84] And the HCPC requires registrants to respect the confidentiality of service users.[85]

7.93   If registrants disclose sensitive information about patients to the regulator as evidence in their case, whether to demonstrate lack of impairment or to challenge the factual basis of allegations against them, they must ensure that the data is appropriately anonymised by either redacting it or by editing it to ensure no breach of either the 1998 Act or their professional standards occurs. Regulators have been known to threaten to add a new charge to the allegations concerning a breach of confidentiality where redaction has not been done properly.

Care Quality Commission

7.94   The Care Quality Commission (CQC) was established in 2009.[86] It is a non-departmental pubic body whose role is to regulate and inspect the providers of social and healthcare in England, this includes, for example, all NHS hospitals, ambulance services, care homes, dentists and providers of care in the home. Its remit therefore overlaps to some extent with the regulators of healthcare registrants.

7.95   All health and adult social care providers are required to register with the CQC and to meet the CQC standards on care provision. The CQC defines its main activities as:

- registration and enforcement;
- encouraging improvement by providing independent, reliable and up-to-date information about the quality of providers' care;
- Mental Health Act visits to monitors the care of people whose rights are restricted under the Mental Health Act 1983; and
- reporting health and adult social care information.

It publishes information on the quality of care to help people make decisions about their care.[87]

7.96   Thus the CQC regulates the provision of care in a number of ways. First, in order to be granted registration, care providers need to demonstrate that they can meet, or are already meeting, the registration

---

84 GDC, *Principles of patient confidentiality*, available at http://www.gdcuk.org/Dentalprofessionals/Standards/Pages/default.aspx.

85 See Point 3 of the HPC, *Standards of conduct, performance and ethics*, July 2008, available at www.hcpc-uk.org/aboutregistration/standards/standardsofconductperformanceandethics.

86 By the Health and Social Care Act 2008.

87 Annex 1 of the Memorandum of Understanding between the CQC and the NMC, as revised May 2011.

requirements, and to maintain their registration they need to demonstrate an ongoing ability to meet the requirements. The CQC undertake inspections of the institutions and publish their results. The CQC presently undertakes notified inspections and also inspects institutions on an unannounced basis, without notification.

7.97   If a care provider is falling short of the expected standards, then the CQC has a number of actions open to it. If the breach of standards is minor, then the CQC undertake compliance action, which requires the provider to send in a report stating how they intend to address the problem and this is then monitored. If the breach is more serious or repeated, then enforcement action can be taken. The CQC has a range of legal powers – it can suspend registration or cancel it, and when people are at immediate risk of significant harm criminal proceedings can be started to issue a warning notice or a caution, or to prosecute.

7.98   The work of the CQC impacts on registrants in the healthcare professions in a number of ways. Registrants will be expected by their workplaces to adhere to the CQC standards, and registrants may also be subjected to inspection when the CQC is at their place of work. The CQC can make a referral to the appropriate regulatory body if they have concerns about a registrant's practice. All the healthcare regulators and the CQC have entered into memorandums of understanding (MoUs) which set out the nature of their relationships and how their work overlaps. All the MoUs embrace a spirit of co-operation between the parties and in particular require the CQC to refer to the relevant regulators any concerns about individual registrants. For example, the NMC MoU states:

> In particular, the CQC will refer to the NMC:
>
> 11.1 Any concerns and relevant information about a registered nurse or midwife which may call into question his or her fitness to practise.
>
> 11.2 Any concerns and relevant information about a health or adult social care organisation which may call into question its suitability as a learning environment for nursing or midwifery students.
>
> 11.3 Any concerns and relevant information relating to the general delivery of nursing and midwifery care at a health or adult social care organisation which may call into question issues of nursing or midwifery leadership.
>
> 11.4 Any investigations into or follow ups of identified risks in which concerns about individual nurses and midwives or nursing and midwifery practice have been identified.[88]

---

88 CQC and NMC MoU May 2011. There is a similar MoU in place between the CQC and all regulators discussed in this book.

Conclusion

7.99   When advising on or conducting a professional disciplinary matter before one of the five councils, the impact of linked litigation must be carefully considered by all advisers and registrants. In particular, criminal and employment proceedings may have a significant impact on how a registrant should conduct himself or herself once a referral to a regulator has been made. The presentation of a case may be assisted by the use of judicial review to challenge a panel's decisions, the use of the FOIA 2000 to obtain information from the registrant's employer or the relevant council and the importance of upholding the data protection principles.

CHAPTER 8

The Independent
Safeguarding Authority

Key points

- Parliament has determined (most recently through the Safeguarding Vulnerable Groups Act (SVGA) 2006) that there are some individuals who pose such a risk to children and/or vulnerable adults that they should be banned entirely from working with such vulnerable groups.
- The scheme established by the SVGA 2006 has been significantly amended by the Protection of Freedoms Act (PFA) 2012, although this has not come into force as of 18 July 2012.
- Decisions as to placement on the adults' and children's barred lists are made by the Independent Safeguarding Agency (ISA), although this body is shortly to become part of a wider Disclosure and Barring Service.
- Although there is no prescribed statutory procedure, the ISA's policies require a five-stage decision-making process for all cases other than those where the most serious criminal offences have been committed.
- The ISA operates on the civil standard of proof and although analysis in terms of a burden of proof may be unhelpful it would be wholly wrong for the ISA to require an individual to disprove any allegations made against them.
- The definitions of 'child' and 'vulnerable adult' are very broadly drawn and the intention of parliament is to prevent unsuitable persons working with any vulnerable people. Any person placed on a barred list who undertakes regulated activity with the relevant vulnerable group will be committing a criminal offence.
- There are four routes under which an individual can be placed on either or both of the barred lists, two relating to criminal convictions or cautions, one relating to inappropriate behaviour that has not led to a criminal conviction and one concerning those individuals deemed to pose an unacceptable risk of harm to vulnerable people.
- Other than for the most serious criminal offences, individuals may make representations to the ISA as to why they should not be placed on one or both of the barred lists. Representations will be invited in writing, but in certain circumstances fairness may require the ISA to hold an oral hearing.
- Upon receipt of any representations the ISA must decide not only whether any factual allegations against an individual are

established but also whether it is 'appropriate' for the individual to be placed on a barred list.

- Any individual placed on a barred list for a reason other than having committed a very serious criminal offence has a right of appeal to the Upper Tribunal, but only on the basis that the ISA has made an error of fact and/or an error of law. The question of whether it was appropriate for an individual to be placed on a barred list is excluded from the tribunal's jurisdiction.
- The emerging case-law shows that the Upper Tribunal should intervene to correct errors of law made by the ISA, including decisions which the Upper Tribunal considers to be disproportionate upon evaluation of all the evidence.
- An individual who is confirmed on the barred list may at present be prevented from seeking a review of his or her inclusion for up to ten years, although this will change once the PFA 2012 comes into force and the ISA already has the power to initiate a review of its own motion.

Introduction

8.1   For some time, the state has taken the view that certain individuals pose such a risk to vulnerable people that they should be barred from working in positions where they will come into contact with these groups. The scheme governing these barring decisions is now found in the Safeguarding Vulnerable Groups Act (SVGA) 2006 and is operated by the Independent Safeguarding Authority (ISA).

8.2   Therefore, in addition to having to engage with the regulatory regimes covered elsewhere in this book, individuals who commit a criminal offence or whose conduct is called into question may find themselves placed on the children's and/or adults' barred lists maintained by the ISA. This chapter sets out the law as to when the ISA may place an individual on one or both of the barred lists and considers the right of appeal established by SVGA 2006 s4. Particular consideration is given to the first decisions of the Upper Tribunal, which give an indication of how it will exercise its jurisdiction to review the ISA's decisions.

8.3   The focus of this chapter is on the barring scheme established by the SVGA 2006, not on the parallel vetting scheme which has caused significant public outcry and is being rolled back by the present government.[1] The SVGA 2006 scheme is subject to significant amendment by the Protection of Freedoms Act (PFA) 2012, which received royal assent on 1 May 2012. Some of the most significant amendments are flagged in this chapter, although as the PFA 2012 generally will come into force by order of the Secretary of State[2] it will be essential to check whether the detail of any of the provisions summarised below has been amended at the relevant time. However, the basic elements of the barring scheme established by the SVGA 2006 are not fundamentally altered by the PFA 2012.

Background – previous barring schemes

8.4   Prior to their consolidation under the SVGA 2006, a number of barred lists had proliferated since at least the 1930s.[3] These included the POCA (Protection of Children Act) and POVA (Protection of Vulnerable Adults) lists, operating under Protection of Children Act 1999 and Care Standards Act 2000. A summary of these arrangements was given by Hedley J in *D v Buckinghamshire CC*.[4] A further list, List 99,[5] was held by the Department for Education in relation to teachers.

8.5   The impetus to amalgamate these disparate barring schemes came from the report of the Bichard Inquiry[6] which followed the Soham murders. The Bichard Inquiry identified systemic failures in the previous barring schemes and recommended a single, national registration scheme for all those working with children or vulnerable adults. Following consultation,[7] the SVGA 2006 was the government's response, and the transitional provisions from the previous regimes to the new barring scheme are set out in Schedule 8[8] to the

---

1   See www.homeoffice.gov.uk/crime/vetting-barring-scheme/ and HM Government, *Vetting and barring scheme remodelling review – report and recommendations*, February 2011. In particular, the PFA 2012, once in force, will remove the present category of 'controlled activity' and abolish the present monitoring requirements, see PFA 2012 ss68–69.
2   By virtue of PFA 2012 s120.
3   See *XY v Independent Safeguarding Authority* [2011] UKUT 289 (AAC) at [6].
4   [2008] EWCA Civ 1372, see judgment at [4]–[7].
5   A list of individuals in relation to whom directions under Education Act 2002 s142 had been made.
6   HC 653, June 2004.
7   'Making safeguarding everybody's business: a post-Bichard vetting scheme', which ran from April to July 2005.
8   Given effect by SVGA 2006 s62.

SVGA 2006. An order made under the SVGA 2006[9] provides that certain individuals who were still subject to the old barring regimes immediately before 12 October 2009 remain subject to them, including in relation to appeals.[10] However, all individuals whose cases were first determined after 12 October 2009 are subject to the new regime under the SVGA 2006.

SVGA 2006 – the present scheme

8.6 The SVGA 2006 applies to England and Wales,[11] and also establishes the equivalent of the ISA for Northern Ireland. Provision is made for information sharing between authorities in England and Wales and in Scotland. The purpose of the new scheme was said to be to 'minimise the risk of harm posed to children and vulnerable adults by those that might seek to harm them through their work'.[12]

The ISA

8.7 The SVGA 2006 begins at section 1 by establishing the ISA[13] and bringing into effect Schedule 1 which imposes requirements, amongst other matters, as to ISA's membership, staffing and funding. The ISA's 'core functions' are determining whether it is appropriate for a person to be included in a barred list, determining whether to remove a person from a barred list and considering representations made on behalf of individuals who may be barred.[14] It is, however, anticipated that under PFA 2012 ss87–88, the Criminal Records Bureau (CRB) and the ISA will be merged with a single, new non-departmental public body created to be known as the Disclosure

---

9 Safeguarding Vulnerable Groups Act 2006 (Commencement No 6, Transitional Provisions and Savings) Order 2009 SI No 2611.

10 See articles 5–7 of the Safeguarding Vulnerable Groups Act 2006 (Commencement No 6, Transitional Provisions and Savings) Order 2009 for the detail of which individuals barred at the relevant date remain subject to the previous regimes.

11 A number of powers to make secondary legislation for Wales under the SVGA 2006 are conferred on the Welsh Ministers rather than the secretary of state – see SVGA 2006 s56.

12 Explanatory notes to the SVGA 2006 at 7.

13 The ISA was originally known as the Independent Barring Board (IBB) but its name was changed by amendment introduced by Policing and Crime Act 2009 s81(3)(m)(i).

14 SVGA 2006 Sch 1 para 8.

and Barring Service (DBS).[15] The planned operational date for the DBS is November 2012.[16] As the new body will simply inherit the ISA's barring functions and its date of operation remains uncertain, the term 'ISA' is used throughout this chapter.

8.8   The ISA's chairman and members must appear to the Secretary of State to have knowledge and experience of child protection or the protection of vulnerable adults,[17] however in practice the day-to-day decision-making of the ISA is delegated to its staff.[18] The Upper Tribunal has described the SVGA 2006 as being 'remarkably silent' as to the decision-making process to be adopted by the ISA.[19] The ISA's board has published guidance notes,[20] but although persuasive in relation to the proper process for the ISA to follow they have no statutory force.[21]

8.9   In the *Royal College of Nursing* case[22] (see paras 8.26–8.27 below) the ISA's witness statement evidence on its decision-making process was summarised by Wyn Williams J,[23] from which the following points can be drawn:

a) The ISA's decision-making process has five stages. At each stage a positive decision is required for the case to progress. The stages are:
   i)   initial assessment;
   ii) information gathering;
   iii) the 'structured judgment process' (SJP) – this involves the application of a risk assessment tool to determine the perceived future risk of harm to children and/or vulnerable adults;
   iv) consideration of representations;
   v)   final barring decision.

---

15 See PFA 2012 chapter 3.
16 See www.homeoffice.gov.uk/crime/vetting-barring-scheme/.
17 SVGA 2006 Sch 1 para 1.
18 Under SVGA 2006 Sch 1 para 6.
19 *XY v Independent Safeguarding Authority* [2011] UKUT 289 (AAC) at [21].
20 *Guidance notes for the barring decision making process*, currently version 3.4, August 2010. See also *Factsheet 2: ISA decision-making process*, published in February 2010 and available on the ISA website at www.isa.homeoffice.gov.uk/PDF/ISA_factsheet_2.pdf.
21 *XY v Independent Safeguarding Authority* [2011] UKUT 289 (AAC) at [21].
22 In *R (Royal College of Nursing and others) v Secretary of State for the Home Department and Independent Safeguarding Authority* [2010] EWHC 2761 (Admin), [2011] PTSR 1193.
23 Judgment at [17]–[21].

b) Where the ISA is proposing to bar an individual under one of the discretionary routes,[24] it will send a 'minded to bar' letter asking for representations.

c) If representations are requested and not received, the individual will be barred.

Burden and standard of proof

8.10   The standard of proof to be applied by the ISA in reaching its decisions is the civil standard of the balance of probabilities.[25] Neither the seriousness of an allegation nor the seriousness of the consequences make any difference to the standard of proof, but the inherent probability of whether a serious incident is likely to have taken place is something for the ISA to take into account.[26] In reaching its decision, the ISA is entitled to take account of all the evidence in the round and assess the probative value of similar fact evidence.[27]

8.11   Although the formal notion of a burden of proof in the ISA's decision-making may be unhelpful, any factual allegations require proof and it would be 'wholly wrong' for the ISA to place the onus on any individual to disprove allegations made against them.[28] The Upper Tribunal has made trenchant criticisms of the use of language in the ISA's decision letters which tends to suggest that the burden of proof has been placed on the barred individual.[29] In one such case, the ISA's counsel described the decision letter as having been 'appallingly drafted'.[30] However, the tribunal has repeatedly looked at the substance not the form of the ISA's decisions[31] and so long as the ISA has not in practice required an individual whom they are minded to bar to prove his or her innocence of any allegation, a decision will

---

24 Currently 'behaviour' or 'risk of harm', see below at paras 8.29–8.35 and 8.36–8.39.

25 *XY v Independent Safeguarding Authority* [2011] UKUT 289 (AAC) at [44].

26 *Re B (Children)* [2008] UKHL 35 at [15] (Lord Hoffmann: 'it is common sense to start with the assumption that most parents do not abuse their children. But this assumption may be swiftly dispelled by other compelling evidence') and [70] (Lady Hale).

27 See *Secretary of State for Children, Schools and Families v J* [2009] EWHC 524 (Admin), a case involving multiple allegations of sexual abuse against different teenagers.

28 *XY v Independent Safeguarding Authority* [2011] UKUT 289 (AAC) at [44].

29 See for example *XY v ISA* [2011] UKUT 289 (AAC) at [115].

30 *XY v Independent Safeguarding Authority* [2011] UKUT 289 (AAC) at [36].

31 See for example *XY v Independent Safeguarding Authority* [2011] UKUT 289 (AAC) at [40].

not be flawed solely by any suggestion to the contrary in a 'minded to bar' letter or decision letter.

Children and 'vulnerable adults'

8.12   The scheme operated by the ISA is intended to protect children and 'vulnerable adults'. Under SVGA 2006 s59(1) (as enacted) a person is a 'vulnerable adult' in a host of specified situations, including that the person:

a) is in residential accommodation or sheltered housing;[32]
b) is or has been a pupil at a residential special school;[33]
c) receives domiciliary care;[34]
d) receives any form of healthcare;[35]
e) receives a welfare service;[36]
f) receives a service as a result of his or her age, disability, physical or mental problem or is an expectant or nursing mother;[37]
g) receives a service funded by way of direct payments made under Health and Social Care Act 2001 s57;[38]
h) is lawfully in custody or under the supervision of a probation officer;[39] or
i) requires assistance in the conduct of his own affairs.[40]

8.13   It can be seen that parliament intended the definition of 'vulnerable adult' to be very broadly drawn, and virtually every person will be a 'vulnerable adult' within the statutory definition at certain points in their life. It is important to note that an adult who as a child attended a residential special school will remain a 'vulnerable adult' for the

32 SVGA 2006 s59(1)(a) and (b).
33 SVGA 2006 s59(2)(b) and (3). A 'welfare service' is a service which provides support, assistance, advice or counseling but is not a community care service within the meaning of National Health Service and Community Care Act 1990 s46 and SVGA 2006 s59(8) and s16(5).
34 SVGA 2006 s59(1)(c). This means any assistance provided to a person by reason of his age, health or disability: SVGA 2006 s59(4) and (5).
35 SVGA 2006 s59(1)(d). This includes any treatment, therapy or palliative care of any description: SVGA 2006 s59(6).
36 SVGA 2006 s59(1)(g).
37 SVGA 2006 s59(1)(h) and (9).
38 SVGA 2006 s59(1)(i).
39 SVGA 2006 s59(1)(e), (f) and (fa). See SVGA 2006 s59(7) for a more detailed definition of 'lawful custody'.
40 SVGA 2006 s59(1)(j) and (10). In short, this means that the person has been held to lack capacity and action has been taken on his behalf under the Mental Capacity Act 2005 or he has an appointee to manage his benefits.

rest of his or her life, regardless of whether the person comes within any of the other categories provided for.

8.14 This complex definition will be replaced with a much simpler definition under PFA 2012 s65, which will omit SVGA 2006 s59 and insert a new definition of 'vulnerable adult' into the interpretation section (SVGA 2006 s60) to the effect that a vulnerable adult is simply an adult to whom an activity which constitutes a 'regulated activity' (see below at paras 8.52–8.60) is provided.

8.15 By contrast to the complexity of the present definition of a 'vulnerable adult', a 'child' is (and will remain) simply a person who has not attained the age of 18 (SVGA 2006 s60(1)). This has obvious and important implications for the ISA's consideration of situations where 'relevant conduct' is alleged in relation to a sexual relationship with a 'child', who may have been aged 16 or 17 at the relevant time and thus over the age of consent. In these cases the requirement on the ISA to consider whether it is appropriate to bar will be particularly important.

Referrals to the ISA

8.16 Regulated activity providers[41] have a duty to refer individuals to ISA if, in short, they consider that any of the tests for inclusion of an individual on one of the barred lists are met (SVGA 2006 s35).[42] If the ISA is considering whether to include an individual on a barred list, or whether to remove the individual from a barred list, it may require regulated activity providers to provide information to the ISA.[43]

8.17 Similarly, local authorities have a duty to refer individuals to the ISA if they think that any of the tests for inclusion of that individual on a barred list are met and they further think that the individual is engaged or may engage in specified activity with children and/

41 SVGA 2006 s6; an individual or organisation responsible for the management or control of regulated activity. This means the person with ultimate responsibility for the regulated activity, not 'every individual in the management chain'; explanatory notes to the SVGA 2006 at 48. A person who makes arrangements for another to engage in regulated activity for the benefit of a child or vulnerable adult who is a member of his or her family or his or her friend is not a regulated activity provider: SVGA 2006 s6(5).

42 The same duty applies to 'personnel suppliers' by virtue of SVGA 2006 s36. A 'personnel supplier' is an employment agency or an education institution who provides a student for work experience: SVGA 2006 s60(1).

43 SVGA 2006 s37. Failure to provide such information without reasonable excuse is an offence: SVGA 2006 s38.

or vulnerable adults (SVGA 2006 s39). Again, local authorities must provide information to the ISA on request.[44]

8.18   Referral duties also apply to professional bodies and supervisory authorities under SVGA 2006 ss41 and 45. The professional bodies governed by this section are specified in a table set out at SVGA 2006 s41(7) and include all those bodies who hold registers of professional members who are likely to work with children and vulnerable adults and the main regulators. These bodies must also provide information to ISA on request.[45]

8.19   The ISA has a duty to consider whether any information it receives from any source is relevant to its consideration as to whether an individual should be included in one of the barred lists (SVGA 2006 Sch 3 para 13(1)). This does not, however, imply any right for an individual to make representations to the ISA other than those found elsewhere in Schedule 3.[46]

Inclusion on the barred lists

8.20   Under SVGA 2006 s2, the ISA must establish and maintain the children's barred list and the adults' barred list. Under SVGA 2006 Sch 3, brought into force by section 2, the ISA must determine whether individuals must be included in the children's barred list (Part 1 of Schedule 3) and/or the adults' barred list (Part 2 of Schedule 3). For both lists there are four routes under which an individual may be barred:

a) automatic inclusion;
b) inclusion subject to consideration of representations;
c) behaviour ('relevant conduct'); and
d) risk of harm.

Each of these barring routes is considered below.

Criminal offences – automatic inclusion

8.21   Parliament has determined that certain criminal offences are so serious that a person who is convicted or cautioned for one of these offences should be automatically included on the relevant barred list; see SVGA 2006 Sch 3 para 1 in relation to children and Sch 3 para 7 in relation to vulnerable adults. These offences are specified in

---

44 SVGA 2006 s40.
45 SVGA 2006 ss42 and 46.
46 A point made explicit by SVGA 2006 Sch 3 para 13(2).

the schedule to the Safeguarding Vulnerable Groups Act 2006 (Prescribed Criteria and Miscellaneous Provisions) Regulations 2009.[47]

8.22   A person convicted or cautioned of one of these offences has no right under the statutory scheme to make representations to the ISA as to why he or she should not be included in the list. Nor does such an individual have any right of appeal to the Upper Tribunal.[48]

8.23   Given that the inclusion prior to representations ('auto-barring with reps') provisions of the SVGA 2006 have been held to be incompatible with articles 6 and 8 (right to a fair trial and right to respect for private life)[49] of the European Convention on Human Rights (ECHR) (see paras 8.26–8.28 below), there is an obvious question as to the compatibility of this barring route with the ECHR – albeit that it may be harder to argue that automatic inclusion without the right to make representations ('auto-barring without reps') is inherently disproportionate when it is confined to a very limited number of extremely serious offences.

Criminal offences – inclusion subject to consideration of representations

8.24   In relation to a much wider category of offences, the SVGA 2006 prescribes that the ISA must place a person who has been convicted or cautioned on the barred lists and then give the person the opportunity to make representations as to why he or she should be removed; see SVGA 2006 Sch 3 para 2 in relation to children and Sch 3 para 8 in relation to vulnerable adults. Again, these offences are specified in the schedule to the Safeguarding Vulnerable Groups Act 2006 (Prescribed Criteria and Miscellaneous Provisions) Regulations 2009.

8.25   These 'auto barring with reps' provisions were considered by Wyn Williams J in *R (Royal College of Nursing and others) v Secretary of State for the Home Department and the Independent Safeguarding Authority*.[50] In that case, the Royal College of Nursing brought proceedings along with four of its nurse members, all of whom had accepted cautions for specified 'auto barring with reps' offences and so had been automatically placed on the barred lists. Wyn Williams J held, applying

---

47 SI No 37.

48 See SVGA 2006 s4(1) for the specified decisions by the ISA against which a right of appeal is granted. The provisions governing automatic inclusion are excluded from this list.

49 In *R (Royal College of Nursing and others) v Secretary of State for the Home Department and Independent Safeguarding Authority* [2010] EWHC 2761 (Admin), [2011] PTSR 1193.

50 [2010] EWHC 2761 (Admin), [2011] PTSR 1193.

the judgment of the House of Lords in *Wright*,[51] that when a person is included in a barred list this determines his or her civil rights so as to engage ECHR article 6 (right to a fair trial).[52] He further concluded that the 'auto barring with reps' provisions were not a 'legitimate and proportionate holding exercise',[53] not least because of the elapse of time in many of the cases between a conviction or caution and an individual's inclusion in one of the lists. As such it was ultimately held that this barring route breached both ECHR articles 6[54] and 8 (right to respect for private life).[55] This conclusion was not challenged through an appeal by the secretary of state.

8.26   Wyn Williams J reached the conclusion that the SVGA 2006 scheme could not be read compatibly with these articles.[56] As such, a 'declaration of incompatibility' was made pursuant to Human Rights Act (HRA) 1998 s4.[57] It is critical to bear in mind that such a declaration leaves the statutory scheme in force and the ISA is required to continue to bar individuals under this route until Parliament remedies the incompatibility. This will be achieved once the PFA 2012 comes into force, as PFA 2012 s67 amends the relevant paragraphs of SVGA 2006 Sch 3 to provide for a right to make representations prior to a barring decision when individuals have committed the lesser class of specified offences.

8.27   However, until the PFA 2012 comes into force this class of individuals will continue to have their ECHR article 6 and 8 rights violated by being included in the barred lists without a right to make representations in advance of their inclusion. The remedy for these individuals lies in an application to the European Court of Human Rights in Strasbourg, where it is likely that the breaches of the convention articles will be found and (particularly where the individual has lost employment or suffered other pecuniary loss) damages will be awarded by way of 'just satisfaction'.

51 *R (Wright) v Secretary of State for Health* [2009] UKHL 3, [2009] AC 739.
52 Judgment at [47] and [57].
53 Judgment at [63].
54 Judgment at [67]. See further the speech of Lady Hale in *R (Wright) v Secretary of State for Health* [2009] UKHL 3, [2009] AC 739 at [28]: 'The [Care Standards Act 2000] scheme does not begin fairly, by offering the care worker an opportunity to answer the allegations made against her, before imposing upon her possibly irreparable damage to her employment or prospects of employment'.
55 Judgment at [68].
56 Judgment at [77].
57 Judgment at [78] and [129].

Behaviour – 'relevant conduct'

8.28 The third route under which the ISA can place an individual on the barred lists is if the person has engaged in 'relevant conduct' and ISA is satisfied that it is appropriate to include them on the list: SVGA 2006 Sch 3 paras 3 and 4 in relation to children and Sch 3 paras 9 and 10 in relation to vulnerable adults.[58]

8.29 Importantly, under this route the ISA is and has always been required to invite representations from the individual *before* determining whether to include him or her on the list: SVGA 2006 Sch 3 paras 3(2) and 9(2).

8.30 The ISA is obliged to include the individual on the list if, having considered any representations, it is satisfied that:

a) he or she engaged in 'relevant conduct';[59] and
b) it appears to the ISA that it is appropriate to include the person in the list.[60]

8.31 It can therefore be seen that it is not sufficient under this barring route for the ISA to make findings of fact that are adverse to the individual and conclude that relevant conduct has occurred. This is merely the first step; the ISA must then go on to consider the separate question of whether it is 'appropriate' to include the individual on the barred list. This calls for an exercise of judgment by the ISA which can be challenged on appeal to the Upper Tribunal on public law principles and (importantly) under the doctrine of proportionality (see paras 8.69–8.78 below).

8.32 'Relevant conduct' is defined similarly in relation to children and vulnerable adults and includes:

- conduct that endangers or is likely to endanger a child or vulnerable adult[61] – this includes harming or attempting to harm a child or vulnerable adult, causing a child or vulnerable adult to be harmed, putting a child or vulnerable adult at risk of harm of inciting another to harm a child or vulnerable adult;[62]

---

58 The wording of the relevant paragraphs of SVGA 2006 Sch 3 governing the 'behaviour' barring route will be subject to relatively minor amendments once PFA 2012 s67 is in force.

59 SVGA 2006 Sch 3 paras 3(3)(a) and 9(3)(a).

60 SVGA 2006 Sch 3 paras 3(3)(b) and 9(3)(b).

61 SVGA 2006 Sch 3 paras 4(1)(a) and 10(1)(a). Conduct in relation to a child is only relevant conduct for the purposes of the children's barred list and conduct in relation to a vulnerable adult is only relevant conduct for the purposes of the adults' barred list.

62 SVGA 2006 Sch 3 paras 4(2) and 10(2).

- conduct which, if repeated, would endanger a child or vulnerable adult or would be likely to endanger him or her;[63]
- possessing sexual material in relation to children (meaning indecent images or material of any form portraying children involved in sexual activity and which is produced for the purposes of giving sexual gratification[64]) or other conduct involving such material;[65]
- possessing sexual images depicting violence against human beings or other conduct involving such images, if it appears to the ISA that such conduct is inappropriate;[66] and
- conduct of a sexual nature involving a child which appears to the ISA to be inappropriate.[67]

8.33   For the purposes of the final two categories of relevant sexual conduct, the ISA must have regard to guidance issued by the secretary of state as to what constitutes inappropriate conduct.[68] The relevant guidance[69] is available on the ISA website.

8.34   Parliament has therefore legislated to bring a very wide range of conduct within the definition of 'relevant conduct' so as to trigger the ISA's barring obligations under this barring route. This is another reason why it is so important that the ISA observes the requirement not only to satisfy itself that relevant conduct has occurred but also that it appears appropriate to include the individual in the barred list or lists.

Risk of harm

8.35   The fourth and potentially most controversial of the barring routes relates to 'risk of harm'. Under this route, an individual may be placed on a barred list despite never having committed an offence or

---

63   SVGA 2006 Sch 3 paras 4(1)(b) and 10(1)(b).
64   SVGA 2006 Sch 3 paras 4(3) and 10(3). An 'image' can be produced by any means and may be of a real or imaginary subject: paras 4(4) and 10(4).
65   SVGA 2006 Sch 3 paras 4(1)(c) and 10(1)(c). It is important to note that this is relevant conduct for the purposes of the adults' barred list, not merely the children's list.
66   SVGA 2006 Sch 3 paras 4(1)(d) and 10(1)(d).
67   SVGA 2006 Sch 3 paras 4(1)(e) and 10(1)(e). Here conduct involving children is only relevant conduct for the purposes of the children's barred list and conduct involving vulnerable adults is only relevant conduct for the purposes of the adults' barred list.
68   SVGA 2006 Sch 3 paras 4(6) and 10(6).
69   *Guidance on inappropriate conduct involving sexually explicit images and conduct of a sexual nature under Schedule 3 of the Safeguarding Vulnerable Groups Act 2006.*

engaged in 'relevant conduct'. Instead, the ISA must place a person on a barred list if is satisfied that:

a) the person presents one of a series of specified risks; and
b) it appears to the ISA that it is appropriate to include the person in the list.[70]

8.36   The risks specified are that the individual may:

a) harm a child or vulnerable adult;[71]
b) cause a child or vulnerable adult to be harmed;[72]
c) put a child or vulnerable adult at risk of harm;[73]
d) attempt to harm a child or vulnerable adult;[74] or
e) incite another to harm a child or vulnerable adult.[75]

8.37   Unsurprisingly, if the ISA proposes to bar an individual under this route, he or she must be first given the opportunity to make representations (SVGA 2006 Sch 3 paras 5(2) and 11(2)).

8.38   No further qualification is imposed by the SVGA 2006 on the ISA's obligations to bar individuals pursuant to the 'risk of harm' route. However, the ISA's case worker guidance[76] states at p92 that the policy is only to conclude that there is a 'risk of harm' where there is 'sufficient and compelling evidence' that an individual poses a risk to a particular vulnerable group.[77] While this guidance does not have statutory force it is nevertheless a helpful indicator that individuals should not be barred under the 'risk of harm' route unless there is substantial and cogent evidence against them. An appeal against a barring decision under this route is likely to raise questions of proportionality (see paras 8.69–8.78 below).

70   SVGA 2006 Sch 3 paras 5(3) and 11(3).
71   SVGA 2006 Sch 3 paras 5(4)(a) and 11(4)(a).
72   SVGA 2006 Sch 3 paras 5(4)(b) and 11(4)(b).
73   SVGA 2006 Sch 3 paras 5(4)(c) and 11(4)(c).
74   SVGA 2006 Sch 3 paras 5(4)(d) and 11(4)(d).
75   SVGA 2006 Sch 3 paras 5(4)(e) and 11(4)(e).
76   It is not understood that this guidance is in the public domain, however the ISA disclosed a redacted version of the guidance to the Supreme Court in *R (G) v Governors of X School* [2011] UKSC 30 and appears to be willing to disclose the same redacted version if requested to do so by the representatives of a barred individual in the context of an appeal to the Upper Tribunal.
77   Reflecting a ministerial speech in parliament on 2 May 2006 (*Hansard* cols GC184 and GC188).

Representations

8.39   As set out above, three of the four routes under which an individual
can be placed on a barred list provide for the individual to make representations to the ISA. In all cases where the ISA proposes to bar an
individual for 'behaviour' ('relevant conduct') or 'risk of harm', the
individual must be given the opportunity to make representations
prior to the barring decision being made (see paras 8.29–8.35 and
8.36–8.39 above). Once the PFA 2012 is in force, individuals who
have committed the less serious categories of specified offences will
also be able to make representations prior to a barring decision in
their case (see para 8.27 above). At the present time such individuals
are only invited to make representations after being placed on the
list.

8.40   The process for making representations is governed by SVGA
2006 Sch 3 para 16. Important points to note are that:

a) The individual must be given the opportunity to make representations in relation to all the information on which the ISA intends
to rely.[78] This must imply an obligation on the ISA to disclose any
information which might not be known to the individual when it
invites representation. If further information comes to light the
ISA must then disclose this and invite further representations.

b) Any requirement to afford an opportunity to make representations
is disapplied where the ISA does not know and cannot reasonably
ascertain the individual's whereabouts.[79]

c) Where a specified 'competent body'[80] has made a finding of fact,
there is no opportunity for an individual to make representations
that that finding of fact was wrongly made.[81]

8.41   If the ISA could not ascertain an individual's whereabouts and the
individual makes representations after the time limit has expired,
the ISA must consider the representations and remove him from the
barred list(s) if it considers in the light of the representations that it is
not appropriate for him or her to be included in the list(s).[82] Similarly, if an individual notified of his or her right to make representations
fails to make representations in time but later submits representations, the ISA *may* consider the late representations and if it does so

78   SVGA 2006 Sch 3 para 16(1).
79   SVGA 2006 Sch 3 para 16(2).
80   See SVGA 2006 Sch 3 para 16(4) – in short, all the relevant regulators.
81   SVGA 2006 Sch 3 para 16(3).
82   SVGA 2006 Sch 3 para 17(1) and (3).

must then remove him from the list(s) if it decides that it is no longer appropriate for him or her to be included.[83] It is immaterial if these representations relate to a time after the person was included on the list[84] – but of course, this only applies if no representations were made prior to the barring decision.

8.42   It is essential that an individual whom the ISA is 'minded to bar' puts in full and detailed representations both on any factual matters which may be in dispute and on why it is (in his or her view) not appropriate for the individual to be included in the barred list(s). A failure to submit sufficiently cogent and detailed representations is highly likely to see the individual included in the barred list(s) subject only to the right of appeal to the Upper Tribunal.

A right to an oral hearing?

8.43   The ISA's practice is in every case to date appears to be to seek representations from an individual whom they are minded to bar in writing. In the *Royal College of Nursing*[85] case, the claimants argued that the absence of a right to an oral hearing before the ISA rendered the SVGA 2006 scheme in breach of ECHR article 6. This argument was rejected by Wyn Williams J,[86] on the basis that there is a right of appeal to the Upper Tribunal where alleged errors of fact and/or law have been made, and this carries with it a right to an oral hearing.[87] However, Wyn Williams J went on to hold that:

> An oral hearing before the ISA is permissible under the statutory scheme and there is no reason to suppose that in an appropriate case the ISA would not hold such a hearing ...[88]

8.44   Despite this conclusion by the High Court, the appellant in *XY v Independent Safeguarding Authority*,[89] the first appeal to be determined by the Upper Tribunal, argued that the ISA's decision was unlawful because he had not been offered an oral hearing before the

---

83   SVGA 2006 Sch 3 para 17(2) and (3).

84   SVGA 2006 Sch 3 para 17(4).

85   *R (Royal College of Nursing and others) v Secretary of State for the Home Department and Independent Safeguarding Authority* [2010] EWHC 2761 (Admin), [2011] PTSR 1193.

86   Judgment at [103].

87   At least of the permission application.

88   Judgment at [103].

89   [2011] UKUT 289 (AAC).

decision was taken.[90] By the time the Upper Tribunal handed down its decision, the Supreme Court had delivered its judgment in *R (G) v Governors of X School*.[91] Unsurprisingly in the light of that judgment,[92] the tribunal held that there was no automatic right to an oral hearing before the ISA[93] and went on to find it was not irrational or unreasonable for the ISA not to have offered an oral hearing on the facts of that case.[94]

8.45   The judgment of the tribunal in *XY* does, however, leave open the possibility that in a future case the tribunal would hold it to have been unlawful for the ISA to have failed to arrange an oral hearing – whether or not an explicit request for such a hearing was made. Indeed, the tribunal held[95] that:

> There may well be circumstances in which the common law duty of procedural fairness *may* point to the need for an oral hearing ... It is true, of course, that there is the possibility of an oral hearing on appeal before the Upper Tribunal. However, it is the unrepresented and vulnerable appellant who is more likely to be at a disadvantage in the appellate process, not least as he or she has to persuade the Upper Tribunal that it is appropriate to grant permission to appeal in the first place. There may well be other situations in which an oral hearing before ISA itself may be desirable, notwithstanding the right of appeal to the Upper Tribunal. [Emphasis as original.]

8.46   So although it has been conclusively established that ECHR article 6 does not require oral hearings as of right before the ISA, the common law may require such a hearing on the facts of an individual case in order for the procedure to be fair. In *XY*, the tribunal invited the ISA to set out a public policy to specify the circumstances in which it would consider it appropriate to hold an oral hearing.[96] This invitation has yet to be accepted by the ISA and so it will remain open to individuals whom the ISA is minded to bar to argue that the particular circumstances of their case mean that an oral hearing is required in order for the ISA's decision-making to be fair.

---

90 *XY v Independent Safeguarding Authority* [2011] UKUT 289 (AAC) at [85]. This argument was particularly surprising because the appellant did not choose to give oral evidence before the tribunal on appeal.

91 [2011] UKSC 30.

92 Described as providing a 'very strong steer ... that an oral hearing will only rarely be necessary in proceedings before ISA': *XY* at [99].

93 Judgment at [103].

94 Judgment at [106].

95 Judgment at [107]–[108].

96 Judgment at [116].

Reviews

8.47 Once confirmed on a barred list, a person may only apply for a review with the permission of the ISA.[97] Such applications can only be made after the expiry of the minimum barred period.[98] These periods are specified in regulations and are presently:

a) one year in relation to a person who has not reached the age of 18;
b) five years for a person aged 18–24; and
c) ten years for a person aged 25 or over.[99]

8.48 In the *Royal College of Nursing*[100] case, Wyn Williams J held that he was persuaded, 'just', that the minimum barring periods were justified and proportionate and therefore a lawful interference with barred individuals' ECHR article 8 rights (right to privacy).[101] The judge invited the secretary of state to consider 'anxiously' whether the minimum barring periods should be reviewed. The government's response to this invitation is found in PFA 2012 s71 which once in force will give the ISA a general power to review a person's inclusion on the barred lists at any time.[102] It is important to note that in meeting this challenge in the *Royal College of Nursing* case, the ISA stated that it was already, in exceptional circumstances, prepared to review individual cases of its own motion where the minimum period of time had not expired.[103]

8.49 Permission should only be granted by the ISA for a review if it thinks the applicant's circumstances have changed since he or she was included on the list (or last applied for permission) and that this change merits permission being granted.[104] If permission is granted,

---

97 SVGA 2006 Sch 3 para 18(1) and (2).
98 SVGA 2006 Sch 3 para 18(3). The date on which time starts to run is specified in SVGA 2006 Sch 3 para 18(6) and includes the date of release where a person is included in the lists because of a conviction (para 18(6)(c)).
99 Safeguarding Vulnerable Groups Act 2006 (Barring Procedure) Regulations 2008 SI No 474 reg 9.
100 *R (Royal College of Nursing and others) v Secretary of State for the Home Department and Independent Safeguarding Authority* [2010] EWHC 2761 (Admin), [2011] PTSR 1193.
101 Judgment at [122].
102 It is important, however, to note that the ISA must only remove the person from the list(s) if it is satisfied that, in the light of information which it did not have at the time of the person's inclusion in the list(s), any change of circumstances relating to the person concerned, or any error by ISA, it is not appropriate for the person to be included in the list.
103 Judgment at [123].
104 SVGA 2006 Sch 3 para 18(4).

the ISA must then consider whether it remains appropriate for the individual to be included on the list(s) and must remove him or her from the list unless it is so satisfied.[105] A refusal by the ISA to review a decision to include an individual on a barred list triggers a further right of appeal to the Upper Tribunal.[106]

Consequences and effect of barring

8.50   If an individual is included in a barred list, the ISA must take all reasonable steps to notify him of this (SVGA 2006 Sch 3 para 14).

Regulated activity

8.51   Under SVGA 2006 s3, a person placed on either or both of the two barred lists is barred from taking part in 'regulated activity' in relation to children and/or vulnerable adults. The term 'regulated activity' is subject to the detailed definitions provided in Schedule 4,[107] Part 1 of which defines regulated activity in relation to children with Part 2 providing the definition in relation to adults. However, in general terms it means activities which 'provide an opportunity for close contact with children or vulnerable adults, other activities in key settings such as schools and care homes and key positions of responsibility'.[108] Given the broad reach of Schedule 4, a barred individual should not engage in any activity which may be in any way related to children and/or vulnerable adults without taking specialist legal advice on the facts of his or her individual case.

8.52   In relation to children, 'regulated activity' includes:

a) a series of specified activities (see below),[109] if carried out frequently;[110]

b) work within a series of specified settings, including schools, nurseries, hospitals, children's homes and children's centres, which gives the person the opportunity to have contact with children;[111]

---

105 SVGA 2006 Sch 3 para 18(5).
106 SVGA 2006 s4(1)(c).
107 In effect by virtue of SVGA 2006 s5. Amendments to these definitions will be made in relation to children (clause 64) and vulnerable adults (clause 66) by the Protection of Freedoms Bill 2011 (bill as at Lords Committee stage).
108 Explanatory notes to the SVGA 2006 at 8.
109 SVGA 2006 Sch 4 paras 1(1) and 2(1).
110 SVGA 2006 Sch 4 para 1(1)(b). Section 64 of the Protection of Freedoms Act 2012 introduces new sub-paras 1A-C, which remove any requirement for frequency in the provision of most personal care and health care services.
111 SVGA 2006 Sch 4 paras 1(2) and 3(1).

    c) paid or voluntary child-minding;[112]

    d) fostering;[113]

    e) holding a series of specified positions, for example school gov-
      ernor, trustee of a children's charity or member of a fostering or
      adoption panel;[114]

    f) acting as an inspector when so acting gives the individual the
      opportunity to have contact with children;[115] and

    g) a series of management and supervisory roles in relation to the
      above.[116]

8.53   The activities specified as regulated activity in relation to children for
    the purposes of SVGA 2006 Sch 4 para 1(1) are:

    a) any form of teaching, training or instruction of children that is
      not merely incidental to the teaching, training or instruction of
      adults[117] – section 64 of the PFA 2012[118] will exclude any form of
      teaching, training or instruction of children where the individual
      is subject to regular day-to-day supervision from the definition of
      regulated activity;

    b) any form of care or supervision of children which is not merely
      incidental to the care or supervision of adults[119] – section 64 of the
      PFA 2012[120] will exclude any form of care where the individual
      carer is subject to regular day-to-day supervision and any care pro-
      vided otherwise than by a healthcare professional from the defin-
      ition of regulated activity;

    c) any form of advice or guidance relating to physical, emotional or
      educational well-being provided wholly or mainly for children;[121]

    d) any form of treatment or therapy provided for a child;[122]

    e) moderating a chatroom[123] which is likely to be used wholly or
      mainly by children;[124]

---

112 SVGA 2006 Sch 4 para 1(2), (3), (6) and (7).
113 SVGA 2006 Sch 4 para 1(5).
114 SVGA 2006 Sch 4 paras 1(9) and 4(1).
115 SVGA 2006 Sch 4 paras 1(9A)–(11).
116 SVGA 2006 Sch 4 para 1(14).
117 SVGA 2006 Sch 4 para 2(1)(a).
118 Inserting new subpara (3A) into para 2 of SVGA 2006 Sch 4.
119 SVGA 2006 Sch 4 para 2(1)(b).
120 Inserting new subpara (3B) into para 2 of SVGA 2006 Sch 4.
121 SVGA 2006 Sch 4 para 2(1)(c).
122 SVGA 2006 Sch 4 para 2(1)(d).
123 Described as a 'public electronic interactive communication service'.
124 SVGA 2006 Sch 4 para 2(1)(e).

f)　driving a vehicle being used solely for the purpose of transporting children and their carers.[125]

8.54　However, doing any of the above with a child in the course of that child's employment is not regulated activity,[126] unless the child is under 16 and the person in question is principally responsible for the child.[127]

8.55　With respect to vulnerable adults, the following presently constitutes regulated activity:[128]

a)　any form of training, teaching or instruction provided wholly or mainly for vulnerable adults;[129]

b)　any form of care or supervision of vulnerable adults;[130]

c)　any form of assistance, advice or guidance provided wholly or mainly for vulnerable adults;[131]

d)　any form of treatment or therapy provided for a vulnerable adult;[132]

e)　moderating a chatroom[133] likely to be used wholly or mainly by vulnerable adults;[134]

f)　driving a vehicle being used solely for the purpose of transporting vulnerable adults and their carers;[135]

g)　anything done on behalf of a vulnerable adult in such circumstances as are prescribed;[136]

h)　any work carried out in a care home which is exclusively or mainly for vulnerable adults which gives the person the opportunity to have contact with vulnerable adults;[137]

125　SVGA 2006 Sch 4 para 2(1)(f).

126　SVGA 2006 Sch 4 para 2(2).

127　SVGA 2006 Sch 4 para 2(3).

128　The activities listed at a)–g) are only 'regulated activity' if carried out 'frequently' or the period condition (see para 8.58 below) is satisfied. There is no statutory definition of 'frequently', but Annex B to the Vetting and Barring Scheme guidance states at B.12 that 'the Government's view is that, in general, relevant activities that are carried out once a week or more frequently on an ongoing basis will satisfy the frequency requirement'.

129　SVGA 2006 Sch 4 para 7(1)(a).

130　SVGA 2006 Sch 4 para 7(1)(b).

131　SVGA 2006 Sch 4 para 7(1)(c).

132　SVGA 2006 Sch 4 para 7(1)(d).

133　Described as a 'public electronic interactive communication service'.

134　SVGA 2006 Sch 4 para 7(1)(e).

135　SVGA 2006 Sch 4 para 7(1)(f).

136　SVGA 2006 Sch 4 para 7(1)(g).

137　SVGA 2006 Sch 4 para 7(4).

i) any management or supervision of a person engaged in any of the above activities;[138]

j) the exercise of inspection functions;[139] and

k) serving in a number of specified positions, including as chief executive of an authority with social services functions, manager of a regulated establishment or agency which provides services to vulnerable adults or as a trustee of a vulnerable adults' charity.[140]

8.56   A specific saving provision in relation to vulnerable adults provides that a person who belongs to a group within which other members engage in regulated activity does not engage in regulated activity if he or she assists that person or does anything on behalf of or under the direction of that person which would otherwise amount to regulated activity.[141]

8.57   When the PFA 2012 comes into force, the above list of regulated activities with respect to vulnerable adults will be replaced with the following:[142]

a) the provision to an adult of healthcare by, or under the direction or supervision of, a healthcare professional;

b) the provision to an adult of relevant personal care;[143]

c) the provision by a social care worker of relevant social work to an adult who is a client or potential client;

d) the provision of assistance in relation to general household matters[144] to an adult who is in need of it by reason of age, illness or disability;

e) any relevant assistance[145] in the conduct of an adult's own affairs;

f) providing transport for vulnerable adults; and

---

138   SVGA 2006 Sch 4 para 7(5).

139   SVGA 2006 Sch 4 para 7(6)–(8A).

140   SVGA 2006 Sch 4 paras 7(9) and 8(1).

141   SVGA 2006 Sch 4 para 7(10).

142   SVGA 2006 Sch 4 new para 7(1), inserted by PFA 2012 s66.

143   Meaning physical assistance, given to a person who is in need of it by reason of age, illness or disability, in connection with i) eating or drinking, ii) toileting, iii) washing or bathing, iv) dressing, v) oral care or vi) the care of skin, hair or nails, or prompting, training, instructing, advising or guiding a person in relation to the above: SVGA 2006 Sch 4 new para 7(3B).

144   Meaning day-to-day assistance in relation to the running of the household of the person concerned where the assistance is the carrying out of one or more of the following activities on behalf of that person: a) managing the person's cash, b) paying the person's bills, c) shopping: SVGA 2006 Sch 4 new para 3D.

145   See the definition of 'relevant assistance' in SVGA 2006 Sch 4 new para 3E – essentially, matters governed by the Mental Capacity Act 2005 or the Mental Health Act 1983.

g) activities involving, or connected with, the provision of healthcare or relevant personal care to adults.

8.58   Where an activity is only 'regulated activity' if it is carried out for a specified period, that period is now more than three days in any period of 30 days.[146]

8.59   Importantly, SVGA 2006 s58 specifies that the Act does not apply to any activity which is carried out in the course of a family relationship[147] or in the course of a personal relationship where money is not involved.[148] A person placed on the barred list(s) does not therefore commit an offence by doing anything within a family or personal relationship, unless the personal relationship involves payment of some kind (for example, paying a friend to look after a child). The example given in the explanatory notes to the SVGA 2006[149] is that a person included in the children's barred list could look after his or her grandchildren without committing an offence.

Criminal offences

8.60   The primary force of the barring scheme stems from SVGA 2006 s7, which specifies that an individual commits an offence if he or she seeks to engage, offers to engage or actually engages in regulated activity from which he or she is barred.[150] This is an 'either way' offence for which the maximum penalty on indictment in the crown court is five years' imprisonment (potentially with a fine)[151] and in the magistrates' court is 12 months (again potentially with a fine).[152] Statutory defences are provided to such a charge, being that:

a) the individual did not know and could not reasonably be expected to have known that he or she was barred from that activity;[153] or

---

146 SVGA 2006 Sch 4 para 10(1). In certain situations specified in para 10(2) the period condition can be satisfied if the activity is carried out at any time between 2am and 6am and the activity gives the person the opportunity for face-to-face contact with children and/or vulnerable adults.

147 Which include relationships between persons who live in the same household and treat each other as though they are members of the same family: SVGA 2006 s57(3).

148 Which includes a relationship between friends: SVGA 2006 s57(4), which itself includes relationships with a member of the person's family: SVGA 2006 s57(5).

149 At [157].

150 SVGA 2006 s7(1). SVGA 2006 s8 creates a further offence where a barred individual engages in regulated activity in and is not subject to monitoring.

151 SVGA 2006 s7(2)(a).

152 SVGA 2006 s7(2)(b).

153 SVGA 2006 s7(3).

b) it was necessary for the individual to engage in that activity to prevent harm to a child or vulnerable adult, it was reasonably believed
that no other person could engage in that activity and he or she
engaged in the activity for no longer than was necessary.[154]

8.61 Both defences are likely to be interpreted strictly, given the protective
purpose of the SVGA 2006. Furthermore, for the purposes of the
criminal offence created by SVGA 2006 s7(1) there is no requirement
for the regulated activity to be carried out frequently.[155]

8.62 SVGA 2006 s9 creates two offences where an individual permits a barred individual to engage in regulated activity.[156] The same
maximum penalties apply in relation to these offences as to the
offence established by SVGA 2006 s7. Regulated activity providers
also commit an offence if they fail to check whether an individual is
barred from regulated activities.[157]

Appeals to the Upper Tribunal

8.63 Decisions made by the ISA to place an individual on one of the barred
lists trigger a right of appeal to the Upper Tribunal. Specifically, an
individual may appeal against:

a) a decision not to remove the individual from a barred list under
SVGA 2006 Sch 3 para 2 or 8 ('auto barring with reps');
b) a decision to include the individual on a barred list under Sch 3
paras 3, 5, 9 or 11 ('behaviour' and 'risk of harm'); or
c) a decision not to remove the individual from a barred list under Sch
3 paras 17 or 18 (decisions on late representations and reviews).

Grounds of appeal

8.64 Appeals are governed by SVGA 2006 s4, which provides at (2) that:

An appeal ... may be made only on the grounds that ISA has made a
mistake –
(a) on any point of law;

---

154 SVGA 2006 s7(4).
155 SVGA 2006 s7(5).
156 The offences relate to individuals and 'personnel suppliers' and are in similar
terms. SVGA 2006 s10 creates offences where providers of regulated activities
allow barred individuals to engage in regulated activity without monitoring.
157 SVGA 2006 s11. This offence is summary-only and is punishable by way of a
fine not exceeding level 5: SVGA 2006 s11(9).

(b) in any finding of fact which it has made an on which the decision mentioned in that subsection was based.

8.65 Importantly, SVGA 2006 s4(3) specifies that 'the decision whether or not it is appropriate for an individual to be included in a barred list' is not a question of fact or law for the purposes of subsection 2 and therefore falls outside the tribunal's jurisdiction.[158] Furthermore, unless the tribunal finds that the ISA has made a mistake of fact or law it must confirm the ISA's decision: SVGA 2006 s4(5).

8.66 As a result of the above, it is clear that parliament did not intend that the Upper Tribunal should be able to conduct a full merits review of the ISA's decision, as was possible under the Care Standards Act 2000 scheme.[159] In the *Royal College of Nursing*[160] case, Wyn Williams J described himself as 'troubled'[161] by the lack of a full merits based appeal but held that this did not entail any breach of ECHR article 6.[162]

8.67 However, both the ISA and the Upper Tribunal are public authorities for the purpose of Human Rights Act (HRA) 1998 s6 and must therefore act in accordance with the ECHR rights contained in HRA 1998 Sch 1. Because there will be an interference with the rights protected by ECHR article 8(1) in very many cases where an individual is placed on a barred list[163] the tribunal must determine whether the interference is proportionate and thereby justified in accordance with

158 Note, however, that in *VT v Independent Safeguarding Authority* [2011] UKUT 427 (AAC), the tribunal held that the exclusion in SVGA 2006 s4(3) only applies to the grounds of appeal which can be advanced by the appellant and considered by the tribunal. In *VT*, having identified an error of law in the decision, the tribunal considered itself entitled to consider all the evidence and find for itself that 'it is not *appropriate* for VT to remain on the children's barred list' (emphasis added); see judgment at [44] and [55].

159 See speech of Lady Hale in *R (Wright) v Secretary of State for Health* [2009] UKHL 3, [2009] AC 739 at [26], describing the premise that permanently to ban a person from a wide variety of care provisions requires a full merits hearing before an independent and impartial tribunal as 'correct'.

160 *R (Royal College of Nursing and others) v Secretary of State for the Home Department and Independent Safeguarding Authority* [2010] EWHC 2761 (Admin), [2011] PTSR 1193.

161 By comparison to the complaint about the lack of an oral hearing before the ISA.

162 Judgment at [104]. This approach was approved by the Upper Tribunal in *SB v Independent Safeguarding Authority* [2011] UKUT 404 (AAC), judgment at [38].

163 See speech of Lady Hale in *R (Wright) v Secretary of State for Health* [2009] UKHL 3, [2009] AC 739 at [36]; and *R (Royal College of Nursing and others) v Secretary of State for the Home Department and Independent Safeguarding Authority* [2010] EWHC 2761 (Admin), [2011] PTSR 1193 at [69].

article 8(2). This was acknowledged by Wyn Williams J in the *Royal College of Nursing*[164] case:

> I do not read section 4(3) of the 2006 Act as precluding a challenge to the ultimate decision on grounds that a decision to include an individual upon a barred list or to refuse to remove him from a list was unreasonable or irrational or, as Mr Grodzinski submits, disproportionate. In my judgment all that section 4(3) precludes is an appeal against the ultimate decision when that decision is not flawed by any error of law or fact.[165]

Proportionality

8.68   The tribunal has now determined two appeals in favour of an appellant where the error of law identified was the disproportionality of the decision. First, in *SB v Independent Safeguarding Authority*,[166] the tribunal considered an appeal by an individual who had been paced on the children's barred list after pleading guilty to 22 counts of possessing indecent images of children. The tribunal found the barring decision to be disproportionate, and in so doing rejected the submission by the ISA that the weight to be given to particular issues falls outside the tribunal's jurisdiction.[167]

8.69   The test which the tribunal in *SB* said should be adopted was taken from the judgment of the Supreme Court in *R (L) v Metropolitan Police Commissioner* and was summarised as follows:

> On an appeal, the Tribunal is entitled to examine the evidence and to allocate weight to it and to decide whether the balance [between the pressing social need that children and vulnerable adults should not be harmed and the individual's right to respect for private life] has been struck in the right place.[168]

164 R *(Royal College of Nursing and others) v Secretary of State for the Home Department and Independent Safeguarding Authority* [2010] EWHC 2761 (Admin); [2011] PTSR 1193.

165 R *(Royal College of Nursing and others) v Secretary of State for the Home Department and Independent Safeguarding Authority* [2010] EWHC 2761 (Admin); [2011] PTSR 1193 at [104].

166 [2011] UKUT 404 (AAC).

167 Judgment at [39]–[45]. See in particular [41]: 'The only way in which a Tribunal can form a view as to whether a decision of the Respondent is disproportionate is to engage in "a weighing of evidence exercise", not so as to ascertain whether the decision is or is not appropriate (that is a matter solely for the Respondent) but so as to ascertain whether it is disproportionate'.

168 Judgment at [44]–[45].

8.70 Having directed itself to this test, the tribunal applied it to the facts of SB's case to conclude that the barring decision was disproportionate and thereby unlawful. The reasons for this included that:

a) the pre-sentence report had identified the risk of further offending to be relatively low;[169]

b) the OASys[170] report concluded that the risk of reoffending was low;[171]

c) there was significant written evidence in support of the appellant, including testimony from his daughter;[172]

d) none of this evidence had been given 'any weight at all' by the ISA;[173] and

e) the conclusion that the appellant poses an unacceptable risk to children could not be justified by the evidence.[174]

8.71 However on the ISA's appeal the Court of Appeal[175] overturned the tribunal's decision and reinstated the ISA's original decision. Maurice Kay LJ approved the finding by Wyn Williams J that proportionality was a proper consideration for the tribunal, describing this as 'undoubtedly correct'.[176] Although the Court of Appeal held that the tribunal was correct to determine the question of proportionality for itself, it erred in (1) failing to accord appropriate weight to the ISA's original decision[177] and (2) failing to specifically address the question of whether public confidence in the barring scheme would be undermined by allowing the appeal.[178] Although the tribunal in *SB* went too far in giving the ISA's decision no weight, it is clear from the Court of Appeal judgment that it would be wrong for the tribunal to give any 'deference'[179] to the ISA's decision.

169 Judgment at [51].

170 The Probation Service's Offender Assessment System.

171 Judgment at [52]–[53].

172 Judgment at [54]–[55].

173 Judgment at [59].

174 Judgment at [62].

175 *ISA v SB (Royal College of Nursing intervening)* [2012] EWCA Civ 977.

176 Judgment at [15].

177 Judgment at [23].

178 Judgment at [25].

179 Judgment at [17]. In support of this conclusion Maurice Kay LJ cited the approach of Lord Bingham in *Huang v Secretary of State for the Home Department* [2007] 2 AC 167 at [16], where assessing proportionality was described as being 'the ordinary judicial task of weighing up the competing considerations on each side and according appropriate weight to the judgment of a person with responsibility for a given subject matter and access to special sources of knowledge and advice'.

8.72   Subsequent to the decision in *SB*, the tribunal also allowed the appeal in *PH v Independent Safeguarding Authority*[180] on a challenge founded solely on proportionality. The facts of *PH* differed markedly from *SB*, in that the appellant was a former teacher who had been convicted of grievous bodily harm in relation to an incident where he assaulted a pupil with a metal dumbbell. However, PH had pleaded guilty at the first opportunity to this offence and had an otherwise unblemished professional record. He produced medical evidence which supported his claim that the index offence was an isolated offence and that the risk he posed to vulnerable adults was low.

8.73   PH did not challenge his inclusion on the children's barred list but appealed against his inclusion on the adult's barred list. By the time of the hearing, the sole outstanding issue was whether the decision to place PH on the adult's barred list was disproportionate. The tribunal directed itself to both the *Royal College of Nursing* case and to its previous judgment in *SB*, but also considered in more detail the leading jurisprudence of the House of Lords and Supreme Court on proportionality, in particular *Huang v Secretary of State for the Home Department*;[181] *Belfast City Council v Miss Behavin' Ltd*[182] and *R (Quila and another) v Secretary of State for the Home Department*.[183]

8.74   From this review of the proportionality case-law, the tribunal accepted[184] the following submissions made by counsel for PH:

a) the Upper Tribunal in *SB* directed itself correctly as to the proper approach to proportionality;

b) the conclusion as to whether or not the ISA's decision is proportionate can only properly be reached by the tribunal after it has conducted its own balancing exercise, weighing all the evidence as it deems appropriate; and

c) it is not for the tribunal to reach its own view on the merits, but rather to ask the four questions identified by Lord Bingham in *Huang*: i) is the legislative objective sufficiently important to justify limiting a fundamental right? ii) are the measures which have been designed to meet it rationally connected to it? iii) are they no more than necessary to accomplish it? and iv) do they strike a fair balance between the rights of the individual and the interests of the community?

180 [2012] UKUT 91 (AAC).
181 [2007] UKHL 11.
182 [2007] UKHL 19.
183 [2011] 3 WLR 836.
184 [2012] UKUT 91 (AAC) at [41] and [43]a.

8.75   The tribunal further rejected the submission by counsel for the ISA that the proportionality case-law could be distinguished in the ISA appeals because of the existence of SVGA 2006 s4(3), which excludes the question of whether it is appropriate for an individual to be placed on one of the barred lists from the tribunal's jurisdiction. As the tribunal stated:

> 'Appropriateness' is a judgement call, and is not subject to any right of appeal. 'Proportionality' is a question of law, and is subject to a challenge based on an error of law.[185]

8.76   Having directed itself to the case-law, the tribunal considered the evidence before it, paying particular regard to the medical evidence obtained by PH, and held that his placement on the adult's barred list was disproportionate because the ISA had 'fundamentally misconstrued'[186] the medical evidence and had failed to carry out the necessary detailed balancing exercise.[187] As in *SB*, the tribunal placed significant weight on PH's own evidence.[188] The tribunal therefore reached the view that the decision did not strike a fair balance between PH's rights and the wider public interest, and was thereby disproportionate and as a result directed that his name should be removed from the adult's barred list.

8.77   The tribunal's decision in *PH* is also the subject of an application for permission to appeal to the Court of Appeal. The tribunal stayed consideration of the application for permission to appeal in *PH* pending the Court of Appeal's judgment in *SB*. Now judgment in *SB* has been handed down the outcome of the application in *PH* should be known shortly.

Other errors

8.78   With respect to errors of fact, the tribunal's jurisdiction extends beyond the limited circumstances where such a mistake establishes an error of law,[189] and the tribunal may allow the appeal if there has been an error by the ISA with respect to any material fact, in other words a fact

---

185 Judgment at [44].

186 Judgment at [48].

187 Judgment at [57].

188 See judgment at [51]: 'we have formed the view that he has now developed insight, that his depressive disorder is under control, and that he now has confidence in himself. He is obviously a very different person to the person who assaulted the school boy in 2009'.

189 As itemised by the Court of Appeal in *R (Iran) v Secretary of State for the Home Department* [2005] EWCA Civ 982 at [9]–[10].

which could have affected the outcome of the barring decision.[190] See, however, *SB v Independent Safeguarding Authority*,[191] where a mistake of fact as to the existence of a purported disqualification order was not held to be a material mistake in the circumstances of that case. Furthermore in *KS v Independent Safeguarding Authority*,[192] the tribunal described itself as 'not influenced either way' by a decision of the Nursing and Midwifery Council (NMC) that the appellant had no case to answer and upheld the ISA's decision on the facts.[193] These cases demonstrate that the tribunal will not leap to the conclusion that the ISA's decisions are invalidated by errors of fact.

8.79   However, in another recent appeal involving child pornography offences, *VW v Independent Safeguarding Authority*,[194] the tribunal held that the ISA's decision was flawed because of a host of errors of both fact and law. The errors of law were held to result from:

a) the ISA's failure to obtain an up-to-date report from the probation service;[195]

b) the ISA's failure to resolve a conflict in the evidence as to the level of risk posed by VW;[196]

c) the absence of any rational basis for the evaluation of evidence provided by the police;[197]

d) the lack of a rational approach to evidence submitted on behalf of VW;[198] and

e) the failure to put evidence from the Criminal Records Bureau, which was given significant weight by the ISA, to the appellant.[199]

8.80   Similarly in *VT v Independent Safeguarding Authority*, the tribunal held that the ISA erred in law by departing from the stated policy in its own guidance that there was a presumption not to bar in the

190 *XY v Independent Safeguarding Authority* [2011] UKUT 289 (AAC) at [53]. In *XY*, the Upper Tribunal suggest that an appeal could be allowed if the appellant could identify that a finding of fact by the ISA was 'plainly wrong'. It is submitted that there is no basis for importing a higher test than that specified in the statute, which is that a finding of fact was (on the balance of probabilities) a 'mistake'.

191 [2011] UKUT 404 (AAC).

192 [2011] UKUT 426 (AAC).

193 Judgment at [26].

194 [2011] UKUT 435 (AAC).

195 Judgment at [47]–[49].

196 Judgment at [50].

197 Judgment at [51].

198 Judgment at [52]–[54].

199 Judgment at [55]–[56].

absence of 'definite concerns' across at least two areas of the structured judgment process and then by failing to refer the case to the board for consideration and final decision in accordance with its guidance.[200] *VW* and *VT* demonstrate that the tribunal will also allow appeals on traditional public law grounds, here essentially irrationality and failure to follow a published policy, in addition to the proportionality grounds advanced in *SB* and *PH*.

Procedural matters

8.81   Appeals to the tribunal must be brought within three months of the ISA's decision,[201] although the tribunal retains a discretion to hear appeals out of time. The appeal form UT10 and accompanying guidance notes can be found on the tribunal website.[202] There is no fee for lodging the appeal. The tribunal may only award costs in very limited circumstances, generally if it considers that either party has acted unreasonably.[203] Therefore an appellant who brings an appeal that is not hopeless or otherwise abusive and complies with tribunal directions in the conduct of his appeal is unlikely to have to pay the ISA's costs if the appeal fails. Conversely, the ISA is unlikely to be ordered to pay the costs of a successful appeal unless the appellant can establish that the ISA acted unreasonably at one or more stages of the proceedings. Legal aid, including full representation, is available in ISA appeals, subject to the usual requirements of financial eligibility.

8.82   Appeals to the tribunal are subject to a permission threshold. The tribunal has generally adopted a relatively generous approach to the grant of permission and will grant permission more readily because of its role in developing practice and giving guidance and the need for the scheme as a whole to comply with ECHR article 6.[204] Any refusal of permission on the papers in a case which raises arguable errors of fact or law should therefore be renewed to an oral hearing.

8.83   The tribunal has held that it should not focus its scrutiny on the decision letter but instead on the ISA's more detailed reasoning as set out in the barring decision-making process document.[205] As such,

---

200 See judgment at [35]–[39].
201 Tribunal Procedure (Upper Tribunal) Rules 2008 SI No 2698 r21(3)(a).
202 See www.justice.gov.uk/global/forms/hmcts/tribunals/aa/index.htm.
203 Tribunal Procedure (Upper Tribunal) Rules 2008 r10.
204 See *SB v Independent Safeguarding Authority* [2011] UKUT 404 (AAC) at [10]–[12].
205 *KS v Independent Safeguarding Authority* [2011] UKUT 426 (AAC) at [47].

it will be necessary to request disclosure of the documentation supporting the ISA's decision at the earliest stage in a proposed appeal, if necessary seeking a direction from the tribunal if this disclosure is not made voluntarily.

8.84   Given the sensitive nature of the subject matter involved, the Upper Tribunal appears to be willing to order anonymity[206] to appellants in appeals against decisions against the ISA.[207] Such an application should be made at the earliest stage in the proceedings, ideally when the appeal papers are first lodged.

Relief and remedy

8.85   SVGA 2006 s4(6) specifies that:

> If the Upper Tribunal finds that ISA has made [a mistake of law or fact] it must –
> (a) direct ISA to remove the person from the list; or
> (b) remit the matter to ISA for a new decision.

8.86   If the tribunal remits a decision back to the ISA, it may set out any findings of fact on which the ISA must base its decision and the individual must be removed from the list(s) until the ISA makes its new decision, unless the tribunal directs otherwise.[208]

8.87   The tribunal therefore has a discretion as to order an individual's removal from the barred list(s) or allow the ISA to reconsider its decision. The way in which the tribunal exercises this discretion will of course be heavily influenced by the nature of the error identified by the tribunal. If the tribunal overturns one material finding of fact in a complex case but upholds the majority of the ISA's factual findings, it may well consider that the proper course is remittal. However, in a decision which is flawed through an error of law or where the entire factual basis on which the ISA's decision rests is rejected, the tribunal may be more likely to take the substantive decision itself; see, for example, the approach of the tribunal in *VT*,[209] where the tribunal took the decision for itself even though the ISA's decision was flawed by a single error of law.

8.88   Importantly, it is submitted that if the tribunal allows an appeal on grounds of proportionality, it must then direct that the individual

---

206 Under Tribunal Procedure (Upper Tribunal) Rules 2008 r14.
207 See, for example *XY v Independent Safeguarding Authority* [2011] UKUT 289 (AAC) at [3].
208 SVGA 2006 s4(7).
209 [2011] UKUT 427 (AAC), see judgment at [50]–[55].

be removed from the list(s) because as a public authority the tribunal must act compatibly with ECHR article 8, HRA 1998 s6. This was the approach taken by the tribunal in both *SB* and *PH*.

8.89   An individual who is wrongly included on a barred list cannot claim damages,[210] save in very limited circumstances where a person provides information to the ISA knowing it to be untrue.[211] However, the saving provision in SVGA 2006 s57(3) means that a court can still award damages under HRA 1998 s8 with respect to unlawful acts of public authorities. As such it may still be open to the Upper Tribunal to award damages on a successful appeal[212] and will be open to the county court to award damages against the ISA on an application made under HRA 1998 s8.

210 SVGA 2006 s57(1).
211 SVGA 2006 s57(2). The intention of this provision is to allow defamation claims to be brought in respect of malicious referrals to the ISA; explanatory notes to the SVGA 2006 at 156.
212 Although it will be necessary to clarify whether the Upper Tribunal has the power to award damages, for instance under the Tribunal, Courts and Enforcement Act 2007, which gives the Upper Tribunal the same powers as the High Court in matters 'incidental to the Upper Tribunal's functions'. It is no more than arguable that awarding damages is 'incidental' to the Upper Tribunal's function of determining whether individuals should remain on the barred lists.

Index

GOC fitness to practise proceedings
continued
Investigation Committee 6.18–
6.34
advice, letters of 6.29
assessments 6.19–6.20, 6.27
bundles 6.84
case examiners 6.21
case management directions
6.20
closing cases 6.26
cooperate, failure to 6.20
evidence 6.19, 6.24, 6.32–6.33
expert assessors 6.19
Fitness to Practise Committee,
referrals to 6.19, 6.21–6.34
further investigations, return
for 6.27
interim orders 6.22
no case to answer 6.24, 6.26
no further action 6.26
not to refer, options following
decisions not to 6.25–6.32
notification of meetings 6.20
public interest 6.24, 6.32
realistic prospect test 6.23
referrals 6.12, 6.19, 6.25–6.34
review of decisions not to refer
6.32–6.34
role 6.24
voluntary performance reviews
6.30
warnings 6.28
jurisdiction 6.5–6.7
Law Commission 6.3–6.4
lay panellists 6.72
legal advisers 6.74–6.77, 6.91,
6.97, 6.103, 6.105–6.107
legal issues 6.91
legal representation 6.47
letters of advice 6.29
location of hearings 6.46, 6.139
London venue 6.46, 6.140
mediation 6.54
medical panellists 6.72
misconduct 6.104, 6.111–6.114,
6.118
mitigation 6.45

no case to answer/no further
action 6.24, 6.26, 6.96–6.98,
6.135
notice of hearings 6.55–6.56, 6.93
notice of interim orders 6.37
notice of meetings 6.20
oaths and affirmations 6.95
one-off incidents 6.56
Opticians Act 1958 6.1, 6.9–6.10,
6.18
Optical Consumer Complaints
Service, mediation by 6.54
own initiative, investigations on
GOC's 6.14
particularisation of allegations
6.57–6.58
pre-hearing conferences 6.88
preparation for hearings 6.84–
6.91
presentation of registrant's case
6.100–6.103
presenting officers 6.75, 6.78,
6.95
private hearings 6.71, 6.83
procedural meetings 6.82
proportionality 6.122
protected titles 6.6
public confidence, maintaining
6.121, 6.132
public hearings 6.83
public interest 6.24, 6.32, 6.41,
6.43, 6.48, 6.69, 6.122, 6.124
public protection 6.36, 6.41, 6.43,
6.119, 6.121–6.122, 6.132,
6.134
questionnaires 6.37, 6.56, 6.81
realistic prospect test 6.23
redactions 6.62, 6.84
referrals 6.12, 6.19, 6.21–6.34
reform 6.3–6.4
registrar, duties of 6.37
regulation, approach to 6.8
representation, right to 6.47, 6.79
representations, making 6.35,
6.17
restoration hearings 6.141
reviews 6.30, 6.32–6.35, 6.42,
6.51, 6.128, 6.136–6.139
rules 6.4, 6.10, 6.49